Windows® Command-Line Administrator's Pocket Consultant, Second Edition

William Stanek

PUBLISHED BY
Microsoft Press
A Division of Microsoft Corporation
One Microsoft Way
Redmond, Washington 98052-6399

Library of Congress Control Number: 2008927283

Printed and bound in the United States of America.

1 2 3 4 5 6 7 8 9 QWE 3 2 1 0 9 8

Distributed in Canada by H.B. Fenn and Company Ltd.

A CIP catalogue record for this book is available from the British Library.

Microsoft Press books are available through booksellers and distributors worldwide. For further information about international editions, contact your local Microsoft Corporation office or contact Microsoft Press International directly at fax (425) 936-7329. Visit our Web site at www.microsoft.com/mspress. Send comments to mspinput@microsoft.com.

Acquisitions Editor: Martin DelRe
Developmental Editor: Karen Szall
Project Editor: Maria Gargiulo
Editorial Production: ICC Macmillan, Inc.
Technical Reviewer: James Johnson, Technical Review services provided by Content Master, a member of CM Group, Ltd
Cover: Tom Draper Design

Body Part No. X14-71538

Contents at a Glance

Table of Contents

List of Tables

Acknowledgments

Wanting to do something fundamentally different from how it's been done before turned out to be much harder than I ever thought—and, I hope, completely rewarding for you. You see, there are plenty of books for Windows administrators—and plenty of books for people who want to script Windows—but no one had sat down before and written an entire book on Windows administration from the command line that was truly focused on administration and not on the commands themselves. I hope that the result of all the hard work is that the book you hold in your hands is something unique. This isn't the kind of command-line book that says, "Here's the Edit command. You use this command to do this and this, and here are its parameters." Sure, some of that is included—as in any book for administrators—but this book focuses on using the command line in the context of everyday administration. It teaches you how to perform the daily administrative procedures and details how those procedures are implemented from the command line. So whether you want to learn how to manage daily operations, track Windows performance, view the event logs, partition disks, configure TCP/IP, or perform hundreds of others tasks, this book has the answers as they relate to the command line.

As I've stated in *Windows Server 2008 Administrator's Pocket Consultant* (Microsoft Press 2008) and in *Internet Information Services (IIS) 7.0 Administrator's Pocket Consultant* (Microsoft Press, 2008), the team at Microsoft Press is top-notch. On this project, I worked with Karen Szall, Devon Musgrave, Maria Gargiulo, and others at Microsoft. They were all very helpful throughout the writing process. Thanks also to Martin DelRe for believing in my work and shepherding it through production.

Unfortunately for the writer (but fortunately for readers), writing is only one part of the publishing process. Next came editing and author review. I must say, Microsoft Press has the most thorough editorial and technical review process I've seen anywhere—and I've written a lot of books for many different publishers. John Pierce was the project editor for the book and helped work the book through the editorial process. This was our first time working together, and it was a good experience. Jim Johnson was the technical editor for the book. Jim was also the technical editor for the first edition of the book, and it was good to work with him again. Becka McKay was the book's copy editor.

I would also like to extend a personal thanks to Lucinda Rowley, Anne Hamilton, and Chris Nelson. They've helped out at many points of my writing career and been there when I needed them the most. Thank you!

I hope I haven't forgotten anyone, but if I have, it was an oversight. *Honest.* ;-)

Introduction

Windows Command-Line Administrator's Pocket Consultant, Second Edition, is designed to be a concise and compulsively usable resource for Windows administrators. This is the readable resource guide that you'll want on your desk or in your pocket at all times. The book discusses everything you need to perform core administrative tasks using the Windows command line. Because the focus is directed toward providing you with maximum value in a pocket-sized guide, you don't have to wade through hundreds of pages of extraneous information to find what you're looking for. Instead, you'll find exactly what you need to get the job done.

In short, the book is designed to be the one resource you consult whenever you have questions regarding Windows command-line administration. To this end, the book concentrates on daily administration procedures, frequently used tasks, documented examples, and options that are representative but not necessarily inclusive. The goal is to keep the content so concise that the book remains compact and easy to navigate, while ensuring that the book is packed with as much information as possible—making it a valuable resource. Thus, instead of a hefty 1,000-page tome or a lightweight 100-page quick reference, you get a valuable resource guide that can help you quickly and easily perform common tasks, solve problems, and implement such advanced administration areas as automated monitoring, memory leak analysis, disk partitioning, Active Directory management, and network troubleshooting.

> **Find Additional Content Online** As new or updated material becomes available that complements your book, it will be posted online on the Microsoft Press Online Windows Server and Client Web site. Based on the final build of Windows Server 2008, the type of material you might find includes updates to book content, articles, links to companion content, errata, sample chapters, and more. This Web site will be available soon at *www.microsoft.com/learning/books/online/serverclient,* and will be updated periodically.

Who Is This Book For?

Windows Command-Line Administrator's Pocket Consultant, Second Edition, covers Windows Server 2008 and Windows Vista. The book is designed for:

- Current Windows Server 2008 administrators
- Support staff who maintain Windows Vista systems
- Accomplished users who have some administrator responsibilities
- Administrators upgrading to Windows Server from previous versions
- Administrators transferring from other platforms

To pack in as much information as possible, I had to assume that you have basic networking skills and a basic understanding of Windows, and that Windows is already installed on your systems. With this in mind, I don't devote entire chapters to understanding Windows architecture, installing Windows, or Windows startup and shutdown. I do, however, cover scheduling tasks, monitoring Windows systems, managing accounts, administering network services, and much more.

I also assume that you are fairly familiar with Windows commands and procedures as well as the Windows user interface. If you need help learning Windows basics, you should read the Windows documentation.

How Is This Book Organized?

Windows Command-Line Administrator's Pocket Consultant, Second Edition, is designed to be used in the daily administration of Windows systems, and as such the book is organized by job-related tasks rather than by Windows features. Speed and ease of reference is an essential part of this hands-on guide. The book has an expanded table of contents and an extensive index for finding answers to problems quickly. Many other quick reference features have been added as well. These features include quick step-by-step instructions, lists, tables with fast facts, and extensive cross-references. The book is organized into both parts and chapters.

Part I, "Windows Command-Line Fundamentals," reviews the fundamental tasks you need for command-line administration. Chapter 1 provides an overview of command-line administration tools, techniques, and concepts. Chapter 2 is designed to help you get the most out of the command shell. It details techniques for starting up the command shell using parameters, how to control command path settings, what redirection techniques are available, and how to use multiple commands in sequences. Chapter 3 discusses the essentials for creating command-line scripts. You'll learn how to set variables, work with conditional controls, and create procedures.

Windows provides many command-line tools to help in the management of daily operations. Part II, "Windows Systems Administration Using the Command Line," discusses the core tools and techniques you'll use to manage Windows systems. Chapter 4 explores techniques for configuring roles, role services, and features on Windows servers. Chapter 5 discusses many of the key administration tools, including those that help you gather system information, work with the Windows registry, configure Windows services, and shut down systems remotely. Chapter 6 examines the logging tools available for Windows systems that can help you identify and track system problems, monitor applications and services, and maintain system security. You'll also learn how to write events to the system and application logs. In Chapter 7, you'll learn about tools and techniques for monitoring applications, examining processes, and maintaining performance. Chapter 8 provides techniques you can use to manage the way logging is performed, centralize event logging across the enterprise, and collect and generate reports on performance data. Chapter 9 discusses ways you can automate tasks to reduce the daily workload.

The book continues with Part III, "Windows File System and Disk Administration Using the Command Line." Users depend on hard disk drives to store their word-processing documents, spreadsheets, and other types of data. If you've worked with Windows Vista or Windows Server 2008 for any length of time, you've probably used the Disk Management tool. The command-line counterpart of Disk Management is the disk partition utility (DiskPart). You can use DiskPart to handle most disk management tasks as well as to perform some additional tasks that cannot be performed in the graphical user interface. Chapter 10 provides an introduction to DiskPart and also discusses FSUtil, ChkDsk, and CHKNTFS. Chapter 11 discusses partitioning basic disks. Chapter 12 examines dynamic disks and how they are used. The chapter also examines implementing, managing, and troubleshooting RAID.

Part IV, "Windows Active Directory Administration Using the Command Line," concentrates on the core commands you'll use for configuring, managing, and troubleshooting Active Directory. Chapter 13 discusses many of the key directory services administration tools, including tools that help you gather directory information. Chapter 14 examines tools that help you create and manage computer accounts in Active Directory. You'll also learn how to configure domain controllers as global catalogs and operations masters. Chapter 15 discusses creating and managing accounts for users and groups in Active Directory.

The final part, Part V, "Windows Network Administration Using the Command Line," examines network printing, TCP/IP networking, and related issues. Chapter 16 examines network printing and print services. Chapter 17 discusses configuring, maintaining, and troubleshooting TCP/IP networking from the command line.

Appendix A provides a quick reference for command-line utilities discussed in the book. In Appendix B, you'll find a quick reference for the contexts and commands available when you are working with the network services shell (Netsh). You can use Netsh to manage the configuration of various network services on local and remote computers.

Conventions Used in This Book

I've used a variety of elements to help keep the text clear and easy to follow. You'll find code terms and listings in monospace type, except when I tell you to actually type a command. In that case, the command appears in bold type. When I introduce and define a new term, I put it in *italics*.

Other conventions include:

- **Notes** To provide details on a point that needs emphasis
- **Best Practices** To examine the best technique to use when working with advanced configuration and administration concepts
- **Cautions** To warn you when there are potential problems you should look out for
- **More Info** To provide more information on the subject
- **Real World** To provide real-world advice when discussing advanced topics
- **Security Alerts** To point out important security issues
- **Tips** To offer helpful hints or additional information

I truly hope you find that *Windows Command-Line Administrator's Pocket Consultant,* Second Edition, provides everything that you need to perform essential administrative tasks as quickly and efficiently as possible. You're welcome to send your thoughts to me at williamstanek@aol.com. Thank you.

Support

Every effort has been made to ensure the accuracy of this book. Microsoft Press provides corrections for books through the World Wide Web at the following address:

http://www.microsoft.com/mspress/support

If you have comments, questions, or ideas about this book, please send them to Microsoft Press using either of the following methods:

Postal Mail:

Microsoft Press
Attn: Editor, *Windows Command-Line Administrator's Pocket Consultant*, Second Edition
One Microsoft Way
Redmond, WA 98052-6399

E-mail:

mspinput@microsoft.com

Please note that product support isn't offered through these mail addresses. For support information, visit Microsoft's Web site at *http://support.microsoft.com/*.

Part I

Windows Command-Line Fundamentals

In this part:

Chapter 1

Overview of the Windows Command Line

The command line is built into the Microsoft Windows operating system and is accessed through the command-shell window. Every version of Windows has had a built-in command line, used to run built-in commands, utilities, and scripts. Although the command line is powerful and versatile, some Windows administrators never use it. If you are happy using the graphical administration tools, you may be able to use them forever without ever having to do anything more than point and click.

However, for proficient Windows administrators, skilled support staff, and committed power users, the Windows command line is inescapable. Knowing how to use the command line properly–including which command-line tools to use when and how to work with the tools effectively–can mean the difference between smooth-running operations and frequent problems. And if you're responsible for multiple domains or networks, learning the time-saving strategies that the command line offers is not just important–it's essential for sustaining day-to-day operations.

In this chapter, I'll explain command line essentials, how to use built-in commands, how to run command-line utilities, and how to work with other support tools. Right up front I should tell you that Windows Vista and Windows Server 2008 have many more command-line tools available by default than their predecessors. In fact, many of the tools that were previously available only when you installed the Windows Support Tools and the Windows Server Resource Kit tools are now available by default.

Real World As you read this chapter, and the rest of the book, keep in mind that this book is written for Windows Server 2008 and Windows Vista. Techniques that you learn in this book can be used on both operating systems unless otherwise noted. In some cases, you might be able to use the techniques discussed with other Windows operating systems, although the options or functions may vary. In any case, you should always test commands, options, and scripts before using them. The best way to do this is in a development or test environment where the systems with which you are working are isolated from the rest of the network.

Command Line Essentials

Each new version of Windows has extended and enhanced the command line. The changes have been dramatic, and they've not only improved the performance capabilities of the command line but its versatility as well. Today you can do things with the Windows command line that you simply could not do in previous versions of Windows. To help you put the available options to use in the fastest, most productive manner, the discussion that follows explores command-shell options and configuration, in addition to providing tips for using the command history.

Understanding the Windows Command Shell

The most commonly used command line is the Windows command shell. The Windows command shell (Cmd.exe) is a 32-bit or 64-bit environment for working with the command line. On 32-bit versions of Windows, you'll find the 32-bit executable in the %SystemRoot%\System32 directory. On 64-bit versions of Windows, you'll find the 32-bit executable in the %SystemRoot%\SysWow64 directory and the 64-bit executable in the %SystemRoot%\System32 directory. Other command lines are available, such as the MS-DOS command shell (Command.com) and Windows PowerShell (powershell.exe) discussed later in this chapter.

> **Note** %SystemRoot% refers to the *SystemRoot* environment variable. The Windows operating system has many environment variables, which are used to refer to user-specific and system-specific values. Often, I'll refer to environment variables using the standard Windows syntax %VariableName%.

You can start the command shell by using the Search box on the Start menu. Click Start, enter **cmd** in the Search box, and then press Enter. Or you can click Start, point to All Programs, point to Accessories, and then choose Command Prompt.

You can initialize the environment for the Windows command shell in several ways, including bypassing startup parameters to Cmd.exe or by using a custom startup file, which is placed in the %SystemRoot%\System32 directory. Figure 1-1 shows a command-shell window. By default, the command line is 80 characters wide and the command shell displays 25 lines of text. When additional text is to be displayed in the command-shell window or you enter commands and the command shell's window is full, the current text is displayed in the window and prior text is scrolled up. If you want to pause the display temporarily when a command is writing output, press Ctrl+S. Afterward, press Ctrl+S to resume or Ctrl+C to terminate execution.

> **Note** Custom startup files are used for MS-DOS programs that require special configurations. These files are named Autoexec.nt and Config.nt, and they are stored in the %SystemRoot%\System32 directory.

In this figure from Windows Server 2008, the display text is

```
Microsoft Windows [Version 6.0.6001]
(C) Copyright 2006 Microsoft Corporation. All rights reserved.

C:\Users\williams>
```

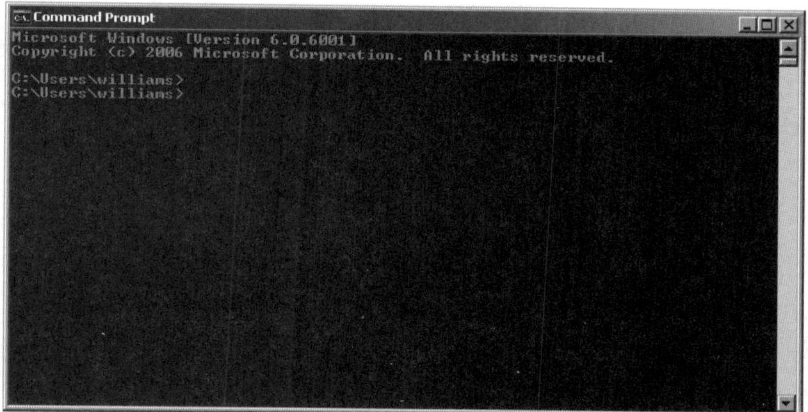

Figure 1-1 The command shell is the primary command-line window you'll use.

Here, the command prompt for the command line shows the current working directory, which by default is %UserProfile%, meaning the user profile directory for the current user. A blinking cursor following the command prompt indicates the command line is in interactive mode. In interactive mode, you can type commands directly after the prompt and press Enter to execute them. For example, type **dir** and then press Enter to get a listing of the current directory.

The command prompt also has a batch mode, which is used when executing a series of commands. In batch mode, the command prompt reads and executes commands one by one. Typically, batch commands are read from a script file, but batch commands can also be entered at the command prompt, such as when you use the FOR command to process each file in a set of files. (You'll learn more about batch scripts, loops, and command controls in Chapter 3, "Command-Line Scripting Essentials.")

Whenever you work with the Windows command line, it is important to keep in mind where the commands you are using come from. Native commands (commands built into the operating system by Microsoft) include:

- Internal commands that exist internally within the command shell and do not have separate executable files
- External commands that have their own executable files and are normally found in the %SystemRoot%\System32 directory

Table 1-1 shows a list of internal commands for the command shell (Cmd.exe). Each internal command is followed by a brief description.

Quick Reference to Internal Commands for the Command Shell (Cmd.exe)

Name	Description
assoc	Displays or modifies the current file extension associations.
break	Sets breaks for debugging.
call	Calls a procedure or another script from within a script.
cd (chdir)	Displays the current directory name or changes the location of the current directory.
cls	Clears the command window and erases the screen buffer.
color	Sets the text and background colors of the command-shell window.
copy	Copies files from one location to another or concatenates files.
date	Displays or sets the system date.
del (erase)	Deletes the specified file, files, or directory.
dir	Displays a list of subdirectories and files in the current or specified directory.
dpath	Allows programs to open data files in specified directories as if they were in the current directory.
echo	Displays text strings to the command line; sets command echoing state (on | off).
endlocal	Ends localization of variables.
exit	Exits the command shell.
for	Runs a specified command for each file in a set of files.
ftype	Displays current file types or modifies file types used in file extension associations.
goto	Directs the command interpreter to a labeled line in a batch script.
if	Performs conditional execution of commands.
md (mkdir)	Creates a subdirectory in the current or specified directory.
mklink	Creates either a symbolic or a hard link for either a file or a directory.
move	Moves a file or files from the current or designated source directory to a designated target directory. Can also be used to rename a directory.
path	Displays or sets the command path the operating system uses when searching for executables and scripts.
pause	Suspends processing of a batch file and waits for keyboard input.
popd	Makes the directory saved by PUSHD the current directory.
prompt	Sets the text for the command prompt.

Table 1-1 Quick Reference to Internal Commands for the Command Shell (Cmd.exe)

Name	Description
pushd	Saves the current directory location and then optionally changes to the specified directory.
rd (rmdir)	Removes a directory or a directory and its subdirectories.
rem	Sets a remark in batch scripts or Config.sys.
ren (rename)	Renames a file or files.
set	Displays current environment variables or sets temporary variables for the current command shell.
setlocal	Marks the start of variable localization in batch scripts.
shift	Shifts the position of replaceable parameters in batch scripts.
start	Starts a separate window to run a specified program or command.
time	Displays or sets the system time.
title	Sets the title for the command-shell window.
type	Displays the contents of a text file.
verify	Causes the operating system to verify files after writing files to disk.
vol	Displays the disk's volume label and serial number.

The syntax for using any internal (and most external commands) can be obtained by typing the command name followed by /? at the prompt, such as

copy /?

You'll find there are many more external commands than internal commands, including ones that are very similar to those built into the command line. Most of these similar commands are extended or enhanced in some way. For example, the external XCOPY command is more versatile than the COPY command because it allows you to copy directory trees as well as files and offers many more parameters. With the external SETX command, you can write environment variable changes directly to the Windows registry, which makes the changes permanent rather than temporary as the SET command does.

> **Tip** SETX is one of many commands that now are available by default in both Windows Vista and Windows Server 2008. You can also use SETX to obtain current Registry key values and write them to a text file.

Beyond this, the difference between internal and external commands isn't very important. Many Windows utilities have command-line extensions that allow parameters to be passed to the utility from the command line, and thus are used like external commands.

Understanding the MS-DOS Command Shell

The MS-DOS command shell (Command.com) includes 16-bit commands for the MS-DOS subsystem and other subsystems. Unlike most earlier Windows releases, 64-bit editions of Windows Server 2008 and Windows Vista do not include the MS-DOS command shell. On 32-bit editions of Windows Server 2008 and Windows Vista, you can start the MS-DOS command shell using the RUN command. Click Start, select Run, and then enter **command** in the Open field. Or, within another command line, type **command** and then press Enter.

> **Tip** If you are using the MS-DOS command shell from within Cmd.exe, the command shell title should change to "Command Prompt – Command" to let you know this. When you finish working with Command.com, you can quit the MS-DOS command shell and return to the Windows command line by typing **exit**.

You can initialize the environment for the MS-DOS command shell in several ways, including passing startup parameters to Command.com and using a Config.nt startup file, which is placed in the %SystemRoot%\System32 folder. As with Cmd.exe, the MS-DOS command window is 80 characters wide and displays at least 25 lines of text by default. When you start an MS-DOS command shell, the standard display text is

```
Microsoft(R) Windows DOS
(C) Copyright Microsoft Corp 1990-2001.

C:\>
```

As with the Windows command shell, the MS-DOS command shell has interactive and batch processing modes. It also has native commands built in by Microsoft. These commands are divided into two categories:

- **Internal configuration commands** Commands used to configure the MS-DOS subsystem, which should be placed in startup or program information files, such as Config.nt or Autoexec.nt. Configuration commands include BUFFERS, COUNTRY, DEVICE, DEVICEHIGH, DOS, DOSONLY, DRIVEPARM, ECHO-CONFIG, FCBS, FILES, INSTALL, LOADHIGH, LASTDRIVE, NTCMDPROMT, SHELL, STACKS, and SWITCHES.
- **Standard external commands** Commands that you can type at the command prompt, place in scripts, and in some cases use in startup files. Standard external commands include APPEND, DEBUG, EDIT, EDLIN, EXE2BIN, EXPAND, FASTOPEN, GRAPHICS, LOADFIX, MEM, NLSFUNC, SETVER, and SHARE.

S-DOS commands can also be run in Cmd.exe.

Configuring Command-Line Properties

If you use the Windows command shell frequently, you'll definitely want to customize its properties. For example, you can add buffers so that text scrolled out of the viewing area is accessible. You can resize the command shell, change its fonts, and more.

To get started, click the command-prompt icon at the top of the command-shell window or right-click the console's display bar, and then select Properties. As Figure 1-2 shows, the Command Prompt Properties dialog box has four tabs:

- **Options** Allows you to configure cursor size, display options, edit options, and command history. Select QuickEdit Mode if you want to use the mouse to cut and paste text within the command window. Clear Insert Mode to use overwrite as the default editing mode. Use the command history to configure how previously used commands are buffered in memory. (You'll find more on the command history in the next section of this chapter, "Working with the Command History.")

  > **Tip** While working in Windows Server 2008 or Windows Vista SP1 with text-only commands and tools, you may want to use Full Screen display mode to reduce the proportion of display space used by the command prompt itself. (To reset the display to command window mode, press Alt+Enter.) Afterward, type **exit** to exit the command prompt and return to the Windows desktop.

- **Font** Allows you to set the font size and face used by the command prompt. Raster font sizes are set according to their pixel width and height. For example, the size 8 x 12 is 8 screen pixels wide and 12 screen pixels high. Other fonts are set by point size, such as 10-point Lucida Console. Interestingly, when you select a point size of *n*, the font will be *n* pixels high; therefore, a 10-point font is 10 screen pixels high. These fonts can be designated as a bold font type as well, which increases their screen pixel width.
- **Layout** Allows you to set the screen buffer size, window size, and window position. Size the buffer height so that you can easily scroll back through previous listings and script output. A good setting is in the range of 1,000 to 2,000. Size the window height so that you can view more of the command-shell window at one time. A good setting is 45 lines on 800 x 600 screens with a 12-point font. If you want the command-prompt window to be in a specific screen position, clear Let System Position Window and then specify a position, in pixels, for the upper-left corner of the command window using Left and Top.
- **Colors** Allows you to set the text and background colors used by the command prompt. Screen Text and Screen Background control the respective color settings for the command-prompt window. The Popup Text and Popup Background options control the respective color settings for any popup dialog boxes generated when running commands at the command prompt.

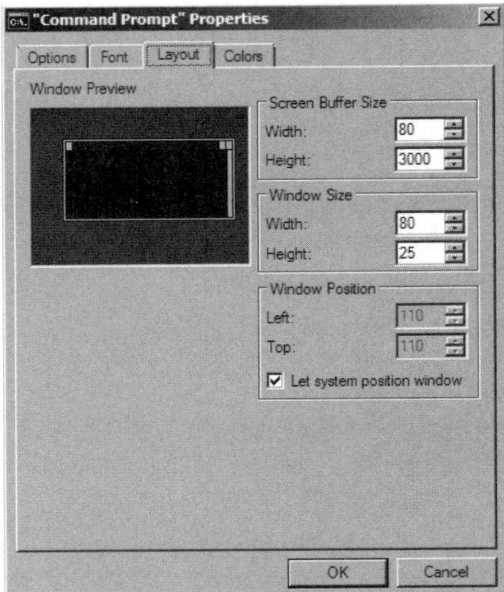

Figure 1-2 Configure the command-line properties for your environment.

When you are finished updating the command-shell properties, click OK to save your settings to your user profile. Your settings only modify the shortcut that started the current window. Any time you start a command line using the applicable shortcut, it will use these settings. If, however, you start a command line using a different shortcut, you'll have the settings associated with that shortcut.

Working with the Command History

The command history buffer is a feature of the Windows command shell (Cmd.exe) that remembers commands you've used in the current command-line session and allows you to access them without having to retype the command text. The maximum number of commands to buffer is set through the command-line Properties dialog box discussed in the previous section. By default, up to 50 commands are stored.

You can change the history size by completing these steps:

1. Right-click the command shell's title bar, select Properties, and then click the Options tab.
2. Use the Buffer Size field to set the maximum number of commands to store in the history and then click OK to save your settings to your user profile.

   Your settings only modify the shortcut that started the current window. Any time you start a command line using the applicable shortcut, it will use these settings.

If, however, you start a command line using a different shortcut, you'll have the settings associated with that shortcut.

You can access commands stored in the history in the following ways:

- **Browsing with the arrow keys** Use the up-arrow and down-arrow keys to move up and down through the list of buffered commands. When you find the command you want to use, press Enter to execute it as previously entered. Or you can modify the displayed command text by adding or changing parameters and then pressing Enter.
- **Browsing the command history pop-up window** Press F7 to display a pop-up window that contains a listing of buffered commands. Next, select a command using the arrow keys. (Alternatively, press F9, then press the corresponding number on the keyboard, and finally press Enter.) Execute the selected command by pressing Enter, or press Esc to close the pop-up window without executing a command.
- **Searching the command history** Enter the first few letters of the command you want to execute and then press F8. The command shell searches through the history for the first command that begins with the characters you've entered. Press Enter to execute it. Or, press F8 again to search the history buffer for the next match in the command history.

As you work with the command history, keep in mind that each instance of Cmd.exe has its own set of command buffers. Thus, buffers are only valid in the related command shell context.

Making Supplemental Components Available

Microsoft designed Windows Vista and Windows Server 2008 with an extensible component architecture. Because of this extensible architecture, Microsoft can make new components available for the operating systems through installer packages. Typically, Microsoft provides such files as individual Microsoft Update Standalone Package (.msu) files.

Installing and configuring new components is a two-part process. First you must register the components on the computer by installing the installer package. Then you must use an appropriate tool to configure the components. After you install a new component on Windows Server 2008, you use an appropriate wizard in Server Manager to install and configure the new role, role service, or feature. Once you install a new component on Windows Vista, you use the Windows Features dialog box to install and configure the new feature. With Windows Vista, one supplemental component that you'll want to install to enable remote administration is the Microsoft Remote Server Administration Tools for Windows Vista.

Using the Microsoft Remote Server Administration Tools for Windows Vista

The Microsoft Remote Server Administration Tools (RSAT) for Windows Vista is a collection of tools for remotely managing the roles and features in Windows Server 2008 from a computer running Windows Vista. RSAT includes support for remote management of Windows Server 2008 regardless of whether the server is running a Server Core installation or a Full Server installation and provides similar functionality to the Windows Server 2003 Administration Tools Pack.

RSAT is available in a 32-bit edition and a 64-bit edition for computers running Windows Vista Business, Windows Vista Enterprise, or Windows Vista Ultimate, provided that you've installed Service Pack 1 (SP1) or later. If your computer is running a 32-bit edition of Windows Vista, you must install the 32-bit edition of RSAT. If your computer is running a 64-bit edition of Windows Vista, you must install the 64-bit edition of RSAT. You can use the tools designed for either architecture to remotely manage both 32-bit and 64-bit editions of Windows Server 2008.

You should not install the Microsoft Remote Server Administration Tools for Windows Vista on a computer that has the Windows Server 2003 Administration Tools Pack or the Windows Server 2000 Administration Tools Pack installed. You must remove all versions of earlier Administration Tools Pack tools from the computer before installing the Microsoft Remote Server Administration Tools for Windows Vista.

Because the installer package for the remote administration tools is provided as an update, Microsoft assigns the installer package an identification number in the Microsoft Knowledge Base. Write down this number. If you need to uninstall or reinstall the installer package, this number will help you locate the update you need to uninstall or reinstall.

Registering the Remote Server Administration Tools Package

You can register the installer package for the Microsoft Remote Server Administration Tools for Windows Vista by completing the following steps:

1. Obtain the version of the Microsoft Remote Server Administration Tools for Windows Vista that is compatible with the architecture and service pack used on your Windows Vista computer. You can obtain the latest version of the tools for the latest Windows Vista service pack by visiting the Microsoft Download site (*http://download.microsoft.com/*).
2. If you've saved this file to a location on your computer or a network share, you can begin the installation process by accessing the file location in Windows Explorer and double-clicking the installer file.

3. When prompted to confirm the installation, click OK. When you are prompted, read the license terms. If you accept the terms, click I Accept to continue. The installer will then install the tools as an update for Windows Vista.
4. When the installer completes the installation of the tools, click Close. Although the installer may not state this explicitly, you may need to restart your computer to finalize the installation. You can confirm whether you need to restart by clicking Start and looking at the power button. If the power button is red and you see a small Windows Update icon within it, you need to restart the computer.

Configuring and Selecting Remote Server Administration Tools

Registering the installer package ensures the remote administration tools are available for selection. You can configure and select the remote server administration tools that you want to use by completing the following steps:

1. Click Start, click Control Panel, and then click Programs.
2. Under Programs And Features, click Turn Windows Features On Or Off.
3. In the Windows Features dialog box, expand Remote Server Administration Tools.
4. Using the options under the Feature Administration Tools and Role Administration Tools nodes, select the remote administration tools that you want to install and then click OK. Keep the following in mind:
   - Active Directory Domain Services Tools includes the directory services consoles and the directory services command-line tools.
   - Distributed File System (DFS) Tools includes the DFS Management console as well as the Dfsradmin, Dfscmd, Dfsdiag, and Dfsutil command-line tools.
   - DNS Server Tools includes the DNS Manager console and the Dnscmd command-line tool.
   - Failover Clustering Tools includes the Failover Cluster Manager console and the Cluster command-line tool.
   - File Server Resource Manager Tools includes the File Server Resource Manager console as well as the Filescrn and Storrept command-line tools.
   - Network Load Balancing Tools includes the Network Load Balancing Manager console as well as the Nlb and the Wlbs command-line tools.
   - Storage Manager For SANs Tools includes the Storage Manager For SANs console and the ProvisionStorage command-line tool.
   - Windows System Resource Manager Tools includes the Windows System Resource Manager console and the Wsrm command-line tool.

After you select the tools you want to use, Windows Vista automatically configures them for use. At the command line, you'll be able to use any command-line tools that Windows Vista has configured for use. The graphical versions of the tools are available on the Administrative Tools menu.

Tip If the Administrative Tools menu isn't available on the Start\All Programs menu already, you can display it to provide quick and easy access to the remote administration tools. Right-click the Start button and then select Properties to display the Taskbar And Start Menu Properties dialog box. On the Start Menu tab, click Customize to the right of the Start Menu option. In the Customize Start Menu dialog box, scroll down until you see the System Administrative Tools options and then select an appropriate option, such as Display On The All Programs Menu And The Start Menu, and then click OK twice.

Removing the Remote Server Administration Tools

You can remove remote server administration tools that you no longer want to use by completing the following steps:

1. Click Start, click Control Panel, and then click Programs.
2. Under Programs And Features, click Turn Windows Features On Or Off.
3. In the Windows Features dialog box, expand Remote Server Administration Tools.
4. Using the options under the Feature Administration Tools and Role Administration Tools nodes, clear the check boxes for any remote administration tool that you want to remove and then click OK.

Removing the Remote Server Administration Tools Package

If you no longer use a computer for remote administration and want to remove the remote administration tools completely, you can remove the entire installer package by completing the following steps:

1. Click Start, click Control Panel, and then click Programs.
2. Under Programs And Features, click View Installed Updates.
3. Click the update you used to install the remote administration tools and then click Uninstall.
4. When prompted to confirm, click Yes.

Chapter 2

Getting the Most from the Command Line

The command shell provides a powerful environment for working with commands and scripts. As discussed in Chapter 1, "Overview of the Windows Command Line," you can run many types of commands at the command line, including built-in commands, Windows utilities, and applications with command-line extensions. Regardless of its source, every command you'll use follows the same syntax rules. These rules state that a command consists of a command name followed by any required or optional arguments. Arguments can also use redirection to specify the sources for inputs, outputs, and errors.

When you execute a command in the command shell, you start a series of events that are similar to the following:

1. The command shell replaces any variables you've entered in the command text with their actual values.
2. Multiple commands that are chained or grouped and passed on a single line are broken into individual commands and separated into command name and related arguments. The individual commands are then processed.
3. If the command name has a file path, the command shell uses this path to find the command. If the command cannot be found in the specified location, the command shell returns an error.
4. If the command name doesn't specify a file path, the command shell tries to resolve the command name internally. A match means that you've referenced a built-in command that can be executed immediately. If no match is found, the command shell looks in the current directory for the command executable, and then searches the command path for the command executable. If the command cannot be found in any of those locations, the command shell returns an error.
5. If the command is located, the command is executed using any specified arguments, including those that specify the inputs to use. Command output and any errors are written to the command window or to the specified destinations for output and error.

As you can see, many factors can affect command execution, including command path settings, redirection techniques used, and whether commands are chained or grouped. In this chapter, we'll use this breakdown of command execution to help you get the most out of the command shell. Before we dive into those discussions, however, let's look at special considerations for starting the command shell and introduce the concept of nesting command shells.

Managing Command Shell Startup

When you previously worked with the command line, you probably started a command prompt by clicking Start, pointing to All Programs, pointing to Accessories, and then choosing Command Prompt. However, because this technique starts the command prompt with standard user privileges rather than administrator privileges, you'll find that you are unable to perform many administrative tasks. To start the command prompt with administrator privileges, you need to click Start, point to All Programs, point to Accessories, right-click Command Prompt, and then select Run As Administrator.

Other ways to start a command line are to use the Search box on the Start menu, the Run dialog box, or type **cmd** in an open command-shell window. These techniques enable you to pass arguments to the command line, including switches that control how the command line works as well as parameters that execute additional commands. For example, you can start the command shell in quiet mode (meaning command echo is turned off) by using the startup command **cmd /q**. If you wanted the command shell to execute a command and then terminate, you could type **cmd /c** followed by the command text enclosed in quotation marks. The following example starts a command shell, sends the output of ipconfig to a file in a subdirectory named data, and then exits the command shell:

```
cmd /c "ipconfig > c:\data\ipconfig.txt"
```

> **Note** The data subdirectory must exist for this command to work. Also note that when you start a command prompt from the Search box on the Start menu or the Run dialog box, the command prompt runs with standard user privileges. This means you will not be able to perform certain administrator tasks or write data to secure system locations. For example, if you were to direct the output to the root of the C drive by typing **c:\ipconfig.txt**, the command prompt would not have sufficient privileges to create the file.

Table 2-1 summarizes the key parameters for the Windows command shell (Cmd.exe). Note that several command-line parameters are set by default. Because of this, the command line normally uses standard ANSI character codes for command output, as opposed to Unicode character codes, and enables command extensions that add features to most built-in commands.

Table 2-1 Essential Parameters for the Command Line

Parameter	Description
/C	Executes the command specified and then exits the command shell.
/K	Executes the command specified and then remains in interactive mode.
/A	Command output to files (or pipes) is set to ANSI format (default).
/U	Command output to files (or pipes) is set to Unicode.
/Q	Turns on quiet mode, meaning command echo is off. By default, command echo is on.
/T:*fg*	Sets the foreground and background colors for the console window, where *fg* are the two values defined in the COLOR command.
/E:ON	Enables command extensions, which is the default.
/E:OFF	Disables command extensions.

Note Some parameters cannot be used with other switches. For example, you can't enable both Unicode and ANSI character codes. If you use both /A and /U, or /E:ON and /E:OFF, the command line applies the last option you passed on the command line.

Sometimes you may want to use different environment settings or parameters for a command line and then go back to your original settings without exiting the console window. To do this, you can use a technique called *nesting*. With nesting, you start a command line within a command line, and the nested command line inherits its environment settings from the current command line. You can then modify the environment as necessary and execute commands and scripts using those settings. When you type **exit** to end the nested command-line instance, you return to the previous command line and the previous environment settings are restored.

Tip As you set out to work with the command shell, keep in mind that some characters have special meanings and that whenever the command shell encounters one of these characters, it attempts to carry out the special procedure associated with that character. Special characters include < > ( ) & | @ ^. If you want to use a special character as a regular character, you must escape the special character for the command shell to look at it literally, without invoking the special procedures with which it is associated. The escape character is the caret (^), which is the character above the 6 key on a standard keyboard, and is placed to immediately precede the special character.

Working with the Command Path

The Windows operating system uses the command path to locate executables. The types of files that Windows considers to be executables are determined by the file extensions for executables. You can also map file extensions to specific applications by using file associations. The two sections that follow discuss techniques for working with the command path, file extensions, and file associations.

Managing the Command Path

You can view the current command path for executables by using the PATH command. Start a command shell, type **path** on a line by itself, and press Enter. If you've installed the Windows PowerShell, the results should look similar to the following:

```
PATH=C:\Windows\system32;C:\Windows;C:\Windows\System32\Wbem;
C:\Windows\System32\PowerShell\v2.0
```

> **Note** Observe the use of the semicolon (;) to separate individual paths. The command shell uses the semicolon to determine where one file path ends and another begins.

The command path is set during logon using system and user environment variables, namely the *%PATH%* variable. The order in which directories are listed in the path indicates the search order used by the command line when looking for executables. In the previous example, the command line searches in this order:

1. C:\Windows\system32
2. C:\Windows
3. C:\Windows\System32\Wbem
4. C:\Windows\System32\PowerShell\v2.0

You can permanently change the command path in the system environment using the SETX command. For example, if you use specific directories for scripts or applications, you may want to update the path information. You can do this by using the SETX command to add a specific path to the existing path, such as **setx PATH "%PATH%;C:\Scripts"**.

> **Note** Observe the use of the quotation marks and the semicolon (;). The quotation marks are necessary to ensure that the value *%PATH%*;C:\Scripts is read as the second argument for the SETX command. And, as discussed previously, the semicolon is used to specify where one file path ends and another begins.

> **Tip** Because the command path is set during logon, you must log off and then log on to see the revised path in your command prompts. If you'd rather not log off, you can verify that you've set the command path properly using the System Properties dialog box. In Control Panel\System, click Advanced System Settings in the Tasks Pane and then click Environment Variables on the Advanced tab of the System Properties dialog box.

In this example, the directory C:\Scripts is appended to the existing command path, and the sample path listed previously would be modified to read as follows:

```
PATH=C:\Windows\system32;C:\Windows;C:\Windows\System32\Wbem;
C:\Windows\System32\PowerShell\v2.0;C:\Scripts
```

Don't forget about the search order that Windows uses. Because the paths are searched in order, the C:\Scripts directory will be the last one searched. This can sometimes slow the execution of your scripts. To help Windows find your scripts faster, you may want C:\Scripts to be the first directory searched. In this case, you could set the command path using the following command:

```
setx PATH "C:\Scripts;%PATH%"
```

Be careful when setting the command path. It is easy to overwrite all path information accidentally. For example, if you don't specify the *%PATH%* environment variable when setting the path, you will delete all other path information. One way to ensure that you can easily re-create the command path is to keep a copy of the command path in a file. To write the current command path to a file, type **path > orig_path.txt**. Keep in mind that if you are using a standard command prompt rather than an administrator command prompt, you won't be able to write to secure system locations. In this case, you can write to a subdirectory to which you have access or your personal profile. To write the command path to the command-shell window, type **path**.

Now you have a listing or a file that contains a listing of the original command path. Not only does the path command list the current command path, it also can be used to set the command path temporarily for the current command shell. For example, type **path %PATH%;C:\Scripts** to append the C:\Scripts directory to the command path in the current command shell.

Managing File Extensions and File Associations

File extensions are what allow you to execute commands by typing just their command name at the command line. Two types of file extensions are used:

- **File extensions for executables** Executable files are defined with the *%PATHEXT%* environment variable. You can view the current settings by typing **set pathext** at the command line. The default setting is PATHEXT=.COM;.EXE;.BAT;.CMD;.VBS;.VBE;.JS;.JSE;.WSF;.WSH;.MSC. With this setting, the command line knows which files are executable and which files are not, so you don't have to specify the file extension at the command line.
- **File extensions for applications** File extensions for applications are referred to as *file associations*. File associations are what enable you to pass arguments to executables and to open documents, spreadsheets, or other application files by double-clicking their file icons. Each known extension on a system has a file association that you can view by typing **assoc** followed by the extension, such as **assoc .exe**. Each file association in turn specifies the file type for the file extension. This can be viewed by typing the FTYPE command followed by the file association, such as **ftype exefile**.

With executables, the order of file extensions sets the search order used by the command line on a per-directory basis. Thus, if a particular directory in the command path has multiple executables that match the command name provided, a .com file would be executed before a .exe file and so on.

Every known file extension on a system has a corresponding file association and file type—even extensions for executables. In most cases, the file type is the extension text without the period followed by the keyword *file*, such as cmdfile, exefile, or batfile, and the file association specifies that the first parameter passed is the command name and that other parameters should be passed on to the application.

You can look up the file type and file association for known extensions using the ASSOC and FTYPE commands. To find the association, type **assoc** followed by the file extension that includes the period. The output of the ASSOC command is the file type. So if you type **ftype *association*** (where *association* is the output of the ASSOC command), you'll see the file type mapping. For example, if you type the following command to see the file associations for .exe executables: **assoc .exe**, you then type **ftype exefile**.

You'll see the file association is set to

```
exefile="%1" %*
```

Thus, when you run an .exe file, Windows knows the first value is the command that you want to run and anything else provided are parameters to pass along.

> **Tip** File associations and types are maintained in the Windows Registry and can be set using the ASSOC and FTYPE commands respectively. To create the file association, type **assoc** followed by the extension setting, such as **assoc .pl=perlfile**. To create the file type, set the file type mapping, including how to use parameters supplied with the command name, such as **perlfile=C:\Perl\Bin\Perl.exe "%1" %***. To learn more about setting file associations and types, refer to the documentation for these two commands in Help And Support Center.

Redirecting Standard Input, Output, and Error

By default, commands take input from the parameters specified when they are called by the command shell and then send their output, including errors, to the standard console window. Sometimes, though, you'll want to take input from another source or send output to a file or other output device such as a printer. You may also want to redirect errors to a file rather than the console window. You can perform these and other redirection tasks using the techniques introduced in Table 2-2 and discussed in the sections that follow.

Table 2-2 Redirection Techniques for Input, Output, and Errors

Redirection Technique	Description
command1 > command2	Sends the output of the first command to be the input of the second command.
command < [path]filename	Takes command input from the specified file path.
command > [path]filename	Sends output to the named file, creating the file if necessary or overwriting it if it already exists.
command >> [path]filename	Appends output to the named file if it exists or creates the file and then writes to it.
command < [path]filename > [path]filename	Gets command input from the specified file and then sends command output to the named file.
command < [path]filename >> [path]filename	Gets command input from the specified file and then appends command output to the named file.
command 2> [path]filename	Creates the named file and sends any error output to it. If the file exists, it is overwritten.
command 2>&1	Sends error output to the same destination as standard output.

Redirecting Standard Output to Other Commands

Most commands generate output that can be redirected to another command as input. To do this, you use a technique called *piping*, whereby the output of a command is sent as the input of the next command. Following this, you can see the general syntax for piping is

```
Command1 | Command2
```

where the pipe redirects the output of Command1 to the input of Command2. But you can also redirect output more than once, such as

```
Command1 | Command2 | Command3
```

The two most common commands that are piped include FIND and MORE. The FIND command searches for strings in files or in text passed to the command as input and then lists the text of matching lines as output. For example, you could obtain a list of all .txt files in the current directory by typing the following command:

```
dir | find /I ".txt"
```

The MORE command accepts output from other commands as input and then breaks this output into sections which can be viewed one console page at a time. For example, you could page through a log file called Dailylog.txt using the following command:

```
type c:\working\logs\dailylog.txt | more
```

Type **find** /? or **more** /? at the command line to get a complete list of the syntax for these commands.

Redirecting I/O to and from Files

Another command redirection technique is to get input from a file using the input redirection symbol (<). For example, the following command sorts the contents of the Usernames.txt file and displays the results to the command line:

```
sort < usernames.txt
```

Just as you can read input from a file, you can also send output to a file. To do this, you can use > to create or overwrite a named file, or >> to create or append data to a named file. For example, if you want to write the current network status to a file, you could use the following command:

```
netstat -a > netstatus.txt
```

Unfortunately, if there is an existing file in the current directory with the same file name, this command overwrites the file and creates a new one. If you want to append this information to an existing file rather than overwrite an existing file, change the command text to read as follows:

```
netstat -a >> netstatus.txt
```

The input and output redirection techniques can be combined as well. You could, for example, obtain command input from a file and then redirect command-output to another file. In this example, a list of user names is obtained from a file and sorted, and then the sorted name list is written to a new file:

```
sort < usernames.txt > usernames-alphasort.txt
```

Redirecting Standard Error

By default, errors from commands are written as output on the command line. If you are running unattended batch scripts or utilities, however, you may want to redirect standard error to a file so that errors are tracked. One way to redirect standard error is to tell the command line that errors should go to the same destination as standard output. To do this, type the **2>&1** redirection symbol as shown in this example:

```
chkdsk /r > diskerrors.txt 2>&1
```

Here, you send standard output and standard error to a file called Diskerrors.txt. If you want to track only errors, you can redirect only the standard error. In this example, standard output is displayed at the command line and standard error is sent to the file Diskerrors.txt:

```
chkdsk /r 2> diskerrors.txt
```

Chaining and Grouping Commands

In previous sections, I discussed redirection techniques that included piping commands. You may have wondered if there were other ways to execute a series of commands. There are. You can chain commands and execute them in sequence, and you can execute commands conditionally based on the success or failure of previous commands. You can also group sets of commands that you want to execute conditionally.

You'll learn more about these techniques in the sections that follow. Before you proceed however, take note of Table 2-3, which provides a quick reference for the basic syntax to use when chaining or grouping commands. Keep in mind that the syntax provided is not intended to be all-inclusive. The chaining syntax can be extended for additional commands to be conditionally executed. The syntax for grouping may vary, depending on the actual situation.

Table 2-3 Quick Reference for Chaining and Grouping Commands

Symbol	Syntax	Description
&	Command1 & Command2	Execute Command1 and then execute Command2.
&&	Command1 && Command2	Execute Command2 if Command1 is completed successfully.
||	Command1 || Command2	Execute Command2 only when Command1 doesn't complete successfully.
( )	(Command1 & Command2) && (Command3)	Use parentheses to group sets of commands for conditional execution based on success.
	(Command1 & Command2) || (Command3)	Use parentheses to group sets of commands for conditional execution based on failure.

Using Chains of Commands

Sometimes, to be more efficient, you'll want to execute commands in a specific sequence. For example, you may want to change to a particular directory and then obtain a directory listing, sorted by date. Using chaining, you can perform both tasks by entering this one line of command text:

```
cd c:\working\docs & dir /O:d
```

In scripts, you'll often need to chain commands such as this to be certain the commands are carried out exactly as you expect. Still, it makes more sense to chain commands when the execution of later commands depends upon whether previous commands succeeded or failed. In this example, a log file is moved only if it exists:

```
dir c:\working\logs\current.log && move current.log d:\history\logs
```

Why would you want to do this? Well, one reason would be so that an error isn't generated as output of a script.

You may also want to perform a task only if a preceding command failed. For example, if you are using a script to distribute files to a group of workstations, some of which have a C:\Working\Data folder and some of which have a C:\Data folder, you could copy sets of files to either folder, regardless of the workstation configuration, using the following commands:

```
cd C:\working\data || cd C:\data
xcopy n:\docs\*.*
```

Grouping Command Sequences

When you combine multiple commands, you may need a way to group commands to prevent conflicts or to ensure that an exact order is followed. You group commands using a set of parentheses. To understand why grouping may be needed, consider the following example. Here, you want to write the host name, IP configuration, and network status to a file, so you use this statement:

```
hostname & ipconfig & netstat -a > current_config.log
```

When you examine the log file, however, you find that it contains only the network status. The reason for this is that the command line executes the commands in the following sequence:

1. hostname
2. ipconfig
3. netstat -a > current_config.log

Because the commands are executed in sequence, the system host name and IP configuration are written to the command line, and only the network status is written to the log file. To write the output of all the commands to the file, you would need to group the commands as follows:

```
(hostname & ipconfig & netstat -a) > current_config.log
```

Here, the output of all three commands is collected and then redirected to the log file. You can also use grouping with conditional success and failure. In the following example, both Command1 and Command2 must succeed for Command3 to execute:

```
(cd C:\working\data & xcopy n:\docs\*.*) && (hostname > n:\runninglog.txt)
```

In the next chapter, you'll see how command grouping is used with *if* and *if...else* constructs.

Chapter 3

Command-Line Scripting Essentials

In a world dominated by whiz-bang graphical user interfaces, you may wonder what command-line scripting has to offer that Windows and point-and-click dialog boxes don't. Well, to be honest, the plain appearance of command-line scripting has more to offer than most people realize, especially considering that most people regard command-line scripts as glorified batch files—the kind you used on computers with 8088 processors and MS-DOS. Today's command-line scripting environment is an extensive programming environment, which includes the following:

- Variables
- Arithmetic expressions
- Conditional statements
- Control flow statements
- Procedures

You can use these programming elements to automate repetitive tasks, perform complex operations while you're away from the computer, find resources that others may have misplaced, and perform many other time-saving activities that you would normally have to type in at the keyboard. Command-line scripts not only have complete access to the command line, they can also call any utilities that have command-line extensions.

Creating Command-Line Scripts

Command-line scripts are text files containing the commands you want to execute. These are the same commands you would normally type into the Windows command shell. However, rather than enter the commands each time you want to use them, you create a script to store the commands for easy execution.

Because scripts contain standard text characters, you can create and edit scripts using a standard text editor, such as Notepad. When you enter commands, be sure to place each command or group of commands that should be executed together on a new line. This ensures proper execution of the commands. When you have finished creating a command-line script, save the script file using the .bat or .cmd extension. Both extensions work with command-line scripts in the same way. For example, if you wanted to create a script to display the system name, the Windows version, and the IP configuration, you could enter these three commands into a file called SysInfo.bat or SysInfo.cmd:

```
hostname
ver
ipconfig -all
```

When you save the script, you can execute it as if it were a Windows utility: Simply type the name of the script in a command shell and press Enter. When you do this, the command shell reads the script file and executes its commands one by one. It stops executing the script when it reaches the end of the file or reads an EXIT command. For the example script, the command line would display output similar to Listing 3-1.

Listing 3-1 Output of Sample Script

```
C:\>hostname
mailer1

C:\>ver
Microsoft Windows [Version 6.0.6001]

C:\>ipconfig -all
Windows IP Configuration
   Host Name . . . . . . . . . . . . : mailer1
   Primary Dns Suffix  . . . . . . . : adatum.com
   Node Type . . . . . . . . . . . . : Hybrid
   IP Routing Enabled. . . . . . . . : No
   WINS Proxy Enabled. . . . . . . . : No
   DNS Suffix Search List. . . . . . : adatum.com

Ethernet adapter Local Area Connection:

   Connection-specific DNS Suffix  . :
   Description . . . . . . . . . . . : Intel(R) PRO/100 VE Network
      Connection
   Physical Address. . . . . . . . . : X0-EF-D7-AB-E2-1E
   DHCP Enabled. . . . . . . . . . . : No
   Autoconfiguration Enabled . . . . : Yes
   Link-local IPv6 Address . . . . . : fe80::2ca3:3d2e:3d46:fe99%9
                                       (Preferred)
   IPv4 Address. . . . . . . . . . . : 192.168.10.50
   Subnet Mask . . . . . . . . . . . : 255.255.255.0
   Default Gateway . . . . . . . . . : 192.168.10.1
   DNS Servers . . . . . . . . . . . : ::1
                                     192.168.10.155
   NetBIOS over Tcpip. . . . . . . . : Enabled
```

If you examine the listing, you'll see that the command prompt and the actual commands are displayed as well as the output of the commands themselves. The reason for this is that the command shell does some extra work behind the scenes while executing scripts in the default processing mode. First, the comman(displays the command prompt. Next, it reads a line from the script, displa) then interprets it. If the command shell reaches the end of the file or reads an EXIT command, execution stops. Otherwise, the command shell starts this process all over again by displaying the prompt and preparing to read the next line in the script.

Although the default processing mode with command echoing turned on can be useful for troubleshooting problems in scripts, you probably don't want to use this display mode with scripts you'll use regularly. Fortunately, you can change the default behavior by turning command echo off, as I'll show you in the section titled "Managing Text Display and Command Echoing" later in the chapter.

Common Statements and Commands for Scripts

So far in this book, I've discussed commands but haven't really introduced what a statement is. While these terms are often used interchangeably, the term *statement* technically refers to the keyword for a command, such as the *rem* statement–but it can also refer to a line of code that includes all the command text on that line. In some programming languages, such as Java, each statement must be terminated with a specific character. With Java, the terminator is a semicolon. The command line doesn't look for a specific terminator other than the end of the line, which is assumed when the command interpreter reads any of the following:

- Line break (such as when you press Shift+Enter)
- Carriage return and line break (such as when you press Enter)
- End-of-file marker

Now that we've discussed how to create scripts, let's look at common statements and commands you'll use in scripts, including the following:

- **Cls** Clears the console window and resets the screen buffer
- **Rem** Creates comments in scripts
- **Echo** Displays messages at the command line and turns command echoing on or off
- **@** Controls command echo on a line-by-line basis
- **Title** Sets the title for the command-shell window
- **Color** Sets the text and background colors used in the command-shell window

Clearing the Command-Shell Window

Clearing the command-shell window before writing script output is usually a good idea. You clear the command-shell window using the CLS command. Why not try it? At the command line, type **cls** and press Enter. The console window clears and the cursor is positioned in the top left corner of the window, immediately following the command prompt. All other text in the screen buffer is cleared.

You could add the CLS command to the sample script listed previously, as shown in this example:

```
cls
hostname
ver
ipconfig -all
```

Adding Comments to Scripts

You use the *rem* statement to add comments to your scripts. Every script you create should have comments that include the following details:

- When the script was created and last modified
- Who created the script
- What the script is used for
- How to contact the script creator
- Whether and where script output is stored

Not only are the answers to the questions of who, what, how, where, and when important for ensuring that the scripts you create can be used by other administrators, they can also help you remember what a particular script does, especially if weeks or months have passed since you last worked with the script. An example of a script that uses comments to answer these questions is shown as Listing 3-2.

Listing 3-2 Updated Sample Script with Comments

```
rem ************************
rem Script: SysInfo.bat
rem Creation Date: 2/28/2008
rem Last Modified: 3/15/2008
rem Author: William R. Stanek
rem E-mail: williamstanek@aol.com
rem ************************
rem Description: Displays system configuration information
rem              including system name, IP configuration
rem              and Windows version.
rem ************************
rem Files: Stores output in c:\data\current-sys.txt.
rem ************************

hostname > c:\data\current-sys.txt
ver >> c:\data\current-sys.txt
ipconfig -all >> c:\data\current-sys.txt
```

Later in this chapter, in the section titled "Passing Arguments to Scripts," I'll show you how to use your comments as automated help documentation. Before we get to that, however, keep in mind that you can also use *rem* statements to

- Insert explanatory text within scripts, such as documentation on how a procedure works.
- Prevent a command from executing. On the command line, add **rem** before the command to comment it out.
- Hide part of a line from interpretation. Add **rem** within a line to block interpretation of everything that follows the *rem* statement.

Managing Text Display and Command Echoing

The ECHO command has two purposes. You use the ECHO command to write text to the output, which can be the command shell or a text file. You also use the ECHO command to turn command echoing on or off. Normally, when you execute commands in a script, the commands as well as the resulting output of the command are displayed in the console window. This is called *command echoing*.

To use the ECHO command to display text, enter **echo** followed by the text to display, such as

```
echo The system host name is:
hostname
```

To use ECHO to control command echoing, type **echo off** or **echo on** as appropriate, such as

```
echo off
echo The system host name is:
hostname
```

Use output redirection to send output to a file rather than the command shell, as follows:

```
echo off
echo The system host name is: > current.txt
hostname >> current.txt
```

To experiment with suppressing command echoing, start a command shell, type **echo off**, and then enter other commands. You'll find that the command prompt is no longer displayed. Instead, you see only what you type into the console window and the resulting output from the commands you've entered. In scripts, the ECHO OFF command turns off command echoing as well as the command prompt. By adding the command ECHO OFF to your scripts, you keep the command-shell window or the output file from getting cluttered with commands when all you care about is the output from those commands.

Tip By the way, if you want to determine whether command echoing is enabled or disabled, type the ECHO command by itself. Give it a try. If command echoing is on, you'll see the message Echo Is On. Otherwise, you'll see the message Echo Is Off. Experiment with the ECHO OFF command in your scripts and you may detect a bit of a problem here. If the ECHO OFF command turns off command echoing, how do you prevent the ECHO OFF command itself from echoing? Don't worry; that's discussed in the next section.

Real World Other command-line programmers frequently ask me how to get a blank line to echo in the command shell. You might think that putting the ECHO command on a line by itself would do the job, but it doesn't. Typing **echo** on a line by itself displays the status of command echoing, as mentioned in the previous tip. Typing **echo** followed by a space doesn't work either, because the Windows command line treats spaces (in this situation) as meaningless, and you get the same results as typing **echo** followed by nothing at all. To get ECHO to display a blank line, you must enter **echo** and a period (**echo.**). The period is part of the command text and there is no space between the period and the ECHO command.

Fine-Tuning Command Echo with @

The @ command prevents commands from echoing to the output on a line-by-line basis; you can think of it as a line-specific *echo off* statement. You could use @ to turn off command echoing like this:

```
@echo The system host name is:
@hostname
```

Using @, the output that shows the command prompt and commands like this:

```
C:\>echo The system host name is:
The system host name is:

C:\>hostname
mailer1
```

becomes

```
The system host name is:
mailer1
```

But the real value of @ is that it allows you to tell the command shell not to display the command prompt or ECHO OFF command, and thereby ensures that the only output of your script is the output of the commands you enter. Here is an example of a script that uses @ to hide the ECHO OFF command so that it isn't displayed in the output:

```
@echo off
echo The system host name is:
hostname
```

The output from this script is

```
The system host name is:
mailer1
```

> **Tip** I recommend using *@echo off* at the beginning of all your command-line scripts. By the way, if you start a command shell and type **@echo off**, you can turn off the display of the command prompt as well.

Setting the Console Window Title and Colors

If you're going to take the time to write a script, you might as well add a few special features to jazz it up. Some of the basic techniques that I've already discussed are using the ECHO OFF command and clearing the console window before you write output. You may also want to set a title for the window or change the colors the window uses.

The title bar for the command shell is located at the top of the console window. Normally, this title bar displays Command Prompt or the file path to the command shell. You can customize the title using the TITLE command. This command works much like the ECHO command in that it displays whatever text follows it on the console's title bar. For example, if you wanted to set the title of the current console to System Information, you would enter the following at the command line:

```
title System Information
```

Not only can you use the TITLE command to show the name of the script that is running, but you can also use TITLE to show the progress of the script as it executes, such as

```
rem add blocks of work commands
title Gathering Information

rem add blocks of logging commands
title Logging System Information
```

By default, the console window displays white text on a black background. As you learned in Chapter 1, "Overview of the Windows Command Line," you can modify this behavior using the Colors tab of the Command Prompt Properties dialog box. You can also set console colors by using the COLOR command. You do this by passing the command a two-digit hexadecimal code. The first digit corresponds to the background color and the second digit corresponds to the text color, as the following example, which sets the text to blue and the background color to green:

```
color 21
```

The color codes you can use with the COLOR command are shown in Table 3-1. Keep in mind that you can't set the text and background colors to the same value. If you try to do this, the color doesn't change. Additionally, you can restore the default colors at any time by using the COLOR command without any arguments, like so:

```
color
```

Table 3-1 Color Codes for the Command-Shell Window

Code	Color	Code	Color
0	Black	8	Gray
1	Blue	9	Light Blue
2	Green	A	Light Green
3	Aqua	B	Light Aqua
4	Red	C	Light Red
5	Purple	D	Light Purple
6	Yellow	E	Light Yellow
7	White	F	Bright White

Passing Arguments to Scripts

As with most command-line utilities, you can pass arguments to scripts when they are started. You use arguments to set special parameters in a script or to pass along information needed by the script. Each argument should follow the script name and be separated by a space (and enclosed in quotation marks if necessary). In the following example, a script named *check-sys* is passed the arguments *mailer1* and *full*:

```
check-sys mailer1 full
```

Each value passed along to a script can be examined using formal parameters. The script name itself is represented by the parameter *%0*. The parameter *%1* represents the first argument passed in to the script, *%2* the second, and so on until *%9* for the ninth argument. For example, if you create a script called *check-sys* and then use the following command to call the script:

```
check-sys mailer1 full actual
```

you would find that the related parameter values are

- *%0 – check-sys*
- *%1 – mailer1*
- *%2 – full*
- *%3 – actual*

You access arguments in scripts using the parameter name: *%0* for the script name, *%1* for the first script parameter, and so on. For example, if you wanted to display the script name and the first argument passed to the script, you could enter the following:

```
echo %0
echo %1
```

If you pass in more than nine parameters, the additional parameters are not lost. Instead, they are stored in a special parameter: %* (percent + asterisk). The %*

parameter represents all arguments passed to the script and you can use the SHIFT command to examine additional parameters. If you call SHIFT without arguments, the script parameters are shifted by 1. This means the related value for *%0* is discarded and replaced by the related value for *%1*, and the related value for *%2* becomes the related value for *%1*, and so on. You can also specify where shifting begins so that you can retain previous parameters if necessary. For example, if you use the following command, *%4* becomes *%3*, *%5* becomes *%4*, and so on. But *%0*, *%1*, and *%2* are unaffected:

```
shift /3
```

Getting Acquainted with Variables

In command-line scripting, what we commonly call variables are more properly called *environment variables*. Environment variables can come from many sources. Some variables are built into the operating system or derived from the system hardware during startup. These variables, called *built-in system variables*, are available to all Windows processes regardless of whether anyone is logged on interactively. System variables can also come from the Windows Registry. Other variables are set during logon and are called *built-in user variables*. The built-in user variables available are the same, no matter who is logged on to the computer. As you might expect, they are valid only during an actual logon session–that is, when a user is logged on.

You can see a listing of all the variables known in the current instance of the command shell by typing **set** at the prompt. In addition to the normal system and user variables, you can create variables whenever Windows is running, which is exactly what you'll do when you program in the command shell. You define variables for the current instance of the command shell using the SET command and the following syntax:

```
set variable_name=variable_value
```

such as

```
set working=C:\Work\Data
set value=5
set string="Hello World"
```

Some variables, including system and user environment variables, have special meaning in the command shell. These variables include *path*, *computername*, *homedrive*, and many other important environment variables. One environment variable that you should learn more about is *errorlevel*, which tracks the exit code of the most recently used command. If the command executes normally, the error level is zero (0). If an error occurs while executing the command, the error level is set to an appropriate nonzero value. Error values include

- **1** Indicates a general error
- **2** Indicates an execution error, meaning the command failed to execute properly

- **–2** Indicates a math error, such as when you create a number that is too large for the command shell to handle

You can work with the *errorlevel* variable in several ways. You can check for a specific error condition, such as

```
if "%ERRORLEVEL%"=="2" echo "An error occurred!"
```

Or, you can use the following special syntax and check for a condition equal to or greater than the specified exit code:

```
if errorlevel 2 echo "An error occurred!"
```

> **Note** You'll see more on *errorlevel* and *if* statements later in the chapter in the sections titled "Substituting Variable Values" and "Command-Line Selection Statements."

When you are finished working with variables, it's good form to dispose of them. You do this to free memory used by the variable and prevent problems or unexpected results if you accidentally refer to the variable in the future. To clear out a variable, you simply set the variable equal to nothing, such as

```
set working=
```

Now the variable is cleared out of memory and is no longer available.

Using Variables in Scripts

In scripts, you'll use variables to store values as you perform various types of operations. Unlike most programming languages, you cannot declare a variable in a command-line script without simultaneously assigning it a value. This makes a certain amount of sense because from a practical point of view, there's no reason to have a variable that contains nothing. The sections that follow discuss key concepts for working with variables, including

- Variable names
- Variable values
- Variable substitution
- Variable scope

Naming Variables

The command shell tracks variable names in the case you use but doesn't care about the case when you are working with the variable. This means variable names aren't case-sensitive but are case-aware. Beyond this, very few restrictions apply to variable names and you can use just about any combination of letters, numbers, and characters to form the variable name. In fact, all the following variable names are technically valid:

```
2six
85
!
?
```

Why in the world you'd want to use such horrendous variable names, however, is beyond me. With that said, how should you name your variables? Well, the most important rule to keep in mind is that variable names should be descriptive.
Use names such as

```
System-name
CurrentStats
mergetotal
Net_Address
```

These descriptive variable names are helpful when you or someone else needs to modify the script. And notice that you have many ways to create multiple-word variable names. Although you are free to use whatever style you like, most programmers format multiword variable names with a lowercase initial letter on the first word and uppercase initial letter on each subsequent word. Why? Simply because this is a standard naming convention. Following this convention, the variable names listed previously would be

```
systemName
currentStats
mergeTotal
netAddress
```

> **Note** Keep in mind that the command shell doesn't care about the case. Variable names are case-aware but they're not case-sensitive. This means that you could refer to the *systemName* variable as *SYSTEMNAME*, *systemname*, or even *sYStemNAMe*.

Setting Variable Values

As discussed previously, you define new variables using the following syntax, where *variable_name* is the variable name and *variable_value* is its related value:

```
set variable_name=variable_value
```

Spaces are valid in both names and values. So only use spaces around the equal sign (=) if you want the name and/or the value to include these spaces.

Unlike many programming languages, the command shell doesn't differentiate between various data types. All variables are stored as character strings. This is true even when you set the variable value to a number. Thus, the following values are stored as strings:

```
Current status:
311
```

```
"Error!"
12.75
```

using commands such as:

```
set varA=Current status:
set varB=311
set varC="Error!"
set varD=12.75
```

Don't forget that some characters are reserved in the command line, including @ < > & | ^. Before you use these characters, you must escape them with the caret symbol (^)– no matter where they occur in the variable value. (This is discussed in Chapter 2, "Getting the Most from the Command Line.") For example, to set these literal string values:

```
2 & 3 = 5
2^3
```

you must set the variable value as follows:

```
2 ^& 3 = 5
2^^3
```

using statements such as

```
set example1=2 ^& 3 = 5
set example2=2^^3
```

> **Note** An odd thing happens if you try to echo the example values. Instead of the equations you expect, you get either an error or an odd value. What is happening here is that when you echo the value, the special characters are reparsed. If you want to set a variable to a value that includes a special character and also be able to display this value to users, you must use three escape codes, meaning that you would use *set example1=2 ^^^& 3 = 5* or *set example2=2^^^^3*. This is necessary because the value is double parsed (once when the value is set and once when the value is displayed).

Substituting Variable Values

Variables wouldn't be very useful if the only way you could access them was with the SET command. Fortunately, you can access variable values in other ways. One of these ways is to use variable substitution to compare a variable name with its actual value. You saw this type of substitution at work in the following line from a previous example in this chapter:

```
if "%ERRORLEVEL%"=="2" echo "An error occurred!"
```

Here, you are determining whether the value of the *errorlevel* environment variable is equal to 2 and, if it is, you display text stating that an error occurred. The percent signs surrounding the variable name tell the command shell you are referencing a variable. Without these percent signs, Windows would perform a literal comparison of

"ERRORLEVEL" and "2". Note also the use of quotation marks in the example. The quotation marks ensure an exact comparison of string values.

Another way to use substitution is to replace a variable name with its actual value. For example, you might want to create a script that can be run on different computers, so rather than hard-coding the path to the system root directory as C:\Windows, you could use the environment variable *systemroot*, which references the system root of the particular computer being accessed. With this in mind, you use the following line of code in your script:

```
cd %SYSTEMROOT%\System32
```

instead of this line of code:

```
cd C:\Windows\System32
```

You can also use variable substitution when you are assigning variable values, such as

```
systemPath=%SystemRoot%\System32
```

Variable substitution can be quite powerful. Consider the code snippet shown in Listing 3-3.

Listing 3-3 Sample Script Header

```
@echo off
@if not "%OS%"=="Windows_NT" goto :EXIT
@if "%1"=="" (set INFO=echo && set SEXIT=1) else (set INFO=rem && set
SEXIT=0)

%INFO% ************************
%INFO% Script: SystemInfo.bat
%INFO% Creation Date: 2/28/2008
%INFO% Last Modified: 3/15/2008
%INFO% Author: William R. Stanek
%INFO% E-mail: williamstanek@aol.com
%INFO% ************************
%INFO% Description: Displays system configuration information
%INFO%              including system name, IP configuration
%INFO%              and Windows version.
%INFO% ************************
%INFO% Files: Stores output in c:\current-sys.txt.
%INFO% ************************

@if "%SEXIT%"=="1" goto :EXIT

@title "Configure Scheduling..."
cls
color 07
```

Listing 3-3 is a standard header that I use in some of my scripts. The first *if* statement checks to see what operating system is running. If it is Windows 2000 or later, the script continues execution. Otherwise a *goto* subroutine is called. The second *if* statement checks the value of the first argument passed in to the script. If the script is called with no arguments, instances of *%INFO%* are replaced with *echo*, which writes the script documentation to the output. If the script is called with one or more arguments, instances of *%INFO%* are replaced with *rem* to designate that the associated lines are comments.

> **Note** Don't worry if you don't understand the example completely. You'll learn all about conditional execution and subroutines in the sections titled, "Command-Line Selection Statements" and "Creating Subroutines and Procedures" later in the chapter.

Localizing Variable Scope

Changes you make to variables in the command shell using *set* are localized, meaning that they apply only to the current command shell instance or to command shells started within the current command shell (nested command shells) and are not available to other system processes. Further, when you exit the command shell in which variables were created, the variables no longer exist.

Sometimes you may want to limit the scope of variables even further than their current command-shell process. To do this, you can create a local scope within a script that ensures that any variable changes are localized to that specific area within the script. Later, you can end the local scope and restore the environment to its original settings.

You can mark the start of a local scope within a script using the SETLOCAL command and then end the local scope with an ENDLOCAL command. Several events take place when you use these commands. The call to SETLOCAL creates a snapshot of the environment. Any changes you make within the scope are then localized and discarded when you call ENDLOCAL. The following example uses SETLOCAL and ENDLOCAL:

```
@echo off
set sysCount=0
set deviceCount=0

rem Start localization
setlocal
set sysCount=5
set deviceCount=5
echo Local count: %sysCount% system edits ^& %deviceCount% device checks
endlocal

echo Count: %sysCount% system edits ^& %deviceCount% device checks
```

The output of the script is

```
Local count: 5 system edits & 5 device checks
Count: 0 system edits & 0 device checks
```

As you can see, local scopes behave much like nested command shells. As with the nested command shells, you can nest several layers of localization. And though each layer inherits the environment settings of its parent, any changes in the nested layer are not reflected in the parent environment.

Using Mathematical Expressions

At times, you'll want to perform some kind of mathematical operation in your scripts and assign the results to a variable. As with most programming languages, the command shell allows you to write mathematical expressions using a variety of operators, including the following:

- Arithmetic operators to perform standard mathematical operations (such as addition, subtraction, multiplication, and division)
- Assignment operators that combine an assignment operation (symbolized by the equal sign) with an arithmetic operation
- Comparison operators that compare values and are usually used with *if* statements
- Bitwise operators that allow you to manipulate the sequences of binary values

Math operations are performed using SET with the */A* (arithmetic) parameter, such as

```
set /a theTotal=18+2
set /a theTotal=18*2
set /a theTotal=18/2
```

All mathematical expressions are evaluated using 32-bit signed integer arithmetic. This allows for values -2^{32} to $2^{32}-1$. If you exceed this range, you'll get an arithmetic error (code −2) instead of the intended value.

The most commonly used operators are those for arithmetic, assignment, and comparison. Arithmetic and assignment operators are discussed in the sections that follow. Comparison operators are discussed in the section titled "Making Comparisons in If Statements" later in this chapter. Pay particular attention to the additional discussions on operator precedence and simulating exponents in scripts.

Working with Arithmetic and Assignment Operators

You use arithmetic operators to perform basic math operations on numerical values. These values can be expressed literally as a number, such as 5, or as a variable that contains the value you want to work with, such as *%TOTAL%*.

Table 3-2 summarizes the available arithmetic and assignment operators. Most of the arithmetic operators are fairly straightforward. You use * in multiplication, / in division, + in addition, and − in subtraction. You use the equal sign (=) to assign values to variables. You use % (modulus) to obtain the remainder from division. For example, if you divide 8 into 60, the answer is 7 Remainder 4; the value 4 is what the result would be if you use the modulus operator.

Examples of working with arithmetic operators follow:

```
set /a theCount=5+3
set /a theCount=%nServers% + %nWstations%
set /a theCount=%nServers% - 1
```

> **Tip** Earlier, I stated that everything stored in a variable is a string, and that remains true. However, the command shell can detect when a string contains only numerals, and this is what allows you to use variables in expressions. The key detail to remember is to use the proper syntax for substitution, which is *%variableName%*.

Table 3-2 Arithmetic and Assignment Operators

Arithmetic Operators	Assignment Operators
+ (Addition)	+= (Increment, or add and assign)
- (Subtraction)	-= (Decrement, or subtract and assign)
* (Multiplication)	*= (Scale up, or multiply and assign)
/ (Division)	/= (Scale down, or divide and assign)
% (Modulus)	%= (Modulus and assign)

You use assignment operators to increment, decrement, scale up, or scale down. These operators combine arithmetic and assignment operation functions. For example, the += operator is used to increment a value and combines the effects of the + operator and the = operator. Thus, the following two expressions are equivalent and yield identical results when entered at the command line:

```
set /a total=total+1
set /a total+=1
```

Understanding Operator Precedence

One thing you should understand when working with mathematic operations is *operator precedence*. Operator precedence determines what happens when the command shell must evaluate an expression that involves more than one operator. For example:

```
set /a total=8+3*4
```

If evaluated from left to right, this expression equals 44 (8+3=11, 11*4=44). But as in standard mathematics, that's not how the command line evaluates the expression. Instead, the command shell evaluates the expression as 20 (3*4=12, 8+12=20) because the precedence of operations is the following:

1. Modulus
2. Multiplication and division
3. Addition and subtraction

Note When an expression contains multiple operations at the same precedence level, these operations are performed from left to right. Hence, set /a total=10-4+2 equals 8 (10-4=6, 6+2=8).

However, as with standard mathematics, you can use parenthetical grouping to ensure that numbers are processed in a certain way. This means you can use the expression

```
set /a total=(8+3)*4
```

to ensure that the command-line interprets the expression as (8+3=11, 11*4=44).

Simulating Exponents

Although you can perform many mathematical operations at the command line, you have no way to raise values to exponents. You can, however, perform these operations manually. For example, the easiest way to get a value for 2^3 is to enter

```
set /a total=2*2*2
```

The result is 8. Similarly, you can get a value for 10^5 by entering

```
set /a total=10*10*10*10*10
```

The result is 100,000.

Command-Line Selection Statements

Now that you know how to work with variables and form expressions, let's look at something more advanced: selection statements used with the command line. When you want to control the flow of execution based upon conditions known only at run time, you'll use

- *if* to execute a statement when a condition is true, such as if the operating system is Windows 2000 or later. Otherwise, the statement is bypassed.
- *if not* to execute a statement when a condition is false, such as if a system doesn't have a C:\Windows directory. Otherwise, the statement is bypassed.
- *if...else* to execute a statement if a condition is matched (true or false) and to otherwise execute the second statement.

Although some of the previous examples in this chapter have used conditional execution, we haven't discussed the syntax for these statements or the associated comparison operators. If your background doesn't include programming, you probably will be surprised by the power and flexibility of these statements.

Using If

The *if* statement is used for conditional branching. It can be used to route script execution through two different paths. Its basic syntax is

```
if condition (statement1) [else (statement2)]
```

Here each statement can be a single command or multiple commands chained, piped, or grouped within parentheses. The condition is any expression that returns a Boolean value of True or False when evaluated. The *else* clause is optional, meaning you can also use the following syntax:

```
if condition (statement)
```

> **Tip** Technically, parentheses aren't required, but using them is a good idea, especially if the condition includes an *echo* statement or a command with parameters. If you don't use parentheses in these instances, everything that follows the statement on the current line will be interpreted as part of the statement, which usually results in an error.

The *if* statement works like this: If the *condition* is true, *statement1* is executed. Otherwise, *statement2* is executed (if the *else* clause is provided). In no case will both the *if* and the *else* clauses be executed. Consider the following example:

```
if "%1"=="1" (echo is one) else (echo is not one)
```

Here, if the first parameter passed to the script is 1, "is one" is written to the output. Otherwise, "is not one" is written to the output.

The command shell expects only one statement after each condition. Typically, the statement is a single command to execute. If you want to execute multiple commands, you'll need to use one of the command piping, chaining, or group techniques, as in this example:

```
if "%1"=="1" (hostname & ver & ipconfig /all) else (netstat -a)
```

Here all three commands between the first set of parentheses will execute if the first parameter value is 1.

Using If Not

When you want to execute a statement only if a condition is false, you can use *if not*. The basic syntax is

```
if not condition (statement1) [else (statement2)]
```

Here the command shell evaluates the *condition*. If it is false, the command shell executes the statement. Otherwise, *statement1* doesn't execute and the command shell proceeds to *statement2*, if present. The *else* clause is optional, meaning you can also use the following syntax:

```
if not condition (statement1)
```

Consider the following example:

```
if not errorlevel 0 (echo An error has occurred!) & (goto :EXIT)
```

Here you check for error conditions other than zero. If no error has occurred (meaning the error level is zero), the command shell continues to the next statement. Otherwise, the command shell writes "An error has occurred!" to the output and exits the script. (You'll learn all about *goto* and subroutines later in the chapter.)

Using If Defined and If Not Defined

The final types of *if* statements you can use are *if defined* and *if not defined*. These statements are designed to help you check for the existence of variables, and their respective syntaxes are

```
if defined variable statement
```

and

```
if not defined variable statement
```

Both statements are useful in your shell scripts. In the first case, you execute a command if the specified variable exists. In the second case, you execute a command if the specified variable does not exist. Consider the following example:

```
if defined numServers (echo Servers: %numServers%)
```

Here, if the *numServers* variable is defined, the script writes output. Otherwise, the script continues to the next statement.

Nesting Ifs

A nested *if* is an *if* statement within an *if* statement. Nested *ifs* are very common in programming, and command-shell programming is no exception. When you nest *if* statements, pay attention to the following points:

- Use parentheses to define blocks of code and the @ symbol to designate the start of the nested *if* statement.
- Remember that an *else* statement always refers to the nearest *if* statement that is within the same block as the *else* statement and that is not already associated with another *else* statement.

Here is an example:

```
if "%1"=="1" (
@if "%2"=="2" (hostname & ver) else (ver)) else (hostname & ver &
netstat -a)
```

The first *else* statement is associated with if "%2"=="2". The final *else* statement is associated with if "%1"=="1".

Making Comparisons in If Statements

Frequently, the expression used to control *if* statements will involve comparison operators, as shown in previous examples. The most basic type of string comparison is when you compare two strings using the equality operator (=), such as

```
if stringA==stringB statement
```

Here, you are performing a literal comparison of the strings; if they are exactly identical, the command statement is executed. This syntax works for literal strings but is not ideal for scripts. Parameters and arguments may contain spaces or there may be no value at all for a variable. In this case, you may get an error if you perform literal comparisons. Instead, use double quotation marks to perform a string comparison and prevent most errors, such as

```
if "%varA%"=="%varB%" statement
```

or

```
if "%varA%"=="string" statement
```

String comparisons are always case-sensitive unless you specify otherwise with the */i* switch. The */i* switch tells the command shell to ignore the case in the comparison, and you can use it as follows:

```
if /I "%1"=="a" (echo A) else (echo is not A)
```

To perform more advanced equality tests, you'll need to use the comparison operators shown in Table 3-3. These operators are used in place of the standard equality operator, such as

```
if "%varA%" equ "%varB" (echo The values match!)
```

Table 3-3 Using Comparison Operators

Operator	Description
equ	Checks for equality and evaluates to true if the values are equal
neq	Checks for inequality and evaluates to true if the values are not equal
lss	Checks for less-than condition and evaluates to true if *value1* is less than *value2*
leq	Checks for less-than or equal-to condition and evaluates to true if *value1* is less than or equal to *value2*
gtr	Checks for greater-than condition and evaluates to true if *value1* is greater than *value2*
geq	Checks for greater-than or equal-to condition, and evaluates to true if *value1* is greater than or equal to *value2*

Command Line Iteration Statements

When you want to execute a command or a series of commands repeatedly, you'll use the *for* statement. The *for* statement is a powerful construct, and before you skip this section because you think you know how the *for* statement works, think again. The *for* statement is designed specifically to work with the command-shell environment and is very different from any other *for* statement you may have worked with in other programming languages. Unlike most other *for* statements, the one in the command line is designed to help you iterate through groups of files and directories, and to parse text files, strings, and command output on a line-by-line basis.

Iteration Essentials

The command shell has several different forms of *for* statements. Still, the basic form of all *for* statements is

```
for iterator do (statement)
```

Here the iterator is used to control the execution of the *for* loop. For each step or element in the iterator, the specified *statement* is executed. The *statement* can be a single command or multiple commands chained, piped, or grouped within parentheses.

The iterator usually consists of an initialization variable and a set of elements to execute against, such as a group of files or a range of values to step through. Initialization variables are essentially placeholders for the values you want to work with. When you work with initialization variables, keep in mind the following:

- Iterator variables only exist within the context of a *for* loop.
- Iterator variable names must be in the range from a to z or A to Z, such as *%%A*, *%%B*, or *%%C*.
- Iterator variable names are case-sensitive, meaning *%%a* is different from *%%A*.

As Table 3-4 shows, the various structures used with *for* statements have specific purposes and forms. When the *for* statement is initialized, iterator variables, such as *%%B*, are replaced with their actual values. These values come from the element set specified in the *for* statement and could consist of a list of files, a list of directories, a range of values, and so on.

Table 3-4 Forms for Iteration

Iteration Purpose	Form Syntax
Sets of files	for *%%variable* in (fileSet) do *statement*
Sets of directories	for /D *%%variable* in (directorySet) do *statement*
Files in subdirectories	for /R [*path*] *%%variable* in (fileSet) do *statement*
Stepping through a series of values	for /L *%%variable* in (*stepRange*) do *statement*
Parsing text files, strings, and command output	for /F ["*options*"] *%%variable* in (*source*) do *statement*

Real World The forms provided are *for* scripts. You can also use *for* statements interactively at the command line. In this case, use *%variable* instead of *%%variable*. Beyond this, *for* statements within scripts or at the command line are handled in precisely the same way.

Stepping Through a Series of Values

The "traditional" way to use *for* statements is to step through a range of values and perform tasks using these values. You can do this in the command shell. The basic syntax of this type of *for* loop is

```
for /l %%variable in (start,step,end) do (statement)
```

This type of *for* statement operates as follows. First, the command shell initializes internal *start*, *step*, and *end* variables to the values you've specified. Next, it compares the start value with the end value to determine whether the statement should be executed, yielding a true condition if the start value can be incremented or decremented as specified in the step and a false condition otherwise. In the case of a true condition, the command shell executes the statement using the start value and then increments or decrements the start value by the step value specified. Afterward it repeats this process. In the case of a false condition, the command shell exits the *for* statement, moving on to the next statement in the script.

Consider the following example that counts from 0 to 10 by increments of 2:

```
for /l %%B in (0,2,10) do echo %%B
```

The output is

```
0
2
4
6
8
10
```

You can also use a negative step value to move through a range in decreasing values. You could count from 10 to 0 by twos as follows:

```
for /l %%B in (10,-2,0) do echo %%B
```

The output is

```
10
8
6
4
2
0
```

Iterating Through Groups of Files

A more powerful way to use *for* statements in the command shell is to use them to work with files and directories. The *for* statement syntax for working with groups of files is

```
for %%variable in (fileSet) do (statement)
```

Here you use *fileSet* to specify a set of files that you want to work with. A file set can be any of the following:

- Individual files as specified by a filename, such as MyFile.txt
- Groups of files specified with wildcards, such as *.txt
- Multiple files or groups of files with spaces separating file names, such as *.txt *.rtf *.doc

Now that you know the basic rules, working with files is easy. For example, if you want to list all text files in an application directory, you can use the following command in a script:

```
for %%B in (C:\Working\*.txt) do (echo %%B)
```

Here *B* is the initialization variable, *C:\Working*.txt* specifies that you want to work with all text files in the C:\Working directory, and the statement to execute is *echo %%B*, which tells the command shell to display the current value of *%%B* each time it iterates through the *for* loop. The result is that a list of the text files in the directory is written to the output.

You could extend this example to examine all .txt, .rtf, and .doc files like this:

```
for %%B in (%AppDir%\*.txt %AppDir%\*.rtf %AppDir%\*.doc) do (echo %%B)
```

You can also use multiple commands using piping, grouping, and chaining techniques, such as

```
for %%B in (%AppDir%\*.txt %AppDir%\*.rtf %AppDir%\*.doc) do (echo %%B &
move C:\Data)
```

Here you list the .txt, .rtf, and .doc files in the location specified by the *AppDir* variable and then move the files to the C:\Data directory.

Iterating Through Directories

If you want to work with directories rather than files, you can use the following *for* statement style:

```
for /d %%variable in (directorySet) do (statement)
```

Here you use *directorySet* to specify the group of directories you want to work with. Iterating directories works exactly like iterating files, except you specify directory paths rather than file paths. If you wanted to list all the base directories under *%SystemRoot%*, you would do this as follows:

```
for /d %%B in (%SystemRoot%\*) do echo %%B
```

On Windows Server 2003, a partial result list would be similar to

```
C:\Windows\AppPatch
C:\Windows\Cluster
C:\Windows\Config
C:\Windows\Cursors
C:\Windows\Debug
```

> **Note** Note that the *for /d* loop iterates through the specified directory set but doesn't include subdirectories of those directories. To access subdirectories (and indeed the whole directory tree structure), you use *for /r* loops, which I'll discuss in a moment.

You can specify multiple base directories by separating the directory names with spaces, such as

```
for /d %%B in (%SystemRoot% %SystemRoot%\*) do echo %%B
```

Here you examine the *%SystemRoot%* directory itself and then the directories immediately below it. So now your list of directories would start with C:\Windows (if this is the system root) and continue with the other directories listed previously.

You can also combine file and directory iteration techniques to perform actions against all files in a directory set, such as

```
for /d %%B in (%APPDATA% %APPDATA%\*) do (
@for %%C in ("%%B\*.txt") do echo %%C)
```

The first *for* statement returns a list of top-level directories under *%APPDATA%*, which also includes *%APPDATA%* itself. The second *for* statement iterates all .txt files in each of these directories. Note the @ symbol before the second *for* statement. As with *if* statements, this indicates the second *for* statement is nested and is required to ensure proper execution. The double quotations with the file set (*"%%B*.txt"*) ensure that directory and filenames containing spaces are handled properly.

Because you'll often want to work with subdirectories as well as directories, the command shell provides *for /r* statements. Using *for /r* statements, you can examine an entire directory tree from a starting point specified as a path. The syntax is

```
for /r [path] %%variable in (fileSet) do (statement)
```

Here *path* sets the base of the directory tree you want to work with, such as C:\. The path is not required, however, and if the path is omitted, the current working directory is assumed.

Using a *for /r* statement, you could extend the previous example to list all .txt files on the C: drive without needing a double *for* loop, as shown here:

```
for /r C:\ %%B in (*.txt) do echo %%B
```

As you can see, *for /r* statements are simpler and more powerful than double *for* loops. You can even combine */r* and */d* without needing a double loop. In this example, you obtain a listing of all directories and subdirectories under *%SystemRoot%*:

```
for /r %SystemRoot% /d %%B in (*) do echo %%B
```

Parsing File Content and Output

Just as you can work with file and directory names, you can also work with the contents of files and the output of commands. To do this, you'll use the following *for* statement style:

```
for /f ["options"] %%variable in (source) do (statement)
```

Here, *options* sets the text-matching options; *source* specifies where the text comes from, which could be a text file, a string, or command output; and *statement* specifies what commands should be performed on matching text. Each line of text in the source is handled like a record, where fields in the record are delimited by a specific character, such as a tab or a space (which are the default delimiters). Using substitution, the command shell then replaces placeholder variables in the statement with actual values.

Consider the following line of text from a source file:

```
William Stanek Engineering Williams@adatum.com 3408
```

One way of thinking of this line of text is as a record with five fields:

- **First Name** William
- **Last Name** Stanek
- **Department** Engineering
- **E-Mail Address** Williams@adatum.com
- **Phone Extension** 3408

To parse this and other similar lines in the associated file, you could use the following *for* statement:

```
for /f "tokens=1-5" %%A in (current-users.txt) do (
@echo Name: %%A %%B Depart: %%C E-mail: %%D Ext: %%E)
```

Here you specify that you want to work with the first five fields (token fields separated by spaces or tabs by default) and identified by iterator variables, starting with *%%A*, which means the first field is *%%A*, the second *%%B*, and so on. The resulting output would look like this:

```
Name: William Stanek Depart: Engineering E-Mail: Williams@adatum.com Ext:
3408
```

Table 3-5 shows a complete list of options that you can use. Examples and descriptions of the examples are included.

Table 3-5 Options for File Content and Command Output Parsing

Option	Option Description	Example	Example Description
eol	Sets the end-of-line comment character. Everything after the end-of-line comment character is considered to be a comment.	"eol=#"	Sets # as the end-of-line comment character.
skip	Sets the number of lines to skip at the beginning of files.	"skip=5"	Tells the command shell to skip lines 1 through 5 in the source file.
delims	Sets delimiters to use for fields. The defaults are space and tab.	"delims=, . :"	Specifies that commas, periods, and colons are delimiters.
tokens	Sets which token fields from each source line are to be used. You can specify up to 26 tokens provided that you start with a or A as the first iterator variable. By default, only the first token is examined.	"tokens=1, 3" "tokens=2-5"	First example sets fields to use as 1 and 3. Second example sets fields 2, 3, 4, and 5 as fields to use.
usebackq	Specifies that you can use quotation marks in the source designator: double quotation marks for file names, back quotation marks for command to execute, and single quotation marks for a literal string.	"*usebackq*"	Enables the option.

To see how additional options can be used, consider the following example:

```
for /f "skip=3 eol=; tokens=3-5" %%C in (current-users.txt) do (
@echo Depart: %%C E-mail: %%D Ext: %%E)
```

Here, three options are used. The *skip* option is used to skip the first three lines of the file. The *eol* option is used to specify the end-of-line comment character as a semicolon (;). Finally, the *tokens* option specifies that tokens 3 through 5 should be placed in iterator variables, starting with *%%C*.

With tokens, you can specify which fields you want to work with in many different ways. Here are some examples:

- **tokens=2,3,7** Use fields 2, 3, and 7.
- **tokens=3-5** Use fields 3, 4, and 5.
- **tokens=*** Examine each line in its entirety and do not break into fields.

When you work with text files, you should note that all blank lines in text files are skipped and that multiple source files can be specified with wild cards or by entering the file names in a space-separated list, such as

```
for /f "skip=3 eol=; tokens=3-5" %%C in (data1.txt data2.txt) do (
@echo Depart: %%C E-mail: %%D Ext: %%E)
```

If a filename contains a space or you want to execute a command, specify the *usebackq* option and quotation marks, such as

```
for /f "tokens=3-5 usebackq" %%C in ("user data.txt") do (
@echo Depart: %%C E-mail: %%D Ext: %%E)
```

or

```
for /f "tokens=3-5 usebackq" %%C in (`type "user data.txt"`) do (
@echo Depart: %%C E-mail: %%D Ext: %%E)
```

> **Tip** Remember the backquote (`) is used with commands and the single quotation mark (') is used with string literals. In print, these characters no doubt look very similar. However, on a standard keyboard, the backquote (`) is on the same key as the tilde (~) and the single quotation mark (') is on the same key as a double quotation mark (").

> **Note** In the second example, I use the TYPE command to write the contents of the file to standard output. This is meant to be an example of using a command with the backquote.

Speaking of quotation marks, you use quotation marks when you want to process strings and variable values. Here, you enclose the string or variable name you want to work with in double quotation marks to ensure that the string or variable can be evaluated properly. You do not, however, need to use the *usebackq* option.

Consider the following example:

```
set value=All,Some,None
for /f "delims=, tokens=1,3" %%A in ("%VALUE%") do (echo %%A %%B)
```

The output is

```
All None
```

Creating Subroutines and Procedures

Normally, the Windows command shell executes scripts line by line, starting at the beginning of the file and continuing until the end of the file. You can change the order of execution. To do this, you use either of the following techniques.

- **Subroutines** With subroutines, you jump to a label within the current script, and execution proceeds to the end of the file.
- **Procedures** With procedures, you call another script and execution of the called script proceeds to the end of its file, and then control returns to the line following the call statement in the original script.

As you can see, the difference between a subroutine and a procedure is primarily in what you want to do. Additionally, while arguments passed in to the script are available in a *goto* subroutine directly, the list of arguments within a called procedure is changed to include the procedure name rather than the script name as argument 0 (*%0*).

Using Subroutines

Subroutines have two parts:

- A *goto* call that specifies the subroutine to which you want to jump
- A label that designates the start of the subroutine

Consider the following subroutine call:

```
if "%1"=="1" goto SUB1
```

Here if the first parameter passed into the script is a 1, the subroutine called *SUB*1 is called and the command shell would jump to the corresponding subroutine label. To create a label, you enter a keyword on a line by itself, beginning with a colon, such as

```
:SUB1
```

Although labels can contain just about any valid type of character, you'll usually want to use alphanumeric characters, which make the labels easy to read when you or someone else is going through the code.

When you use *goto*, execution of the script resumes at the line following the target label and continues to the end of the file, unless it's necessary to process any procedure calls or *goto* statements encountered along the way. If the label is before the current position in the script, the command shell can go back to an earlier part of the script. This can create an endless loop (unless there is a control to bypass the *goto* statement). Here's an example of an endless loop:

```
:START
.
.
.
goto START
```

If the label is after the *goto* statement, you can skip commands and jump ahead to a new section of the script, such as

```
goto MIDDLE
.
.
.
:MIDDLE
```

Here, execution of the script jumps to the *:MIDDLE* label and continues to the end of the file. You cannot go back to the unexecuted commands unless you use another *goto* statement.

Sometimes you may not want to execute the rest of the script and instead will want to exit the script after executing subroutine statements. To do this, create an exit label and then go to the exit at the end of the routine, such as

```
goto MIDDLE
.
.
.
:MIDDLE
.
.
.
goto EXIT
.
.
.
:EXIT
```

Listing 3-4 shows a detailed example of working with *goto* and labels. In this example, the value of the script's first parameter determines what subroutine is executed. The first *if* statement handles the case when no parameter is passed in by displaying an error message and exiting. The *goto EXIT* statement following the *if* statements handles the case when an invalid parameter is passed in. Here, the script simply goes to the *:EXIT* label.

Listing 3-4 Using goto

```
>@echo off
if "%1"=="" (echo Error: No parameter passed with script!) & (goto
EXIT)
if "%1"=="1" goto SUBROUTINE1
if "%1"=="2" goto SUBROUTINE2
if "%1"=="3" goto SUBROUTINE3
goto EXIT

:SUBROUTINE1
echo In subroutine 1
goto EXIT

:SUBROUTINE2
```

```
echo In subroutine 2
goto EXIT

:SUBROUTINE3
echo In subroutine 3
goto EXIT

:EXIT
echo Exiting...
```

Tip Remember that if the label you call doesn't exist, you'll get an error when the end of the file is reached during the search for the nonexistent label, and then the script will exit without executing the other subsequent commands. Old-school command-shell programmers who have been at this for a long time, like me, like to use *goto EXIT* and then provide an actual *:EXIT* label, as shown in the previous example. However, the command interpreter also supports a target label of *:EOF*, which transfers control to the end of the file. This makes *:EOF* an easy way to exit a batch script without defining a label.

Using Procedures

You use procedures to call other scripts without exiting the current script. When you do this, the command shell executes the named script, executing its commands, and then control returns to the original script, starting with the first line following the original call. Consider the following example:

```
if "%1"=="1" call system-checks
if "%1"=="2" call C:\scripts\log-checks
```

Caution If you forget to use the *call* statement and reference a script name within a script, the second script executes, but control isn't returned to the caller.

Here the first call is made to a script expected to be in the current working directory or in the command path. The second call is made to a script with the file path c:\scripts\log-checks.

Any arguments passed to the original script are passed to the called script with one change: The list of arguments is updated to include the procedure name as argument 0 (%0). These procedure-specific arguments remain in effect until the end of the file is reached and control returns to the original script.

You can also pass arguments to the called script, such as

```
set Arg1=mailer1
set Arg2=dc2
set Arg3=web3
call system-checks Arg1 Arg2 Arg3
```

Now within the called script, the variables *Arg1*, *Arg2*, and *Arg3* are available.

Part II

Windows Systems Administration Using the Command Line

In this part:

Chapter 4

Deploying Windows Servers

When you are working with Windows Server 2008, you have many more configuration options than when you are working with Windows Vista. In this chapter, we'll look at these additional configuration options with a goal of helping you successfully deploy Windows servers using command-line tools or a combination of command-line and graphical tools.

Managing Server Configurations

With Windows Server 2008, you should carefully plan the server architecture before you deploy any new servers. As part of your planning, you should look closely at the software configuration that will be used and modify the hardware configuration accordingly to meet the related requirements of each individual server. You prepare servers for use by installing the operating system using one of two installation types:

- **Full-server installation** A full-server installation provides full functionality. You can configure a server using any allowed combination of roles, role services, and add-on features, and a full user interface is provided for management of the server. Use this installation option for deployments of Windows Server 2008 in which the server role may change over time.
- **Core-server installation** A core-server installation provides minimal functionality. You can configure a server using only a limited set of roles and a minimal user interface is provided for local management of the server. Use this installation option when you have dedicated servers for a specific server role or combination of roles and want to reduce the overhead caused by other services.

You choose the installation type when you install Windows Server 2008. While you can manage both installations remotely using any available and permitted remote administration technique, full-server and core-server installations are completely different when it comes to local console administration. Keep the following in mind:

- With a full-server installation, you have a full user interface that includes a full desktop environment for local console management of the server, and you can deploy servers with any permitted combination of roles, role services, and features.
- With a core-server installation, you have a minimal install that supports a limited set of roles and role combinations. The supported roles include Active Directory Domain Services (AD DS), Domain Name Service (DNS) Server, Dynamic Host Configuration Protocol (DHCP) Server, File Services, and Print Services. Additionally, as currently implemented, a core-server installation is not a platform for running server applications.

Tip You install servers using Windows Setup (setup.exe). During installation, on the Where Do You Want To Install Windows page, you can access a command prompt by pressing Shift+F10. This gives you access to many of the same command-line tools that are available in a standard installation of Windows Server 2008, including DiskPart.

Because core-server installations have a minimal user interface with a limited desktop, you manage them in a different way than full-server installations. The minimal interface includes:

- Windows Logon screen for logging on and logging off
- Command Prompt for administration via the command line
- Notepad for editing files
- Regedit for managing the registry
- Task Manager for managing tasks and starting new tasks

When you start a server with a core-server installation, you can use the Windows Logon screen to log on just as you do with a full-server installation. In a domain, the standard restrictions apply for logging on to servers and anyone with appropriate user rights and logon permissions can log on to the server. On servers that are not acting as domain controllers and in workgroup environments, you can use the NET USER command to add users and the NET LOCALGROUP command to add users to local groups for the purposes of logging on locally.

After you log on to a core-server installation, you have a limited desktop environment with an Administrator command prompt. You can use this command prompt for administration of the server. If you accidentally close the command prompt, you can start a new command prompt by following these steps:

1. Press Ctrl+Shift+Esc to display Task Manager.
2. On the Applications tab, click New Task.
3. In the Create New Task dialog box, type **cmd** in the Open field and then click OK.

You can use this technique to open additional Command Prompt windows as well. Although you can work with Notepad and Regedit by typing **notepad.exe** or **regedit.exe** instead of **cmd**, you can also start Notepad and Regedit directly from a command prompt by entering **notepad.exe** or **regedit.exe** as appropriate.

When you are logged on, you can display the Windows Logon screen at any time by pressing Ctrl+Alt+Delete. The Windows Logon screen has the same options as a full-server installation, allowing you to lock the computer, switch users, log off, change a password, or start Task Manager. At the command prompt, you'll find that you have all the standard commands and command-line utilities available for managing the server. However, keep in mind that commands, utilities, and programs will only run if all of the components on which they depend are available in the core-server installation.

While core-server installations support a limited set of roles and role services, you can install most features. The key exceptions are those that depend on the Microsoft .NET Framework. Because the .NET Framework is not supported in the original implementation, you cannot add features such as Windows PowerShell. This limitation may change with future updates or service packs. As with any full-server installation, you can use Terminal Services to manage a core-server installation remotely.

Working with Roles, Role Services, and Features

After you've installed a server, you can manage the server configuration by installing and configuring the following components:

- **Server roles** Server roles are related sets of software components that allow servers to perform specific functions for users and other computers on networks. A server can be dedicated to a single role, such as File Services, or a server can have multiple roles.
- **Role services** Role services are software components that provide the functionality of server roles. While some server roles have a single function and installing the role installs this function, most server roles have multiple, related role services and you are able to choose which role services to install.
- **Features** Features are software components that provide additional functionality. Features are installed and removed separately from roles and role services. A computer can have multiple features installed or none, depending on its configuration.

You manage roles, role services, and features using ServerManagerCmd, a command-line administration tool, or Server Manager, a graphical administration tool. Because only one instance of either ServerManagerCmd or Server Manager can add or remove components at the same time, you can't use ServerManagerCmd at the same time you are using one of the Server Manager's add or remove wizards.

Table 4-1 provides an overview of the primary roles and the related role services that you can deploy on a server running Windows Server 2008. In addition to roles and features that are included with Windows Server 2008 by default, Server Manager and ServerManagerCmd enable integration of additional roles and features that are available on the Microsoft Download Center as optional updates to Windows Server 2008.

Table 4-1 Primary Roles and Related Role Services for Windows Server 2008

Role	Description
Active Directory Certificate Services (AD CS)	AD CS provides functions necessary for issuing and revoking digital certificates for users, client computers, and servers. Includes these role services: Certification Authority, Certification Authority Web Enrollment, Online Certificate Status Protocol, and Microsoft Simple Certificate Enrollment Protocol (MSCEP).
Active Directory Domain Services (AD DS)	AD DS provides functions necessary for storing information about users, groups, computers, and other objects on the network and makes this information available to users and computers. Domain controllers give network users and computers access to permitted resources on the network.
Active Directory Federation Services (AD FS)	AD FS complements the authentication and access management features of AD DS by extending them to the World Wide Web. Includes these role services and subservices: Federation Service, Federation Service Proxy, AD FS Web Agents, Claims-aware Agent, and Windows Token-based Agent.
Active Directory Lightweight Directory Services (AD LDS)	AD LDS provides a data store for directory-enabled applications that do not require AD DS and do not need to be deployed on domain controllers. Does not include additional role services.
Active Directory Rights Management Services (AD RMS)	AD RMS provides controlled access to protected e-mail messages, documents, intranet Web pages, and other types of files. Includes these role services: Active Directory Rights Management Server and Identity Federation Support.
Application Server	Application Server allows a server to host distributed applications built using ASP.NET, Enterprise Services, and .NET Framework 3.0. Includes more than a dozen role services, which are discussed in detail in *Internet Information Server 7.0 Administrator's Pocket Consultant* (Microsoft Press, 2007).
DHCP Server	DHCP provides centralized control over Internet Protocol (IP) addressing. DHCP servers can assign dynamic IP addresses and essential TCP/IP settings to other computers on a network. Does not include additional role services.
DNS Server	DNS is a name resolution system that resolves computer names to IP addresses. DNS servers are essential for name resolution in Active Directory domains. Does not include additional role services.

Table 4-1 Primary Roles and Related Role Services for Windows Server 2008

Role	Description
Fax Server	Fax Server provides centralized control over sending and receiving faxes in the enterprise. A Fax Server can act as a gateway for faxing and allows you to manage fax resources, such as jobs and reports, and fax devices on the server or on the network. Does not include additional role services.
File Services	File Services provide essential services for managing files and the way they are made available and replicated on the network. A number of server roles require some type of File Service. Includes these role services and subservices: File Server, Distributed File System, DFS Namespace, DFS Replication, File Server Resource Manager, Services for Network File System (NFS), Windows Search Service, Windows Server 2003 File Services, File Replication Service (FRS), and Indexing Service.
Network Policy And Access Services (NPAS)	NPAS provides essential services for managing routing and remote access to networks. Includes these role services: Network Policy Server (NPS), Routing And Remote Access Services (RRAS), Remote Access Service, Routing, Health Registration Authority, and Host Credential Authorization Protocol (HCAP).
Print Services	Print Services provide essential services for managing network printers and print drivers. Includes these role services: Print Server, LPD Service, and Internet Printing.
Terminal Services	Terminal Services provide services that allow users to run Windows-based applications that are installed on a remote server. When users run an application on a Terminal Server, the execution and processing occur on the server, and only the data from the application is transmitted over the network. Includes these role services: Terminal Server, TS Licensing, TS Session Broker, TS Gateway, and TS Web Access.
Universal Description Discovery Integration (UDDI) Services	UDDI provides capabilities for sharing information about Web services both within an organization and between organizations. Includes these role services: UDDI Services Database and UDDI Services Web Application.

Table 4-1 Primary Roles and Related Role Services for Windows Server 2008

Role	Description
Web Server (IIS)	Web Server (IIS) is used to host Web sites and Web-based applications. Web sites hosted on a Web server can have both static content and dynamic content. You can build Web applications hosted on a Web server using ASP.NET and .NET Framework 3.0. When you deploy a Web server, you can manage the server configuration using IIS 7 modules and administration tools. Includes several dozen role services, which are discussed in detail in *Internet Information Server 7.0 Administrator's Pocket Consultant*.
Windows Deployment Services	Windows Deployment Services provides services for deploying Windows computers in the enterprise. Includes these role services: Deployment Server and Transport Server.
Windows SharePoint Services	Windows SharePoint Services enables team collaboration by connecting people and information. A SharePoint server is essentially a Web server running a full installation of IIS and using managed applications that provide the necessary collaboration functionality.
Windows Server Update Services	Microsoft Windows Server Update Services (WSUS) allows you to distribute updates that are released through Microsoft Update to computers in your organization using centralized servers rather than individual updates.

Table 4-2 provides an overview of the primary features that you can deploy on a server running Windows Server 2008. Unlike earlier releases of Windows, some important server features are not installed automatically. For example, you must add Windows Server Backup to use the built-in backup and restore features of the operating system.

Table 4-2 Primary Features for Windows Server 2008

Feature	Description
.NET Framework 3.0	Provides .NET Framework 3.0 APIs for application development. Additional subfeatures include .NET Framework 3.0 Features, XPS Viewer, and Windows Communication Foundation (WCF) Activation Components.
BitLocker Drive Encryption	Provides hardware-based security to protect data through full-volume encryption that prevents disk tampering while the operating system is offline. Computers that have Trusted Platform Module (TPM) can use BitLocker Drive Encryption in Startup Key or TPM-only mode. Both modes provide early integrity validation.

Table 4-2 Primary Features for Windows Server 2008

Feature	Description
Background Intelligent Transfer Service (BITS) Server Extensions	Provides intelligent background transfers. When this feature is installed, the server can act as a BITS server that can receive file uploads by clients. This feature isn't necessary for downloads to clients using BITS.
Connection Manager Administration Kit (CMAK)	Provides functionality for generating Connection Manager profiles.
Desktop Experience	Provides additional Windows Vista desktop functionality on the server. Windows Vista features added include Windows Media Player, desktop themes, and Windows Photo Gallery. Although these features allow a server to be used like a desktop computer, they can reduce the server's overall performance.
Failover Clustering	Provides clustering functionality that allows multiple servers to work together to provide high availability for services and applications. Many types of services can be clustered, including file and print services. Messaging and database servers are ideal candidates for clustering.
Group Policy Management	Installs the Group Policy Management Console (GPMC), which provides centralized administration of Group Policy.
Internet Printing Client	Provides functionality that allows clients to use HTTP to connect to printers on Web print servers.
Internet Storage Name Server (iSNS)	Provides management and server functions for Internet SCSI (iSCSI) devices, allowing the server to process registration requests, de-registration requests, and queries from iSCSI devices.
Line Printer Remote (LPR) Port Monitor	Installs the LPR Port Monitor, which allows printing to devices attached to UNIX-based computers.
Message Queuing	Provides management and server functions for distributed message queuing. A group of related subfeatures is available as well.
Multipath I/O (MPIO)	Provides functionality necessary for using multiple data paths to a storage device.
Network Load Balancing (NLB)	NLB provides failover support and load balancing for IP-based applications and services by distributing incoming application requests among a group of participating servers. Web servers are ideal candidates for load balancing.

Table 4-2 Primary Features for Windows Server 2008

Feature	Description
Peer Name Resolution Protocol (PNRP)	Provides Link-Local Multicast Name Resolution (LLMNR) functionality that allows peer-to-peer name-resolution services. When you install this feature, applications running on the server can register and resolve names using LLMNR.
Remote Assistance	Allows a remote user to connect to the server to provide or receive Remote Assistance.
Remote Server Administration Tools (RSAT)	Installs role-management and feature-management tools that can be used for remote administration of other Windows Server 2008 systems. Options for individual tools are provided or you can install tools by top-level category or subcategory.
Removable Storage Manager (RSM)	Installs the Removable Storage Manager tool, which you can use to manage removable media and removable media devices.
Remote Procedure Call (RPC) over HTTP Proxy	Installs a proxy for relaying RPC messages from client applications over HTTP to the server. RPC over HTTP is an alternative to having clients access the server over a VPN connection.
Simple TCP/IP Services	Installs additional TCP/IP services, including Character Generator, Daytime, Discard, Echo, and Quote of the Day.
Simple Mail Transfer Protocol (SMTP) Server	SMTP is a network protocol for controlling the transfer and routing of e-mail messages. When this feature is installed, the server can act as a basic SMTP server. For a full-featured solution, you'll need to install a messaging server such as Microsoft Exchange Server 2007.
Simple Network Management Protocol (SNMP) Services	SNMP is a protocol used to simplify management of TCP/IP networks. You can use SNMP for centralized network management if your network has SNMP-compliant devices. You can also use SNMP for network monitoring via network management software.
Storage Manager For SANs	Installs the Storage Manager For SANs console. This console provides a central management interface for Storage Area Network (SAN) devices. You can view storage subsystems, create and manage logical unit numbers (LUNs), and manage iSCSI target devices. The SAN device must support Visual Disk Services (VDS).

Table 4-2 Primary Features for Windows Server 2008

Feature	Description
Subsystem for UNIX-based Applications (SUA)	Provides functionality for running UNIX-based programs. You can download additional management utilities from the Microsoft Web site.
Windows Internal Database	Installs SQL Server 2005 Compact edition. This allows the server to use relational databases with Windows roles and features that require an internal database, such as AD RMS, UDDI Services, Windows Server Update Services (WSUS), Windows SharePoint Services, and Windows System Resource Manager.
Windows PowerShell	Installs Windows PowerShell, which provides an enhanced command-line environment for managing Windows systems.
Windows Process Activation Service	Provides support for distributed Web-based applications that use HTTP and non-HTTP protocols.
Windows Server Backup	Allows you to back up and restore the operating system, system state, and any data stored on a server.
Windows System Resource Manager (WSRM)	Allows you to manage resource usage on a per-processor basis.
WINS Server	WINS is a name-resolution service that resolves computer names to IP addresses. Installing this feature allows the computer to act as a WINS server.
Wireless Networking	Allows the server to use wireless networking connections and profiles.

Microsoft designed Server Manager and ServerManagerCmd to be extensible. This makes it easier to provide supplemental roles, role services, and features for the operating system. Some additional components are available as downloads from the Microsoft Web site, including Windows Media Services for Windows Server 2008 and Windows SharePoint Services 3.0.

You can make these components available for installation and configuration by completing the following steps:

1. Download the installer package or packages from the Microsoft Web site. Typically, these are provided as a set of Microsoft Update Standalone Packages (.msu) files.
2. Double-click each installer package to register it for use.
3. If Server Manager is running on the server, restart or refresh Server Manager to make the new components available.
4. In Server Manager, use the appropriate wizard to install and configure the supplemental role, role service, or feature.

Managing Roles, Role Services, and Features

When you want to manage server configuration from the command-line, Server-ManagerCmd is the primary tool you'll use. Not only can you use ServerManagerCmd to add or remove roles, role services, and features, but you can also use ServerManager-Cmd to view the configuration details and status for these software components.

ServerManagerCmd Essentials

Whenever you work with ServerManagerCmd, you should use an elevated administrator command prompt. You can manage roles, role services, and features using the following parameters and command-line syntaxes:

- **Servermanagercmd -query** Lists the server's current state with regard to roles, role services, and features. If SaveFile.xml is specified, the query results are displayed and saved to the named file, in XML format. Optionally, you can use -q instead of -query.

```
ServerManagerCmd -query [SaveFile.xml] [-logPath LogFile.txt]
```

- **Servermanagercmd -install** Installs the named role, role service, or feature. The -AllSubFeatures or -A parameter allows you to install all subordinate role services and features of the named component. The -Setting or -S parameter allows you to configure required settings to specific values. Optionally, you can use -i instead of -install.

```
ServerManagerCmd -install ComponentName
[-setting SettingName=SettingValue] [-allSubFeatures]
[-resultPath Results.xml] [-restart] | -whatIf]
[-logPath LogFile.txt]
```

- **Servermanagercmd –inputPath** Adds or removes roles, role services, and features as specified in an XML answer file. Optionally, you can use -ip instead of -inputPath.

```
ServerManagerCmd -inputPath AnswerFile.xml [-resultPath
Results.xml] [-restart] | -whatIf]
[-logPath LogFile.txt]
```

- **Servermanagercmd –remove** Removes the named role, role service, or feature. Optionally, you can use -r instead of -remove.

```
ServerManagerCmd -remove ComponentName [-resultPath Results.xml]
[-restart] | -whatIf] [-logPath LogFile.txt]
```

- **Servermanagercmd -version** Lists the version of ServerManagerCmd you are using. Optionally, you can use -v instead of -version.

```
ServerManagerCmd -version
```

Each of the main parameters accepts additional parameters and parameter values. When applicable, you can:

- Use the -LogPath or -L parameter to log error details to a named log file.
- Use the -Restart parameter to restart the computer automatically (if restarting is necessary to complete the operation).
- Use the -ResultPath or -Rp parameter to write standard output results to a named file in XML format.
- Use the -Whatif or -W parameter to display the operations that would be performed if the command were executed.

The parameter values that you can use include:

- **AnswerFile.xml** Uses the XML-formatted answer file to determine what components to add or remove.
- **ComponentName** Identifies the role, role service, or feature to work with.
- **LogFile** Sets the name of the text file to which log error details should be written.
- **Results.xml** Saves the results of the install or remove operation to a named file in XML format. Results are still displayed.
- **SaveFile.xml** Saves the standard output results to a named file in XML format. The results are still displayed and it is important to note that results do not include errors, which are written separately to standard error output.
- **SettingName** Identifies a required setting by its name.
- **SettingValue** Sets the configuration value for a setting.

Most installable roles, role services, and features have a corresponding component name that identifies the component so that you can manipulate it from the command-line. This also is true for supplemental components you've made available by downloading and installing their installer packages from the Microsoft Web site.

Table 4-3 provides a hierarchical listing of the component names associated with roles, related role services, and related subcomponents. When you are installing a role, you can use the -AllSubFeatures parameter to install all the subordinate role services and features listed under the role. When you are installing a role service, you can use the -AllSubFeatures parameter to install all the subordinate features listed under the role service.

Table 4-3 Component Names for Key Roles and Role Services

Component Name	Role	Service	Feature
AD-Certificate	Active Directory Certificate Services		
ADCS-Cert-Authority		Certification Authority	
ADCS-Web-Enrollment		Certification Authority Web Enrollment	
ADCS-Online-Cert		Online Responder	
ADCS-Device-Enrollment		Network Device Enrollment Service	
	Active Directory Domain Services		
ADDS-Domain-Controller		Active Directory Domain Controller	
ADDS-Identity-Mgmt		Identity Management For UNIX	
ADDS-NIS			Server For Network Information Services
ADDS-NIS			Password Synchronization
ADDS-IDMU-Tools			Administration Tools
	Active Directory Federation Services		
ADFS-Federation		Federation Service	
ADFS-Proxy		Federation Service Proxy	
ADFS-Web-Agents		AD FS Web Agents	
ADFS-Claims			Claims-aware Agent
ADFS-Windows-Token			Windows Token-based Agent
ADLDS	Active Directory Lightweight Directory Services		
DHCP	DHCP Server		
DNS	DNS Server		
Fax	Fax Server		
	File Services		
FS-FileServer		File Server	
FS-DFS		Distributed File System	
FS-DFS-Namespace			DFS Namespaces
FS-DFS-Replication			DFS Replication
FS-Resource-Manager		File Server Resource Manager	

Table 4-3 Component Names for Key Roles and Role Services

Component Name	Role	Service	Feature
FS-NFS-Services		Services For Network File System	
FS-Search-Service		Windows Search Service	
FS-Win2003-Services		Windows Server 2003 File Services	
FS-Replication			File Replication Service
FS-Indexing-Service			Indexing Service
Hyper-V	Hyper-V		
NPAS	Network Policy And Access Services		
NPAS-Policy-Server		Network Policy Server	
NPAS-RRAS-Services		Routing And Remote Access Services	
NPAS-RRAS			Remote Access Service
NPAS-Routing			Routing
NPAS-Health		Health Registration Authority	
NPAS-Host-Cred		Host Credential Authorization Protocol	
Print-Services	Print Services		
Print-Server		Print Server	
Print-LPD-Service		LPD Service	
Print-Internet		Internet Printing	
Terminal-Services	Terminal Services		
TS-Terminal-Server		Terminal Server	
TS-Licensing		TS Licensing	
TS-Session-Broker		TS Session Broker	
TS-Gateway		TS Gateway	
TS-Web-Access		TS Web Access	
WDS	Windows Deployment Services		
WDS-Deployment		Deployment Server	
WDS-Transport		Transport Server	

Table 4-4 provides a hierarchical listing of the component names associated with features and related subfeatures. When you are installing a feature, you can use the -AllSubFeatures parameter to install all the subordinate second-level and third-level features listed under the feature. When you are installing a second-level feature, you can use the -AllSubFeatures parameter to install all the subordinate third-level features listed under the second-level feature.

Note An asterisk following the feature command indicates the feature has unlisted subordinate features that generally are installed together by adding the -AllSubFeatures parameter.

Table 4-4 Component Names for Key Features and Subfeatures

Component Name	Feature	Second-Level Feature	Third-Level Feature
NET-Framework*	.NET Framework 3.0 Features		
BitLocker	BitLocker Drive Encryption		
BITS	BITS Server Extensions		
CMAK	Connection Manager Administration Kit		
Desktop-Experience	Desktop Experience		
Failover-Clustering	Failover Clustering		
GPMC	Group Policy Management Console		
Internet-Print-Client	Internet Printing Client		
ISNS	Internet Storage Name Server		
LPR-Port-Monitor	LPR Port Monitor		
MSMQ*	Message Queuing		
Multipath-IO	Multipath I/O		
NLB	Network Load Balancing		
PNRP	Peer Name Resolution Protocol		
qWave	Quality Windows Audio Video Experience		
Remote-Assistance	Remote Assistance		
RDC	Remote Differential Compression		
RSAT	Remote Server Administration Tools		
RSAT-Role-Tools		Role Administration Tools	
RSAT-ADCS*			Active Directory Certificate Services Tools
RSAT-ADDS*			Active Directory Domain Services Tools
RSAT-ADLDS			Active Directory Lightweight Directory Services Tools

Table 4-4 Component Names for Key Features and Subfeatures

Component Name	Feature	Second-Level Feature	Third-Level Feature
RSAT-RMS			Active Directory Rights Management Services Tools
RSAT-DHCP			DHCP Server Tools
RSAT-DNS-Server			DNS Server Tools
RSAT-Fax			Fax Server Tools
RSAT-File-Services*			File Services Tools
RSAT-NPAS*			Network Policy And Access Services Tools
RSAT-Print-Services			Print Services Tools
RSAT-TS*			Terminal Services Tools
RSAT-UDDI			UDDI Services Tools
RSAT-Web-Server			Web Server (IIS) Tools
RSAT-WDS			Windows Deployment Services Tools
RSAT-Feature-Tools		Feature Administration Tools	
RSAT-BitLocker			BitLocker Drive Encryption Tools
RSAT-Bits-Server			BITS Server Extensions Tools
RSAT-Clustering			Failover Clustering Tools
RSAT-NLB			Network Load Balancing Tools
RSAT-SMTP			SMTP Server Tools
RSAT-WINS			WINS Server Tools
Removable-Storage	Removable Storage Manager		
RPC-over-HTTP-Proxy	RPC over HTTP Proxy		
Simple-TCPIP	Simple TCP/IP Services		
SMTP-Server	SMTP Server		

Table 4-4 Component Names for Key Features and Subfeatures

Component Name	Feature	Second-Level Feature	Third-Level Feature
SNMP-Services	SNMP Services		
SNMP-Service		SNMP Service	
SNMP-WMI-Provider		SNMP WMI Provider	
Storage-Mgr-SANS	Storage Manager For SANs		
Subsystem-UNIX-Apps	Subsystem For UNIX-based Applications		
Telnet-Client	Telnet Client		
Telnet-Server	Telnet Server		
TFTP-Client	TFTP Client		
Windows-Internal-DB	Windows Internal Database		
PowerShell	Windows PowerShell		
Backup-Features	Windows Server Backup Features		
Backup		Windows Server Backup	
Backup-Tools		Command-line Tools	
WSRM	Windows System Resource Manager		
WINS-Server	WINS Server		
Wireless-Networking	Wireless LAN Service		

Querying Installed Roles, Role Services, and Features

At an elevated command prompt, you can determine the roles, roles services, and features that are installed on a server by typing **servermanagercmd -query**. ServerManagerCmd then lists the configuration status of each available role, role service, and feature. Installed roles, role services, and features are highlighted and marked as being installed. In the output, roles and role services are listed before features as shown in the following example:

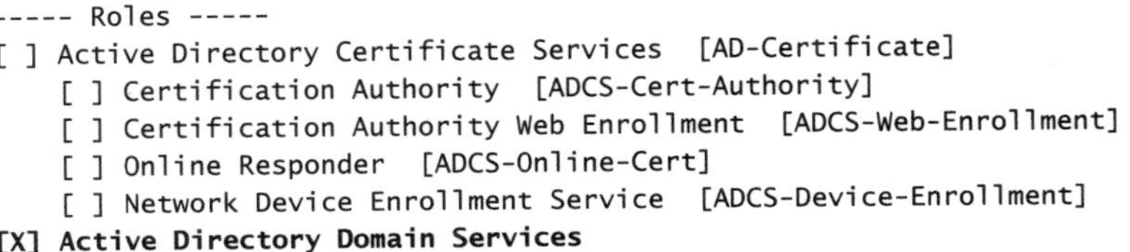

```
----- Roles -----
[ ] Active Directory Certificate Services  [AD-Certificate]
    [ ] Certification Authority  [ADCS-Cert-Authority]
    [ ] Certification Authority Web Enrollment  [ADCS-Web-Enrollment]
    [ ] Online Responder  [ADCS-Online-Cert]
    [ ] Network Device Enrollment Service  [ADCS-Device-Enrollment]
[X] Active Directory Domain Services
```

```
    [X] Active Directory Domain Controller  [ADDS-Domain-Controller]
    [ ] Identity Management for UNIX  [ADDS-Identity-Mgmt]
        [ ] Server for Network Information Services  [ADDS-NIS]
        [ ] Password Synchronization  [ADDS-Password-Sync]
        [ ] Administration Tools  [ADDS-IDMU-Tools]

...

----- Features -----
[ ] .NET Framework 3.0 Features  [NET-Framework]
    [ ] .NET Framework 3.0  [NET-Framework-Core]
    [ ] XPS Viewer  [NET-XPS-Viewer]
    [ ] WCF Activation  [NET-Win-CFAC]
        [ ] HTTP Activation  [NET-HTTP-Activation]
        [ ] Non-HTTP Activation  [NET-Non-HTTP-Activ]
[X] BitLocker Drive Encryption  [BitLocker]
[X] BITS Server Extensions  [BITS]
[ ] Connection Manager Administration Kit [CMAK]
[X] Desktop Experience [Desktop-Experience]
```

In addition to helping you determine at a glance what components are installed, Servermanagercmd –query can help you document a server's configuration. To do this, you can save the output in a file as standard text using the redirection symbol (>) as shown in this example:

```
servermanagercmd -query > ServerConfig06-15-2008.txt
```

In this example, you save the output to a text file named ServerConfig06-15-2008.txt. If you want to save the results as an XML-formatted file instead of a text file, simply follow the -query command with the name of the XML file, such as:

```
servermanagercmd -query MySaveFile.xml
```

Saving the output to an XML file makes the file easier to manipulate using automation techniques.

Installing Roles, Role Services, and Features

At an elevated command prompt, you can install roles, role services, and features by typing **servermanagercmd -install *ComponentName***, where *ComponentName* is the name of the component to install as listed in Table 4-3 or Table 4-4. You can install subordinate components by including the -AllSubFeatures parameter as shown in the following example:

```
servermanagercmd -install fs-dfs -allsubfeatures
```

Here, you install the Distributed File System role service as well as the subordinate DFS Namespaces and DFS Replication role services. The output for a successful installation should look similar to the following:

```
Start Installation...
[Installation] Succeeded: [File Services] Distributed File System.
[Installation] Succeeded: [File Services] DFS Namespaces.
[Installation] Succeeded: [File Services] DFS Replication.
<100/100>

Success: Installation succeeded.
```

If a restart is required to complete an installation, you can have ServerManagerCmd restart the computer by including the -Restart parameter. To test the installation prior to performing that actual operation, you can use the -Whatif parameter. If you are trying to install components that are already installed you'll see a note stating no changes were made, such as:

```
NoChange: No changes were made because the roles, role services and featur
es specified are already installed, or have already been removed from the
local computer.
```

If an error occurs and ServerManagerCmd is not able to perform the operation specified, you'll see an error. Generally, error text is shown in red and includes an error flag and error text, such as:

```
WriteError: Failed to write the log file: . Access to the path 'C:\Windows
\logs\ServerManager.log' is denied.
```

This error indicates that ServerManagerCmd couldn't perform the operation because it couldn't gain write access to the log file. When you install components, Server-ManagerCmd writes extended logging information to %SystemRoot%\logs\server-manager.log. This logging information details every operation performed by ServerManagerCmd. You can write the detailed information to an alternate location by including the -LogPath or -L parameter. In this example, you write the logging information to c:\logs\install.log:

```
servermanagercmd -install fs-dfs -allsubfeatures
-logPath c:\logs\install.log
```

Other common errors you'll see are related to invalid arguments passed on the command-line, such as:

```
ArgumentNotValid: Invalid parameters. Only specify either -install or
-remove.
ArgumentNotValid: Invalid role, role service, or feature: 'fs-
dfsd". The name was not found.
```

Here, you can resolve the problem using the correct parameters. Finally, if you forget to run the command prompt as an administrator, you'll see an error stating Server-ManagerCmd can be run only by a member of the built-in Administrators group on the local computer. You'll need to run the command prompt with elevated permissions to resolve this error.

Removing Roles, Role Services, and Features

At an elevated command prompt, you can uninstall roles, role services, and features by typing **servermanagercmd -remove *ComponentName***, where *ComponentName* is the name of the component to uninstall as listed in Table 4-3 or Table 4-4. You can uninstall subordinate components by including the -AllSubFeatures parameter as shown in the following example:

```
servermanagercmd -remove fs-dfs -allsubfeatures
```

Here, you uninstall the Distributed File System role service as well as the subordinate DFS Namespaces and DFS Replication role services and the output for a successful removal should look similar to the following:

```
Start Removal...
[Removal] Succeeded: [File Services] Distributed File System.
[Removal] Succeeded: [File Services] DFS Namespaces.
[Removal] Succeeded: [File Services] DFS Replication.
<100/100>

Success: Removal succeeded.
```

If a restart is required to complete a removal, you can have ServerManagerCmd restart the computer by including the -Restart parameter. As with installation, you can test the removal prior to performing that actual operation using the -Whatif parameter. If you are trying to remove components that aren't installed, you'll see a note stating no changes were made, such as:

```
NoChange: No changes were made because the roles, role services and featur
es specified are already installed, or have already been removed from the
local computer.
```

If an error occurs and ServerManagerCmd is not able to perform the operation specified, you'll see an error. During the removal process, ServerManagerCmd writes extended logging information to %SystemRoot%\logs\servermanager.log. As with the installation process, you can write the detailed information to an alternate location by including the -LogPath or -L parameter.

Chapter 5

Managing Windows Systems

Your job as an administrator is to plan, organize, and track the details that keep the network running. If you're to survive without just muddling through, you need to learn how to do those jobs quickly and efficiently. Fortunately, Windows supplies plenty of command-line tools to help you with these tasks, and this chapter discusses some of the more important tools for daily systems management.

Examining System Information

Often when you are working with a user's computer or a remote server, you'll want to examine some basic system information, such as who is logged on, the current system time, or the location of a certain file. Commands that help you gather basic system information include the following:

- **DATE** Displays and sets the current system date
- **TIME** Displays and sets the current system time
- **WHOAMI** Displays the name of the user currently logged on the system, such as adatum\administrator
- **WHERE** Searches for files using a search pattern and returns a list of matching results

To use DATE or TIME, simply type the command in a command shell window followed by the /T parameter and press Enter. The output of date /t is the current date, such as **Wed 03/19/2008**. The output of time /t is the current time, such as **04:35 PM**. To set the date or time, simply follow the command name with the desired date or time. You enter the current date in MM-DD-YY format, where MM is for the two-digit month, DD is for the two-digit day, and YY is for the two-digit year, such as entering **03-20-08** for March 20, 2008.

You enter the current time in HH:MM or HH:MM:SS format, where HH is for the two-digit hour, MM is for the two-digit minute, and SS is for the two-digit second. If you enter the time without designating A.M. or P.M., the TIME command assumes you are using a 24-hour clock, where hours from 00 to 11 indicate A.M. and hours from 12 to 23 indicate P.M. All of the following examples set the time to 4:45 P.M.:

```
time 04:45 PM
time 04:45:00 PM
time 16:45:00
```

To use WHOAMI to determine who is logged on, simply type the command in a command shell window and press Enter. If the computer is part of a workgroup, the output includes the name of the computer followed by a backward slash and the name of the logged-on user, such as computer84\deanr. If the computer is part of a domain, the output includes the name of the domain followed by a backward slash and the name of the logged-on user, such as adatum\williams.

By default, WHERE searches the current directory and in the paths specified by the PATH environment variable. This means you can quickly search for an executable in the current path simply by typing **where** followed by the executable you want to find. For example, if you want to find CMD.EXE, you can type the following:

```
where cmd.exe
```

The output is the full file path to CMD.EXE, such as:

```
C:\Windows\System32\cmd.exe
```

With WHERE, the other most common syntax you'll use is

```
where /r baseDir filename
```

Here, /r is for a recursive search starting from the specified directory (*BaseDir*) and including all subdirectories, and *filename* is the name or partial name of the file to search for, which can include wildcard characters. Use ? as a wildcard to match a single character and * as a wildcard to match multiple characters, such as data???.txt or data*.*. In the following example, you search the C:\ directory and all subdirectories for text files that begin with *data*, as follows:

```
where /r C:\ data*.txt
```

You can also search for files of all types that begin with *data*, as in this example:

```
where /r C:\ data*.*
```

Sometimes when you are working with a computer, you'll want to obtain information on the system configuration or the system environment. With mission-critical systems, you may want to save or print this information for easy reference. Commands that help you gather system information include the following:

- **DRIVERQUERY** Displays a list of all installed device drivers and their properties, including module name, display name, driver type, and driver link date. With verbose output, the command also lists the driver status, state, start mode, memory usage, and file system path. Use the /V parameter to get verbose output of all unsigned drivers.
- **SYSTEMINFO** Displays detailed system configuration information, including operating system version, system type, system manufacturer, processor, BIOS version, memory size, locale setting, time zone setting, and network card configuration. This command also shows the hotfixes that have been installed.

To use these commands on a local computer, simply type the command name in a command shell window and press Enter. With DRIVERQUERY, use the /V parameter to get verbose output for unsigned drivers, and the /Si parameter to display properties of signed drivers, such as

```
driverquery /si
```

With the DRIVERQUERY and SYSTEMINFO commands, you can also specify the remote computer to query and the Run As permissions. To do this, you must use the expanded syntax, which includes the following parameters:

```
/S Computer /U [Domain\]User [/P Password]
```

where *Computer* is the remote computer name or IP address, *Domain* is the optional domain name in which the user account is located, *User* is the name of the user account whose permissions you want to use, and *Password* is the optional password for the user account. If you don't specify the domain, the current domain is assumed. If you don't provide the account password, you are prompted for the password.

To see how the computer and user information can be added to the syntax, consider the following examples:

Use the account adatum\wrstanek when querying MAILER1 for driver settings:

```
driverquery /s mailer1 /u adatum\wrstanek
```

Use the account adatum\administrator when querying CORPSERVER01 for system information:

```
systeminfo /s corpserver01 /u adatum\administrator
```

> **Tip** The basic output of these commands is in table format. You can also format the output as a list or lines of comma-separated values using /Fo List or /Fo Csv, respectively. You may wonder why you should use the various formats. That's a good question. For SYSTEMINFO, I recommend using the list format (/ Fo List) when you want to see all details about system configuration, and for DRIVERQUERY I recommend the verbose list format (/Fo List /V) when you are troubleshooting unsigned drivers. Further, I recommend using comma-separated values when you want to store the output in a file that may later be exported to a spreadsheet or flat-file database. Remember you can redirect the output of the DRIVERQUERY and SYSTEMINFO commands to a file by using output redirection (> or >>).

Working with the Registry

The Windows registry stores configuration settings. Using the Reg command-line utility, you can view, add, delete, compare, and copy registry entries. Because the Windows registry is essential to the proper operation of the operating system, make changes to the registry only when you know how these changes will affect the system. Before you edit the registry in any way, perform a complete system backup and create a system recovery data snapshot. This way, if you make a mistake, you can recover the registry and the system.

> **Caution** Improperly modifying the Windows registry can cause serious problems. If the registry becomes corrupted, you might have to reinstall the operating system. Double-check the commands you use before executing them. Make sure that they do exactly what you intend.

Understanding Registry Keys and Values

The Windows registry stores configuration settings for the operating system, applications, users, and hardware. Registry settings are stored as keys and values, which are placed under a specific root key controlling when and how the keys and values are used.

Table 5-1 lists the registry root keys as well as a description and the reference name you will use to refer to the root key when working with the REG command. Under the root keys, you'll find the main keys that control system, user, application, and hardware settings. These keys are organized into a tree structure, with folders representing keys. For example, under HKEY_LOCAL_MACHINE\SYSTEM\CurrentControlSet\Services, you'll find folders for all services installed on the system. Within these folders are the registry keys that store important service configuration settings and their subkeys.

Table 5-1 Keys in the Windows Registry

Root Key	Reference Name	Description
HKEY_CURRENT_USER	HKCU	Stores configuration settings for the current user.
HKEY_LOCAL_MACHINE	HKLM	Stores system-level configuration settings.
HKEY_CLASSES_ROOT	HKCR	Stores configuration settings for applications and files. Also ensures that the correct application is opened when a file is accessed.
HKEY_USERS	HKU	Stores default-user and other-user settings by profile.
HKEY_CURRENT_CONFIG	HKCC	Stores information about the hardware profile being used.

Keys that you want to work with must be designated by their folder path. For example, the path to the DNS key is HKEY_LOCAL_MACHINE\SYSTEM\CurrentControlSet\Services\DNS and, using the abbreviated path HKLM\SYSTEM\CurrentControlSet\Services\DNS, you can view and manipulate this key.

Key values are stored as a specific data type. Table 5-2 provides a summary of the main data types used with keys.

Table 5-2 Registry Key Values and Data Types

Data Type	Description	Example
REG_BINARY	Identifies a binary value. Binary values are stored using base-2 (0 or 1 only) but are displayed and entered in hexadecimal (base-16) format.	01 00 14 80 90 00 00 9c 00
REG_DWORD	Identifies a binary data type in which 32-bit integer values are stored as four byte-length values in hexadecimal.	0x00000002
REG_EXPAND_SZ	Identifies an expandable string value, which is usually used with directory paths.	%SystemRoot%\dns.exe
REG_MULTI_SZ	Identifies a multiple string value.	Tcpip Afd RpcSc
REG_NONE	Identifies data without a particular type. This data is written as binary values but displayed and entered in hexadecimal (base-16) format.	23 45 67 80
REG_SZ	Identifies a string value containing a sequence of characters.	DNS Server

As long as you know the key path and understand the available key data types, you can use the REG command to view and manipulate keys in a variety of ways. REG has several different subcommands, and we'll explore some of them. The sections that follow discuss each of the following REG subcommands:

- **REG add** Adds a new subkey or entry to the registry
- **REG delete** Deletes a subkey or entries from the registry
- **REG query** Lists the entries under a key and the names of subkeys (if any)

- **REG compare** Compares registry subkeys or entries
- **REG copy** Copies a registry entry to a specified key path on a local or remote system
- **REG flags** Displays and manages the current flags of a specified key
- **REG restore** Writes saved subkeys, entries, and values back to the registry
- **REG save** Saves a copy of specified subkeys, entries, and values to a file

The following sections will also discuss the following commands for performing advanced registry manipulation:

- **REG import** Imports a specified hive file into the registry
- **REG export** Exports specified subkeys, entries, and values to a registry file
- **REG load** Loads a specified hive file into the registry
- **REG unload** Unloads a specified hive file into the registry

Note The REG command is run using the permissions of the current user. If you want to use a different set of permissions, the easiest way is to log on as that user.

Querying Registry Values

Using REG query, you can read registry values by referencing the full path and name of a key or key value that you want to examine. The basic syntax is

```
reg query KeyName [/v ValueName]
```

where *KeyName* is the name of the key you want to examine and *ValueName* is an optional parameter that specifies a specific key value. In the following example, you query the DNS key under the current control set:

```
reg query HKLM\SYSTEM\CurrentControlSet\Services\DNS
```

Alternatively, if you know the specific key value you want to examine, you can limit the query results using the /V parameter. In this example, you list the value of the ImagePath entry for the DNS key:

```
reg query HKLM\SYSTEM\CurrentControlSet\Services\DNS /v ImagePath
```

The key path can also include the UNC name or IP address of a remote computer that you want to examine, such as \\Mailer1 or \\192.168.1.100. However, keep in mind that on a remote computer, you can only work with the HKLM and HKU root keys. In this example, you examine the DNS key on MAILER1:

```
reg query \\Mailer1\HKLM\SYSTEM\CurrentControlSet\Services\DNS
```

Note If you specify a nonexistent key or value, an error message is displayed. Typically, it reads: ERROR: The system was unable to find the specified registry key or value.

Comparing Registry Keys

With REG compare, you can compare registry entries and values between two systems or between two different keys on the same system. Performing registry comparisons is useful in the following situations:

- **When you are trying to troubleshoot service and application configuration issues** At such times, it is useful to compare the registry configurations between two different systems. Ideally, these systems include one that appears to be configured properly and one that you suspect is misconfigured. You can then perform a comparison of the configuration areas that you suspect are causing problems.
- **When you want to ensure that an application or service is configured the same way on multiple systems** Here you would use one system as the basis for testing the other system configurations. Ideally, the basis system is configured exactly as expected before you start comparing its configuration to other systems.

The basic syntax for REG compare is

```
reg compare KeyName1 KeyName2 [/v ValueName]
```

where *KeyName1* and *KeyName2* are the names of the subkeys that you want to compare and *ValueName* is an optional parameter that specifies a specific key value to compare. The key name can include the UNC name or IP address of a remote computer that you want to examine. In the following example, you compare the DNS key under the current control set on MAILER1 and MAILER2:

```
reg compare \\Mailer1\HKLM\SYSTEM\CurrentControlSet\Services\DNS
\\Mailer2\HKLM\SYSTEM\CurrentControlSet\Services\DNS
```

If the keys are configured the same, the output is

```
Results Compared: Identical
The operation completed successfully.
```

If the keys are configured differently, the output shows the differences. Any differences that begin with the < character pertain to the first key specified and differences that begin with the > character pertain to the second key specified. The output will also state

```
Results Compared: Different
The operation completed successfully.
```

> **Tip** Differences are displayed because the /Od parameter is assumed by default. Using additional parameters, you can also specify that you want to see all differences and matches (/Oa), only matches (/Os), or no results (/On).

Additionally, if you want to compare all subkeys and entries recursively, you can add the /S parameter, as shown in the following example:

```
reg compare \\Mailer1\HKLM\SYSTEM\CurrentControlSet\Services\DNS
\\Mailer2\HKLM\SYSTEM\CurrentControlSet\Services\DNS /s
```

Now the key, all subkeys, and all related entries for the DNS key on MAILER1 and MAILER2 are compared.

Saving and Restoring Registry Keys

Before you modify registry entries, it is a good idea to save the keys you will use. If anything goes wrong, you can restore those keys to their original settings. To save a copy of a registry subkey and all its related subkeys and values, use REG save, as shown here:

```
reg save KeyName "FileName"
```

where *KeyName* is the path to the subkey you want to save and *FileName* is the text name of the registry hive file you want to create. The subkey path can include the UNC name or IP address of a remote computer. However, on a remote computer, you can only work with the HKLM and HKU root keys. Additionally, the filename should be enclosed in double quotation marks and should end in the .hiv extension to indicate it is a registry hive file, as shown in the following example:

```
reg save HKLM\SYSTEM\CurrentControlSet\Services\DNS "DNSKey.hiv"
```

Here, you are saving the DNS subkey and its related subkeys and values to the file named Dnskey.hiv. The filename can also include a directory path, as shown in this example:

```
reg save \HKLM\SYSTEM\CurrentControlSet\Services\DNS
"\\Mailer1\SavedData\DNSKey.hiv"
```

If the registry hive file exists, you will be prompted to overwrite the file. Press Y to overwrite. If you want to force overwrite without prompting, use the /Y parameter.

To restore a registry key that you saved previously, use Reg restore. The syntax for REG restore is

```
reg restore KeyName "FileName"
```

where *KeyName* is the path to the subkey you want to save and *FileName* is the text name of the registry hive file you want to use as the restore source. Unlike REG copy, REG restore can be used only on a local computer, meaning you cannot restore registry keys on a remote computer using the command. You can, however, start a remote desktop session on the remote computer and then use the remote desktop logon to restore the registry key on the local computer.

An example using REG restore is shown here:

```
reg restore HKLM\SYSTEM\CurrentControlSet\Services\DNS "DNSKey.hiv"
```

Here, you are restoring the DNS key saved previously to the DNSKey.hiv file.

Adding Registry Keys

To add subkeys and values to the Windows registry, use REG add. The basic syntax for creating a key or value is

```
reg add KeyName /v ValueName /t DataType /d Data
```

where *KeyName* is the name of the key you want to examine, *ValueName* is the subkey or key value to create, *DataType* is the type of data, and *Data* is the actual value you are inserting. That seems like a lot of values, but it is fairly straightforward. Consider the following example:

```
reg add HKLM\SYSTEM\CurrentControlSet\Services\DNS /v DisplayName
/t REG_SZ /d "DNS Server"
```

Here, you add a key value called DisplayName to the DNS key in the registry. The key entry is a string with the "DNS Server" value. Note the double-quotation marks. The quotation marks are necessary in this example because the string contains a space. If the key or value you are attempting to add already exists, you are prompted to overwrite the existing data. Enter Y to overwrite, or N to cancel. To force overwriting an existing registry key or value without a prompt, use the /F parameter.

When you set expandable string values (REG_EXPAND_SZ), you must use the caret (^) to escape the percent symbols (%) that designate the environment variable you use. Consider the following example:

```
reg add HKLM\SYSTEM\CurrentControlSet\Services\DNS /v ImagePath
/t REG_EXPAND_SZ /d ^%SystemRoot^%\System32\dns.exe
```

Here, you enter **^%SystemRoot^%** so that the SystemRoot environment variable is properly entered and interpreted.

When you set non-string values, you don't need to use quotation marks, as shown in this example:

```
reg add HKLM\SYSTEM\CurrentControlSet\Services\DNS /v ErrorControl
/t REG_DWORD /d 0x00000001
```

Copying Registry Keys

Using REG copy, you can copy a registry entry to a new location on a local or remote system. The basic syntax for REG copy is

```
reg copy KeyName1 KeyName2
```

where *KeyName1* is the path to the subkey you want to copy and *KeyName2* is the path to the subkey destination. Although the subkey paths can include the UNC name or IP address of a remote computer, REG copy is limited in scope with regard to which root keys you can use when working with remote source or destination keys, as follows:

- A remote source subkey can use only the HKLM or HKU root keys.
- A remote destination subkey can use only the HKLM or HKU root keys.

In the following example, you copy the DNS subkey on the local system to the DNS subkey on MAILER2:

```
reg copy HKLM\SYSTEM\CurrentControlSet\Services\DNS
    \\Mailer2\HKLM\SYSTEM\CurrentControlSet\Services\DNS
```

By adding the /S parameter, you can copy the specified subkey as well as all subkeys and key entries under the specified subkey. In this example, the DNS subkey and all related subkey and values are copied:

```
reg copy HKLM\SYSTEM\CurrentControlSet\Services\DNS
    \\Mailer2\HKLM\SYSTEM\CurrentControlSet\Services\DNS /s
```

If values exist at the destination path, REG copy will prompt you to confirm that you want to overwrite each existing value. Press Y or N as appropriate. You can also press A to overwrite all existing values without further prompting.

> **Note** If you don't want prompts to be displayed, you can use the /F parameter to force overwrite without prompting. However, before you copy over an existing registry key, you may want to save the key so that it can be restored if problems occur. To do this, use REG save and REG restore as discussed earlier in the section of this chapter titled "Saving and Restoring Registry Keys."

Deleting Registry Keys

To delete subkeys and values from the Windows registry, use REG delete. REG delete has several different syntaxes. If you want to delete a subkey and all subkeys and entries under the subkey, use the following syntax:

```
reg delete KeyName
```

where *KeyName* is the name of the subkey you want to delete. Although the subkey path can include the UNC name or IP address of a remote computer, a remote source subkey can use only the HKLM or HKU root keys. Consider the following example:

```
reg delete \\Mailer1\HKLM\SYSTEM\CurrentControlSet\Services\DNS2
```

Here you delete the DNS2 subkey and all subkeys and entries under the subkey on MAILER1.

If you want to limit the scope of the deletion, specify that only a specific entry under the subkey should be deleted using the following syntax:

```
reg delete KeyName /v ValueName
```

where *KeyName* is the name of the subkey you want to work with and *ValueName* is the name of the specific entry to delete. As before, the subkey path can include the UNC name or IP address of a remote computer. However, a remote source subkey can use only the HKLM or HKU root keys. In this example, you delete the Description entry for the DNS2 subkey on MAILER2:

```
reg delete \\Mailer2\HKLM\SYSTEM\CurrentControlSet\Services\DNS2 /v
Description
```

> **Tip** In both cases, you will be prompted to confirm that you want to delete the specified entry permanently. Press Y to confirm the deletion. You can force deletion without prompting using the /F parameter. Another useful parameter is /Va. Using the /Va parameter, you can specify that only values under the subkey should be deleted. In this way, subkeys under the designated subkey are not deleted.

Exporting and Importing Registry Keys

Sometimes you might find it necessary or useful to copy all or part of the registry to a file and then use this copy on another computer. For example, if you've installed a component that requires extensive configuration, you might want to use it on another computer without having to go through the whole configuration process again. To do this, you would install and configure the component, export the component's registry settings from the computer, copy the settings to another computer, and then import the registry settings so that the component is properly configured. Of course, this technique works only if the complete configuration of the component is stored in the registry, but you can see how useful being able to export and import registry data can be.

When you use the REG export and REG import commands, exporting and importing registry data is fairly easy. This includes branches of data stemming from a particular root key as well as individual subkeys and the values they contain. When you export data, you create a .reg file that contains the designated registry data. This registry file is a script that can then be loaded back into the registry of this or any other computer by importing it.

Because the registry script is written as standard text, you could view it and, if necessary, modify it in any standard text editor as well. To export registry data to a file in the current directory, use the following syntax:

```
reg export KeyName FileName
```

where *KeyName* is the name of the subkey you want to work with and *FileName* is the name of the file in which to store the registry data. As before, the subkey path can include the UNC name or IP address of a remote computer. However, a remote source subkey can use only the HKLM or HKU root keys. In this example, you export the MSDTC subkey on MAILER1:

```
reg export \\Mailer1\HKLM\SOFTWARE\Microsoft\MSDTC msdtc-regkey.reg
```

You can export keys at any level of the registry. For example, you export the HKLM root key and all its subkeys using the following command line:

```
reg export HKLM hklm.reg
```

Tip Add the /Y parameter to force REG export to overwrite an existing file. You can export the entire registry at the command line by typing **regedit /e *SaveFile***, where *SaveFile* is the complete file path to the location where you want to save the copy of the registry. For example, if you wanted to save a copy of the registry to C:\Save\Regdata.reg, you would type **regedit /e C:\Save\Regdata.reg**.

Importing registry data adds the contents of the registry script file to the registry of the computer you are working with, either creating new keys and values if they didn't previously exist or overwriting keys and values if they did previously exist. You can import registry data using the REG import command and the following syntax:

```
reg import FileName
```

where *FileName* is the name of the registry file in the current directory you want to import, such as:

```
reg import msdtc-regkey.reg
```

You cannot perform imports remotely or use non-local files for imports. When you are importing registry keys, you must be logged on locally to the computer and the file must exist on the local computer.

Loading and Unloading Registry Keys

Just as you sometimes must export or import registry data, you'll sometimes need to work with individual hive files. The most common reason for doing this is when you must modify a user's profile to correct an issue that prevents the user from accessing or using a system. For example, you may need to load and modify the settings for a user profile because the user inadvertently changed the display mode to an invalid setting and can no longer access the computer locally. With the user profile data loaded into the registry, you could edit the registry to correct the problem and then save the changes so that the user can once again log on to the system.

Another reason for loading registry keys is to change a particular part of the registry on a remote system. Loading and unloading hives affects only HKEY_LOCAL_MACHINE and HKEY_USERS, and you can perform these actions only when one of these root keys is selected. Rather than replacing the selected root key, the hive you are loading then becomes a subkey of that root key. HKEY_LOCAL_MACHINE and HKEY_USERS are of course used to build all the logical root keys used on a system, so you could in fact work with any area of the registry.

The file to be loaded must have been saved by the REG save command. You can load a previously saved hive file using the REG load command and the following syntax:

```
reg load RootKey\KeyName FileName
```

where *RootKey* is the root key under which the temporary key will be created, *KeyName* is the name of the temporary subkey you want to create, and *FileName* is the name of the saved hive file to load. You must create the temporary subkey under HKLM or HKU. In the following example, you create a temporary key called CurrTemp under HKLM and load the Working.hiv hive file into this key:

```
reg load HKLM\CurrTemp Working.hiv
```

You cannot perform loads remotely or use non-local files for loads. When you are loading registry keys, you must be logged on locally to the computer and the file must exist on the local computer.

Once you load a registry key, you can manipulate its subkeys and values using the techniques discussed previously. When you are finished modifying the key, you can save the key to a new registry file using REG save. After you save the key, you can unload the hive file and remove it from the computer's memory and the working registry by using the REG unload command and the following syntax:

```
reg unload RootKey\KeyName
```

where *RootKey* is the root key under which the temporary key was created and *KeyName* is the name of the temporary subkey you want to unload. In the following example, you unload the temporary key called CurrTemp under HKLM:

```
reg unload HKLM\CurrTemp
```

> **Note** You can't work with hive files that are already being used by the operating system or another process. You can, however, make a copy of the hive and then work with it. At the command line, type **reg save** followed by the abbreviated name of the root key to save and the filename to use for the hive file. For example, type **reg save hkcu c:\currhkcu.hiv** to save HKEY_LOCAL_MACHINE to a file called Currhkcu.hiv on the root folder of drive C. Although you can save the logical root keys (HKCC, HKCR, HKCU) in this manner, you can save only subkeys of HKLM and HKU for use in this technique.

Following these rules, if you needed to repair an area of the registry on a remote computer, you could:

1. Access the remote computer and save the registry hive to a file using the REG save command.
2. Copy the registry file to a folder on your computer using XCOPY or a similar command.
3. Load the related hive file into the registry of your computer using the REG load command.
4. Make any necessary changes and then save the changes using the REG save command.

5. Import the registry hive on the remote computer to repair the problem using the REG import command.
6. After you test the changes on the remote computer, unload the registry hive from your computer using the REG unload command.

Managing System Services

Services provide key functions to workstations and servers. To manage system services on local and remote systems, you'll use the service controller command SC, which has several subcommands, only some of which are explored here. The sections that follow discuss each of these subcommands:

- **SC config** Configures service startup and logon accounts
- **SC query** Displays the list of all services configured on the computer
- **SC qc** Displays the configuration of a specific service
- **SC start** Starts services
- **SC stop** Stops services
- **SC pause** Pauses services
- **SC continue** Resumes services
- **SC failure** Sets the actions to take upon failure of a service
- **SC qfailure** Views the actions to take upon failure of a service

With all commands, you can specify the name of the remote computer whose services you want to work with. To do this, insert the UNC name or IP address of the computer before the subcommand you want to use. This makes the syntax

```
sc ServerName Subcommand
```

Viewing Configured Services

To get a list of all services configured on a system, type the following command at the command prompt:

```
sc query type= service state= all
```

or

```
sc ServerName query type= service state= all
```

where *ServerName* is the UNC name or IP address of the remote computer, such as \\Mailer1 or \\192.168.1.100, as shown in the following examples:

```
sc \\Mailer1 query type= service state= all
sc \\192.168.1.100 query type= service state= all
```

Note You must include a space after the equal sign (=) as used with type= *service* and *state= all*. If you don't use a space, the command will fail.

With the *state* flag, you can also use the value *active* (to show running services only) or *inactive* (to show all paused or stopped services). Consider the following examples:

```
sc \\Mailer1 query type= service state= active
sc \\Mailer1 query type= service state= inactive
```

In the first example, you query MAILER1 for a list of all services that are running. In the second example, you query MAILER1 for a list of all services that are stopped.

The output of SC query shows the services and their configurations. Each service entry is formatted as follows:

```
SERVICE_NAME: W3SVC
DISPLAY_NAME: World Wide Web Publishing Service
        TYPE               : 20  WIN32_SHARE_PROCESS
        STATE              : 4  RUNNING
                                (STOPPABLE, PAUSABLE, ACCEPTS_SHUTDOWN)
        WIN32_EXIT_CODE    : 0  (0x0)
        SERVICE_EXIT_CODE  : 0  (0x0)
        CHECKPOINT         : 0x0
        WAIT_HINT          : 0x0
```

As an administrator, the fields you will work with the most are

- **Service Name** The abbreviated name of the service. Only services installed on the system are listed here. If a service you need isn't listed, you'll need to install it.
- **Display Name** The descriptive name of the service.
- **State** The state of the service as Running, Paused, or Stopped.

As you'll see if you run the SC query command, the output is very long and is best used with a filter to get only the information you want to see. For example, if you use the following command, you clean up the output to show only the most important fields:

```
sc query type= service | find /v "x0"
```

Here you pipe the output of SC query through the FIND command and clean up the output so the service entries appear, as shown in this example:

```
SERVICE_NAME: W3SVC
DISPLAY_NAME: World Wide Web Publishing Service
        TYPE               : 20  WIN32_SHARE_PROCESS
        STATE              : 4  RUNNING
                                (STOPPABLE, PAUSABLE, ACCEPTS_SHUTDOWN)
```

Note The parameter /V "x0" tells the FIND command to display only lines of output that do not contain the text x0, which is the common text on the WIN32_Exit_Code, Service_Exit_Code, Checkpoint, and Wait_Hint fields. By specifying that you don't want to see lines of output that contain this value, you therefore remove these unwanted fields from the display.

If you know the name of a service you want to work with, you can use SC qc to display its configuration information. The syntax is

```
sc qc ServiceName
```

where *ServiceName* is the name of the service you want to examine. The output for individual services looks like this:

```
SERVICE_NAME: w3svc
        TYPE               : 20  WIN32_SHARE_PROCESS
        START_TYPE         : 2   AUTO_START
        ERROR_CONTROL      : 1   NORMAL
        BINARY_PATH_NAME   : C:\WINDOWS\System32\svchost.exe -k iissvcs
        LOAD_ORDER_GROUP   :
        TAG                : 0
        DISPLAY_NAME       : World Wide Web Publishing Service
        DEPENDENCIES       : RPCSS
                           : HTTPFilter
                           : IISADMIN
        SERVICE_START_NAME : LocalSystem
```

Note that the output doesn't tell you the current status of the service. It does, however, tell you the following:

- **Binary Path Name** The file path to the executable for the service
- **Dependencies** Services that cannot run unless the specified service is running
- **Display Name** The descriptive name of the service
- **Service Start Name** The name of the user account the service logs on as
- **Start Type** The startup configuration of the service

  Note Services that are configured to start automatically are listed as AUTO_START. Services that are configured to start manually are listed as DEMAND_START. Services that are disabled are listed as DISABLED.

- **Type** The type of service and whether it is a shared process

Note When you are configuring a service logon, it is sometimes important to know whether a process runs in its own context or is shared. Shared processes are listed as WIN32_SHARE_PROCESS. Processes that run in their own context are listed as WIN32_OWN_PROCESS.

Starting, Stopping, and Pausing Services

As an administrator, you'll often have to start, stop, or pause Windows services. The related SC commands and their syntaxes are

Start a service:

```
sc start ServiceName
```

Pause a service:

```
sc pause ServiceName
```

Resume a paused service:

```
sc continue ServiceName
```

Stop a service:

```
sc stop ServiceName
```

where *ServiceName* in each case is the abbreviated name of the service you want to work with, such as

```
sc start w3svc
```

As with all SC commands, you can also specify the name of the remote computer whose services you want to work with. For example, to start the w3svc on MAILER1, you would use the following command:

```
sc \\Mailer1 start w3svc
```

The state listed in the results should show START_PENDING. With stop, pause, and continue you'll see STOP_PENDING, PAUSE_PENDING, and CONTINUE_PENDING respectively as well. If an error results, the output states FAILED and error text is provided to describe the reason for the failure in more detail. If you are trying to start a service that is already started, you'll see the error

```
An instance of the service is already running.
```

If you are trying to stop a service that is already stopped, you'll see the error

```
The service has not been started.
```

Configuring Service Startup

You can set Windows services to start manually or automatically. You can also turn them off permanently by disabling them. You configure service startup using

```
sc config ServiceName start= flag
```

where *ServiceName* is the abbreviated name of the service you want to work with and flag is the startup type to use. For services, valid flag values are

- **Auto** Starts service at system startup
- **Demand** Allows the services to be started manually
- **Disabled** Turns off the service
- **Delayed-Auto** Delays the start of the service until all non-delayed automatic services have started

Following this, you can configure a service to start automatically by using

```
sc config w3svc start= auto
```

or

```
sc \\Mailer1 config w3svc start= auto
```

> **Note** You must include a space after the equal sign (=) as used with *start= auto*. If you don't use a space, the command will fail. Note also the command only reports SUCCESS or FAILURE. It won't tell you that the service was already configured in the startup mode you've specified.
>
> Disabling a service doesn't stop a running service. It only prevents it from being started the next time the computer is booted. To ensure that the service is disabled and stopped, run SC stop and then SC config.

Configuring Service Logon

You can configure Windows services to log on as a system account or as a specific user. To ensure a service logs on as the LocalSystem account, use

```
sc config ServiceName obj= LocalSystem
```

where *ServiceName* is the name of the service you are configuring to use the Local-System account. If the service provides a user interface that can be manipulated, add the flags **type= interact type= own**, as shown in the following example:

```
sc config w3svc obj= LocalSystem type= interact type= own
```

The *type= interact* flag specifies that the service is allowed to interact with the Windows desktop. The *type= own* flag specifies that the service runs in its own process. In the case of a service that shares its executable files with other services, you would use the *type= share* flag, as shown in this example:

```
sc config w3svc obj= LocalSystem type= interact type= share
```

> **Tip** If you don't know whether a service runs as a shared process or in its own context, use SC qc to determine the service's start type. This command is discussed in the section titled "Viewing Configured Services," earlier in this chapter.

Services can also log on using named accounts. To do this, use

```
sc config ServiceName obj= [Domain\]User password= Password
```

where *Domain* is the optional domain name in which the user account is located, *User* is the name of the user account whose permissions you want to use, and *Password* is the password of that account. Consider the following example:

```
sc config w3svc obj= adatum\webbies password= blue5!CraZy
```

Here, you configure W3svc to use the Webbies account in the Adatum domain. The output of the command should state SUCCESS or FAILED. The change will fail if the account name is invalid or doesn't exist, or if the password for the account is invalid.

> **Note** If a service has been previously configured to interact with the desktop under the LocalSystem account, you cannot change the service to run under a domain account without using the type= own flag. The syntax therefore becomes sc config **ServiceName** obj= [**Domain**\]**User** password= Password type= own.

> **Real World** As an administrator, you should keep track of any accounts that are used with services. These accounts can be the source of huge security problems if they're not configured properly. Service accounts should have the strictest security settings and as few permissions as possible while allowing the service to perform necessary functions. Typically, accounts used with services don't need many of the permissions you would assign to a normal user account. For example, most service accounts don't need the right to log on locally. Every administrator should know what service accounts are used (so that he or she can better track use of these accounts), and the accounts should be treated as if they were administrator accounts. This means secure passwords, careful monitoring of account usage, careful application of account permissions and privileges, and so on.

Configuring Service Recovery

Using the SC failure command, you can configure Windows services to take specific actions when a service fails. For example, you can attempt to restart the service or run an application.

You can configure recovery options for the first, second, and subsequent recovery attempts. The current failure count is incremented each time a failure occurs. You can also set a parameter that specifies the time that must elapse before the failure counter is reset. For example, you could specify that if 24 hours have passed since the last failure, the failure counter should be reset.

Before you try to configure service recovery, check the current recovery settings using SC qfailure. The syntax is

```
sc qfailure ServiceName
```

where *ServiceName* is the name of the service you want to work with, such as

```
sc qfailure w3svc
```

You can of course specify a remote computer as well, such as

```
sc \\Mailer1 qfailure w3svc
```

or

```
sc \\192.168.1.100 qfailure w3svc
```

In the output, the failure actions are listed in the order they are performed. In the following example output, W3svc is configured to attempt to restart the service the first and second time the service fails and to restart the computer if the service fails a third time:

```
[SC] QueryServiceConfig2 SUCCESS

SERVICE_NAME: w3svc
        RESET_PERIOD (in seconds)    : 86400
        REBOOT_MESSAGE               :
        COMMAND_LINE                 :
         FAILURE_ACTIONS               : RESTART -- Delay = 1 milliseconds.
                                         RESTART -- Delay = 1 milliseconds.
                                         REBOOT -- Delay = 1000 milliseconds.
```

> **Note** Windows automatically configures recovery for some critical system services during installation. Typically, these services are configured so that they attempt to restart the service. A few services are configured so that they run programs. For example, the IIS Admin service is configured to run a program called Iisreset.exe if the service fails. This program is an application that corrects service problems and safely manages dependent IIS services while working to restart the IIS Admin service.

The command you use to configure service recovery is SC failure and its basic syntax is

```
sc failure ServiceName reset= FailureResetPeriod actions= RecoveryActions
```

where *ServiceName* is the name of the service you are configuring, *FailureResetPeriod* specifies the time, in seconds, that must elapse without failure in order to reset the failure counter, and *RecoveryActions* are the actions to take when failure occurs plus the delay time (in milliseconds) before that action is initiated. The available recovery actions are

- **Take No Action (indicated by an empty string "")** The operating system won't attempt recovery for this failure but might still attempt recovery of previous or subsequent failures.
- **Restart The Service** Stops and then starts the service after a brief pause.
- **Run A Program** Allows you to run a program or a script in case of failure. The script can be a batch program or a Windows script. If you select this option, set the full file path to the program you want to run and then set any necessary command-line parameters to pass in to the program when it starts.

- **Reboot The Computer** Shuts down and then restarts the computer after the specified delay time is elapsed.

Best Practices When you configure recovery options for critical services, you might want to try to restart the service on the first and second attempts and then reboot the server on the third attempt.

When you work with SC failure, keep the following in mind:

- **The reset period is set in seconds.** Reset periods are commonly set in multiples of hours or days. An hour is 3,600 seconds and a day is 86,400 seconds. For a two-hour reset period, for example, you'd use the value 7,200.
- **Each recovery action must be followed by the time to wait (in milliseconds) before performing the action.** For a service restart you'll probably want to use a short delay, such as 1 millisecond (no delay), 1 second (1,000 milliseconds), or 5 seconds (5,000 milliseconds). For a restart of the computer, you'll probably want to use a longer delay, such as 15 seconds (15,000 milliseconds) or 30 seconds (30,000 milliseconds).
- **Enter the actions and their delay times as a single text entry with each value separated by a forward slash (/).** For example, you could use the value: restart/1000/restart/1000/ reboot/15000. Here, on the first and second attempts the service is restarted after a 1-second delay, and on the third attempt the computer is rebooted after a 15-second delay.

Consider the following examples:

```
sc failure w3svc reset= 86400 actions= restart/1/restart/1/reboot/30000
```

Here, on the first and second attempts the service is restarted almost immediately, and on the third attempt the computer is rebooted after a 30-second delay. In addition, the failure counter is reset if no failures occur in a 24-hour period (86,400 seconds). You can also specify a remote computer by inserting the UNC name or IP address as shown in previous examples.

If you use the Run action, you specify the command or program to run using the *Command=* parameter. Follow the *Command=* parameter with the full file path to the command to run and any arguments to pass to the command. Be sure to enclose the command path and text in double quotation marks, as in the following example:

```
sc failure w3svc reset= 86400 actions= restart/1/restart/1/run/30000
command= "c:\restart_w3svc.exe 15"
```

Restarting and Shutting Down Systems from the Command Line

You'll often find that you need to shut down or restart systems. One way to do this is to use the Shutdown utility, which you can use to work with both local and remote systems. Another way to manage system shutdown or restart is to schedule a shutdown. Here, you can use Schtasks to specify when shutdown should be run or you can create a script with a list of shutdown commands for individual systems.

Real World Although Windows systems usually start up and shut down without problems, they can occasionally stop responding during these processes. If this happens, try to determine the cause. Some of the reasons systems might stop responding include the following:

1. The system is attempting to execute or is running a startup or shutdown script that has not completed or is itself not responding (and in this case, the system might be waiting for the script to time out).
2. A startup initialization file or service may be the cause of the problem and if so, you might need to troubleshoot startup items using the System Configuration Utility (Msconfig). Disabling a service, startup item, or entry in a startup initialization file might also solve the problem.
3. The system may have an antivirus program that is causing the problem. In some cases, the antivirus program may try to scan the removable media drives when you try to shut down the system. To resolve this, configure the antivirus software so that it doesn't scan the removable media drives or other drives with removable media on shutdown. You could also try temporarily disabling or turning off the antivirus program.
4. Improperly configured sound devices can cause startup and shutdown problems. To determine what the possible source is, examine each of these devices in turn. Turn off sound devices and then restart the computer. If the problem clears up, you have to install new drivers for the sound devices you are using or you may have a corrupted Start Windows or Exit Windows sound file.
5. Improperly configured network cards can cause startup and shutdown problems. Try turning off the network adapter and restarting. If that works, you might need to remove and then reinstall the adapter's driver or obtain a new driver from the manufacturer.
6. Improperly configured video adapter drivers can cause startup and shutdown problems. From another computer, remotely log on and try to roll back the current video drivers to a previous version. If that's not possible, try uninstalling and then reinstalling the video drivers.

Managing Restart and Shutdown of Local Systems

On a local system, you can manage shutdown and restart using the following commands:

Shutdown local system:

```
shutdown /s /t ShutdownDelay /l /f
```

Restart local system:

```
shutdown /r /t ShutdownDelay /l /f
```

Cancel delayed shutdown of local computer:

```
shutdown /a
```

where /T *ShutdownDelay* is used to set the optional number of seconds to wait before shutdown or restart, /L optionally logs off the current user immediately, and /F optionally forces running applications to close without warning users in advance. In this example, the local system is restarted after a 60-second delay:

```
shutdown /r /t 60
```

> **Best Practices** In most network environments, system uptime is of the utmost importance. Systems that are restarting or shutting down aren't available to users, which might mean someone won't be able to finish her work and might get upset as a result. Rather than shut down systems in the middle of business hours, consider performing shutdowns before or after normal business hours. But if you need to shut down a system during business hours, warn users beforehand if possible, allowing them to save current work and log off the system as necessary.

Managing Restart and Shutdown of Remote Systems

With remote systems, you need to specify the UNC name or IP address of the system you want to shut down or restart using the /M parameter. Thus, the basic syntax for shutdown, restart, and cancel delayed shutdown needs to be modified as shown in these examples:

Shutdown remote system:

```
shutdown /s /t ShutdownDelay /l /f /m \\System
```

Restart remote system:

```
shutdown /r /t ShutdownDelay /l /f /m \\System
```

Cancel delayed shutdown of remote computer:

```
shutdown /a /m \\System
```

In this example, MAILER1 is restarted after a 30-second delay:

```
shutdown /r /t 30 /m \\Mailer1
```

In this example, the system with the IP address 192.168.1.105 is restarted immediately and running applications are forced to stop running:

```
shutdown /r /f /m \\192.168.1.105
```

Adding Shutdown or Restart Reasons and Comments

In most network environments, it's a good idea to document the reasons for shutting down or restarting computers. Following an unplanned shutdown, you can document the shutdown in the computer's system log by expanding the syntax to include the following parameters:

```
/e /c "UnplannedReason" /d MajorCode:MinorCode
```

where /E replaces the /R switch, */C "UnplannedReason"* sets the detailed reason (which can be up to 512 characters in length) for the shutdown or restart, and */D MajorCode:MinorCode* sets the reason code for the shutdown. Reason codes are arbitrary, with valid major codes ranging from 0 to 255 and valid minor reason codes ranging from 0 to 65,535.

For a planned restart, consider the following example:

```
shutdown /r /m \\Mailer1 /c "System Reset" /d 5:15
```

In this example, you are restarting MAILER1 and documenting the reason for the unplanned restart as a "System Reset" using the reason code 5:15.

Table 5-3 summarizes the common reasons and codes for shutdowns and restarts for Windows Vista and Windows Server 2008. As the table shows, Windows can generate the prefix code E for Expected, U for Unexpected, and P for planned as well as various combinations of these prefix codes.

Table 5-3 Common Reasons and Codes for Shutdowns and Restarts

Prefix Code	Major Code	Minor Code	Shutdown or Restart Type
U	0	0	Other (Unplanned)
E	0	0	Other (Unplanned)
E P	0	0	Other (Planned)
U	0	5	Other Failure: System Unresponsive
E	1	1	Hardware: Maintenance (Unplanned)
E P	1	1	Hardware: Maintenance (Planned)
E	1	2	Hardware: Installation (Unplanned)
E P	1	2	Hardware: Installation (Planned)
P	2	3	Operating System: Upgrade (Planned)
E	2	4	Operating System: Reconfiguration (Unplanned)
E P	2	4	Operating System: Reconfiguration (Planned)
P	2	16	Operating System: Service pack (Planned)
U	2	17	Operating System: Hotfix (Unplanned)
P	2	17	Operating System: Hotfix (Planned)
U	2	18	Operating System: Security fix (Unplanned)
P	2	18	Operating System: Security fix (Planned)
E	4	1	Application: Maintenance (Unplanned)
E P	4	1	Application: Maintenance (Planned)
E P	4	2	Application: Installation (Planned)
E	4	5	Application: Unresponsive
E	4	6	Application: Unstable

Table 5-3 Common Reasons and Codes for Shutdowns and Restarts

Prefix Code	Major Code	Minor Code	Shutdown or Restart Type
U	5	15	System Failure: Stop error
E	5	19	Security issue
U	5	19	Security issue
E P	5	19	Security issue (Planned)
E	5	20	Loss of network connectivity (Unplanned)
U	6	11	Power Failure: Cord Unplugged
U	6	12	Power Failure: Environment
P	7	0	Legacy API shutdown (Planned)

For the SHUTDOWN command, only the P: and the U: prefixes are accepted. For example, with planned shutdowns and restarts, prefix the reason codes with **p:** to indicate a planned shutdown, as shown here:

```
/c "PlannedReason" /d p:MajorCode:MinorCode
```

For instance, consider the following code:

```
shutdown /r /m \\Mailer1 /c "Planned Application Upgrade" /d p:4:2
```

In this example, you are restarting MAILER1 and documenting the reason for the planned restart as a "Planned Application Upgrade" using the reason code 4:2.

Chapter 6

Event Logging, Tracking, and Monitoring

Up to this point, we have focused on tools and techniques used to manage local and remote systems from the command line. Now let's look at how the event logs can be used for monitoring and optimization. Monitoring is the process by which systems are regularly checked for problems. Optimization is the process of fine-tuning system performance to maintain or achieve its optimal capacity.

This chapter examines the logging tools available for Windows systems that can help you to identify and track system problems, monitor applications and services, and maintain system security. When systems slow down, behave erratically, or experience other problems, you may want to look to the event logs to identify the potential source of the problem. Once you've identified problem sources or issues, you can perform maintenance or preventative tasks to resolve or eliminate them. Using performance monitoring, you can watch for events to occur and take appropriate action to resolve them.

Windows Event Logging

In Microsoft Windows, an *event* is any significant occurrence in the operating system that requires users or administrators to be notified. Events are recorded in the Windows event logs and provide important historical information to help you monitor systems, maintain system security, solve problems, and perform diagnostics. It's not just important to sift regularly through the information collected in these logs, it is essential. Administrators should closely monitor the event logs of every business server and ensure that workstations are configured to track important system events. On servers, you want to ensure that systems are secure, that applications and services are operating normally, and that the server isn't experiencing errors that could hamper performance. On workstations, you want to ensure that the events you need to maintain systems and resolve problems are being logged, and that the logs are accessible to you as necessary.

The Windows service that manages event logging is called the Windows Event Log service. When this service is started, Windows logs important information. The logs available on a system depend on the system's role and the services installed. Two general types of log files are used:

- **Windows Logs** Logs that the operating system uses to record general system events related to applications, security, setup, and system components
- **Applications And Services Logs** Logs that specific applications and services use to record application-specific or service-specific events

Logs you may see include the following:

- **Application** This log records significant incidents associated with specific applications. For example, Exchange Server logs events related to mail exchange, including events for the information store, mailboxes, and service states. By default, this log is stored in %SystemRoot%\System32\Winevt\Logs\Application.Evtx.
- **Directory Service** On domain controllers, this log records incidents from Active Directory Domain Service (AD DS), including events related to directory startup, global catalogs, and integrity checking. By default, this log is stored in %SystemRoot%\System32\Winevt\Logs\Directory Service.Evtx.
- **DNS Server** On DNS servers, this log records DNS queries, responses, and other DNS activities. By default, this log is stored in %SystemRoot%\System32\Winevt\Logs\DNS Server.Evtx.
- **DFS Replication** On domain controllers using DFS replication, this log records file replication activities on the system, including events for service status and control, scanning data in system volumes, and managing replication sets. By default, this log is stored in %SystemRoot%\System32\Winevt\Logs\DFS Replication.Evtx.
- **File Replication Service** This log records file replication activities on the system. By default, this log is stored in %SystemRoot%\System32\Winevt\Logs\File Replication Service.Evtx.
- **Forwarded Events** When event forwarding is configured, this log records forwarded events from other servers. The default location is %SystemRoot%\System32\Winevt\Logs\FordwardedEvents.Evtx.
- **Hardware Events** When hardware subsystem event reporting is configured, this log records hardware events reported to the operating system. The default location is %SystemRoot%\System32\Winevt\Logs\HardwareEvent.Evtx.
- **Microsoft\Windows** A group of logs that track events related to specific Windows services and features. Logs are organized by component type and event category.
- **Security** This log records events related to security such as logon/logoff, privilege use, and resource access. By default, this log is stored in %System-Root%\System32\Winevt\Logs\Security.Evtx.

> **Note** To gain access to security logs, users must be granted the user right Manage Auditing And Security Log. By default, members of the administrators group have this user right. You can learn more about assigning user rights in the section titled "Configuring User Rights Policies," in Chapter 10, "Creating User and Group Accounts," of the *Windows Server 2008 Administrator's Pocket Consultant* (Microsoft Press, 2008).

- **Setup** This log records events logged by the operating system or its components during setup and installation. The default location is: %SystemRoot%\System32\Winevt\Logs\Setup.Evtx.
- **System** This log records events from the operating system or its components, such as the failure of a service to start, driver initialization, system-wide messages, and other messages that relate to the system in general. By default, this log is stored in %SystemRoot%\System32\Winevt\Logs\System.Evtx.
- **Windows PowerShell** This log records activities related to the use of the Windows PowerShell. The default location is %SystemRoot%\System32\Winevt\Logs\Windows PowerShell.Evtx.

Events range in severity from informational messages to general warnings to serious incidents such as critical errors and failures. The category of an event is indicated by its event level. Event levels include

- **Information** Indicates an informational event has occurred, which is generally related to a successful action.
- **Warning** Indicates a general warning. Warnings are often useful in preventing future system problems.
- **Error** Indicates a critical error, such as the failure of a service to start.
- **Audit Success** Indicates the successful execution of an action that you are tracking through auditing, such as privilege use.
- **Audit Failure** Indicates the failed execution of an action that you are tracking through auditing, such as failure to log on.

> **Note** Of the many event types, the two you'll want to monitor closely are warnings and errors. Whenever these types of events occur and you're unsure of the reason, you should take a closer look to determine whether you need to take further action.

In addition to level, each event has the following common properties associated with it:

- **Date and Time** Specifies the date and time the event occurred.
- **Source** Identifies the source of the event, such as an application, service, or system component. The event source is useful for pinpointing the cause of an event.
- **Event ID** Details the specific event that occurred with a numeric identifier. Event IDs are generated by the event source and used to uniquely identify the event.
- **Task Category** Specifies the category of the event, which is sometimes used to further describe the related action. Each event source has its own event categories. For example, with the security source, categories include logon/logoff, privilege use, policy change, and account management.

- **User** Identifies the user account that caused the event to be generated. Users can include special identities, such as Local Service, Network Service, and Anonymous Logon, as well as actual user accounts. The user account can also be listed as N/A to indicate that a user account is not applicable in this situation.
- **Computer** Identifies the computer that caused the event to occur.
- **Description** Provides a detailed description of the event and may also include details about where to find more information to resolve or handle an issue. This field is available when you double-click a log entry in Event Viewer.
- **Data** Any data or error code output by the event

The graphical tool you use to manage events is Event Viewer. You can start this tool by typing **eventvwr** at the command line for the local computer, or **eventvwr *ComputerName***, where *ComputerName* is the name of the remote computer whose events you wish to examine. As with most GUI tools, Event Viewer is easy to use and you will want to continue to use it for certain management tasks. For example, you must use Event Viewer to control the size of the event logs, to specify how logging is handled, and to archive event logs. You cannot perform these tasks at the command line.

Windows Vista and Windows Server 2008 provide several different tools and techniques for working with the event logs at the command line, including the following:

- **Powershell Get-Eventlog** Searches event logs and collects event entries that match specific criteria. In a script, you could use Powershell Get-Eventlog to examine events in multiple logs and then store the results in a file, making it easier to track information as well as warnings and errors.
- **Eventcreate** Creates custom events in the event logs. Whenever you run custom scripts on a schedule or as part of routine maintenance, you may want to record the action in the event logs and Eventcreate provides a way to do this.
- **Custom views** Uses XPath queries to create custom or filtered views of event logs, allowing you to quickly and easily find events that match specific criteria. Because XPath queries can be used on any compatible system, you can re-create custom and filtered views on other computers simply by running the query on a target computer.

Real World Monitoring system events isn't something you should do haphazardly. Rather, it is something you should do routinely and thoroughly. With servers, you will want to examine event logs at least once a day. With workstations, you will want to examine logs on specific workstations as necessary, such as when a user reports a problem.

Viewing and Filtering Event Logs

Using the Windows PowerShell Get-Eventlog cmdlet, you can obtain detailed information from the event logs. When working with Get-Eventlog, don't overlook the power of automation. You don't have to run the command manually each time from a Windows PowerShell prompt. Instead, you can create a script to query the event logs and then save the results to a file. If you copy that file to a published folder on an intranet server, you can use your Web browser to examine event listings. Not only will that save you time, it will also give you a single location for examining event logs and determining whether any issues require further study.

> **Note** In this book, I discuss tools that provide the best way to get the job done using the command line. In this instance, the best way to extract information from the event logs at the command line is to use Windows PowerShell. Although I introduce Windows PowerShell and discuss key cmdlets in this book, this book does not provide in-depth information on Windows PowerShell. For in-depth information on Windows PowerShell, I recommend *Windows PowerShell Administrator's Pocket Consultant* (Microsoft Press, 2008).

Viewing Events

You run Get-Eventlog at a Windows PowerShell prompt. The basic syntax for Get-Eventlog is

```
get-eventlog "LogName"
```

where *LogName* is the name of the log you want to work with, such as "Application," "System," or "Directory Service." In this example, you examine the Application log:

```
get-eventlog "Application"
```

> **Note** Technically, the quotation marks are necessary only when the log name contains a space, as is the case with the DNS Server, Directory Service, and File Replication Service logs. However, I recommend using the quotation marks all the time. That way, you won't forget them when they are needed and they won't cause your scripts or scheduled tasks to fail.

The output of this query would look similar to the following:

```
Index Time          Type Source                EventID Message
----- ----          ---- ------                ------- -------
15959 Mar 20 16:56  Erro MSExchange System...     4001 A transient failure
 has occurred. The problem may resolve its...
15958 Mar 20 16:55  Erro MSExchange System...     4001 A transient failure
 has occurred. The problem may resolve its...
15957 Mar 20 16:54  Erro MSExchange System...     4001 A transient failure
 has occurred. The problem may resolve its...
15956 Mar 20 16:53  Erro MSExchange System...     4001 A transient failure
 has occurred. The problem may resolve its...
```

As you can see, the output shows the Index, Time, Type, Source, Event ID, and Message properties of events. Because the index is the position of the event in the log, this example lists events 15,956 to 15,959. When you follow Get-Eventlog with the log name, the –Logname parameter is implied. You can also specify the –Logname parameter directly as shown in this example:

```
get-eventlog -logname "security"
```

By default, Get-Eventlog returns every event in the specified event log from newest to oldest. In most cases, this is simply too much information and you'll need to filter the events to get a usable amount of data. One way to filter the event logs is to specify that you only want to see details about the newest events. For example, you might want to see only the 100 newest events in a log.

Using the –Newest parameter, you can limit the return to the newest events. The following example lists the 100 newest events in the security log:

```
get-eventlog "security" -newest 50
```

Unlike previous command-line utilities that we've worked with, Get-Eventlog is a Windows PowerShell cmdlet. If this is your first time working with Windows PowerShell, you'll need to ensure that the feature is installed on your computer. If you don't want to invoke a separate Windows PowerShell instance, you can invoke Windows PowerShell only to run the Get-Eventlog cmdlet, as shown in this example:

```
powershell.exe get-eventlog -logname "security"
```

You also could insert this command in a batch script. In a batch script, this command would invoke Windows PowerShell, execute the Get-Eventlog cmdlet, and then exit Windows PowerShell.

Filtering Events

One of the key reasons for using Get-Eventlog is its ability to group and filter events in the result set. When you group events by type, you can more easily separate informational events from critical, warning, and error events. When you group by source, you can more easily track events from specific sources. When you group by event ID, you can more easily correlate the recurrence of specific events.

You can group events by source, eventid, entrytype, and timegenerated using the following technique:

1. Get the events you want to work with and store them in the *$e* variable by entering:

   ```
   $e = get-eventlog -newest 100 -logname "application"
   ```

2. Use the Group-Object cmdlet to group the event objects stored in *$e* by a specified property. In this example, you group by eventid:

   ```
   $e | group-object -property eventid
   ```

Another way to work with events is to sort them according to a specific property. You can sort by source, eventid, entrytype, or timegenerated using the following technique:

1. Get the events you want to work with and store them in the *$e* variable by entering:

   ```
   $e = get-eventlog -newest 100 -logname "application"
   ```

2. Use the Sort-Object cmdlet to sort the event objects stored in *$e* by a specified property. In this example, you sort by entrytype:

   ```
   $e | sort-object -property entrytype
   ```

Typically, you won't want to see every event generated on a system. More often, you will want to see only warnings or critical errors, and that is precisely what filters are for. Using filters, you can include only events that match the criteria you specify. To do this, you would search the EntryType property for occurrences of the word *error*. Here is an example:

1. Get the events you want to work with and store them in the *$e* variable by entering:

   ```
   $e = get-eventlog -newest 500 -logname "application"
   ```

2. Use the Where-Object cmdlet to search for specific text in a named property of the event objects stored in *$e*. In this example, you match events with the error entry type:

   ```
   $e | where-object {$_.EntryType -match "error"}
   ```

The Where-Object cmdlet uses a search algorithm that is not case-sensitive, meaning you could enter Error, error, or ERROR to match error events. You can also search for warning, critical, and information events. Because Where-Object considers partial text matches to be valid, you don't want to enter the full entry type. You could also search for warn, crit, or info, such as:

```
$e = get-eventlog -newest 100 -logname "application"
$e | where-object {$_.EntryType -match "warn"}
```

You can use Where-Object with other event object properties as well. The following example searches for event sources containing the text MSDTC:

```
$e = get-eventlog -newest 500 -logname "application"
$e | where-object {$_.Source -match "MSDTC}
```

The following example searches for event ID 15001:

```
$e = get-eventlog -newest 500 -logname "application"
$e | where-object {$_.EventID -match "15001"}
```

You can automate the event querying process by creating a Windows PowerShell script that obtains the event information you want to see and then writes it to a text file. Consider the following example:

```
$e = get-eventlog -newest 100 -logname "system"
$e | where-object {$_.EntryType -match "error"} > currentlog.txt
```

```
$e = get-eventlog -newest 500 -logname "application"
$e | where-object {$_.EntryType -match "error"} >> currentlog.txt

$e = get-eventlog -newest 500 -logname "directory service"
$e | where-object {$_.EntryType -match "error"} >> currentlog.txt
```

Here, you are examining the system, application and directory service event logs and writing any resulting output to a network share on CorpIntranet01. If any of the named logs have error events among the 500 most recent events in the logs, the errors are written to the Currentlog.txt file. Because the first redirection is overwrite (>) and the remaining entries are append (>>), any existing Currentlog.txt file is overwritten each time the script runs. This ensures that only current events are listed. To take the automation process a step further, you can create a scheduled task that runs the script each day or at specific intervals during the day.

Windows PowerShell script files have the .ps1 filename extension. (Note that this is the letter P, the letter S, and the digit one.) To run a script at the Windows PowerShell prompt, you type the name of the script and optionally, the filename extension. You must specify the full qualified path to the script file, even if the script is in the current directory. To indicate the current directory, type the directory name or use the dot (.) to represent the current directory. Following this, if you saved the Windows PowerShell script as a file called CheckEvents.ps1 in the current directory, you could run the script by entering **.\checkevents.ps1** at the Windows PowerShell prompt.

Writing Custom Events to the Event Logs

Whenever you work with automated scripts, scheduled tasks, or custom applications, you might want those scripts, tasks, or applications to write custom events to the event logs. For example, if a script runs normally, you might want to write an informational event in the application log that specifies this so it is easier to determine that the script ran and completed normally. Similarly, if a script doesn't run normally and generates errors, you might want to log an error or warning event in the application log so that you'll know to examine the script and determine what happened.

> **Tip** You can track errors that occur in scripts using *%ErrorLevel%*. This environment variable tracks the exit code of the most recently used command. If the command executes normally, the error level is zero (0). If an error occurs while executing the command, the error level is set to a nonzero value. To learn moreabout working with error levels, see the section titled "Getting Acquainted with Variables" in Chapter 3, "Command-Line Scripting Essentials."

To create custom events, you'll use the Eventcreate utility. Custom events can be logged in any available log except the security log, and can include the event source, ID, and description you want to use. The syntax for Eventcreate is

```
eventcreate /l LogName /so EventSource /t EventType /id EventID
/d EventDescr
```

where

- **LogName** Sets the name of the log to which the event should be written. Use quotation marks if the log name contains spaces, as in "DNS Server."

  Tip You cannot write custom events to the security log. You can, however, write custom events to the other logs. Start by writing a dummy event using the event source you want to register for use with that log. The initial event for that source will be written to the application log. You can then use the source with the specified log and your custom events.

- **EventSource** Specifies the source to use for the event and can be any string of characters. If the string contains spaces, use quotation marks, as in "Event Tracker." In most cases, you'll want the event source to identify the application, task, or script that is generating the error.

  Caution Carefully plan the event source you want to use before you write events to the logs using those sources. Each event source you use must be unique and cannot have the same name as an existing source used by an installed service or application. Further, you shouldn't use event source names used by Windows roles, role services, or features. For example, you shouldn't use DNS, W32Time, or Ntfrs as sources because these sources are used by Windows Server 2008. Additionally, once you use an event source with a particular log, the event source is registered for use with that log on the specified system. For example, you cannot use "EventChecker" as a source in the application log and in the system log on MAILER1. If you try to write an event using "EventChecker" to the system log after writing a previous event with that source to the application log, you will see the following error message: "ERROR: Source already exists in 'Application' log. Source cannot be duplicated."

- **EventType** Sets the event type as Information, Warning, or Error. "Success Audit" and "Failure Audit" event types are not valid; these events are used with the security logs and you cannot write custom events to the security logs.
- **EventID** Specifies the numeric ID for the event and can be any value from 1 to 1,000. Before you assign event IDs haphazardly, you may want to create a list of the general events that can occur and then break these down into categories. You could then assign a range of event IDs to each category. For example, events in the 100s could be general events, events in the 200s could be status events, events in the 500s could be warning events, and events in the 900s could be error events.
- **EventDescr** Sets the description for the event and can be any string of characters. Be sure to enclose the description in quotation marks.

Note Eventcreate runs by default on the local computer with the permissions of the user who is currently logged on. As necessary, you can also specify the remote computer whose tasks you want to query and the Run As permissions using /S *Computer* /u [*Domain*\]*User* [/P *Password*], where *Computer* is the remote computer name or IP address, *Domain* is the optional domain name in which the user account is located, *User* is the name of the user account whose permissions you want to use, and *Password* is the optional password for the user account.

To see how you can use Eventcreate, consider the following examples:

Create an information event in the application log with the source Event Tracker and event ID 209:

```
eventcreate /l "application" /t information /so "Event Tracker"
/id 209 /d "evs.bat script ran without errors."
```

Create a warning event in the system log with the source CustApp and event ID 511:

```
eventcreate /l "system" /t warning /so "CustApp" /id 511 /d
"sysck.exe didn't complete successfully."
```

Create an error event in the system log on MAILER1 with the source "SysMon" and event ID 918:

```
eventcreate /s Mailer1 /l "system" /t error /so "SysMon" /id 918
/d "sysmon.exe was unable to verify write operation."
```

Creating and Using Saved Queries

For Windows Vista and Windows Server 2008, Microsoft significantly enhanced Event Viewer's filtering and query capabilities. Because of these enhancements, Event Viewer now supports XPath queries for creating custom views and filtering event logs. XPath is a non-XML language used to identify specific parts of XML documents. Event Viewer uses XPath expressions that match and select elements in a source log and copy them to a destination log to create a custom or filtered view.

When you are creating a custom or filtered view in Event Viewer, you can copy the XPath query and save it to an Event Viewer Custom View file. By running this query again, you can re-create the custom view or filter on any computer running Windows Vista or Windows Server 2008. For example, if you create a filtered view of the application log that helps you identify a problem with Microsoft SQL Server, you could save the related XPath query to a Custom View file so that you can create the filtered view on other computers in your organization.

Event Viewer creates several filtered views of the event logs for you automatically. Filtered views are listed under the Custom Views node. When you select the Administrative Events node, you'll see a list of all errors and warnings for all logs. When you expand the Server Roles node and then select a role-specific view, you'll see a list of all events for the selected role.

You can create and save your own custom view by following these steps:

1. Start Event Viewer by clicking Start, clicking Administrative Tools, and then clicking Event Viewer.
2. Select the Custom Views node. In the Actions pane or on the Action menu, click Create Custom View.
3. In the Create Custom View dialog box, shown in Figure 6-1, use the Logged list to select the included time frame for logged events. You can choose to include events from Anytime, the Last Hour, Last 12 Hours, Last 24 Hours, Last 7 Days, or Last 30 Days.

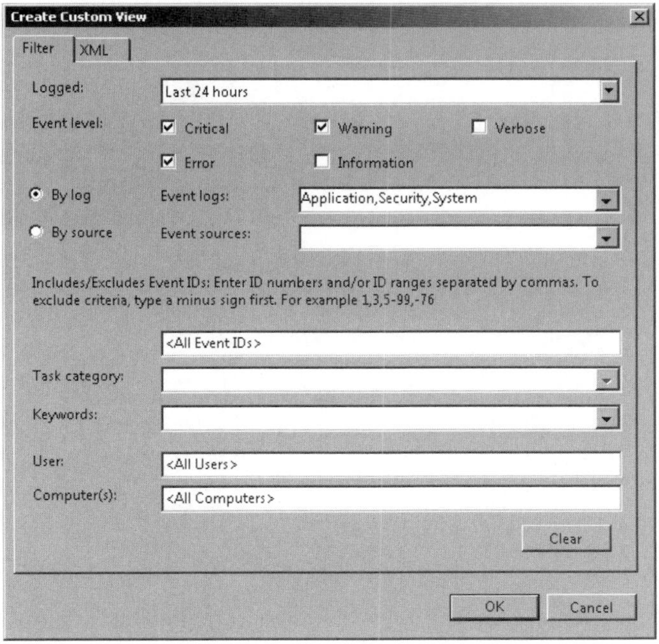

Figure 6-1 Create a filter to specify the types of events to display.

4. Use the Event Level check boxes to specify the level of events to include. Select Verbose to get additional detail.
5. You can create a custom view for either a specific set of logs or a specific set of event sources:
   - Use the Event Logs list to select event logs to include. You can select multiple event logs by selecting their related check boxes. If you select specific event logs, all other event logs are excluded.
   - Use the Event Sources list to select event sources to include. You can select multiple event sources by selecting their related check boxes. If you select specific event sources, all other event sources are excluded.
6. Optionally, use the User and Computer(s) boxes to specify users and computers that should be included. If you do not specify the users and computers to be included, events generated by all users and computers are included.
7. Click the XML tab to display the related XPath query, as shown in Figure 6-2.

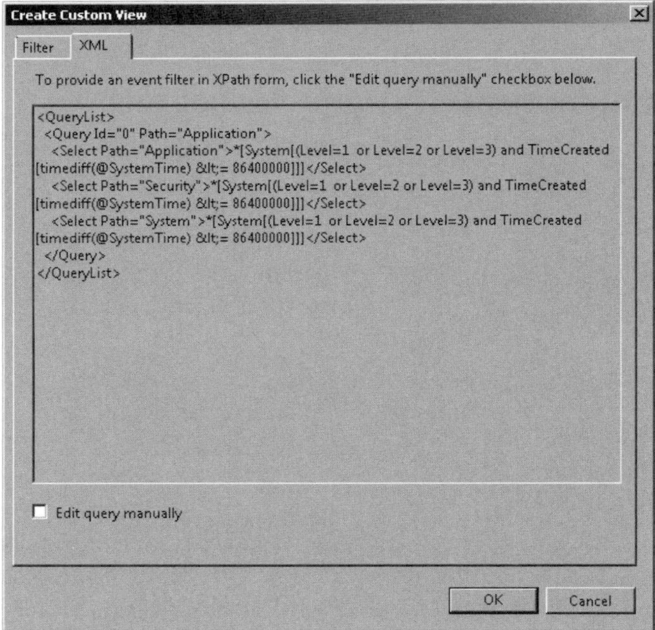

Figure 6-2 Review the related XPath query.

8. Click OK to close the Create Custom View dialog box. In the Save Filter To Custom View dialog box, shown in Figure 6-3, type a name and description for the custom view.

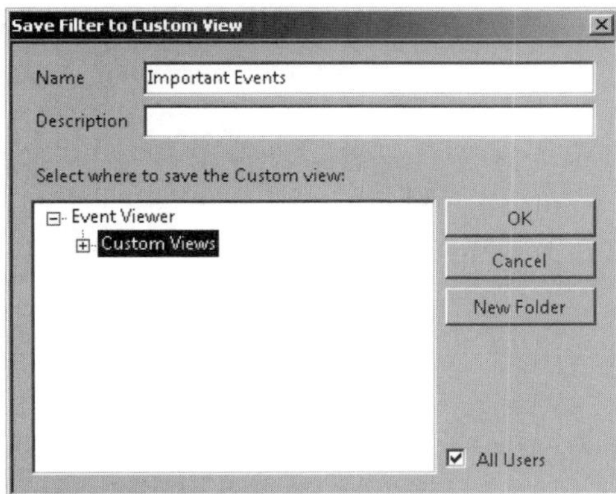

Figure 6-3 Save the filtered view.

9. Select where to save the custom view. By default, custom views are saved under the Custom View node. You can create a new node by clicking New Folder, entering the name of the new folder, and then clicking OK.
10. Click OK to close the Save Filter To Custom View dialog box. You should now see a filtered list of events.
11. Right-click the custom view and then select Export Custom View. Use the Save As dialog box to select a save location and enter a filename for the Event Viewer Custom View file.

The Custom View file contains the XPath query that was displayed on the XML tab previously. Members of the Event Log Readers group, administrators, and others with appropriate permissions can run the query to view events on remote computers using the following syntax:

```
eventvwr ComputerName /v: QueryFile
```

where *ComputerName* is the name of the remote computer whose events you wish to examine and *QueryFile* is the name or full path to the Custom View file containing the XPath query, such as:

```
eventvwr mailserver25 /v: importantevents.xml
```

When Event Viewer starts, you'll find the custom view under the Custom Views node.

Monitoring Performance: The Essentials

Now that you know how to view, filter, and create events, let's look at techniques that you can use to monitor a computer's performance. Windows Vista and Windows Server 2008 have several tools for this purpose and in this section, we'll look at the Typeperf command-line utility. In the next chapter, you'll learn about other tools for monitoring performance.

Understanding Performance Monitoring at the Command Line

Typeperf is a tool designed to track and display performance information in real time. It gathers information on any performance parameters you've configured for monitoring and presents it on the command line. Each performance item you want to monitor is defined by the following three components:

- **Performance object** Represents any system component that has a set of measurable properties. A performance object can be a physical part of the operating system, such as the memory, the processor, or the paging file; a logical component, such as a logical disk or print queue; or a software element, such as a process or a thread.
- **Performance object instance** Represents single occurrences of performance objects. If a particular object has multiple instances, such as when a computer has multiple processors or multiple disk drives, you can use an object instance to track a specific occurrence of that object. You could also elect to track all instances of an object, such as whether you want to monitor all processors on a system.
- **Performance counter** Represents measurable properties of performance objects. For example, with a paging file, you can measure the percentage utilization using the %Usage counter.

In a standard installation of Windows Vista or Windows Server 2008, many performance objects are available for monitoring. As you add services, applications, and components, additional performance objects can become available. For example, when you install the Domain Name System (DNS) on a server, the DNS object becomes available for monitoring on that computer.

The most common performance objects you'll want to monitor are summarized in Table 6-1. Like all performance objects, each performance object listed here has a set of counters that you can track. The most commonly tracked performance objects are Memory, PhysicalDisk, and Processor.

Table 6-1 Commonly Tracked Performance Objects

Performance Object	Description
Cache	Monitors the file system cache, which is an area of physical memory that indicates application I/O activity.
Database ==> Instances	Monitors performance for instances of the embedded database management system used by the operating system.
IPv4	Monitors IPv4 communications and related activities.
IPv6	Monitors IPv6 communications and related activities.
LogicalDisk	Monitors the logical volumes on a computer.
Memory	Monitors memory performance for system cache (including pooled, paged memory and pooled, nonpaged memory), physical memory, and virtual memory.

Table 6-1 Commonly Tracked Performance Objects

Performance Object	Description
Network Interface	Monitors the network adapters configured on the computer.
Objects	Monitors the number of events, mutexes, processes, sections, semaphores, and threads on the computer.
Paging File	Monitors page file current and peak usage.
PhysicalDisk	Monitors hard disk read/write activity as well as data transfers, hard faults, and soft faults.
Print Queue	Monitors print jobs, spooling, and print queue activity.
Process	Monitors all processes running on a computer.
Processor	Monitors processor idle time, idle states, usage, deferred procedure calls, and interrupts.
Server	Monitors communication between the computer and the network as well as important usage statistics, including logon errors, access errors, and user sessions.
Server Work Queues	Monitors threading and client requests.
System	Monitors system-level counters, including processes, threads, context switching of threads, file system control operations, system calls, and system uptime.
TCPv4	Monitors TCPv4 communications and related activities.
TCPv6	Monitors TCPv6 communications and related activities.
Thread	Monitors all running threads and allows you to examine usage statistics for individual threads by process ID.
UDPv4	Monitors UDPv4 communications and related activities.
UDPv6	Monitors UDPv6 communications and related activities.

Tracking Performance Data

Using Typeperf, you can write performance data to the command line or to a log file. The key to using Typeperf is to identify the pathnames of the performance counters you want to track. The performance counter path has the following syntax:

ComputerName***ObjectName******ObjectCounter***

where *ComputerName* is the computer name or IP address of the local or remote computer you want to work with, *ObjectName* is the name of a counter object, and *ObjectCounter* is the name of the object counter to use. For example, if you wanted to track the available memory on FileServer42, you'd type the following:

```
typeperf "\\fileserver42\memory\available mbytes"
```

Note Enclosing the counter path in double quotation marks is required in this example because the counter path includes spaces. Although double quotation marks aren't always required, it is good form to always use them.

You can also easily track all counters for an object by using an asterisk (*) as the counter name, such as in the following example:

```
typeperf "\\fileserver42\Memory\*"
```

Here, you track all counters for the Memory object.

When objects have multiple instances, such as the Processor or LogicalDisk object, you must specify the object instance you want to work with. The syntax for this is as follows:

```
\\ComputerName\ObjectName(ObjectInstance)\ObjectCounter
```

Here, you follow the object name with the object instance in parentheses. When an object has multiple instances, you can work with all instances of that object using _Total as the instance name. You can work with a specific instance of an object by using its instance identifier. For example, if you want to examine the Processor\%Processor Time counter, you can use this command line to work with all processor instances:

```
typeperf "\\fileserver42\Processor(_Total)\%Processor Time"
```

or this command line to work with a specific processor instance:

```
typeperf "\\fileserver42\Processor(0)\%Processor Time"
```

Here, Processor(0) identifies the first processor on the system.

Typeperf has many available parameters, as summarized in Table 6-2.

Table 6-2 Parameters for Typeperf

Parameter	Description
–cf <*filename*>	Identifies a file containing a list of performance counters to monitor.
–config <*filename*>	Identifies a settings file containing command options.
–f <CSV|TSV|BIN|SQL>	Sets the output file format. The default is .csv for comma-separated values.
–o <*filename*>	Sets the path of an output file or SQL database.
–q [*object*]	Lists installed counters for the specified object.
–qx [*object*]	Lists installed counters with instances.
–s <*ComputerName*>	Sets the remote computer to monitor if no computer is specified in the counter path.
–sc <*samples*>	Sets the number of samples to collect.
–si <[[hh:]*mm*:]*ss*>	Sets the time between samples. The default is 1 second.
–y	Answers Yes to all questions without prompting.

Typeperf writes its output to the command line in a comma-delimited list by default. You can redirect the output to a file using the –O parameter and set the output format using the –F parameter. The output format indicators are CSV for a comma-delimited text file, TSV for a tab-delimited text file, BIN for a binary file, and SQL for an SQL binary file. Consider the following example:

```
typeperf "\\fileserver42\Memory\*" -o memperf.bin -f bin
```

Here, you track all counters for the Memory object and write the output to a binary file called MemPerf.bin in the current directory.

If you need help determining the available counters for an object, type **typeperf –q** followed by the object name for which you want to view counters. For example, if you enter the following command:

```
typeperf -q Memory
```

you'll see a list of available counters similar to the following:

```
\memory\Page Faults/sec
\memory\Available Bytes
\memory\Committed Bytes
\memory\Commit Limit
\memory\Write Copies/sec
\memory\Transition Faults/sec
\memory\Cache Faults/sec
\memory\Demand Zero Faults/sec
\memory\Pages/sec
\memory\Pages Input/sec
\memory\Page Reads/sec
\memory\Pages Output/sec
\memory\Pool Paged Bytes
\memory\Pool Nonpaged Bytes
\memory\Page Writes/sec
\memory\Pool Paged Allocs
\memory\Pool Nonpaged Allocs
\memory\Free System Page Table Entries
\memory\Cache Bytes
\memory\Cache Bytes Peak
\memory\Pool Paged Resident Bytes
\memory\System Code Total Bytes
\memory\System Code Resident Bytes
\memory\System Driver Total Bytes
\memory\System Driver Resident Bytes
\memory\System Cache Resident Bytes
\memory\% Committed Bytes In Use
\memory\Available KBytes
\memory\Available MBytes
\memory\Transition Pages RePurposed/sec
\memory\Free & Zero Page List Bytes
```

```
\memory\Modified Page List Bytes
\memory\Standby Cache Reserve Bytes
\memory\Standby Cache Normal Priority Bytes
\memory\Standby Cache Core Bytes
```

If an object has multiple instances, you can list the installed counters with instances by using the –Qx parameter, such as in the following:

```
typeperf -qx PhysicalDisk
```

The output is a long list of available counters according to their object instances, such as:

```
\PhysicalDisk(0 E: C:)\Current Disk Queue Length
\PhysicalDisk(1 D:)\Current Disk Queue Length
\PhysicalDisk(2 I:)\Current Disk Queue Length
\PhysicalDisk(3 J:)\Current Disk Queue Length
\PhysicalDisk(4 K:)\Current Disk Queue Length
\PhysicalDisk(5 L:)\Current Disk Queue Length
\PhysicalDisk(6 N:)\Current Disk Queue Length
\PhysicalDisk(7 O:)\Current Disk Queue Length
\PhysicalDisk(8 P:)\Current Disk Queue Length
\PhysicalDisk(9 Q:)\Current Disk Queue Length
\PhysicalDisk(_Total)\Current Disk Queue Length
\PhysicalDisk(0 E: C:)\% Disk Time
\PhysicalDisk(1 D:)\% Disk Time
\PhysicalDisk(2 I:)\% Disk Time
\PhysicalDisk(3 J:)\% Disk Time
\PhysicalDisk(4 K:)\% Disk Time
\PhysicalDisk(5 L:)\% Disk Time
\PhysicalDisk(6 N:)\% Disk Time
\PhysicalDisk(7 O:)\% Disk Time
\PhysicalDisk(8 P:)\% Disk Time
\PhysicalDisk(9 Q:)\% Disk Time
\PhysicalDisk(_Total)\% Disk Time
\PhysicalDisk(0 E: C:)\Avg. Disk Queue Length
\PhysicalDisk(1 D:)\Avg. Disk Queue Length
\PhysicalDisk(2 I:)\Avg. Disk Queue Length
\PhysicalDisk(3 J:)\Avg. Disk Queue Length
\PhysicalDisk(4 K:)\Avg. Disk Queue Length
\PhysicalDisk(5 L:)\Avg. Disk Queue Length
\PhysicalDisk(6 N:)\Avg. Disk Queue Length
\PhysicalDisk(7 O:)\Avg. Disk Queue Length
\PhysicalDisk(8 P:)\Avg. Disk Queue Length
\PhysicalDisk(9 Q:)\Avg. Disk Queue Length
...
\PhysicalDisk(0 E: C:)\% Idle Time
\PhysicalDisk(1 D:)\% Idle Time
\PhysicalDisk(2 I:)\% Idle Time
\PhysicalDisk(3 J:)\% Idle Time
\PhysicalDisk(4 K:)\% Idle Time
```

```
\PhysicalDisk(5 L:)\% Idle Time
\PhysicalDisk(6 N:)\% Idle Time
\PhysicalDisk(7 O:)\% Idle Time
\PhysicalDisk(8 P:)\% Idle Time
\PhysicalDisk(9 Q:)\% Idle Time
\PhysicalDisk(_Total)\% Idle Time
\PhysicalDisk(0 E: C:)\Split IO/Sec
\PhysicalDisk(1 D:)\Split IO/Sec
\PhysicalDisk(2 I:)\Split IO/Sec
\PhysicalDisk(3 J:)\Split IO/Sec
\PhysicalDisk(4 K:)\Split IO/Sec
\PhysicalDisk(5 L:)\Split IO/Sec
\PhysicalDisk(6 N:)\Split IO/Sec
\PhysicalDisk(7 O:)\Split IO/Sec
\PhysicalDisk(8 P:)\Split IO/Sec
\PhysicalDisk(9 Q:)\Split IO/Sec
\PhysicalDisk(_Total)\Split IO/Sec
```

You can use this counter information as input to Typeperf as well. Add the –O parameter and write the output to a text file, such as in the following:

```
typeperf -qx PhysicalDisk -o perf.txt
```

Then edit the text file so that only the counters you want to track are included. You can then use the file to determine which performance counters are tracked by specifying the –Cf parameter followed by the file path to this counter file. Consider the following example:

```
typeperf -cf perf.txt -o c:\perflogs\perf.bin -f bin
```

Here, Typeperf reads the list of counters to track from Perf.txt and then writes the performance data in binary format to a file in the C:\perflogs directory.

By default, Typeperf samples data once every second until you tell it to stop by pressing Ctrl+C. This may be okay when you are working at the command line and actively monitoring the output. However, it doesn't work so well when you have other things to do and can't actively monitor the output—which is probably most of the time. Therefore, you'll usually want to control the sampling interval and duration.

To control the sampling interval and set how long to sample, you can use the –Si and –Sc parameters, respectively. For example, if you wanted Typeperf to sample every 120 seconds and stop logging after 100 samples, you could type this:

```
typeperf -cf perf.txt -o c:\perflogs\perf.bin -f bin -si 120 -sc 100
```

Chapter 7

Monitoring Processes and Maintaining Performance

An important part of every administrator's job is to monitor network systems and ensure that everything is running smoothly—or as smoothly as can be expected, anyway. As you learned in the previous chapter, watching the event logs closely can help you detect and track problems with applications, security, and essential services. Often when you detect or suspect a problem, you'll need to dig deeper to search out the cause of the problem and correct it. Hopefully, by pinpointing the cause of a problem, you can prevent it from happening again.

Managing Applications, Processes, and Performance

Whenever the operating system or a user starts a service, runs an application, or executes a command, Windows starts one or more processes to handle the related program. Several command-line utilities are available to help you manage and monitor programs. These utilities include the following:

- **Task List (Tasklist)** Lists all running processes by name and process ID. Includes information on the user session and memory usage.
- **Task Kill (Taskkill)** Stops running processes by name or process ID. Using filters, you can also halt processes by process status, session number, CPU time, memory usage, user name, and more.
- **Powershell get-process** Displays performance statistics, including memory and CPU usage, as well as a list of all running processes. Used to get a detailed snapshot of resource usage and running processes. Available when you install Windows PowerShell.

In the sections that follow, you'll find detailed discussions on how these command-line tools are used. First, however, let's look at the ways processes are run and the common problems you may encounter when working with them.

Understanding System and User Processes

Generally, processes that the operating system starts are referred to as *system processes*; processes that users start are referred to as *user processes*. Most user processes are run in interactive mode. That is, a user starts a process interactively with the keyboard or mouse. If the application or program is active and selected, the related interactive process has control over the keyboard and mouse until you switch control by terminating the program or selecting a different one. When a process has control, it's said to be running "in the foreground."

Processes can also run in the background, independently of user logon sessions. Background processes do not have control over the keyboard, mouse, or other input devices and are usually run by the operating system. Using the Task Scheduler, users can run processes in the background as well, however, and these processes can operate regardless of whether the user is logged on. For example, if Task Scheduler starts a scheduled task while the user is logged on, the process can continue even when the user logs off.

Windows tracks every process running on a system by image name, process ID, priority, and other parameters that record resource usage. The image name is the name of the executable that started the process, such as Msdtc.exe or Svchost.exe. The process ID is a numeric identifier for the process, such as 2588. The process ID is a priority-indicator of how much of the system's resources the process should get relative to other running processes. With priority processing, a process with a higher priority gets preference over processes with lower priority and may not have to wait to get processing time, access memory, or work with the file system. A process with lower priority, on the other hand, usually must wait for a higher-priority process to complete its current task before gaining access to the CPU, memory, or the file system.

In a perfect world, processes would run perfectly and would never have problems. The reality is, however, that problems occur and they often appear when you'd least want them to. Common problems include the following:

- Processes become nonresponsive, such as when an application stops processing requests. When this happens, users may tell you that they can't access a particular application, that their requests aren't being handled, or that they were kicked out of the application.
- Processes fail to release the CPU, such as when you have a runaway process that is using up CPU time. When this happens, the system may appear to be slow or nonresponsive because the runaway process is hogging processor time and is not allowing other processes to complete their tasks.
- Processes use more memory than they should, such as when an application has a memory leak. When this happens, processes aren't properly releasing memory that they're using. As a result, the system's available memory may gradually decrease over time and as the available memory gets low, the system may be slow to respond to requests or it may become nonresponsive. Memory leaks can also make other programs running on the same system behave erratically.

In most cases, when you detect these or other problems with system processes, you'll want to stop the process and start it again. You would also want to examine the event logs to see whether you can determine the cause of the problem. In the case of memory leaks, you want to report the memory leak to the developers and see whether an update that resolves the problem is available.

A periodic restart of an application with a known memory leak is often useful. Restarting the application should allow the operating system to recover any lost memory.

Examining Running Processes

When you want to examine processes that are running on a local or remote system, you can use the Tasklist command-line utility. With Tasklist, you can do the following:

Obtain the process ID, status, and other important information about processes running on a system.

- View the relationship between running processes and services configured on a system.
- View lists of DLLs used by processes running on a system.
- Use filters to include or exclude processes from Tasklist queries.

Each of these tasks is discussed in the sections that follow.

Obtaining Detailed Information on Processes

On a local system, you can view a list of running tasks simply by typing **tasklist** at the command prompt. As with many other command-line utilities, Tasklist runs by default with the permissions of the currently logged-on user, and you can also specify the remote computer whose tasks you want to query and the Run As permissions. To do this, use the expanded syntax, which includes the following parameters:

/s *Computer* /u [*Domain*\]*User* [/p *Password*]

where *Computer* is the remote computer name or IP address, *Domain* is the optional domain name in which the user account is located, *User* is the name of the user account whose permissions you want to use, and *Password* is the optional password for the user account. If you don't specify the domain, the current domain is assumed. If you don't provide the account password, you are prompted for the password.

To see how you can add computer and user information to the syntax, consider the following examples:

Query Mailer1 for running tasks:

```
tasklist /s mailer1
```

Query 192.168.1.5 for running tasks using the account adatum\wrstanek:

```
tasklist /s 192.168.1.5 /u adatum\wrstanek
```

The basic output of these commands is in table format. You can also format the output as a list or lines of comma-separated values using /Fo List or /Fo Csv, respectively. Remember that you can redirect the output to a file using output redirection (> or >>), such as tasklist /s mailer1 >> current-tasks.log.

Regardless of whether you are working with a local or remote computer, the output should be similar to the following:

```
Image Name                     PID Session Name        Session#    Mem Usage
========================= ======== ================ =========== ============
System Idle Process              0 Services                   0         28 K
System                           4 Services                   0     28,952 K
smss.exe                       488 Services                   0        776 K
csrss.exe                      560 Services                   0      5,272 K
wininit.exe                    608 Services                   0      4,056 K
csrss.exe                      620 Console                    1     13,004 K
services.exe                   652 Services                   0      7,456 K
lsass.exe                      664 Services                   0      1,852 K
lsm.exe                        680 Services                   0      6,400 K
svchost.exe                    836 Services                   0      7,228 K
winlogon.exe                   868 Console                    1      5,544 K
svchost.exe                    932 Services                   0      9,440 K
svchost.exe                    984 Services                   0     23,304 K
svchost.exe                   1048 Services                   0     12,208 K
svchost.exe                   1100 Services                   0     71,696 K
svchost.exe                   1132 Services                   0     36,920 K
dwm.exe                       2832 Console                    1     65,456 K
explorer.exe                  2892 Console                    1     25,624 K
```

The Tasklist fields provide the following information:

- **Image Name** The name of the process or executable running the process.
- **PID** The process identification number.
- **Session Name** The name of the session from which the process is being run. An entry of *console* means the process was started locally.
- **Session #** A numerical identifier for the session.
- **Memory Usage** The total amount of memory being used by the process at the specific moment that Tasklist was run.

If you want more detailed information you can specify that verbose mode should be used by including the /V parameter. Verbose mode adds the following columns of data:

- **Status** Current status of the process as Running, Not Responding, or Unknown. A process can be in an Unknown state and still be running and responding normally. A process that is Not Responding, however, more than likely must be stopped or restarted.

- **User Name** User account under which the process is running, listed in domain\user format. For processes started by Windows, you will see the name of the system account used, such as SYSTEM, LOCAL SERVICE, or NETWORK SERVICE, with the domain listed as NT AUTHORITY.
- **CPU Time** The total amount of CPU-cycle time used by the process since its start.
- **Window Title** Windows display name of the process if available. Otherwise, the display name is listed as *N/A* for not available. For example, the HelpPane.exe process is listed with the title Windows Help And Support Center

If you use Tasklist to examine running processes, you'll note two unique processes: System and System Idle Process. System shows the resource usage for the local system process. System Idle Process tracks the amount of CPU processing time that isn't being used. Thus, a 99 in the CPU column for the System Idle Process means 99 percent of the system resources currently aren't being used. If you believe that a system is overloaded, you should monitor the idle process. Watch the CPU usage and the total CPU time. If the system consistently has low idle time (meaning high CPU usage), you may want to consider upgrading the processor or even adding processors.

As you examine processes, keep in mind that a single application might start multiple processes. Generally, these processes are dependent on a central process, and from this main process a process tree containing dependent processes is formed. When you terminate processes, you'll usually want to target the main application process or the application itself rather than dependent processes. This ensures that the application is stopped cleanly.

Viewing the Relationship Between Running Processes and Services

When you use Tasklist with the /Svc parameter, you can examine the relationship between running processes and services configured on the system. In the output, you'll see the process image name, process ID, and a list of all services that are using the process, similar to that shown in the following example:

```
Image Name                     PID Services
========================= ======== ============================================
System Idle Process              0 N/A
System                           4 N/A
smss.exe                       488 N/A
csrss.exe                      560 N/A
wininit.exe                    608 N/A
csrss.exe                      620 N/A
services.exe                   652 N/A
lsass.exe                      664 KeyIso, ProtectedStorage, SamSs
lsm.exe                        680 N/A
svchost.exe                    836 DcomLaunch, PlugPlay
winlogon.exe                   868 N/A
```

```
svchost.exe                   932 RpcSs
svchost.exe                   984 WinDefend
svchost.exe                  1048 Audiosrv, Dhcp, Eventlog, lmhosts, wscsvc
svchost.exe                  1100 AudioEndpointBuilder, CscService, EMDMgmt,
                                  Netman, PcaSvc, SysMain,
                                  TabletInputService, TrkWks, UmRdpService,
                                  UxSms, WdiSystemHost, Wlansvc, WPDBusEnum,
                                  wudfsvc
svchost.exe                  1132 AeLookupSvc, BITS, Browser, CertPropSvc,
                                  EapHost, gpsvc, IKEEXT, iphlpsvc,
                                  LanmanServer, MMCSS, ProfSvc, RasMan,
                                  Schedule, seclogon, SENS, SessionEnv,
                                  ShellHWDetection, Themes, Winmgmt, wuauserv
svchost.exe                  1384 EventSystem, fdPHost, FDResPub,
                                  LanmanWorkstation, netprofm, nsi, SSDPSRV,
                                  upnphost, W32Time, WebClient
svchost.exe                  1520 CryptSvc, Dnscache, KtmRm, NlaSvc, TapiSrv,
                                  TermService
spoolsv.exe                  1776 Spooler
svchost.exe                  1800 BFE, DPS, MpsSvc
dwm.exe                      2832 N/A
explorer.exe                 2892 N/A
```

By default, the output is formatted as a table, and you cannot use the *list* or *CSV* format. Beyond formatting, the important thing to note here is that services are listed by their abbreviated names, which is the naming style used by Sc, the service controller command-line utility, to manage services.

You can use the correlation between processes and services to help you manage systems. For example, if you think you are having problems with the World Wide Web Publishing Service (W3svc), one step in your troubleshooting process is to begin monitoring the service's related process or processes. You would want to examine the following:

- Process status
- Memory usage
- CPU time

By tracking these statistics over time, you can watch for changes that could indicate the process has stopped responding or is a runaway process hogging CPU time, or that there is a memory leak.

Viewing Lists of DLLs Being Used by Processes

When you use Tasklist with the /M parameter, you can examine the relationship between running processes and DLLs configured on the system. In the output, you'll see the process image name, process ID, and a list of all DLLs that the process is using, as shown in the following example:

```
Image Name                     PID Modules
========================= ======== ============================================
System Idle Process              0 N/A
System                           4 N/A
smss.exe                       488 N/A
csrss.exe                      560 N/A
wininit.exe                    608 N/A
csrss.exe                      620 N/A
services.exe                   652 N/A
lsass.exe                      664 N/A
lsm.exe                        680 N/A
svchost.exe                    836 N/A
winlogon.exe                   868 N/A
svchost.exe                    932 N/A
svchost.exe                    984 N/A
svchost.exe                   1048 N/A
svchost.exe                   1100 N/A
svchost.exe                   1132 N/A
dwm.exe                       2832 ntdll.dll, kernel32.dll, ADVAPI32.dll,
                                   RPCRT4.dll, GDI32.dll, USER32.dll,
                                   msvcrt.dll, ole32.dll, OLEAUT32.dll,
                                   UxTheme.dll, IMM32.dll, MSCTF.dll,
                                   dwmredir.dll, SLWGA.dll, urlmon.dll,
                                   SHLWAPI.dll, iertutil.dll, WTSAPI32.dll,
                                   slc.dll, LPK.DLL, USP10.dll, comctl32.dll,
                                   NTMARTA.DLL, WLDAP32.dll, WS2_32.dll,
                                   NSI.dll, PSAPI.DLL, SAMLIB.dll,
                                   milcore.dll, dwmapi.dll, uDWM.dll,
                                   WindowsCodecs.dll, ctagent.dll, d3d9.dll,
                                   VERSION.dll, d3d8thk.dll, nvd3dum.dll,
                                   IconCodecService.dll
explorer.exe                  2892 ntdll.dll, kernel32.dll, ADVAPI32.dll,
                                   RPCRT4.dll, GDI32.dll, USER32.dll,
                                   msvcrt.dll, SHLWAPI.dll, SHELL32.dll,
                                   ole32.dll, OLEAUT32.dll, SHDOCVW.dll,
                                   UxTheme.dll, POWRPROF.dll, dwmapi.dll,
                                   gdiplus.dll, slc.dll, PROPSYS.dll,
                                   BROWSEUI.dll, IMM32.dll, MSCTF.dll,
                                   DUser.dll, LPK.DLL, USP10.dll,
                                   comctl32.dll, WindowsCodecs.dll,
                                   apphelp.dll, CLBCatQ.DLL, cscui.dll,
                                   CSCDLL.dll, CSCAPI.dll,
                                   IconCodecService.dll, Secur32.dll,
                                   rsaenh.dll, msiltcfg.dll, VERSION.dll,
                                   msi.dll, NTMARTA.DLL, WLDAP32.dll,
                                   WS2_32.dll, NSI.dll, PSAPI.DLL, SAMLIB.dll,
                                   SFC.DLL, sfc_os.dll, SETUPAPI.dll,
                                   timedate.cpl, ATL.DLL, NETAPI32.dll,
                                   OLEACC.dll, actxprxy.dll, USERENV.dll
```

Knowing which DLL modules a process has loaded can further help you pinpoint what may be causing a process to become nonresponsive, to fail to release the CPU, or to use more memory than it should. In some cases, you might want to check DLL versions to ensure that they are the correct DLLs that the system should be running. Here, you would need to consult the Microsoft Knowledge Base or manufacturer documentation to verify DLL versions and other information.

If you are looking for processes using a specified DLL, you can also specify the name of the DLL you are looking for. For example, if you suspect that the printer spooler driver Winspool.drv is causing processes to hang up, you can search for processes that use Winspool.drv instead of Winspool32.drv and check their status and resource usage.

The syntax that you use to specify the DLL to find is

```
tasklist /m DLLName
```

where *DLLName* is the name of the DLL to search for. Tasklist matches the DLL name without regard to the letter case, and you can enter the DLL name in any letter case. Consider the following example:

```
tasklist /m winspool.drv
```

In this example, you are looking for processes using Winspool.drv. The output of the command would show the processes using the DLL along with their process IDs, as shown in the following example:

```
Image Name                     PID Modules
========================= ======== ============================================
explorer.exe                  2892 WINSPOOL.DRV
rundll32.exe                  3308 WINSPOOL.DRV
acrotray.exe                  3340 WINSPOOL.DRV
IAAnotif.exe                  3464 WINSPOOL.DRV
IntelHCTAgent.exe             3584 WINSPOOL.DRV
DrgToDsc.exe                  3636 WINSPOOL.DRV
WINWORD.EXE                   4836 WINSPOOL.DRV
```

Filtering Task List Output

Using the /Fi parameter of the Tasklist utility, you can filter task lists using any of the information fields available, even if the information field isn't normally included in the output because of the parameters you've specified. This means you can specify that you want to see only processes listed with a status of Not Responding, only information for Svchost.exe processes, or only processes that use a large amount of CPU time.

You designate how a filter should be applied to a particular Tasklist information field using filter operators. The following filter operators are available:

- **Eq** Equals. If the field contains the specified value, the process is included in the output.
- **Ne** Not equals. If the field contains the specified value, the process is excluded from the output.

- **Gt** Greater than. If the field contains a numeric value and that value is greater than the value specified, the process is included in the output.
- **Lt** Less than. If the field contains a numeric value and that value is less than the value specified, the process is included in the output.
- **Ge** Greater than or equal to. If the field contains a numeric value and that value is greater than or equal to the value specified, the process is included in the output.
- **Le** Less than or equal to. If the field contains a numeric value and that value is less than or equal to the value specified, the process is included in the output.

As Table 7-1 shows, the values that you can use with filter operators depend on the task list information field you use. Remember that all fields are available even if they aren't normally displayed with the parameters you've specified. For example, you can match the status field without using the */V* (verbose) flag.

Table 7-1 Filter Operators and Valid Values for Tasklist

Filter Field Name	Valid Operators	Valid Values
CPUTime	eq, ne, gt, lt, ge, le	Any valid time in the format hh:mm:ss
Services	eq, ne	Any valid string of characters
ImageName	eq, ne	Any valid string of characters
MemUsage	eq, ne, gt, lt, ge, le	Any valid integer, expressed in kilobytes (KB)
Modules	eq, ne	DLL name
PID	eq, ne, gt, lt, ge, le	Any valid positive integer
Session	eq, ne, gt, lt, ge, le	Any valid session number
SessionName	eq, ne	Any valid string of characters
Status	eq, ne	Running, Not Responding, Unknown
Username	eq, ne	Any valid user name, with user name only or in domain\user format
WindowTitle	eq, ne	Any valid string of characters

You must use double quotation marks to enclose the filter string. Consider the following examples to see how you can use filters:

Look for processes that are not responding:

```
tasklist /fi "status eq not responding"
```

When working with remote systems, you can't filter processes by status or window title. A workaround for this in some cases is to pipe the output through the FIND command, such as **tasklist /v /s Mailer1 /u adatum\wrstanek | find /i "not**

responding". Note that in this case, the field you are filtering must be in the output, which is why the /V parameter was added to the example. Further, you should specify that the FIND command should ignore the letter case of characters by using the /I parameter.

Look for processes on Mailer1 with a CPU time of more than 30 minutes:

```
tasklist /s Mailer1 /fi "cputime gt 00:30:00"
```

Look for processes on Mailer1 that use more than 20,000 KB of memory:

```
tasklist /s Mailer1 /u adatum\wrstanek /fi "memusage gt 20000"
```

Enter multiple /Fi "Filter" parameters to specify that output must match against multiple filters:

```
tasklist /s Mailer1 /fi "cputime gt 00:30:00" /fi "memusage gt 20000"
```

Monitoring System Resource Usage and Processes

When you are working with processes, you'll often want to get a snapshot of system resource usage, which will show you exactly how memory is being used. One way to get such a snapshot is to use the Typeperf command to display current values for key counters of the memory object. As discussed in Chapter 6, "Event Logging, Tracking, and Monitoring," the Memory object is one of many performance objects available, and you can list its related performance counters by typing **typeperf -q Memory** at a command line.

Table 7-2 provides a summary of key counters of the Memory object. Most counters of the Memory object display the last observed value or the current percentage value rather than an average.

Table 7-2 Key Counters of the Memory Object

Memory Object Counter	Counter Description
% Committed Bytes In Use	The ratio of Committed Bytes to the Commit Limit. Committed memory is the physical memory in use for which space has been reserved in the paging file if it needs to be written to disk. The commit limit is determined by the size of the paging file. If Windows increases the paging file size, the commit limit increases as well, and the ratio is reduced.

Table 7-2 Key Counters of the Memory Object

Memory Object Counter	Counter Description
Available MBytes	The amount of physical memory, in megabytes, immediately available for allocation to a process or for system use. This is physical memory not currently being used and available for use. It is equal to the sum of memory assigned to the standby (cached), free, and zero page lists. When less than five percent of memory is free, the system is low on memory and performance can suffer.
Cache Bytes	The sum of the System Cache Resident Bytes, System Driver Resident Bytes, System Code Resident Bytes, and Pool Paged Resident Bytes counters. This provides information on the memory used by the operating system kernel. Critical portions of kernel memory must operate in physical memory and can't be paged to virtual memory; the rest of kernel memory can be paged to virtual memory.
Cache Bytes Peak	The maximum number of bytes used by the file system cache since the system was last restarted.
Cache Faults/sec	The rate at which faults occur when a page sought in the file system cache is not found and must be retrieved from elsewhere in memory (a soft fault) or from disk (a hard fault). The file system cache is an area of physical memory that stores recently used pages of data for applications.
Commit Limit	The amount of virtual memory, measured in bytes, that can be committed without having to extend the paging file(s). As the number of committed bytes grows, the paging file is allowed to grow up to its maximum size, which can be determined by subtracting the total physical memory on the system from the commit limit. If you set the initial paging file size too small, the system will repeatedly extend the paging file and this requires system resources. It is better to set the initial page size as appropriate for typical usage or simply use a fixed paging file size.
Committed Bytes	The amount of committed virtual memory, in bytes. Committed memory is the physical memory in use for which space has been reserved in the paging file if it needs to be written to disk. Each physical drive can have one or more paging files. If a system is using too much virtual memory relative to the total physical memory on the system, you might need to add physical memory.
Demand Zero Faults/sec	The rate at which a zeroed page is required to satisfy a fault, according to the difference between the values observed in the last two samples, divided by the duration of the sample interval. Pages emptied of previously stored data and filled with zeros are a security feature of Windows that prevent processes from seeing data stored by earlier processes that used the memory space.
Free & Zero Page List Bytes	The amount of physical memory, in bytes, that is assigned to the free and zero page lists. This memory does not contain cached data and is immediately available for allocation to a process or for system use.

Table 7-2 Key Counters of the Memory Object

Memory Object Counter	Counter Description
Free System Page Table Entries	The number of page table entries not currently in use by the system.
Modified Page List Bytes	The amount of physical memory, in bytes, that is assigned to the modified page list. Areas of memory on the modified page list contain cached data and code that is not actively in use by processes, the system, or the system cache. Windows needs to write out this memory before it will be available for allocation to a process or for system use.
Page Faults/sec	The number of pages faulted per second. This counter includes both hard and soft faults. Soft faults result in memory lookups. Hard faults require access to disk.
Page Reads/sec	The number of read operations required per second to resolve hard page faults. Hard page faults occur when a requested page isn't in memory and the computer has to go to disk to get it. Too many hard faults can cause significant delays and hurt performance.
Page Writes/sec	The number of page writes to disk to free up space in physical memory. Pages are written to disk only if they are changed while in physical memory.
Pages Input/sec	The rate at which pages are read from disk to resolve hard page faults. Hard page faults occur when a requested page isn't in memory and the computer has to go to disk to get it. Too many hard faults can cause significant delays and hurt performance.
Pages Output/sec	The rate at which pages are written to disk to free up space in physical memory. If the computer has to free up memory too often, this is an indicator that the system doesn't have enough physical memory (RAM).
Pages/sec	The number of memory pages that are read from disk or written to disk to resolve hard page faults. It is the sum of Pages Input/sec and Pages Output/sec.
Pool Non-paged Allocs	The number of calls to allocate space in the nonpaged pool. The nonpaged pool is an area of system memory area for objects that cannot be written to disk, and must remain in physical memory as long as they are allocated.
Pool Non-paged Bytes	The size, in bytes, of the nonpaged pool, an area of system memory for objects that cannot be written to disk, but must remain in physical memory as long as they are allocated. If the size of the nonpaged pool is large relative to the total amount of virtual memory allocated to the computer, you might want to increase the virtual memory size. If this value slowly increases in size over time, a kernel mode process might have a memory leak.

Table 7-2 Key Counters of the Memory Object

Memory Object Counter	Counter Description
Pool Paged Allocs	The number of calls to allocate space in the paged pool. The paged pool is an area of system memory for objects that can be written to disk when they are not being used.
Pool Paged Bytes	The total size, in bytes, of the paged pool. The paged pool is an area of system memory for objects that can be written to disk when they are not being used. If the size of the paged pool is large relative to the total amount of physical memory on the system, you might need to add memory to the system. If this value slowly increases in size over time, a kernel mode process might have a memory leak.
Pool Paged Resident Bytes	The size, in bytes, of the paged pool that is currently resident and actively being used. Typically, the resident bytes in the paged pool is a smaller amount than the total bytes assigned to the paged pool.
Standby Cache Core Bytes	The amount of physical memory, in bytes, that is assigned to the core standby cache page lists. A standby cached page list is an area of memory that contains cached data and code that is not actively in use by processes, the system, or the system cache. It is immediately available for allocation to a process or for system use. If the system runs out of available free–and-zero memory, memory on lower priority standby cache page lists will be repurposed before memory on higher priority standby cache page lists.
System Cache Resident Bytes	The size, in bytes, of the pageable operating system code in the file system cache. This value includes only current physical pages and does not include any virtual memory pages not currently resident.
System Code Resident Bytes	The size, in bytes of the operating system code currently in physical memory that can be written to disk when not in use.
System Code Total Bytes	The size, in bytes, of the pageable operating system code currently in virtual memory. It is a measure of the amount of physical memory being used by the operating system that can be written to disk when not in use and does not include code that must remain in physical memory and cannot be written to disk.
System Driver Resident Bytes	The size, in bytes, of the pageable physical memory being used by device drivers. It is the working set (physical memory area) of the drivers.
System Driver Total Bytes	The size, in bytes, of the pageable memory and pageable virtual memory currently being used by device drivers. It includes physical memory and code and data paged to disk.
Transition Faults/sec	The rate at which page faults are resolved by recovering pages that were being used by another process sharing the page, or were on the modified page list or the standby list, or were being written to disk at the time of the page fault. The pages were recovered without additional disk activity.

Table 7-2 Key Counters of the Memory Object

Memory Object Counter	Counter Description
Transition Pages RePurposed/sec	The rate at which the number of transition cache pages were reused for a different purpose. These pages would have otherwise remained in the page cache to provide a soft fault in the event the page was accessed in the future. These pages can contain private or sharable memory.
Write Copies/sec	The rate at which page faults are caused by attempts to write that have been satisfied by copying the page from elsewhere in physical memory.

Sample 7-1 provides an example of how you can use Typeperf to get a snapshot of memory usage. In this example, you use a counter file called Perf.txt to specify the counters you want to track. You collect five samples with an interval of 30 seconds between samples and save the output in a file called SaveData.txt. If you import the data into a spreadsheet or convert it to a table in a Microsoft Office Word document, you can make better sense of the output and will know exactly how the computer is using memory.

> **Note** I chose to track these counters because they give you a good overall snapshot of memory usage. If you save the command line as a script, you can run the script as a scheduled task to get a snapshot of memory usage at various times of the day.

Sample 7-1 Getting a snapshot of memory usage

Command-line

```
typeperf -cf c:\logs\perf.txt -o c:\logs\savedata.txt -sc 5 -si 30
```

Source for Perf.txt

```
\memory\% Committed Bytes In Use
\memory\Available MBytes
\memory\Cache Bytes
\memory\Cache Bytes Peak
\memory\Committed Bytes
\memory\Commit Limit
\memory\Page Faults/sec
\memory\Pool Nonpaged Bytes
\memory\Pool Paged Bytes
```

Sample output

```
"(PDH-CSV 4.0)","\\SERVER12\memory\% Committed Bytes In Use","
\\SERVER12\memory\Available MBytes","\\SERVER12\memory\Cache Bytes","
\\SERVER12\memory\Cache Bytes Peak","\\SERVER12\memory\Committed Bytes","
\\SERVER12\memory\Commit Limit","\\SERVER12\memory\Page Faults/sec","
\\SERVER12\memory\Pool Nonpaged Bytes","\\SERVER12\memory\Pool Paged
Bytes"
```

```
"03/25/2008 14:24:28.033","22.860837","2023.000000","260632576.000000","
280514560.000000","1636175872.000000","7157112832.000000","80.494007","
73240576.000000","152875008.000000"
"03/25/2008 14:24:30.033","22.861294","2023.000000","260653056.000000","
280514560.000000","1636208640.000000","7157112832.000000","70.997253","
73240576.000000","152875008.000000"
"03/25/2008 14:24:32.033","22.861294","2023.000000","260653056.000000","
280514560.000000","1636208640.000000","7157112832.000000","3.000142","
73261056.000000","152875008.000000"
"03/25/2008 14:24:34.033","22.861581","2023.000000","260673536.000000","
280514560.000000","1636229120.000000","7157112832.000000","15.999741","
73154560.000000","152875008.000000"
"03/25/2008 14:24:36.033","22.861695","2023.000000","260681728.000000","
280514560.000000","1636237312.000000","7157112832.000000","6.499981","
73134080.000000","152875008.000000"
```

You can obtain detailed information about running processes using the Windows PowerShell Get-Process cmdlet. See Table 7-3 for a summary of this cmdlet's significant properties. At a Windows PowerShell prompt, you can view important statistics for all processes by following these steps:

1. Get all the processes running on the server and store them in the *$a* variable by entering:

   ```
   $a =  get-process
   ```

2. Use the InputObject parameter to pass the process objects stored in *$a* to Get-Process and then pass the objects to the format-table cmdlet along with the list of properties you want to see by entering:

   ```
   get-process -inputobject $a | format-table -property ProcessName,
   BasePriority, HandleCount, Id, NonpagedSystemMemorySize,
   PagedSystemMemorySize, PeakPagedMemorySize, PeakVirtualMemorySize,
   PeakWorkingSet, SessionId, Threads, TotalProcessorTime,
   VirtualMemorySize, WorkingSet, CPU, Path
   ```

The order of the properties in the comma-separated list determines the display order. If you want to change the display order, simply move the property to a different position in the list.

When you know the process you want to examine, you don't need to use this multistep procedure. Simply enter the name of the process without the .exe or .dll instead of using –inputobject $a. In the following example, you list details about the winlogon process:

```
get-process winlogon | format-table -property ProcessName, BasePriority,
HandleCount, Id, NonpagedSystemMemorySize, PagedSystemMemorySize,
PeakPagedMemorySize, PeakVirtualMemorySize, PeakWorkingSet, SessionId,
Threads, TotalProcessorTime, VirtualMemorySize, WorkingSet, CPU, Path
```

You can enter part of a process name as well using an asterisk as a wildcard to match a partial name. In this example, Get-Process lists any process with a name that starts with winl:

```
get-process winl* | format-table -property ProcessName, BasePriority,
HandleCount, Id, NonpagedSystemMemorySize, PagedSystemMemorySize,
PeakPagedMemorySize, PeakVirtualMemorySize, PeakWorkingSet, SessionId,
Threads, TotalProcessorTime, VirtualMemorySize, WorkingSet, CPU, Path
```

> **Tip** By default, many properties that measure memory usage are defined as 32-bit values. When working with Get-Process on 64-bit systems, you'll find that these properties have both a 32-bit and 64-bit version. On 64-bit systems with more than 4 GB of RAM, you'll need to use the 64-bit versions to ensure you get accurate values.

Table 7-3 Properties of Get-Process and How They Are Used

Property Name	Property Description
BasePriority	Shows the priority of the process. Priority determines how much of the system resources are allocated to a process. The standard priorities are Low (4), Below Normal (6), Normal (8), Above Normal (10), High (13), and Real-Time (24). Most processes have a Normal priority by default, and the highest priority is given to real-time processes.
CPU	Shows the percentage of CPU utilization for the process. The System Idle Process shows what percentage of CPU power is idle. A value of 99 for the System Idle Process means 99 percent of the system resources currently aren't being used. If the system has low idle time (meaning high CPU usage) during peak or average usage, you might consider upgrading to faster processors or adding processors.
Description	Shows a description of the process.
FileVersion	Shows the file version of the process's executable.
HandleCount	Shows the number of file handles maintained by the process. The number of handles used is an indicator of how dependent the process is on the file system. Some processes have thousands of open file handles. Each file handle requires system memory to maintain.
Id	Shows the run-time identification number of the process.
MinWorkingSet	Shows the minimum amount of working set memory used by the process.
Modules	Shows the executables and dynamically linked libraries used by the process.

Table 7-3 Properties of Get-Process and How They Are Used

Property Name	Property Description
NonpagedSystem-MemorySize / NonpagedSystem-MemorySize64	Shows the amount of virtual memory for a process that cannot be written to disk. The nonpaged pool is an area of RAM for objects that can't be written to disk. You should note processes that require a high amount of nonpaged pool memory. If the server doesn't have enough free memory, these processes might be the reason for a high level of page faults.
PagedSystem-MemorySize / PagedSystem-MemorySize64	Shows the amount of committed virtual memory for a process that can be written to disk. The paged pool is an area of RAM for objects that can be written to disk when they aren't used. As process activity increases, so does the amount of pool memory the process uses. Most processes have more paged pool than nonpaged pool requirements.
Path	Shows the full path to the executable for the process.
PeakPageMemorySize / PeakPageMemorySize64	Shows the peak amount of paged memory used by the process.
PeakVirtualMemorySize / PeakVirtualMemorySize64	Shows the peak amount of virtual memory used by the process.
PeakWorkingSet / PeakWorkingSet64	Shows the maximum amount of memory the process used, including both the private working set and the non-private working set. If peak memory is exceptionally large, this can be an indicator of a memory leak.
PriorityBoostEnabled	Shows a Boolean value that indicates whether the process has the PriorityBoost feature enabled.
PriorityClass	Shows the priority class of the process.
PrivilegedProcessorTime	Shows the amount of kernel-mode usage time for the process.
ProcessName	Shows the name of the process.
ProcessorAffinity	Shows the processor affinity setting for the process.
Responding	Shows a Boolean value that indicates whether the process responded when tested.
SessionId	Shows the identification number user (session) within which the process is running. This corresponds to the ID value listed on the Users tab in Task Manager.
StartTime	Shows the date and time the process was started.

Table 7-3 Properties of Get-Process and How They Are Used

Property Name	Property Description
Threads	Shows the number of threads that the process is using. Most server applications are multithreaded, which allows concurrent execution of process requests. Some applications can dynamically control the number of concurrently executing threads to improve application performance. Too many threads, however, can actually reduce performance, because the operating system has to switch thread contexts too frequently.
TotalProcessorTime	Shows the total amount of CPU time used by the process since it was started. If a process is using a lot of CPU time, the related application might have a configuration problem. This could also indicate a runaway or nonresponsive process that is unnecessarily tying up the CPU.
UserProcessorTime	Shows the amount of user-mode usage time for the process.
VirtualMemorySize / VirtualMemorySize64	Shows the amount of virtual memory allocated to and reserved for a process. Virtual memory is memory on disk and is slower to access than pooled memory. By configuring an application to use more physical RAM, you might be able to increase performance. To do this, however, the system must have available RAM. If it doesn't, other processes running on the system might slow down.
WorkingSet / WorkingSet64	Shows the amount of memory the process is currently using, including both the private working set and the non-private working set. The private working set is memory the process is using that cannot be shared with other processes. The non-private working set is memory the process is using that can be shared with other processes. If memory usage for a process slowly grows over time and doesn't go back to the baseline value, this can be an indicator of a memory leak.

Stopping Processes

When you want to stop processes that are running on a local or remote system, you can use the Taskkill command-line utility. With Taskkill, you can stop processes by process ID using the /Pid parameter or image name using the /Im parameter. If you want to stop multiple processes by process ID or image name, you can enter multiple /Pid or /Im parameters as well. With image names, however, watch out, because Taskkill will stop all processes that have that image name. Thus if three instances of Helpctr.exe are running, all three processes would be stopped if you use Taskkill with that image name.

As with Tasklist, Taskkill runs by default with the permissions of the user who is currently logged on, and you can also specify the remote computer whose tasks you want to query, and the Run As permissions. To do this, you use the expanded syntax, which includes the following parameters:

/s *Computer* /u [*Domain*\]*User* [/p *Password*]

where *Computer* is the remote computer name or IP address, *Domain* is the optional domain name in which the user account is located, *User* is the name of the user account whose permissions you want to use, and *Password* is the optional password for the user account. If you don't specify the domain, the current domain is assumed. If you don't provide the account password, you are prompted for the password.

Note Sometimes it is necessary to force a process to stop running. Typically, this is necessary when a process stops responding while opening a file, reading or writing data, or performing other read/write operations. To force a process to stop, you use the /F parameter. This parameter is only used with processes running on local systems. Processes stopped on remote systems are always forcefully stopped.

Tip As you examine processes, keep in mind that a single application might start multiple processes. Generally, these processes depend on a central process, and from this main process a process tree containing dependent processes is formed. Occasionally, you may want to stop the entire process tree, starting with the parent application process and including any dependent processes. To do this, you can use the /T parameter.

Consider the following examples to see how you can use Taskkill:

Stop process ID 208:

```
taskkill /pid 208
```

Stop all processes with the image name Cmd.exe:

```
taskkill /im cmd.exe
```

Stop processes 208, 1346, and 2048 on MAILER1:

```
taskkill /s Mailer1 /pid 208 /pid 1346 /pid 2048
```

Force local process 1346 to stop:

```
taskkill /f /pid 1346
```

Stop a process tree, starting with process ID 1248 and including all child processes:

```
taskkill /t /pid 1248
```

To ensure that only processes matching specific criteria are stopped, you can use all the filters listed in Table 7-1 except SessionName. For example, you can use a filter to specify that only instances of Cmd.exe that are not responding should be stopped rather than all instances of Cmd.exe (which is the default when you use the /Im parameter).

As with Tasklist, Taskkill provides a Modules filter with operators EQ and NE to allow you to specify DLL modules that should be excluded or included. As you may recall, you use the Tasklist /M parameter to examine the relationship between running processes and DLLs configured on the system. Using the Taskkill Modules filter with the EQ operator, you could stop all processes using a specific DLL. Using the Taskkill Modules filter with the NE operator, you ensure that processes using a specific DLL are not stopped.

> **Tip** When you use filters, you don't have to specify a specific image name or process ID to work with. This means you can stop processes based solely on whether they match filter criteria. For example, you can specify that you want to stop all processes that aren't responding.

As with Tasklist, you can also use multiple filters. Again, you must use double quotation marks to enclose the filter string. Consider the following examples to see how you can use filters with Taskkill:

Stop instances of Cmd.exe that are not responding:

```
taskkill /im cmd.exe /fi "status eq not responding"
```

Stop all processes with a process ID greater than 4 if they aren't responding:

```
taskkill /fi "pid gt 4" /fi "status eq not responding"
```

Stop all processes using the Winspool.drv DLL:

```
taskkill /fi "modules eq winspool.drv"
```

Although the /Im and /Pid flags are not used in the second example, the process IDs are filtered so that only certain processes are affected. You don't want to stop the system or system idle process accidentally. Typically, these processes run with process IDs of 4 and 0 respectively, and if you stop them, the system will stop responding or shut down.

Detecting and Resolving Performance Issues Through Monitoring

At the command line, Tasklist and Windows PowerShell Get-Process provide everything you need for detecting and resolving most performance issues. However, you'll often need to dig deep to determine whether a problem exists and if so, what is causing the problem.

Monitoring Memory Paging and Paging to Disk

Often, you'll want to get detailed information on hard and soft page faults that are occuring. A page fault occurs when a process requests a page in memory and the system can't find it at the requested location. If the requested page is elsewhere in memory, the fault is called a soft page fault. If the requested page must be retrieved from disk, the fault is called a hard page fault.

To see page faults that are occurring in real time, enter the following at the command line:

```
typeperf "\memory\Page Faults/sec" -si 5
```

To stop Typeperf, press Ctrl+C. Page faults are shown according to the number of hard and soft faults occuring per second. Other counters of the Memory object that you can use for tracking page faults include:

- Cache Faults/sec
- Demand Zero Faults/sec
- Page Reads/sec
- Page Writes/sec
- Write Copies/sec
- Transition Faults/sec
- Transition Pages RePurposed/sec

Pay particular attention to the Page Reads/sec and Page Writes/sec, which provide information on hard faults. Although developers will be interested in the source of page faults, administrators are more interested in how many page faults are occurring.

Most processors can handle large numbers of soft faults. A soft fault simply means the system had to look elsewhere in memory for the requested memory page. With a hard fault, on the other hand, the requested memory page must be retrieved from disk, which can cause significant delays. If you are seeing a lot of hard faults, you may need to increase the amount of memory or reduce the amount of memory being cached by the system and applications.

In addition to counters of the Memory object discussed previously, you can use the following objects and counters to check for disk paging issues:

- **Paging File(*)\% Usage** The percentage of the paging file currently in use. If this value approaches 100 percent for all instances, you should consider either increasing the virtual memory size or adding physical memory to the system. This will ensure that the computer has additional memory if it needs it, such as when the computer load grows.
- **Paging File(*)\% Usage Peak** The peak size of the paging file as a percentage of the total paging file size available. A high value can mean that the paging file isn't large enough to handle increased load conditions.
- **PhysicalDisk(*)\% Disk Time** The percentage of time that the selected disk spent servicing read and write requests. Keep track of this value for the physical disks that have paging files. If you see this value increasing over several monitoring periods, you should more closely monitor paging file usage and you might consider adding physical memory to the system.
- **PhysicalDisk(*)\Avg. Disk Queue Length** The average number of read and write requests that were waiting for the selected disk during the sample interval. Keep track of this value for the physical disks that have paging files. If you see this value increasing over time and the Memory\Page Reads/Sec is also increasing, the system is having to perform a lot of paging file reads.

The asterisks in parentheses are placeholders for the object instance. If a particular object has multiple instances, such as when a computer has multiple physical disks or multiple paging files, you can use an object instance to track a specific occurrence of that object. You could also elect to track all instances of an object, such as whether you want to monitor all physical disks on a system. Specify _Total to work with all counter instances, or specify individual counter instances to monitor.

Sample 7-2 provides an example of how you can use Typeperf to get a snapshot of disk paging. In this example, you use a counter file called PagePerf.txt to specify the counters you want to track. You collect five samples with an interval of 30 seconds between samples and save the output in a file called SavePageData.txt. If you import the data into a spreadsheet or convert it to a table in a Word document, you can make better sense of the output and a better understanding of how the computer is using the page file and paging to disk.

Sample 7-2 Checking disk paging

Command line

```
typeperf -cf c:\logs\pageperf.txt -o c:\logs\savepagedata.txt -sc 5
-si 30
```

Source for PagePerf.txt

```
\memory\Pages/Sec
\Paging File(_Total)\% Usage
\Paging File(_Total)\% Usage Peak
\PhysicalDisk(_Total)\% Disk Time
\PhysicalDisk(_Total)\Avg. Disk Queue Length
```

Monitoring Memory Usage and the Working Memory Set for Individual Processes

You can use Tasklist to get basic memory usage for a process. The syntax you can use is:

```
tasklist /fi "pid eq ProcessID"
```

where *ProcessID* is the id number of the process you want to work with. The output from Tasklist will show you how much memory the process is currently using. For example, if you were tracking process ID 7292, your output might look like the following:

```
Image Name      PID       Session Name      Session#    Mem Usage
============== ======== ================ =========== ============
jvappm.exe      7292                             1      7,424 K
```

In this example, the process is using 7,424 KB of memory. By watching the memory usage over time, you can determine whether the memory usage is increasing. If memory usage is increasing compared to a typical baseline, the process might have a memory-related problem.

Sample 7-3 provides the source for a command-line script that checks the memory usage of a process over a timed interval. The script expects the process ID you want to work with to be passed as the first parameter. If you do not supply a process ID, error text is written to the output.

Sample 7-3 Viewing memory usage at the command line

MemUsage.bat

```
@echo off
if "%1"=="" (echo Error: please enter Process ID to track) & (goto
EXIT)

tasklist /fi "pid eq %1"
timeout /t 600
```

```
tasklist /fi "pid eq %1"
timeout /t 600
tasklist /fi "pid eq %1"
:EXIT
```

Sample output

```
Image Name                     PID Session Name        Session#    Mem Usage
====================== ======= ================ ========== ============
jvapm.exe                     7292                            1      7,452 K

Waiting for  0 seconds, press a key to continue ...

Image Name                     PID Session Name        Session#    Mem Usage
====================== ======= ================ ========== ============
jvapm.exe                     7292                            1      7,452 K

Waiting for  0 seconds, press a key to continue ...

Image Name                     PID Session Name        Session#    Mem Usage
====================== ======= ================ ========== ============
jvapm.exe                     7292                            1      7,452 K
```

In Sample 7-3, the process's memory usage does not change over the sampled interval. Because of this, it is unlikely the process has a memory leak, but to be sure you'd need to sample over a longer period.

You can use the Windows PowerShell Get-Process cmdlet to track detailed memory usage for individual processes. The syntax you can use is

```
get-process ProcessName | format-table -property
NonpagedSystemMemorySize, PagedSystemMemorySize, VirtualMemorySize,
PeakVirtualMemorySize, MinWorkingSet, WorkingSet, PeakWorkingSet
```

where *ProcessName* is the name of the process without the .exe or .dll. In a Windows PowerShell script, such as the one shown as Sample 7-4, you could combine the Get-Process cmdlet with the start-sleep cmdlet to view the memory usage for a process at timed intervals.

Sample 7-4 Viewing detailed memory usage

MemUsage.ps1

```
get-process msdtc | format-table -property NonpagedSystemMemorySize,
PagedSystemMemorySize, VirtualMemorySize, PeakVirtualMemorySize,
MinWorkingSet, WorkingSet, PeakWorkingSet

start-sleep -seconds 600

get-process msdtc | format-table -property NonpagedSystemMemorySize,
PagedSystemMemorySize, VirtualMemorySize, PeakVirtualMemorySize,
MinWorkingSet, WorkingSet, PeakWorkingSet
```

```
start-sleep -seconds 600

get-process msdtc | format-table -property NonpagedSystemMemorySize,
PagedSystemMemorySize, VirtualMemorySize, PeakVirtualMemorySize,
MinWorkingSet, WorkingSet, PeakWorkingSet
```

Sample output

```
   Nonpaged PagedSystem     Virtual        Peak     Working       Peak
     System      Memory      Memory     Virtual         Set    Working
 MemorySize        Size        Size  MemorySize                    Set
----------- ----------- ----------- ---------- ---------- ----------
       6304       70544    41766912   63631360    6287360    6344704

   Nonpaged PagedSystem     Virtual        Peak     Working       Peak
     System      Memory      Memory     Virtual         Set    Working
 MemorySize        Size        Size  MemorySize                    Set
----------- ----------- ----------- ---------- ---------- ----------
       8123       96343    56243535   97423424    9147256    9348942

   Nonpaged PagedSystem     Virtual        Peak     Working       Peak
     System      Memory      Memory     Virtual         Set    Working
 MemorySize        Size        Size  MemorySize                    Set
----------- ----------- ----------- ---------- ---------- ----------
      17564      129645    48934246   97423424    9987384   10344706
```

Note Windows PowerShell script files have the .ps1 filename extension. To run a script at the Windows PowerShell prompt, you type the name of the script and, optionally, the filename extension. You must specify the fully qualified path to the script file, even if the script is in the current directory. To indicate the current directory, type the directory name or use the dot (.) to represent the current directory. With the MemUsage.ps1 script in the current directory, you can run the script by entering **.\memusage.ps1** at the Windows PowerShell prompt.

The Get-Process properties examined in Sample 7-4 provide the following information:

- **NonPagedSystemMemorySize** Shows the amount of allocated memory that can't be written to disk
- **PagedSystemMemorySize** Shows the amount of allocated memory that is allowed to be paged to the hard disk
- **VirtualMemorySize** Shows the amount of virtual memory allocated to and reserved for a process
- **PeakVirtualMemorySize** Shows the peak amount of paged memory used by the process
- **WorkingSetSize** Shows the amount of memory allocated to the process by the operating system
- **PeakWorkingSet** Shows the peak amount of memory used by the process

When you focus on these properties, you are zeroing in on the memory usage of a specific process. The key aspect to monitor is the working memory set. The working set of memory shows how much memory is allocated to the process by the operating system. If the working set increases over time and doesn't eventually go back to baseline usage, the process may have a memory leak. With a memory leak, the process isn't properly releasing memory that it's using, which can lead to reduced performance of the entire system.

In Sample 7-4, the process's memory usage changes substantially over the sampled interval. While it is most likely the process is simply actively being used by users or the computer itself, the process should eventually return to a baseline memory usage. If this doesn't happen, the process may have a memory-related problem.

Resolving Performance Bottlenecks

Because memory is usually the primary performance bottleneck on both workstations and servers, I've discussed many techniques previously in this chapter that you can use to help identify problems with memory. Memory is the resource you should examine first to try to determine why a system isn't performing as expected.

However, memory isn't the only bottleneck. Processor bottlenecks can occur if a process's threads need more processing time than is available. If a system's processors are the performance bottleneck, adding memory, drives, or network connections won't solve the problem. Instead, you might need to upgrade the processors to faster clock speeds or add processors to increase the computer's upper capacity. With servers, you could also move processor-intensive applications to another server.

Typeperf counters you can use to check for processor bottlenecks include the following:

- **System\Processor Queue Length** Records the number of threads waiting to be executed. These threads are queued in an area shared by all processors on the system. The processor queue grows because threads have to wait to get processing time. As a result, the system response suffers and the system appears sluggish or nonresponsive. Here, you might need to upgrade the processors to faster clock speeds or add processors to increase the server's upper capacity.
- **Processor(*)\% Processor Time** Records the percentage of time the selected processor is executing a non-idle thread. You should track this counter separately for each processor instance on the server. If the % Processor Time values for all instances are high (above 75 percent) while the network interface and disk input/output (I/O) throughput rates are relatively low, you might need to upgrade the processors to faster clock speeds or add processors to increase the server's upper capacity.
- **Processor(*)\% User Time** Records the percentage of time the selected processor is executing a non-idle thread in User mode. *User mode* is a processing mode for applications and user-level subsystems. A high value for all processor instances

might indicate that you need to upgrade the processors to faster clock speeds or add processors to increase the server's upper capacity.

- **Processor(*)\% Privileged Time** Records the percentage of time the selected processor is executing a non-idle thread in Privileged mode. *Privileged mode* is a processing mode for operating system components and services, allowing direct access to hardware and memory. A high value for all processor instances might indicate that you need to upgrade the processors to faster clock speeds or add processors to increase the computer's upper capacity.
- **Processor(*)\Interrupts/sec** Records the average rate, in incidents per second, that the selected processor received and serviced hardware interrupts. If this value increases substantially over time without a corresponding increase in activity, the system might have a hardware problem. To resolve this problem, you must identify the device or component that is causing the problem. Each time drivers or disk subsystem components such as hard disk drives or network components generate an interrupt, the processor has to stop what it is doing to handle the request because requests from hardware take priority. However, poorly designed drivers and components can generate false interrupts, which tie up the processor for no reason. System boards or components that are failing can generate false interrupts as well.

Note The asterisks in parentheses are placeholders for the object instance. On multiprocessor systems, you might need to rule out processor affinity as a cause of a processor bottleneck. By using processor affinity, you can set a program or process to use a specific processor to improve its performance. Assigning processor affinity can, however, block access to the processor for other programs and processes.

A system's hard disks are rarely the primary reason for a bottleneck. If a system is having to do a lot of disk reads and writes, it is usually because there isn't enough physical memory available and the system has to page to disk. Because reading from and writing to disk is much slower than reading and writing memory, excessive paging can degrade the server's overall performance. To reduce the amount of disk activity, you want the system to manage memory as efficiently as possible and page to disk only when necessary.

You can use these counters to monitor disk reads and writes:

- **PhysicalDisk(*)\% Disk Time** Records the percentage of time the physical disk is busy. Track this value for all hard disk drives on the system in conjunction with Processor(*)\% Processor Time and Network Interface(*)\Bytes Total/sec. If the % Disk Time value is high and the processor and network connection values aren't high, the system's hard disk drives might be creating a bottleneck.
- **PhysicalDisk(*)\Current Disk Queue Length** Records the number of system requests that are waiting for disk access. A high value indicates that the disk-waits are impacting system performance. In general, you want very few waiting requests.

- **PhysicalDisk(*)\Avg. Disk Write Queue Length** Records the number of write requests that are waiting to be processed.
- **PhysicalDisk(*)\Avg. Disk Read Queue Length** Records the number of read requests that are waiting to be processed.
- **PhysicalDisk(*)\Disk Writes/sec** Records the number of disk writes per second, which indicates the amount of disk I/O activity. By tracking the number of writes per second and the size of the write queue, you can determine how write operations are impacting disk performance.
- **PhysicalDisk(*)\Disk Reads/sec** Records the number of disk reads per second, which indicates the amount of disk I/O activity. By tracking the number of reads per second and the size of the read queue, you can determine how read operations are impacting disk performance.

Networking components can also cause bottlenecks. A delay between when a request is made, the time the request is received, and the time a user gets a response can cause users to think that systems are slow or nonresponsive. Unfortunately, in many cases, the delay users experience when working over the network is beyond your control. This is because the delay is a function of the type of connection the user has and the route the request takes. The total capacity of a computer to handle requests and the amount of bandwidth available to a computer are factors you can control, however. Network capacity is a function of the network cards and interfaces configured on the computers. Network bandwidth availability is a function of the network infrastructure and how much traffic is on it when a request is made.

You can use the following counters to check network activity and look for bottlenecks:

- **Network Interface(*)\Bytes Received/Sec** Records the rate at which bytes are received over a network adapter.
- **Network Interface(*)\Bytes Sent/Sec** Records the rate at which bytes are sent over a network adapter.
- **Network Interface(*)\Bytes Total/Sec** Records the rate at which bytes are sent and received over a network adapter. Check the network card configuration if you think there's a problem.
- **Network Interface(*)\Current Bandwidth** Estimates the current bandwidth for the selected network adapter in bits per second. Check to ensure the current bandwidth matches the type of network card configured on the computer. Most computers use 10 megabit, 100 megabit, or 1 gigabit network cards. Keep in mind that if the computer has a 1 gigabit network card, the networking devices to which the computer connects must also support this speed.

Chapter 8

Managing Event and Performance Logging

Proactively maintaining and monitoring systems is an important part of any administrator's job. Unfortunately, most administrators don't have time to perform routine maintenance and monitoring of all the systems for which they are responsible. For this reason, I'm going to dig even deeper into automated maintenance and monitoring, showing you techniques that you can use to reduce the administrative workload and save time.

In the previous chapters, I've shown you how to track and work with the event logs, how to automate monitoring, how to monitor processes, and how to troubleshoot performance issues. Now let's look at techniques you can use to manage the way logging is performed, centralize event logging across the enterprise, and collect and generate reports on performance data. Administrators and others with appropriate permissions can read event logs, configure event logs, and manage performance logging.

Managing the Event Logs

Often, you'll want to manage the configuration of event logs on local and remote systems to ensure that logs are configured in a specific way. For example, your organization's security policies may require that you ensure that security logs are never overwritten. Rather than logging on locally or remotely to every computer that you want to configure, you can use the command line or command-line scripts to configure the security log and any other logs exactly as needed. Your tool of choice for configuring event logs is the Windows Events Command Line Utility (Wevtutil). You can use Wevtutil to view and modify the configuration of event logs, read events, export and archive event logs, and clear event logs.

Getting Started with Wevtutil

Wevtutil provides a number of commands and options for managing event logs and their configurations. Before you start working with this utility you should take a moment to learn about the available subcommands and options. Subcommands and options have both an abbreviated short form and a long form. When you are just starting out with Wevtutil or for clarity within scripts, you may want to use the long form, which clearly names the tasks you are performing and reduces any possible confusion. Otherwise, you'll typically want to use the short form to save time and keystrokes.

The basic syntax for Wevtutil is:

```
wevtutil Command Argument [[Argument] …] [/Option:Value [/Option:Value] …]
```

where *Command* is a command listed in Table 8-1, *Argument* is a command argument, and *Value* is a value for an option.

Table 8-1 Commands Available with Wevtutil

Long Form	Short Form	Description
archive-log	Al	Archives an exported log.
clear-log	Cl	Clears a log and permanently deletes all of its events.
enum-logs	El	Lists all available logs by name.
enum-publishers	Ep	Lists all registered event publishers, which includes all Windows services and other components configured to write to the event logs.
export-log	Epl	Exports a log in Windows Event Log (.evtx) format.
get-log	Gl	Gets log configuration information.
get-log-info	Gli	Gets log status information.
get-publisher	Gp	Gets publisher configuration information.
install-manifest	Im	Installs event publishers and logs from manifests.
query-events	Qe	Queries events from a log or log file.
set-log	Sl	Modifies the configuration of a log.
uninstall-manifest	Um	Uninstalls event publishers and logs from manifest.

While each Wevtutil command has a slightly different set of available options, all commands have common options, as shown in Table 8-2. Wevtutil runs by default with the permissions of the user who is currently logged on. You can also specify the remote computer you want to work with and the Run As permissions. To do this, you use the expanded syntax, which includes the following parameters:

```
/r:Computer /u:[Domain\]User [/p:Password]
```

where *Computer* is the remote computer name or IP address, *Domain* is the optional domain name in which the user account is located, *User* is the name of the user account whose permissions you want to use, and *Password* is the optional password for the user account. If you don't specify the domain, the current domain is assumed. If you don't provide the account password, you are prompted for the password.

Note Options and option values are separated by colons. Do not insert a space after the colon.

Table 8-2 Wevtutil Command Options

Long Form	Short Form	Description
/remote:	/r:	Specifies the remote computer on which to run the command. You cannot use this option with im (install-manifest) or um (uninstall-manifest).
/username:	/u:	Specifies a different user to log on to a remote computer in the form Domain\User or user. Only applicable when working with a remote computer.
/password:	/p:	Sets the password for the specified user. If you don't specify a password, or if you use "*", you are prompted to enter a password. The option is only applicable when a different logon user is specified when working with a remote computer.
/authentication:	/a:	Sets the authentication type for connecting to a remote computer. You can set this option to Default, Negotiate, Kerberos, or NTLM. The default is Negotiate.
/unicode:	/uni:	Sets the display output in Unicode or ASCII text. You can set this option to true for Unicode or false for ASCII text. The default is ASCII text.

Listing Available Logs and Registered Publishers

As discussed previously in Chapter 6, "Event Logging, Tracking, and Monitoring," the event logs available on a system depend on the role and the services installed. The same is true for the registered event log publishers, which includes all Windows services and other components configured to write to the event logs.

You can list all available logs on a computer by entering **wevtutil el** at a command prompt. Because this list typically is very long, you may want to redirect the output through the FIND command to help you look for a specific log. You can use FIND with Wevtutil as shown in the following example:

```
wevtutil el | find /i "FindText"
```

where *FindText* is the search text you want to use to filter the output. For example, if you wanted to determine whether a specific log is associated with the Encrypting File System (EFS), you could filter the output as shown in the following example:

```
wevtutil el | find /i "efs"
```

Because the /I parameter tells the FIND command to ignore the letter case of characters in the output text, the resulting output would then include any log names with "EFS" in any letter case, such as:

```
Microsoft-Windows-EFS/Debug
```

You can list registered event log publishers by entering **wevtutil ep** at a command prompt. Again, because the output typically will be a fairly long list, you can filter the output using the FIND command. For example, if you wanted to determine whether the Netlogon service is a registered event log publisher, you could enter the following command at a command prompt:

```
wevtutil ep | find /i "netlogon"
```

Because Windows services, system components, and other add-ons to a computer can be registered as event log publishers, you may want to know exactly how event publishers write events to the event logs. To do this, you can list publisher configuration information using Wevtutil gp and the following syntax:

```
wevtutil gp Publisher
```

where *Publisher* is the full name of the registered event log publisher that you want to work with. For example, after you determine that the Netlogon service was a registered publisher, you might want to know where it records its events. You could do this by entering **wevtutil gp netlogon** at a command prompt. In this case, the output would be similar to the following:

```
name: netlogon
guid: 00000000-0000-0000-0000-000000000000
helpLink: http://go.microsoft.com/fwlink/events.asp?CoName=
Microsoft%20Corporation&ProdName=Microsoft%c2%ae%20Windows%c2
%ae%20Operating%20System&ProdVer=6.0.6000.16386&FileName=netmsg.
dll&FileVer=6.0.6000.16386
parameterFileName: %SystemRoot%\System32\kernel32.dll
messageFileName: %SystemRoot%\System32\netmsg.dll
message:
channels:
  channel:
    name: System
    id: 8
    flags: 1
    message:
levels:
opcodes:
tasks:
keywords:
```

The name value listed within the Channels details lists the log or logs to which the publisher writes. In some cases, you can also obtain a complete list of all the events the publisher uses when writing to event logs. To do this, set the /Ge parameter to true as shown in the following example:

```
wevtutil gp Microsoft-Windows-TaskScheduler /ge:true
```

If the publisher has registered specific events, Wevtutil lists these after the standard publisher configuration information. Don't forget that you can specify a remote computer and logon credentials. In the following example, you can examine the Microsoft-Windows-TaskScheduler publisher on FileServer25:

```
wevtutil gp Microsoft-Windows-TaskScheduler /r:fileserver25
/u:cpandl\williams /p:Cab!@#45898
```

Viewing and Changing Log Configuration

Log configuration options allow you to control the size of the event logs as well as how logging is handled. By default, event logs are set with a maximum file size. Then, when a log reaches this limit, events are overwritten to prevent the log from exceeding the maximum file size. You also can configure logs for autobackup and strict retention. With autobackup enabled, Windows archives an event log when it reaches its maximum size by saving a copy of the log in the default directory and then creating a new log for storing current events. With strict retention enabled, Windows discards any new events and generates error messages telling you the event log is full when it reaches its maximum size.

You can list a log's current configuration using Wevtutil gl and the following syntax:

```
wevtutil gl LogName
```

where *LogName* is the name of the log you want to examine. For example, if you wanted to view the configuration of the application log, you'd enter:

```
wevtutil gl application
```

and the output would be similar to the following:

```
name: application
enabled: true
type: Admin
owningPublisher:
isolation: Application
channelAccess: O:BAG:SYD:(A;;0xf0007;;;SY)(A;;0x7;;;BA)
logging:
  logFileName: %SystemRoot%\System32\Winevt\Logs\application.evtx
  retention: false
  autoBackup: false
  maxSize: 20971520
publishing:
```

The main items you want to focus on are the enabled status of the log and the default logging settings. In this example, the log is enabled, the full path to the log file is %SystemRoot%\System32\Winevt\Logs\application.evtx, retention is disabled, autobackup is disabled, and the maximum log size is 20,971,520 bytes (20,480 KB).

> **Real World** The isolation property provides valuable information about the log security. If you set the isolation property to Application, the log has the same security permissions for writing to the log as the Application log. If you set the isolation property to System, the log has the same security permissions for writing to the log as the System log. In either case, the security on the log is not restricted unless access is controlled through Group Policy. If you set the isolation property to Custom, the log has a custom security and access to the log is restricted to those who are a member of the group or groups granted access to the log. For example, the Security log has Custom isolation and its related security descriptor restricts access to only those who are granted the user right Manage Auditing And The Security Log—a user right granted to administrators by default. Because of the access controls on the Security log, you have to use an elevated, administrator-level command prompt to work with the local computer's security log at the command line.

Whether a log is enabled or disabled is important. A disabled log is turned off so that it is not being used and as a result you cannot get the log's status details. To learn more about an enabled log, you can list its status information using Wevtutil gli. If you were to enter **Wevtutil gli application**, you'd list status information for the application log and the output would contain similar information to the following:

```
creationTime: 2006-06-11T23:39:52.078Z
lastAccessTime: 2006-06-11T23:39:52.078Z
lastWriteTime: 2008-03-28T17:35:14.547Z
fileSize: 20975616
attributes: 32
numberOfLogRecords: 43293
oldestRecordNumber: 27607
```

The key information in the log output includes:

- creationTime, which lists the time and date the log was created.
- lastWriteTime, which lists the last time and date an event was written to the log.
- fileSize, which lists the current log size in bytes.
- numberOfLogRecords, which lists the number of events in the log.
- oldestRecordNumber, which lists the oldest record number.

> **Note** If the oldest record number is 1, Windows has not overwritten events in the log. If the older record number is greater than 1, Windows is overwriting events in the log and the number of events overwritten is equal to the oldest record number. In the example, the oldest record number is 27,607, indicating the events have been extensively overwritten since Windows created the log.

If you want to modify the configuration of a log, you can use the Wevtutil sl command to change the log settings. You can set the maximum log size in bytes using the /Ms parameter. You can enable or disable a log using the /E parameter. Use /e:true to enable a log or /e:false to disable a log. If you want to ensure that the log is never overwritten, you can enable log retention using /r:true. When you enable retention, Windows discards any new events and generates error messages telling you the event log is full when it reaches its maximum size. The only exception is when autobackup also is enabled. To ensure that a log is automatically backed up when it reaches its maximum size, you can enable autobackup using /ab:true. When you enable autobackup, you must also enable retention.

Consider the following examples to see how you can configure event logs:

Set the System log to a maximum size of 20,971,520 bytes (20,480 KB):

```
Wevtutil sl System /ms:20971520
Wevtutil sl System /maxsize:20971520
```

Disable the Windows RPC debug log:

```
Wevtutil sl Microsoft-Windows-RPC/Debug /e:false
Wevtutil sl Microsoft-Windows-RPC/Debug /enabled:false
```

Enable retention of the application log on FileServer86:

```
Wevtutil sl application /s:FileServer86 /rt:true
Wevtutil sl application /s:FileServer86 /retention:true
```

Enable retention and autobackup of the Security log on DomainServer18:

```
Wevtutil sl security /s:DomainServer18 /rt:true /ab:true
Wevtutil sl security /s:DomainServer18 /retention:true
/autobackup:true
```

Note When you are working with the Security log, remote systems, or both, you'll usually want to configure logs using an elevated, administrator command prompt. With remote systems, you may also need to use alternate credentials.

Exporting and Manipulating Event Logs

Typically, you'll want to keep several months' worth of logs for all critical systems. While it isn't always practical to set the maximum log size to accommodate this, several workarounds are available. You can allow Windows to periodically archive the event logs as discussed in the previous section. Or you can export logs to a save location using the command line or command-line scripts.

Using the Wevtutil epl command, you can export logs to a file in Windows Event Log (.evtx) format. The basic syntax for exporting a log is:

```
wevtutil epl LogName SaveLocation
```

where *LogName* is the name of the event log to export to a file and *SaveLocation* is the full file path to the location where the exported file is to be saved. For example, you could export the Application log to C:\Logs\AppLog092908.evtx using the following command:

```
wevtutil epl Application C:\Logs\AppLog092908.evtx
```

> **Note** You can more easily locate logs if you create a dedicated archive directory. You should also name the log file so that you can easily determine the log file type and the period of the archive. For example, if you're archiving the Application log file for June 2009, you might want to use AppLogJune2009.evtx as the filename.

When you export logs in this way, Windows exports the full contents of the named log to the designated file, but does not clear the existing event log. Clearing the event log is a separate action accomplished with the Wevtutil cl command as discussed in the section titled "Clearing Event Logs" later in this chapter.

If you want to export a subset of events rather than all events in a log, you can do this using a saved XPath query. In the section titled "Creating and Using Saved Queries" in Chapter 6, I discussed the basics of XPath queries and how you can create custom views using them. To use XPath queries to export a subset of events, you must create a query containing a filter rather than a custom view. The easiest way to do this is to use Event Viewer and follow these steps:

1. Start Event Viewer by clicking Start, clicking Administrative Tools, and then clicking Event Viewer.

   > **Note** If you are not logged on locally to the computer you want to work with, right-click the Event Viewer node and then select Connect To Another Computer. In the Select Computer dialog box, enter the host name, IP address, or fully qualified domain name of the computer in the Another Computer text box. As necessary, you can use alternate credentials to connect to the remote computer. To establish the connection, click OK.

2. Select the log you want to filter. In the Actions pane or on the Action menu, click Filter Current Log.

3. In the Filter Current Log dialog box, shown in Figure 8-1, use the Logged list to select the included time frame for logged events. You can choose to include events from Anytime, the Last Hour, Last 12 Hours, Last 24 Hours, Last 7 Days, or Last 30 Days.

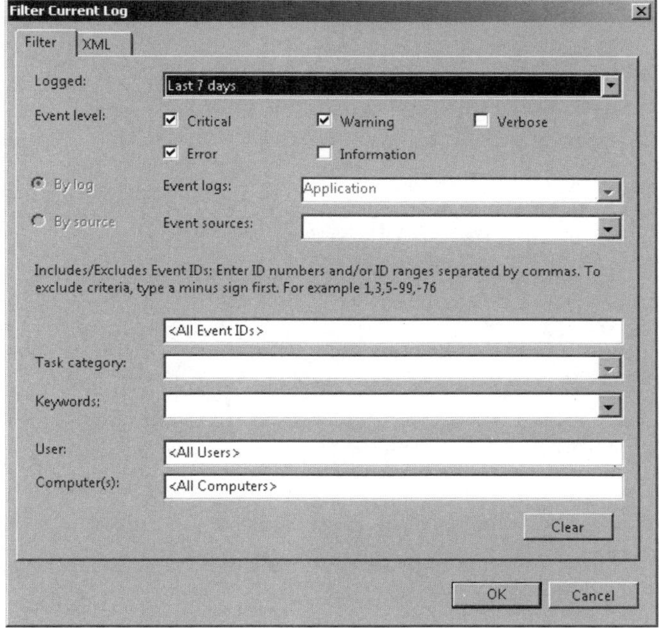

Figure 8-1 Create a filter to specify the types of events to display.

4. Use the Event Level check boxes to specify the level of events to include. Select Verbose to get additional detail.

5. You can create a filter for all event sources or a specific set of event sources. Use the Event Sources list to select event sources to include. You can select multiple event sources by selecting their related check boxes. Keep in mind that when you select specific event sources, all other event sources are excluded.

6. Optionally, use the User and Computer(s) boxes to specify users and computers that should be included. If you do not specify the users and computers to include, events generated by all users and computers are included.

7. Click the XML tab to display the related XPath query as shown in Figure 8-2.

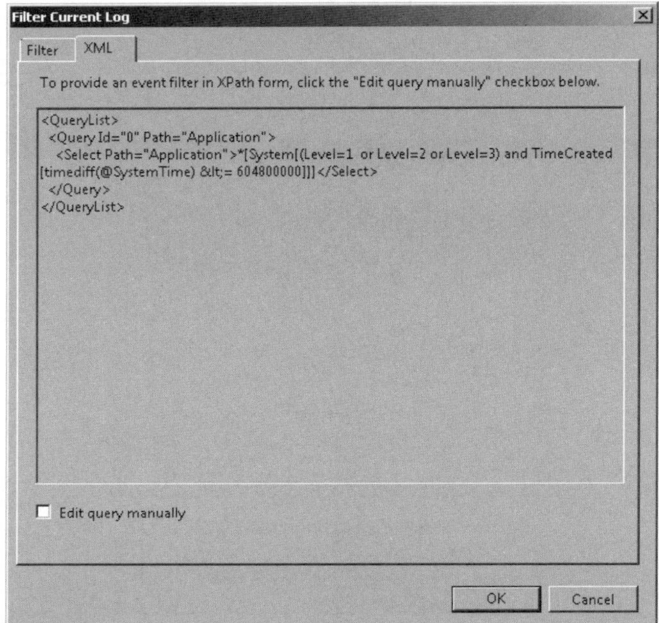

Figure 8-2 Review the related XPath query.

8. Select the query by clicking in the query and pressing Ctrl+A, and then copy the query to the clipboard by pressing Ctrl+C.
9. Open Notepad by clicking Start, clicking All Programs, clicking Accessories, and then clicking Notepad.
10. Paste the copied query into Notepad by pressing Ctrl+V.
11. On the File menu, click Save As. In the Save As dialog box, select a save location and then type a name for the saved query in the File Name text box. Be sure to specify .xml as the file extension.
12. In the Save As Type list, select All Files (*.*) to ensure that Notepad doesn't try to append the .txt file extension to the filename you entered.
13. Click Save to close the Save As dialog box.
14. Click OK to close the Filter Current Log dialog box and preview your filter in Event Viewer.

The following is a sample query that filters recent Critical, Error, and Warning events in the Application log:

```
<QueryList>
  <Query Id="0" Path="Application">
    <Select Path="Application">*[System[(Level=1  or Level=2 or Level=3)
and TimeCreated[timediff(@SystemTime) &lt;= 604800000]]]</Select>
  </Query>
</QueryList>
```

You tell Wevtutil that you want to use a query by setting the /Structuredquery (/Sq) parameter to true. When you do this, you no longer need to specify the log you want to export because this is defined in the filter; instead you must tell Wevtutil about the query using the following syntax:

```
wevtutil epl QueryPath SaveLocation /sq:true
```

where *QueryPath* is the name of an XML query in the current directory, or the full file path to an XML query, and *SaveLocation* is the full file path to the location where the exported file is to be saved. For example, you could use the query defined in the C:\Queries\AppQuery.xml file to export a filtered Application log to C:\Logs\AppLogFiltered092908.evtx using the following command:

```
wevtutil epl C:\Queries\AppQuery.xml C:\Logs\AppLogFiltered092908.evtx
/sq:true
```

In Event Viewer, you can open saved logs by selecting the Event Viewer node, choosing Open Saved Log on the Action menu or in the Actions pane, and then using the Open Saved Log dialog box to select the log to open. With Wevtutil, you can use the qe command to view the contents of either a current or an archived log. The best syntax to use when working with logs is the following:

```
wevtutil qe LogName /c:NumEvents /rd:true /f:text
```

where *LogName* is the name of an event log or the full file path to an archived log, *NumEvents* is the number of events to read, /rd:true specifies that you want to work with the most recent events, and /f:text sets the output format as text rather than XML. Following this, you could read the 50 most recent events in the Application log using this command:

```
wevtutil qe Application /c:50 /rd:true /f:text
```

You can also use XPath queries to filter a current log. As with the Wevtutil epl command, you specify that you want to use a query by setting the /Structuredquery (/Sq) parameter to true–then you no longer need to specify the log you want to query because this is defined in the filter. Thus, the syntax for filtering events using a query is:

```
wevtutil qe QueryPath /sq:true
```

where *QueryPath* is the name of an XML query in the current directory, or the full file path to an XML query, such as:

```
wevtutil qe C:\Queries\AppQuery.xml /sq:true
```

You can use the /C, /Rd, and /F parameters as well to restrict the output as discussed previously and shown in the following example:

```
wevtutil qe C:\Queries\AppQuery.xml /sq:true /c:50 /rd:true /f:text
```

You can also use the /R, /U, and /P parameters to query events on a remote computer as discussed previously and shown in the following example:

```
wevtutil qe C:\Queries\AppQuery.xml /sq:true /c:50 /rd:true /f:text/
r:PrintServer23 /u:adatum\williams /p:Fiber
```

Clearing Event Logs

When an event log is full, you need to clear it. You can clear a log using the Wevtutil cl command and the following syntax:

```
wevtutil cl LogName
```

where *LogName* is the name of an event log to clear, such as:

```
wevtutil cl Application
```

If you haven't already archived a log that you are clearing, you may also want to back up the log so that you have a saved copy of its contents. You can specify that you want to back up a log before clearing it by using the /Backup (/Bu) parameter. Follow the /Backup (/Bu) parameter with the backup filename or file path. Be sure to always include the .evtx file extension as shown in the following example:

```
wevtutil cl Application /bu:C:\Logs\AppLogFiltered.evtx
```

Centralizing Event Logging Across the Enterprise

In Chapter 6 as well as in this chapter, I've shown you many techniques you can use to work with event logs. Although you can create command-line scripts to examine logs on multiple computers and copy this information to a central save location for easy viewing, you also can centralize event logging by configuring event forwarding. With event forwarding, you can forward all events or specific types of events to a designated central logging computer. For example, you might want to configure all workstations and servers in the organization to forward Audit Failure events from the Security log to a central logging computer, and then you could analyze these events in real time to detect someone trying to break into your organization's computers. On your critical servers, you might also want to forward all critical and error events from the Application and System logs to a central logging computer and then analyze these events in real time to detect application failures and other issues that need administrator attention.

Configuring centralized event logging is a multi-step process. First, you must configure event forwarding and collection. Then, on your designated central event logging computers, you must create subscriptions that specify on a per source-computer basis the types of events to forward and the logs from which events will be forwarded. On your central logging computers, forwarded events are collected in the Forwarded Events log by default.

Configuring Event Forwarding and Collection

The event forwarding architecture is very flexible. You can configure a central logging computer to in turn forward events to another central logging computer. Because the forwarding protocol (WS-Management) makes use of the standard Hypertext Transfer Protocol (HTTP) and Secure HTTP (HTTPS) protocols, you can forward across firewalls as long as the related TCP ports are open. In a standard configuration, this means TCP port 80 must be open for HTTP and TCP port 443 must be open for HTTPS.

Using event forwarding involves configuring and enabling event forwarding on the appropriate computers and then creating subscriptions to the forwarded events on your central logging computer or computers. In a domain, you can configure event forwarding and collection of forwarded events by following these steps:

1. To configure forwarding on a computer running Windows Vista or Windows Server 2008, you must log on to all source computers and do the following:
   - Set the Windows Remote Management (WinRM) service to delayed auto start.
   - Start the WinRM service.
   - Create WinRM listener.
   - Enable the WinRM firewall exception (if Windows Firewall is turned on).

   Rather than perform all these tasks through separate actions, you can type **winrm quickconfig** at an elevated command prompt to perform these tasks and create a WinRM listener on HTTP://* to accept WS-Management requests to any IP address on the source computer. You will then be prompted to confirm. Press Y.
2. To configure collection, log on to your central logging computers and type **wecutil qc** at an elevated command prompt. This starts the Windows Event Collector service and configures this service to use the delayed-start mode. When prompted to confirm, press Y.
3. In Active Directory, create a global group for your collector computers and then add the collector computers to this group as discussed in the sections titled "Adding Group Accounts" and "Managing Group Accounts" in Chapter 15, "Managing Active Directory Users and Groups."

4. Add the global group for the collector computers to the local Administrators group on each of the source computers. At an elevated command prompt, you can do this using net localgroup. Type **net localgroup Administrators *CollectorGroup* /add** where *CollectorGroup* is the name of the global group you created for the collector computers, such as **net localgroup Administrators Collectors /add**.

Creating Subscriptions

The easiest way to create subscriptions is to use Event Viewer and follow these steps:

1. Start Event Viewer by clicking Start, clicking Administrative Tools, and then clicking Event Viewer. If you aren't logged on to the central logging computer, right-click the Event Viewer node and then select Connect To Another Computer. In the Select Computer dialog box, enter the host name, IP address, or fully qualified domain name of the computer in the Another Computer text box. As necessary, you can use alternate credentials to connect to the remote computer. To establish the connection, click OK.
2. Right-click the Subscriptions node and select Create Subscription.
3. In the Subscription Properties dialog box, shown in Figure 8-3, type a name for the subscription, such as **All File Servers**. The name you enter is set as the Subscription Identifier. Optionally, enter a description.

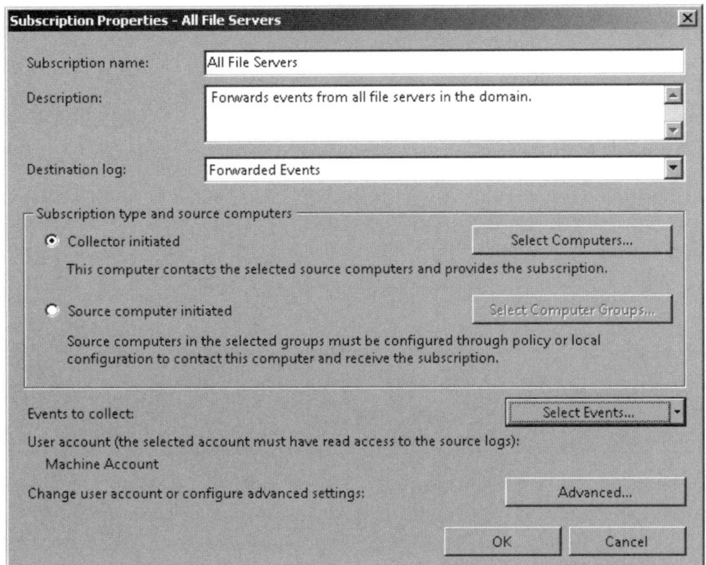

Figure 8-3 Create a subscription to forward events.

4. By default, the Forwarded Events log is selected as the destination log. If you are making extensive use of event forwarding and forwarding to a computer dedicated to event collection, you may want to forward to other logs. However, if you do this, you should ensure that the query you create is only for that specific log, which will help reduce any possible confusion.
5. Collector-initiated event forwarding is the easiest to configure, and is the default setting. To specify the computers that forward events to the server, click Select Computers. In the Computers dialog box, click Add Domain Computers. In the Select Computer dialog box, type the account name of a computer that is forwarding events and then click OK twice. Repeat this process as necessary.
6. Click Select Events. This displays the Query Filter dialog box.
7. Use the Event Level check boxes to specify the level of events to include. Select Verbose to get additional detail.
8. In most cases, you'll want to create a filter for a single log or for multiple logs, so ensure that By Log is selected and then use the Event Logs lists to select the log or logs to filter.
9. If you want to filter the selected log or logs for specific event sources rather than all event sources, use the Event Sources list to select event sources to include. You can select multiple event sources by selecting their related check boxes. Keep in mind that when you select specific event sources, all other event sources are excluded. Also, do not select the By Source option because doing so will remove your log selections.
10. By default, the Windows Event Collector Service uses the central logging computer's machine account to read the source logs. To use other credentials, click Advanced. In the Advanced Subscription Settings dialog box, select Specific User and then click the User And Password button. In the Credentials For Subscription Source dialog box, enter the user name and password of the account to use and then click OK twice. You can enter the user name in Domain\user format to specify the user's logon domain, such as **cpandl\williams**.
11. Click OK to create the subscription. Once the subscription is created and the selected computer or computers begin forwarding events, you'll see the forwarded events when you access the destination log.

Now that you know how to create subscriptions using Event Viewer, let's look at how you can perform this complex task at the command line. You can create and manage subscriptions on a central logging computer using the Wecutil commands summarized in Table 8-3. As with Wevtutil, Wecutil commands have both long and short forms.

Table 8-3 Commands Available with Wecutil

Long Form	Short Form	Description
enum-subscription	Es	Lists existing subscriptions on the computer.
get-subscription	Gs	Displays subscription configuration details.
get-subscriptionruntimestatus	Gr	Displays the subscription runtime status.
set-subscription	Ss	Modifies the subscription configuration.
create-subscription	Cs	Creates a new subscription.
delete-subscription	Ds	Deletes a subscription.
retry-subscription	Rs	Retries all sources of a subscription.
quick-config	Qc	Enables and configures the Windows Event Collector service.

You create subscriptions using the Wecutil cs command and an XML configuration file. The configuration file contains an XPath query that defines the events you want to forward, identifies the source computer and assigns the subscription a subscription identifier. As when you are creating subscriptions in Event Viewer, collector-initiated event forwarding is the easiest to configure and is the default setting.

You can display a sample XML configuration file that you can copy and paste into a text editor by typing **wecutil cs /?** at a command prompt. The sample configuration file will look similar to the following:

```
<Subscription xmlns="http://schemas.microsoft.com/2006/03/windows/events/
subscription">
  <Uri>http://schemas.microsoft.com/wbem/wsman/1/windows/EventLog</Uri>
  <!-- Use Normal (default), Custom, MinLatency, MinBandwidth -->
  <ConfigurationMode>Normal</ConfigurationMode>
  <Description>Forward Sample Subscription</Description>
  <SubscriptionId>SampleSubscription</SubscriptionId>
  <Query><![CDATA[
    <QueryList>
        <Query Path="Application">
          <Select>*</Select>
        </Query>
    </QueryList>
  ]]></Query>
  <EventSources>
    <EventSource Enabled="true">
      <Address>mySource.myDomain.com</Address>
```

```
      <UserName>myUserName</UserName>
      <Password>*</Password>
    </EventSource>
  </EventSources>
  <CredentialsType>Default</CredentialsType>
  <Locale Language="EN-US"></Locale>
</Subscription>
```

Once you copy and paste the sample configuration file into your text editor, you'll need to edit the file. The key data you want to edit includes the description, subscription identifier, XPath query, and event sources.

The description provides a general description of the subscription to help administrators determine how the subscription is used and is defined in the XML file using the Description element. You can change the descriptive text between the begin <Description> tag and the end </Description> tag as necessary. Here is an example:

```
<Description>Forwards important events from file servers</Description>
```

The subscription identifier is a unique id for the subscription on a specified central logging computer and is defined in the SubscriptionID element. You can change the descriptive text between the begin <SubscriptionId> tag and the end </SubscriptionId> tag as necessary. Here is an example:

```
<SubscriptionId>All File Servers</SubscriptionId>
```

The QueryList element within the Query element defines the XPath query. You can copy and paste in any existing XPath query that defines an event log filter. However, because event forwarding occurs in real time, you will want to remove any part of the query that filters by the time the event was created.

Unlike when you work with Wevtutil and a single event log, you'll usually want to create a single query that works with multiple logs because this reduces the number of subscriptions you must create. The following is a sample query that filters Critical, Error, and Warning events in the Application, System, and DNS Server logs:

```
<QueryList>
  <Query Id="0" Path="Application">
    <Select Path="Application">*[System[(Level=1  or Level=2 or Level=3)]]
</Select>
    <Select Path="System">*[System[(Level=1  or Level=2 or Level=3)]]
</Select>
    <Select Path="DNS Server">*[System[(Level=1  or Level=2 or Level=3)]]
</Select>
  </Query>
</QueryList>
```

Individual EventSource elements within the EventSources element identify the source computers. Each computer that will forward events based on the previously entered query must have its own EventSource element and that element must specify the computer's fully qualified domain name or IP address. In this example, you are enabling event forwarding for FileServer24, FileServer26, and FileServer28 in the Cpandl.com domain:

```
<EventSources>
  <EventSource Enabled="true">
    <Address>fileserver24.cpandl.com</Address>
  </EventSource>
  <EventSource Enabled="true">
    <Address>fileserver26.cpandl.com</Address>
  </EventSource>
  <EventSource Enabled="true">
    <Address>fileserver28.cpandl.com</Address>
  </EventSource>
</EventSources>
```

By default, the Windows Event Collector Service uses the central logging computer's machine account to read the source logs. To use other credentials, you must provide the logon information. One way to do this is as part of the EventSource element, as shown in the following example:

```
<EventSource Enabled="true">
  <Address>fileserver24.cpandl.com</Address>
    <UserName>williams</UserName>
    <Password>*</Password>
</EventSource>
```

Here, you specify the credentials to use for FileServer24. Because the password is specified as *, you are prompted for the necessary credentials when you create the subscription. Any credentials you provide when prompted are associated with the subscription and stored securely.

> **Note** When you define other credentials in the configuration file, you'll almost always want to use * for the password rather than entering the password. Entering passwords directly into the configuration file is a poor security practice.

Elements not in the sample configuration file but set to default values include:

- **ConfigurationMode** Sets the delivery optimization method as either Normal, MinLatency, or MinBandwidth and uses the begin <ConfigurationMode> tag and the end </ConfigurationMode> tag.
- **DeliveryMode** Sets the delivery method as either Push or Pull (Pull is the default) and uses the begin <DeliveryMode> tag and the end </DeliveryMode> tag.
- **ReadExistingEvents** Specifies whether existing events or only new events are read and uses the begin <ReadExistingEvents> tag and the end </ReadExisting-Events> tag. By default, this element has a value of False, meaning only new events are read.

- **LogFile** Specifies the log file to which events are forwarded and uses the begin <LogFile> tag and the end </LogFile> tag. When you specify a log name, be sure to remove any spaces in the name. Thus Forwarded Events becomes ForwardedEvents.
- **TransportName** Specifies the transport to use as either HTTP or HTTPS and uses the begin <TransportName> tag and the end </TransportName> tag. When you specify HTTPS as the transport, you must also configure a WinRM listener for HTTPS on the source computers.
- **TransportPort** Specifies the transport port to use and uses the begin <TransportPort> tag and the end </TransportPort> tag. You need to use the same port you configured for the WinRM listener on the source computers. Typically, this means using port 80 for HTTP and port 443 for HTTPS.

Sample 8-1 shows a configuration file for Wecutil that uses the elements and options we've discussed so far.

Sample 8-1 Working configuration file for Wecutil

```
<Subscription xmlns="http://schemas.microsoft.com/2006/03/windows/
events/subscription">
  <Uri>http://schemas.microsoft.com/wbem/wsman/1/windows/EventLog</
Uri>
  <!-- Use Normal (default), Custom, MinLatency, MinBandwidth -->
  <ConfigurationMode>Normal</ConfigurationMode>
  <Description>Forwards events from file servers in the domain</
Description>
  <SubscriptionId>All Servers</SubscriptionId>
  <DeliveryMode>Pull</DeliveryMode>
  <ReadExistingEvents >False</ReadExistingEvents>
  <LogFile>ForwardedEvents</LogFile>
  <TransportName>HTTPS</TransportName>
  <TransportPort>443</TransportPort>
  <QueryList>
    <Query Id="0" Path="Application">
      <Select Path="Application">*[System[(Level=1  or Level=2 or
Level=3)]]</Select>
      <Select Path="System">*[System[(Level=1  or Level=2 or Level=
3)]]</Select>
      <Select Path="DNS Server">*[System[(Level=1  or Level=2 or Level
=3)]]</Select>
    </Query>
  </QueryList>
  <EventSources>
    <EventSource Enabled="true">
      <Address>fileserver24.cpandl.com</Address>
    </EventSource>
    <EventSource Enabled="true">
```

```
      <Address>fileserver26.cpandl.com</Address>
    </EventSource>
    <EventSource Enabled="true">
      <Address>fileserver28.cpandl.com</Address>
    </EventSource>
  </EventSources>
  <CredentialsType>Default</CredentialsType>
  <Locale Language="EN-US"></Locale>
</Subscription>
```

Once you've created an XML configuration file, you can create a subscription with the Wecutil cs command. Use the following syntax:

```
wecutil cs ConfigFile
```

where *ConfigFile* is the name of a configuration file in the current directory, or the full file path to a configuration file in another directory. For example, if you wanted to create a subscription using the C:\Evtforwarding\config1.xml file, you could use the following command:

```
wecutil cs c:\evtforwarding\config1.xml
```

When you create a subscription, you can specify shared credentials to use rather than any credentials specified in the configuration file using the /Cun and /Cup parameters. The /Cun parameter sets the user name and the /Cup parameter sets the password as shown in this example:

```
wecutil cs c:\evtforwarding\config1.xml /cun:cpandl\williams /cup:Rover
```

Managing Subscriptions

Once you've created a subscription and the selected computer or computers begin forwarding events, you'll see the forwarded events when you access the destination log. When you select the Subscriptions node in Event Viewer, you'll see the subscriptions you've created. Event Viewer lists each subscription by name, status, type, number of source computers, destination log, and description. When you select a subscription by clicking it, you can manage the subscription using these options in the Actions pane or on the Action menu:

- **Properties** Displays the Subscription Properties dialog box, which you can use to modify the subscription. The options available are similar to those discussed in the previous procedure except that you cannot change the subscription name or type.
- **Disable** Disables the subscription so that events are not forwarded or collected. The subscription status changes to Disabled.
- **Enable** Enables the subscription so that events are forwarded or collected. The subscription status changes to Active.

- **Runtime Status** Displays the run-time status of the subscription, including whether the subscription is active or inactive as well as whether collection errors are on the source computers. If a source computer has an error status, you can select the entry to see additional details. With the source computer's entry selected, you can also disable or enable event forwarding on the selected source computer.
- **Delete** Deletes the subscription permanently.

Wecutil provides commands to perform these tasks as well. To list all subscriptions on a computer by name, enter **wecutil es** at a command prompt. To list the configuration details for a specific subscription, enter **wecutil gs** followed by the subscription name. If the subscription name includes spaces, you should enclose the subscription name in quotation marks, such as:

```
wecutil gs "All File Servers"
```

As shown in the following example, the output shows you exactly how the subscription is configured:

```
Subscription Id: all servers
SubscriptionType: CollectorInitiated
Description: all servers in the domain
Enabled: false
Uri: http://schemas.microsoft.com/wbem/wsman/1/windows/EventLog
ConfigurationMode: Normal
DeliveryMode: Pull
DeliveryMaxLatencyTime: 900000
HeartbeatInterval: 900000
Query: <QueryList><Query Id="0"><Select Path="Application">*[System[(Level=1
  or
 Level=2 or Level=3)]]</Select><Select Path="System">*[System[(Level=1
or Level =2
or Level=3)]]</Select><Select Path="DNS Server">*[System[(Level=1  or
Level=2
 or Level=3)]]</Select></Query></QueryList>
ReadExistingEvents: false
TransportName: HTTP
TransportPort: 80
ContentFormat: RenderedText
Locale: en-US
LogFile: Microsoft-Windows-DateTimeControlPanel/Operational
PublisherName:
CredentialsType: Default

EventSource[0]:
        Address: MAILSERVER84.cpandl.com
        Enabled: true
EventSource[1]:
        Address: ROOM5.cpandl.com
        Enabled: true
```

You can modify the settings of a subscription using the Wecutil ss command. When you work with the Wecutil ss command, you can use the individual parameters available to modify the subscription configuration. However, the easiest way to modify a subscription is to create a new configuration file or simply make the changes in the original configuration file and then run Wecutil ss with the following syntax:

```
wecutil ss SubscriptionName ConfigFile
```

where *SubscriptionName* is the name of the subscription and *ConfigFile* is the name of a configuration file in the current directory, or the full file path to a configuration file in another directory. For example, if you wanted to create a subscription using the C:\Evtforwarding\config1.xml file, you could use the following command:

```
wecutil ss "All File Servers" c:\evtforwarding\config1.xml
```

When you are modifying a subscription, you can specify shared credentials to use rather than any existing credentials or credentials specified in the configuration file using the /Cun and /Cup parameters. The /Cun parameter sets the user name and the /Cup parameter sets the password as shown in this example:

```
wecutil ss "All File Servers" c:\evtforwarding\config1.xml
/cun:cpandl\williams /cup:Rover
```

You also use the Wecutil ss command to enable or disable a subscription. Set the /E parameter to True to enable the subscription or False to disable the subscription. In this example, you disable the "All File Servers" subscription:

```
wecutil ss "All File Servers" /e:false
```

To get the run-time status of a subscription, enter **wecutil gr** followed by the subscription name at a command prompt. The output provides details on recent errors and the enabled or disabled status of event forwarding on each source computer. Here is an example:

```
Subscription: all servers
        RunTimeStatus: Disabled
        LastError: 0
        EventSources:
                MAILSERVER84.cpandl.com
                        RunTimeStatus: Disabled
                        LastError: 0
                ROOM5.cpandl.com
                        RunTimeStatus: Disabled
                        LastError: 0
```

If you no longer want a subscription to be used, you can permanently remove it using the Wecutil ds command. At a command line, enter **wecutil ds** followed by the name of the subscription to remove, such as **wecutil ds "all file servers"**.

Performance Logging

Windows Vista and Windows Server 2008 use data collector sets and reports. Data collector sets allow you to specify sets of performance objects and counters that you want to track. When you've created a data collector set, you can easily start or stop monitoring the performance objects and counters included in the set. In a way, this makes data collector sets similar to the performance logs used in earlier releases of Windows. However, data collector sets are much more sophisticated and flexible.

Getting Started with Data Collector Sets

You can create and work with several different types of data collector sets. Data collector set types include:

- **Alert** The Alert type is for data collectors that notify you when certain events occur or when certain performance conditions are reached.
- **API** The API type is for data collectors that record data whenever events related to their source providers occur.
- **Configuration** The Configuration type is for data collectors that record changes to particular registry paths.
- **Counter** The Counter type is for data collectors that record data on selected counters when a predetermined interval has elapsed.
- **Trace** The Trace type is for data collectors that record performance data whenever related events occur.

Windows Vista and Windows Server 2008 use event traces to track a wide variety of performance statistics. Some event traces are configured to start automatically with the operating system. These event traces are called Startup Event Traces. The two types of data collectors you'll use the most are counters and alerts, and these are the types of data collectors you'll learn about in this section.

In the graphical user interface, you create and manage data collectors in Reliability And Performance Monitor. Under the Data Collector Sets node, you'll see nodes for user-defined data collectors, system-defined data collectors, event trace sessions, and startup event trace sessions. By expanding these nodes, you can view the related entries for data collectors and traces.

You use Logman to work with data collectors at the command line. In most cases, Logman requires an elevated, administrator command prompt. You can view a computer's currently configured data collector sets by typing **logman** or **logman**

query at a command prompt. You'll then see a list of data collector sets by name, type, and status as shown in the following example:

```
Data Collector Set        Type                Status
---------------------------------------------------
High CPU                  Alert               Started
Memory Usage              Alert               Stopped
```

You can run the command on a remote computer using the following syntax:

```
logman query -s RemoteComputer
```

where *RemoteComputer* is the host name or IP address of the remote computer to examine. Because your current user credentials are used to determine whether you are granted access, you'll need to ensure that you are logged on with an account that has appropriate permissions to access the remote computer. In most cases, you'll also need to use an elevated command prompt.

To view details about a specific data collector, enter **logman query** followed by the name of the data collector. You'll then see a detailed status listing similar to the following:

```
Name:                  cpu
Status:                Stopped
Root Path:             %systemdrive%\PerfLogs\Admin\CPU
Segment:               Off
Schedules:             On
Run as:                SYSTEM

Name:                  cpu\DataCollector01
Type:                  Alert
Sample Interval:       15 second(s)
Event Log:             Off

Thresholds:
  \Processor(_Total)\% Processor Time>98
```

Working with Data Collector Sets

When working with Reliability And Performance Monitor, you can start or stop logging for a data collector by right-clicking the data collector and then selecting either Start or Stop as appropriate. At the command line, you can perform these same tasks using the Logman Start and Logman Stop commands respectively. The syntax for starting a data collector is:

```
logman start CollectorName
```

where *CollectorName* is the name of the data collector to start, such as:

```
logman start "General Activity Monitor"
```

The syntax for stopping a data collector is:

```
logman stop CollectorName
```

where *CollectorName* is the name of the data collector to stop, such as:

```
logman stop "General Activity Monitor"
```

In Reliability And Performance Monitor, you can save a data collector as a template that can be used as the basis of other data collectors by right-clicking the data collector and selecting Save Template. In the Save As dialog box, select a directory, type a name for the template, and then click Save. The data collector template is saved as an XML file that can be copied to other systems. The template is also available when you are creating new data collectors.

To export data collector settings into an XML file at the command line, you use the Logman export command and the following syntax:

```
logman export CollectorName -xml OutputFile
```

where *CollectorName* is the name of the data collector to work with and *OutputFile* is the name of the XML file to which you want to write the data collector settings, such as:

```
logman export "General Activity Monitor" -xml GeneralCollectorConfig.xml
```

You can use a template to import and create or recreate a data collector using the Logman import command. As shown here, the syntax is similar to an export:

```
logman import CollectorName -xml InputFile
```

where *CollectorName* is the name of the data collector to work with and *InputFile* is the name of the XML file from which you are reading data collector settings. Use the –S parameter to specify a remote computer and the –U parameter to specify a user whose credentials you want to use. Although you can follow the user name with a password, you can also leave the password blank or enter * to be prompted for a password. In this example, you import a data collector on a remote computer (FileServer86) using the user account WilliamS:

```
logman import "General Activity Monitor" -xml GeneralCollectorConfig.xml
-s FileServer86 -u Williams
```

In Reliability And Performance Monitor, you can delete a user-defined data collector by right-clicking it and then selecting Delete. If a data collector is running, you'll need to stop collecting data first and then delete the collector. Deleting a collector deletes the related reports as well.

At the command line, you can delete a user-defined data collector with the Logman delete command. The syntax for deleting a data collector is:

```
logman delete CollectorName
```

where *CollectorName* is the name of the data collector to delete, such as:

```
logman delete "General Activity Monitor"
```

Because you cannot delete a running data collector, you must stop a data collector before you can delete it. Using the –S parameter, you can delete data collectors on remote computers. As necessary, provide alternate credentials using the –U parameter. Keep in mind the syntax for –U is:

```
-u UserName Password
```

where *UserName* is the account name to use for accessing the remote computer and Password is the optional password for that account.

Collecting Performance Counter Data

You can use data collectors to record performance data on the selected counters at a specific sample interval. For example, you could sample performance data for the CPU every 15 minutes. The default location for logging is %SystemDrive%\PerfLogs\Admin. Log files can grow in size very quickly. If you plan to log data for an extended period, be sure to place the log file on a drive with lots of free space. Remember, the more frequently you update the log file, the greater the drive space and CPU resource usage on the system.

Collect performance counter data by following these steps:

1. In Reliability And Performance Monitor, under the Data Collector Sets node, right-click the User-Defined node in the left pane, point to New, and then choose Data Collector Set.
2. In the Create New Data Collector Set wizard, type a name for the data collector, such as **General Activity Monitor**. Then select the Create Manually (Advanced) option and click Next.
3. On the What Type Of Data Do You Want To Include page, the Create Data Logs option is selected by default. Select the Performance Counter check box and then click Next.
4. On the Which Performance Counters Would You Like To Log page, click Add. This displays the Add Counter dialog box, which you can use to select the performance counters to track. When you are finished selecting counters, click OK.
5. On the Which Performance Counters Would You Like To Log page, shown in Figure 8-4, type in a sample interval and select a time unit in seconds, minutes, hours, days, or weeks. The sample interval specifies when new data is collected. For example, if you sample every 30 seconds, the data log is updated every 30 seconds. Click Next when you are ready to continue.

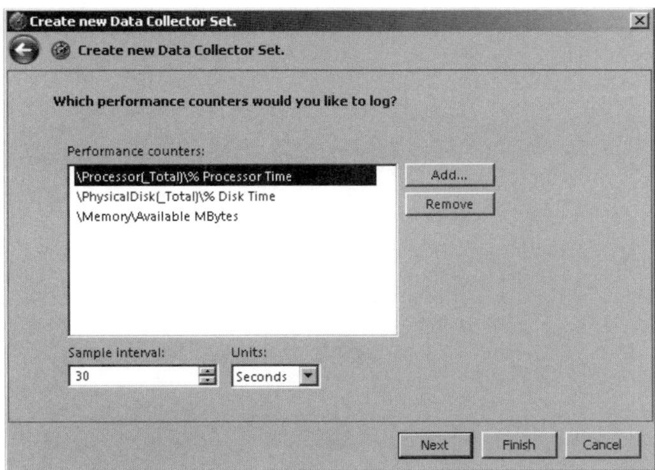

Figure 8-4 Set the sample interval.

6. On the Where Would You Like The Data To Be Saved page, type the root path to use for logging collected data. Alternatively, you can click Browse and then use the Browse For Folder dialog box to select the logging directory. Click Next when you are ready to continue.

7. On the Create New Data Collector Set page, the Run As box lists <Default> as the user to indicate that the log will run under the privileges and permissions of the default system account. To run the log with the privileges and permissions of another user, click Change. Type the user name and password for the desired account, and then click OK. User names can be entered in Domain\user format, such as **adatum\williams** for the WilliamS account in the Adatum domain.

8. Select the Open Properties For This Data Collector Set option and then click Finish. This saves the Data Collector Set, closes the wizard, and then opens the related Properties dialog box.

9. By default, logging is configured to start manually. To configure a logging schedule, click the Schedule tab and then click Add. You can now set the Active Range, Start Time, and run days for data collection as shown in Figure 8-5.

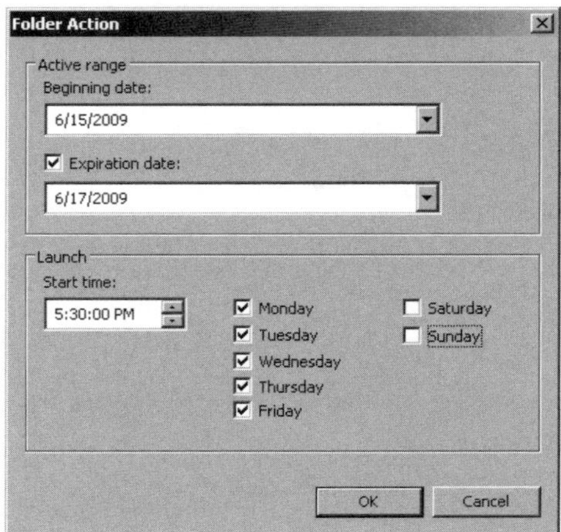

Figure 8-5 Configure a run schedule for performance logging.

10. By default, logging only stops if you set an expiration date as part of the logging schedule. Using the options on the Stop Condition tab, you can configure the log file to stop manually after a specified period of time, such as seven days, or when the log file is full (if you've set a maximum size limit).

11. Click OK when you've finished setting the logging schedule and stop conditions. You can manage the data collector as explained in the section titled "Working with Data Collector Sets" earlier in the chapter. If you want Windows to run a scheduled task when data collection stops, configure the tasks on the Task tab in the Properties dialog box.

12. In Reliability And Performance Monitor, select the data collector for the alert in the left pane, right-click the data collector in the main pane, and then select Properties. On the Performance Counters tab, you can add or remove performance counters, set the sample interval, and specify the maximum number of samples. On the File tab, you can set the log file name, format, and log mode as overwrite or append. Click OK to save your settings.

At a command line, you create data collectors to record performance data using the Logman create counter command and update data collector settings using the Logman update counter command. As summarized in Table 8-4, both commands have a similar set of available parameters. With many parameters, you can negate previously set values using an extra dash. For example, to stop using logon credentials previously specified with –U, you can use --U.

Table 8-4 Parameters for Logman create counter and Logman update counter

<table>
<tr><th>Parameter</th><th>Description</th><th>Can Be Negated</th></tr>
<tr><td>-a</td><td>Appends output to an existing log file.</td><td>Yes</td></tr>
<tr><td>-b <mm/dd/yyyy h:mm:ss[AM|PM]></td><td>Schedules the data collector to begin at a specified time.</td><td></td></tr>
<tr><td>-c <<em>path</em> [<em>path</em> [...]]></td><td>Identifies the performance counters to collect when not using a counter file.</td><td></td></tr>
<tr><td>-cf <<em>filename</em>></td><td>Identifies a counter file containing performance counters to collect with one counter per line.</td><td></td></tr>
<tr><td>-cnf <[[hh:]mm:]ss></td><td>Creates a new file when the specified time has elapsed or when the maximum size is exceeded.</td><td>Yes</td></tr>
<tr><td>–config <<em>filename</em>></td><td>Specifies a settings file containing command options.</td><td></td></tr>
<tr><td>-e <mm/dd/yyyy h:mm:ss[AM|PM]></td><td>Schedules the data collector to end at a specified time.</td><td></td></tr>
<tr><td>-f <bin|bincirc|csv|tsv|sql></td><td>Sets the output format for log files.</td><td></td></tr>
<tr><td>-m <[start] [stop] [[start] [stop] [...]]></td><td>Changes to manual start or stop instead of a scheduled begin or end.</td><td></td></tr>
<tr><td>-max <value></td><td>Sets the maximum log file size in megabytes (MB) or number of records for SQL logs.</td><td>Yes</td></tr>
<tr><td>-o <path|dsn!log></td><td>Specifies the path of the output log file, or the DSN and log set name in a SQL database.</td><td></td></tr>
<tr><td>-ow</td><td>Overwrites an existing log file.</td><td>Yes</td></tr>
<tr><td>-r</td><td>Specifies that you want to repeat the data collector daily at the specified begin and end times.</td><td>Yes</td></tr>
<tr><td>-rc <command></td><td>Runs the command specified each time the log is closed.</td><td>Yes</td></tr>
<tr><td>-rf <[[hh:]mm:]ss></td><td>Sets the run duration for the data collector.</td><td></td></tr>
<tr><td>-s <<em>computer</em>></td><td>Performs the command on the specified remote computer.</td><td></td></tr>
<tr><td>-sc <<em>value</em>></td><td>Sets the maximum number of samples to collect.</td><td></td></tr>
</table>

Table 8-4 Parameters for Logman create counter and Logman update counter

Parameter	Description	Can Be Negated
-si <[[hh:]mm:]ss>	Sets the sample interval for performance counters.	
-u *<user>* [*<password>*]	Sets the logon user for a remote computer and an optional password. If the password isn't provided, you are prompted to provide one.	Yes
-v <nnnnnn|mmddhhmm>	Adds file versioning information to the end of the log name.	Yes
–y	Answers Yes to all questions without prompting.	

The easiest way to use Logman create counter to create a data collector for a performance counter is to use this syntax:

```
logman create counter DataCollectorName -c Counter
```

where *DataCollectorName* sets the unique name of the data collector and *Counter* sets the relative counter path. A relative counter path is different from the absolute counter path discussed in the section titled "Tracking Performance Data" in Chapter 6. With a relative counter path, you do not specify the computer you want to work with, which is why the counter path is said to be relative to the local or remote computer with which you are working.

Performance counter files use relative paths, as discussed in Chapter 7, "Monitoring Processes and Maintaining Performance." The syntax for a relative counter path is:

```
\ObjectName\ObjectCounter
```

where *ObjectName* is the name of a counter object and *ObjectCounter* is the name of the object counter to use. Thus, if you wanted to create a data collector to track the available memory counter, you could type:

```
logman create counter MemCounterCollector -c "\memory\available mbytes"
```

While this command line creates the data collector, Logman does not start the counter. You must either manually start and stop as discussed previously, or set a scheduled start time and end time that is later than the current date and time. In the following example, you start the counter at 5:30 P.M. on 6/15/2009 and stop the counter at 9:30 P.M. on 6/17/2009:

```
logman create counter MemCounterCollector -c "\memory\available mbytes"
 -b 06/15/2009 05:30PM -e 06/17/2009 09:30PM
```

If you make a mistake and inadvertently set the wrong start time and end time, you can modify the data collector settings using Logman counter update. When you set the start time without setting the end time, you are specifying that the data collector should run indefinitely. In contrast, you must always set a start time whenever you set an end time. Keep in mind that if the start time is before the current time, the data collector will not start automatically.

If you do not set a sample interval or a maximum number of samples, the data collector will collect an unlimited number of samples every 15 seconds. You can set the sample interval using the –Si parameter and the sample count using the –Sc parameter. The following example creates a new counter and sets a sample interval of 10 minutes and a maximum sample count of 1,000:

```
logman create counter MemCounterCollector -c "\memory\available mbytes"
-si 00:10:00 -sc 1000
```

The following example modifies an existing counter and sets a sample interval of 1 hour and a maximum sample count of 10,000:

```
logman update counter MemCounterCollector -si 01:00:00 -sc 10000
```

Using the –Cf parameter, you can specify a counter file containing a list of counters for which you want to collect data. In the counter file, each counter should be on a separate line. Sample 8-2 provides an example of how you can use a counter file with Logman create counter. In this example, the counter file is in the current directory, but you could also specify the full file path to a counter file in another directory.

Sample 8-2 Collecting performance data

Command line

```
logman create counter GenPerformanceDataCollector -cf collector.txt
 -b 06/15/2009 05:30PM -e 06/17/2009 09:30PM
-si 00:10:00 -sc 1000
```

Source for Collector.txt

```
\memory\% Committed Bytes In Use
\memory\Available MBytes
\memory\Cache Bytes
\memory\Cache Bytes Peak
\memory\Committed Bytes
\memory\Commit Limit
\memory\Page Faults/sec
\memory\Pool Nonpaged Bytes
\memory\Pool Paged Bytes
```

Configuring Performance Counter Alerts

You can configure alerts to notify you when certain events occur or when certain performance thresholds are reached. You can send these alerts as events that are logged in the application event log. You can also configure alerts to start tasks and performance logs.

Configure an alert by following these steps:

1. In Reliability And Performance Monitor, under the Data Collector Sets node, right-click the User-Defined node in the left pane, point to New, and then choose Data Collector Set.
2. In the Create New Data Collector Set wizard, type a name for the data collector, such as **Processor Usage Alert**. Then select the Create Manually (Advanced) option and click Next.
3. On the What Type Of Data Do You Want To Include page, select the Performance Counter Alert option and then click Next.
4. On the Which Performance Counters Would You Like To Monitor page, click Add to display the Add Counters dialog box. Use the Add Counters dialog box to add counters that trigger the alert. Click OK when you're finished.
5. In the Performance Counters panel, select the first counter and then use the Alert When text box to set the occasion when an alert for this counter is triggered. Alerts can be triggered when the counter is above or below a specific value. Select Above or Below, and then set the trigger value. The unit of measurement is whatever makes sense for the currently selected counter(s). For example, to alert if processor time is over 98 percent, you would select Over and then type **98**. Repeat this process to configure other counters you've selected.
6. On the Create New Data Collector Set page, the Run As box lists <Default> as the user to indicate that the alert will run under the privileges and permissions of the default system account. To run the alert with the privileges and permissions of another user, click Change. Type the user name and password for the desired account, and then click OK. User names can be entered in Domain\user format, such as **adatum\williams** for the WilliamS account in the Adatum domain.
7. Select the Open Properties For This Data Collector Set option and then click Finish. This saves the data collector set, closes the wizard, and then opens the related Properties dialog box.
8. By default, alerting is configured to start manually. To configure a time interval for alerting on the selected performance counters, click the Schedule tab and then click Add. You can now set the Active Range, Start Time, and run days for alerting.
9. By default, alerting only stops if you set an expiration date as part of the logging schedule. Using the options on the Stop Condition tab, you can configure alerting to stop manually after a specified period of time, such as seven days, or when the log file is full (if you've set a maximum size limit).

10. Click OK when you've finished setting the alerting schedule and stop conditions. You can manage the data collector as explained in the section titled "Working with Data Collector Sets" earlier in the chapter.
11. In Reliability And Performance Monitor, select the data collector for the alert in the left pane, right-click the data collector in the main pane and then select Properties. On the Alerts tab, you can configure the performance counters used for alerts as necessary.
12. On the Alert Action tab, select the Log An Entry In The Application Event Log check box to write alert events to the application event log. If you want to start another data collector when an alert is triggered, use the Start A Data Collector Set list to select that data collector.
13. On the Alert Task tab, you can choose a Windows Management Instrumentation (WMI) task to run when an alert is triggered and specify arguments to pass to the task on start up.
14. Click OK to save your settings.

At a command line, you create data collectors for performance alerts using the Logman create alert command and update data collector settings using the Logman update alert command. As summarized in Table 8-5, both commands have a similar set of available parameters. With many parameters, you can negate previously set values using an extra dash. For example, to stop writing alert events to the application log, you can use –El.

Table 8-5 Parameters for Logman create alert and Logman update alert

Parameter	Description	Can Be Negated
-a	Appends output to an existing log file.	Yes
-b <mm/dd/yyyy h:mm:ss[AM|PM]>	Schedules the data collector to begin at a specified time.	
-cnf <[[hh:]mm:]ss>	Creates a new file when the specified time has elapsed or when the max size is exceeded.	Yes
–config <*filename*>	Specifies a settings file containing command options.	
-e <mm/dd/yyyy h:mm:ss[AM|PM]>	Schedules the data collector to end at a specified time.	
-el	Enables event log reporting.	Yes
-m <[start] [stop] [[start] [stop] [...]]>	Changes to manual start or stop instead of a scheduled begin or end.	

Table 8-5 Parameters for Logman create alert and Logman update alert

Parameter	Description	Can Be Negated
-max <value>	Sets the maximum log file size in MB or number of records for SQL logs.	Yes
-o <path|dsn!log>	Specifies the path of the output log file, or the DSN and log set name in a SQL database.	
-ow	Overwrites an existing log file.	Yes
-r	Specifies that you want to repeat the data collector daily at the specified begin and end times.	Yes
-rc <command>	Runs the command specified each time the log is closed.	Yes
-rdcs *<collector>*	Identifies a data collector to run when alert is triggered.	Yes
-rf <[[hh:]mm:]ss>	Sets the run time for the data collector.	
-s *<computer>*	Performs the command on the specified remote computer.	
-si <[[hh:]mm:]ss>	Sets the sample interval for performance counters.	
-targ	Identifies the arguments to pass to a task run when alert is triggered.	Yes
-th *<path>thr* [*<path>thr* [...]]	Identifies the performance counters to collect and the alert threshold. Use < for alerting below a value and > for alerting above a value.	
-tn *<task>*	Identifies a task to run when alert is triggered.	Yes
-u *<user>* [*<password>*]	Sets the logon user for a remote computer and an optional password. If the password isn't provided, you are prompted to provide one.	Yes
-v <nnnnnn|mmddhhmm>	Adds file versioning information to the end of the log name.	Yes
–y	Answers Yes to all questions without prompting.	

The basic syntax for creating a data collector for performance alerting is:

```
logman create alert DataCollectorName -th Counter>Threshold
```

where *DataCollectorName* sets the unique name of the data collector, *Counter* sets the relative counter path, and *Threshold* sets the threshold for the alert. When specifying the threshold, you use < for alerting below a value and > for alerting above a value. For example, to create an alert when the processor utilization time is above 98 percent, you could use the following command:

```
logman create alert ProcessorAlert
-th "\Processor(_Total)\% Processor Time>98"
```

To create an alert when the available memory goes below 64 MB, you could use this command:

```
logman create alert LowMemAlert -th "\Memory\Available Mbytes<64"
```

With the –Th parameter, you can specify multiple alerts. Simply separate each alert with a space as shown in the following example:

```
logman create alert CoreAlerts
-th "\Processor(_Total)\% Processor Time>98" "\Memory\Available Mbytes<64"
```

Creating an alert in this way does not start performance alerting. You must either manually start and stop as discussed previously, or set a scheduled start time and end time that is later than the current date and time. In the following example, you start the data collector at 7:30 A.M. on 5/10/2009:

```
logman create alert ProcessorAlert
-th "\Processor(_Total)\% Processor Time>98"
 -b 05/10/2009 07:30AM
```

If you make a mistake and inadvertently set the wrong start time, end time, or both, you can modify the data collector settings using Logman alert update. When you set the start time without setting the end time, you are specifying that the data collector should run indefinitely.

To write alert events to the application log, you enable event log reporting using the –El parameter. If you don't specify this when creating the data collector, you can update the data collector. This example enables event log reporting:

```
logman update alert ProcessorAlert -el
```

This example disables event log reporting:

```
logman update alert ProcessorAlert --el
```

Viewing Data Collector Reports

When you're troubleshooting problems, you'll often want to log performance data over an extended period of time and then review the data to analyze the results. For each data collector that has been or is currently active, you'll find related data collector reports. As with data collector sets themselves, data collector reports usually are organized into two general categories: user-defined and system.

To view data collector reports in Reliability And Performance Monitor, expand the Reports node and then expand the individual report node for the data collector you want to analyze. Under the data collector's report node, you'll find individual reports for each logging session. A logging session begins when logging starts and ends when logging is stopped.

Logs are numbered sequentially with the most recent log having the highest log number. To view a log and analyze its related data graphically, double-click it. Keep in mind that if a data collector is actively logging, you won't be able to view the most recent log. You can stop collecting data by right-clicking a data collector set and selecting Stop. Collected data is shown by default in a graph view from the start of data collection to the end of data collection. Only counters that you selected for logging will be available. If a report doesn't have a counter that you want to work with, you'll need to modify the data collector properties, restart the logging process, and then check the logs again.

You can modify the report details using the following techniques:

1. In Reliability And Performance Monitor, right-click the Performance Monitor node and then select Properties. In the Performance Monitor Properties dialog box, click the Source tab.
2. Specify data sources to analyze. Under Data Source, select Log Files and then click Add to open the Select Log File dialog box. You can now select an additional log file to analyze.
3. Specify the time window that you want to analyze. Click Time Range, and then drag the Total Range bar to specify the appropriate starting and ending times. Drag the left edge to the right to move up the start time. Drag the right edge to the left to move down the end time.
4. Click the Data tab. You can now select counters to view. Select a counter and then click Remove to remove it from the graph view. Click Add to display the Add Counter dialog box, which you can use to select the counters that you want to analyze.
5. Click OK. In the monitor pane, click the Change Graph Type button to select the type of graphing.

You can generate similar reports at the command line using Tracerpt. Tracerpt processes data collector logs and allows you to generate trace analysis reports and dump files for the events generated. The parameters for Tracerpt are summarized in Table 8-6.

Table 8-6 Parameters for Tracerpt

Parameter	Description
–config <*filename*>	Specifies a settings file containing command options.
-df <*filename*>	Sets the name of a Microsoft-specific counting/reporting schema file that should be used for processing the trace.
–export <*filename*>	Sets the name of the event schema export file. The default is Report.xsl.
-f <XML|HTML>	Sets the report file format as .xml or .html.
-gmt	Converts the timestamps to GMT time.
-i <*path*>	Sets the provider image path with each path value separated by semicolons (;).
-int <*filename*>	Sets the name of a dump file for the interpreted event structure.
-lr	Sets less restrictive output so that events not matching the schema can be displayed using a best effort approach.
–o [*filename*]	Sets the text output file to which the parsed data should be written. The default is Dumpfile.xml.
-of <CSV|EVTX|XML>	Sets the dump file format as .csv, .evtx, or .xml.
-pdb <*path*>	Sets the symbol server path with each path value separated by semicolons (;).
–report [*filename*]	Sets the name of the text file to which a detailed report of the data should be written. The default is Workload.xml.
-rl <*level*>	Sets the system report level from 1 to 5. The default value is 1.
–rt <*session_name* [*session_name* [...]]>	Sets the real-time event trace session data source to use instead of a converted log file.
-rts	Adds the raw timestamp from the event trace header to the output. Can only be used with –O and not with –Report or –Summary.
–summary [*filename*]	Sets the name of the text file to which a summary report of the data should be written. The default is Summary.txt.
-tmf <*filename*>	Sets the name of the Trace Message Format (TMF) definition file that should be used for processing the trace.
-tp <*path*>	Sets the TMF file search path with each path value separated by semicolons (;).
–y	Answers Yes to all questions without prompting.

One way to use Tracerpt is to specify the name of the data collector log to use. By default data collector logs are written to a restricted subdirectory of C:\PerfLogs, so if a log in this directory was named DataCollector01.blg, you could analyze it by typing the following:

```
tracerpt "C:\Perflogs\Admin\Process Monitor\000001\DataCollector01.blg"
```

Here, two files are created in the current directory: The parsed output is written to Dumpfile.xml, and a summary report is written to Summary.txt. To get a detailed report and the associated schema file, add the –Report and –Export parameters as shown in the following example:

```
tracerpt "C:\Perflogs\Admin\Process Monitor\000001\DataCollector01.blg"
-report -export
```

Here, four files are created in the current directory: The parsed output is written to Dumpfile.xml, a summary report is written to Summary.txt, a detailed report is written to Workload.xml, and an event schema report file is written to Report.xsl.

You could also specify the exact files to use for output as shown in the following example:

```
tracerpt "C:\Perflogs\Admin\Process Monitor\000001\DataCollector01.blg"
 -o c:\PerfLogs\dumpfile.csv  -summary c:\PerfLogs\summary.txt
 -report report.txt
```

Chapter 9

Scheduling Tasks to Run Automatically

As an administrator, you probably find yourself repeatedly performing the same or similar tasks every day. You may also find that you have to come in to work early or stay late to perform tasks during nonbusiness hours. These tasks might be routine maintenance activities, such as deleting temporary files so that disks don't run out of space, or backing up important data. These tasks might also be more involved processes, such as searching the event logs on all business servers for problems that need to be resolved. The good news is that if you can break down these tasks into a series of steps, chances are that you can also automate these tasks, and Windows provides a couple of ways to do this:

- **Schtasks** An advanced command-line utility for running commands, scripts, and programs on a scheduled basis. You can schedule tasks to run one time only, on a minute-by-minute basis, at a specific interval (such as hourly, daily, weekly, or monthly), at system startup, at logon, or whenever the system is idle.
- **Task Scheduler** A graphical utility for running commands, scripts, and programs on a scheduled basis. Task Scheduler performs the same operations as the Schtasks command-line utility, allowing you to use Task Scheduler and Schtasks together, and to manage tasks created in either utility by using one tool or the other.

Because you can use Schtasks and Task Scheduler interchangeably, this chapter discusses how to use both utilities to automate the running of programs, command-line utilities, and scripts. In most cases, you'll find that it is useful to understand both utilities, and that even when you use Task Scheduler for point-and-click convenience, you'll still work with the command line.

Scheduling Tasks on Local and Remote Systems

Whatever you can execute at the command line can be configured as a scheduled task, including command-line utilities, scripts, applications, shortcuts, and documents. You can also specify command-line arguments. Sometimes when you schedule tasks, you'll do so for the computer to which you are currently logged on (that is, a local system). More typically, however, when you schedule tasks you'll do so for remote systems throughout your network from your local computer (that is, a remote computer).

Introducing Task Scheduling

The Task Scheduler service enables local and remote task scheduling. This service must be running for each system on which you want to schedule tasks. Task Scheduler logs on as the LocalSystem account by default and usually doesn't have adequate permissions to perform administrative tasks. Because of this, you should configure each task individually to use an account with adequate user privileges and access rights to run the tasks you want to schedule. You should also make sure that the Task Scheduler service is configured to start automatically on all the systems for which you want to schedule tasks. Be sure to set the Task Scheduler startup and logon account options appropriately.

You use the Task Scheduler console to view and work with scheduled tasks. To access Task Scheduler, click Start, click Administrative Tools, and then click Task Scheduler. Any user can schedule a task on the local computer, and can view and change scheduled tasks. Administrators can schedule, view, and change all tasks on the local computer except for restricted system tasks. To schedule, view, or change tasks on remote computers, you must be a member of the Administrators group on the remote computer, or you must be able to provide the credentials of an Administrator of the remote computer when prompted.

In Task Scheduler, the Task Scheduler Library contains all the tasks defined on the computer. Unlike earlier versions of Windows, Windows Vista and Windows Server 2008 both make extensive use of scheduled tasks. Many tasks are created automatically when you install and configure the operating system for the first time. When you install roles, role services, features, and applications, those components can create additional tasks as well. In Figure 9-1, the Task Scheduler Library shows the following:

- **Name** The name of the task. Task names can be any string of characters and, like other task properties, are set when you create the task.
- **Status** The current status of the task. "Running" indicates the task has been started by the task scheduler and is running. "Ready" indicates the task is enabled and ready to be triggered. "Disabled" means that task has been disabled and will not run. "Failed" indicates the task could not be started and that there is a problem with the task.
- **Triggers** Lists the triggers associated with the task.
- **Next Run Time** The next date and time the task will run. "Never" indicates the task will not run again after the scheduled run time and is probably a one-time task.
- **Last Run Time** The last date and time the task ran. "Never" indicates the task has not run for the first time.
- **Last Run Result** The exit error code. An error code of zero indicates no error occurred. Any other value indicates some type of error occurred.

- **Author** The user name of the person who created the scheduled task.
- **Created** The date and time the task was created.

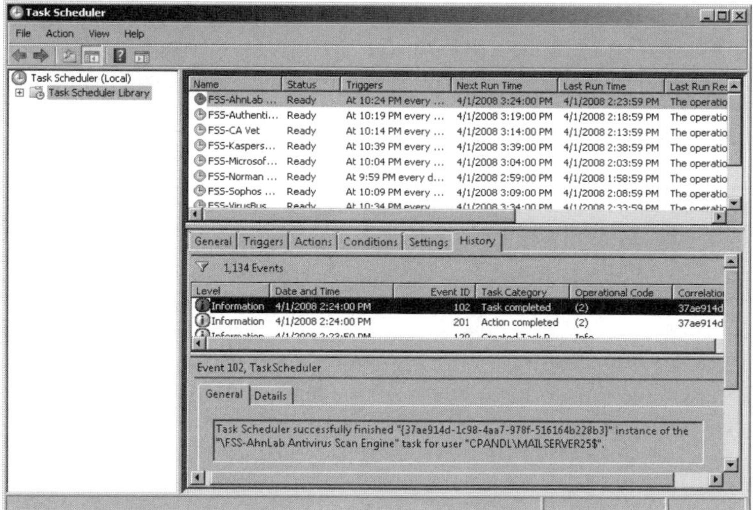

Figure 9-1 Use Task Scheduler to work with scheduled tasks in the graphical interface.

Windows Vista and Windows Server 2008 have two general types of scheduled tasks:

- **Standard tasks** Automate routine tasks and perform housekeeping. These tasks are visible to users and can be modified if necessary.
- **Hidden tasks** Automate special system tasks. These tasks are hidden from users by default and should not be modified in most cases. Some hidden tasks are created and managed through a related program, such as Windows Defender.

> **Note** You can display hidden tasks by selecting Show Hidden Tasks on the View menu.

In the Task Scheduler Library, you'll find system tasks under Microsoft\Windows and Microsoft\Windows Defender. Tasks under Microsoft\Windows handle many of the background housekeeping tasks on your computer. Tasks under Microsoft\Windows Defender are used to automate malware scans. Windows Defender is the default malware tool used with Windows Vista and can be added to Windows Server 2008 by installing the Desktop Experience feature.

Although you can create tasks at any level within the Task Scheduler Library, you will in most cases want to create tasks at the top level within the library. You do this by selecting the Task Scheduler node rather than a lower-level node when creating a task.

To help organize your tasks, you can create folders within the Task Scheduler Library. These folders then appear as nodes within the library hierarchy and act as containers for your tasks. In a large enterprise, you may even want to create your own subhierarchy within the Task Scheduler Library. You can create a new folder to contain your tasks by following these steps:

1. In Task Scheduler, select the top-level node that will contain your folder. For example, if you want your folder to appear as a subnode of the Task Scheduler Library node, you'd select this node.
2. On the Action menu or in the Actions pane, select New Folder. In the dialog box provided, type a unique name for the folder and then click OK.

Task Scheduler is fully integrated with the Windows security model implemented in both Windows Vista and Windows Server 2008. When you define a task, you specify the user account under which the task runs. By default, the task runs with the user's standard privileges. If the task requires higher privileges, however, you don't want Windows to block the task and display a User Account Control prompt. For this reason, you can specify that you want Windows to always run the task with the highest user privileges available. When you run with highest user privileges, Task Scheduler prompts you for the password of the user account under which the task will run. This password is then stored securely on the system.

> **Note** In the revised Task Scheduler, Microsoft has changed the way user credentials are used with tasks as well. Previously, when the password for a user account changed, you needed to modify the password settings associated with each task that used the user account. In Windows Vista and Windows Server 2008, you never have to update the passwords of user accounts associated with tasks that only access local resources. The password change doesn't affect the task and it will continue to work. If the task accesses external resources, however, you'll need to update the password associated with just one task on each computer that uses those credentials.

Tasks can have many properties associated with them, including:

- Triggers that specify the circumstances under which a task begins and ends
- Actions that define what the task does when it is started
- Conditions that qualify the conditions under which a task is started or stopped
- Settings that affect the behavior of the task
- History that shows events generated while a task is running or attempting to run

Unlike task scheduling for earlier versions of Windows, you can specify more than one trigger and more than one action. This means each scheduled task can run multiple programs, utilities, or scripts, and can be configured to run in a number of ways, including:

- At a specific time and date, such as at 5:45 P.M. on October 25, 2009

- At a specified interval, such as every Monday, Wednesday, and Friday at 5:45 P.M.
- When a specific system event occurs, such as when someone logs on to the system
- Any combination of the previous examples, as well as other ways not listed

Task triggers deserve special attention because they don't always work as you might expect and include tasks triggered by the following events:

- **System Start** If you schedule a task to run at startup, Task Scheduler runs the task as a noninteractive process whenever the computer is started. The task will continue to run until it finishes, is terminated, or the system is shut down. Keep in mind that only the owner of the task or an administrator can terminate running tasks.
- **System Logon** If you schedule a task to run when a user logs on, you can configure the task to run whenever anyone logs on (regardless of who configured the task to run) or only when a specified user logs on. Task Scheduler will then continue to run until the task finishes, is terminated, or the user logs off. Logon tasks can run interactively or noninteractively, depending on how they are configured.

  Tip If a user configures an interactive task using his or her logon and someone else logs on, the task runs with the original user's permissions and may not terminate when the other user logs off (because it is owned by someone else and the current user may or may not have appropriate permissions to terminate the task). Further, with Fast User Switching, logon tasks do not run when you switch users. Logon tasks only run when someone logs on while all users are logged off.

- **System Idle** If you schedule a task to run when the system is idle, Task Scheduler runs the task whenever no user activity occurs for a specified amount of time. For example, you might create a task that runs only when the system has been idle for five minutes. Keep in mind, however, that subsequent user activity will not terminate the task. The task will continue to run until it finishes or is terminated.
- **Windows Event** If you schedule a task to run based on a Windows event, Task Scheduler runs the task whenever Windows writes an event with the identifier you specify to a particular event log. In the basic configuration, you can specify a single event identifier, an optional source, and a single event log to monitor. With a custom configuration, you can define an event filter that works like the filters we've discussed in previous chapters and allows you to monitor multiple logs, multiple sources, or both for multiple types of events.

- **User Session** If you schedule a task to run when a user establishes a Terminal Services user session, Task Scheduler runs the task when a user creates a user session by connecting from the local computer or from a remote computer. You can also schedule a task to run when a user ends a Terminal Services user session from the local computer or from a remote computer.

Although you can define multiple actions for a task, you can create a command-line script that runs multiple commands, programs, and utilities and performs other necessary tasks as well. Here, you'll want the script to run with specific user or administrator credentials to ensure that the script has the necessary permissions and access rights. The script should also configure whatever user settings are necessary to ensure that everything it does is under its control and that domain user settings, such as drive mappings, are available as necessary.

> **Real World** When you configure tasks to run, you can specify the user account and logon password to use when the task runs. With recurring tasks, this tactic can lead to problems, especially if permissions or passwords change—and they inevitably do. If account permissions or passwords change and the task works with remote resources, you'll need to edit the properties of at least one task that uses those credentials and supply the new credentials for the account.

Monitoring Scheduled Tasks

Task Scheduler doesn't verify the information you provide or the availability of programs, commands, or utilities. If you don't specify the correct information, the task simply won't run or will generate errors when it does run. One way to check tasks is to view their status and last result in the Task Scheduler. This information pertains to the last time the scheduled task ran. If the Last Run Result is an error, you'll need to resolve the referenced problem so that the task can run normally. Check a task's properties by clicking its entry in Task Scheduler.

A task that is listed as Running might not in fact be running but instead might be a nonresponsive or runaway process. You can check for nonresponsive or runaway processes using Last Run Time, which tells you when the task was started. If a task has been running for more than a day, a problem usually needs to be corrected. A script might be waiting for input, it might have problems reading or writing files, or it might simply be a runaway task that needs to be stopped. To stop the task, right-click it in Task Scheduler and then select End.

The Last Run Result won't tell you, however, if there were problems running tasks prior to the last run time. To dig deep and get a better understanding of how tasks are running, you should periodically check the Task Scheduler operational log. In Event Viewer, this log is stored under Applications And Services Logs\Microsoft\Windows\TaskScheduler\Operational. If you examine the task scheduler log, you'll find the following information:

- Entries that record when the Task Scheduler Service was started and when the service exited (was stopped).
- Entries that record when tasks are started, when they finished running, and the exit error or result code. An exit error or result code of zero (0) means that the task executed normally. Any other exit or result code indicates an error may have occurred.
- Entries that record warnings and errors that occurred when Task Scheduler tried to start an event.

Tip The command-line name for the Task Scheduler operational log is Microsoft-Windows-TaskScheduler/Operational. By default the log is stored in the %SystemRoot%\System32\Winevt\Logs folder with the name Microsoft-Windows-TaskScheduler/Operational.evtx. Using the techniques discussed in Chapter 6, "Event Logging, Tracking, and Monitoring," and Chapter 8, "Managing Event and Performance Logging," you can manipulate this log as you would any other log.

Task Scheduler has custom filtered views of the operational log. When you select the Task Scheduler node in Task Scheduler, the main pane has several panels, including Task Status and Active Tasks. Using the options on the Task Status panel, you can view a summary status for all scheduled tasks in the last hour, last 24 hours, last 7 days, or last 30 days. On the Active Tasks panel, you can view summary information about running tasks. If you double-click a running task, you'll access the task definition within the Task Scheduler Library.

When you select a task definition in the Task Scheduler and then click the History tab, you'll see a filtered view of the Task Scheduler operational log with events specific to that task. If you select a specific event in turn, you'll see detailed information about the event in the lower pane.

You may also want a more detailed understanding of what happens when scripts run. To do this, you may want to record the output of commands and utilities in a separate log file, thereby giving you the opportunity to determine that those commands and utilities produced the expected results. You can write command output to a named file by redirecting standard output and standard error. In the following examples, the output of the DEFRAG command is appended to Stat-log.txt and any DEFRAG errors are written to this file as well:

```
defrag c: >> c:\logs\stat-log.txt 2>&1
defrag d: >> c:\logs\stat-log.txt 2>&1
```

Caution If you are working with a directory, as shown in these examples, the directory must already exist. It will not be created for you, and any errors resulting from the lack of a directory will not be written to the log file.

Real World Writing command output to a log file won't help you resolve every problem that can occur, but it goes a long way toward ensuring that scheduled tasks run as expected. If you are trying to troubleshoot problems, keep in mind that tasks can fail to run for many reasons, some of which are beyond your control. For example, scheduled tasks won't run if the system is shut down when the task is scheduled to run. If you want to ensure that a task runs even if the scheduled start time is missed, you must access the Settings tab in the task's Properties dialog box and select Run Task As Soon As Possible After A Scheduled Start Is Missed. With this feature enabled, Windows runs a scheduled task as soon as possible if you missed a task because the system was shut down.

Scheduling Tasks with Task Scheduler

You can use Task Scheduler to create basic and advanced tasks. Basic tasks include triggers and actions that are meant to help you quickly schedule a common task. Advanced tasks include triggers, actions, conditions, and settings that are meant to be used by advanced users or administrators.

Creating Basic Tasks

Basic tasks have many default settings and are easy to create. By default, basic tasks you create run under your logon account and will run only when you are logged on. These tasks run with standard user privileges rather than the highest possible privileges and are configured for compatibility with Windows Vista and Windows Server 2008. These tasks only start if the computer is on AC power and stop when the computer switches to battery power. Additionally, basic tasks stop when they've been running for longer than three days.

You can create a basic task by completing these steps:

1. Open Task Scheduler by clicking Start, clicking Administrative Tools, and then clicking Task Scheduler. You are connected to the local computer by default. If you want to view logs on a remote computer, right-click the Task Scheduler entry in the console tree (left pane) and then select Connect To Another Computer. Then, in the Select Computer dialog box, enter the name or IP address of the computer that you want to access and click OK.
2. You can create tasks at any level within the Task Scheduler Library. Right-click the node you want the task to be stored in and then select Create Basic Task. This starts the Create Basic Task Wizard.
3. On the Create A Basic Task page, shown in Figure 9-2, type a name and description of the task. The name should be short but descriptive so that you can quickly determine what the task does. The optional description can provide a detailed explanation of the task's purpose. Click Next.

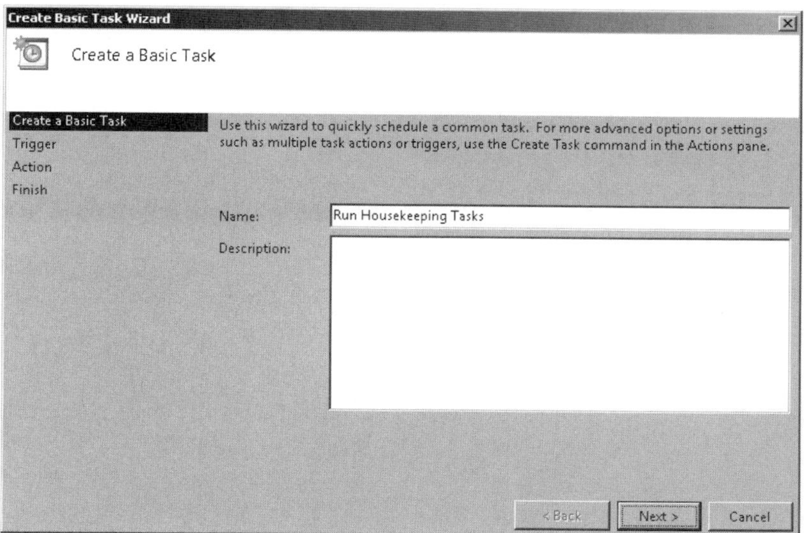

Figure 9-2 Create a basic task using the Create Basic Task Wizard.

4. On the Task Trigger page, select a run schedule for the task. You can schedule tasks to run one time, periodically (daily, weekly, or monthly), when a specific event occurs when the computer starts, or when the task's user logs on. Click Next. The next page you see depends on when the task is scheduled to run.

5. If you've selected a daily running task, the wizard displays the Daily page. Configure the task using the following fields and then click Next:

   - **Start** Use the Start options to set a start date and time.
   - **Universal Time** Select this option to schedule the task according to Greenwich Mean Time (GMT) instead of local time. GMT is the time at 0 degrees meridian and it is the time zone for Greenwich, London, England.
   - **Recur** Allows you to run the task every day, every other day, or every nth day, beginning with the start date you set. For example, if you want the task to run every other day, you'd set the Recur . . . Days text box to 2 days.

6. If you've selected a weekly running task, the wizard displays the Weekly page. Configure the task using the following fields and then click Next:

   - **Start** Use the Start options to set a start date and time.
   - **Universal Time** Select this option to schedule the task according to GMT instead of local time.

- **Recur** Allows you to run the task every week, every other week, or every nth week.
- **Days of the Week** Sets the day(s) of the week when the task runs, such as on Tuesday, or on Tuesday and Friday.

7. If you've selected a monthly running task, the wizard displays the Monthly page. Configure the task using the following fields and then click Next:
   - **Start** Use the Start options to set a start date and time.
   - **Months** Use this selection list to choose which months the task runs. You can select all months, or one or more individual months.
   - **Days** Sets the day(s) of the month the task runs. For example, if you select 2 and 8, the task runs on the second and eighth days of the month.
   - **On** Sets the task to run on the nth occurrence of a day in a month, such as the second Monday, or the first and third Tuesday of every month.
8. If you've selected One Time for running the task, the wizard displays the One Time page. Use the Start options to set a start date and time. Click Next.
9. If you've selected When A Specific Event Is Logged, the wizard displays the When A Specific Event Is Logged page. You'll need to select the event log to monitor and the specific event source, event ID, or both. Click Next.
10. If you've selected When I Log On or When The Computer Starts, clicking Next takes you immediately to the Action page.
11. On the Action page, specify the task to perform. You can start a program, send an e-mail, or display a message. The next page you see depends on the action you selected. Click Next.
12. If you've selected Start A Program, the wizard displays the Start A Program page. Click Browse to display the Open dialog box and then select the program or script to run. Click Next.
13. If you've selected Send An E-mail, the wizard displays the Send An E-mail page. You can then configure the automated e-mail to send by completing the From, To, Subject, and Text fields of the e-mail message. In the SMTP Server text box, enter the fully qualified domain name of the mail server through which you will send your message. Click Next.
14. If you've selected Display A Message, the wizard displays the Display A Message page. You can then configure the message to display on the desktop when the task is started. Enter the title and text of your message in the text boxes provided. Click Next.
15. On the Summary page, review the task details and then click the Finish button. Once the task is created, you can modify the basic task's default settings by accessing its Properties dialog box.

Creating Advanced Tasks

With advanced tasks, you configure the task settings directly in a dialog box similar to the standard properties dialog box for tasks. Advanced tasks have the same default settings initially as basic tasks.

You can create an advanced task by completing these steps:

1. Open Task Scheduler by clicking Start, clicking Administrative Tools, and then clicking Task Scheduler. You are connected to the local computer by default. If you want to view logs on a remote computer, right-click the Task Scheduler entry in the console tree (left pane) and then select Connect To Another Computer. Then, in the Select Computer dialog box, enter the name or IP address of the computer that you want to access and then click OK.
2. You can create tasks at any level within the Task Scheduler Library. Right-click the node you want the task to be stored in and then select Create Task. This opens the Create Task dialog box.
3. On the General tab, shown in Figure 9-3, type a name and description of the task. The name should be short but descriptive so that you can quickly determine what the task does. The optional description can provide a detailed explanation of the task's purpose.

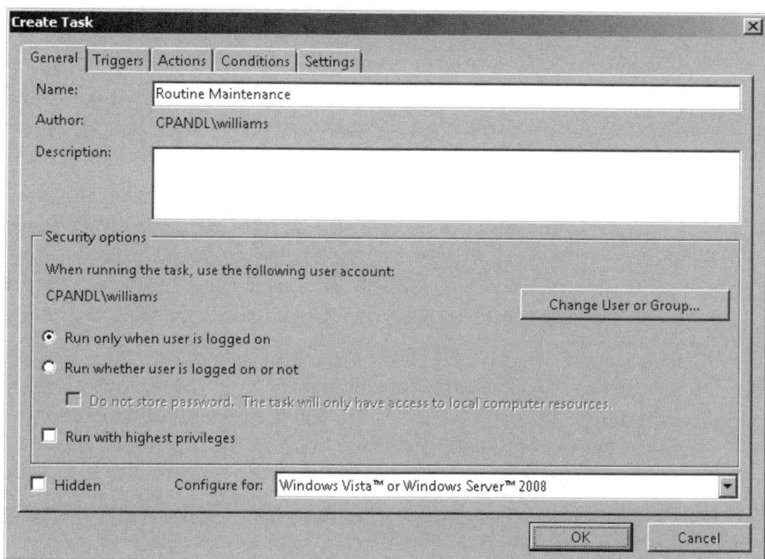

Figure 9-3 Create an advanced task using the Create Task dialog box.

4. By default, the task runs under your user account. To run the task under a different user account, click Change User Or Group and then use the dialog box provided to select the user or group under which the task should run.
5. By default, the task runs only when you or another specified user is logged on. If you want to run the task regardless of whether you are logged on, select Run Whether User Is Logged On Or Not. With this setting, Task Scheduler stores your credentials or the specified user's credentials.

   Note If don't want Task Scheduler to store the password associated with these credentials, select the Do Not Store Password check box. Keep in mind, however, that this setting will allow the task to be used to access local computer resources but will prevent the task from being used to access remote computer resources.

6. By default, the task runs with standard user privileges rather than the highest possible privileges associated with your account or the specified user's account. If the task requires administrative privileges to run, select the Run With Highest Privileges check box.
7. By default, Task Scheduler always displays the task. To identify the task as a hidden task, select the Hidden check box. This hides the task from the default view and requires users to elect to display hidden tasks if they want to view the task.
8. By default, the task is created for use with Windows Vista or Windows Server 2008. If you are creating a task to export and then import to an earlier version of Windows, on the Configure list, select Windows Server 2003, Windows XP, or Windows 2000.
9. On the Triggers tab, create and manage triggers using the options provided. Using triggers, you can schedule tasks to run one time, periodically (daily, weekly, or monthly), or when a specific event occurs, such as when the computer starts or when the task's user logs on. To create a trigger, click New, use the options provided to configure the trigger, and then click OK. You can define multiple triggers.
10. On the Actions tab, create and manage actions using the options provided. You can start a program, send an e-mail, or display a message. To create an action, click New, use the options provided to configure the action, and then click OK. You can define multiple actions.
11. On the Conditions tab, specify any limiting conditions for starting or stopping the task.
12. On the Settings tab, choose any additional optional settings for the task.
13. Click OK to create the task. Once the task is created, you can modify the task's settings by accessing its Properties dialog box.

Managing Task Properties

You can access and work with the tasks configured on your computer through Task Scheduler. Select a task to view its properties using the tabs provided in the lower portion of the main pane. Note the task status, last run time, and last run result. On a task's History tab, you'll see a detailed history of the task. Use the history information to help you resolve problems with the task. If you want to change a task's properties, you can double-click the task and then use the Properties dialog box to make the necessary changes.

Enabling and Disabling Tasks

You can enable or disable tasks as needed, depending on your preference. If you temporarily don't want to use a task, you can disable it. When you are ready to use the task again, you can enable it. By enabling and disabling tasks rather than deleting them, you save the time involved in reconfiguring task settings. To disable a task, right-click the task and then select Disable. To enable a task, right-click the task and then select Enable.

Copying Tasks to Other Computers

The import and export options in Task Scheduler make it very easy to copy tasks from one computer to another. You can copy a task to another computer by following these steps:

1. Open Task Scheduler by clicking Start, clicking Administrative Tools, and then clicking Task Scheduler.
2. If you aren't logged on to the source computer with the task you want to copy, right-click the Task Scheduler node and then select Connect To Another Computer. Use the Connect To Another Computer to connect to the source computer.
3. Right-click the task you want to copy and then select Export Task. In the Save As dialog box, select a save location and filename for the task's XML configuration file, and then click Save.
4. Right-click the Task Scheduler node and then select Connect To Another Computer. Use the Select Computer dialog box to connect to the destination computer.
5. Right-click the Task Scheduler node and then select Import Task. In the Open dialog box, access the save location of the task's XML configuration file. Click the configuration file to select it and then click Open.
6. Task Scheduler reads the configuration file and then opens the Create Task dialog box with the task's settings preconfigured. Using the Create Task dialog box, modify the task's original settings as necessary for the destination computer. Click OK.

Running Tasks Immediately

You don't have to wait for the scheduled time to run a task. To run a task at any time, access the Task Scheduler, right-click the task you want to run, and then select Run.

Removing Unwanted Tasks

If you no longer need a task, you can delete it permanently by accessing the Scheduled Tasks folder, right-clicking the task you want to delete, and then selecting Delete.

Scheduling Tasks with Schtasks

With Schtasks, you can perform the same task scheduling operations as with the Task Scheduler wizard. Any tasks you create using Schtasks are displayed as scheduled tasks in the Task Scheduler and can be managed from the command line or from the graphical user interface (GUI).

Schtasks has several different sets of subcommands and is one of the more complex utilities available at the command line. The sections that follow discuss each of the following subcommands:

- **Schtasks /Create** Use to create scheduled tasks.
- **Schtasks /Change** Use when you want to change the properties of existing tasks.
- **Schtasks /Query** Use to display scheduled tasks on the local or named computer.
- **Schtasks /Run** Use to start a scheduled task immediately.
- **Schtasks /End** Use to stop a running task.
- **Schtasks /Delete** Use to remove scheduled tasks that are no longer wanted.

Creating Scheduled Tasks with Schtasks /Create

With Schtasks /Create, you can create one-time-only tasks, recurring tasks, and tasks that run based on specific system events, such as logon and startup. The basic syntax for defining these types of tasks is as follows:

```
schtasks /create /tn TaskName /tr TaskToRun /sc ScheduleType
[/mo Modifier]
```

where *TaskName* sets the task name string, *TaskToRun* specifies the file path to the program, command-line utility, or script that you want to run, *ScheduleType* specifies the run schedule, and *Modifier* is an optional value that modifies the run schedule based on the schedule type. Any tasks you create using this syntax are created on the local computer and use your user permissions. Further, if you don't provide your account password, you are prompted for your user password when you create tasks.

Valid values for *ScheduleType* are shown in Table 9-1. Note the usage and modifiers that the various schedule types accept. I'll discuss each schedule type and modifier in detail later in the chapter. Note the following as well:

- You can enter days of the week in a comma-separated list, such as Mon, Wed, Fri, or with a hyphen to specify a sequence of days, such as Mon-Fri for Monday through Friday.
- You can enter months of the year in a comma-separated list, such as Jan, Mar, Jun, or with a hyphen to specify a sequence of months, such as Jan-Jun for January through June.
- With week of the month, you can only enter one value, such as FIRST or LAST.

Table 9-1 Schedule Types for Schtasks /Create

Schedule Type	Description	Modifier Values
MINUTE	Task runs at a specified interval in minutes. By default, tasks run once a minute.	/mo 1-1439; the number of minutes between each run of the task. The default modifier is 1.
HOURLY	Task runs at a specified interval in hours. By default, tasks run once an hour.	/mo 1-23; the number of hours between each run of the task. The default modifier is 1.
DAILY	Task runs every day or every *n* days. By default, tasks run once a day.	/mo 1-365; the number of days between each run of the task. The default modifier is 1.
WEEKLY	Task runs every week or every *n* weeks, on designated days. By default, tasks run once a week on Mondays.	/mo 1-52; the number of weeks between each run of the task. Optionally, use /d to specify the days of the week to run. Use MON, TUE, WED, THU, FRI, SAT, and SUN to specify days. Use * for every day of the week.
MONTHLY	Task runs every month or every *n* months on designated days. By default, tasks run the first day of every month.	/mo 1-12; the number of months between each run of the task. Optionally, use /d MON-SUN; sets day of the week to run during the month. Use * to have the task run every day.
	Second monthly variant for specific day of month. Use /mo and /m, or /m and /d.	/mo LASTDAY; last day of month. /m JAN, FEB, . . ., DEC; sets the month(s). /d 1-31; day of month.

Table 9-1 Schedule Types for Schtasks /Create

Schedule Type	Description	Modifier Values
	Third monthly variant for specific week of the month.	/mo FIRST | SECOND | THIRD | FOURTH | LAST; sets week of month. /d MON-SUN; sets day of week. /m JAN, FEB, . . ., DEC; sets month(s).
ONCE	Task runs once at a specified date and time.	—
ONEVENT	Tasks run when a specified event or events occur in a specified event log.	/mo *XPathString* where *XPath-String* is the XPath event query string that identifies the event on which the scheduled task is triggered.
ONSTART	Task runs whenever the system starts.	—
ONLOGON	Task runs whenever a user logs on.	—
ONIDLE	Task runs whenever the system is idle for a specified period of time.	/i 1-999; the number of minutes the system has to be idle before the task starts.

To see how you can use Schtasks /Create, consider the following examples:

Task runs once immediately and then doesn't run again:

```
schtasks /create /tn "SysChecks" /tr c:\scripts\sch.bat /sc once
```

Task runs when the system starts:

```
schtasks /create /tn "SysChecks" /tr c:\scripts\sch.bat /sc onstart
```

Task runs whenever the system is idle for more than 10 minutes:

```
schtasks /create /tn "SysChecks" /tr c:\scripts\sch.bat /sc
onidle /i 10
```

Task runs every 15 minutes on the local computer:

```
schtasks /create /tn "SysChecks" /tr c:\scripts\sch.bat /sc minute
/mo 15
```

Task runs every five hours on the local computer:

```
schtasks /create /tn "SysChecks" /tr c:\scripts\sch.bat /sc hourly
/mo 5
```

Task runs every two days on the local computer:

```
schtasks /create /tn "SysChecks" /tr c:\scripts\sch.bat /sc daily
/mo 2
```

Task runs every two weeks on Monday (the default run day):

```
schtasks /create /tn "SysChecks" /tr c:\scripts\sch.bat /sc weekly
/mo 2
```

Task runs every week on Monday and Friday:

```
schtasks /create /tn "SysChecks" /tr c:\scripts\sch.bat /sc weekly
/d mon,fri
```

Task runs on the first day of every month:

```
schtasks /create /tn "SysChecks" /tr c:\scripts\sch.bat /sc monthly
```

Task runs on the fifth day of every other month:

```
schtasks /create /tn "SysChecks" /tr c:\scripts\sch.bat /sc monthly
/mo 2 /d 5
```

Task runs the last day of every month:

```
schtasks /create /tn "SysChecks" /tr c:\scripts\sysch.bat
/sc monthly./mo lastday
```

Task runs the first Monday of April, August, and December:

```
schtasks /create /tn "SysChecks" /tr c:\scripts\sysch.bat /sc
monthly /mo first /d mon /m apr,aug,dec
```

When the path of the specified task includes a space, enclose the file path in double quotation marks as shown in the following example:

```
schtasks /create /tn "SysChecks" /tr "c:\My Scripts\sch.bat" /sc onstart
```

If you do not enclose the file path in quotation marks, an error will occur when Schtasks attempts to run the task. Further, if you want to pass arguments to a program, utility, or script, simply follow the Task To Run file path with the arguments you want to use. Any argument that contains spaces should be enclosed in quotation marks so that it is properly interpreted as a single argument rather than multiple arguments. Here are examples:

```
schtasks /create /tn "SysChecks" /tr c:\scripts\sch.bat 1 Y LAST
/sc onstart

schtasks /create /tn "SysChecks" /tr "c:\My Scripts\sch.bat" Y N
/sc onstart

schtasks /create /tn "SysChecks" /tr "c:\My Scripts\sch.bat" "Full Checks"
```

You can also schedule tasks for remote computers as well as tasks that should run with different user permissions. The key detail to remember when scheduling tasks on remote computers is that the computer you are using should be in the same domain as the remote computer or in a domain that the remote computer trusts. To do this, you must use the expanded syntax, which includes the following parameters:

```
/s Computer /u [Domain\]User [/p Password]
```

where *Computer* is the remote computer name or IP address, *Domain* is the optional domain name in which the user account is located, *User* is the name of the user account whose permissions you want to use, and *Password* is the optional password for the user account. If you don't specify the domain, the current domain is assumed. If you don't provide the account password, you are prompted for the password.

To see how you can add the computer and user information to the syntax, consider the following examples:

Use the account adatum\wrstanek when creating the task on the local computer:

```
schtasks /create /tn "SysChecks" /tr c:\scripts\sch.bat /sc onstart
/u adatum\wrstanek /p RoverSays
```

Set the remote computer as mailer01 and the account to use as adatum\wrstanek:

```
schtasks /create /tn "SysChecks" /tr c:\scripts\sch.bat /sc onstart
/s mailer01 /u adatum\wrstanek /p RoverSays
```

Using the /Ru and /Rp parameters, you can specify the credentials for the user account under which the task should run. If you want a task to run only when a specific user is logged on, use the optional /It parameter, which specifies that the task should run interactively and only when the user who owns the task is logged on. With tasks that work only with local resources, you can use the /Np parameter to specify that no password should be saved with a user's credentials. When you don't allow Task Scheduler to save a password, the task only has access to local resources and runs non-interactively as the specified user.

Tasks run with standard user privileges by default. If you want a task to run with the highest privileges of the specified user, such as may be necessary for administrative tasks, you can set the /Rl parameter to Highest rather than the default value Limited.

To see how you can add alternate credentials and privileges to the syntax, consider the following examples:

Configure the task to run using the credentials of adatum\thomasv:

```
schtasks /create /tn "CleanUp" /tr c:\scripts\cleanup.bat /sc onlogon
/ru adatum\thomasv /rp DingoE
```

Set the remote computer as server18, the account to use for creating the task as adatum\wrstanek, and configure the task to run using the credentials of adatum\thomasv:

```
schtasks /create /tn "CleanUp" /tr c:\scripts\cleanup.bat /sc onlogon
/s server18 /u adatum\wrstanek /p RoverSays /ru adatum\thomasv
/rp DingoE
```

Run the task without saving the user password on server18 using the account adatum\wrstanek:

```
schtasks /create /tn "CleanUp" /tr c:\scripts\cleanup.bat /sc onlogon
/s server18 /u adatum\wrstanek /np
```

Run the task with the highest privileges:

```
schtasks /create /tn "SysChecks" /tr c:\scripts\sch.bat /sc onlogon
/rl highest
```

Finally, if desired, you can add specific start times and dates, as well as end times and dates, using the following values:

- /st *StartTime*, where *StartTime* is in 24-hour clock format (HH:MM), such as 15:00 for 3:00 P.M. This parameter is required with /Sc ONCE.
- /et *EndTime*, where *EndTime* is in 24-hour clock format (HH:MM), such as 15:00 for 3:00 P.M. This parameter is not applicable for schedule types ONSTART, ONLOGON, ONIDLE, and ONEVENT.
- /du *Duration*, where *Duration* is the number of hours and minutes to run, in the form HHHH:MM. This parameter is not applicable with /Et and for schedule types ONSTART, ONLOGON, ONIDLE, and ONEVENT.
- /sd *StartDate*, where *StartDate* is the start date using the default system format for dates, such as MM/DD/YYYY. This parameter is not applicable for schedule types ONCE, ONSTART, ONLOGON, ONIDLE, and ONEVENT.
- /ed *EndDate*, where *EndDate* is the end date using the default system format for dates, such as MM/DD/YYYY. This parameter is not applicable for schedule types ONCE, ONSTART, ONLOGON, ONIDLE, and ONEVENT.

Tip If you specify an end date or time, you can also specify the /Z parameter, which tells Task Scheduler to delete the task upon completion of its schedule.

To see how you can use specific start times and dates, as well as end times and dates, consider the following examples:

Start the hourly task at midnight:

```
schtasks /create /tn "SysChecks" /tr c:\scripts\sch.bat /sc hourly
/st 00:00
```

Start the hourly task at 3:00 A.M. and stop it at 7:00 A.M.:

```
schtasks /create /tn "SysChecks" /tr c:\scripts\sch.bat /sc hourly
/st 03:00 /et 07:00
```

Start the weekly task at 3:00 A.M. on February 20, 2009:

```
schtasks /create /tn "SysChecks" /tr c:\scripts\sch.bat /sc weekly
/st 03:00 /sd 02/20/2009
```

Start the weekly task at 3:00 A.M. on February 20, 2009 and end at 2:59 A.M. on March 15, 2009:

```
schtasks /create /tn "SysChecks" /tr c:\scripts\sch.bat /sc weekly
/st 03:00 /sd 02/20/2009 /et 02:59 /ed 03/15/2009
```

> **Note** Date and time formats are determined by the Regional And Language Options settings used by the computer. In these examples, the date format preference is English (United States).

Creating Scheduled Tasks Triggered by Windows Events

With Schtasks /Create, you can create scheduled tasks that start when the operating system or a Windows component writes specific events or types of events to one of the event logs. The basic syntax for event-triggered tasks is as follows:

```
schtasks /create /tn TaskName /tr TaskToRun /sc ONEVENT
/ec LogName /MO EventString
```

where *TaskName* sets the task name string, *TaskToRun* specifies the file path to the program, command-line utility, or script that you want to run, *LogName* sets the name of the event log to monitor, and *EventString* sets the XPath event query string that identifies the event or events on which the scheduled task is triggered.

Using /Sc ONEVENT with the schedule task definition is what schedules the task to trigger based on an event. With the /Ec parameter, you specify the command-line compatible name of the event log to monitor. As discussed in the section titled "Listing Available Logs and Registered Publishers" in Chapter 8, you can use the Wevtutil el command to list all available event logs on a computer in a command-line compatible format. With the /Mo parameter, you specify the XPath event query string. An XPath event query string is the query string at the heart of the XPath queries discussed in Chapter 8.

You don't have to try to create query strings from scratch. Instead, use Event Viewer to create a filter that identifies the exact event or events you want to monitor. Then, as discussed in the section titled "Exporting and Manipulating Event Logs" in Chapter 8, copy the related XPath query to Notepad or any standard text editor. Once you've copied the query to Notepad, you should save the query so that you have the original settings and then try to extract the necessary event query string. Generally, the event query string you need is the text between the begin <Select> tag and the end </Select> tag within the Query element. Consider the following example:

```
<QueryList>
  <Query Id="0" Path="Application">
    <Select Path="Application">*[System[(Level=1  or Level=2 or Level=3)]]
</Select>
  </Query>
</QueryList>
```

In this example, the event query string is:

```
*[System[(Level=1  or Level=2 or Level=3)]]
```

This query string creates a filter that looks for critical, warning, and error events in the applicable event log. The following example uses this query to create a scheduled task called Track Application Issues to run Event Viewer whenever critical, warning, and error events are written to the applicable event log:

```
schtasks /create /tn "Track Application Issues" /tr wevtvwr.msc /
sc ONEVENT
/ec Application /MO "*[System[(Level=1  or Level=2 or Level=3)]]"
```

Note that because the task name and the query string contain spaces, they are enclosed in double quotation marks. While this type of query string is probably too broad, it is a good example of what a query string looks like. A better query is one that identifies a specific event by its event identifier. The event query string syntax for specifying a single event identifier is:

```
*[System[(EventID=EventNumber)]]
```

where *EventNumber* is the identifier number of the event to monitor. In the following example, you create a scheduled task that runs whenever event id 3210 is written to the System log:

```
schtasks /create /tn "Computer Authentication Issues" /tr wevtvwr.msc
/sc ONEVENT /ec System /MO "*[System[(EventID=3210)]]"
```

Real World Events with Event ID 3210 are written to the System log when a computer is unable to authenticate in the domain. This error can occur because the computer's password needs to be reset, as discussed in the section titled "Resetting Locked Computer Accounts" in Chapter 14, "Managing Computer Accounts and Domain Controllers." This error can also occur if another computer on the network has the same name.

By extending the query string with *or* statements, you can enter multiple event identifiers. The extended syntax looks like this:

```
*[System[(EventID=EventNumber or EventID=EventNumber or ...)]]
```

In the following example, you create a scheduled task that runs whenever event id 3210 or event id 5722 are written to the System log:

```
schtasks /create /tn "Computer Authentication Issues" /tr wevtvwr.msc
/sc ONEVENT /ec System /MO "*[System[(EventID=3210 or EventID=5722)]]"
```

Real World Events with Event ID 5722 are written to the System log when a computer is denied access to a resource. This error can occur because the computer account has been disabled or deleted. See the sections titled "Creating a Computer Account" and "Disabling and Enabling Computer Accounts" in Chapter 14 for more information.

Changing Scheduled Tasks with Schtasks /Change

You use Schtasks /Change to change key parameters associated with scheduled tasks. The basic syntax of Schtasks /Change is

```
schtasks /change /tn TaskName ParametersToChange
```

where *TaskName* is the name of the task you want to change and *ParametersToChange* are the parameters you want to change. Parameters you can work with include the following:

- /ru *Domain\User* changes the user under which the task runs, such as /ru adatum\wrstanek. For the system account, valid values are "", "NT AUTHORITY\SYSTEM", or "SYSTEM". For tasks configured to work with Windows Vista or Windows Server 2008, you can also use "NT AUTHORITY\LOCALSERVICE" and "NT AUTHORITY\NETWORKSERVICE".
- /rp *Password* sets the password for the previously specified or newly designated runas user account. To prompt for the password, use "*" or leave blank. This password is ignored for the system account. You can only set the runas user password when you also specify the runas user account.
- /tr *TaskToRun* changes the program, command-line utility, or script that is run for the named task.

- /st *StartTime* sets the start time for minute or hourly tasks. *StartTime* is in 24-hour clock format (HH:MM), such as 15:00 for 3:00 P.M. This parameter is required if /Sc ONCE was specified during task schedule creation.
- /ri *Interval* sets the repetition interval in minutes, with a valid range of 1–599,940 minutes. This parameter is not applicable for schedule types MINUTE, HOURLY, ONSTART, ONLOGON, ONIDLE, and ONEVENT. If either /Et or /Du is specified, the repetition interval defaults to 10 minutes.
- /et *EndTime* sets the end time for minute or hourly tasks. *EndTime* is in 24-hour clock format (HH:MM), such as 15:00 for 3:00 P.M. This parameter is not applicable for schedule types ONSTART, ONLOGON, ONIDLE, and ONEVENT.
- /du *Duration* sets the number of hours and minutes to run the task, in the form HHHH:MM. This parameter is not applicable with /Et and for schedule types ONSTART, ONLOGON, ONIDLE, and ONEVENT.
- /sd *StartDate* sets the start date for the task using the default system format for dates, such as MM/DD/YYYY. This parameter is not applicable for schedule types ONCE, ONSTART, ONLOGON, ONIDLE, and ONEVENT.
- /ed *EndDate* sets the end date for the task using the default system format for dates, such as MM/DD/YYYY. This parameter is not applicable for schedule types ONCE, ONSTART, ONLOGON, ONIDLE, and ONEVENT.
- /k specifies that the task should not be started again when the end time or duration interval is reached, but it doesn't stop the task if it is already running. (The current run will be the last one.) This parameter is not applicable for schedule types ONSTART, ONLOGON, ONIDLE, and ONEVENT. Either /Et or /Du must be specified.
- /it specifies that the task should run only when the user who owns the task is logged on.
- /rl *Level* sets the run level for the task as Limited for standard user privileges or Highest for the highest possible privileges of the runas user.
- /delay *DelayTime* sets the time delay for running a task after it is triggered. *DelayTime* is set in the form mmmm:ss and can only be set for schedule types ONSTART, ONLOGON, and ONEVENT.
- /enable enables the schedule task, allowing the task to run according to its schedule.
- /disable disables the schedule task, preventing the task from running.
- /z marks the task for deletion after its final, scheduled run.

To see how you can change tasks, consider the following examples:

Change the script that is run:

```
schtasks /change /tn "SysChecks" /tr c:\scripts\systemchecks.bat
```

Change the runas user and password:

```
schtasks /change /tn "SysChecks" /ru adatum\hthomas /rp gophers
```

Change task to start weekly at 7:00 A.M. on March 1, 2009 and end at 6:59 A.M. on March 30, 2009:

```
schtasks /change /tn "SysChecks" /st 07:00 /sd 03/01/2009 /et 06:59
/ed 03/30/2009
```

> **Note** As mentioned previously, date and time formats are determined by the Regional And Language Options settings used by the computer. Here, the date format is English (United States).

When you change a task, Schtasks displays a message that states whether the changes succeeded or failed, such as:

```
SUCCESS: The parameters of the scheduled task "SysChecks" have been changed.
```

If you are working with a remote computer or aren't logged in with a user account that has permission to change the task, you can specify the computer and account information as necessary. The syntax is

`schtasks /change /tn` *`TaskName`* `/s` *`Computer`* `/u [`*`Domain`*`\]`*`User`* `[/p` *`Password`*`]`

where *Computer* is the remote computer name or IP address, *Domain* is the optional domain name in which the user account is located, *User* is the name of the user account whose permissions you want to use, and *Password* is the optional password for the user account. If you don't specify the domain, the current domain is assumed. If you don't provide the account password, you are prompted for the password.

In the following example, the remote computer is mailer01 and the user account that has authority to change the SysChecks task is wrstanek's Adatum domain account:

```
schtasks /change /tn "SysChecks" /tr c:\scripts\systemchecks.bat
/s mailer01 /u adatum\wrstanek
```

Because a password isn't specified, Schtasks will prompt for one.

You can also quickly enable or disable tasks by name. Use the following syntax to enable tasks:

```
schtasks /change /tn TaskName /enable
```

Use this syntax to disable tasks:

```
schtasks /change /tn TaskName /disable
```

where *TaskName* is the name of the task you want to enable or disable, such as:

```
schtasks /change /tn "SysChecks" /disable
```

Querying for Configured Tasks with Schtasks /Query

You can quickly determine what tasks are configured on a computer by typing **schtasks /query** at the command prompt and, as necessary for a remote computer, you can specify the computer and the account information needed to access the computer using the following form:

```
schtasks /query /s Computer /u [Domain\]User [/p Password]
```

where *Computer* is the remote computer name or IP address, *Domain* is the optional domain name in which the user account is located, *User* is the name of the user account with appropriate access permissions on the remote computer, and *Password* is the optional password for the designated user account.

In the following example, the remote computer is mailer01 and the user account is wrstanek's Adatum domain account:

```
schtasks /query /s mailer01 /u adatum\wrstanek
```

Because a password isn't specified, Schtasks will prompt for one.

The basic output of Schtasks /Query is in table format and provides TaskName, Next Run Time, and Status columns. You can also format the output as a list or lines of comma-separated values using /Fo List or /Fo Csv, respectively. The list output works best with the /V (verbose) parameter, which provides complete details on all task properties and which you can use as shown in the following example:

```
schtasks /query /s mailer01 /u adatum\wrstanek /fo list /v
```

Another useful parameter is /Nh, which specifies that table-formatted or CSV-formatted output should not have headings.

> **Tip** You may wonder why you'd want to use the various formats. It's a good question. I recommend using the verbose list format (/Fo List /V) when you want to see all details about tasks configured on a system and when you are troubleshooting, and I recommend using comma-separated values when you want to store the output in a file that may later be exported to a spreadsheet or flat-file database. Remember that you can redirect the output of Schtasks to a file using output redirection (> or >>).

Creating Tasks Using XML Configuration Files

The /Xml parameter is one of the parameters we haven't talked about for Schtasks / Create. When you use this parameter with Schtasks /Create, you can specify the XML configuration file that defines the new task you are creating. The basic syntax is:

```
schtasks /create /tn TaskName /xml XmlFile
```

where *TaskName* is the name of the task to create and *XmlFile* specifies the name or full file path to the XML configuration file containing the task settings, such as:

```
schtasks /create /tn "Housekeeping Task" /xml housekeepingtask.xml
```

As at other times when you are creating tasks, you can use the /S parameter to specify a remote computer, /U to specify the user context for creating the task, and /P to specify the user password. Although the XML configuration file for a task can define alternate credentials under which the task runs, you can also specify the alternate credentials using the /Ru and /Rp parameters.

Rather than having the actual user password in the file, you may want to set the password to blank or "*". If you do this, you can specify the required password when you create the task using the /Rp parameter.

The following is an XML configuration file that defines a scheduled task and its settings:

```
<?xml version="1.0" encoding="UTF-16"?>
<Task version="1.2" xmlns="http://schemas.microsoft.com/windows/2009/02/
mit/task">
  <RegistrationInfo>
    <Date>2009-10-01T18:10:12</Date>
    <Author>WilliamS</Author>
  </RegistrationInfo>
  <Triggers>
    <EventTrigger>
      <StartBoundary>2009-10-01T18:10:00</StartBoundary>
      <Enabled>true</Enabled>
      <Subscription>&lt;QueryList&gt;&lt;Query&gt;&lt;Select Path='system'
&gt;*[System[(Level=1  or Level=2 or Level=3)]
]&lt;/Select&gt;&lt;/Query&gt;&lt;/QueryList&gt;</Subscription>
    </EventTrigger>
  </Triggers>
  <Settings>
    <IdleSettings>
      <Duration>PT10M</Duration>
      <WaitTimeout>PT1H</WaitTimeout>
      <StopOnIdleEnd>true</StopOnIdleEnd>
      <RestartOnIdle>false</RestartOnIdle>
    </IdleSettings>
    <MultipleInstancesPolicy>IgnoreNew</MultipleInstancesPolicy>
    <DisallowStartIfOnBatteries>true</DisallowStartIfOnBatteries>
```

```
    <StopIfGoingOnBatteries>true</StopIfGoingOnBatteries>
    <AllowHardTerminate>true</AllowHardTerminate>
    <StartWhenAvailable>false</StartWhenAvailable>
    <RunOnlyIfNetworkAvailable>false</RunOnlyIfNetworkAvailable>
    <AllowStartOnDemand>true</AllowStartOnDemand>
    <Enabled>true</Enabled>
    <Hidden>false</Hidden>
    <RunOnlyIfIdle>false</RunOnlyIfIdle>
    <WakeToRun>false</WakeToRun>
    <ExecutionTimeLimit>PT72H</ExecutionTimeLimit>
    <Priority>7</Priority>
  </Settings>
  <Actions Context="Author">
    <Exec>
      <Command>wevtvwr.msc</Command>
    </Exec>
  </Actions>
  <Principals>
    <Principal id="Author">
      <UserId>ADATUM\WILLIAMS</UserId>
      <LogonType>InteractiveToken</LogonType>
    </Principal>
  </Principals>
</Task>
```

As you can see, this file is fairly complex, but don't worry. You don't have to create the XML configuration file from scratch. Using the techniques discussed in the section titled "Copying Tasks to Other Computers" earlier in this chapter, you can export the settings for an existing task into an XML configuration file and then use this file to create the same task on other computers.

At the command line, you can display a task's status and its XML configuration using Schtasks /Query. Simply use the /Tn parameter followed by the name of the task to work with and the /Xml parameter to display the XML configuration as well as the status. This example displays the status and XML configuration for the "Computer Authentication" task:

```
schtasks /query /tn "Computer Authentication" /xml
```

If you redirect this output to a file with the .xml extension and then edit this file to remove the status details, you'll have a complete XML configuration file that you can use to create the task. In the following example, the configuration for the "Computer Authentication" task is written to a file called ComputerAuthTask.xml:

```
schtasks /query /tn "Computer Authentication" /xml > ComputerAuthTask.xml
```

When working with remote computers, you can use the /S parameter to specify a remote computer, /U to specify the user context for creating the task, and /P to specify the user password.

Once you gain a working knowledge of how the XML configuration files work, you may want to start manually editing XML configuration files as necessary. When you do, make sure to test your changes on a test or development system rather than a production system. That said, let's go through the essentials.

The RegistrationInfo element specifies when the task was originally created and by whom:

```
<RegistrationInfo>
  <Date>2009-10-01T18:10:12</Date>
  <Author>WilliamS</Author>
</RegistrationInfo>
```

The Triggers element specifies under which conditions the task runs. Within this element, the following is true:

- EventTrigger elements define tasks triggered by events.
- TimeTrigger elements define tasks triggered by one-time or periodic tasks.
- BootTrigger elements define tasks triggered at startup.
- IdleTrigger elements define tasks triggered when the computer is idle.
- RegistrationTrigger elements define tasks triggered when the task is created or modified.

Boot, idle, and registration triggers are the easiest to define because they are either enabled or not enabled, as shown in this example:

```
<Triggers>
  <BootTrigger>
    <Enabled>true</Enabled>
  </BootTrigger>
</Triggers>
```

Actions elements define the commands to run, the e-mail to send, or the message to display. Commands to run are defined within Exec elements. The following example runs a script called CleanUp.bat:

```
<Actions Context="Author">
  <Exec>
    <Command>c:\scripts\cleanup.bat</Command>
  </Exec>
</Actions>
```

E-mail messages to send are defined within SendEmail elements. The following example defines an e-mail message to send to admins@adatum.com via the mailer15.adatum.com mail server:

```
<Actions Context="Author">
  <SendEmail>
    <Server>mailer15.adatum.com</Server>
```

```
      <Subject>Possible Database Outage</Subject>
      <To>admins@adatum.com</To>
      <From>williams@adatum.com</From>
      <Body>The CRM Database appears to be down.</Body>
      <HeaderFields />
    </SendEmail>
  </Actions>
```

Messages to display on the desktop are defined within ShowMessage elements. The following example displays a warning about a possible application outage:

```
  <Actions Context="Author">
    <ShowMessage>
      <Title>Application Outage Warning</Title>
      <Body>The CRMComms application is having write errors.</Body>
    </ShowMessage>
  </Actions>
```

Finally, the Principals element defines the user context under which the task runs, including whether the task can run interactively, and the run level. In the following example, the task runs interactively with least privileges under the user account of WilliamS:

```
  <Principals>
    <Principal id="Author">
      <UserId>CPANDL\williams</UserId>
      <LogonType>InteractiveToken</LogonType>
      <RunLevel>LeastPrivilege</RunLevel>
    </Principal>
  </Principals>
```

You can configure the task to run whether the user is logged on or not, or to run with highest privileges. To run whether the user is logged on or not, you set LogonType to Password. To run with highest privileges, you set RunLevel to HighestAvailable. Here is an example using these options:

```
  <Principals>
    <Principal id="Author">
      <UserId>CPANDL\williams</UserId>
      <LogonType>Password</LogonType>
      <RunLevel>HighestAvailable</RunLevel>
    </Principal>
  </Principals>
```

If you don't want Task Scheduler to store the password associated with the user account, you can set the LogonType to S4U, as shown in this example:

```
  <Principals>
    <Principal id="Author">
      <UserId>CPANDL\williams</UserId>
      <LogonType>S4U</LogonType>
```

```
      <RunLevel>HighestAvailable</RunLevel>
    </Principal>
  </Principals>
```

Running Tasks Immediately with Schtasks /Run

You can run a task at any time using the following syntax:

```
schtasks /run /tn TaskName
```

where *TaskName* is the name of the task you want to run, such as

```
schtasks /run /tn "SysChecks"
```

Running a task does not affect its schedule and does not change the next run time for the task. If the task can be successfully started, you should see a message stating this. Additionally, you can specify the name of the remote computer on which the task is configured and, as necessary, the account to run the task as, including an optional password, as in the following examples:

```
schtasks /run /tn "SysChecks" /s 192.168.1.100
schtasks /run /tn "SysChecks" /s 192.168.1.100 /u adatum\wrstanek
```

> **Note** If you specify a user and don't provide a password, you will be prompted immediately to enter the password.

Stopping Running Tasks with Schtasks /End

You can stop a task at any time using the following syntax:

```
schtasks /end /tn TaskName
```

where *TaskName* is the name of a task that is currently running and should be stopped, such as

```
schtasks /end /tn "SysChecks"
```

The task is only stopped if it is running. If successful, the output message should be similar to the following:

```
SUCCESS: The scheduled task "SysChecks" has been terminated successfully.
```

You can also specify the name of the remote computer on which the task is configured and, as necessary, the account with authority to stop the task, including an optional password, such as

```
schtasks /end /tn "SysChecks" /s 192.168.1.100
```

or

```
schtasks /end /tn "SysChecks" /s 192.168.1.100 /u adatum\wrstanek
```

Because a password isn't specified, Schtasks will prompt you for one.

Deleting Tasks with Schtasks /Delete

You can delete tasks by name on local and remote computers using the following syntax:

```
schtasks /delete /tn TaskName [/s Computer /u [Domain/]User [/p Password]]
```

where *TaskName* is the name of a task that should be deleted and the rest of the parameters optionally identify the remote computer, the user account to use when deleting the task, and the password for the account, such as

```
schtasks /delete /tn "SysChecks"
```

or

```
schtasks /delete /tn "SysChecks" /s 192.168.1.100 /u adatum\wrstanek
/p frut5
```

> **Note** If you specify a user name and don't provide a password, you will be prompted immediately to enter the password.

After entering the Schtasks /Delete command, you should see a warning asking you to confirm that you want to remove the task. Press the appropriate letter on your keyboard. If you don't want to see a warning prompt use the /F parameter, such as

```
schtasks /delete /tn "SysChecks" /f
```

Here, you force Schtasks to delete the task without a warning.

In addition, if you want to delete all scheduled tasks on the local computer or the specified remote computer, enter an asterisk (*) as the task name, such as

```
schtasks /delete /tn *
```

Confirm the action when prompted.

Part III

Windows File System and Disk Administration Using the Command Line

In this part:

Chapter 10

Configuring and Maintaining Disks

In this chapter, you'll learn techniques for configuring and maintaining disks–and there's a lot more to this than most people realize. Windows Server 2008 and Windows Vista support hard disk drives as well as removable storage devices. Hard disk drives can be configured with two disk types, basic and dynamic, and two disk partition types, Master Boot Record (MBR) and GUID Partition Table (GPT). Removable storage devices have the Removable disk type.

Getting Started with DiskPart

DiskPart is the tool of choice for working with disks, partitions, and volumes. Key tasks you'll use DiskPart for are to convert disk types, create partitions and volumes, and to configure RAID. Beyond this, you can also use DiskPart to configure automounting of new disks as well as to assign drive letters and drive paths. DiskPart can now be used for formatting disks; for this, you'll use the FORMAT command, as discussed in the section of Chapter 11, "Partitioning Basic Disks," titled "Formatting Partitions."

DiskPart Basics

Unlike all the other commands we've worked with so far in this book, DiskPart isn't a simple command-line utility that you invoke using a command line and parameters. Rather, it is a text-mode command interpreter that you invoke so that you can manage disks, partitions, and volumes using a separate command prompt and commands that are internal to DiskPart. You invoke the DiskPart interpreter by typing **diskpart** in a command window and pressing Enter.

DiskPart is designed to work with the physical hard disks installed on a computer, which can be internal, external, or a mix of both. Although DiskPart will list other types of disks, such as CD/DVD drives, removable media, and universal serial bus (USB)–connected flash random access memory (RAM) devices, and allow you to perform some minimal tasks, such as assigning a drive letter, you cannot fully manage these devices using DiskPart.

Before you can use DiskPart commands, you must first list and then select the disk, partition, or volume you want to work with to give it focus. When a disk, partition, or volume has focus, any DiskPart commands that you type will act on that disk, partition, or volume.

List the available disks, partitions, and volumes by using the following list commands:

- **list disk** Lists all physical hard disks on the computer
- **list volume** Lists all volumes on the computer (including hard disk partitions and logical drives)
- **list partition** Lists partitions, but only on the disk that has focus

When you use the list commands, an asterisk (*) appears next to the disk, volume, or partition with focus. You select a disk or partition by its number, or a volume by its number or drive letter, such as disk 0, partition 1, volume 2, or volume D.

When you are finished working with DiskPart, type **exit** at the DiskPart prompt to return to the standard command line.

DiskPart: An Example

To see how you can work with DiskPart, consider the following example, which invokes DiskPart, lists the available disks, and then gives focus to disk 2:

1. Type **diskpart** at the command prompt to invoke DiskPart.
2. The command prompt changes to

   DISKPART>
3. This tells you that you are in the text-mode interpreter for DiskPart. To list available disks, type **list disk** after the command prompt.
4. The output of list disk shows you the available disks and their status, size, and free space:

   ```
   Disk ###      Status      Size       Free       Dyn    Gpt
   --------      ----------  -------    -------    ---    ---
   Disk 0        Online      466 GB     1528 KB
   Disk 1        Online      466 GB     1528 KB
   Disk 2        Online      233 GB     0 B         *
   ```
5. Because disk 2 is the one we want to work with, we give it focus by typing **select disk 2** at the command prompt.
6. DiskPart reports:

   Disk 2 is now the selected disk.
7. Work with the disk, and when you are finished, exit the DiskPart prompt by typing **exit** after the command prompt.

Understanding Focus and What It Means

When you select a disk, partition, or volume, the focus remains on that object until you select a different object. In the previous example, the focus is set on disk 2, but if you were to select volume 2 on disk 0, the focus would shift from disk 2 to disk 0, volume 2. In some cases, the focus changes automatically, based on the command you use. For example, when you create a partition or volume, the focus automatically switches to the new partition or volume.

You can only give focus to a partition on the currently selected disk. When a partition has focus, the related volume, if any, also has focus. When a volume has focus, the related disk and partition also have focus if the volume maps to a single specific partition. If the volume doesn't map to a single specific partition, only the volume has focus.

DiskPart Commands and Scripts

LIST and SELECT are only two of the many commands that DiskPart has to offer. A complete list of DiskPart commands is shown in Table 10-1. Many of the commands listed accept *Noerr* as an additional parameter. The *Noerr* parameter is used with DiskPart scripts to indicate that when an error is encountered, DiskPart should continue to process commands in the script. Without *Noerr*, an error causes DiskPart to exit with an error code, which halts execution of the script.

- Commands that use *Noerr* and exit with error codes are ADD, ASSIGN, ATTRIBUTES, AUTOMOUNT, BREAK, CONVERT, CREATE, DELETE, EXTEND, IMPORT, OFFLINE, ONLINE, RECOVER, REMOVE, REPAIR, SAN, SETID, SHRINK, and UNIQUEID.
- Commands that don't use *Noerr* or exit with error codes are ACTIVE, CLEAN, DETAIL, EXIT, FILESYSTEMS, GPT, HELP, INACTIVE, LIST, REM, RESCAN, RETAIN, and SELECT.

Table 10-1 DiskPart Command Summary

Command	Description	Syntax
ACTIVE	On MBR disks, marks the partition with current focus as the active system partition, meaning it is the partition containing the operating system startup files.	Active
ADD	Creates a mirrored volume on the selected dynamic disk.	add disk=*n* where *n* is the disk number that will contain the mirror add disk=*n* [align=*nn*]
ASSIGN	Assigns a drive letter or mount point to the selected partition, logical drive, or volume.	assign letter=*x* assign mount=*path*

Table 10-1 DiskPart Command Summary

Command	Description	Syntax
ATTRIBUTES	Displays or manages attributes on a disk or volume.	attributes disk [set| clear] [readonly] (Note that the pre-SP1 version of Windows Vista does not support the *disk* subcommand.) attributes volume [set | clear] [hidden | readonly | nodefaultdriveletter | shadowcopy] (Note that the pre-SP1 version of Windows Vista does not support the *nodefaultdriveletter* or the *shadow-copy* subcommand.)
AUTOMOUNT	Controls whether Windows automatically mounts new basic volumes that are added to the system and assigns them drive letters.	automount [enable | disable | scrub]
BREAK	Breaks a mirror set. Add Nokeep to specify that only one volume should be retained, which means the other volume is deleted (Windows Server 2008 only).	break disk=*n* break disk=*n* nokeep
CLEAN	Removes all partition or volume formatting on the disk that has focus. With CLEAN ALL, all disk sectors are set to zero.	clean clean [all]
CONVERT	Converts between different disk formats.	convert basic | dynamic convert gpt | mbr
CREATE	Creates a partition or volume of a specific type.	create partition efi | extended | logical | msr | primary create volume simple | raid | stripe
DELETE	Deletes the disk, partition, or volume that has focus.	delete disk | partition | volume
DETAIL	Provides details about the disk, partition, or volume that has focus.	detail disk | partition | volume
EXIT	Exits the DiskPart interpreter.	exit

Table 10-1 DiskPart Command Summary

Command	Description	Syntax
EXTEND	Extends the simple volume on the selected disk or spans the simple volume across multiple disks.	extend size=*n* disk=*n* extend filesystem
FILESYSTEMS	Displays current and supported filesystem types on the volume.	filesystems
FORMAT	Formats a selected volume.	format [[format fs=*type*] [revision] | [recommended] [label=*label*] [unit=*n*] [quick] [compress] [override] [nowait]
GPT	Changes GPT attributes on the partition with focus.	gpt attributes=*n*, where *n* is a 16-digit hexadecimal value
HELP	Displays a list of commands or help for the specified command.	help help *command name*
IMPORT	Imports a foreign disk.	import
INACTIVE	On MBR disks, marks the partition with focus as inactive, meaning the computer won't boot from the system partition and will instead look for the next boot option in firmware.	inactive
LIST	Displays a list of disks or volumes and information about them, or a list of partitions on the disk that has focus.	list disk | partition | volume
ONLINE	Brings the selected disk or volume online. Resynchronizes the mirrored or RAID-5 volume that has focus.	online disk online volume
OFFLINE	Takes the selected disk offline (Windows Server 2008 only).	offline disk

Table 10-1 DiskPart Command Summary

Command	Description	Syntax
RECOVER	Attempts to recover and resynchronize the RAID-5 volumes associated with a selected dynamic disk (Windows Server 2008 only).	recover
REM	Marks the start of a comment in a DiskPart script.	rem *comment*
REMOVE	Removes a drive letter or mount point from the currently selected volume. Optionally, you can add the Dismount parameter.	remove letter=*x* remove mount=*path* *remove all*
REPAIR	Repairs the RAID-5 volume with focus by replacing that volume with the designated dynamic disk (Windows Server 2008 only).	repair disk=*n [align=nn]*
RESCAN	Looks for new disks that may have been added to the computer.	rescan
RETAIN	Prepares the selected simple volume to be used as the boot or system volume.	retain
SAN	Displays or sets the Storage Area Network (SAN) policy for the currently booted operating system (Windows Vista SP1 or later and Windows Server 2008 only).	san san policy=*value*
SELECT	Selects a disk, partition, or volume, giving it focus.	select disk | partition | volume
SETID	Sets the partition type on the selected partition.	set id=*value* [override]
SHRINK	Reduces the size of the selected volume by making free disk space available from unused space at the end of the volume.	shrink [desired=*n*] [nowait] shrink [minimum=*n*] [nowait] shrink querymax

Table 10-1 DiskPart Command Summary

Command	Description	Syntax
UNIQUEID	Displays or sets GPT identifier or MBR signature of a disk (Windows Vista SP1 or later and Windows Server 2008 only).	uniqueid disk [id=*value*]

Speaking of DiskPart scripts, the way you use scripts with DiskPart is a bit different from the way you use them with other commands. The reason is that DiskPart is a text-mode interpreter, not a standard utility. When you invoke DiskPart (by typing **diskpart** at the command prompt), you tell the interpreter about the script you want to use by adding the */S* parameter as shown here:

```
diskpart /s ScriptName.txt
```

where *ScriptName*.txt is the name of the text file that contains the script you want to use. By default, the output from DiskPart is written to the current command prompt. You can redirect the output to a file as shown here:

```
diskpart /s ScriptName.txt > LogFile.log
```

or

```
diskpart /s ScriptName.txt >> LogFile.log
```

where *LogFile*.log is the name of the text file to which DiskPart output should be written.

Note Remember that > is used to create or overwrite a file using output redirection and that >> is used to create or append to an existing file.

Tip The advantage of using scripts over directly inputting commands is that you can automate disk-related tasks so that they can be performed repeatedly and in exactly the same way each time. Scripting disk management tasks also is useful if you are deploying Windows using an unattended setup technique.

When you work with DiskPart scripts, look for the following error codes:

- **0** Indicates that no errors occurred; execution proceeded without failure
- **1** Indicates that a fatal exception occurred and there may be a serious problem
- **2** Indicates that the parameters you specified for a command were incorrect
- **3** Indicates that DiskPart was unable to open the specified script or output file
- **4** Indicates that a service that DiskPart uses returned an error code or reported a failure
- **5** Indicates that a command syntax error occurred, typically because a disk, partition, or volume was improperly selected or was invalid for use with the command

DiskPart: A Script Example

When you use DiskPart scripts, you should complete all the operations you want to perform as part of a single session. The script should contain all of the DiskPart commands you want to execute. It is not necessary to include the EXIT command because the text-mode interpreter exits automatically at the end of the script. Consider the following example script in Listing 10-1:

Listing 10-1 Sample DiskPart Script

```
rem Select disk 2
select disk 2

rem Create the primary partition on the disk and assign the drive letter
create partition primary size=4096assign letter=s
format fs=ntfs label="primary"
rem Create extended partition with 2 logical drives
create partition extended size=4096
create partition logical size=2048
assign letter=u
format fs=ntfs label="extended1"create partition logical size=2047
assign letter=vformat fs=ntfs label="extended2"
```

Here, you create a primary and an extended partition on disk 2. The primary partition is set to 4096 megabytes (MB) in size, is assigned the drive letter S, and formatted with NTFS as the file system. The extended partition is created, set to 4096 MB in size, and two logical partitions are added. The first logical partition is 2048 MB in size, is assigned drive letter U, and formatted with NTFS as the file system. The second logical partition is 2047 MB in size, is assigned drive letter V, and formatted with NTFS as the file system. The sizes are set this way on the logical partitions because you lose some space because of the partitioning. You could have also created a single logical partition that was 4096 MB in size.

> **Note** Creating partitions and assigning drive letters as shown in this example doesn't make the partitions available for use. You must still format them using the FORMAT command within DiskPart. For more information on formatting partitions and volumes, see the section of Chapter 11 titled "Formatting Partitions."

> **Tip** Because DiskPart must make and then apply changes, you shouldn't run multiple DiskPart scripts back to back. Instead, you should wait for 10 to 15 seconds between running scripts or handle all tasks in a single DiskPart session. Not only does this help ensure that the last command issued by the previous DiskPart session is completed, but it also ensures that the previous DiskPart session is shut down before the next session begins.

You can run the example script by typing **diskpart /s *ScriptName***, such as **diskpart /s disk2config.txt**. When you run the script, you should expect the following output:

```
Disk 2 is now the selected disk.
DiskPart succeeded in creating the specified partition.
DiskPart successfully assigned the drive letter or mount point.
DiskPart successfully formatted the volume.
DiskPart succeeded in creating the specified partition.
DiskPart succeeded in creating the specified partition.
DiskPart successfully assigned the drive letter or mount point.
DiskPart successfully formatted the volume.
DiskPart succeeded in creating the specified partition.
DiskPart successfully assigned the drive letter or mount point.
DiskPart successfully formatted the volume.
```

As you can see, DiskPart reports step-by-step success or failure. Keep in mind that the script doesn't have to be on the local computer. If the DiskPart script was saved to the network share \\corpserver01\scripts, you can invoke it by typing

diskpart /s \\corpserver01\scripts\disk2config.txt

This assumes that the network share is available to the local system. You can also map network drives at the command line with the NET USE command. The format is

```
net use DriveLetter: \\ComputerName\ShareName
```

such as in this example:

```
net use X: \\corpserver01\scripts
```

> **Note** The NET USE command also accepts user name and password information provided in the form /USER:*Domain\User*. You can also specify whether the mapped drive is persistent (that is, whether the network share mapping should remain when the computer is restarted). Use the parameter */Persistent:Yes*. Persistent network share mappings can be deleted by typing **net use *ComputerName**ShareName* /DELETE**.

By default, if DiskPart encounters an error while executing a command, it stops processing the script and displays an error code. If you specify the *Noerr* parameter for each applicable command, however, DiskPart will report the error and continue execution of the script. Additionally, you don't have to type the command line that invokes DiskPart directly at the command prompt. The command could be part of a larger script, which I'll refer to as a master script. A sample master script is shown as Listing 10-2.

Listing 10-2 Sample Master Script

```
@echo off
@if not "%OS%"=="Windows_NT" goto :EXIT
@if "%1"=="" (set INFO=echo && set SEXIT=1) else (set INFO=rem && set
 SEXIT=0)

%INFO% ************************
%INFO% Script: Disk2Setup.bat
%INFO% Creation Date: 3/3/2008
%INFO% Last Modified: 3/15/2008
%INFO% Author: William R. Stanek
%INFO% Email: williamstanek@aol.com
%INFO% ************************
%INFO% Description: Configures the standard partitions on workstations
%INFO%              with a third hard drive. The script is configured so
%INFO%              that it will only run if you pass in a parameter,
%INFO%              which  can be any value. This is meant as a
%INFO%              safeguard to help prevent accidental formatting
%INFO%              of disks.
%INFO% ************************
@if "%SEXIT%"=="1" goto :EXIT

@title "Configuring Disk 2..."
cls
color 07

net use x: \\corpserver01\scripts
diskpart /s x:\disk2config.txt

rem perform other necessary tasks here
:EXIT
echo Exiting...
```

That's it for the introduction to DiskPart. The remainder of this chapter discusses the specifics of using DiskPart and related commands such as CHKDSK and DEFRAG to create, manage, and maintain disks, partitions, and volumes.

Installing and Managing Hard Disk Drives

A key reason for using DiskPart is to help you to configure and maintain hard disk drives. Key management tasks include checking for new drives, determining drive status, and managing partition table styles.

Installing and Checking for a New Drive

Windows operating systems support both hot-swappable and non-hot-swappable drives. *Hot swapping* is a feature that allows you to remove devices without shutting off the computer. In most cases, hot-swappable drives are installed and removed from the front of the computer, and if a computer supports hot swapping, you can install drives to the computer without having to shut down. After you hot swap drives, start DiskPart and then type **rescan** to find the new drives. New drives that are found are added as disks of the appropriate type—either basic or dynamic. If a drive that you've added isn't found, reboot the computer.

If the computer doesn't support the hot swapping of drives, you must turn the computer off and then install the new drives. Afterward you can scan for new drives as previously described, if necessary.

Checking Drive Status and Configuration

You can use DiskPart to check the status of drives by typing **list disk** from the DiskPart prompt. Typical output from list disk looks like this:

```
Disk ###        Status      Size        Free        Dyn     Gpt
--------        ----------  -------     -------     ---     ---
Disk 0          Online      466 GB      1528 KB
Disk 1          Online      466 GB      1528 KB
Disk 2          Offline     233 GB      230 GB       *
```

As you can see, list disk shows each configured disk on the system by the following categories:

- **Disk ###** The number of the disk.
- **Status** The current status of the disk.
- **Size** The total capacity of the disk.
- **Free** The available space for partitioning (not the amount of actual free space on the disk).
- **Dyn** An asterisk in this column indicates that the disk type is dynamic. Otherwise, the disk is the basic disk type.
- **Gpt** An asterisk in this column indicates that the disk partition table type is GPT. Otherwise, the partition type is MBR.

In the previous example, the computer had three basic disks that used the MBR partition type. Although disks 0 and 1 were online, disk 2 was offline and could be brought online by changing the focus to disk 2 (by typing **select disk 2**) and then typing **online**.

As you can see, knowing the drive status is useful when you install new drives but also when you want to troubleshoot drive problems. Table 10-2 summarizes the most common status values.

Table 10-2 Common Drive Status Values and Their Meaning

Status	Description	Resolution
Audio CD	An audio CD is in the CD/DVD drive.	The drive doesn't have any known problems.
Foreign	The dynamic disk has been moved to your computer but hasn't been imported for use. A failed drive brought back online might sometimes be listed as Foreign.	Use the IMPORT command to add the disk to the system.
Initializing	A temporary status that occurs when you convert a basic disk to a dynamic disk.	When initialization is complete, the status should change to Online automatically.
Missing	The dynamic disk is corrupted, turned off, or disconnected. This value appears as the disk identifier instead of in the Status column.	Reconnect or turn on the missing disk, and then use RESCAN to locate the volume. If the disk won't be used again, use DELETE DISK to delete the disk from the disk list.
No Media	No media have been inserted into the CD- ROM or removable drive. Only CD-ROM and removable disk types display this status.	Insert a CD-ROM, floppy disk, or removable media to bring the disk online.
Not Initialized	The disk does not contain a valid signature. Windows writes the MBR or GPT for the disk the first time you start Disk Management using a wizard that shows the new disks detected. If you cancel the wizard before the disk signature is written, this status occurs.	If you haven't started Disk Management yet, do so, and then use the Initialize Disk Wizard to write the disk signature. Otherwise, right-click the disk in Disk Management and then select Initialize Disk.
Offline	The dynamic disk isn't accessible and might be corrupted or temporarily unavailable. If the disk name changes to Missing, the disk can no longer be located or identified on the system.	Check for problems with the drive, its controller, and cables. Make sure that the drive has power and is connected properly. Use the ONLINE command to bring the disk back online (if possible).
Online	The normal disk status. It means the disk is accessible and doesn't have problems. Both dynamic disks and basic disks display this status.	The drive doesn't have any known problems.

Table 10-2 Common Drive Status Values and Their Meaning

Status	Description	Resolution
Online (Errors)	Input/output (I/O) errors have been detected on a dynamic disk.	You can try to correct temporary errors using the ONLINE command. Use the RECOVER command to resynchronize mirrored and RAID-5 volumes.
Unreadable	The disk isn't currently accessible, which can occur when rescanning disks. Both dynamic and basic disks display this status.	If the drives aren't being scanned, the drive might be corrupt or have I/O errors. Use the RESCAN command to rescan the disk and read it (if possible). You might also want to reboot the system.
Unrecognized	The disk is of an unknown type and can't be used on the system. A drive from a non-Windows system might display this status.	You can't use the drive on the computer. Try a different drive.

Changing Drive Partition Styles

After you install a drive on a computer, you'll need to configure it for use. You configure the drive by partitioning it and creating file systems in the partitions, as needed. Two partition styles are used for disks: Master Boot Record (MBR) and GUID Partition Table (GPT).

MBR and GPT Partition Styles

MBR contains a partition table that describes where the partitions are located on the disk. With this partition style, the first sector on a hard disk contains the master boot record and a binary code file called the master boot code that's used to boot the system. This sector is unpartitioned and hidden from view to protect the system.

With the MBR partitioning style, disks support volumes of up to 4 terabytes and use one of two types of partitions:

- Primary
- Extended

Each MBR drive can have up to four primary partitions or three primary partitions and one extended partition. Primary partitions are drive sections that you can access directly for file storage. You make a primary partition accessible to users by creating a file system on it. Unlike primary partitions, extended partitions can't be accessed directly. Instead, you can configure extended partitions with one or more logical drives that are used to store files. Being able to apportion extended partitions into logical drives allows you to apportion a physical drive into more than four sections.

Both 32-bit and 64-bit editions of Windows Server 2008 and Windows Vista support MBR and GPT. GPT was originally developed for high-performance Itanium-based computers. GPT is recommended for disks larger than 2 terabytes on x86 and x64 systems, or any disks used on Itanium-based computers. The key difference between the GPT partition style and the MBR partition style is how partition data is stored. With GPT, critical partition data is stored in the individual partitions, and redundant primary and backup partition tables are used for improved structural integrity.

A GPT-based disk has two required partitions, one data partition and one or more optional (OEM or data) partitions:

- EFI system partition (ESP)
- Microsoft Reserved partition (MSR)
- At least one data partition

Additionally, GPT disks support volumes of up to 18 exabytes (EB) and as many as 128 partitions. Although there are underlying differences between the GPT and MBR partitioning styles, most disk-related tasks are performed in the same way.

Converting Partition Table Styles

Using the CONVERT command, DiskPart can help you change partition table styles from MBR to GPT or from GPT to MBR. Changing partition table styles is useful when you do the following:

- Move disks between computers that need to use a different partition table style
- Receive new disks that are formatted for the wrong partition table style

You can only convert partition table styles on empty disks, however. This means the disks must either be new or newly formatted. You can, of course, empty the disk by removing any existing partitions or volumes on the disk that you want to convert.

> **Note** DiskPart provides the CLEAN command for wiping out all the volume or partition information on a disk. When you give a disk focus and then use the CLEAN command, all partition or volume information on the disk is removed. On MBR disks, this means that the MBR partition and hidden sector information are overwritten. On GPT disks, the GPT partition information, including the protected MBR, is overwritten. You can also use CLEAN ALL to specify that each and every sector on the disk should be set to zero.

> **Caution** If you haven't backed up the data on the drives you want to convert, don't delete any partitions or volumes. Doing so will clear all data on the disk.

To convert the partition table style, use the following procedure:

1. Invoke DiskPart by typing **diskpart** at the command prompt.
2. Select the disk to work with to give it focus, such as

   DISKPART> **select disk 2**

3. Convert the disk, as follows:
   - To convert a disk from MBR to GPT, type **convert gpt** at the command prompt.
   - To convert a disk from GPT to MBR, type **convert mbr** at the command prompt.

Working with Basic and Dynamic Disks

Windows Server 2008 and Windows Vista support two types of hard disk configurations:

- **Basic** The standard disk type used in previous versions of Windows. Basic disks are partitioned and can be used with current and previous versions of Windows.
- **Dynamic** An enhanced disk type that can be updated without having to restart the system (in most cases). Dynamic disks are apportioned into one or more volumes and can be configured with software RAID.

Note You can't use dynamic disks on portable computers or with removable media.

Understanding Basic and Dynamic Disks

When you upgrade to Windows Vista or Windows Server 2008, disks with partitions are initialized as basic disks. When you install Windows Vista or Windows Server 2008 on a new system with unpartitioned drives, you have the option of initializing the drives as either basic or dynamic.

You can't create fault-tolerant drive sets using the basic disk type. Because of this, if you want to set up software RAID, you must convert to dynamic disks and then create volumes that use mirroring or striping. The fault-tolerant features and the ability to modify disks without having to restart the computer are the key capabilities that distinguish basic disks from dynamic disks.

Although you can use both basic and dynamic disks on the same computer, disk configuration tasks that you can perform with basic and dynamic disks are different. With basic disks, you work with partitions, which means that you can perform the following tasks:

- Format partitions and mark them as active
- Create and delete primary and extended partitions
- Create and delete logical drives within extended partitions
- Convert from a basic disk to a dynamic disk

With dynamic disks, you work with volumes, which means that you can perform the following tasks:

- Create standard and fault-tolerant volumes
- Remove a mirror from a mirrored volume
- Extend simple or spanned volumes
- Split a volume into two volumes
- Repair mirrored or RAID-5 volumes
- Reactivate a missing or offline disk
- Revert to a basic disk from a dynamic disk (which requires deleting all existing volumes prior to doing so)

With either disk type, you can perform the following tasks:

- View properties of disks, partitions, and volumes
- Make drive letter assignments
- Configure security and drive sharing

Whether you're working with basic or dynamic disks, you need to keep in mind five special types of drive sections:

- **Active** The active partition or volume is the drive section for system cache and startup. Some devices with removable storage may be listed as having an active partition.
- **Boot** The boot partition or volume contains the operating system and its support files. The system and boot partition or volume can be the same.
- **Crash Dump** The partition to which the computer attempts to write dump files in the event of a system crash. By default, dump files are written to the *%SystemRoot%* folder, but they can be located on any desired partition or volume.
- **Page File** A partition containing a paging file used by the operating system. Because a computer can page memory to multiple disks, according to the way virtual memory is configured, a computer can have multiple page file partitions or volumes.
- **System** The system partition or volume contains the hardware-specific files needed to load the operating system. The system partition or volume can't be part of a striped or spanned volume.

Setting the Active Partition

On a disk with the MBR partition style, you can mark a partition as active, which means the partition is the drive section from which the computer starts. You can't mark dynamic disk volumes as active. When you convert a basic disk containing the active partition to a dynamic disk, this partition becomes a simple volume that's active automatically. Before you mark a partition as active, be sure that the necessary startup files are on the primary partition that you want to make the active partition.

Follow these steps to designate the active partition:

1. Invoke DiskPart by typing **diskpart** at the command prompt.
2. Select the disk that contains the partition you want to make active, such as

   DISKPART> **select disk 0**
3. List the partitions on the disk by typing **list partition** at the command prompt.
4. Select the partition you want to work with, such as

   DISKPART> **select partition 0**
5. Make the selected partition the active partition by typing **active** at the command prompt.

> **Caution** The disk and partition numbers used in the steps are arbitrary and meant only to demonstrate the procedure. Make sure you've selected the right disk and partition in steps 2 and 4. If you incorrectly mark a partition as active and it does not contain the operating system startup files, your computer might not start.

Changing the Disk Type: Basic to Dynamic or Vice Versa

Windows Vista and Windows Server 2008 support both basic and dynamic disk types. At times, you'll need to convert one disk type to the other, and Windows provides the tools you'll need to do this. When you convert a basic disk to a dynamic disk, partitions are changed to volumes of the appropriate type automatically. You can't change these volumes back to partitions on a basic disk, however. Instead, you must delete the volumes on the dynamic disk and then change the disk back to a basic disk. Deleting the volumes destroys all the information on the disk.

Converting a Basic Disk

Converting a basic disk to a dynamic disk is a straightforward process but includes lots of stipulations. To start with, consider the following:

- With MBR disks, you should ensure that the disk has 1 MB of free space at the end of the disk. Without the free space at the end of the disk, the conversion will fail. Both Disk Management and DiskPart reserve this space automatically; it is primarily when you use third-party disk-management utilities that you need to be concerned about whether this space is available.
- With GPT disks, you must have contiguous, recognized data partitions. If the GPT disk contains partitions that Windows doesn't recognize, such as those created by another operating system, you won't be able to convert to a dynamic disk.

In addition, with either type of disk, the following is true:

- You can't convert drives that use sector sizes larger than 512 bytes. If the drive has large sector sizes, you'll need to reformat before converting.
- You can't use dynamic disks on portable computers or with removable media. You can only configure these drives as basic drives with primary partitions.
- You can't convert a disk if the system or boot partition is part of a spanned, striped, mirrored, or RAID-5 volume. You'll need to stop the spanning, mirroring, or striping before you convert.
- You can, however, convert disks with other types of partitions that are part of spanned, striped, mirrored, or RAID-5 volumes. These volumes become dynamic volumes of the same type and you must convert all drives in the set together.

You can convert a basic disk to a dynamic disk by completing the following steps:

1. Invoke DiskPart by typing **diskpart** at the command prompt.
2. Select the disk that you want to convert to a dynamic disk, such as

   DISKPART> **select disk 0**
3. Convert the disk by typing **convert dynamic** at the command prompt.

Converting a Dynamic Disk

Once you convert a basic disk to a dynamic disk, the only way to revert to a basic disk is to remove all the volumes on the disk. This ensures that the disk is empty and that all data it contains is removed. DiskPart does provide a command, named CLEAN, for wiping out all the volume or partition information on a disk. When you give a disk focus and then type the CLEAN command, all partition or volume information on the disk is removed.

On MBR disks, this means that the MBR partition and hidden sector information are overwritten. On GPT disks, the GPT partition information, including the protected MBR, is overwritten. You can also use CLEAN ALL to specify that every sector on the disk should be set to zero, which completely deletes all data contained on the disk.

You can convert an empty dynamic disk to a basic disk by following these steps:

1. Invoke DiskPart by typing **diskpart** at the command prompt.
2. Select the disk that you want to convert to a basic disk, such as

   DISKPART> **select disk 0**
3. Convert the disk by typing **convert basic** at the command prompt.

This changes the dynamic disk to a basic disk and you can then create new partitions and logical drives on the disk.

Maintaining Disks

Many command-line utilities are available to help you maintain disks. Some of these utilities include FSUtil, ChkDsk, and Defrag.

Obtaining Disk Information and Managing File Systems with FSUtil

One tool we haven't examined until now is the File System Utility (FSUtil).

FSUtil: An Overview

FSUtil has a fairly complex command structure, but it all basically boils down to the fact that you need to type a command string containing a command and a subcommand to get FSUtil to do what you want it to do. The available FSUtil commands are summarized in Table 10-3.

Table 10-3 FSUtil Commands and Their Usage

BEHAVIOR	Use the related subcommands to view and control how short (MS-DOS) filenames are generated, whether the last access timestamp on NTFS volumes is updated, how frequently quota events are written to the system log, the internal cache levels of NTFS paged pool and NTFS non-paged pool memory, and the amount of disk space reserved for the Master File Table (MFT).
DIRTY	Use the related subcommands to query or set a volume's dirty bit. If a volume is dirty, that means it is suspected to have errors and the next time the computer is restarted, a program called AUTOCHK will check the disk and run Check Disk if necessary to repair any errors.
FILE	Use the related subcommands to find a file by user name (only if disk quotas are enabled), check a file for sparse regions, set a file's valid data length, and zero out portions of sparse files.
FSINFO	Use the related subcommands to list a computer's drives, to query drive type, and to obtain volume information.
HARDLINK	Use the related subcommands to create hard links so that a single file can appear in multiple directories (or even in the same directory with multiple names). Programs can open any of the links to modify the file and the file is deleted from the file system only after all links to it have been deleted.
OBJECTID	Use the related subcommands to manage object identifiers for files and directories.
QUOTA	Use the related subcommands to manage disk quotas on NTFS volumes.

Table 10-3 FSUtil Commands and Their Usage

REPARSEPOINT	Use the related subcommands to view or delete reparse points. Primarily, reparse points are used for directory junction points and volume mount points.
REPAIR	Use the related subcommands to view and change the self-healing state. By default, self-healing is enabled on both Windows Vista and Windows Server 2008.
RESOURCE	Use the related commands to manage transactional resource managers. A transaction is a series of operations that is treated as a single unit, where all the operations occur or none of the operations occur.
SPARSE	Use the related subcommands to manage sparse files. A sparse file is a file with one or more regions of unallocated data in it.
TRANSACTION	Use the related commands to manage transactions.
USN	Use the related subcommands to manage the update sequence number (USN) change journal. The USN change journal provides a persistent log of all changes made to files on the volume.
VOLUME	Use the related subcommands to dismount a volume or query to see how much free space is available.

Using FSUtil

Although FSUtil has many very advanced applications, such as allowing you to remove reparse points on disks, manage disk quotas, and designate sparse files, it also has some basic applications that you'll find useful if you want to obtain disk information.

Obtaining Drive Lists for a Computer To obtain a list of drives on a computer by drive letter, type

fsutil fsinfo drives

The output shows you the drives available in alphabetical order, as follows:

```
Drives: A:\ C:\ D:\ F:\ G:\ T:\ U:\
```

Obtaining Drive Type Once you know about the drives, you can obtain the drive type for a particular drive by typing **fsutil fsinfo drivetype** followed by the drive designator, such as

```
C:\>fsutil fsinfo drivetype g:
g: - CD-ROM Drive
```

Here, the G: drive is a CD-ROM drive. Of course, you could obtain similar information for all disks on the computer using DiskPart's list volume command. Still, this is another way to obtain information that you might find useful.

Obtaining Detailed Drive Information To obtain detailed information about a drive, type **fsutil fsinfo volumeinfo** followed by the drive designator. Provide the drive letter followed by a colon, such as

```
C:\>fsutil fsinfo volumeinfo c:
```

FSUtil then lists the volume name, serial number, file system type, and the features supported, such as

```
Volume Name : Primary
Volume Serial Number : 0x23b36g45
Max Component Length : 255
File System Name : NTFS
Supports Case-sensitive filenames
Preserves Case of filenames
Supports Unicode in filenames
Preserves & Enforces ACL's
Supports file-based Compression
Supports Disk Quotas
Supports Sparse files
Supports Reparse Points
Supports Object Identifiers
Supports Encrypted File System
Supports Named Streams
Supports Transactions
```

Obtaining Sector and Cluster Information for Drives If you want to determine an NTFS disk's sector or cluster information, type **fsutil fsinfo ntfsinfo** followed by the drive designator, such as

```
C:\>fsutil fsinfo ntfsinfo c:
```

FSUtil then lists detailed information on the number of sectors and clusters, including the total clusters used, free clusters and reserved clusters, such as

```
NTFS Volume Serial Number :            0x23b36g45
Version :    3.1
Number Sectors :        0x0000000008fcf7c3
Total Clusters :        0x0000000000eb9f38
Free Clusters  :        0x0000000000d12400
Total Reserved :        0x0000000000000000
Bytes Per Sector  :        512
Bytes Per Cluster :        4096
Bytes Per FileRecord Segment                 :     1024
Clusters Per FileRecord Segment              :     0
```

Obtaining Free Space Information for a Drive You can also use FSUtil to determine the amount of free space on a disk. Type **fsutil volume diskfree** followed by the drive designator, such as

```
C:\>fsutil volume diskfree c:
```

FSUtil will then report the total bytes on the disk as well as the total number of bytes free and available, such as

```
Total # of free bytes          : 52231667712
Total # of bytes               : 60028059648
Total # of avail free bytes    : 52231667712
```

Determining Whether a Volume Is Dirty One way to tell whether an NTFS volume has been marked as dirty is to use FSUtil. Type **fsutil dirty query** followed by the drive letter and a colon, such as

```
fsutil dirty query c:
```

If the volume has errors that should be fixed (or has been marked as dirty), FSUtil reports:

```
Volume - c: is Dirty
```

If the volume doesn't have any known errors, FSUtil reports:

```
Volume - c: is NOT Dirty
```

Checking Disks for Errors and Bad Sectors

When you want to check disks for errors and bad sectors, you can use the Check Disk (Chkdsk.exe) command-line utility. This utility checks the integrity of both basic and dynamic disks. You can use it to check for and optionally repair problems found on FAT, FAT32, and NTFS volumes.

Check Disk can check for and correct many kinds of errors. The utility primarily looks for inconsistencies in the file system and its related metadata. One of the ways Check Disk locates errors is by comparing the volume bitmap to the disk sectors assigned to files in the file system. Check Disk can't repair corrupted data within files that appear to be structurally intact, however.

Analyzing a Disk Without Repairing It

You can test the integrity of a drive by typing the command name followed by the drive letter and a colon. For instance, to check the integrity of the C drive, type **chkdsk c:**

With FAT and FAT32 volumes, Check Disk displays a report similar to the following:

```
The type of the file system is FAT32.
The volume is in use by another process. Chkdsk
might report errors when no corruption is present.
Volume TRAVELDRIVE created 4/21/2008 12:32 AM
Volume Serial Number is DFGA-9871
Windows is verifying files and folders...
File and folder verification is complete.
Windows has checked the file system and found no problems.
    8,043,504 KB total disk space.
           20 KB in 5 folders.
```

```
    3,739,684 KB in 85 files.
    4,303,796 KB are available.

        4,096 bytes in each allocation unit.
    2,010,876 total allocation units on disk.
    1,075,949 allocation units available on disk.
```

Here ChkDsk examines each record in the file allocation table for consistency. It confirms all the file and folder records currently allocated and determines the starting cluster for each using the root directory table. It checks each file and notes any discrepancies in the output. Any clusters marked as in use by files or folders but that weren't actually in use are noted, and during repair the clusters can be marked as available. Any other discrepancies noted in the output can be fixed during repair as well.

With NTFS, Check Disk performs analysis in multiple phases and reports its progress during each phase. The following is an example check of an NTFS volume:

```
The type of the file system is NTFS.
WARNING!  F parameter not specified.
Running CHKDSK in read-only mode.

CHKDSK is verifying files (stage 1 of 3)...
  73088 file records processed.
File verification completed.
  123 large file records processed.
  0 bad file records processed.
  0 EA records processed.
  0 reparse records processed.
CHKDSK is verifying indexes (stage 2 of 3)...
  269869 index entries processed.
Index verification completed.
  5 unindexed files processed.
CHKDSK is verifying security descriptors (stage 3 of 3)...
  73088 security descriptors processed.
Security descriptor verification completed.
  3511 data files processed.
CHKDSK is verifying Usn Journal...
  26911912 USN bytes processed.
Usn Journal verification completed.
Windows has checked the file system and found no problems.

 488384000 KB total disk space.
 353648812 KB in 69111 files.
     25836 KB in 3512 indexes.
         0 KB in bad sectors.
    180660 KB in use by the system.
     65536 KB occupied by the log file.
 134528692 KB available on disk.
```

```
      4096 bytes in each allocation unit.
 122096000 total allocation units on disk.
  33632173 allocation units available on disk.
```

As you can see, the Check Disk operation is performed in three stages. During the first stage, Check Disk verifies file structures:

```
CHKDSK is verifying files (stage 1 of 3)...
  73088 file records processed.
File verification completed.
  123 large file records processed.
  0 bad file records processed.
  0 EA records processed.
  0 reparse records processed.
```

This means Check Disk examines each file's record in the MFT for consistency. It confirms all the file records currently allocated and determines which clusters the file records are stored in and then compares this with the volume's cluster bitmap metadata file. Any discrepancies are noted in the Check Disk output. For example, any clusters marked as in use by files but that weren't actually in use are noted. During repair the clusters can be marked as available.

During the second stage, Check Disk verifies disk index entries:

```
CHKDSK is verifying indexes (stage 2 of 3)...
  269869 index entries processed.
Index verification completed.
  5 unindexed files processed.
```

This means Check Disk verifies directory structure by examining directory indexes, starting with the volume's root directory index, which is stored in the index metadata file. Check Disk examines index records, making sure that each index record corresponds to an actual directory on the disk and that each file that is supposed to be in a directory is in the directory. It also checks for files that have an MFT record but that don't actually exist in any directory. During repair these lost files can be recovered.

If there are lost files identified as a result of verifying the disk index entries, Check Disk will recover the lost files if the /F switch was provided. Typically, the recovered files would then be stored as .chk files in the root folder of the associated disk drive. Additionally, if Check Disk finds unindexed files, it will process and then index those files.

During the third stage, Check Disk verifies security descriptors:

```
CHKDSK is verifying security descriptors (stage 3 of 3)...
  73088 security descriptors processed.
Security descriptor verification completed.
  3511 data files processed.
```

This means Check Disk verifies the consistency of security descriptors for each file and directory object on the volume using the security metadata file. It does this by validating that the security descriptors work. It doesn't actually check to see whether the users or groups as signed in the security descriptors exist.

Check Disk also verifies the update sequence numbers (USNs) in the USN change journal. A change journal provides a complete log of all changes made to the volume. It records additions, deletions, and modifications regardless of who made them or how the additions, deletions, and modifications occurred. The change log is persistent, so it isn't reset if you shut down and restart the operating system. If USN errors are found as a result of verifying the change journal entries, Check Disk can make corrections.

Finally, Check Disk completes the process by reporting whether any problems were found and includes a report on the disk:

```
Windows has checked the file system and found no problems.

 488384000 KB total disk space.
 353648812 KB in 69111 files.
     25836 KB in 3512 indexes.
         0 KB in bad sectors.
180660 KB in use by the system.
     65536 KB occupied by the log file.
 134528692 KB available on disk.

     4096 bytes in each allocation unit.
 122096000 total allocation units on disk.
  33632173 allocation units available on disk.
```

Fixing Disk Errors

When you analyze a disk, you are checking it but aren't really fixing anything. To check the disk and repair any problems found, you'll use the /F switch, which tells Check Disk to check for and fix errors:

```
chkdsk /f C:
```

Check Disk can't repair volumes that are in use. If the volume is in use, Check Disk displays a prompt that asks if you want to schedule the volume to be checked the next time you restart the system. Alternatively, you can use the /R and /X switches (note that the /X switch applies only to NTFS volumes), and each implies the /F switch. The /R switch is used to locate bad disk sectors and recover readable information, and the /X switch is used to force the NTFS volume to dismount if necessary.

Real World If you use the /R parameter, Check Disk will perform an additional step in the analysis and repair that involves checking each sector on the disk to be sure it can be read from and written to correctly. If it finds a bad sector, Check Disk will mark it so that data won't be written to that sector. If the sector was part of a cluster that was being used, Check Disk will move the good data in that cluster to a new cluster.

The data in the bad sector can be recovered only if there's redundant data from which to copy it. The bad sector won't be used again, so at least it won't cause problems in the future. Checking each sector on a disk is a time-intensive process. Because of this, you'll typically use ChkDsk /F to check for and repair common errors rather than ChkDsk /R.

For NTFS volumes, you can force Check Disk to reevaluate clusters it has marked as bad using the /B parameter. This parameter implies the /R parameter, and Check Disk will again attempt to determine whether it can correctly read from and write to a cluster marked bad. If the cluster can be read from and written to correctly, Check Disk marks the cluster as good so it can be used by the disk subsystem.

You can tell Check Disk to display more information about what it is doing using the verbose switch (/V). On NTFS, you can tell Check Disk to perform limited checks of disk index entries using the /I switch and to skip checking of cycles within folder structures using /C. A cycle is a very rarely occurring type of error in which a directory contains a pointer to itself, causing an infinite loop.

To see how Check Disk can be used, consider the following examples:

Find and repair errors that are found on the C drive:

```
chkdsk /f C:
```

Locate bad sectors and repair them on the C drive:

```
chkdsk /r C:
```

Perform minimum checks on the C drive, an NTFS volume:

```
chkdsk /i /c C:
```

Controlling Auto Check on Startup

By default, Windows Server 2008 and Windows Vista check all disks on startup and if necessary start Check Disk to repair any errors. Two different programs control automatic disk checking on startup: AUTOCHK and CHKNTFS. Auto Check is used by the operating system to initiate automatic checking of drives on startup. You can't invoke Auto Check directly, but you can control how it works using Check NTFS. With Check NTFS, you can determine whether a disk will be checked next time the computer starts and change options for automatic checking.

Determining Auto Check Status

To determine whether a disk will be checked next time the computer starts, type

chkntfs *Volume*:

where *Volume:* is the drive letter to check followed by a colon, such as

```
chkntfs c:
```

You can specify multiple drive designators as well. Separate each drive designator with a space. In this example, you determine the Check Disk status of drive C, D, and E:

```
chkntfs c: d: e:
```

Check NTFS reports the file system type and whether the disk is dirty or not dirty, as shown in this example:

```
The type of the file system is NTFS.
C: is not dirty.
The type of the file system is NTFS.
D: is dirty.
```

Here, the C drive is not dirty and Auto Check won't trigger Check Disk to run on the drive. The D drive is dirty, on the other hand, which indicates the drive may have errors and Auto Check will trigger Check Disk to run when the computer is started.

Configuring Auto Check Parameters

Using Check NTFS, you can configure Auto Check to work in several key ways. When the computer reboots, the operating system displays a countdown timer that allows the user to cancel the Auto Check operation before it begins. Using the /T parameter, you can set the length of the countdown timer in the form

```
chkntfs /t:NumSeconds
```

where *NumSeconds* is the number of seconds for the timer, such as

```
chkntfs /t:15
```

To exclude a volume or volumes from being checked when the computer starts, even if the volume is marked as requiring Check Disk, you can use the /X parameter. Follow the /X parameter with the drive designators as shown in this example:

```
chkntfs /x d: e:
```

Here, the computer will skip checking of the D and E drives even if they were marked as dirty.

To include a volume for checking when the computer starts (which is the normal configuration for Auto Check), use the /C parameter. Follow the /C parameter with the drive designators, as shown in this example:

```
chkntfs /c c: d:
```

Here, the computer will Auto Check the C and D drives when it starts to determine their status as dirty or not dirty.

The final parameter you can use is /D, which restores the default Auto Check settings, except for the countdown timer. The default behavior is to Auto Check all drives when the computer starts.

Defragmenting Disks

Whenever you add files, move files, or remove files, the data on a computer's drives can become fragmented. When a drive is fragmented, large files can't be written to a single contiguous area on the disk. As a result, large files must be written to several smaller areas of the disk and more time is spent reading the file from the disk whenever it is accessed. To reduce fragmentation, you should periodically analyze and defragment disks. Although you can configure both Windows Vista and Windows Server 2008 to automatically defragment disks, you can also use the Defrag command-line utility to check for and correct volume fragmentation problems on FAT, FAT32, and NTFS volumes.

Understanding and Using Defrag

Typically, defragmentation is performed in two steps. First, the disk is analyzed to determine the level of fragmentation and whether the disk should be defragmented. You can perform both steps simply by typing **defrag** followed by the drive letter and a colon, such as

```
defrag c:
```

Defrag will analyze the disk and, if the disk needs to be defragmented, then begin defragmenting it. If the disk doesn't need to be defragmented, Defrag will stop after the analysis phase and report that the disk doesn't need to be defragmented.

Defrag requires at least 15 percent free space to defragment a disk completely. Defrag uses this space as a sorting area for file fragments. If a volume has less than 15 percent free space, Defrag will only partially defragment it. Additionally, you cannot defragment disks that the file system has marked as dirty, which indicates that the disk has errors. In this case, you must run Check Disk and repair the errors before you can defragment the disk.

Defrag accepts several parameters, including –a, which tells Defrag to analyze the disk but not to defragment it. Defrag has two defragmentation modes: partial, specified with the –r flag, and full, specified with the –w flag. By default, defrag performs partial defragmentation only by attempting to consolidate file fragments smaller than 64 megabytes (MB). With the –w flag, defrag attempts to perform a full defragmentation by consolidating all file fragments regardless of their size.

Two additional switches you can use with Defrag are –v for verbose output and –f to force defragmentation of a disk even if free space is low. Forcing defragmentation on such a disk, however, could mean that defragmentation will take a very long time or won't be completely finished.

Performing Defrag Analysis Only

Sometimes you'll only want to analyze a disk to determine whether you should defragment it later. Defrag has two analysis modes: summary, specified using the –a flag without the –v flag, and full, specified using the –a flag with the –v flag.

To perform a summary analysis of a disk without defragmenting it, type the **defrag –a** command followed by the disk letter and a colon. Defrag will then report whether the disk should be defragmented. The following is an analysis of a disk that doesn't need to be defragmented:

```
C:\>defrag -a c:
Windows Disk Defragmenter
Copyright (c) 2006 Microsoft Corp.

Analysis report for volume C:
    Volume size                             = 457 GB
    Free space                              = 358 GB
    Largest free space extent               = 209 GB
    Percent file fragmentation              = 2 %
    Note: On NTFS volumes, file fragments larger than 64MB are not
included in the fragmentation statistics

    You do not need to defragment this volume.
```

As you can see, the disk is only 2 percent fragmented. Because fragmentation is so low, the disk doesn't need to be defragmented. On the other hand, the following disk analysis shows a disk that is heavily fragmented:

```
C:\>defrag -a d:
Windows Disk Defragmenter
Copyright (c) 2006 Microsoft Corp.

Analysis report for volume D:
    Volume size                             = 466 GB
    Free space                              = 131 GB
    Largest free space extent               = 74.69 GB
    Percent file fragmentation              = 29 %
    Note: On NTFS volumes, file fragments larger than 64MB are not included
in the fragmentation statistics
    You should defragment this volume.
```

Here, Defrag recommends that you defragment the disk and you could schedule this as necessary maintenance.

To perform a full analysis of a disk without defragmenting it, type **defrag –a –v** followed by the disk letter and a colon. Defrag will then report whether the disk should be defragmented. The following is an analysis of a disk that needs to be defragmented:

```
C:\>defrag -a -v d:
Windows Disk Defragmenter
Copyright (c) 2006 Microsoft Corp.

Analysis report for volume D:

    Volume size                                  = 466 GB
    Cluster size                                 = 4 KB
    Used space                                   = 335 GB
    Free space                                   = 131 GB
    Percent free space                           = 28 %

File fragmentation
    Percent file fragmentation                   = 29 %
    Total movable files                          = 72,608
    Average file size                            = 5 MB
    Total fragmented files                       = 18,200
    Total excess fragments                       = 91,257
    Average fragments per file                   = 1.64
    Total unmovable files                        = 10

Free space fragmentation
    Free space                                   = 131 GB
    Total free space extent                      = 552
    Average free space per extent                = 243 MB
    Largest free space extent                    = 74.69 GB

Folder fragmentation
    Total folders                                = 3,504
    Fragmented folders                           = 15
    Excess folder fragments                      = 35
Master File Table (MFT) fragmentation
    Total MFT size                               = 71 MB
    MFT record count                             = 72,757
    Percent MFT in use                           = 99
    Total MFT fragments                          = 8

     Note: On NTFS volumes, file fragments larger than 64MB are not
included in the fragmentation statistics

    You should defragment this volume.
```

The type of volume you are working with determines the areas in the report. Report areas can include the following:

- **File Fragmentation** Provides an overview of file-level fragmentation showing the percentage of used space that is fragmented, the total number of files on the volume that are movable, the average size of those files, how many files are fragmented, the total number of excess fragments, the average number of fragments per file, and the total number of unmovable files. Ideally, you want the percent fragmentation to be 10 percent or less and the number of fragments per file to be as close to 1.00 as possible.
- **Free Space Fragmentation** Provides an overview of fragmentation on a volume's unused space showing how much free space is available on the volume, the number of extents on which free space is located, the average free space per extend, and the largest free space extent.
- **Folder Fragmentation** Provides an overview of folder-level fragmentation showing the total number of folders on the volume and how many folders are fragmented.
- **Master File Table (MFT) Fragmentation** For NTFS volumes only, gives an overview of fragmentation in the MFT, showing the current size of the MFT, the number of records it contains, the percentage of the MFT in use, and the total number of fragments in the MFT. In this example, the MFT has some fragmentation. But the real concern is that it is at 99 percent of its maximum size. Because of this, the MFT could become more fragmented over time—there is still 28 percent free space on the volume, and if it needs to grow it will grow into the free space.

Here, you could resolve fragmentation issues by running Defrag again without the –a parameter. Add the –w parameter to perform a full defrag (rather than the default, partial defrag). Although neither technique will clear up all fragmentation, either will help so that disk space is used more efficiently—and on a fragmented volume like the one shown, you should see some performance improvements after defragmentation as well.

Chapter 11

Partitioning Basic Disks

When you install a new computer or update an existing computer, you'll often need to partition the hard disk drives on the computer. DiskPart can use the Master Boot Record (MBR) or GUID Partition Table (GPT) partition style. When you use the MBR partition style, a drive can have up to four primary partitions or three primary partitions and one extended partition. When you use the GPT partition style on Windows Vista or Windows Server 2008, there are two required partitions on bootable or system disks (the EFI system partition and the Microsoft Reserved partition), and one or more optional OEM or data partitions for a total of as many as 128 partitions.

Obtaining Partition Information

When you work with DiskPart, you can obtain partition information on the selected disk by using the LIST PARTITION command. As shown in the following example, LIST PARTITION lists information on all partitions of the selected disk. For example, if you typed **select disk 2** and then type **list partition**, you would see a list of partitions on disk 2, such as

```
Partition ###  Type          Size       Offset
-------------  -----------   ---------  -------
Partition 1    Primary        706 MB      32 KB
Partition 2    Primary        706 MB     706 MB
Partition 3    Primary        706 MB    1412 MB
Partition 4    Extended      1004 MB    2118 MB
Partition 5    Logical        502 MB    2118 MB
Partition 6    Logical        502 MB    2620 MB
```

Note An asterisk at the beginning of an entry means the partition is currently selected and has focus.

As you can see, LIST PARTITION shows

- **Partition ###** The number of the partition. You can use **select partition** *n* to work with the partition.
- **Type** The layout type. Partition layouts include primary, extended, and logical.
- **Size** The total storage size of the partition.
- **Offset** The byte offset of the partition, which is always rounded to the nearest cylinder boundary.

Note A cylinder is a section of a drive within a partition. A cylinder is in turn apportioned into tracks; the tracks are apportioned into sectors; and finally the sectors are made up of individual data bytes. For example, a 4-gigabyte (GB) drive could have 525 cylinders with 255 tracks per cylinder. Each track in turn could have 63 sectors and the sectors could have 512 bytes. In this example, a cylinder is about 8 megabytes (MB) in size, so the byte offset of the partition would always be rounded to the nearest 8 MB. The exception is for the first partition on the disk, which starts at the beginning of the first available cylinder.

Creating Partitions

How you create partitions on basic disks depends on the partition style of the disk. Because you create different types of partitions with MBR disks than you do with GPT disks, the following sections separate the discussions about creating partitions for MBR and GPT disks.

Creating Partitions for MBR Disks

With MBR disks, you can use DiskPart to create primary and extended partitions. A primary partition can fill an entire disk, or you can size it as appropriate for the computer you're configuring. Each physical drive can have one extended partition. This extended partition can contain one or more logical drives, which are simply sections of the partition with their own file system. Although you can size the logical drive any way you want, you might want to consider how you'll use logical drives on the current workstation or server. Generally, you use logical drives to divide a large physical drive into manageable sections. With this in mind, you might want to apportion a 60-GB extended partition into three logical drives of 20 GB each.

Creating Primary Partitions

Before you add a primary partition to a disk, you should assess the amount of free space on the disk and also check the current partition configuration. Follow these steps to perform these tasks:

1. Invoke DiskPart by typing **diskpart** at the command prompt.
2. List the disks on the computer by typing **list disk** and check the free space:

```
Disk ###  Status      Size     Free     Dyn  Gpt
--------  ----------  -------  -------  ---  ---
Disk 0    Online      56 GB    0 B
Disk 1    Online      29 GB    0 B
Disk 2    Online      37 GB    37 GB
```

3. In this example, disk 2 has 37 GB of free space for partitioning and no currently assigned partitions because the size of the disk is also 37 GB. If the disk size and free space aren't the same, however, some space has been assigned to partitions.

If you wanted to work with disk 2, you would select the disk and then check the partitions on the disk by typing **select disk 2**, and then typing **list partition**.

Once you select a disk to work with and give the disk focus, you can create the primary partition using the command

```
create partition primary size=n
```

where *n* is the size of the space to allocate in megabytes. If no size is given, the partition is created to fill the unallocated space on the disk.

> **Note** Here, the partition is created at the beginning of the first free space on the disk. DiskPart accomplishes this by automatically setting the offset parameter to the appropriate value. It is important to note that the offset is rounded to the closest cylinder boundary. The value is therefore rounded up or down as appropriate to coincide with the closest cylinder boundary, which can change the final size of the partition or logical drive.

> **Tip** With RAID Logical Unit Number (LUN) arrays, you may find that you want to align all the starting points for a volume or partition to the nearest alignment boundary to improve performance. You can do this with the Align parameter. Use the syntax **align=*n***, where *n* is the number of kilobytes from the beginning of the disk to the closest alignment boundary, such as **align=64**.

After you create the partition, it will automatically have focus, meaning it will be selected. The partition will not yet have a drive letter or mount point. You must use the ASSIGN command to do this. To finalize the partition, you must also format it using the FORMAT command. For more information, see the sections "Assigning Drive Letters or Mount Points" and "Formatting Partitions" later in this chapter.

Creating Extended Partitions with Logical Drives

Each disk drive can have one extended partition. As with primary partitions, you should assess the amount of free space on the disk and also check the current partition configuration before creating an extended partition. After you do this, you can create the extended partition in the unallocated space on the disk you've selected (meaning that you have given that disk focus).

You create an extended partition using the command

```
create partition extended size=n
```

where *n* is the size of the space to allocate in megabytes. If no size is given, the partition is created to fill the unallocated space on the disk.

After you create the extended partition, it will automatically have focus, meaning that it will be selected. Unlike primary partitions, you don't assign drive letters or format extended partitions directly. Instead, you create one or more logical drives within the extended partition space and these drives are the ones to which you assign drive letters and then format.

You can create a logical drive within an extended partition using the command

```
create partition logical size=n
```

where *n* is the size of the space to allocate in megabytes. If no size is given, the logical drive will use all the available space in the extended partition. When you specify the size of logical drives, remember that the sum of the sizes of all logical drives within the partition must be less than the size of the extended partition. That's why, in Chapter 10, "Configuring and Maintaining Disks," we created an extended partition of 4,096 MB and logical drives within the partition of 2,048 MB and 2,047 MB, respectively.

After you create a logical drive, it will automatically have focus, but will not yet have a drive letter or mount point. You must use the ASSIGN command to assign the drive letter or mount point you want to use and then finalize the logical drive by formatting it.

Creating Partitions for GPT Disks

GPT disks can have the following types of partitions:

- EFI system partition (ESP)
- Microsoft Reserved (MSR) partition
- Primary partition
- Logical Disk Manager (LDM) Metadata partition
- LDM Data partition
- OEM or Unknown partition

As with MBR disks, before you add partitions to GPT disks, you should assess the amount of free space on the disk and also check the current partition configuration. Once you select a disk to work with and give the disk focus, you can create any necessary partition.

Creating EFI System Partitions

A computer with EFI must have one GPT disk that contains an ESP. This partition is similar to the system volume on an x86-based computer in that it contains the files that are required to start the operating system. Windows Server 2008 creates the ESP during setup, formats it by using FAT, and sizes it so that it is at least 100 MB in size or 1 percent of the disk up to a maximum size of 1,000 MB.

On the system disk used to load the operating system, the EFI system partition should be the first partition and the MSR partition should be the second partition. Because GPT disks that are not used for startup don't contain EFI system partitions, the MSR partition should be the first partition on nonsystem disks.

Although the ESP normally is created for you automatically when you install Windows Server 2008 on a computer with EFI, in some limited instances you might need to create an ESP after installing an additional GPT disk on a server, such as when you want to use the new disk as a boot device rather than the existing boot device.

You can create an EFI system partition using the command

```
create partition efi size=n
```

where *n* is the size of the space to allocate in megabytes. The partition you create will automatically have focus, meaning that it will be selected. The partition will not yet have a drive letter or mount point, which is needed for EFI and data partitions. To finalize an EFI partition, you must also format it. Normally, you format EFI partitions as FAT.

DiskPart automatically sets the offset parameter to mark the partition as an EFI system partition; you shouldn't set the byte offset manually in most cases. The globally unique identifier (GUID) for an EFI system partition is:

```
c12a7328-f81f-11d2-ba4b-00a0c93ec93b
```

> **Real World** If for some reason, the GUID is unset or set incorrectly, you can use the SETID command to correctly identify the partition and reestablish it as the MSR partition. Because doing so could cause the computer to fail or be unable to start up, only experienced administrators with a solid understanding of GPT disks should attempt to use SETID. Further, you should only use SETID as a measure of last resort when you are unable to otherwise create the MSR partition using the CREATE PARTITION MSR command. SETID doesn't work on dynamic disks and is meant to be used only by OEMs. Finally, keep in mind that DiskPart doesn't check the GUID to ensure that it is valid.

Creating Microsoft Reserved Partitions

A computer with EFI must have an MSR partition on every GPT disk. The MSR partition contains additional space that might be needed by the operating system to perform disk operations. For example, when you convert a basic GPT disk to a dynamic GPT disk, the Windows operating system takes 1 MB of the MSR partition space and uses it to create the LDM Metadata partition, which is required for the conversion.

The Windows operating system creates the MSR partition automatically. For the boot disk, it is created along with the ESP when you install the operating system. An MSR partition is also created automatically when a disk is converted from MBR to GPT and any time you access a GPT disk that doesn't already have an MSR partition.

If a GPT disk contains an ESP as the first partition on the disk, the MSR partition is usually the second partition on the disk. If a GPT disk does not contain an ESP, the MSR partition is typically the first partition on the disk. However, if a disk already has a primary partition at the beginning of the disk, the MSR partition is placed at the end of the disk.

The MSR partition is sized according to the size of the associated disk. For disks up to 16 GB in size, it normally is 32 MB in size. For all other disks, it normally is 128 MB in size.

You can create an MSR partition using the command

```
create partition msr size=n
```

where *n* is the size of the space to allocate in megabytes. The partition you create will automatically have focus, meaning that it will be selected. The partition will not have a drive letter or mount point. Windows does not mount MSR partitions, and you cannot store data on them or delete them. Further, you do not need to format the MSR partition. Windows uses the partition without formatting.

DiskPart automatically sets the offset parameter to mark the partition as the MSR partition; you shouldn't set the byte offset manually in most cases. The GUID for an MSR partition is

```
e3c9e316-0b5c-4db8-817d-f92df00215ae
```

Creating Primary Partitions

On basic disks, you create primary partitions to store your data. GPT disks support up to 128 partitions, which can be a mix of required and optional partitions. Every primary partition you create appears in the GUID partition entry array within the GPT header. If you convert a basic disk that contains primary partitions to a dynamic disk, the primary partitions become simple volumes, and information about them is then stored in the dynamic disk database and not in the GUID partition entry array.

You can create a primary partition using the command

```
create partition primary size=n
```

where *n* is the size of the space to allocate in megabytes. The partition you create will automatically have focus, meaning that it will be selected. The partition will not yet have a drive letter or mount point, which is needed for primary partitions. To finalize the primary partition, you must also format it. You can format the partition using any supported file system, such as FAT32 or NTFS.

DiskPart automatically sets the offset parameter to mark the partition as a primary partition; you shouldn't set the byte offset manually in most cases. The GUID for a primary partition is

```
ebd0a0a2-b9e5-4433-87c0-68b6b72699c7
```

Creating LDM Metadata and LDM Data Partitions

Windows creates LDM Metadata and LDM Data partitions when you convert a basic GPT disk to a dynamic GPT disk. The LDM Metadata partition is 1 MB in size and is used to store the partitioning information needed for the conversion. The LDM Data partition is the partition in which the actual dynamic volumes are created.

The LDM Data partition represents sections of unallocated space on the converted disk as well as sections that had basic partitions that are now dynamic volumes. For example, if a disk had a primary boot partition that spanned the whole disk, the converted disk will have a single LDM Data partition. If a disk had a boot partition and other primary partitions, it will have two LDM Data partitions after the conversion: one for the boot volume and one for all other partitions. Although the LDM Metadata and LDM Data partitions do not receive drive letters or mount points, you are able to use this space by creating primary partitions as discussed in the previous section.

The GUID for an LDM Metadata partition on a dynamic disk is

```
5808c8aa-7e8f-42e0-85d2-e1e90434cfb3
```

The GUID for an LDM Data partition on a dynamic disk is

```
af9b60a0-1431-4f62-bc68-3311714a69ad
```

Managing Drive Letters and Mount Points

After partitioning a drive, you can assign each partition a drive letter or mount point and then format the partition so that it is ready to store data. Generally, the drive letters E through Z are available for use, with drive letters A to D reserved or already in use in most cases. On many systems, drive letter A is for the system's floppy, drive letter B is reserved for a removable disk drive, drive letter C is the primary disk drive, and drive letter D is for the CD-ROM or DVD drive.

If you need additional partitions, you can create them using mount points, which allow you to mount disks to a file system path, such as C:\Data. The only restriction for drive paths is that you must mount them to empty folders on NTFS drives.

Assigning Drive Letters or Mount Points

To assign a drive letter or mount point, follow these steps:

1. Invoke DiskPart by typing **diskpart** at the command prompt.
2. List the volumes on the computer and check the current assignments by typing **list volume**.

> **Note** Only the LIST VOLUME command shows drive letter and mount point assignments, and it does so for all partitions, logical drives, and volumes on the computer. That's why you use this command instead of the LIST PARTITION command. Seems illogical, but that's how it works. The good news is that you use this same technique when assigning drive letters and mount points to volumes on dynamic disks.

3. Assign the drive letter or mount point as follows:
   - To assign a drive letter, type **assign letter=***x* where *x* is the drive letter to use, such as

     ```
     DISKPART> assign letter=f
     ```

   - To assign a mount point, type **assign mount=***Path* where *Path* is the path to the empty NTFS folder to use as the mount point, such as

     ```
     DISKPART> assign mount=c:\data
     ```

Changing Drive Letters or Mount Points

The ASSIGN command can also be used to change an existing drive letter or mount point assignment. Simply select the partition to work with and use ASSIGN to set the new drive letter or mount point. DiskPart will change the drive letter and report that you must reboot the computer before the changes take effect:

```
DiskPart assigned the drive letter, but your computer needs to be rebooted
before the changes take effect.
```

With a mount point, DiskPart will report that it made the requested change without requiring a reboot:

```
DiskPart successfully assigned the drive letter or mount point.
```

Removing Drive Letters or Mount Points

You can remove a drive letter or mount point from a partition that has focus by using the REMOVE command. Follow these steps:

1. Invoke DiskPart by typing **diskpart** at the command prompt.
2. List the volumes on the computer by typing **list volume**, and check the current assignments. Remember, only the LIST VOLUME command shows drive letter and mount point assignments, and it does so for all partitions, logical drives, and volumes on the computer.
3. Select the partition you want to work with by typing **select volume** followed by the number of the volume representing the desired partition. Again, it seems illogical to do this with partitions, but this is the easiest way.
4. Remove the current drive letter or mount point assignment from the select partition by typing **remove**.

When entered without any parameters, this command removes the first drive letter or mount point it encounters and reports:

```
DiskPart successfully removed the drive letter or mount point.
```

This technique is fine when the partition only has a single drive letter or mount point. If a partition has multiple drive letters or mount points, you'll want to specify the drive letter to remove by typing the parameter **letter=*x*** or the mount point to remove by typing the parameter **mount=*Path***, such as

```
DISKPART> remove letter=d
```

or

```
DISKPART> remove mount=D:\Data
```

You can also specify that all drive letters and mount points should be removed and that DiskPart should close all open handles to the volume and then dismount it after removing the drive letter or mount point. To do this, you use the All and Dismount parameters, as shown in these examples:

Remove all drive letters and mount points:

```
DISKPART> remove all
```

Remove all drive letters and mount points and then dismount the related volumes:

```
DISKPART> remove all dismount
```

Remove the volume mounted as d: and dismount it:

```
DISKPART> remove letter=d dismount
```

> **Note** On MBR disks, you cannot remove the drive letter from the system or boot partition, or any partition that contains the active paging file or crash dump (memory dump). On GPT disks, you cannot remove the drive letter for any EFI, OEM, unrecognized, or non-data partition. You can, however, use this command to remove the drive letter from a removable drive.

Formatting Partitions

Formatting creates a file system in a partition and permanently deletes any existing data. Windows Vista and Windows Server 2008 support hard disk drives with FAT, FAT32, and NTFS file systems. FAT is the file system type supported by MS-DOS and early releases of Windows. FAT32 is a 32-bit version of FAT. NTFS is the native file system type for Windows NT, Windows 2000, Windows XP, Windows Vista, Windows Server 2003, and Windows Server 2008.

Windows Vista SP1 or later and Windows Server 2008 support hot-pluggable media that use exFAT and NTFS volumes. This means you have more options with removable storage devices and can format USB flash devices and other similar media with exFAT, FAT16, FAT32, or NTFS. The exFAT file system is the next generation file system in the FAT family and is designed so that it can be used with any compliant operating system or device.

Using FORMAT

Unlike earlier releases, the version of DiskPart in Windows Vista and Windows Server 2008 has an internal FORMAT command. This means that while you are using DiskPart, you can format a partition that has focus without having to exit the utility. In fact, if you type **format** and press Enter without providing any additional parameters, the selected partition is automatically formatted using the default file system type and allocation unit size. However, rather than using the default values, you'll typically want to specify the desired formatting. The basic syntax of the DiskPart FORMAT command is

```
format fs=FileSystem label=Label unit=UnitSize
```

where *FileSystem* sets the file system type, *Label* sets the descriptive text name, and *UnitSize* sets the allocation unit size for bytes per disk cluster. A disk cluster is a small section of a disk made up of contiguous 512-byte sectors. The volume label is a text descriptor for a drive and is used with drive letters, not mount points. If you don't set the allocation unit size, FORMAT chooses one for you based on the size of the volume. Valid allocation unit sizes include the following:

- **512** Sets 512 bytes per cluster
- **1024** Sets 1,024 bytes per cluster
- **2048** Sets 2,048 bytes per cluster
- **4096** Sets 4,096 bytes per cluster
- **8192** Sets 8,192 bytes per cluster
- **16K** Sets 16 kilobytes per cluster
- **32K** Sets 32 kilobytes per cluster
- **64K** Sets 64 kilobytes per cluster

To see how the FORMAT command is used, consider the following examples:

Format the selected volume using the FAT32 file system and label it AppData:

```
format fs=fat32 label=AppData
```

Format the selected volume using the NTFS file system and 512 bytes per disk cluster:

```
format fs=ntfs unit=512
```

Format the selected volume using the NTFS file system and label it AppData:

```
format fs=ntfs label=AppData
```

> **Caution** If there's an existing file system, FORMAT does not provide a prompt. As a result, if you aren't careful in your volume selection, you could accidentally format a volume and destroy all its contents.

In some cases, you might need to dismount the volume before you can format it. You can do this with the Override parameter. In addition, if you are working with a previously formatted drive that doesn't have any known problems, you could perform a quick format instead of a thorough format using the Quick parameter. With a quick format, FORMAT prepares the file system for use without checking for errors. With large partitions, this option can save you a few minutes. However, it doesn't allow FORMAT to mark bad sectors on the disk and lock them out.

When FORMAT starts, it will display the format progress by default. You can force the command to return immediately while the format is still in progress using the Nowait parameter. However, you shouldn't try to work with the volume in DiskPart until the formatting is complete.

DiskPart's FORMAT command provides several other useful parameters, including Compress, Revision, and Recommended. You can use the Compress parameter to mark an NTFS volume as compressed, which means files created on the volume will be compressed using NTFS compression. You can use the Revision parameter to set the file system revision as applicable and necessary, such as when you are formatting CD/DVD media and want to use a specific version of Universal Disk Format (UDF). You can use the Recommended parameter to use the recommended file system type and revision instead of the default values if a recommendation exists.

Using FILESYSTEMS

When you are preparing to format disks, you can use the FILESYSTEMS command to display current and supported file systems on a selected volume. Consider the following sample output:

```
Current File System

  Type                    : FAT32
```

```
  Allocation Unit Size : 32K

File Systems Supported for Formatting

  Type                 : NTFS
  Allocation Unit Sizes: 512, 1024, 2048, 4096 (Default), 8192, 16K, 32K,
64K

  Type                 : FAT
  Allocation Unit Sizes: 512, 1024, 2048, 4096, 8192, 16K, 32K, 64K (Defau
lt)

  Type                 : FAT32 (Default)
  Allocation Unit Sizes: 512, 1024, 2048, 4096, 8192, 16K, 32K (Default),
64K
```

In this example, the current file system type is FAT32 and the allocation unit size is 32 KB. The volume can be formatted with FAT, FAT32, or NTFS by using any of the allocation units listed. With this volume, the default allocation unit is 64 KB for FAT, 32 KB for FAT32, and 4,096 bytes for NTFS.

When you are working with Windows Server 2008 or Windows Vista SP1 or later, you'll find that exFAT is listed as an additional formatting option with most types of removable storage devices. You may also find that standard FAT (FAT 12/16) is no longer available as an option. Here is sample output for FILESYSTEMS with a removable storage device:

```
Current File System

  Type                 : FAT32
  Allocation Unit Size : 4096

File Systems Supported for Formatting

  Type                 : NTFS
  Allocation Unit Sizes: 512, 1024, 2048, 4096 (Default), 8192, 16K, 32K,
64K

  Type                 : FAT32 (Default)
  Allocation Unit Sizes: 512, 1024, 2048, 4096 (Default), 8192, 16K, 32K,
64K

  Type                 : exFAT
  Allocation Unit Sizes: 512, 1024, 2048, 4096, 8192, 16K, 32K (Default),
64K,
128K, 256K, 1024K, 2048K, 4096K, 8192K, 16384K, 32768K
```

When you are working with Windows Server 2008 or Windows Vista SP1 or later, you can use DiskPart to format blank CDs and DVDs. Here is sample output for FILESYSTEMS with a blank DVD:

```
Current File System

  Type                 : RAW
  Allocation Unit Size : 2048

File Systems Supported for Formatting

  Type                 : UDF [Revision 1.50]
  Allocation Unit Sizes: 2048 (Default)

  Type                 : UDF [Revision 2.00]
  Allocation Unit Sizes: 2048 (Default)

  Type                 : UDF [Revision 2.01] (Default)
  Allocation Unit Sizes: 2048 (Default)

  Type                 : UDF [Revision 2.50]
  Allocation Unit Sizes: 2048 (Default)
```

In this example, the type RAW indicates that the media is unformatted. Once you format the media, you'll see UDF as the file system type. UDF replaces the standard CD File System (CDFS) used previously. Although you can continue to use disks formatted with CDFS, UDF has many advantages. UDF is a live file system that works like any other type of removable storage, such as a USB flash drive or a removable disk drive. You can copy files to the disk immediately without having to burn them, simply by copying and pasting files or by dragging and dropping files. If the disk is re-recordable, you can remove files simply by selecting them and deleting them. If you eject the disk, you can insert it into your CD/DVD drive later and continue to use it like removable storage. Although compliant computers can read UDF discs, most home and car CD/DVD players cannot read UDF data disks.

UDF versions that Windows Vista and Windows Server 2008 support include the following:

- **UDF 1.50** A format compatible with Windows 2000 and later versions of Windows. It might not be compatible with Windows 98 or Apple computers.
- **UDF 2.00** A format compatible with Windows XP and later versions of Windows. It might not be compatible with Windows 98, Windows 2000, or Apple computers.
- **UDF 2.01** The default format, which includes an important update that you'll want to take advantage of in most cases. This format is compatible with

Windows XP and later versions of Windows. It might not be compatible with Windows 98, Windows 2000, or Apple computers.

- **UDF 2.50** A format optimized for Windows Vista. It might not be compatible with earlier versions of Windows or Apple computers.

When you are formatting a blank CD or DVD, you can use the Revision parameter to set the desired UDF version. Be sure to enclose the revision number in either single or double quotation marks as shown in the following examples:

```
format fs=udf revision='1.50'
format fs=udf revision='2.00'
format fs=udf revision='2.01'
format fs=udf revision='2.50'
```

You should always use the full version identifier as shown.

Formatting: An Example

You can format a volume that has focus by using the FORMAT command. Follow these steps:

1. Invoke DiskPart by typing **diskpart** at the command prompt.
2. List the volumes on the computer by typing **list volume**. Before you continue, note the type, status, and file system of each volume. The volume type is listed as Partition for partitions, Removable for removable storage devices, CD_ROM for CD-only devices, and DVD-ROM for CD/DVD drives. If you haven't inserted media for removable storage or CD/DVD drives, the volume status typically is listed as No Media.
3. Select the volume you want to work with by typing **select volume** followed by the number of the desired volume. If you type **list volume** again, an asterisk next to the volume number will confirm your selection. Always confirm your selection before continuing.
4. Type **format** followed by the desired parameters and parameter values, such as: **format fs=ntfs label='secondary data' unit=4096**.

DiskPart will then show you the progress of the formatting. When DiskPart finishes, the output should look similar to the following:

```
  100 percent completed
DiskPart successfully formatted the volume.
```

If an error occurs and DiskPart is unable to format the volume, you'll see an error, such as:

```
DiskPart encountered an unexpected error.
Check the system event log for more information on the failure.
```

Errors can occur for a variety of reasons. If an error occurs, you can use FILESYSTEMS to ensure you are using compatible file system settings. In some cases, you may need to use OVERRIDE to force a volume to dismount prior to formatting.

Managing Partitions

Common management tasks for partitions include converting FAT and FAT32 partitions to NTFS, changing volume labels, shrinking partitions, extending partitions, and deleting partitions. These tasks are discussed in this section.

Converting a Partition or Volume to NTFS

If you created a partition or volume using FAT or FAT32, you can convert it to NTFS without having to reformat. The advantage of this is that the file and directory structure is preserved and no data is lost. To convert from FAT or FAT32 to NTFS, use the command-line CONVERT command. (The DiskPart CONVERT command serves an entirely different purpose.)

Conversion: Preliminary Checks

Before you use CONVERT, you should do the following:

- **Check to see whether the partition is being used as the active boot partition or a system partition containing the operating system.** On systems with MBR disks, you can convert the active boot partition to NTFS. If you do this, however, CONVERT must have exclusive access to the partition, which can only be obtained during startup. So if you attempt to convert the active boot or system partition to NTFS, you will see a prompt asking whether you want to schedule the drive to be converted the next time the system starts. If you click Yes, you can restart the system to begin the conversion process. Just keep in mind that it usually takes several restarts to completely convert the active boot partition.
- **Check to see whether the drive has enough free space to perform the conversion.** You'll need a block of free space that's roughly equal to 25 percent of the total space used by the partition or volume. For example, if a 300 GB partition stores 200 GB of data, CONVERT will need about 50 GB of free space. CONVERT checks for this free space before running and stops if there isn't enough.

Caution There isn't a utility for converting NTFS to FAT. The only way to go from NTFS to FAT or NTFS to FAT32 is to delete the partition or volume and then to re-create the partition as a FAT or FAT32 volume.

Handling Basic Conversions

CONVERT is run at the command prompt. If you want to convert a drive, use the following syntax:

```
convert volume /FS:NTFS
```

where *volume* is the drive letter followed by a colon, drive path, or volume name. For example, if you wanted to convert the D drive to NTFS, you'd use the following command:

```
convert D: /FS:NTFS
```

> **Tip** For volumes converted from FAT or FAT32 to NTFS, the Master File Table (MFT) is created in a different location than on a volume originally formatted with NTFS, which can result in a slowdown in performance. For optimal performance, you might want to use a designated conversion area as discussed in "Using the CvtArea Parameter" later in the chapter.

On converted boot and system volumes, CONVERT applies the same default security that is applied during Windows setup. On other volumes, CONVERT sets security so that the Users group has access but doesn't give access to the special group Everyone. To give Everyone access to the data on the disk, you can remove the security settings by using the /NoSecurity parameter, such as

```
convert D: /FS:NTFS /nosecurity
```

> **Caution** The /NoSecurity parameter removes all security attributes and makes all files and directories on the disk accessible to the group Everyone.

CONVERT has several additional parameters. You can use the verbose switch (/V) to get more detailed information during the conversion, and the force dismount switch (/X) to force the partition or volume to dismount before the conversation if necessary. The main reason for dismounting a drive prior to conversion is to ensure that no application or process tries to use the drive while it is being converted. You can't, however, dismount a boot or system drive. These drives will be converted when the system is restarted.

The basic conversion procedure works well with most types of disks. Sometimes, however, you may find that this procedure doesn't yield ideal results. For example, a converted drive could actually slow instead of accelerate. To work around this problem, you can use the /CvtArea parameter, which sets the name of a contiguous file in the root directory to be a placeholder for NTFS system files.

Using the CvtArea Parameter

Ideally, the more often a file is accessed, the closer it should be placed to the beginning of the drive to decrease the amount of time required to find and read the file. When a drive is formatted, certain NTFS system files should be placed at the beginning of the drive precisely for this reason. However, when you use the basic conversion process, Windows is unable to place the new NTFS system files at the beginning of the disk because that space is already used by other files that need to be retained. As a result, a converted drive could perform somewhat slower than it did when formatted as FAT or FAT32.

Windows Server 2008 and Windows Vista resolve this problem by allowing you to designate a conversion area using the CvtArea parameter followed by the name of a temporary file to use. The syntax is

```
convert volume /FS:NTFS /CVTAREA:FileName
```

where *volume* is the drive letter followed by a colon and *FileName* is a file created in advance for use as a temporary location, such as

```
convert C: /FS:NTFS /CVTAREA:temp.txt
```

This specifies that the Master File Table (MFT) and other NTFS metadata files are written to an existing, contiguous placeholder file called temp.txt. When you use CONVERT without the CvtArea parameter, the FAT system files at the beginning of the disk aren't moved. They are deleted and subsequent regular files are placed in the location of the old system files. When you use CONVERT with the CvtArea parameter, CONVERT looks for the listed filename and puts a placeholder at the beginning of the disk instead of placing regular files in that location. When the drive is converted to NTFS, CONVERT deletes the CvtArea file and replaces it with the newly completed NTFS system files. Thus, using the /CvtArea parameter can result in a less fragmented file system after conversion.

You create the placeholder file by using the FSUTIL command prior to running CONVERT. CONVERT does not create this file for you. For optimal results, the size of this file should be 1 KB multiplied by the number of files and directories in the file system. The easiest way to determine the number of files and directories in the file system is to check the properties of each of the top-level folders on the drive, record the total number of files and folders, and then compute the totals for all top-level folders. To do this, follow these steps:

1. Start Windows Explorer, right-click a top-level folder on the drive, and then select Properties.
2. Note the total number of files and folders for the Contains entry, and then click OK.
3. Repeat this procedure for each top-level folder, and then add the totals.

Once you have the total number of file and folders, multiply this by 1 KB to determine the size of the placeholder file. For example, if you have 1,000 files and folders, the placeholder file's size needs to be 1,000 KB. To create the placeholder file, type

```
fsutil file createnew FileName ByteSize
```

where *FileName* is the name of the file to create and *ByteSize* is the size of the file in bytes. To create a 1,000 KB file named Temp.txt, we would create a file with 1,024,000 bytes (each KB is 1024 bytes), such as

```
fsutil file createnew temp.txt 1024000
```

> **Note** Keep in mind that CONVERT overwrites this file with NTFS metadata. After conversion, any unused space in this file is freed.

Changing or Deleting the Volume Label

The volume label is a text descriptor for a volume that has a drive letter. With FAT and FAT32, the volume label can be up to 11 characters in length and can include spaces. With NTFS, the volume label can be up to 32 characters in length. Additionally, although FAT and FAT32 don't allow you to use some special characters, including * / \ [ ] : ; | = , . + " ? < >, NTFS does allow you to use these special characters.

The volume label is displayed when the drive is accessed in various utilities, such as Windows Explorer. You can change or delete a volume label using the LABEL command at a command prompt. (LABEL is not available within DiskPart as a command for changing or deleting an existing label, but there is a Label parameter available for DiskPart's FORMAT command.)

You can change the volume's label by using the syntax

```
label drive: label
```

where *drive:* is the drive letter followed by a colon and *label* is the text description to assign, such as

```
label f: AppData
```

> **Note** A useful command when working with volume labels is VOL. VOL lists the current volume name (if any).

Shrinking Partitions or Volumes

The technique for shrinking partitions on basic disks—and volumes on dynamic disks—is the same. If you create a volume that's too large, you may sometimes want to reduce its size to free up space for another volume. You can shrink volumes regardless of whether you are working with a basic disk or a dynamic disk. In shrinking a volume, you remove areas of unused space from the existing volume.

Several limitations apply to shrinking volumes. You can only shrink formatted volumes when the file system is NTFS; you can't shrink volumes that are formatted with FAT or FAT32. Although you can shrink volumes that were not previously formatted, you can't shrink striped volumes.

Follow these steps to shrink a partition:

1. Invoke DiskPart by typing **diskpart** at the command prompt.
2. List the disks on the computer by typing **list disk**, and check the free space.
3. Select the disk you want to work with, such as disk 2, by typing **select disk 2**.
4. List the partitions on the selected disk by typing **list partition**.
5. Select the partition you want to work with. For instance, type **select partition 2**.
6. Type **shrink querymax** to determine the maximum amount of space you can remove from the volume.

   Tip In most cases, you won't want to reduce the disk by the maximum allowed. Instead, you'll want to keep sufficient free space to allow the volume to perform well during read and write operations. I recommend keeping at least 10 percent free space. When working with boot and system volumes as well as volumes with page files or shadow copies, you may need to retain much more free space.

7. Shrink the partition by typing **shrink desired=*n***

   where *n* is the desired amount of space to remove in megabytes, such as

   ```
   DISKPART> shrink desired=1000
   ```

Note The size is rounded to the nearest cylinder boundary, which typically results in slightly more or slightly less disk space being removed.

DiskPart will reduce the volume by the desired amount, provided that you have enough free space to do so. Otherwise, DiskPart will reduce the volume by the maximum free space available on the volume.

You can use SHRINK in several other ways as well. If you simply type **shrink** after selecting a volume, DiskPart will reduce the volume by the maximum free space available on the volume. You can use the Nowait parameter to force DiskPart to return immediately while the shrinking process is still in progress. However, you shouldn't try to work with the volume in DiskPart until the shrink operation is complete.

Additionally, you can use the Minimum parameter to specify the minimum amount of space in megabytes to remove. When you specify a minimum reduction, however, DiskPart will either shrink the volume by at least that amount or the shrink will fail completely. In this example, I set the desired shrink value to 2,400 MB and the minimum shrink value to 1,200 MB:

```
shrink desired=2400 minimum=1200
```

Here DiskPart will attempt to shrink the volume by at least 1,200 MB. If DiskPart is unable to do this, DiskPart doesn't remove any space from the disk.

Extending Partitions or Volumes

The technique for extending partitions on basic disks and volumes on dynamic disks is the same. If you create a volume that's too small, you'll sometimes want to be able to extend it. You can extend volumes regardless of whether you are working with a basic disk or a dynamic disk. In extending a volume, you convert areas of unallocated space and add them to the existing volume. For spanned volumes on dynamic disks, the space can come from any available dynamic disk, not only those on which the volume was originally created. Thus you can combine areas of free space on multiple dynamic disks and use those areas to increase the size of an existing volume.

As with shrinking volumes, several limitations apply to extending volumes. You can extend formatted volumes when the file system is NTFS; you can't extend volumes that are formatted with FAT or FAT32. Although you can extend volumes that were not previously formatted, you can't extend striped volumes. You can't extend a system or boot volume, regardless of its configuration. Additionally, on basic disks, the free space must be on the same disk as the volume or partition you've selected and must also immediately follow that volume or partition. This means the free space must start at the next sector offset.

Follow these steps to extend a volume:

1. Invoke DiskPart by typing **diskpart** at the command prompt.
2. List the disks on the computer by typing **list disk,** and check the free space.
3. Select the disk you want to work with, such as disk 2, by typing **select disk 2**.
4. List the volumes on the selected disk by typing **list volume**.
5. Select the volume you want to work with. For instance, type **select volume 6**.
6. Extend the volume by typing **extend size=*n***

   where *n* is the amount of space to add in megabytes, such as

   ```
   DISKPART> extend size=1000
   ```

Note The size is rounded to the nearest cylinder boundary, which typically results in a slightly larger or smaller disk space being added. If no size is given, the volume is extended to fill the unallocated space on the disk.

Deleting Partitions

To change the configuration of a drive that's fully allocated, you might need to delete existing partitions. Deleting a partition removes the associated file system, and all data in the file system is lost. Before you delete a partition, therefore, you should back up any files and directories that the partition contains.

On a basic disk, you can delete the partition with focus using DELETE PARTITION. You cannot, however, use this command to delete the system or boot partition, or any partition that contains the active paging file or crash dump (memory dump). To see how DELETE PARTITION is used, consider the following example:

1. Invoke DiskPart by typing **diskpart** at the command prompt.
2. List the disks on the computer by typing **list disk** and pressing Enter. Select the basic disk you want to work with by typing **select disk** followed by the disk number.
3. List the partitions on the selected disk by typing **list partition**.
4. Select the partition to delete by typing **select partition** followed by the partition number, and then delete it by typing **delete partition**.

> **More Info** DiskPart allows you to delete only known data partitions. You can override this behavior if you are certain you know what you are doing. To do this, add the Override parameter to the DELETE PARTITION command.

The technique for deleting partitions on basic disks and deleting volumes on dynamic disks is *not* the same. Don't use the DELETE PARTITION command to delete volumes on a dynamic disk. Instead, use the DELETE VOLUME command as discussed in "Deleting Volumes" in Chapter 12, "Managing Volumes and RAID on Dynamic Disks."

Chapter 12

Managing Volumes and RAID on Dynamic Disks

When you work with dynamic disks, you create volumes instead of partitions. A volume is simply a disk section that you can use for storing data directly. Although you create volumes in much the same way as you create partitions, volumes have many additional capabilities. You can

- Create a volume on a single drive, called a *simple* volume.
- Extend volumes to fill empty space on a disk, which creates an *extended* volume.
- Create a single volume that spans multiple drives, called a *spanned* volume.
- Configure RAID (a redundant array of independent disks). Windows Server 2008 supports RAID-0, RAID-1, and RAID-5. Windows Vista supports only RAID-0.

Because volumes and RAID arrays are created on dynamic drives, they are accessible only by Windows 2000, Windows XP, Windows Vista, Windows Server 2003, and Windows Server 2008. So if you dual-boot a computer to an earlier version of Windows, the dynamic drives are unavailable. Over a network, however, dynamic drives can be accessed as you would access any other drive. This means that computers running earlier versions of Windows can access the drives over the network.

Obtaining Volume Information and Status

When you are working with DiskPart and want to check the status of partitions and volumes, you can use the LIST VOLUME command. As shown in the following example, LIST VOLUME lists the current statistics of all volumes, partitions, and logical drives on the computer:

```
DISKPART> list volume
Volume ### Ltr  Label        Fs     Type        Size     Status     Info
---------- ---  -----------  -----  ----------  -------  ---------  --------
Volume 0    N                        Removable      0 B  No Media
Volume 1    F   Blank Disc   CDUDF   DVD-ROM     2048 B  Healthy
Volume 2    J                        Removable      0 B  No Media
Volume 3    I                        Removable      0 B  No Media
Volume 4    L                        Removable      0 B  No Media
Volume 5    G                        DVD-ROM        0 B  No Media
Volume 6    E   Recovery     NTFS    Simple         9 GB Healthy
Volume 7    C                NTFS    Mirrored     457 GB Healthy    System
Volume 8    D                NTFS    Mirrored     457 GB Healthy
```

```
Volume 9   O         NTFS  RAID-5    466 GB Healthy
Volume 10  Q         NTFS  RAID-5    466 GB Healthy
Volume 11  P         NTFS  RAID-5    466 GB Healthy
Volume 12  K         NTFS  Simple    477 GB Healthy
```

As you can see, LIST VOLUME shows the following:

- **Volume ###** The number of the volume. You can type **select volume** *n* to work with the volume.
- **Ltr** The drive letter of the volume.
- **Label** The volume label.
- **Fs** The file system type, such as CDUDF, FAT, FAT32, or NTFS.
- **Type** The layout type. With dynamic disks, volume layout type tells you the configuration of the volume as simple, spanned, mirrored, striped, or RAID-5.
- **Size** The total storage size of the volume.
- **Status** The state of the volume, shown as Healthy, Failed Redundancy, and so on.
- **Info** Provides additional information related to the volume, such as whether the volume is the system volume.

One of the more important statistics provided is the volume status. Understanding the volume status is useful when you install new volumes or try to troubleshoot problems. Table 12-1 summarizes status values, which are primarily associated with dynamic volumes. In DiskPart, you can use the following commands to perform related tasks: ONLINE to attempt to bring a volume online, RECOVER to attempt recovery on disks and attempt to resynchronize, REPAIR to repair a failed RAID-5 member, and RESCAN to rescan the computer's disks and volumes.

Table 12-1 Understanding and Resolving Volume Status Issues

Status	Description	Resolution
Data Incomplete	Spanned volumes on a foreign disk are incomplete. You must have forgotten to add the other disks from the spanned volume.	Move over the disks that contain the rest of the spanned volume, and then import all the disks at one time.
Data Not Redundant	Fault-tolerant volumes on a foreign disk are incomplete (not redundant). You must have forgotten to add the other disks from a mirror or RAID-5 set.	Add the remaining disk(s), and then import all the disks at one time.

Table 12-1 Understanding and Resolving Volume Status Issues

Status	Description	Resolution
Failed	A disk-error status. The disk is inaccessible or damaged.	Ensure that the related dynamic disk is online. If necessary, rescan for volumes or try to bring the volume online. You can also attempt to recover the volume.
Failed Redundancy	A disk-error status. One of the disks in a mirror or RAID-5 set is offline.	Ensure that the related dynamic disk is online. If necessary, try to bring the volume online. You can also attempt to recover the volume. If the volume cannot be brought online, you might need to replace a failed mirror or repair a failed RAID-5 volume.
Formatting	A temporary status that indicates that the volume is being formatted.	The progress of the formatting is indicated as the percentage completed. On successful completion, the volume will be set to Healthy status.
Healthy	The normal volume status.	The volume doesn't have any known problems.
Healthy (At Risk)	Windows had problems reading from or writing to the physical disk on which the dynamic volume is located. This status appears when Windows encounters errors.	Ensure that the related dynamic disk is online. If necessary, rescan for volumes or try to bring the volume online. You can also attempt to recover the volume. If the disk continues to have this status or has this status periodically, the disk might be failing and you should back up all data on the disk.
Healthy (Unknown Partition)	Windows does not recognize the partition. This can occur because the partition is from a different operating system or is a manufacturer-created partition used to store system files.	No corrective action is necessary.
Initializing	A temporary status that indicates the disk is being initialized.	The drive status should change after a few seconds.

Table 12-1 Understanding and Resolving Volume Status Issues

Status	Description	Resolution
Regenerating	A temporary status that indicates that a mirrored volume is being added or imported, or data and parity for a RAID-5 volume are being regenerated.	Progress is indicated as the percentage completed. The volume should return to Healthy status.
Resynching	A temporary status that indicates that a mirror set is being resynchronized.	Progress is indicated as the percentage completed. The volume should return to Healthy status.
Stale Data	Data on foreign disks that are fault tolerant are out of sync.	Rescan the disks or attempt to resynchronize the mirrored or RAID-5 volumes, and then check the status. A new status should be displayed, such as Failed Redundancy.
Unknown	The volume cannot be accessed. It might have a corrupted boot sector.	The volume might have a boot sector virus. Check it with an up-to-date antivirus program. Rescan the disks or restart the computer, and then check the status.

Creating and Managing Simple Volumes

With dynamic disks, you can use DiskPart to create simple volumes. A simple volume is the most basic type of dynamic volume. Unlike partitions, a simple volume can fill an entire disk, or you can size a simple volume as appropriate for the computer you're configuring.

Creating Simple Volumes

Before you add a simple volume to a disk, you should assess the amount of free space on the disk and also check the current volume configuration. Follow these steps to perform these tasks:

1. Invoke DiskPart by typing **diskpart** at the command prompt.
2. List the disks on the computer and check the free space, as follows:

```
DISKPART> list disk

Disk ###  Status  Size     Free     Dyn  Gpt
--------  ------  -------  -------  ---  ---
Disk 0    Online  372 GB   0 B
Disk 1    Online  329 GB   204 GB    *
Disk 2    Online  337 GB   37 GB     *
```

In this example, disk 1 and disk 2 are formatted as dynamic disks (denoted by the asterisk in the Dyn column) using MBR partitioning (denoted by a blank entry in the Gpt column). Disk 1 has 204 gigabytes (GB) of free space and disk 2 has 37 GB of free space available.

Once you identify the disk you want to work with, you can create the simple volume using the command

```
create volume simple size=n disk=n
```

where *size=n* sets the size of the volume in megabytes (MB) and *disk=n* specifies the disk you want to work with.

After you create the volume, the volume will automatically have focus, meaning it will be selected. The volume will not yet have a drive letter or mount point. You must use the ASSIGN command to do this. Then to finalize the partition, you must also format it using the FORMAT command. These tasks are performed in the same way for volumes and partitions. See the sections of Chapter 11, "Partitioning Basic Disks," titled "Assigning Drive Letters or Mount Points" and "Formatting Partitions," respectively.

Extending Simple Volumes

If you find that you need more space on a simple volume, you can extend it in two ways. First, you can extend a simple volume within the same disk, creating what is called an *extended volume*. Or you can extend a simple volume onto other disks, creating what is called a *spanned volume*. In either case, the volume must be formatted as NTFS.

The steps you follow to extend a simple volume are as follows:

1. Invoke DiskPart by typing **diskpart** at the command prompt.
2. List the disks on the computer and check the free space, as follows:

   ```
   DISKPART> list disk
   ```

3. List the volumes on the computer, as follows:

   ```
   DISKPART> list volume
   ```

4. Select the volume you want to extend, such as volume 5:

   ```
   DISKPART> select volume 5
   ```

5. Extend the volume.
   - To extend the volume on the current disk, use the following command:

     ```
     DISKPART> extend size=n
     ```

     where *size=n* is the amount of space to add in megabytes. For example, you could extend the previously selected volume by 1,004 MB by using the command

     ```
     DISKPART> extend size=1004 disk=2
     ```

Note The size is rounded to the nearest cylinder boundary, which typically results in a slightly larger or smaller disk space being added.

- To extend the volume onto another dynamic disk, use the following command:

  ```
  DISKPART> extend size=n disk=n
  ```

  where *size=n* is the amount of space to add in megabytes and *disk=n* sets the disk onto which the volume should be extended. For example, if the volume were on disk 0 and you wanted to extend it onto disk 1, you would use the command

  ```
  DISKPART> extend size=2008 disk=1
  ```

  Here, you extend disk 0 onto disk 1. The size of the extended area on disk 1 is 2,008 MB.

Caution When extending volume sets, many things are not possible. You can't extend boot or system volumes. You can't extend volumes that use mirroring or striping (RAID-0, RAID-1, or RAID-5). You can't extend a volume onto more than 32 disks, either. Additionally, you can't extend FAT or FAT32 volumes; you must first convert them to NTFS.

Bringing Dynamic Disks Online

Dynamic disks are much more versatile than basic disks. You can easily resolve errors and return drives that have gone offline to service. You can also check for drive configuration changes and import disks moved from one computer to another.

As discussed in Chapter 10, "Configuring and Maintaining Disks," the LIST DISK command shows the status of each disk available on a system. If the status of a dynamic disk displays as Online (Errors) or Offline, you can often use the ONLINE command to correct the problem. Using DiskPart, simply designate the disk you want to work with, such as by typing **select disk 0**, and then by typing **online**. If the drive status doesn't change, you might need to reboot the computer. If a reboot still doesn't resolve the problem, check the drive, its controller, cables, and power supply to make sure everything is connected properly. ONLINE also resynchronizes mirrored or RAID-5 volumes.

If the drive configuration has changed or a disk has been added to the computer, you can use the RESCAN command to rescan all drives on the computer and to check for updates to the drive configuration. A rescan can sometimes resolve a problem with drives that show a status of Unreadable.

If you moved a dynamic disk from one computer to another, the disk might be marked as Foreign. A disk can also be marked as Foreign if it failed and you brought it back online. To bring the disk online using DiskPart, select the disk you want to work with, by typing **select disk 0** for example, and then typing **import**.

Deleting Volumes

You should not use the DELETE PARTITION command on a dynamic disk because this could delete all the dynamic volumes on the disk. If you want to delete a volume with focus on a dynamic disk, use the DELETE VOLUME command. As with DELETE PARTITION, you cannot use this command to delete the system or boot volume, or any volume that contains the active paging file or crash dump (memory dump).

To see how DELETE VOLUME is used, consider the following example:

1. Invoke DiskPart by typing **diskpart** at the command prompt.
2. List the volumes on the computer, as follows:

   ```
   DISKPART> list volume
   ```

3. Select the volume to delete and then delete it as follows:

   ```
   DISKPART> select volume 5
   DISKPART> delete volume
   ```

More Info By default, DiskPart allows you to delete only known data volumes. As with partitions, you can override this behavior by adding the Override parameter to the DELETE VOLUME command.

Providing Fault Tolerance with RAID on Dynamic Disks

With RAID, you can give important data increased protection from drive failures. RAID can be implemented at the hardware or software level. Hardware RAID is implemented and managed using the tools provided by the hardware vendor. Software RAID is implemented and managed by the operating system.

On dynamic disks, Windows Vista supports RAID-0 and Windows Server 2008 supports three software RAID levels:

- **RAID-0** Disk striping. Here, two or more volumes, each on a separate drive, are configured as a stripe set. Data is broken into blocks, called stripes, and then blocks of data are sequentially written to all drives in the stripe set. RAID-0 provides a speed and performance enhancement but is not fault-tolerant.
- **RAID-1** Disk mirroring or duplexing. Here, two volumes on two drives are configured identically. Data is written to both drives. If one drive fails, no data is lost because the other drive also contains the data. RAID-1 gives redundancy and better write performance than disk striping with parity (RAID-5).

- **RAID-5** Disk striping with parity. Here, you use three or more volumes, each on a separate drive, to create a stripe set with parity error checking. In the case of failure, data can be recovered. RAID-5 gives fault tolerance with less overhead than mirroring and better read performance than disk mirroring.

Implementing RAID-0: Disk Striping

With RAID-0, also known as disk striping, two or more volumes–each on a separate drive–are configured as a striped set. Data written to the striped set is separated into blocks that are called *stripes*. These stripes are written sequentially to all drives in the striped set. Although you can place volumes for a striped set on up to 32 drives, in most circumstances sets with two to five volumes offer the best performance improvements and beyond this the performance improvement decreases significantly.

Using RAID-0

One of the key reasons for using RAID-0 is speed improvement. Because data can be accessed on multiple disks using multiple drive heads, read performance improves considerably. However, it also increases the chances of catastrophic failure. If any hard disk drive in the striped set fails, the striped set can no longer be used and all data in the striped set is lost. To recover, you would need to re-create the striped set and restore the data from backups. Data backup and recovery is discussed in Chapter 16 of the *Windows Server 2008 Administrator's Pocket Consultant* (Microsoft Press, 2008).

When you create striped sets, you'll want to keep the following in mind:

- The boot and system volumes can't be part of a striped set. Don't use disk striping with these volumes.
- The overall size of the striped set is based on the smallest volume size. Because of this, you should use volumes that are approximately the same size.
- You can maximize performance by using disks that are on separate disk controllers. This allows the system to simultaneously access the drives.

Running the LIST DISK or DETAIL DISK command on a disk with RAID-0 shows a volume type of STRIPED. If you run the DETAIL VOLUME command on the striped volume, DiskPart shows you all the simple volumes that are part of the striped set.

A disk status of Missing appears any time a striped volume is broken. You can use the DETAIL DISK command on one of the remaining drives, which should show a status of Failed, indicating that the redundancy has failed. If you see a status of Failed but don't know which other disk was part of the striped set, you can track down the problem disk by running DETAIL DISK on each of the other disks on the computer. The status of the problem disk should appear as Missing.

Fixing the striped set typically involves removing the failed disk, replacing it with a new one, and then configuring the new disk to be part of a new striped set. To do this, you would run DiskPart, select the new disk, and then run CONVERT DYNAMIC to convert the disk type. Afterward, you would need to format the new disk and assign a drive letter. Then you would need to use DiskPart to remove the volumes on the drives that were part of the broken striped set and create a striped set using the command CREATE VOLUME STRIPE. When the process is complete, you should be able to select the striped volume and use LIST VOLUME to view its status. The status should show as Healthy.

> **Caution** All data is removed from the drives when you remove the volumes. You will need to re-create the data from backup. If you don't have a backup of the disks, don't overwrite the drives. You might be able to salvage some of the data by using third-party recovery utilities.

Configuring the Stripe Set

To implement RAID-0, follow these steps:

1. Invoke DiskPart by typing **diskpart** at the command prompt.
2. List the disks on the computer, check the free space, and ensure that the disks you want to work with are all configured as dynamic disks, as follows:

   ```
   DISKPART> list disk
   ```
3. Create the stripe set as follows:

   ```
   DISKPART> create volume stripe size=n disk=n,n,n,...
   ```

   where *size=n* is the amount of space in megabytes that the volume will use on each disk. If no size is given, DiskPart uses all the remaining free space on the smallest disk and then uses the same amount of space on the remaining disks. The parameter disk=n,n,n,... sets the disks onto which the volume should be striped. You need to use at least two dynamic disks.

Consider the following examples:

Create a striped volume on disks 0, 1, and 2 using all available space on the smallest disk and then using the same amount of space on the remaining disks:

```
create volume stripe disk=0,1,2
```

Create a striped volume on disks 0, 1, and 2 using 80 GB (81,920 MB) of space on each disk:

```
create volume stripe size=81920 disk=0,1,2
```

Note When you are combining software RAID with hardware RAID, you may find that you want to align the starting point for a volume or partition to the nearest alignment boundary to improve performance. You can do this with the Align parameter. Use the syntax **align=*n*,** where *n* is the number of kilobytes from the beginning of the disk to the closest alignment boundary, such as **align=64**. Keep in mind that the value is rounded up or down as appropriate to coincide with the closest cylinder boundary, which can change the final size of the partition or logical drive.

Implementing RAID-1: Disk Mirroring and Duplexing

With RAID-1, also known as disk mirroring, you use identically sized volumes on two different drives to create a redundant data set. Here the mirrored drives contain identical sets of information, which means you read data from the primary mirror only but write data to both drives. Because it is necessary to write the data twice, each mirrored drive often is given its own disk controller, which allows the data to be written simultaneously to both drives. When you use two disk controllers, the drives are said to be *duplexed*. Thus, the difference between disk mirroring and disk duplexing lies in whether there is one disk controller or two (and for the remainder of this section, I won't distinguish between the two).

Using RAID-1

One of the key reasons to use disk mirroring is that if one of the disks fails, the other disk can be used automatically for reading and writing data. You can also use the working drive to regenerate the failed drive onto the same or another disk. You'll need to break the mirror before you can fix it. To learn how, see the section of this chapter titled "Managing RAID and Recovering from Failure."

As you probably guessed, disk mirroring comes with a trade-off: Disk mirroring effectively cuts the amount of storage space in half. For example, to mirror a 750 GB drive, you need another 750 GB drive. That means you use 1,500 GB of space to store 750 GB of information.

Note Unlike disk striping, with disk mirroring you can mirror any type of simple volume. This means that you can mirror the boot and system volumes if you choose.

Running the LIST DISK or DETAIL DISK commands on a disk with RAID-1 shows a volume type of Mirrored. If you run the DETAIL VOLUME command on the mirrored volume, DiskPart shows details on both volumes in the mirrored set.

A disk status of Missing appears any time a mirrored volume is broken. You can use the DETAIL DISK command on one of the remaining disks, which should show a status of Failed Redundancy, indicating that the redundancy has failed. If you see a status of Failed Redundancy but don't know which other disk was part of the mirrored set, you can track down the problem drive by running DETAIL DISK on each of the other disks on the computer. The status of the problem disk should appear as Missing.

Fixing the mirrored set typically involves removing the failed disk, replacing it with a new one, and then configuring the new disk to be a part of the mirrored set. To do this, you would run DiskPart, select the new disk, and then run CONVERT DYNAMIC to convert the disk type. Afterward, you would need to break the existing mirror using the BREAK DISK command and then use the ADD DISK command, designating the new disk as the disk to add to the new mirrored set. When the process is complete, you should be able to select the mirrored volume and use the LIST VOLUME command to view its status, which should appear as Healthy.

Configuring Mirroring or Duplexing

To create a mirrored set, you select the simple volume that you want to mirror and then add a disk to use as the second drive in the mirrored set. The secondary drive must have unallocated space at least as large as the size of the selected volume. Follow these steps:

1. Invoke DiskPart by typing **diskpart** at the command prompt.
2. List the disks on the computer, check the free space, and ensure that the disks you want to work with are all configured as dynamic disks, as follows:

   ```
   DISKPART> list disk
   ```
3. Select the disk you want to mirror. In this example, you select disk 0:

   ```
   DISKPART> select disk 0
   ```
4. Add a disk to use as the second drive in the mirrored set. In this example, you add disk 1:

   ```
   DISKPART> add disk=1
   ```

When you do this, the operating system begins the mirror creation process and you'll see a status of Resynching on both volumes. If you'd prefer for DiskPart to wait until the volume finishes synchronizing before returning, you can use the Wait parameter. Additionally, as with disk striping, you can use the Align parameter to align the start of the volume or partition to the nearest alignment boundary.

Implementing RAID-5: Disk Striping with Parity

With RAID-5, known as disk striping with parity, you use a minimum of three hard disk drives to set up fault tolerance using identically sized volumes. One of the key reasons to use RAID-5 is that it protects a computer from a single disk failure. If two disks fail, the parity information isn't sufficient to recover the data, and you'll need to rebuild the striped set from backup.

Using RAID-5

You can think of RAID-5 as an enhanced version of RAID-0, in which you gain the performance benefits of striping and add fault tolerance. Thus, unlike RAID-0, the failure of a single drive won't bring down the entire drive set. Instead, the set continues to function with disk operations directed at the remaining volumes in the set. These remaining volumes can also be used to regenerate the striped set onto a new disk or the restored disk that you've recovered as discussed in the section of this chapter titled "Managing RAID and Recovering from Failure."

> **Caution** The boot and system volumes cannot be part of a striped set. Don't use disk striping with parity on these volumes.

Running the LIST DISK or DETAIL DISK command on a disk with RAID-5 shows a volume type of RAID-5. If you run the DETAIL VOLUME command on the RAID-5 volume, DiskPart shows you all the volumes that are part of the set.

A disk status of Missing appears whenever a RAID-5 volume is broken. You can use the DETAIL DISK command on one of the remaining drives, which should show a status of Failed Redundancy, indicating that the redundancy has failed. If you see a status of Failed Redundancy, but don't know which other disk was part of the RAID-5 set, you can track down the problem disk by running DETAIL DISK on each of the applicable disks in the RAID-5 set. The status on the problem disk should appear as Missing.

Fixing the RAID-5 set typically involves removing the failed disk, replacing it with a new one, and then configuring the new disk to be a part of the RAID-5 set. To do this, you would run DiskPart, select the new disk, and then run CONVERT DYNAMIC to convert the disk type. Afterward, you would select the RAID-5 volume using SELECT DISK and then run REPAIR DISK, designating the new disk as the disk to use. This re-creates the RAID-5 set and makes the new disk a member of the set. When the process is complete, you should be able to select the RAID-5 volume and use LIST VOLUME to view its status. The status should appear as Healthy.

Configuring Disk Striping with Parity

To implement RAID-5, select three dynamic disks with enough unallocated space to create the RAID set of the desired size. Follow these steps:

1. Invoke DiskPart by typing **diskpart** at the command prompt.
2. List the disks on the computer, check the free space, and ensure that the disks you want to work with are all configured as dynamic disks, as follows:

   ```
   DISKPART> list disk
   ```
3. Create the RAID-5 set as follows:

   ```
   DISKPART> create volume raid size=n disk=n,n,n,...
   ```

where size=n is the amount of space in megabytes that the volume set will use on each disk. If no size is given, DiskPart uses all the remaining free space on the smallest disk and then uses the same amount of space on the remaining disks. The parameter disk=*n*,*n*,*n*,... sets the disks for the RAID-5 set. You need to use at least three dynamic disks.

Consider the following examples:

Create a RAID-5 set on disks 2, 3, and 4 using all available space on the smallest disk and then using the same amount of space on the remaining disks:

```
create volume raid disk=2,3,4
```

Create a RAID-5 volume on disks 2, 3, and 4 using 80 GB (81,920 MB) of space on each disk:

```
create volume raid size=81920 disk=2,3,4
```

Note Additionally, as with disk striping and disk mirroring, you can use the Align parameter to align the start of the volume or partition to the nearest alignment boundary. However, you can't expand a RAID-5 set after you create it. Because of this, you should consider the setup carefully before you implement it.

Managing RAID and Recovering from Failure

You don't manage mirrored drives and stripe sets in the same way as you manage other types of volumes. If a mirrored drive or stripe set fails, it must be recovered in a specific way. If you want to stop using disk mirroring, you must break the mirrored set. If you want to stop using RAID-5, you must delete the entire volume set.

Breaking a Mirrored Set

Breaking a mirrored set is a standard procedure that you'll use when you want to stop using drive mirroring or when you need to rebuild the mirrored set. If you no longer want to mirror your drives, you can break the mirror and use the data on only one drive. This allows you to use the space on the other drive for a different purpose. If one of the mirrored drives in a set fails, disk operations continue using the remaining disk drive. To fix the mirror, you must first break the mirror set and then re-establish it.

Tip Although breaking a mirror doesn't delete the data in the set, you should always back up the data before breaking a mirrored set. This ensures that if you have problems, you can recover your data.

You can break a mirrored set by following these steps:

1. Invoke DiskPart by typing **diskpart** at the command prompt.
2. List the disks on the computer to determine which disks are part of the mirrored set, as follows:

   ```
   DISKPART> list disk
   ```

3. Break the mirror on the designated disk. The disk that you specify when breaking the mirror does not retain the drive letter or mount point. For example, if disks 0 and 1 are mirrored and you want users to continue using disk 0, you can break the mirror by typing

   ```
   DISKPART> break disk=1
   ```

   Once you break the mirror, you have two drives containing the same information. Only disk 0, however, has a usable drive letter or mount point. If you want to break the mirror, discard the duplicate information on the second disk, and return all of its space to the unallocated space, you can do this by adding the Nokeep parameter, such as

   ```
   DISKPART> break disk=1 nokeep
   ```

Resynchronizing and Repairing a Mirrored Set

When one of the drives in a mirrored set fails, the mirrored set will need to be repaired before mirroring can be restored. You do this by breaking the mirrored set and then re-establishing mirroring on a new drive, or the newly recovered drive if you've recovered the failed drive. Sometimes, however, you won't have an outright failure; rather, you'll have a case in which data is out of sync. In such a situation, one of the drives in the set has probably gone offline for some reason, and as a result data was written to only one of the drives.

To recover the mirrored set, you need to get both drives in the mirrored set online and the corrective action you take depends on the failed volume's status, as follows:

- If the status is Missing, Offline, or Healthy (At Risk), be sure that the drive has power and is connected properly. Afterward, start DiskPart and use the RESCAN command to attempt to detect the volume. Then use ONLINE to attempt to bring the disk online. The drive status should change to Regenerating and then to Healthy. If the volume doesn't return to Healthy status, try recovering the volume. If this doesn't work, try breaking the mirror and then adding the recovered disk to re-establish the mirror.
- If the status is Online (Errors), Stale Data, Failed, Failing, or Failed Redundancy, use the RECOVER command to refresh the state of the mirrored set, attempt recovery as necessary, and then resynchronize the mirrored volume. The drive status should change to Regenerating or Resynching and then to Healthy. If the

volume doesn't return to Healthy status, use BREAK to stop mirroring and then use ADD to re-establish the mirror on the recovered disk or a new disk.

- If one of the drives shows as Unreadable, use RESCAN to rescan the drives on the system. If the drive status doesn't change, you might need to reboot the computer.
- If one of the drives still won't come back online, break the mirror, designating the failed disk as the one to remove. Replace or repair the disk, and then use ADD to re-establish the mirror.

Real World The failure of a mirrored drive might prevent your system from booting. This usually happens when you're mirroring the system or boot volume and the primary mirror drive has failed. In this case, you need to modify the boot configuration data so that the secondary drive in the mirror set is used for startup. See Chapter 13 of the *Windows Server 2008 Administrator's Pocket Consultant*.

Repairing a RAID-0 Striped Set Without Parity

As discussed previously, RAID-0 is not fault-tolerant. If a drive that's part of a RAID-0 set fails, the entire striped set is unusable. Before you try to restore the striped set, you should repair or replace the failed drive. Once you do this, you will need to re-create the RAID-0 set and then recover the data it contained from backup.

Regenerating a RAID-5 Striped Set with Parity

RAID-5 allows you to recover the striped set if a single drive fails. You'll know that a drive has failed because the set's status will change to Failed Redundancy and the corrective action you take depends on the failed volume's status:

- If the status is Missing, Offline, or Healthy (At Risk), be sure that the drive has power and is connected properly. Afterward, start DiskPart and then use ONLINE to attempt to bring the volume online. The drive's status should change to Regenerating and then to Healthy. If the drive's status doesn't return to Healthy, try recovering the volume. If this doesn't work, you'll need to use the REPAIR command.
- If the status is Online (Errors), Stale Data, Failed, Failing, or Failed Redundancy, use the RECOVER command to refresh the state of the RAID-5 set, attempt recovery as necessary, and then resynchronize the set. The drive status should change to Regenerating or Resynching and then to Healthy. If the drive's status doesn't return to Healthy, you'll need to use the REPAIR command.
- If one of the drives shows as Unreadable, use RESCAN to rescan the drives on the system. If the drive status doesn't change, you might need to reboot the computer.

- If one of the drives still won't come back online, you need to use the REPAIR command.

You can repair RAID-5 using the REPAIR command. If possible, you should back up the data before you perform this procedure. This ensures that if you have problems, you can recover your data. Follow these steps to resolve problems with the RAID-5 set:

1. Invoke DiskPart by typing **diskpart** at the command prompt.
2. List the disks on the computer to confirm that the RAID-5 set failed, as follows:

   ```
   DISKPART> list disk
   ```

3. Remove and replace the failed drive if necessary and possible. Then specify the new drive that should be part of the RAID set using the REPAIR command as follows:

   ```
   DISKPART> repair disk=n
   ```

   where n specifies the dynamic disk that will replace the failed RAID-5 drive. Keep in mind the specified disk must have free space equal to or larger than the total size used on the failed RAID disk. Additionally, you can use the Align parameter to align the start of a volume or partition on the new volume to the nearest alignment boundary.

Part IV

Windows Active Directory Administration Using the Command Line

In this part:

Chapter 13

Core Active Directory Services Administration

One of the more important areas of Windows networking has to do with Active Directory Domain Services. Active Directory is an extensible and scalable directory service that provides a network-wide database for storing account and resource information. Using Active Directory, you have a consistent way to name, describe, locate, manage, and secure information for resources. This means that you can use Active Directory to work with user, group, and computer accounts as easily as you can use it to work with applications, files, printers, and other types of resources. You can use Active Directory to help you manage the network infrastructure, perform system administration, and control the user environment.

Active Directory is only available in Windows domains with domain controllers. A *domain controller* is a Windows server on which you've installed and configured the Active Directory Domain Services role. Active Directory acts as the central authority for security; unlike the Security Accounts Manager (SAM), however, Active Directory also acts as the integration point for bringing together diverse systems. Active Directory consolidates management tasks into a single set of Windows-based management tools, and their counterparts are the directory service command-line tools discussed in this chapter.

> **Note** To manage Active Directory from a computer running the Business, Enterprise, or Ultimate edition of Windows Vista, you must install the Microsoft Remote Server Administration Tools for Windows Vista. See the section "Using the Microsoft Remote Server Administration Tools for Windows Vista" in Chapter 1, "Overview of the Windows Command Line," for more information.

Controlling Active Directory from the Command Line

A basic understanding of Active Directory and its structures is all that you need to take advantage of the many command-line tools that are available to manage Active Directory. Microsoft designed Active Directory to use Domain Name System (DNS) as a naming system. With DNS, you organize network resources using a hierarchical structure that matches how you manage the resources. This hierarchy of domains, or domain tree, is the backbone of the Active Directory environment and looks much like a directory structure used with files. Another name for such a hierarchy or tree is a *namespace*. Every organization that uses Active Directory domains has an Active Directory hierarchy or namespace.

Understanding Domains, Containers, and Objects

The first Active Directory domain that you create is the *root* of the tree and the *parent* of all domains below it. Domains below the root are called *child domains*. Suppose, for example, that the root domain is cpandl.com. You can then decide to break down your organization geographically or functionally into child domains. Grouping geographically, you might have seattle.cpandl.com, ny.cpandl.com, and la.cpandl.com child domains. Grouping functionally, you might have sales.cpandl.com, support.cpandl.com, and tech.cpandl.com child domains. The key here is that child domains must have a name that extends from the parent domain. If the name doesn't extend from the parent domain, the domain is in a separate namespace. For example, microsoft.com, msn.com, and hotmail.com are all in different namespaces from cpandl.com.

You can create additional levels within the namespace if you choose. Under the la.cpandl.com child domain, you might have sales.la.cpandl.com, tech.la.cpandl.com, and support.la.cpandl.com. If this isn't enough, you can add another level, and then another and another to the namespace. Keep in mind that Active Directory manages the relationships within the tree and creates the appropriate trust relationships between domains.

In Active Directory, trusts are automatically two-way and transitive. Simply creating a child domain, such as tech.la.cpandl.com, creates a two-way trust relationship between tech.la.cpandl.com and la.cpandl.com. The trust continues up and down the tree as well, meaning that because la.cpandl.com trusts cpandl.com, tech.la.cpandl.com has an automatic trust relationship with cpandl.com, as well as with all the other domains in the same namespace.

Active Directory uses *objects* to represent network resources, such as users, groups, and computers. It also uses specialized objects called *containers* to organize network resources according to geographic, business, or functional needs. Typically, containers are used to group objects that have similar attributes. For example, you might want to apply a specific set of permissions to all engineers, and putting these users together in the same container will make this easier.

Each container represents a grouping of objects, and each individual resource is represented by a unique Active Directory object. The most common type of Active Directory container is an organizational unit, or OU. Objects placed in an OU can only come from the related domain. For example, OUs associated with tech.la.cpandl.com contain objects for this domain only. This means you can't add objects from support.la.cpandl.com, la.cpandl.com, or tech.ny.cpandl.com to these containers.

Each Active Directory object class, such as container, user, group, or printer, is assigned a set of attributes that describes the individual resource. For example, user objects have attributes that describe user accounts including contact information along with their permissions and privileges. This means that user object attributes are related to first names, last names, display names, telephone numbers, e-mail addresses, passwords, and so on.

Because each object within Active Directory is really a record in a database, it is possible to expand the attribute set to meet the needs of individual organizations. This allows you to add custom attributes to help describe objects. For example, you can add an attribute to include an employee's identification code.

Understanding Logical and Physical Structures in Active Directory

So far we've talked about Active Directory structures that are used to organize directory data logically, including domains, subdomains, and OUs. You use these structures to organize Active Directory according to business or functional needs. You can also use them to specify geographic breakdowns, such as would occur if you had ny.cpandl.com, la.cpandl.com, and seattle.cpandl.com domains.

Insofar as Active Directory is concerned, however, domains, subdomains, and OUs have no mapping to the real world–even if you create geographic breakdowns for domains or OUs. They are simply locations within the directory where related data is stored and, as far as Active Directory is concerned, they could all have one physical location, which is how Active Directory sees things until you tell the directory about the physical structures associated with your logical breakdowns of domains, subdomains, and OUs.

In the real world, any of these logical structures could span more than one physical location. It doesn't matter whether we are talking about different floors in a single building, different buildings entirely, or different cities; these are all different physical locations. To tell Active Directory about these multiple locations, you must define subnets and sites. A *subnet* is a network group with a specific IP address range and network mask. A *site* is a group of one or more subnets that maps your network's physical structure. Because site mappings are independent from logical domain structures, there's no necessary relationship between a network's physical structure and its logical domain structure.

You can create multiple sites within a single domain and you can create a single site that serves multiple domains. For example, if you group subdomains geographically, you might have seattle.cpandl.com, ny.cpandl.com, and la.cpandl.com child domains and corresponding sites named Seattle-Site, NY-Site, and LA-Site. But if your organization has only one office and you group subdomains functionally, you might have sales.cpandl.com, support.cpandl.com, and tech.cpandl.com child domains and a single site called Main-Site.

Understanding Distinguished Names

Every object in Active Directory has an associated distinguished name, or DN. The DN uniquely identifies the object by its common name and its location within the namespace. An object's common name is the plain-English name given to the object when you created it. You identify an object's common name using CN=*Name*, where *Name* is the common name of the object, such as:

```
CN=William Stanek
```

The common name is also referred to as an object's relative DN (RDN). This refers to the fact that this portion of the object's full name relates to its location in Active Directory. An object's location is determined by the names of the container objects and domains that contain the object. You identify OU containers using OU= and domain components using DC=. Each level within the domain tree is broken out as a separate domain component. Consider the following example:

```
OU=Engineering, DC=ny, DC=tech, DC=cpandl, DC=com
```

Here, you specify the DN for the Engineering OU in the ny.tech.cpandl.com domain. You use commas to separate each name component, and the name components go from the lowest level of the tree to the highest level (that is, from the OU that contains the actual object you want to work with), to the child domain, to the parent domain, and finally to the root domain.

What makes the DN so important is that it specifies the exact location of an object; and the DN is what Active Directory uses to search for, retrieve, and manage objects within the database. Knowing the DN for an object allows you to perform these same tasks.

All objects have associated containers and domain components. Although the container for users, computers, groups, and other types of objects typically is an OU, this isn't always the case, because Active Directory includes several default containers where objects can be stored. These default containers are identified by their common name using CN= and include

- **Builtin** A container for built-in security groups
- **Computers** The default container for member servers and workstations in a domain
- **ForeignSecurityPrincipals** A container for objects from a trusted external domain
- **Users** The default container for users

Note The Domain Controllers container is created as an OU. This means you would use OU=Domain Controllers as the name identifier.

Knowing this, you can identify an object in any of these containers. For example, if you wanted to identify an object in the Users container for the tech.cpandl.com domain, you would use

```
CN=Users,DC=tech,DC=cpandl,DC=com
```

If the object is the user account for William Stanek, the complete DN would be

```
CN=William Stanek,CN=Users,DC=tech,DC=cpandl,DC=com
```

If the user account is later moved to the Engineering OU, its DN would become

```
CN=William Stanek,OU=Engineering,DC=tech,DC=cpandl,DC=com
```

Getting Started with the Active Directory Command-Line Tools

Once you know the basic structures of Active Directory and can identify the DN for the objects you want to use, you are ready to control Active Directory from the command line. You'll find that the key advantage of doing so is in the additional flexibility you gain. You can, in fact, perform many tasks easily from the command line that are either much more difficult to perform in the graphical tools or simply cannot be performed. For example, you might search for all computer accounts that have been inactive for more than a week and then disable them. Or you might modify the properties of multiple user accounts at the same time using a single command.

When you are working with Windows domains, Windows Server 2008 includes a set of command-line tools that you can use to manage Active Directory. With the Business, Ultimate, or Enterprise editions of Windows Vista, you can use the Active Directory tools if you've installed the Windows Server 2008 Administration Tools Pack. These tools include

- **DSADD** Adds objects to Active Directory
- **DSGET** Displays properties of objects registered in Active Directory
- **DSMOD** Modifies properties of objects that already exist in Active Directory
- **DSMOVE** Moves a single object to a new location within a single domain or renames the object without moving it
- **DSQUERY** Finds objects in Active Directory using search criteria
- **DSRM** Removes objects from Active Directory

Each of the various command-line utilities is designed to work with a specific set of objects in Active Directory. Table 13-1 provides an overview of the utilities and the objects they are designed to work with.

Table 13-1 Active Directory Command-Line Utilities and the Objects They Work With

Object	Dsquery	Dsget	Dsadd	Dsmod
Computer	Yes	Yes	Yes	Yes
Contact	Yes	Yes	Yes	Yes
Group	Yes	Yes	Yes	Yes
Partition	Yes	Yes	No	Yes
Quota	Yes	Yes	Yes	Yes
Server	Yes	Yes	No	Yes
Site	Yes	Yes	No	No
Subnet	Yes	Yes	No	No
User	Yes	Yes	Yes	Yes
OU	Yes	Yes	Yes	Yes

In most cases, Active Directory objects are manipulated with a set of parameters specific to the type of object you are working with and the subcommand name used to access these parameters is the same as the object name. For example, if you wanted to add a computer to the domain, you would use DSADD COMPUTER and its related parameters. If you wanted to add a user account to the domain, you would use DSADD USER and its related parameters.

> **Note** DSMOVE and DSRM aren't listed in the table because they are designed to work with any object in the directory. You move or remove objects based on their DNs. In addition, by using an asterisk (*) as the object name for DSQUERY, you can find any objects in the directory with criteria that match your query.

Making Directory Queries Using the DSQUERY Command

You use the DSQUERY command to search Active Directory for objects matching a specific set of criteria. For instance, you could search for all computer accounts that start with "D" or all user accounts that are disabled and DSQUERY would return a list of objects that match the criteria.

DSQUERY Subcommands and Syntax

You make directory queries using the following subcommands and command-line syntaxes:

- **DSQUERY COMPUTER** Searches for computer accounts matching criteria you've specified

```
dsquery computer [{StartNode | forestroot | domainroot}]
[-o {dn | rdn | samid}] [-scope {subtree | onelevel | base}]
[-name Name] [-desc Description] [-samid SAMName]
[-inactive NumberOfWeeks] [-stalepwd NumberOfDays] [-disabled]
[{-s Server | -d Domain}] [-u UserName] [-p {Password | *}] [-q] [-r]
[-gc] [-limit NumberOfObjects] [{-uc | -uco | -uci}]
```

- **DSQUERY CONTACT** Searches for contacts matching criteria you've specified

```
dsquery contact [{StartNode | forestroot | domainroot}]
[-o {dn | rdn}] [-scope {subtree | onelevel | base}] [-name Name]
[-desc Description] [{-s Server | -d Domain}] [-u UserName]
[-p {Password | *}] [-q] [-r] [-gc] [-limit NumberOfObjects]
[{-uc | -uco | -uci}]
```

- **DSQUERY GROUP** Searches for group accounts matching criteria you've specified

```
dsquery group [{StartNode | forestroot | domainroot}]
[-o {dn | rdn | samid}] [-scope {subtree | onelevel | base}]
[-name Name] [-desc Description] [-samid SAMName]
[{-s Server / -d Domain}] [-u UserName] [-p {Password | *}] [-q] [-r]
[-gc] [-limit NumberOfObjects] [{-uc | -uco | -uci}]
```

- **DSQUERY OU** Searches for organizational units matching criteria you've specified

```
dsquery ou [{StartNode | forestroot | domainroot}] [-o {dn | rdn }]
[-scope {subtree | onelevel | base}] [-name Name] [-desc Description]
[{-s Server | -d Domain}] [-u UserName] [-p {Password | *}] [-q]
[-r] [-gc] [-limit NumberOfObjects] [{-uc | -uco | -uci}]
```

- **DSQUERY PARTITION** Searches for Active Directory partitions matching criteria you've specified

```
dsquery partition [-o {dn | rdn}] [-part Filter]
[-desc Description] [{-s Server | -d Domain}]
[-u UserName] [-p {Password | *}] [-q] [-r] [-limit NumberOfObjects]
[{-uc | -uco | -uci}]
```

- **DSQUERY QUOTA** Searches for object quotas matching criteria you've specified

```
dsquery quota {domainroot | ObjectDN} [-o {dn | rdn}] [-acct Name]
[-qlimit Filter] [-desc Description] [{-s Server | -d Domain}]
[-u UserName] [-p {Password | *}] [-q] [-r] [-limit NumberOfObjects]
[{-uc | -uco | -uci}]
```

- **DSQUERY SERVER** Searches for domain controllers matching criteria you've specified

```
dsquery server [-o {dn | rdn}] [-forest] [-domain DomainName]
[-site SiteName] [-name Name] [-desc Description]
[-hasfsmo {schema | name | infr | pdc | rid}] [-isgc]
[-isreadonly] [{-s Server | -d Domain}] [-u UserName]
[-p {Password | *}] [-q] [-r] [-gc] [-limit NumberOfObjects]
[{-uc | -uco | -uci}]
```

- **DSQUERY SITE** Searches for Active Directory sites matching criteria you've specified

  ```
  dsquery site [-o {dn | rdn}] [-name Name] [-desc Description]
  [{-s Server | -d Domain}] [-u UserName] [-p {Password | *}]
  [-q] [-r] [-gc] [-limit NumberOfObjects] [{-uc | -uco | -uci}]
  ```

- **DSQUERY SUBNET** Searches for subnet objects matching criteria you've specified

  ```
  dsquery subnet [-o {dn | rdn}] [-name Name] [-desc Description]
  [-loc Location] [-site SiteName] [{-s Server | -d Domain}]
  [-u UserName] [-p {Password | *}] [-q] [-r] [-gc]
  [-limit NumberOfObjects] [{-uc | -uco | -uci}]
  ```

- **DSQUERY USER** Searches for user accounts matching criteria you've specified

  ```
  dsquery user [{StartNode | forestroot | domainroot}]
  [-o {dn | rdn | upn | samid}] [-scope {subtree | onelevel | base}]
  [-name Name] [-namep namephonetic] [-desc Description] [-upn UPN]
  [-samid SAMName] [-inactive NumberOfWeeks] [-stalepwd NumberOfDays]
  [-disabled] [{-s Server | -d Domain}] [-u UserName]
  [-p {Password | *}] [-q] [-r] [-gc] [-limit NumberOfObjects]
  [{-uc | -uco | -uci}]
  ```

- **DSQUERY *** Searches for any Active Directory objects matching criteria you've specified

  ```
  dsquery * [{StartNode | forestroot | domainroot}]
  [-scope {subtree | onelevel | base}] [-filter LDAPFilter]
  [-attr {AttributeList | *}] [-attrsonly] [-l]
  [{-s Server | -d Domain}] [-u UserName] [-p {Password | *}]
  [-q] [-r] [-gc] [-limit NumberOfObjects] [{-uc | -uco | -uci}]
  ```

At first glance, the syntax is almost overwhelming. Don't let this put you off of using DSQUERY. Most DSQUERY subcommands share a standard syntax and include only a few extensions to the standard syntax that are specific to the type of object with which you are working. The best way to learn the DSQUERY subcommands is to dive right in. So here goes.

Searching Using Names, Descriptions, and SAM Account Names

Regardless of the other parameters you use, the search parameters should include the name, description, or SAM account name on which you want to search. When you type the –Name parameter, you search for the specified type of object whose name matches the given value. You can use an asterisk as a wildcard to make matches using partial names; for example, typing **–name Will*** to match *William Stanek*. A simple search on a name looks like this:

```
dsquery user -name Will*
```

The resulting output from this query is the DN of any matching user account or accounts, such as

```
"CN=William R. Stanek,CN=Users,DC=cpandl,DC=com"
```

That's all there is to a basic search. And you only had to use one parameter to get the results you needed.

> **Note** Keep in mind that with users, the –Name parameter searches on the Display Name as listed in the user's properties dialog box. In this example, the account display name is William R. Stanek. With other types of objects, this would be the value in the Name field on the General tab in the object's associated Properties dialog box.

The asterisk can appear in any part of the search criteria. If you know a user's last name but not the user's first name, you can search on the last name, such as

```
dsquery user -name *Stanek
```

You can also search using a partial beginning and ending of a name, such as

```
dsquery user -name W*Stanek
```

When you type the **-desc** parameter, you search for the specific type of object whose description matches the given value. Use an asterisk as a wildcard to make matches using partial descriptions, such as typing **-desc Eng*** to match Engineering Workstation. Consider the following example:

```
dsquery computer -desc Server*
```

The resulting output from this query is the DN of any matching computer account or accounts, such as

```
"CN=CORPSVR02,OU=Domain Controllers,DC=cpandl,DC=com"
```

> **Note** The –Desc parameter searches on the Description field as listed in the object's associated properties dialog box. In the previous example, the computer account description began with the word *Server*.

When you use the –Samid parameter, you search for the specific type of object whose SAM account name matches the given value. Use an asterisk as a wildcard to make matches using partial SAM account names, such as typing **-samid wr*** to match *wrstanek*.

> **Note** In the user's properties dialog box, the SAM account name is listed on the Account tab as the User Logon Name. For computers and groups, the SAM account name is the same as the related account name.

Setting Logon and Run As Permissions for Searches

By default when you use DSQUERY you are connected to a domain controller in your logon domain. You can connect to a specific domain controller in any domain in the forest by using the –S parameter. Follow the –S parameter with the DNS name of the server, such as

```
-s corpdc01.cpandl.com
```

Here, you are connecting to the corpdc01 domain controller in the cpandl.com domain.

> **Note** Technically, you don't have to use the fully qualified domain name (DNS name) of the server. You can use only the server name if you want. However, this slows the search because Active Directory must perform a DNS lookup to obtain the full name and then make the query.

Rather than connect to a specific domain controller in a domain, you can connect to any available domain controller. To do this, you can use the –D parameter. Follow the parameter with the DNS name of the domain, such as

```
-d tech.cpandl.com
```

Here, you connect to any available domain controller in the tech.cpandl.com domain. Keep in mind that you can't use the –S and the –D parameters together. This means you either connect to a specific domain controller or any available domain controller in a given domain.

As with many other types of commands, you can authenticate yourself if necessary by specifying a user name and password. To do this, you use the following parameters:

```
-u [Domain\]User [-p Password]
```

where Domain is the optional domain name in which the user account is located, *User* is the name of the user account whose permissions you want to use, and *Password* is the optional password for the user account. If you don't specify the domain, the current domain is assumed. If you don't provide the account password, you are prompted for the password.

To see how these parameters can all be used together, consider the following examples:

Connect to the corpsvr02 domain controller in the tech.cpandl.com domain using the Wrstanek user account in the cpandl logon domain and search for a user account whose display name ends with Stanek:

```
dsquery user -name *Stanek -s corpsvr02.tech.cpandl.com -u
cpandl\wrstanek
```

Connect to any domain controller in the tech.cpandl.com domain using the Wrstanek user account in the cpandl logon domain and search for a user account whose display name begins with Will:

```
dsquery user -name Will* -d tech.cpandl.com -u cpandl\wrstanek
```

Setting the Start Node, Search Scope, and Object Limit

In the command syntax, the start node is denoted by {*StartNode* | **forestroot** | **domainroot**} or it may include *ObjectDN*. This specifies the node where the search will start. You can specify the forest root (type **forestroot**), domain root (type **domainroot**), or a node's DN (*StartNode*), such as: **"CN=Users,DC=cpandl,DC=com"**. If you specify by typing **forestroot**, the search is done using the global catalog. The default value is **domainroot**. This means that the search begins in the top container for the logon domain for the user account you are using. Some subcommands can be passed the actual DN of the object you want to work with (*ObjectDN*), such as: **"CN=William Stanek,CN=Users,DC=cpandl,DC=com"**.

> **Note** You may have noticed that I'm using double-quotes to enclose both object DNs. This is a good technique because it is required if the DN contains a space, as is the case for the second object DN used.

When you want to perform exhaustive searches, you will want to specify a node's DN, and the real value of doing so becomes apparent when you want to return complete object sets. You can, for example, return a list of all objects of a specific type in a specific container simply by specifying the start node to use and not specifying –Name, –Desc, or –Samid parameters.

To see how start nodes can be used, consider the following examples:

Return a list of all computer accounts in the domain:

```
dsquery computer "DC=cpandl,DC=com"
```

Return a list of all computer accounts in the Computers container:

```
dsquery computer "CN=Computers,DC=cpandl,DC=com"
```

Return a list of all computers in the Domain Controllers OU:

```
dsquery computer "OU=Domain Controllers,DC=cpandl,DC=com"
```

Return a list of all users in the domain:

```
dsquery user "DC=cpandl,DC=com"
```

Return a list of all users in the Users container:

```
dsquery user "CN=Users,DC=cpandl,DC=com"
```

Return a list of all users in the Tech OU:

```
dsquery user "OU=Tech,DC=cpandl,DC=com"
```

In addition to being able to specify the start node, you can specify the scope for the search. The search scope is denoted by {–scope **subtree** | **onelevel** | **base**} in the command syntax. By default, the **subtree** search scope is used, which means the scope is the **subtree** rooted at the start node. For **domainroot**, this means the search scope is the entire domain. For **forestroot**, this means the search scope is the entire forest. For a specific container, this means the search scope is the specified container and any child containers. For example if the start node is set as "OU=Tech,DC=cpandl, DC=com", Active Directory would search the Tech OU and any OUs within it.

You use a value of **onelevel** to set the scope for the specified start node and its immediate children. With **domainroot**, for example, this would mean that the domain and its top-level containers and OUs would be included. However, if any of the OUs contained additional (child) OUs these would not be searched.

If you use a value of **base**, this sets the scope to the single object represented by the start node. For example, you would only search the specified OU and not its child OUs.

> **Note** **subtree** is the only valid value for the scope when **forestroot** is set as the start node.

To see how search scopes can be used, consider the following examples:

Search the Tech OU and any OUs below it for computer accounts:

```
dsquery computer "OU=Tech,DC=cpandl,DC=com"
```

> **Note** The default scope is for a subtree, which means **–scope subtree** is implied automatically.

Search only the Tech OU for computer accounts:

```
dsquery computer "OU=Tech,DC=cpandl,DC=com" -scope base
```

Search the Tech OU as well as OUs immediately below it for computer accounts:

```
dsquery computer "OU=Tech,DC=cpandl,DC=com" -scope onelevel
```

Another optional parameter you can use is –Limit. This parameter sets the maximum number of objects to return in the search results. By default, if this parameter is not specified, the first 100 results are displayed. If you want to set a different limit, follow the parameter with the number of objects to return. For example, if you wanted only the first 10 results to be displayed, you can type **–limit 10**. To remove the limit and have all matching results displayed, you use a value of 0, typing **–limit 0**, for example.

> **Tip** In a large organization where there are potentially thousands of objects, you shouldn't remove the limit. Instead, set a specific limit on the number of objects that can be returned or simply accept the default. This will ensure that your queries don't unnecessarily burden the domain controller you are working with.

Setting the Output Format for Names

With DSQUERY, you can set the output format for the name values returned as well as the format for individual characters. In the command syntax, the output format for names is denoted by **–o** followed by one of these elements: {dn | rdn | upn | samid}. By default, the output format is as a DN (designated as **–o dn**), such as **"CN=William R. Stanek,CN=Users,DC=cpandl,DC=com"**. You may also be able to specify the output format as a relative DN (by typing **–o rdn**), user principal name (by typing **–o upn**), or SAM account name (by typing **–o samid**).

The RDN is the common name of the object, taken from the lowest level name part of the DN. With users, the RDN is the same as the Display Name as listed in the associated properties dialog box. With other types of objects, this would be the value in the Name field on the General tab in the object's associated properties dialog box. Some examples of RDNs include

- "William R. Stanek"
- "CORPSVR01"
- "Administrators"

UPNs are applicable only to user accounts. In Active Directory, there is an actual field with this name, which is used for logon and authentication. In the user's properties dialog box, you'll find the user logon name and logon domain on the Account tab. An example of a UPN is wrstanek@cpandl.com. Here, wrstanek is the logon name and @cpandl.com is the logon domain information.

The SAM account name applies to users, computers, and groups. Again, there is an actual field with this name in Active Directory but you can navigate the properties dialog to find it as well. For users, the SAM account name is the pre–Windows 2000 account name as designated on the Account tab of the related properties dialog box. For groups, the SAM account name is the same as the value listed in the name field on the General tab. For computers, the SAM account name is the same as the value listed in the name field on the General tab with a dollar sign ($) as a suffix.

> **Note** The dollar sign ($) is part of the actual computer account name but is normally hidden and isn't referenced. Active Directory uses $ to allow you to have a user account and a computer account with the same name. This allows, for example, the user JAMESW to have a computer named JAMESW, which wasn't possible with pre–Windows 2000 computers.

To learn more about name formats, consider the following examples:

Return the RDN for computers matching the search criteria:

```
dsquery computer -name corp* -o rdn
```

Return the SAM account name for the users matching the search criteria:

```
dsquery user -name Wi* -o samid
```

Return the UPN for the users matching the search criteria:

```
dsquery user "OU=Tech,DC=cpandl,DC=com" -o upn
```

Return the DN for the users matching the search criteria:

```
dsquery user "CN=Users,DC=cpandl,DC=com"
```

> **Note** The default format is as a DN, which means **–o dn** is implied automatically.

Using DSQUERY with Other Active Directory Command-Line Tools

Because DSQUERY returns the DN of matching objects, the result set it returns is useful for piping as input to other Active Directory command-line utilities. Consider the following example where you search for all user accounts whose names begin with *Willia*:

```
dsquery user -name Willia*
```

The resulting output from this query is the DN of any matching account or accounts, such as

```
"CN=William R. Stanek,CN=Users,DC=cpandl,DC=com"
```

You could then pipe the result set as input for DSGET USER to display a list of groups of which this user is a member, such as

```
dsquery user -name Willia* | dsget user -memberof -expand
```

The resulting output would show the group memberships according to their DNs, such as

```
"CN=Domain Admins,CN=Users,DC=cpandl,DC=com"
"CN=Enterprise Admins,CN=Users,DC=cpandl,DC=com"
"CN=Administrators,CN=Builtin,DC=cpandl,DC=com"
"CN=Domain Users,CN=Users,DC=cpandl,DC=com"
"CN=Users,CN=Builtin,DC=cpandl,DC=com"
```

Searching for Problem User and Computer Accounts

DSQUERY USER and DSQUERY COMPUTER include several syntax extensions designed to help you search for problem accounts. You can use the –Disabled parameter to find accounts that have been disabled. To search the entire domain for disabled user accounts, type **dsquery user –disabled**.

The resulting output shows any computer accounts that have been disabled according to their DN, such as

```
"CN=Guest,CN=Users,DC=cpandl,DC=com"
"CN=SUPPORT_456945a0,CN=Users,DC=cpandl,DC=com"
"CN=krbtgt,CN=Users,DC=cpandl,DC=com"
```

Another very useful command option is –Stalepwd. This option lets you search for accounts that have not changed their password for at least the number of days specified. So for instance, you could search for all user accounts whose passwords haven't been changed for at least 15 days by typing **dsquery user –stalepwd 15**.

The resulting output is a list of users by DNs:

```
"CN=Administrator,CN=Users,DC=cpandl,DC=com"
"CN=Guest,CN=Users,DC=cpandl,DC=com"
"CN=SUPPORT_456945a0,CN=Users,DC=cpandl,DC=com"
"CN=krbtgt,CN=Users,DC=cpandl,DC=com"
"CN=William R. Stanek,CN=Users,DC=cpandl,DC=com"
"CN=Howard Smith,CN=Users,DC=cpandl,DC=com"
```

Real World You can set password policies that require users to change passwords regularly, as discussed in Chapter 10 of the *Windows Server 2008 Administrator's Pocket Consultant* (Microsoft Press, 2008). These policies only apply when users log on to the domain. If a user is on vacation or otherwise unavailable, the last time the password changed could exceed the limit (but normally the user would have to change his password on the next login). Most disabled accounts will also show up on your stale password list.

Finally, you might also want to search for computer or user accounts that have been inactive for at least the number of weeks specified. An inactive account is one that hasn't logged on to the domain within the specified time period. For example, if you wanted to find out which user accounts haven't logged on to the domain for at least two weeks, you could type **dsquery user –inactive 2**.

Generally, users don't log on to the domain because they are out of the office, which means they could be on vacation, sick, or working off-site. With computer accounts, being inactive means the computers have been shut down or disconnected from the network. For example, if a user goes on vacation and takes her laptop with her but doesn't connect to the office remotely while away, the related computer account would be inactive for that period of time.

Renaming and Moving Objects

Renaming and moving objects within a domain is handled with the DSMOVE command. Why one command instead of two? Because when you rename an object, you actually move it from its current DN to a new DN. Remember, a DN has two parts: a common name or RDN, and a location.

The syntax for DSMOVE is as follows:

```
dsmove ObjectDN [-newname NewName] [-newparent ParentDN]
[{-s Server | -d Domain}] [-u UserName] [-p {Password | *}] [-q]
[{-uc | -uco | -uci}]
```

To rename a user, computer, group, or other Active Directory object, you must specify the object's DN and then use the –Newname parameter to specify the new relative name. You could rename a user object from William Stanek to William R. Stanek, by typing **dsmove "CN=William Stanek,OU=Tech, DC=cpandl,DC=Com" –newname "William R. Stanek"**.

To move a user, computer, group, or other Active Directory object within a domain, you must specify the object's current DN and then use the –Newparent parameter to specify the new location or parent DN of the object. Suppose, for instance, that you want to move a user account from the Tech OU to the Engineering OU. Here, you specify the object's DN, such as **"CN=William Stanek,OU=Tech,DC=cpandl, DC=com"**, and provide the DN for the new location, such as **"OU=Engineering, DC=cpandl,DC=com"**. The related command would look like this:

```
dsmove "CN=William Stanek,OU=Tech,DC=cpandl,DC=com"
-newparent OU=Engineering,DC=cpandl,DC=com
```

To rename an object while moving it, you simply add the –Newname parameter to give the object a new name. Consider the following example:

```
dsmove "CN=William Stanek,OU=Tech,DC=cpandl,DC=com"
-newparent OU=Engineering,DC=cpandl,DC=com -newname "William R. Stanek"
```

Here, you move the William Stanek user account to the Engineering OU and rename it William R. Stanek.

In any of these examples, we could have obtained the object DN by means of the DSQUERY command. To do this, you simply pipe the output of DSQUERY to DSMOVE, as shown in this example:

```
dsquery user -name "William Stanek" | dsmove -newname "William R. Stanek"
```

Here, the object DN, "CN=William Stanek,OU=Tech,DC=cpandl,DC=Com", is obtained from DSQUERY USER and used as input to DSMOVE, which results in the renaming of the User object.

> **Tip** Want to move objects between domains? Use the Active Directory Migration Tool, which is available online at the Microsoft Downloads Web site (*http://downloads.microsoft.com*). Be sure to get the version compatible with Windows Server 2008.

Removing Objects from Active Directory

If you no longer want an object to be in Active Directory, you can delete it permanently using the DSRM command. The syntax for DSRM is

```
dsrm ObjectDN ... [-subtree [-exclude]] [-noprompt] [{-s Server |
-d Domain}] [-u UserName] [-p {Password | *}] [-c] [-q] [{-uc | -uco |
-uci}]
```

> **Caution** Don't use DSRM unless you've experimented first on an isolated test domain. This command is powerful. It will delete any object you pass to it, including object containers.

The best way to use DSRM is to pass it a specific object to remove. In this example, you delete the engcomp18 computer account from the Eng OU in the cpandl.com domain:

```
dsrm "CN=engcomp18,OU=Eng,DC=cpandl,DC=com"
```

By default, DSRM prompts you to confirm the deletion:

```
Are you sure you wish to delete CN=engcomp18,OU=Eng,DC=cpandl,DC=com (Y/N)?
```

You can disable the prompt using the *-noprompt* switch, such as in the following example:

```
dsrm "CN=engcomp18,OU=Eng,DC=cpandl,DC=com" -noprompt
```

However, you should only do this when you are absolutely certain that DSRM will delete only the object you expect it to.

DSRM can be used to delete objects in containers or OUs as well as the containers and OUs themselves. If the container or OU is empty, you would delete it by its DN, such as

```
dsrm "OU=Eng,DC=cpandl,DC=com"
```

If the container or OU is not empty, it cannot be deleted in this way, however, and DSRM will report:

```
Failed: The operation cannot be performed because child objects exist. Thi
s operation can only be performed on a leaf object.
```

To delete the container and all the objects it contains, you can use the –Subtree parameter. Consider the following example:

```
dsrm "OU=Eng,DC=cpandl,DC=com" -subtree
```

Here, you use –Subtree to delete all the objects (regardless of type) from the Eng OU as well as the container itself. To delete all the objects in the container but not the container itself, you can use the –Subtree and –Exclude parameters. Consider the following example:

```
dsrm "OU=Eng,DC=cpandl,DC=com" -subtree -exclude
```

Here, you use –Subtree to delete all the objects (regardless of type) from the Eng OU and use the –Exclude parameter to exclude the Eng OU as one of the objects to delete.

Chapter 14

Managing Computer Accounts and Domain Controllers

The focus of this chapter is on managing domain computer accounts, which control access to the network and its resources. Like user accounts, domain computer accounts have attributes that you can manage, including names and group memberships. You can add computer accounts to any container or OU in Active Directory. However, the best containers to use are Computers, Domain Controllers, and any OUs that you've created. The standard Microsoft Windows tool for working with computer accounts is Active Directory Users And Computers. At the command line, you have many commands, each with a specific use. Whether you are logged on to a Windows Vista or Windows Server 2008 system, you can use the techniques discussed in this chapter to manage computer accounts and domain controllers.

Overview of Managing Computer Accounts from the Command Line

Two sets of command-line utilities are available for managing domain computer accounts. The first set can be used with any type of computer account, including workstations, member servers, and domain controllers. The second set of commands is used only with domain controllers and designed to help you manage their additional features and properties.

In addition to DSQUERY COMPUTER discussed in the previous chapter, the general computer account commands include

- **DSADD COMPUTER** Creates a computer account in Active Directory.

```
dsadd computer ComputerDN [-samid SAMName] [-desc Description]
[-loc Location] [-memberof GroupDN ...] [{-s Server | -d Domain}]
[-u UserName] [-p {Password | *}] [-q] [{-uc | -uco | -uci}]
```

- **DSGET COMPUTER** Displays the properties of a computer account using one of two syntaxes. The syntax for viewing the properties of multiple computers is

```
dsget computer ComputerDN ... [-dn] [-samid] [-sid] [-desc] [-loc]
[-disabled] [{-s Server | -d Domain}] [-u UserName]
[-p {Password | *}] [-c] [-q] [-l] [{-uc | -uco | -uci}]
[-part PartitionDN] [-qlimit] [-qused]]
```

The syntax for viewing the membership information of a single computer is

```
dsget computer ComputerDN [-memberof [-expand]]
[{-s Server | -d Domain}][-u UserName]
[-p {Password | *}] [-c] [-q] [-l] [{-uc | -uco | -uci}]
```

- **DSMOD COMPUTER** Modifies attributes of one or more computer accounts in the directory.

```
dsmod computer ComputerDN ... [-desc Description] [-loc Location]
[-disabled {yes | no}] [-reset] [{-s Server | -d Domain}]
[-u UserName] [-p {Password | *}] [-c] [-q] [{-uc | -uco | -uci}]
```

Tip For any of the computer and server commands, you can use input from DSQUERY to specify the object or objects you want to work with. If you want to type the distinguished names (DNs) for each object you want to work with, you can do this as well. Simply separate each DN with a space.

In addition to DSQUERY SERVER, discussed in the previous chapter, the utilities for managing the additional features of domain controllers include

- **DSGET SERVER** Displays the various properties of domain controllers using one of three syntaxes. The syntax for displaying the general properties of a specified domain controller is

```
dsget server ServerDN ... [-dn] [-desc] [-dnsname] [-site]
[-isgc] [{-s Server | -d Domain}] [-u UserName]
[-p {Password | *}] [-c] [-q] [-l] [{-uc | -uco | -uci}]
```

The syntax for displaying a list of the security principals who own the largest number of directory objects on the specified domain controller is

```
dsget server ServerDN ... [{-s Server | -d Domain}] [-u UserName]
[-p {Password | *}] [-c] [-q] [-l] [{-uc | -uco | -uci}]
[-topobjowner NumbertoDisplay]
```

The syntax for displaying the DNs of the directory partitions on the specified server is

```
dsget server ServerDN ... [{-s Server | -d Domain}] [-u UserName]
[-p {Password | *}] [-c] [-q] [-l] [{-uc | -uco | -uci}] [-part]
```

- **DSMOD SERVER** Modifies properties of a domain controller.

```
dsmod server ServerDN ... [-desc Description] [-isgc {yes | no}]
[{-s Server | -d Domain}] [-u UserName] [-p {Password | *}] [-c]
[-q] [{-uc | -uco | -uci}]
```

Note Another useful command for working with domain controllers and Active Directory is NTDSUtil. NTDSUtil is a text-mode command interpreter that you invoke so that you can manage directory services using a separate command prompt and internal commands. You invoke the NTDSUtil interpreter by typing **ntdsutil** in a command window and pressing Enter.

Creating Computer Accounts in Active Directory Domains

You can create a computer account for a workstation or server that you want to add to the domain using DSADD COMPUTER. When you do this, you create the computer account in advance so that it is available when the computer joins the domain. To create computer accounts, you must have the appropriate permissions. Most users can create a computer account in their logon domain. Group Policy and other permissions can change this.

Creating a Computer Account

When you create a computer account, the only required information is the account's DN. As you may recall from the previous chapter, a DN specifies the full name of an object in Active Directory and includes the path to the object's location. Because of this, when you provide a DN for a computer account, you specify the computer account name and the container in which the account should be created. Consider the following example:

```
dsadd computer "CN=CORPSERVER05,OU=Domain Controllers,DC=cpandl,
DC=com"
```

Tip The DN specifies where, within the domain hierarchy, the computer account is created. You can create computer accounts in any domain in the forest for which you have appropriate access permissions. In some cases, you might need to log on directly to a domain controller in the domain you want to work with. Use –S Server to connect to a specific domain controller in any domain in the forest. Use –D Domain to connect to any available domain controller in the specified domain.

Here you create the CORPSERVER05 computer account in the Domain Controllers container within Active Directory. If the account creation is successful, DSADD COMPUTER reports:

```
dsadd succeeded:CN=CORPSERVER05,OU=Domain Controllers,DC=cpandl,
DC=com
```

Use –U *UserName* and –P *Password* to set the Run As permissions.

Account creation isn't always successful, however. The most common reason is that you specified an incorrect DN. For example, if you were to use the command

```
dsadd computer "CN=CORPSERVER05,CN=Domain Controllers,DC=cpandl,
DC=com"
```

DSADD COMPUTER would report

```
dsadd failed:CN=CORPSERVER05,CN=Domain Controllers,DC=cpandl,
DC=com:Directory object not found.
```

This error occurred because Domain Controllers is created as an organizational unit (OU), not as a generic container. That is, we improperly used CN=Domain Controllers instead of correctly using OU=Domain Controllers.

Another common reason for failure is the instance when an account already exists with the name you attempt to use. In this case, select a different computer account name.

Customizing Computer Account Attributes and Group Memberships

When you provide only a DN, several parameters are set for you automatically. Group membership is set so that the computer is a member of Domain Computers. The SAM account name is derived from the common name attribute used in the computer's DN. Basically, the DSADD COMPUTER command adds a dollar sign as a suffix to this name. In the previous example, the common name is CORPSERVER05, so the SAM account name is CORPSERVER05$.

If you want to customize the computer account attributes when you create a computer account, you can do this using these additional parameters:

- **–Samid** Use –Samid to set the SAM account name, which must end in a dollar sign, such as **–samid CORPSERVER05$**.
- **–Desc** Use –Desc to set the description of the computer you want to add, such as **–desc "CNMember Server"**.
- **–Loc** Use –Loc to provide a text description of the physical location of the computer you want to add. Typically, this is the office and building in which the computer is located. For example, if the computer is located in office 110 of building E you could type **–loc "E/110"**.

You set group memberships for a new computer account by using the –Memberof parameter. This parameter accepts a space-separated list of DNs representing the groups in which you want the computer as a member. For example, if you wanted a new computer account to be a member of the Engineering group and the DN for this group was CN=Engineering,OU=Eng,DC=cpandl,DC=com, you could use a command line similar to the following:

```
dsadd computer "CN=CORPSERVER05,OU=Domain Controllers,DC=cpandl,DC=com"
-memberof "CN=Engineering,OU=Eng,DC=cpandl,DC=com"
```

If you wanted a new computer account to be a member of the Engineering and Tech groups and the DNs for these groups were CN=Engineering,OU=Eng, DC=cpandl,DC=com and CN=Tech,CN=Users,DC=cpandl,DC=com respectively, you could use a command line similar to the following:

```
dsadd computer "CN=CORPSERVER05,OU=Domain Controllers,DC=cpandl,DC=com"
-memberof "CN=Engineering,OU=Eng,DC=cpandl,DC=com"
"CN=Tech,CN=Users,DC=cpandl,DC=com"
```

Note You don't have to specify Domain Computers as a group membership. New computer accounts are automatically members of Domain Computers as well as any other groups you specify.

Managing Computer Account Properties

Managing computer accounts from the command line is slightly different from managing them in Active Directory Users And Computers, chiefly because you have more options, especially when it comes to working with multiple computer accounts at the same time.

Viewing and Finding Computer Accounts

As discussed in Chapter 13, "Core Active Directory Services Administration," you can use the DSQUERY COMPUTER command to search for computers. Not only can you search by Active Directory account name, SAM account name, and description, but you can also use wildcards in any of these fields to facilitate matches. The output of DSQUERY COMPUTER contains the DN of computers that match the search criteria and can be piped as input to other commands, including DSGET COMPUTER, which you can use in turn to display computer account properties.

DSGET COMPUTER is best used with DSQUERY COMPUTER. Here, you use DSQUERY COMPUTER to obtain the DNs for one or more computers and then use DSGET COMPUTER to display the properties for the related accounts. Properties you can display are set with the search parameters:

- **–Dn** Displays the DN of matching computer accounts in the output.
- **–Samid** Displays the SAM account name of matching computer accounts in the output.

- **–Sid** Displays the security identifier for matching computer accounts in the output.
- **–Desc** Displays the description of matching computer accounts in the output.
- **–Loc** Displays the location attribute of matching computer accounts in the output.
- **–Disabled** Displays a Yes/No value indicating whether the computer account is disabled.

DSGET COMPUTER displays output in table format. Generally speaking, you will always want to use –Dn, –Samid, or –Sid as a parameter to help you make sense of and identify the computers in the output. For example, if you wanted to search for all engineering computers that were disabled, you could use the command line

```
dsquery computer -name engcomp* | dsget computer -dn -disabled
```

Here, the results display the DN and the disabled status:

```
  dn                                          disabled
  CN=engcomp18,OU=Eng,DC=cpandl,DC=com        yes
  CN=engcomp19,OU=Eng,DC=cpandl,DC=com        yes
  CN=engcomp20,OU=Eng,DC=cpandl,DC=com        no
  CN=engcomp21,OU=Eng,DC=cpandl,DC=com        no
  CN=engcomp22,OU=Eng,DC=cpandl,DC=com        no
dsget succeeded
```

You could also display the SAM account name as shown in this example:

```
dsquery computer -name engcomp* | dsget computer -samid -disabled

  samid             disabled
  ENGCOMP18$        yes
  ENGCOMP19$        yes
  ENGCOMP20$        no
  ENGCOMP21$        no
  ENGCOMP22$        no
dsget succeeded
```

Or the security identifier:

```
dsquery computer -name engcomp* | dsget computer -sid -disabled

  sid                                              disabled
  S-1-5-21-4087030303-3274042965-2323426166-1119   yes
  S-1-5-21-4087030303-3274042965-2323426166-1120   yes
  S-1-5-21-4087030303-3274042965-2323426166-1122   no
  S-1-5-21-4087030303-3274042965-2323426166-1123   no
  S-1-5-21-4087030303-3274042965-2323426166-1124   no
dsget succeeded
```

Either way, you have an identifier that makes it easier to differentiate the computer account entries. You can use the second syntax for DSGET COMPUTER to obtain the group membership of computers. For example, if you want to see what groups ENGCOMP18 is a member of, you could type the command

```
dsquery computer -name engcomp18 | dsget computer -memberof
```

or

```
dsget computer "CN=engcomp18,OU=Eng,DC=cpandl,DC=com" -memberof
```

Both commands work the same way. In the first example, you use DSQUERY COMPUTER to obtain the DN of the computer account. In the second example, you specify the DN directly. Either way, the output would show the group memberships, such as

```
"CN=Tech,CN=Users,DC=cpandl,DC=com"
"CN=Engineering,OU=Eng,DC=cpandl,DC=com"
"CN=Domain Computers,CN=Users,DC=cpandl,DC=com"
```

Here, the computer is a member of the Tech, Engineering, and Domain Computers groups.

While this technique could be used to display the membership of multiple computers, there is no way to display a DN or SAM account name for the associated computers. Thus, you get a list of group memberships, and the only indicator that the memberships are for different computers are the blank lines separating the responses. For example, if you used the query

```
dsquery computer -name engcomp* | dsget computer -memberof
```

the output might look like this:

```
"CN=Domain Computers,CN=Users,DC=cpandl,DC=com"

"CN=Engineering,OU=Eng,DC=cpandl,DC=com"
"CN=Domain Computers,CN=Users,DC=cpandl,DC=com"

"CN=Domain Computers,CN=Users,DC=cpandl,DC=com"

"CN=Domain Computers,CN=Users,DC=cpandl,DC=com"

"CN=Tech,CN=Users,DC=cpandl,DC=com"
"CN=Engineering,OU=Eng,DC=cpandl,DC=com"
"CN=Domain Computers,CN=Users,DC=cpandl,DC=com"
```

Here, you have output for five computer accounts (you can tell this because of the blank links separating each group membership listing), but you have no indication to which computer accounts the entries specifically relate.

Real World Don't overlook the importance of being able to use DSQUERY COMPUTER to document the current computer account configuration. A sample command line for documenting computer accounts follows:

```
dsquery computer "DC=cpandl,DC=com" | dsget computer -dn
-samid -sid -desc -loc -disabled > domaincomputers.txt
```

Here, the command is used to list all the computer accounts in the cpandl.com domain as well as their properties and save this information to a file.

Setting or Changing a Computer's Location or Description Attribute

From the command line, it is fast and easy to set or change computer account locations and descriptions using the DSMOD COMPUTER command. You can, in fact, set the location or description for 1, 10, 100, or more computers at the same time. Suppose that you want all 500 computers in the Engineering OU to have their description say "Engineering Computer" and their location say "Engineering Dept." You could do this with a single command line, as follows:

```
dsquery computer "OU=Engineering,DC=cpandl,DC=com" | dsmod computer
-loc "Engineering Dept." -desc "Engineering Computer"
```

The DSMOD COMPUTER command would then report the individual success or failure of each change:

```
dsmod succeeded:CN=Engineeringcomp01,OU=Engineering,DC=cpandl,DC=com
dsmod succeeded:CN=Engineeringcomp02,OU=Engineering,DC=cpandl,DC=com
dsmod succeeded:CN=Engineeringcomp03,OU=Engineering,DC=cpandl,DC=com
...
dsmod succeeded:CN=Engineeringcomp499,OU=Engineering,DC=cpandl,DC=com
dsmod succeeded:CN=Engineeringcomp500,OU=Engineering,DC=cpandl,DC=com
```

Although changing these values in the GUI could take you hours, the entire process from the command takes only a few minutes. You simply type the command line and let DSMOD COMPUTER do the work for you.

Disabling and Enabling Computer Accounts

You can enable or disable computer accounts from the command line using the DSMOD COMPUTER command and the –Disabled parameter. Type **–disabled yes** to disable the computer account and type **–disabled no** to enable the computer account.

In the following example, you disable all computers in the TestLab OU:

```
dsquery computer "OU=TestLab,DC=cpandl,DC=com" | dsmod computer
-disabled yes
```

The DSMOD COMPUTER command would then report the individual success or failure of each change:

```
dsmod succeeded:CN=TestLabcomp01,OU=TestLab,DC=cpandl,DC=com
dsmod succeeded:CN=TestLabcomp02,OU=TestLab,DC=cpandl,DC=com
dsmod succeeded:CN=TestLabcomp03,OU=TestLab,DC=cpandl,DC=com
```

Resetting Locked Computer Accounts

Just like user accounts, computer accounts have passwords. Unlike user accounts, however, computer-account passwords are managed and maintained automatically. Computer accounts use two passwords: a standard password, which by default is changed every 30 days, and a private-key password for establishing secure communications with domain controllers, which is also changed by default every 30 days.

Both passwords must be synchronized. If synchronization of the private-key password and the computer-account password lapses, the computer won't be allowed to log on to the domain and a domain authentication error message will be logged for the Netlogon service with an event ID of 3210 or 5722. If this happens, the computer-account password is said to be "stale," and you'll need to reset the account to get the passwords back in sync.

You use different techniques for workstations and servers. To reset a password that is out of sync on a workstation, use DSMOD COMPUTER and the –Reset parameter. Consider the following example:

```
dsmod computer
"CN=Engineeringcomp01,OU=Engineering,DC=cpandl,DC=com" -reset
```

Here, you reset the password for the Engineeringcomp01 computer in the Engineering organization unit of the cpandl.com domain.

You could just as easily reset all computer accounts in the Engineering OU. To do this, you would use DSQUERY COMPUTER to obtain a list of all computers in the domain and DSMOD COMPUTER to reset their passwords, such as

```
dsquery computer "OU=Engineering,DC=cpandl,DC=com" | dsmod computer
-reset
```

Real World One way to determine that a computer account has a stale password is to use the DSQUERY COMPUTER command with the -Stalepwd parameter. If you are using the default value of 30 days for computer-account passwords, you would find stale passwords by using a value of -Stalepwd 30. Here is an example:

```
dsquery computer -stalepwd 30
```

The resulting output shows a list of computers with passwords older than 30 days, which could mean the passwords are stale or simply that the computers have been inactive.

With member servers and domain controllers, you should use NETDOM RESETPWD instead of DSMOD COMPUTER -RESET. You can reset the computer account password of a member server or domain controller by completing the following steps:

1. Log on locally to the server. If you are resetting the password of a domain controller, you must stop the Kerberos Key Distribution Center service and set its startup type to Manual.
2. At an elevated command prompt, type **netdom resetpwd /s:*ComputerName* /ud:*domain\user* /pd:*** where *ComputerName* is the name of a domain controller in the computer account's logon domain, *domain\user* is the name of an

administrator account with the authority to change the computer account password, and * tells NETDOM to prompt you for the account password before continuing.

3. When you enter your password, NETDOM will change the computer account password locally and on the appropriate domain controller. That domain controller will then distribute the password change to other domain controllers.
4. When NETDOM completes this task, restart the computer and verify that the password has been successfully reset. If you reset a domain controller's password, restart the Kerberos Key Distribution Center service and set its startup type to Automatic.

Real World As part of the troubleshooting process, you should always check the status of the computer account in Active Directory. You should check the storage location of the computer and its group membership. Computer accounts, like user accounts, are placed in a specific container in Active Directory and can be made members of specific groups. The container in which a computer is placed determines how Active Directory policy settings are applied to the computer. Moving a computer to a different container or OU can affect the way policy settings are applied.

Check group membership as well. The group membership of a computer determines many permissions with regard to security and resource access. Changing a computer's group membership also can affect security and resource access. With Kerberos authentication, a computer's system time can affect authentication. If a computer's system time deviates outside the permitted values set in group policy, the computer will fail authentication.

Joining Computer Accounts to a Domain

Any authenticated user can join a computer to a domain using the NETDOM JOIN command. If the related computer account hasn't been created, running NETDOM JOIN also creates the computer account. When a computer joins a domain, the computer establishes a trust relationship with the domain. The computer's security identifier is changed to match that of the related computer account in Active Directory, and the computer is made a member of the appropriate groups in Active Directory. Typically, this means the computer is made a member of the Domain Computers group. If the computer is later made a domain controller, the computer will be made a member of the Domain Controllers group instead.

Note NETDOM is available on Windows Server 2008 but not on Windows Vista (unless you've installed it). Before joining a computer to a domain, you should verify the computer's network configuration. If the network configuration is not correct, you will need to modify the settings before attempting to join the computer to the domain. Additionally, if the computer account was created previously, only a user specifically delegated permission or an administrator can join the computer to a domain. Users must also have local administrator permissions on the local computer.

You can join a computer to a domain in two ways:

- Log on to the computer you want to join to a domain and run NETDOM JOIN.
- Run NETDOM JOIN from another computer and connect to the computer you want to join to a domain.

When logged on to the computer you want to join to a domain, you can use NETDOM JOIN to simultaneously join a computer to a domain and create a computer account in the domain with the following command syntax:

```
netdom join ComputerName /Domain:DomainName /UserD:DomainUser
/PasswordD:UserPassword
```

where *ComputerName* is the name of the computer, *DomainName* is the name of the Active Directory domain to join, *DomainUser* is the name of a domain user account authorized to join the computer to the domain (and create the related computer account if necessary), and *UserPassword* is the password for the user account. The domain user account should be specified in the form DOMAIN*UserName*, such as CPANDL\WilliamS. Consider the following example:

```
netdom join corpsvr32 /domain:cpandl.com /userd:CPANDL\williams
/passwordd:2892389383234
```

Here, you join CorpSvr32 to the cpandl.com domain and create the related computer account in the default Computers container. The full path to this computer object is CN=CorpSvr32,CN=Computers,DC=cpandl,DC=com.

Additionally, you can use the /Ou parameter to specify the distinguished name of the OU into which the computer account should be placed. If you want to shut down and restart the computer after joining the domain, use the /Reboot parameter. Consider the following example:

```
netdom join corpsvr32 /domain:cpandl.com
/ou:OU=Engineering,DC=cpandl,DC=com
/userd:CPANDL\williams /passwordd:2892389383234 /reboot
```

Here, you join CorpSvr32 to the cpandl.com domain, create the related computer account in the Engineering OU, and then reboot the computer. The full path to this computer object is CN=CorpSvr32,OU=Engineering,DC=cpandl,DC=com.

When running NETDOM JOIN from another computer and connecting to the computer you want to join to a domain, you use the following command syntax to join a domain:

```
netdom join ComputerName /Domain:DomainName /UserD:DomainUser
/PasswordD:UserPassword /UserO:ComputerUser
/PasswordO:ComputerPassword
```

where *ComputerUser* is the name of a local user account on the computer you are joining to the domain and *ComputerPassword* is the password for that local user account. As before, this command will create the related computer account if necessary and you optionally can use the /Ou parameter to specify the distinguished name of the OU into which the computer account should be placed.

Consider the following example:

```
netdom join desktop267 /domain:cpandl.com /ou:OU=Services,DC=cpandl,DC=com
/userd:CPANDL\williams /passwordd:2892389383234 /usero:sammiep
/passwordo:383478478722
```

Here, you join Desktop267 to the cpandl.com domain and create the related computer account in the Services OU. The full path to this computer object is CN=Desktop267, OU=Services,DC=cpandl,DC=com.

Renaming Computers and Computer Accounts

Using the NETDOM RENAMECOMPUTER command, you can easily rename workstations and member servers. If the workstation or member server is joined to a domain, the computer's account is renamed as well. You should not, however, use NETDOM RENAMECOMPUTER to rename domain controllers, servers running Certificate Services, or servers running any other services that require a specific, fixed server name.

When you are logged on locally, you can rename a workstation or member server using the following command syntax:

```
netdom renamecomputer ComputerName /NewName:NewName /UserD:DomainUser
/PasswordD:UserPassword
```

where *ComputerName* is the current name of the computer, *NewName* is the new name for the computer, *DomainUser* is the name of a domain user account authorized to rename the computer in the domain, and *UserPassword* is the password for the user account. The domain user account should be specified in the form: DOMAIN\ *UserName*, such as CPANDL\WilliamS. Consider the following example:

```
netdom renamecomputer desktop16 /newname:wkstn75 /userd:CPANDL\williams
/passwordd:2892389383234
```

Here, you rename Desktop16 as Wkstn75 and use the WilliamS account to make the changes in the domain. If you want to shutdown and restart the computer after renaming, use the /Reboot parameter.

When running NETDOM RENAMECOMPUTER from another computer and connecting to the computer you want to rename, you use the following command syntax:

```
netdom renamecomputer ComputerName /NewName:NewName /UserD:DomainUser
/PasswordD:UserPassword /UserO:ComputerUser /PasswordO:ComputerPassword
```

where *ComputerUser* is the name of a user account authorized to connect to the computer you are renaming and *ComputerPassword* is the password for that user account. Consider the following example:

```
netdom renamecomputer desktop143 /newname:wkstn76 /userd:CPANDL\williams
/passwordd:2892389383234 /usero:sammiep /passwordo:383478478722
```

Here, you rename Desktop143 as Wkstn76, use the WilliamS account to make the changes in the domain, and use the SammieP account to connect to the computer you are renaming.

Moving Computer Accounts

Computer accounts are normally placed in the Computers, Domain Controllers, or customized OU containers. You can move a computer account to a different container or OU within its current domain using DSMOVE. Specify the computer account's current DN and then use the –Newparent parameter to specify the new location or parent DN of the computer accounts. If you wanted to move the CORPSVR03 computer account from the Tech OU to the Engineering OU, you would specify the computer account's DN, such as "CN=CORPSVR03,OU=Tech, DC=cpandl,DC=com," and provide the parent DN for the new location, such as "OU=Engineering,DC=cpandl,DC=com." The related command would look like this:

```
dsmove "CN=CORPSVR03,OU=Tech,DC=cpandl,DC=com"
-newparent "OU=Engineering,DC=cpandl,DC=com"
```

We could have also obtained the computer account DN using the DSQUERY COMPUTER command. To do this, you simply pipe the output of DSQUERY COMPUTER to DSMOVE, as shown in this example:

```
dsquery computer -name "CORPSVR03" | dsmove
-newparent "OU=Engineering,DC=cpandl,DC=com"
```

Here, the computer account DN, "CN=CORPSVR03,OU=Tech,DC=cpandl, DC=com," is obtained from DSQUERY COMPUTER and used as input to DSMOVE. This example works regardless of whether the computer account is for a workstation, member server, or domain controller.

Deleting Computer Accounts

If you no longer need a computer account, you can delete it permanently from Active Directory using the DSRM command. In most cases, you'll want to delete only a specific computer account, such as Corpserver03. If this is the case, you remove the account by passing DSRM the DN of the computer account, such as

```
dsrm "CN=corpserver03,OU=Eng,DC=cpandl,DC=com"
```

By default, DSRM prompts you to confirm the deletion. If you don't want to see the prompt, use the –Noprompt parameter, such as

```
dsrm "CN=corpserver03,OU=Eng,DC=cpandl,DC=com" -noprompt
```

Working with Domain Controllers

Computers running Windows Server 2008 can act as member servers or domain controllers. Although everything discussed in the previous sections of this chapter applies to any type of computer account, the discussion in this section applies only to domain controllers.

Installing and Demoting Domain Controllers

Windows Server 2008 supports two types of domain controllers: read-writable domain controllers (RWDCs) and read-only domain controllers (RODCs). RWDCs host writable replicas of the Active Directory data store. RODCs host read-only replicas of the Active Directory data store.

Domain controllers perform many important tasks in Active Directory domains. You make a member server a domain controller by installing the Active Directory Domain Services role using **servermanagercmd –install adds-domain-controller** and then running the DCPROMO command, which installs directory services and promotes the member server to be a domain controller. If you run DCPROMO a second time on the server, you will demote the domain controller so that it acts once again as a member server only.

> **Real World** The DCPROMO command starts a graphical utility. It does, however, accept several command-line parameters, including /Answer:*FileName* and /Adv. With the /Answer parameter, you can provide the name of an answer file that scripts the directory services installation. If you are automating the installation of an entire server, you would add a GUIRunOnce entry in the Unattend.txt file to automatically start DCPROMO at the end of the Unattended Setup. With the /Adv parameter, you tell DCPROMO to run in advanced mode, which gives you the option to create the domain controller from installation media or from media backup. To be able to copy domain information from either, you will first need to create installation media or a media backup for a domain controller running Windows Server 2008 in the same domain as the member server you want to promote, and then you start an advanced installation of Active Directory using DCPROMO.

Finding Domain Controllers in Active Directory

When you want to work strictly with domain controllers rather than all computer accounts, you can use the DSQUERY SERVER and DSGET SERVER commands. By default when you use DSQUERY SERVER, you search your logon domain. In fact, if you type **dsquery server** on a line by itself and press Enter, you'll get a list of all domain controllers in your logon domain. As necessary, you can specify the domain to search using the –Domain parameter. Consider the following example:

```
dsquery server -domain tech.cpandl.com
```

Here, you obtain a list of all the domain controllers in the tech.cpandl.com domain. If you want a list of all domain controllers in the entire forest, you can do this as well. Simply type **dsquery server –forest**.

In all these examples, the resulting output is a list of DNs for domain controllers. Unlike previous DNs that we've worked with, these DNs include site configuration information, such as:

```
"CN=CORPSVR02,CN=Servers,CN=Default-First-Site-
Name,CN=Sites,CN=Configuration,DC=cpandl,DC=com"
```

This additional information is provided by DSQUERY SERVER to specify the site associated with the server. Remember, domains can span more than one physical location, and the way you tell Active Directory about these physical locations is to use sites and subnets. In this example, the associated site is Default-First-Site-Name in the Sites configuration container.

Sometimes, you'll want to find the domain controllers in a particular site and you can specify a site to examine using the –site parameter. In the following example, you look for all domain controllers in a site called Seattle-First-Site:

```
dsquery server -site Seattle-First-Site
```

> **Note** DSQUERY SERVER has additional parameters that help you search for global catalogs, operations masters, and read-only domain controllers. These parameters are discussed in the sections of this chapter titled "Finding Global Catalog Servers," "Finding Operations Masters," and "Finding Read-Only Domain Controllers" respectively.

As with the computer-related commands, DSQUERY SERVER and DSGET SERVER are best used together. Here, you use DSQUERY SERVER to obtain the DNs for one or more domain controllers and then use DSGET SERVER to display the properties for the related accounts. Properties you can display are specified with the following parameters:

- **–Dn** Displays the DN of matching domain controllers in the output.
- **–Desc** Displays the description of matching domain controllers in the output.
- **–Dnsname** Displays the fully qualified domain name of the domain controller.
- **–Isgc** Displays a Yes/No value indicating whether the domain controller is a global catalog server as well.

For example, if you wanted a detailed summary of all domain controllers in the forest, you could type the command

```
dsquery server -forest | dsget server -desc -dnsname -isgc
```

To save this information, direct the output to a file, such as

```
dsquery server -forest | dsget server -desc -dnsname -isgc >
forest-dcs.txt
```

Designating Global Catalog Servers

A domain controller designated as a global catalog stores a full replica of all objects in Active Directory for its host domain and a partial replica for all other domains in the domain forest. Global catalogs are used during logon and for information searches. In fact, if the global catalog is unavailable, normal users can't log on to the domain. The only way to change this behavior is to cache universal group membership on local domain controllers. By default, the first domain controller installed in a domain is designated as the global catalog. You can also add global catalogs to a domain to help improve response time for logon and search requests. The recommended technique is to have one global catalog per site within a domain.

Any domain controller hosting a global catalog should be well connected to the network and to domain controllers acting as infrastructure masters. Infrastructure master is one of the five operations master roles that you can assign to a domain controller and it is responsible for updating object references. The infrastructure master does this by comparing its data with that of a global catalog. If the infrastructure master finds outdated data, it requests the updated data from a global catalog. The infrastructure master then replicates the changes to the other domain controllers in the domain.

> **Tip** When there's only one domain controller in a domain, you can assign the infrastructure master role and the global catalog to the same domain controller. When there are two or more domain controllers in the domain, however, the global catalog and the infrastructure master shouldn't be on the same domain controller because this can affect the infrastructure master's ability to determine that directory data is out of date.

Finding Global Catalog Servers

Want to determine where the global catalogs are? For your current (logon) domain, just type **dsquery server –isgc**. The resulting output is a list of DNs for global catalogs, such as

```
"CN=CORPSVR02,CN=Servers,CN=Default-First-Site-
Name,CN=Sites,CN=Configuration,DC=cpandl,DC=com"
```

DSQUERY SERVER can also be used to locate global catalogs in a specific domain. To do this, use the –Domain parameter, and type **dsquery server -domain tech.cpandl.com -isgc**.

Here, you search for global catalog servers in the tech.cpandl.com domain. If you wanted to search the entire forest, you can do this as well. Just type **dsquery server -forest –isgc**.

You can also search for global catalog servers by site, but to do this, you must know the full site name, and you cannot use wildcards. For example, if you wanted to find all the global catalog servers for Default-First-Site-Name, you would have to type **dsquery server –site Default-First-Site-Name**.

> **Note** Being able to search site by site is important because you typically want at least one global catalog server per site. If you search a site and don't find a global catalog, you should consider adding one.

Adding or Removing a Global Catalog

You can designate a domain controller as a global catalog using DSMOD SERVER. Specify the DN of the server you want to work with and type **–isgc yes** to make it a global catalog server, such as

```
dsmod server "CN=corpdc05,OU=Eng,DC=cpandl,DC=com" -isgc yes
```

Another way to perform this task would be to use DSQUERY SERVER to obtain a list of servers that you want to work with. Let's say the tech.cpandl.com domain has three domain controllers and you want them all to be global catalogs. You could do this using the following command line:

```
dsquery server -domain tech.cpandl.com | dsmod server -isgc yes
```

Here, you use DSQUERY SERVER to obtain the DNs for all domain controllers in the tech.cpandl.com domain and pass this information as input to DSMOD SERVER, which in turn sets each domain controller as a global catalog.

If you later want a server to stop acting as a global catalog, use the parameter –isgc no. In this example, you no longer want the corpdc04 server in the tech.cpandl.com domain to host the global catalog:

```
dsmod server "CN=corpdc04,OU=Tech,DC=cpandl,DC=com" -isgc no
```

Checking Caching Settings and Global Catalog Preferences

Different levels of domain and forest functionality are available depending on the network configuration. If all domain controllers in your domain or forest are running at least Windows 2000 Server and the functional level is set to Windows 2000 Native mode, your organization can take advantage of the many additional features of Active Directory but can no longer use Windows NT primary domain controllers (PDC) and backup domain controllers (BDC). One of the features enabled in this mode is the caching of universal group membership.

In the event that no global catalog is available when the user tries to log on, caching of universal group membership makes it possible for normal users to log on. Caching is enabled or disabled on a per-site basis and you can determine whether caching is enabled using DSGET SITE. To do this, provide the DN of the site you want to work with and pass the –Cachegroups parameter as shown in the following example:

```
dsget site "CN=Default-First-Site-
Name,CN=Sites,CN=Configuration,DC=cpandl,DC=com" -cachegroups
```

If universal group membership caching is enabled, the output is:

```
  cachegroups
  yes
dsget succeeded
```

Otherwise, the output is:

```
  cachegroups
  no
dsget succeeded
```

Another way to perform this search would be to use the DSQUERY SITE command. If you type **dsquery site** on a line by itself, the command will return a list of all sites in the forest. To limit the result set, you can use the –Name parameter and either specify the common name of the site or use wildcards to specify a part of the name, such as:

```
dsquery site -name *First*
```

Here, you are looking for any site with the letters "First" in the common name.

To put this together, you could use the following command to determine the caching setting for all sites in the forest:

```
dsquery site | dsget site -cachegroups
```

What you'll get is a list of "yes" and "no" answers similar to the following:

```
  cachegroups
  yes
  yes
  no
  no
  yes
dsget succeeded
```

To make the output more meaningful, you would add the –Dn parameter to display the DNs of the related sites, such as

```
  dn                                                                cachegroups
  CN=Seattle-Site-Name,CN=Sites,CN=Configuration,DC=cpandl,DC=com  yes
  CN=LA-Site-Name,CN=Sites,CN=Configuration,DC=cpandl,DC=com       yes
  CN=NY-Site-Name,CN=Sites,CN=Configuration,DC=cpandl,DC=com       yes
  CN=Chicago-Site-Name,CN=Sites,CN=Configuration,DC=cpandl,DC=com  yes
  CN=Detroit-Site-Name,CN=Sites,CN=Configuration,DC=cpandl,DC=com  yes
dsget succeeded
```

If universal group membership caching has been enabled, a domain with multiple global catalogs per site can have a preferred global catalog. This preferred global catalog is the one specifically used to refresh universal group membership caching for the site's domain controllers. You can determine the preferred global catalog using the –Prefgcsite parameter. For example, you could type **dsquery site | dsget site –cache groups –prefgcsite** to return the complete caching configuration for all global catalogs in the forest. You'll see a "yes" or "no" value if preferred global catalogs are configured. If preferred global catalogs aren't configured, you'll see a value of "Not Configured."

Designating Operations Masters

In Active Directory, five distinct operations master roles are defined, each of which has a critical part in ensuring network operations. Although certain roles can be assigned only once in a domain forest, others must be defined once in each domain.

The forest-wide roles that must be assigned are schema master and domain naming master. The schema master controls updates and modifications to directory schema. The domain naming master controls the addition or removal of domains in the forest. As these forest-wide roles must be unique in the forest, you can assign only one schema master and domain naming master in a forest.

The domain roles that must be assigned are relative ID master, PDC emulator master, and infrastructure master. As the name implies, the relative ID master allocates relative IDs to domain controllers. Whenever you create a user, group, or computer object, domain controllers assign a unique security ID to the related object. The security ID consists of the domain's security ID prefix and a unique relative ID, which was allocated by the relative ID master. The PDC emulator processes password changes for users, computers, and trusts. The infrastructure master updates object references by comparing its directory data with that of a global catalog. If the data is outdated, the infrastructure master requests the updated data from a global catalog and then replicates the changes to the other domain controllers in the domain. These domain-wide roles must be unique in each domain. This means you can assign only one relative ID master, PDC emulator master, and infrastructure master in each domain.

Finding Operations Masters

When you install a new network, the first domain controller in the first domain is assigned all the operations master roles. If you later create a new child domain or a root domain in a new tree, the first domain controller in the new domain is assigned operations master roles automatically as well. In a new domain forest, the domain controller is assigned all operations master roles. If the new domain is in the same forest, the assigned roles are relative ID master, PDC emulator master, and infrastructure master. The schema master and domain naming master roles remain in the first domain in the forest. Operations master roles can be transferred by administrators if necessary.

You can determine the current operations masters for your logon domain by typing the following at a command prompt:

```
netdom query fsmo
```

As shown here, the output lists each role owner by its fully qualified domain name:

```
Schema master              CorpServer18.cpandl.com
Domain naming master       CorpServer35.cpandl.com
PDC                        CorpServer23.eng.cpandl.com
RID pool manager           CorpServer23.eng.cpandl.com
Infrastructure master      CorpServer49.eng.cpandl.com
```

From the output in this example, you can also determine that the forest root domain is cpandl.com and the current logon domain is eng.cpandl.com. If you want to determine the operations masters for a specific domain, use the following command:

```
netdom query fsmo /d:DomainName
```

where *DomainName* is the name of the domain, such as eng.cpandl.com.

You can determine which domain controllers in a forest or domain have a designated operation's master role using the -Hasfsmo parameter of the DSQUERY SERVER command. Use the following values with this parameter:

- **schema** Returns the DN for the schema master of the forest.
- **name** Returns the DN for the domain naming master of the forest.
- **infr** Returns the DN for the infrastructure master of the domain. If no domain is specified with the –Domain parameter, the current domain is used.
- **pdc** Returns the DN for the PDC emulator master of the domain. If no domain is specified with the –Domain parameter, the current domain is used.
- **rid** Returns the DN for the relative ID master of the domain. If no domain is specified with the –Domain parameter, the current domain is used.

Schema master and domain naming master are forest-wide roles. When you type **dsquery server –hasfsmo schema** or **dsquery server –hasfsmo name**, you always obtain the DN for the related operations master in the Active Directory forest.

Infrastructure master, PDC emulator master, and relative ID master are domain-wide roles. When you type **dsquery server –hasfsmo infr**, **dsquery server –hasfsmo pdc**, or **dsquery server –hasfsmo rid**, you always obtain the DN for the related operations master in your logon domain. If you want the DN for an operations master in another domain, you must use the – Domain parameter. Consider the following example:

```
dsquery server -hasfsmo rid -domain tech.cpandl.com
```

Here, you obtain the DN for the relative ID master in the tech.cpandl.com domain. If there are multiple domains in the forest, you might also want a list of all the domain controllers that have a particular role on a per domain basis. To do this, use the -Forest parameter, such as

```
dsquery server -hasfsmo rid -forest
```

Configuring Operations Master Roles Using the Command Line

Although you can use the directory services commands to check where the operations masters are located, you cannot use them to configure operations master roles. To configure operations master roles, you must use NTDSUtil. NTDSUtil is a text-mode command interpreter that you invoke so that you can manage directory services using a separate command prompt and internal commands. You invoke the NTDSUtil interpreter by typing **ntdsutil** in a command window and pressing Enter.

Using NTDSUtil, you can transfer operations master roles from one domain controller to another and seize roles when a role cannot be transferred gracefully. For example, a domain controller acting as the infrastructure master might have a drive failure that takes down the entire server. If you're unable to get the server back online, you might need to seize the infrastructure role and assign this role to another domain controller. You should never seize a role on a domain controller you plan to bring back online eventually. Once you seize a role, the old server is permanently out of service and the only way to bring the original server master back online is to format the boot disk and reinstall Windows Server 2008. Therefore, only seize a role as a last resort.

Before seizing a role and forcibly transferring it, you should determine how up-to-date the domain controller that will take over the role is with respect to the previous role owner. Active Directory tracks replication changes using Update Sequence Numbers (USNs). Because of replication latency, domain controllers might not all be up-to-date. If you compare a domain controller's USN to that of other servers in the domain, you can determine whether the domain controller is the most up-to-date with respect to changes from the previous role owner. If the domain controller is up-to-date, you can transfer the role safely. If the domain controller isn't up-to-date, you can wait for replication to occur and then transfer the role to the domain controller.

Windows Server 2008 includes REPADMIN for working with Active Directory replication. To display the highest sequence number for a specified naming context on each replication partner of a designated domain controller, type the following at a command prompt:

```
repadmin /showutdvec DomainControllerName NamingContext
```

where *DomainControllerName* is the fully qualified domain name of the domain controller, and *NamingContext* is the distinguished name of the domain in which the server is located, such as:

```
repadmin /showutdvec corpserver45 dc=cpandl,dc=com
```

The output shows the highest USN on replication partners for the domain partition:

```
Main-Site\corpserver18    @ USN    967382 @ Time 2008-05-15 10:12:22
Main-Site\corpserver92    @ USN    970043 @ Time 2008-05-15 10:12:25
```

In this example, if CorpServer18 was the previous role owner and the domain controller you are examining has an equal or larger USN for CorpServer18, the domain controller is up-to-date. However, if CorpServer18 was the previous role owner and the domain controller you are examining has a lower USN for CorpServer18, the domain controller is not up-to-date, and you should wait for replication to occur before seizing the role. You could also use REPADMIN /SYNCALL to force the domain controller that is the most up-to-date with respect to the previous role owner to replicate with all of its replication partners.

You can transfer roles at the command line by following these steps:

1. Log on to the server you want to assign as the new operations master, then start a command prompt.
2. At the command prompt, type **ntdsutil** to invoke the text-mode command interpreter for NTDSUtil.
3. At the *ntdsutil* prompt, type **roles**. This puts the utility in Operations Master Maintenance mode and the prompt changes to

   ```
   fsmo maintenance:
   ```

4. At the *fsmo maintenance* prompt, type **connections** to get to the *server connections* prompt. Then type **connect to server** followed by the fully qualified domain name of the current schema master for the role, such as

   ```
   connect to server corpdc01.eng.cpandl.com
   ```

5. Once a successful connection is established, type **quit** to exit the *server connections* prompt, and then at the *fsmo maintenance* prompt, type **transfer** and then type the identifier for the role to transfer. The identifiers are
   - *pdc*—For the PDC emulator master role
   - *rid master*—For the relative ID master role
   - *infrastructure master*—For the infrastructure master role
   - *schema master*—For the schema master role
   - *naming master*—For the domain naming master role
6. The role is transferred. Type **quit** at the *fsmo maintenance* prompt and type **quit** at the *ntdsutil* prompt.

If you can't transfer the role gracefully because the current server holding the role is offline or otherwise unavailable, you can seize the role by following these steps:

1. Ensure that the current domain controller with the role you want to seize is permanently offline. If the server can be brought back online, don't perform this procedure unless you intend to completely reinstall this server.
2. Log on to the server you want to assign as the new operations master, then start a command prompt.
3. At the command prompt, type **ntdsutil** to invoke the text-mode command interpreter for NTDSUtil.
4. At the *ntdsutil* prompt, type **roles**. This puts the utility in Operations Master Maintenance mode and the prompt changes to:

   ```
   fsmo maintenance:
   ```

5. At the *fsmo maintenance* prompt, type **connections** and then, at the *server connections* prompt, type **connect to server** followed by the fully qualified domain name of the current schema master for the role, such as

   ```
   connect to server corpdc01.eng.cpandl.com
   ```

6. Once a successful connection is established, type **quit** to exit the *server connections* prompt and then, at the *fsmo maintenance* prompt, type **seize** and then type the identifier for the role to seize. The identifiers are
   - *pdc*–For the PDC emulator master role
   - *rid master*–For the relative ID master role
   - *infrastructure master*–For the infrastructure master role
   - *schema master*–For the schema master role
   - *naming master*–For the domain naming master role
7. The role is seized. Type **quit** at the *fsmo maintenance* prompt and type **quit** at the *ntdsutil* prompt.

Finding Read-Only Domain Controllers

Want to determine where the read-only domain controllers are? For your current (logon) domain, just type **dsquery server –isreadonly**. The resulting output is a list of DNs for read-only domain controllers, such as

```
"CN=CORPSVR48,CN=Servers,CN=Default-First-Site-
Name,CN=Sites,CN=Configuration,DC=cpandl,DC=com"
```

DSQUERY SERVER can also be used to locate read-only domain controllers in a specific domain. To do this, use the –Domain parameter, and type

```
dsquery server -domain seattle.cpandl.com -isreadonly
```

Here, you search for read-only domain controllers in the seattle.cpandl.com domain. If you want to search the entire forest, you can do this as well. Just type **dsquery server -forest -isreadonly**

You can also search for read-only domain controllers by site, but to do this, you must know the full site name and you cannot use wildcards. For example, if you wanted to find all the read-only domain controllers for Default-First-Site-Name, you would have to type **dsquery server −site Default-First-Site-Name -isreadonly**.

Chapter 15

Managing Active Directory Users and Groups

The heart of an administrator's job is creating and managing user and group accounts. In this chapter, you'll first learn how to create and manage user accounts from the command line. You'll then see how to create and manage groups from the command line. The focus of this chapter is on working with Active Directory users and groups.

Overview of Managing User Accounts from the Command Line

In Windows Server 2008, two types of user accounts are defined:

- **Domain user accounts** User accounts are defined in Active Directory and can access resources throughout the domain. You create and manage domain user accounts using the directory services commands.
- **Local user accounts** User accounts are defined on a local computer and must authenticate themselves before they can access network resources. You create and manage local user accounts with the network services commands.

> **Note** Local machine accounts are used primarily in workgroup configurations rather than in Windows domains. Still, every computer on the network has one or more local machine accounts. The only exceptions are domain controllers, which do not have local machine accounts. When you want to work with local machine accounts, you use the network services commands.

The directory services commands that are used to manage domain user accounts include:

- **DSADD USER** Creates a user account in Active Directory. The syntax is

```
dsadd user UserDN [-samid SAMName] [-upn UPN] [-fn FirstName]
[-mi Initial] [-ln LastName] [-display DisplayName]
[-empid EmployeeID]
[-pwd {Password | *}] [-desc Description] [-memberof Group ...]
[-office Office] [-tel PhoneNumber] [-email EmailAddress]
[-hometel HomePhoneNumber] [-pager PagerNumber]
[-mobile CellPhoneNumber] [-fax FaxNumber] [-iptel IPPhoneNumber]
[-webpg WebPage] [-title Title] [-dept Department]
[-company Company] [-mgr Manager] [-hmdir HomeDirectory]
[-hmdrv DriveLetter:] [-profile ProfilePath] [-loscr ScriptPath]
[-mustchpwd {yes | no}] [-canchpwd {yes | no}]
```

```
[-reversiblepwd {yes | no}] [-pwdneverexpires {yes | no}]
[-acctexpires NumberOfDays] [-disabled {yes | no}]
[{-s Server | -d Domain}]
[-u UserName] [-p {Password | *}] [-q] [{-uc | -uco | -uci}]
[-fnp FirstNamePhonetic] [-lnp LastNamePhonetic]
[-displayp DisplayNamePhonetic]
```

- **DSGET USER** Displays the properties of user accounts using one of two syntaxes. The syntax for viewing the properties of multiple users is

```
dsget user UserDN ... [-dn] [-samid] [-sid] [-upn] [-fn] [-mi]
[-ln] [-display] [-fnp] [-lnp] [-displayp] [-effectivepso]
[-empid] [-desc] [-office] [-tel] [-email] [-hometel] [-pager]
[-mobile] [-fax] [-iptel] [-webpg] [-title] [-dept] [-company]
[-mgr] [-hmdir] [-hmdrv] [-profile] [-loscr]
[-mustchpwd] [-canchpwd] [-pwdneverexpires] [-disabled]
[-acctexpires] [-reversiblepwd] [{-uc | -uco | -uci}]
[-part PartitionDN [-qlimit] [-qused]] [{-s Server | -d Domain}]
[-u UserName] [-p {Password | *}] [-c] [-q] [-l]
```

  The syntax for viewing the group membership for users is

```
dsget user UserDN [-memberof [-expand]] [{-s Server | -d Domain}]
[-u UserName] [-p {Password | *}] [-c] [-q] [-l]
[{-uc | -uco | -uci}]
```

- **DSMOD USER** Modifies attributes of one or more user accounts in the directory. The syntax is

```
dsmod user UserDN ... [-upn UPN] [-fn FirstName] [-mi Initial]
[-ln LastName] [-display DisplayName] [-empid EmployeeID]
[-pwd {Password | *}] [-desc Description] [-office Office]
[-tel PhoneNumber] [-email EmailAddress] [-hometel HomePhoneNumber]
[-pager PagerNumber] [-mobile CellPhoneNumber] [-fax FaxNumber]
[-iptel IPPhoneNumber] [-webpg WebPage] [-title Title]
[-dept Department] [-company Company] [-mgr Manager]
[-hmdir HomeDirectory] [-hmdrv DriveLetter:] [-profile ProfilePath]
[-loscr ScriptPath] [-mustchpwd {yes | no}] [-canchpwd {yes | no}]
[-reversiblepwd {yes | no}] [-pwdneverexpires {yes | no}]
[-acctexpires NumberOfDays] [-disabled {yes | no}]
[{-s Server | -d Domain}] [-u UserName] [-p {Password | *}] [-c] [-q]
[{-uc | -uco | -uci}] [-fnp FirstNamePhonetic]
[-lnp LastNamePhonetic] [-displayp DisplayNamePhonetic]
```

> **Tip** These user commands accept input from DSQUERY USER to set the distinguished name (DN) for the user or users you want to work with. You can also type the DNs for each user you want to work with. When you do this, make sure to separate each DN with a space.

At first glance, the user commands seem extraordinarily complex. Actually, the user commands aren't complex so much as they are versatile. They allow you to add, view, or modify user accounts and include an extensive set of user account properties that you can work with. The parameter for working with a particular property is the same whether you are adding, viewing, or modifying an account. For example, when you create an account, you can set the user's office telephone number with the –Tel parameter. To determine a user's telephone number, use the –Tel parameter of DSGET USER; if you need to modify a user's telephone number, use the –Tel parameter of DSMOD USER.

To manage local machine user accounts, use the NET USER command, which is one of several network services commands. NET USER has several syntaxes, and the syntax you use depends on what you want to do, as follows:

Display or modify local user accounts:

```
net user [UserName [Password | *] [/active:{no | yes}] [/comment:
"DescriptionText"] [/countrycode:NNN] [/expires:{{MM/DD/YYYY |
DD/MM/YYYY | mmm,dd,YYYY} | never}] [/fullname:"Name"]
[/homedir:Path] [/passwordchg:{yes | no}] [/passwordreq:{yes |
no}] [/profilepath:[Path]] [/scriptpath:Path] [/times:{Day[-Day]
[,Day[-Day]] ,Time[-Time] [,Time[-Time]] [;...] | all}]
[/usercomment:"Text"] [/workstations:{ComputerName[,...] | *}]
```

Create local user accounts:

```
net user [UserName {Password | *} /add [/active:{no | yes}]
[/comment:"DescriptionText"] [/countrycode:NNN] [/expires:
{{MM/DD/YYYY | DD/MM/YYYY | mmm,dd,YYYY} | never}] [/fullname:"Name"]
[/homedir:Path] [/passwordchg:{yes | no}] [/passwordreq:{yes | no}]
[/profilepath:[Path]] [/scriptpath:Path] [/times:{Day[-Day]
[,Day[-Day]] ,Time[-Time] [,Time[-Time]] [;...] | all}]
[/usercomment:"Text"] [/workstations:{ComputerName[,...] | *}]]
```

Delete local user accounts:

```
net user UserName /delete
```

As you can see, NET USER lets you work with a fairly narrow set of user account properties. These account properties are best suited for working with local user accounts.

> **Note** You can also use NET USER to work with domain accounts in your logon domain. However, beyond the current (logon) domain, you have no access, in contrast to the directory services commands, which let you create and manage domain user accounts in any domain in the Active Directory forest.

Adding User Accounts

Each user that wants to access resources on the network must have a user account. The type of account needed depends on your network configuration. With Active Directory domains, you use domain user accounts. With workgroups, you use local user accounts that pertain only to specific computers.

Creating Domain User Accounts

When you create a domain user account, you pass the user's DN to DSADD USER. The common name component of the DN sets the user's name. The rest of the DN specifies where in Active Directory the user account is to be located, which includes the container in which the user account is to be created and the related domain. For example, you could create a user account for Lisa Andrews in the Sales organizational unit of the cpandl.com domain by typing: **dsadd user "CN=Lisa Andrews,OU=Sales,DC=cpandl,DC=com"**. The account would be created with Lisa Andrews as the user logon name, but because no other properties would be set, the account would be disabled automatically for security reasons.

User names aren't case-sensitive and can be as long as 64 characters. Typically, in addition to the user account's DN, you'll want to specify the following:

- First name as set with the –Fn parameter.
- Middle initial as set with the –Mi parameter.
- Last name as set with the –Ln parameter.
- Display name as set with the –Display parameter.

> **Note** In most cases, you should set the display name to the same value as the common name of the user account. This ensures that the account is easier to manage: If you know the user's display name, you also know the common name component of the distinguished name.

- SAM account name (also referred to as the *logon name*) as set with the –Samid parameter.
- Password as set with the –Pwd parameter. The password must follow the complexity requirements enforced through Group Policy (if any).

> **Note** By default, the first 20 characters of the common name are used to set the SAM account name of the user account, which is also referred to as the pre–Windows 2000 user logon name. The SAM account name must be unique in the domain, and if there is overlap you might want the user's SAM account name to be different from its display name. In this case, you would need to set the SAM account name using the –Samid parameter.

Unlike an account you create in the Active Directory Users And Computers administrative tool, you do not use the user's first name, middle initial, and last name values to set the user's display name. You must set this value using the –Display parameter. The display name is the name Windows displays in dialog boxes. The common name component of the user account name and the domain name component of the distinguished name are used to set the user's fully qualified logon name. The fully qualified logon name is used for logon and authentication. For example, if the user's logon domain is cpandl and the logon name is lisaandrews, the fully qualified logon name is cpandl\lisaandrews.

To create an account for Lisa A. Andrews that uses these parameters, you can use the following command:

```
dsadd user "CN=Lisa Andrews,OU=Sales,DC=cpandl,DC=com" -fn Lisa -mi A
-ln Andrews -samid "lisaandrews" -display "Lisa Andrews" -pwd dg56$2#
```

Note Note the use of double quotation marks in this example. Whenever a parameter value contains a space, you must enclose that parameter value in double quotation marks. I recommend always using double quotation marks with the user DN, samid, and display name values. That way, you get used to using double quotation marks and if any of those values contains a space, the command will execute successfully. Otherwise, you might forget to use double quotation marks and, in such a case, account creation will fail.

If you have problems creating the account, you'll see a warning and you'll need to check your syntax, ensuring that all the values are set appropriately and that the DN values are valid. Otherwise, DSADD USER should report DSADD SUCCEEDED.

Real World The most confusing thing about creating accounts at the command line, whether for users or for groups, is that the accounts have so many different name values. To be clear, the common name of the account, also referred to as the *relative distinguished name*, is the name component you assign using the first CN= component of the DN, such as CN=Lisa Andrews. User accounts also have a display name. The user display name is the value used in Windows dialog boxes. Typically, the display name is the user's full name and you may see references to a user's full name rather than to his or her display name. Both user and group accounts also have a pre–Windows 2000 name. For users, this name is used for domain logon and authentication so it is also referred to as the pre–Windows 2000 logon name.

Customizing Domain User Account Attributes and Group Memberships

All new domain users are members of the group Domain Users, and their primary group is specified as Domain Users. You can add group memberships using the

–Memberof parameter. Follow the parameter name with the group DNs. If a group DN contains a space, it should be enclosed in quotation marks, such as

```
dsadd user "CN=Lisa Andrews,OU=Sales,DC=cpandl,DC=com"
-memberof "CN=Backup Operators,CN=Builtin,DC=cpandl,DC=com" "CN=DHCP
Administrators,CN=Builtin,DC=cpandl,DC=com"
```

> **Note** Pay particular attention to the space used between the group DNs. If you don't use a space, group membership will not be properly configured and an error will occur.

Here, the user account is created and then added as a member of the Backup Operators and DHCP Administrators groups. This is a two-stage process: account creation happens first and then group memberships are configured. If an error occurs when you are adding group membership, DSADD USER will specify that the object was created successfully but that an error occurred after creation. Check the syntax you used when specifying the group DNs, then use DSMOD USER to configure the user's group membership correctly.

For security reasons, you might want to consider setting these parameters as well when creating user accounts:

- **–mustchpwd {yes | no}** By default, the user doesn't have to change his or her password upon first logon, which means **–mustchpwd no** is assumed. If you set **–mustchpwd yes** the user must change his or her password upon first logon.
- **–canchpwd {yes | no}** By default, the user can change his or her password, which means **–canchpwd yes** is assumed. If you set **–canchpwd no**, the user can't change the password.
- **–pwdneverexpires {yes | no}** By default, **–pwdneverexpires no** is assumed and the user password expires according to the group policy settings. If you set **–pwdneverexpires yes**, the password for this account never expires.

  > **Note** Using –pwdneverexpires yes overrides the domain account policy. Generally it isn't a good idea to set a password so that it doesn't expire. This defeats the purpose of having passwords in the first place.

- **–disabled {yes | no}** By default, as long as you create an account with a password, the account is created and enabled for use (meaning **–disabled no** is assumed). If you set **–disabled yes**, the account is disabled and can't be used. This temporarily prevents anyone from using the account.

Consider the following examples to learn more about DSADD USER:

Create an account for Scott L. Bishop in the Users container of the cpandl.com domain. Set the password so that it must be changed upon first logon:

```
dsadd user "CN=Scott L.
Bishop,CN=Users,DC=cpandl,DC=com" -fn Scott -mi L -ln Bishop -samid
"scottb" -display "Scott L. Bishop" -pwd acornTree -mustchpwd yes
```

Create an account for Bob Kelly in the Engineering OU of the ny.cpandl.com domain. Set the password so that it never expires, but disable the account:

```
dsadd user "CN=Bob
Kelly,OU=Engingeering,DC=ny,DC=cpandl,DC=com" -fn Bob -ln Kelly -
samid "bkelly" -display "Bob Kelly" -pwd dazedOne
-pwdneverexpires yes -disabled
```

Create an account for Eric F. Lang in the Marketing OU of the cpandl.com domain. Set the password so that it can't be changed:

```
dsadd user "CN=Eric F.
Lang,OU=Marketing,DC=cpandl,DC=com" -fn Eric -mi F -ln Lang -samid
"eflang" -display "Eric F. Lang" -pwd albErt -canchpwd no
```

> **Tip** You can create accounts in any domain in the forest for which you have appropriate access permissions. In some cases, you might need to log on directly to a domain controller in the domain you want to work with. Use –S *Server* to connect to a specific domain controller in any domain in the forest. Use -D *Domain* to connect to any available domain controller in the specified domain.

Most of the time, the parameters discussed in this section will be the only ones you'll use when creating accounts. As you've seen, based on the DSADD USER syntax, there are many other user account parameters. You can set these properties for user accounts as discussed later in the chapter.

Creating Local User Accounts

Local machine accounts are created on individual computers. If you want to create a local machine account for a particular computer, you must log on locally or use a remote logon to access a local command prompt. Once you are logged on to the computer you want to work with, you can create the required account using NET USER. In some cases, local computer policy might allow you to create an account using only the name of the account to create and the /Add parameter, such as

```
net user wrstanek /add
```

Note You can't create local user accounts on domain controllers. Domain controllers do not have local machine accounts.

Here, you create a local account with the logon name **wrstanek** and use a blank password. Although you might be able to use a blank password, you risk the computer's and possibly the network's security by doing so. Therefore, at a minimum, I recommend that you provide a user name and password for new local user accounts. The password follows the account name as shown in the following example:

```
net user wrstanek dg56$2# /add
```

Here, you create the local machine account for **wrstanek** and set the password to **dg56$2#**.

If the account creation is successful, NET USER will state "Command Completed Successfully." However, if you encounter problems creating the account, NET USER won't display an error message per se. Instead, it will display the command syntax. In this case, check your syntax and ensure that all the values are set appropriately.

Other values and parameters you might want to use with local user accounts include

- **/comment:"*DescriptionText*"** Sets a description of the user account. Normally, you would type the user's job title or department.
- **/fullname:"*Name*"** Sets the full name of the user account. The full name is also referred to as the display name.
- **/passwordchg {yes | no}** By default, users can change their passwords, which means / **passwordchg yes** is assumed. If you set /**passwordchg no**, users won't be able to change their passwords.
- **/passwordreq {yes | no}** By default, users are required to have a password for their accounts. This means /**passwordreq yes** is assumed, so a user's account must have a password and that password cannot be blank.
- **/active {yes | no}** By default, user accounts are enabled when they are created, which means /**active yes** is assumed. If you set /**active no** the account is disabled and can't be used. Use this parameter to temporarily prevent anyone from using an account.

Consider the following examples to learn more about using NET USER:

Create a local machine account for the Desktop Support team with a full name and description:

```
net user dsupport squ5 /fullname:"Desktop Support"
/comment:"Desktop Support Account" /add
```

Create a local machine account for Phil Spencer, include a full name and description, and require a password:

```
net user pspencer magma2 /fullname:"Phil Spencer"
/comment:"Offsite Sales Manager" /passwordreq yes /add
```

Create a local machine account for Chris Preston, include a full name and description. Set a password but don't let the user change it:

```
net user chrisp apples /fullname:"Chris Preston" /comment:"PR
Manager" /passwordchg no /add
```

Managing User Accounts

Managing user accounts from the command line is different from managing them in the Active Directory Users And Computers administrative tool, chiefly because you have more options and it is easier to work with multiple user accounts at the same time.

Viewing and Finding User Accounts

You can use the DSQUERY USER command to search for users. Not only can you search by common name, SAM account name, and description, but you can also use wildcards in any of these fields to facilitate matches. The output of DSQUERY USER contains the DNs of users that match the search criteria and can be piped as input to other commands, including DSGET USER, which you can use in turn to display user account properties.

DSQUERY USER and DSGET USER are best used together. Here, you use DSQUERY USER to obtain the DNs for one or more users, and then use DSGET USER to display the properties for the related accounts. Using DSGET USER, properties you can display are specified by using parameters, including

- **–display** Displays the full name attribute of matching user accounts in the output
- **–desc** Displays the description of matching user accounts in the output
- **–dn** Displays the distinguished name of matching user accounts in the output
- **–empid** Displays the employee ID attribute of matching user accounts in the output
- **–fn** Displays the first name attribute of matching user accounts in the output

- **–mi** Displays the middle initial attribute of matching user accounts in the output
- **–ln** Displays the last name attribute of matching user accounts in the output
- **–samid** Displays the SAM account name of matching user accounts in the output
- **–sid** Displays the security identifier for matching user accounts in the output
- **–disabled** Displays a Yes/No value indicating whether the user account is disabled
- **–effectivepso** Displays the effective Password Settings Object (PSO) of matching user accounts

Note Active Directory defines three types of account policies: password policies, account lockout policies, and Kerberos policies. You use PSOs to define secondary account policy settings for a domain. PSOs are available when a domain is running in Windows Server 2008 functional level.

DSGET USER displays output in table format. Generally speaking, you will always want to use –Dn, –Samid, or –Display as a parameter to help you make sense of and identify the users in the output. For example, if you wanted to search for all engineering users that were disabled, you can use the command line

```
dsquery user "OU=Eng,DC=cpandl,DC=com" | dsget user -dn -disabled
```

Here, you list the disabled status of each user in the Engineering OU of the cpandl.com domain, such as

```
  dn                                     disabled
  CN=edwardh,OU=Eng,DC=cpandl,DC=com     yes
  CN=jacobl,OU=Eng,DC=cpandl,DC=com      yes
  CN=maryk,OU=Eng,DC=cpandl,DC=com       yes
  CN=ellene,OU=Eng,DC=cpandl,DC=com      yes
  CN=williams,OU=Eng,DC=cpandl,DC=com    yes
dsget succeeded
```

Instead, you could display the SAM account name as shown in this example:

```
dsquery user -name william* | dsget user -samid -disabled
  samid    disabled
  williamb    yes
  williamd    yes
  williams    no
dsget succeeded
```

Here, you search for all user accounts whose common name begins with William, then display the SAM account name and disabled status of each.

Determining Group Membership for Individual User Accounts

You can use the second syntax for DSGET USER to obtain the group membership of individual user accounts. For example, if you wanted to see what groups WilliamS is a member of, you could type the command

```
dsquery user -name williams | dsget user -memberof
```

or

```
dsget user "CN=William Stanek,OU=Eng,DC=cpandl,DC=com" -memberof
```

Both commands work the same way. In the first example, you use DSQUERY USER to obtain the DN of the user account. In the second example, you specify the DN directly. Either way, the output would show the group memberships, such as

```
"CN=Tech,CN=Users,DC=cpandl,DC=com"
"CN=Engineering,OU=Eng,DC=cpandl,DC=com"
"CN=Domain Users,CN=Users,DC=cpandl,DC=com"
```

Here, the user is a member of the Tech, Engineering, and Domain Users groups.

While you could use this technique to display the membership of multiple users, displaying a DN or SAM account name for the associated users is not possible. Thus, you get a list of group memberships and the only indicator that the memberships are for different users are the blank lines in the listing. For example, if you used the query

```
dsquery user -name bill* | dsget user -memberof
```

the output might look like this:

```
"CN=Tech,CN=Users,DC=cpandl,DC=com"
"CN=Engineering,OU=Eng,DC=cpandl,DC=com"
"CN=Domain Users,CN=Users,DC=cpandl,DC=com"

"CN=Domain Users,CN=Users,DC=cpandl,DC=com"

"CN=Tech,CN=Users,DC=cpandl,DC=com"
"CN=Engineering,OU=Eng,DC=cpandl,DC=com"
"CN=Domain Users,CN=Users,DC=cpandl,DC=com"

"CN=Engineering,OU=Eng,DC=cpandl,DC=com"
"CN=Domain Users,CN=Users,DC=cpandl,DC=com"

"CN=Tech,CN=Users,DC=cpandl,DC=com"
"CN=Engineering,OU=Eng,DC=cpandl,DC=com"
"CN=Domain Users,CN=Users,DC=cpandl,DC=com"

"CN=Domain Users,CN=Users,DC=cpandl,DC=com"

"CN=Domain Users,CN=Users,DC=cpandl,DC=com"
```

Here, you have output for seven user accounts. You can tell this because of the blank lines separating each group membership listing. But you have no indication to which user accounts the entries specifically relate.

Setting or Changing User Account Attributes

From the command line, setting or changing user account attributes is swift and easy using the DSMOD USER command. You can, in fact, set attributes for one or many users at the same time. Suppose that you want all 150 users in the Sales OU to have their department attribute set as "Sales & Marketing," their company attribute set as "City Power and Light," and their title set to "Customer Sales." You can do this with a single command-line entry:

```
dsquery user "OU=Sales,DC=cpandl,DC=com" | dsmod user -dept "Sales
& Marketing" -company "City Power and Light" -title "Customer Sales"
```

The DSMOD USER command would then report the individual success or failure of each change:

```
dsmod succeeded:CN=edwardh,OU=Sales,DC=cpandl,DC=com    no
dsmod succeeded:CN=erinp,OU=Sales,DC=cpandl,DC=com    no
dsmod succeeded:CN=jayo,OU=Sales,DC=cpandl,DC=com    no
dsmod succeeded:CN=johng,OU=Sales,DC=cpandl,DC=com    yes
...
dsmod succeeded:CN=williams,OU=Sales,DC=cpandl,DC=com    yes
```

Although changing these values in the GUI could take you hours, the entire process from the command line takes only a few minutes. You simply type the command-line entry and let DSMOD USER do the work for you.

Other parameters that you'll work with frequently include

- **–webpg** Sets an intranet or Internet address that will appear in the directory listing for the associated user, such as \\Intranet\Sales.
- **–profile** Sets the path to the user's profile, which provides the environment settings for user accounts, such as \\Gamma\Profiles\wrstanek.
- **–hmdrv** Sets the drive letter of the user's home directory, such as X:. The user's home directory will be mapped to this drive letter.
- **–hmdir** Sets the home directory for the user, such as \\Gamma\Users\wrstanek.

Caution Generally, you don't want to change user profile paths, home drives, or home directories when users are logged on, because this might cause problems. So you might want to update this information outside of normal business hours or ask the user to log off for a few minutes and then log back on.

Tip By default, if an error occurs when processing changes, DSMOD USER will halt execution and report the error. Generally, this is the behavior you want, because you don't want to make improper changes. You can, however, use the –C parameter to tell DSMOD USER to report the error but continue.

These parameters accept the special value *$username$*. This value lets you assign paths and filenames that are based on individual user names. For example, if you assign the home directory path as \\Gamma\Users\$username$\ or C:\Home*$username$*, Windows replaces the *$username$* value with the actual user name–and it does so for each user you're managing. This would mean if you are working with the accounts for erinb, sandyr, miked, and kyler, they would all be assigned unique home directories–either \\ Gamma \Users\erinb, \\ Gamma \Users\sandyr, \\ Gamma \Users\miked, and \\ Gamma \Users\kyler; or C:\Home\erinb, C:\Home\sandyr, C:\Home\miked, and C:\Home\kyler. In these examples, \\ Gamma \Users is a path to a network share and C:\Home represents a directory on the user's computer.

Following this, you could set the Web page, profile, home drive, and home directory for all users in the Sales OU by typing

```
dsquery user "OU=Sales,DC=cpandl,DC=com" | dsmod user -webpg
\\Intranet\Sales\$username$ -profile "\\corpdc02\sales\$username$"
-hmdrv "X:" -hmdir "\\corpserver01\users\$username$"
```

Real World With the Active Directory Users And Computers administrative tool, you enter the value *%username%* to get paths and filenames based on individual user names. Don't use this value with the special parameters discussed here. *%username%* is an environment variable and the GUI knows to replace the environment variable on a per-user basis. The command line interprets this and other environment variables based on the currently logged-on user, however. So in this case the value of *%username%* is the SAM account name of the user account under which you run the command.

Disabling and Enabling User Accounts

You can enable or disable users accounts from the command line using the DSMOD USER command and the –Disabled parameter. Use **–disabled yes** to disable the user account and **–disabled no** to enable the user account.

In the following example, you disable all users in the OffsiteUsers OU:

```
dsquery user "OU=OffsiteUsers,DC=cpandl,DC=com" | dsmod user -disabled yes
```

The DSMOD USER command would then report the individual success or failure of each change.

Resetting Expired User Accounts

You can set domain user accounts with a specific expiration date. You can check the account expiration date using DSGET USER with the –Acctexpires parameter. For example, if you wanted to check the expiration date of all user accounts in the Sales OU, you can type

```
dsquery user "OU=Sales,DC=cpandl,DC=com" | dsget user -dn -acctexpires
```

The resulting output would show you the account expiration dates of each account in the Sales OU according to the distinguished name of the account, such as

```
  dn    acctexpires
  CN=Lisa Andrews,OU=Sales,DC=cpandl,DC=com    never
  CN=Joseph Brad,OU=Sales,DC=cpandl,DC=com    11/15/2010
  CN=Ann Beebe,OU=Sales,DC=cpandl,DC=com    never
  CN=Jeanne Bosworth,OU=Sales,DC=cpandl,DC=com    12/31/2010
dsget succeeded
```

Here, accounts without expiration dates have an account expires value of "never" and other accounts have a specific expiration date, such as 11/15/2010.

If you need to extend or change the account expiration date to allow a user to log on to the domain, you can do this with DSMOD USER. Set the –Acctexpires parameter to the number of days for which the account should be valid. For example, if an account should be valid for the next 60 days, you would type **– acctexpires 60**, such as

```
dsquery user -name johnw | dsmod user -acctexpires 60
```

or

```
dsmod user "CN=John Woods,OU=Sales,DC=cpandl,DC=com" -acctexpires 60
```

In these examples you change the account expiration for John Woods.

If you want to remove an account expiration date, use a value of 0 to specify that the account never expires, such as

```
dsquery user -name johnw | dsmod user -acctexpires 0
```

> **Note** To set an account so that it is past the expiration date, you can type a negative value, such as –**acctexpires -1**.

Controlling and Resetting User Passwords

Using DSGET USER, you can check the password settings on user accounts. Typically, you'll want to know whether a user can change his or her password, whether the password expires, and whether the password uses reversible encryption. You can check for these settings using the –Canchpwd, –Pwdneverexpires, and –Reversiblepwd parameters respectively. You might also want to know whether the account is set so that the user must change his or her password on next logon. To do this, you can use the –Mustchpwd parameter. For example, if you wanted to check these values for all user accounts in the Users container, you can type

```
dsquery user "CN=Users,DC=cpandl,DC=com" | dsget user -samid -canchpwd
-pwdneverexpires -reversiblepwd -mustchpwd
```

The resulting output would show you the related password settings of each account in the Users container according to the SAM account name, such as

```
  samid     mustchpwd     canchpwd     reversiblepwd     pwdneverexpires
  andya     no     yes     no     no
  billg     no     yes     no     no
  bobh     yes     yes     no     no
  brianw     no     yes     no     no
  conniej     no     yes     yes     yes
dsget succeeded
```

DSMOD USER provides several parameters for controlling these and other password settings. You can use the –Pwd parameter to set the password for a particular user account. You can then configure how the password is used as follows:

- Use **–mustchpwd yes** to force users to change the password after their next logon.
- Use **–canchpwd no** to set the account so users can't change the password for their accounts.
- Use **–pwdneverexpires yes** to set the account so that the password never expires, which overrides Group Policy settings.

The wonderful thing about the command line is that you can control passwords for many user accounts as easily as for one user. Say you wanted to change the password for every user in the TempEmployee OU to Time2ChangeMe and force these users to change their passwords on next logon. You can do this by typing the command

```
dsquery user "OU=TempEmployee,DC=cpandl,DC=com" | dsmod user -pwd
Time2ChangeMe -mustchpwd yes
```

Moving User Accounts

User accounts are normally placed in the Users container or in OUs. You can move a user account to a different container or OU within its current domain using DSMOVE. Specify the user account's current DN and then use the –Newparent parameter to specify the new location or parent DN of the user account. For instance if you wanted to move the William Stanek user account from the Tech OU to the Engineering OU, you would specify the user account's DN, such as "**CN=William Stanek,OU=Tech, DC=cpandl,DC=com**", and provide the parent DN for the new location, such as "**OU=Engineering,DC=cpandl, DC=com**". The related command would look like this:

```
dsmove "CN=William Stanek,OU=Tech,DC=cpandl,DC=com" -newparent
"OU=Engineering,DC=cpandl,DC=com"
```

You could have also obtained the user account DN using the DSQUERY USER command. To do this, you simply pipe the output of DSQUERY USER to DSMOVE, as shown in this example:

```
dsquery user -name "William Stanek" | dsmove
-newparent "OU=Engineering,DC=cpandl,DC=com"
```

Here, the user account DN, "CN=William Stanek,OU=Tech,DC=cpandl, DC=com", is obtained from DSQUERY USER and used as input to DSMOVE.

Renaming User Accounts

Although moving user accounts is fairly straightforward, you don't want to rename user accounts without some planning. When you rename a user account, you give the account a new common name. You'll find that you might have to rename accounts in cases of marriage, divorce, or adoption. For example, if Nancy Anderson (nancya) gets married, she might want her user name to be changed to Nancy Freehafer (nancyf). When you rename her account, all associated privileges and permissions will reflect the name change. Thus, if you view the permissions on a file that nancya had access to, nancyf will now have access (and nancya will no longer be listed).

You rename user accounts using the DSMOVE command. Specify the user's DN and then use the –Newname parameter to specify the new common name. You can rename a user object from Nancy Anderson to Nancy Freehafer by typing

```
dsmove "CN=Nancy Anderson,OU=Marketing,DC=cpandl,DC=com"
-newname "Nancy Freehafer"
```

You could obtain the user DN by means of DSQUERY USER as well. Consider the following example:

```
dsquery user -name N*Anderson | dsmove -newname "Nancy Freehafer"
```

Here you use DSQUERY USER to find an account that begins with the letters "N" and ends with "Anderson." You then use DSMOVE to rename this account.

Renaming the user account doesn't change any of the other account properties. Because some properties may reflect the old last name, you will need to update these properties to reflect the name change using DSMOD USER. The parameters you might want to modify include

- **–Ln** Used to change the last name for the user account.
- **–Display** Used to change the user account's Display Name.
- **–Samid** Used to change the SAM account name.
- **–Profile** Used to change the profile path for the account. Afterward, you'll need to rename the corresponding directory on disk.

- **–Loscr** If you use individual logon scripts for each user, you can use –Loscr to change the logon script name property. Afterward, you'll need to rename the logon script on disk.
- **–Hmdir** Used to change the home directory path. Afterward, you'll need to rename the corresponding directory on disk.

> **Note** In most cases, you won't want to modify this information while a user is logged on because this might cause problems. Instead, update this information outside of normal business hours or ask the user to log off for a few minutes and then log back on.

Consider the following example:

```
dsquery user -name N*Freehafer | dsmod -samid nancyf -ln Freehafer
-display "Nancy Freehafer"
```

Here, you change the SAM account name, last name, and display name to match the previous name change for the user Nancy Freehafer.

> **Real World** User names are used to make managing and using accounts easier. Behind the scenes, Windows Server 2008 actually uses the account's security identifier (SID) to identify, track, and handle the account independently from the user name. SIDs are unique identifiers that are generated when accounts are created. Because SIDs are mapped to account names internally, you don't need to change the privileges or permissions on renamed accounts. Windows Server 2008 simply maps the SID to the new account name as necessary.

Deleting User Accounts

If you no longer need a user account, you can delete it permanently from Active Directory using the DSRM command. In most cases, you'll want to delete only a specific user account, such as the account for Lisa Andrews. If this is the case, you remove the account by passing DSRM the DN of the user account, such as

```
dsrm "CN=Lisa Andrews,OU=Sales,DC=cpandl,DC=com"
```

By default, DSRM prompts you to confirm the deletion. If you don't want to see the prompt, use the –Noprompt parameter, such as

```
dsrm "CN=Lisa Andrews,OU=Sales,DC=cpandl,DC=com" -noprompt
```

> **Note** Even though you delete a user's account, Windows Server 2008 won't delete the user's profile, personal files, or home directory. If you want to delete these files and directories, you'll have to do it manually. If this is a task you perform routinely, you might want to create a script that performs the necessary tasks for you. Keep in mind you should back up files or data that might be needed before you do this.

Overview of Managing Group Accounts from the Command Line

Group accounts help you manage privileges for multiple users. Windows Server 2008 has three types of groups:

- **Security groups** Groups that have security descriptors associated with them and are used to help manage access permissions. You create and manage security groups with the directory services commands.
- **Distribution groups** Groups used as e-mail distribution lists, which don't have security descriptors associated with them. You create and manage distribution groups with the directory services commands.
- **Local groups** Groups used on the local computer only. You create and manage local groups with the network services commands.

Security and distribution groups are used with domains. This makes them available throughout the directory. Local groups, however, are available only on the computer on which they are created. The general domain group account command-line utilities include

- **DSADD GROUP** Creates a group account in Active Directory. The syntax is

  ```
  dsadd group GroupDN [-secgrp {yes | no}] [-scope {l | g | u}]
  [-samid SAMName] [-desc Description] [-memberof Group ...]
  [-members Member ...] [{-s Server | -d Domain}] [-u UserName]
  [-p {Password | *}] [-q] [{-uc | -uco | -uci}]
  ```

- **DSGET GROUP** Displays the properties of group accounts using one of two syntaxes. The syntax for viewing the properties of multiple groups is

  ```
  dsget group GroupDN ... [-dn] [-samid] [-sid] [-desc] [-secgrp]
  [-scope] [{-s Server | -d Domain}] [-u UserName]
  [-p {Password | *}] [-c] [-q] [-l] [{-uc | -uco | -uci}]
  [-part PartitionDN [-qlimit] [-qused]]
  ```

  The syntax for viewing the group membership information for an individual group is

  ```
  dsget group GroupDN [{-memberof | -members} [-expand]] [
  {-s Server | -d Domain}] [-u UserName] [-p {Password | *}] [-c]
  [-q] [-l] [{-uc | -uco | -uci}]
  ```

- **DSMOD GROUP** Modifies attributes of one or more group accounts in the directory. The syntax is

  ```
  dsmod group GroupDN ... [-samid SAMName] [-desc Description]
  [-secgrp {yes | no}] [-scope {l | g | u}] [{-addmbr | -rmmbr |
  -chmbr} MemberDN ...] [{-s Server | -d Domain}] [-u UserName]
  [-p {Password | *}] [-c] [-q] [{-uc | -uco | -uci}]
  ```

Tip You can use input from DSQUERY GROUP to set the DN for the security group or groups you want to work with. You can also type the DNs for each group you want to work with. When you do this, make sure to separate each DN with a space.

To manage local group accounts, you use the NET LOCALGROUP command. This command has several different syntaxes. The syntax you use depends on what you want to do, as follows:

- **Create local group accounts** net localgroup [*GroupName* {/add [/comment:"*Text*"]}
- **Modify local group accounts** net localgroup [*GroupName Name* [...] {/add | /delete}]
- **Delete local group accounts** net localgroup [*GroupName* {/delete [/comment:"*Text*"]}

Note NET LOCALGROUP can be used to add a local group to a group in the current (logon) domain. In some limited situations you might want to consider doing this, but ordinarily you wouldn't use this technique to grant access permissions for regular users. For example, if you created a local group called DevTesters you can add this group to the Developers domain group. This would give local machine users who are members of the DevTesters group the same domain permissions as other members of the Developers domain group. Here, developers who are testing local system configurations need access to the domain.

Adding Group Accounts

The type of group you need depends on your network configuration. In domains, you'll typically work with security and distribution groups. In workgroups, you'll typically work with local groups that pertain only to specific computers.

Creating Security and Distribution Groups

As discussed previously, security groups are used to manage access permissions for groups of users, and distribution groups are used for mail distribution lists. Regardless of which type of group you create, the way the group is used depends on the scope. Scope controls the areas in which the groups are valid. The defined scopes are

- **Domain local groups** Groups used to grant permissions within a single domain. This group's members can include only accounts (both user and computer accounts) and groups from the domain in which they're defined.
- **Global groups** Groups used to grant permissions to objects in any domain in the domain tree or forest. This group's members can include only accounts and groups from the domain in which they're defined.

- **Universal groups** Groups used to grant permissions on a wide scale throughout a domain tree or forest. This group's members can include accounts, global groups, and other universal groups from any domain in the domain tree or forest.

Note Universal security groups are available only when Active Directory is running at the Windows 2000 native functional level or higher, and are more useful on larger networks than on smaller ones. Primarily this is because they add another level of group hierarchy for administrators to manage; therefore, their benefits are clearer in large installations where you need more control over groups.

Table 15-1 summarizes the capabilities of groups based on the scope and the operations mode. As the table shows, both affect what you can and can't do with groups.

Table 15-1 Group Capabilities with Regard to Functional Level and Scope

Group Capability	Domain Local Scope	Global Scope	Universal Scope
Windows 2000 Native functional level or higher	Members can include user accounts, global groups, and universal groups from any domain; domain local groups from the same domain only.	Members can include only user accounts from the same domain and global groups from the same domain.	Members can include user accounts from any domain, as well as groups from any domain regardless of scope.
Windows 2000 Mixed functional level	Members can include user accounts and global groups from any domain.	Members can include only user and group accounts from the same domain.	Universal security groups can't be created in mixed-mode domains.
Member Of	Can be put into other domain local groups and assigned permissions only in the same domain.	Can be put into other groups and assigned permissions in any domain.	Can be put into other groups and assigned permissions in any domain.

When you create groups, you pass DSADD GROUP the group's DN. The common name component of the DN sets the group's display name. The rest of the DN specifies where in Active Directory the group is to be located, which includes the container in which the group is to be created and the related domain. By default, if you provide no other parameters, a global security group is created. For example, you could create a global security group called Sales in the Sales organizational unit of the cpandl.com domain by typing **dsadd group "CN=Sales,OU=Sales,DC=cpandl,DC=com"**. The group would be created with Sales as the group's display name and the same value as the SAM account name. No other properties would be set, however.

Group names aren't case-sensitive and can be as long as 64 characters. In most cases, you'll want to specify the group type and scope directly. You use the –Secgrp parameter to specify whether the group is a security group, as follows:

- Type **–secgrp yes** to specify that you are creating a security group.
- Type **–secgrp no** to specify that you are creating a distribution group.

To set the group scope, use the –Scope parameter, as follows:

- Type **–scope l** to create a local domain group.
- Type **–scope g** to create a global group.
- Type **–scope u** to create a universal group. For security groups, the universal group scope is valid only when running at the Windows 2000 functional level or higher.

> **Note** By default, groups are created as security groups with a global scope. Therefore, even if you create a security group with a different scope, you don't have to specify **–secgrp yes** because this is the default.

The first 20 characters of the group name are used to set the SAM account name of the group, which is also referred to as the pre–Windows 2000 group name. The SAM account name must be unique in the domain, and if there is overlap you might want the group's SAM account name to be different from its display name. In this case, you would need to set the SAM account name using the –Samid parameter.

You can also specify the group membership when you create the group. If the group you are creating should be a member of an existing group, you can use the –Memberof parameter to specify the DNs for these groups. If the group should have users or other groups as its members, you can specify the DNs for these members using the –Members parameter. However, it is much easier to use DSMOD GROUP to configure group membership. Why? You can pass DSMOD GROUP a list of DNs as input from DSQUERY USER. This saves you from having to type several dozen and sometimes hundreds of DNs.

Consider the following examples to see how groups can be created:

Create a domain local security group called Engineering. Add the group to the Engineering OU in the tech.cpandl.com domain:

```
dsadd group "CN=Engineering,OU=Engineering,DC=tech,DC=cpandl,
DC=com" -scope l
```

Create a global security group called Engineering Global in the Users container of the cpandl.com domain. Set the SAM account name to gEngineering:

```
dsadd group "CN=Engineering Global,CN=Users,DC=cpandl,DC=com"
-samid "gEngineering"
```

Create a universal distribution group called Engineering All in the Engineering OU of the cpandl.com domain. Set the SAM account name to allEngineering:

```
dsadd group "CN=Engineering All,OU=Engineering,DC=cpandl,DC=com"
-samid "allEngineering" -secgrp no -scope u
```

If you encounter problems creating the group, you'll see a warning and you'll need to check your syntax to ensure that all the values are set appropriately and that the DN values are valid. Otherwise, DSADD GROUP should report DSADD SUCCEEDED. Once the group is created, you can add members and set additional properties, as discussed later in this chapter.

Creating a Local Group and Assigning Members

Local groups are created on individual computers to help manage permissions for users that log on locally instead of logging on to the domain. To create a local group, you'll need to log on to the computer you want to work with or use a remote logon to access a local command prompt. Once you are logged on to the computer, you can create the required local group account using NET LOCALGROUP.

You can create the local group simply by following the command name with the name of the group and then using the /Add parameter. Consider the following example:

```
net localgroup localDevs /add
```

> **Note** You can't create local group accounts on domain controllers. Domain controllers do not have local machine accounts.

Here, you create a group called localDevs on the local computer. If you wanted, you could also use the /Comment parameter to add a description of the group, such as

```
net localgroup localDevs /comment:"Local Developers and Testers" /add
```

If the account creation is successful, NET LOCALGROUP will state "Command Completed Successfully." However, if you encounter problems creating the account, NET LOCALGROUP won't display an error message per se. Instead, it will display the command syntax. In this case, check your syntax and ensure that all the values are set appropriately.

When you create a local group, you can also specify a list of local user accounts which should be members of the group. This list of names follows the group name as shown in this example:

```
net localgroup localDevs williams johng edwardh /add
```

Here, you create a group called localDevs and add WilliamS, JohnG, and EdwardH as members.

If you want to add members to a local group later rather than when you create the group, you can do this as well. The syntax is the same as for creating the group. For example, if you create a group called custSupport by typing

```
net localgroup custSupport /add
```

You could later add members to this group by typing

```
net localgroup custSupport williams johng edwardh /add
```

Here, you add WilliamS, JohnG, and EdwardH as members to the custSupport group.

Managing Group Accounts

Managing group accounts from the command line is different from managing them in Active Directory Groups And Computers, chiefly because the command line offers more options and it is easier to work with multiple group accounts at the same time.

Viewing and Finding Group Accounts

When you want to obtain information about group accounts, you can use the DSQUERY GROUP command. This command lets you search by common name, SAM account name, and description. It also accepts wildcards in any of these fields. The output of DSQUERY GROUP contains the distinguished name of groups that match the search criteria and can be piped as input to other commands, including DSGET GROUP.

Typically, you'll use DSQUERY GROUP and DSGET GROUP together. You start by using DSQUERY GROUP to obtain the distinguished names of one or more groups and then use DSGET GROUP to display the properties for the related accounts. DSGET GROUP parameters that you might find useful include

- **–Desc** Displays the description of matching group accounts in the output
- **–Dn** Displays the distinguished name of matching group accounts in the output
- **–Samid** Displays the SAM account name of matching group accounts in the output
- **–Scope** Displays the scope of matching groups as domain local, global, or universal

- **–Secgrp** Displays yes if a group is a security group and no if a group is a distribution group
- **–Sid** Displays the security identifier for matching group accounts in the output

As with the other DSGET commands, DSGET GROUP displays output in table format and you will usually want to include –Dn or –Samid as a parameter to help you make sense of and identify the groups in the output. For example, if you wanted to search for all marketing groups that were available, you could use the command line

```
dsquery group -name marketing* | dsget group -dn -scope -secgrp
```

Here, the results display the DN, the scope, and security group information:

```
  dn     scope    secgrp
  CN=MarketingAll,OU=Sales,DC=cpandl,DC=com    universal    no
  CN=Marketing Global,OU=Sales,DC=cpandl,DC=com    global    no
  CN=Marketing Local,OU=Sales,DC=cpandl,DC=com    domain local    no
dsget succeeded
```

Determining Group Membership

When you want to determine group membership, you use the second syntax for DSGET GROUP, which includes two special parameters: –Members and –Memberof. You use the –Members parameter to determine which users and groups belong to a specific group. You use the –Memberof parameter to determine the groups to which the specified group belongs. How do these parameters work? Let's suppose that you wanted to see the current members of a group called AllUsers. You could do this by typing

```
dsquery group -name AllUsers | dsget group -members
```

Or you could type the group DN directly, such as

```
dsget group "CN=AllUsers,CN=Users,DC=cpandl,DC=com" -members
```

Here the group is in the Users container of the cpandl.com domain. Either way, the output would show the DNs for members of this group, such as

```
"CN=Tech,OU=Tech,DC=cpandl,DC=com"
"CN=Engineering,OU=Eng,DC=cpandl,DC=com"
"CN=Sales,OU=Sales,DC=cpandl,DC=com"
"CN=Domain Users,CN=Users,DC=cpandl,DC=com"
```

As the listing shows, the AllUsers group has as its members the Tech, Engineering, Sales, and Domain Users groups. The AllUsers group could have also had user accounts as its members.

If you want to determine to which groups a group belongs, you can use the –Memberof parameter. For example, the group DevUsers could be a member of the Domain

Administrators group and the Developers group, and you could display this membership information by typing

```
dsquery group -name devusers | dsget group -memberof
```

or

```
dsget group "CN=devusers,OU=Dev,DC=cpandl,DC=com" -memberof
```

Both commands work the same. In the first example, you use DSQUERY GROUP to obtain the DN of the group account. In the second example, you specify the DN directly. Either way the output would be a list of groups in which DevUsers is a member.

Note You could use both techniques to display the membership information of multiple groups. However, you have no way to display a DN or SAM account name for the associated groups because the second syntax for DSGET GROUP doesn't allow this.

Changing Group Type or Scope

Sometimes after you create a group you'll want to change the group type or scope. This isn't as easy as you might think, because a number of controls are in place to prevent arbitrary changes that can affect access throughout the organization. First of all, you cannot change group type or scope in Windows 2000 Mixed or Windows Server 2003 Interim functional levels. In Windows 2000 Native, Windows Server 2003, or Windows Server 2008 functional level, the following is true:

- **Domain Local Groups** Can be converted to universal scope, provided the group doesn't have as its member another group having domain local scope.
- **Global Groups** Can be converted to universal scope, provided the group is not a member of any other group having global scope.
- **Universal Groups** Can be converted to any other group scope. Keep in mind a global group cannot have a universal group as a member and that local groups can only be members of other local groups.

With these restrictions in mind, you can use DSMOD GROUP and its –Secgrp parameter to change the group type as follows:

- Change a distribution group to a security group by including **– secgrp yes**.
- Change a security group to a distribution group by including **– secgrp no**.

Consider the following examples:

Convert the Engineering security group to a distribution group:

```
dsquery group -name Engineering | dsmod group -secgrpno
```

Convert the AllMarketing distribution group to a security group:

```
dsmod group "CN=AllMarketing,OU=Marketing,DC=cpandl,DC=com"
-secgrp yes
```

You change the group scope using the –Scope parameter of DSMOD GROUP as follows:

- Set the scope as domain local by including **–scope l**.
- Set the scope as global by including **–scope g**.
- Set the scope as universal by including **–scope u**.

Consider the following examples:

Set the scope of the Marketing group to domain local:

```
dsquery group -name Marketing | dsmod group -scope l
```

Set the scope of the Sales group to global:

```
dsmod group "CN=Sales,CN=Users,DC=cpandl,DC=com" -scope g
```

Adding, Removing, or Replacing Group Members

Using the command line, you can easily change the membership of any group. As with the GUI, you can easily add or remove users, groups, or computers as members of a group. But the command-line utilities take this a step further in making it easy to add or remove multiple members. You can also replace the existing membership list entirely.

Adding Members to a Group

You can, for example, use a single command line to add all 100 users in the Sales organizational unit to the AllSales group. To do this, you would use DSQUERY USER to obtain a list of user accounts that you want to work with and then pass this list as input to DSMOD GROUP. The parameter for adding group members is –Addmbr so the command would look like this:

```
dsquery user "OU=Sales,DC=ny,DC=cpandl,DC=com" | dsmod group "CN=AllSales,
OU=Sales,DC=ny,DC=cpandl,DC=com" -addmbr
```

Here, you obtain a list of all user accounts in the Sales OU of the ny.cpandl.com domain and pass this as input to DSMOD GROUP. DSMOD GROUP then adds these users as members to the AllSales group, which is located in the Sales container of the ny.cpandl.com domain.

Another way to use –Addmbr is to specify the DNs of the objects you want to add. For example, if you wanted to add the SalesLocal and SalesGlobal groups to the AllSales group, you could do so with the following command-line entry:

```
dsquery group -name AllSales | dsmod group
-addmbr "CN=SalesLocal,OU=Sales,DC=ny,DC=cpandl,DC=com"
"CN=SalesGlobal,OU=Sales,DC=ny,DC=cpandl,DC=com"
```

> **Note** Remember, the object DNs could include user and group accounts as well as computer accounts.

Removing Members from a Group

The counterpart to –Addmbr is –Rmmbr, which you use to remove members from groups. As with –Addmbr, –Rmmbr accepts object DNs from input or in a space-separated list. So if you wanted to remove all marketing and customer support users from the AllSales group, one way to do this is to use the following commands:

```
dsquery user "OU=Marketing,DC=ny,DC=cpandl,DC=com" | dsmod group
"CN=AllSales,OU=Sales,DC=ny,DC=cpandl,DC=com" -rmmbr

dsquery user "OU=CustSupport,DC=ny,DC=cpandl,DC=com" | dsmod group
"CN=AllSales,OU=Sales,DC=ny,DC=cpandl,DC=com" -rmmbr
```

Here, the first command obtains a list of all users in the Marketing OU and then passes this as input to DSMOD GROUP so that these users can be removed from the AllSales group. The second command obtains a list of all users in the CustSupport OU and then passes this as input to DSMOD GROUP so that these users can be removed from the AllSales group.

> **Tip** A problem is introduced if the two lists of users don't match exactly to the current membership for the AllSales group. For example, if new marketing users have started working and they've been added to the Marketing OU but not been granted access to Sales information, they wouldn't be in the AllSales group. In this case, when the DSMOD GROUP command finds the first mismatch, it will exit and report an error. But you don't want that to happen because of a slight mismatch. So to prevent this, add the –C parameter. This parameter says to report errors but continue processing changes.

As with –Addmbr, you can also specify the DNs of the objects you want to remove directly. Say you wanted to remove the SalesLocal and SalesGlobal groups from the AllSales group. You could do this with the following command-line entry:

```
dsquery group -name AllSales | dsmod group
-rmmbr "CN=SalesLocal,OU=Sales,DC=ny,DC=cpandl,DC=com"
"CN=SalesGlobal,OU=Sales,DC=ny,DC=cpandl,DC=com"
```

Note With the formatting of the page, you might not notice it, but there is a space between each of the group DNs. The space is necessary so that each group DN is interpreted correctly.

Replacing All Members in a Group

The command line takes the notion of adding and removing group members a step further than the GUI by allowing you to replace the entire membership list of a group. For example, if the group membership for the AllUsers group wasn't up to date and it would be hard to add and remove members manually, you might want to replace the existing membership and start over.

You replace the existing group members with a list of your choosing with the –Chmbr parameter of the DSMOD GROUP command. This parameter accepts input that is passed from DSQUERY USER or a space-separated list of DNs. So one way to replace the existing membership list and add all users in the organization to the AllUsers group is to type the following command:

```
dsquery user -name * | dsmod group
"CN=AllUsers,CN=Users,DC=seattle,DC=cpandl,DC=com" -chmbr
```

Here, DSMOD GROUP first removes all the existing objects that are members and then adds the objects passed as input. If any error occurs in either part of the processing, the command will fail and no changes will occur.

Note Although you can use the –C parameter to ensure that the operation continues even in the event of errors, this can result in the group having an empty membership. What happens is that the DSMOD GROUP command removes the current members without any problems but fails when trying to add members. The removal of members requires only the proper administrative permissions. The addition of members, however, depends on the input you provide.

Moving Group Accounts

As with user accounts, you can easily move a group account to a different container or OU within its current domain. To do this, you use the DSMOVE command to specify the group account's current DN and then use the –Newparent parameter to specify the new location or parent DN of the group account. For instance, if you wanted to move the ProdDev group from the Users container to the Developers organizational unit, you would specify the group account's DN, such as **"CN=ProdDev,CN=Users, DC=cpandl,DC=com"**, and provide the parent DN for the new location, such as **"OU=Developers,DC=cpandl,DC=com"**. The related command would look like this:

```
dsmove "CN=ProdDev,CN=Users,DC=cpandl,DC=com"
-newparent "OU=Developers,DC=cpandl,DC=com"
```

DSQUERY GROUP can also save you some typing by sending the group DN to DSMOVE as input, as shown in this example:

```
dsquery group -name "ProdDev" | dsmove
-newparent "OU=Developers,DC=cpandl,DC=com"
```

Here, the group account DN, "CN=ProdDev,CN=Users,DC=cpandl,DC=com", is obtained from DSQUERY GROUP and used as input to DSMOVE.

Renaming Group Accounts

As with users, groups have security identifiers. This allows you to change a group name without having to change the access permissions later on individual resources, such as files and folders. When you rename a group, you change its common name.

You rename groups using the DSMOVE command. Specify the group's DN and then use the –Newname parameter to specify the new common name. You can rename a group object from ProdDevs to TechDevs by typing

```
dsmove "CN=ProdDevs,OU=Developers,DC=cpandl,DC=com" -newname "TechDevs"
```

As when moving groups, you can also obtain the group DN from DSQUERY GROUP. Consider the following example:

```
dsquery group -name ProdDevs | dsmove -newname "TechDevs"
```

Here you use DSQUERY GROUP to obtain the DN for the ProdDevs group, and then use DSMOVE to rename the group.

Because renaming a group doesn't change the pre–Windows 2000 group name or description associated with the group, you'll need to change these properties next. To do this, use the DSMOD GROUP command. The –Samid parameter sets the pre–Windows 2000 group name and the –Desc parameter sets the description. Consider the following example:

```
dsquery group -name TechDevs | dsmod -samid techdevs
-desc "Technical Developers Group"
```

Here, you change the pre–Windows 2000 group name to **techdevs** and the description to "Technical Developers Group."

Deleting Group Accounts

To delete a group permanently from Active Directory, you can use the DSRM command. In most cases, you'll want to delete only a named group rather than, for example, all groups whose names start with "M." If this is the case, you remove the group by passing DSRM the DN of the group account, such as

```
dsrm "CN=AllSales,OU=Sales,DC=chicago,DC=cpandl,DC=com"
```

By default, DSRM prompts you to confirm the deletion. If you don't want to see the prompt, use the –Noprompt parameter, such as

```
dsrm "CN=AllSales,OU=Sales,DC=chicago,DC=cpandl,DC=com" -noprompt
```

In some limited situations, you might want to remove several groups at once. For example, if your marketing department is outsourced as the result of a company-wide reorganization, you might find that you no longer need marketing-related groups. If the group names begin with the keyword *Marketing*, you could delete them by typing

```
dsquery group -name Marketing* | dsrm -c
```

Here, you pass as input to DSRM the group DNs for all groups that begin with the keyword *Marketing*. The –C parameter is added to allow the operation to continue if an error occurs.

> **Caution** Even though input is passed to the command from DSQUERY GROUP, you can't use DSRM by itself. For example, you couldn't type **dsquery group –name Marketing* | dsrm**. The reason for this is that the command line still expects the DN of the object or a parameter to follow the DSRM command. Therefore, you would have to use some parameter, and –C is the safest because it only tells DSRM to continue in the event of an error. –Noprompt, on the other hand, tells DSRM go ahead and delete everything without prompting the user, which could lead to many more groups than expected being deleted and no way to cancel the operation.

Part V

Windows Network Administration Using the Command Line

In this part:

Chapter 16

Administering Network Printers and Print Services

Most organizations have a mix of high-volume and low-volume, low-cost printers. Typically, the high-volume printers handle the heavy, daily loads of multiple users, and the low-volume, low-cost printers handle the print loads of small groups or individual users. Regardless of usage, the print server needs sufficient memory and processing power to handle the print services. In a high-volume environment or an environment in which very large or complex documents are routinely printed, the server may need to be specially configured or dedicated to print services only. Otherwise, print servers typically aren't expensive or dedicated computers. In fact, many print servers are standard desktop systems that handle other network jobs as well. Just keep in mind that Windows Server 2008 and Windows Vista give higher priority to file sharing than to print sharing, so if a system handles both services, printing might be slowed to accommodate file services and prevent any file access performance problems.

Print servers must have sufficient disk space to handle print jobs as well. The amount of disk space required depends on the size of the print jobs and how long the print queue gets. For best performance, the printer's spool folder should be on a dedicated drive that isn't used for any other purpose. A key part of print services administration is maintenance. To maintain and support print services properly, you should keep track of print spooler information and usage statistics. This information helps you determine how print services are performing. Although you are focused on performance issues, you'll find that several useful command-line utilities can help you maintain print servers and troubleshoot printer issues. These utilities are discussed in this chapter.

Obtaining Support and Troubleshooting Information for Printers

Printers are often purchased and deployed without much thought given to how the printers will be used. Someone sees that a printer is needed in an area and a printer is ordered and installed. Sometimes it's not even an administrator that does the printer ordering and installation, so when you try to manage and maintain it, you may be flying blind. Regardless of how printers are obtained, the administration or support teams should maintain information about each printer's configuration, including what drivers are available and which drivers are used. You need to periodically check how busy the printer is and if it is handling the workload. You'll also want to track the printer status, the number of jobs queued, and other important information that can help you determine any problems. In many cases, this information is also useful for capacity planning.

Working with Printers at the Command Line

Working with printers at the command line is different from working with other components and hardware. The key reason is that the tools you need are stored in subdirectories that aren't part of the command path by default. You either need to change to these directories to use the related tools, or update the command path as discussed in the section titled "Managing the Command Path" in Chapter 2, "Getting the Most from the Command Line." In a locale-specific subfolder of %SystemRoot%\System32\Printing_Admin_Scripts, such as c:\Windows\System32\Printing_Admin_Scripts\en-us, you'll find the following Windows Scripts:

- **prncnfg.vbs** Allows you to list and manage printer configuration settings
- **prndrvr.vbs** Allows you to list, install, and manage printer drivers
- **prnjobs.vbs** Allows you to list and manage print jobs in a print queue
- **prnmngr.vbs** Allows you to install, list, and remove printers
- **prnport.vbs** Allows you to add, configure, and remove TCP/IP ports used by printers
- **prnqctl.vbs** Allows you to manage print queues
- **pubprn.vbs** Allows you to publish a printer in Active Directory

If this is your first time working with Windows scripts from the computer's command line, or if you've configured WScript as the primary script host, you will need to set CScript as the default script host. You do this by typing **cscript //h:cscript //s** at the command prompt. You will then work with the command-line script host rather than the graphical script host. Keep in mind that the script host is set on a per-user basis. Thus, if you are running a script as a specific user, that user might not have CScript configured as the default script host and you might want to type **cscript //h:cscript //s** as a line in your script.

With any of these scripts, you can specify the remote computer to work with by using the –S parameter and specifying logon credentials with the –U and –W parameters. Use the –U parameter to specify the user account for logon and the –W parameter to specify the password for that account. In the following example, you set the remote computer as PrintServer43 and use the credentials of WilliamS:

```
-s PrintServer43 -u WilliamS -w Rover
```

> **Note** As with most other commands, you can specify the user domain as well as the user account. Use the form *Domain\User*.

Another useful tool is the Printer Backup and Migration utility (Printbrm.exe). When you install the Print Services tools for Remote Server Administration or add the Print Services role to a Windows server, you'll find Printbrm in the %SystemRoot%\System32\Spool\Tools folder. You can use Printbrm to do the following:

- List summary configuration information for printers.
- Back up and restore a print server's configuration.
- Convert LPR ports to standard TCP/IP ports on restore.
- Migrate printers and print queues from one computer to another.
- Publish all available printers in Active Directory.

Because Printbrm is a command-line utility, you don't need to execute it via a script host. When you are using Printbrm, you can use the –S parameter to specify a remote computer to work with. However, because you cannot specify alternate credentials, you'll want to ensure that you are using an elevated command prompt and are logged on with an account that has appropriate privileges for working with printers, print drivers, and print queues.

Tracking Print Drivers and Printer Information

To get a better understanding of how printers are configured and used on a print server, you'll want to track detailed information about the printers installed. One tool you can use to get information about installed printers and their drivers is the Prndrvr utility. Using Prndrvr with the –L parameter, you can list all printers installed on the local computer along with their print driver configuration. As Listing 16-1 shows, the print driver and printer information is very detailed.

Listing 16-1 Output from Prndrvr -l

```
Server name PrintServer43
Driver name magicolor 2300 DL,3,Windows NT x86
Version 3
Environment Windows NT x86
Monitor name MLMON__B.DLL
Driver path C:\Windows\system32\spool\DRIVERS\W32X86\3\MIMFN5_B.DLL
Data file C:\Windows\system32\spool\DRIVERS\W32X86\3\MSDMLT_B.SDD
Config file C:\Windows\system32\spool\DRIVERS\W32X86\3\MNT5UI_B.DLL
Help file C:\Windows\system32\spool\DRIVERS\W32X86\3\MSDMLT_B.HLP
Dependent files
 C:\Windows\system32\spool\DRIVERS\W32X86\3\MSPL32_B.EXE
 C:\Windows\system32\spool\DRIVERS\W32X86\3\MSPOOL_B.DLL
 C:\Windows\system32\spool\DRIVERS\W32X86\3\MIMFPR_B.DLL
 C:\Windows\system32\spool\DRIVERS\W32X86\3\MIMF32_B.DLL
 C:\Windows\system32\spool\DRIVERS\W32X86\3\MSDIMF_B.DLL
 C:\Windows\system32\spool\DRIVERS\W32X86\3\MQDPRT_B.DLL
 C:\Windows\system32\spool\DRIVERS\W32X86\3\MSD32__B.DLL
 C:\Windows\system32\spool\DRIVERS\W32X86\3\MSR32__B.DLL
```

```
C:\Windows\system32\spool\DRIVERS\W32X86\3\MDDM32_B.DLL
C:\Windows\system32\spool\DRIVERS\W32X86\3\MCMM___B.DLL
C:\Windows\system32\spool\DRIVERS\W32X86\3\MICM___B.DLL
C:\Windows\system32\spool\DRIVERS\W32X86\3\MGDI32_B.DLL
C:\Windows\system32\spool\DRIVERS\W32X86\3\MDDMUI_B.DLL
C:\Windows\system32\spool\DRIVERS\W32X86\3\MTAG32_B.DLL
C:\Windows\system32\spool\DRIVERS\W32X86\3\MLTSRV_B.DLL
C:\Windows\system32\spool\DRIVERS\W32X86\3\MSUMLT_B.DLL
C:\Windows\system32\spool\DRIVERS\W32X86\3\MSUMLT_B.INI
C:\Windows\system32\spool\DRIVERS\W32X86\3\MSDMLT_B.DLL
C:\Windows\system32\spool\DRIVERS\W32X86\3\MICM6__B.ICM
C:\Windows\system32\spool\DRIVERS\W32X86\3\MICM12_B.ICM
C:\Windows\system32\spool\DRIVERS\W32X86\3\MICM24_B.ICM
C:\Windows\system32\spool\DRIVERS\W32X86\3\MICM6L_B.ICM
C:\Windows\system32\spool\DRIVERS\W32X86\3\MICM12LB.ICM
C:\Windows\system32\spool\DRIVERS\W32X86\3\MICM24LB.ICM
C:\Windows\system32\spool\DRIVERS\W32X86\3\MSEP01_B.SEP
C:\Windows\system32\spool\DRIVERS\W32X86\3\MUINST_B.EXE
C:\Windows\system32\spool\DRIVERS\W32X86\3\MUNZ___B.UNM
```

If you examine the detailed driver information, you'll see that the following information is included:

- **The printer driver name, such as magicolor 2300 dl** The printer driver name is the name used by Windows to track the printer driver. The driver used for a printer should match the actual type of printer being used. In this case, the printer is a Minolta QMS Magicolor 2300 DL series printer. When you print a document, the application from which you are printing uses the printer driver to translate the document into a file format understandable by the physical print device. If you were having problems with a printer and suspected the wrong driver was loaded, this would be one of the best indicators.
- **The printer driver mode** Printer drivers either operate in Type 2 (kernel) mode or Type 3 (user) mode. In the output, these modes are referred to as Version 2 for kernel mode or Version 3 for user mode. In kernel mode, the driver operates like other programs run directly by the operating system. In user mode, the driver runs like programs run by users. Stop errors from kernel-mode printer drivers are typically more detailed than those from user-mode printer drivers. However, printer drivers operating in kernel mode are more likely to cause system instability if they have problems. In Windows Vista and Windows Server 2008, user mode drivers are preferred to help ensure the stability of the operating system.
- **Available driver environments** When you share a printer, Windows automatically makes drivers available so that users can download them when they first connect to the printer. Typically, only Type 3 x86 drivers are available by default. Type 3 x86 drivers can be used with 32-bit editions of Windows. To make drivers available for additional environments, you'll need to install and enable them. For example, if your organization has X64 or IA64 computers, you can install print drivers available for these computers.

- **The print monitor being used** Each print device has an associated print monitor. Printers that support bidirectional printing have a language monitor that handles two-way communication between the printer and the print spooler as well as a port monitor that controls the I/ O port to the printer. These collectively are referred to as the *print monitor for a print device*. If a printer has an associated language monitor, the name of this monitor is specified and that name is the same as its filename, without the .dll extension. If a printer doesn't have an associated language monitor, the value (Null) is specified or no name is specified. When a document reaches the top of the printer stack, the print monitor is responsible for sending it to the print device. The print device is the physical hardware on which the document is actually printed. Most print devices have their own print monitors, which were created by the manufacturer of the device. Windows has a default print monitor as well. A print monitor is required to print to a print device. If the print monitor is corrupted or missing, you might need to reinstall it.
- **The print spooler DLL and related data files** The specific DLL for the print spooler is specified by the driver path. The spooler has associated data, config, and help files. The print spooler is what passes documents that users want printed to the print processor. The print processor in turn creates the raw print data necessary for printing on the print device. This data is in turn passed back to the print spooler so that it can be routed.
- **The printer driver stack files** All the stack files associated with a particular printer driver are listed as dependent files. Documents are routed (using the print router) from the print spooler to the printer stack, which is also called the print queue. Once in the print queue, documents are referred to as print jobs, which essentially means the documents are tasks for the print spooler to handle.

To use Prndrvr to return driver information for remote print servers and network printers, use the –S parameter followed by the domain name of the server, such as

```
prndrvr -s corpserver01
```

Here, you are examining printer driver information on CorpServer01.

Several details are missing from the Prndrvr output that would give you a complete picture regarding printer configuration. To get this additional information, you can use Printbrm with the –Q parameter. Although the output from Printbrm –Q is similar to that provided with Prndrvr –l, it provides important additional information. Consider the following example output:

```
Operation mode: query
Target server: local machine
Queue publish mode: none
Overwrite Mode: keep existing settings
```

```
LISTING PRINT QUEUES
hp laserjet 9500 on second floor
magicolor 2300 main floor
Adobe PDF

LISTING PRINTER DRIVERS
hp laserjet 9500 series, Windows NT x86, HP_PRNMON.DLL
magicolor 2300 DL, Windows NT x86, MLMON__B.DLL
Adobe PDF Converter, Windows NT x86, None

LISTING PRINT PROCESSORS
hpzpplhn Windows NT x86 hpzpplhn.dll
MIMFPR_B Windows NT x86 MIMFPR_B.DLL

LISTING PRINTER PORTS
192.168.0.90, TCP
192.168.1.90, TCP

Displaying print hierarchy.
hp laserjet 9500 on second floor
        hp laserjet 9500 (Windows NT x86) #1
        192.168.1.80 #1
magicolor 2300 main floor
        magicolor 2300 DL (Windows NT x86) #1
        192.168.1.90 #1
Adobe PDF
        Adobe PDF Converter (Windows NT x86) #1
Unassociated:
        192.168.0.70 #0
```

In the output, you'll find the following information:

- A list of all available print queues with each queue listed by name
- A list of print drivers for installed printers listed by print driver name, driver environments enabled, and associated print monitor
- A list of configured ports for network printers listed by IP address and type
- A list of the print hierarchy on the computer that correlates print queues to their associated print drivers and, if applicable, printer ports

Note Printers directly connected to a print server use LPT, COM, or USB ports. Network-attached printers usually have an IP address and a TCP port.

Getting Detailed Print Statistics for Capacity Planning and Troubleshooting

Tracking print queue information and usage statistics can help you answer these important questions about the print services in your organization:

- How busy is the print server on average?
- What is the average size of print jobs?
- How many print jobs are queued and waiting?
- What is the current printer status?
- How long has the print spooler been running?
- How long has the printer been up?
- How long has the print server been up?

Why are the answers to these questions important? They're important because if you can answer these questions, you can proactively manage and maintain your organization's print services. You can also plan for future needs. Thus, rather than being a firefighter who responds only to problems, you'll be able to stay a step ahead of any major issues, thereby providing a better experience for users throughout your organization.

The key tool you'll use to track print spool information and usage statistics is the Print Queue counter object, accessed with the TYPEPERF command. This performance counter object has many performance counters that you can use to track print queues and usage statistics. As discussed in Chapters 6 through 9, you can use a number of techniques to work with and automatically monitor performance objects at the command line.

When working with the Print Queue object, you'll want to track counters of the _Total instance to determine how busy the print server is overall as well as individual instances to determine how busy a particular print queue is. Important counters to track to determine usage include:

- **Bytes Printed/sec** Lists the number of bytes printed per second and gives you a good idea of how much data the printer is handling and how busy a printer is. Compare the Bytes Printed/sec value to the printer server's up time to get a good indicator of how much data the printer is handling on an hourly or daily basis.

> **Note** In some printer configurations, print jobs are saved after they've been queued. This allows a user to resubmit a document to the printer from the print queue instead of from an application. If you configure a printer to keep print jobs, you'll want to keep close tabs on Bytes Printed/sec and Total Jobs Printed. This helps you determine how much disk space will be required to maintain print services and gives you a good indicator of how frequently you might need to clear old jobs from the print queue.

> **Tip** Most printers have internal memory. Ideally you want that memory to be large enough so that entire print jobs can be handed off to the print device. If you find that a printer is being used routinely for large or complex print jobs, you probably want to add memory to the print device. Note that you need to refer to the printer's config page (which can be printed on the printer itself) to determine its installed RAM.

- **Jobs** Shows the number of printer jobs queued and waiting to print. Busy printers will typically have several jobs queued and waiting, especially at peak usage times. If you frequently see many jobs waiting to print, however, the printer may be overloaded. You could help improve this situation by letting users know about other available printers or perhaps setting different default printers for some of these users.
- **Jobs Spooling** Lists the current number of print jobs being spooled to the print queue. These are incoming print jobs.
- **Max Jobs Spooling** Lists the peak number of print jobs being spooled to the print queue.
- **References** Lists the current number of handles open to a print queue. This is important to track because each open handle uses resources, and open handles can be from clients that aren't actively printing.
- **Max References** Lists the peak number of handles open to a print queue.
- **Total Jobs Printed** Shows how many printer jobs have been processed since the last restart of the print server. This is a relative indicator of how busy a printer is. Compare the total number of printer jobs to the printer server's up time to get a good indicator of how busy the printer really is.
- **Total Pages Printed** Lists the total number of pages printed on a print queue since the last restart. This is a relative indicator of how busy a printer is.

Sample 16-1 provides an example of how you can use TYPEPERF to get a snapshot of the relative print load of multiple print servers across the enterprise. In this example, you use a counter file called Perf.txt to specify the counters you want to track. In addition to the print queue counters, you track the System Up Time counter of the System object to determine the elapsed time in seconds that the computer has been running since it was last started. You collect one sample from each print server and save the output in a file called SaveData.txt. If you import the data into a spreadsheet or convert it to a table in a Word document, you can make better sense of the output and will know exactly how busy each printer server is.

Sample 16-1 Getting usage statistics for print servers

Command line

```
typeperf -cf c:\printers\perf.txt -o c:\printers\savedata.txt -sc 1 -y
```

Source for perf.txt

```
\\printserver14\system\System Up Time
\\printserver14\print queue(_Total)\Bytes Printed/Sec
\\printserver14\print queue(_Total)\Jobs Spooling
\\printserver14\print queue(_Total)\Max Jobs Spooling
\\printserver14\print queue(_Total)\Jobs
\\printserver14\print queue(_Total)\References
\\printserver14\print queue(_Total)\Max References
\\printserver14\print queue(_Total)\Total Jobs Printed
\\printserver14\print queue(_Total)\Total Pages Printed
\\printserver21\system\System Up Time
\\printserver21\print queue(_Total)\Bytes Printed/Sec
\\printserver21\print queue(_Total)\Jobs Spooling
\\printserver21\print queue(_Total)\Max Jobs Spooling
\\printserver21\print queue(_Total)\Jobs
\\printserver21\print queue(_Total)\References
\\printserver21\print queue(_Total)\Max References
\\printserver21\print queue(_Total)\Total Jobs Printed
\\printserver21\print queue(_Total)\Total Pages Printed
\\printserver32\system\System Up Time
\\printserver32\print queue(_Total)\Bytes Printed/Sec
\\printserver32\print queue(_Total)\Jobs Spooling
\\printserver32\print queue(_Total)\Max Jobs Spooling
\\printserver32\print queue(_Total)\Jobs
\\printserver32\print queue(_Total)\References
\\printserver32\print queue(_Total)\Max References
\\printserver32\print queue(_Total)\Total Jobs Printed
\\printserver32\print queue(_Total)\Total Pages Printed
```

Sample output

```
"(PDH-CSV 4.0)","\\printserver14\system\System Up Time","
\\printserver14\print queue(_Total)\Bytes Printed/
Sec","\\printserver14\print queue(_Total)\Jobs Spooling","
\\printserver14\print queue(_Total)\Max Jobs Spooling","\\printserver14\
print queue(_Total)\Jobs","\\printserver14\print queue(_Total)
\References","\\printserver14\print queue(_Total)\Max References","
\\printserver14\print queue(_Total)\Total Jobs Printed","
\\printserver14\print queue(_Total)\Total Pages Printed"
"10/12/2009 08:20.509","15535.955367","96.827000","3.000000","19.000000",
"8.000000","93.000000","151.000000","267.000000","2413.000000"

"(PDH-CSV 4.0)","\\printserver21\system\System Up Time","
\\printserver21\print queue(_Total)\Bytes Printed/Sec","
\\printserver21\print queue(_Total)\Jobs Spooling","
```

```
\\printserver21\print queue(_Total)\Max Jobs Spooling","
\\printserver21\print queue(_Total)\Jobs","
\\printserver21\print queue(_Total)\References","
\\printserver21\print queue(_Total)\Max References","
\\printserver21\print queue(_Total)\Total Jobs Printed","
\\printserver21\print queue(_Total)\Total Pages Printed"
"10/12/2009 08:21.002","2487384.875323","124.393923","17.000000","
39.000000","12.000000", "165.000000","223.000000","17897.000000","
35672.000000"

"(PDH-CSV 4.0)","\\printserver34\system\System Up Time","
\\printserver34\print queue(_Total)\Bytes Printed/Sec","
\\printserver34\print queue(_Total)\Jobs Spooling","
\\printserver34\print queue(_Total)\Max Jobs Spooling","
\\printserver34\print queue(_Total)\Jobs","
\\printserver34\print queue(_Total)\References","
\\printserver34\print queue(_Total)\Max References","
\\printserver34\print queue(_Total)\Total Jobs Printed","
\\printserver34\print queue(_Total)\Total Pages Printed"
"10/12/2009 08:21.535","96375.673823","24.975632",
"2.000000","7.000000","3.000000", "42.000000","67.000000",
"514.000000","5785.000000"
```

Here, you examine the print queues on three print servers. For this example, let's assume that each print server has one primary print queue or that all of the active print queues on an individual print server are for the same physical printer. If you examine the usage statistics for PrintServer14 as shown in the sample output, you find the following to be true:

- On average, the server prints about 62 jobs an hour. That is 267 total print jobs on a print spooler that's been up for 4.3 hours (259 minutes). You can calculate this by dividing the Total Jobs Printed value by the System Up Time value (expressed as a number of hours rather than seconds).
- The average print job is about two pages long. You can calculate this by dividing the total pages printed by the total number of print jobs.
- Currently, the print server is fairly active with 3 jobs being spooled, 8 jobs in the queue, and a peak number of jobs being spooled of 19.

If you examine the usage statistics for PrintServer21 as shown in the sample output, you find the following to be true:

- On average, the server prints about 26 jobs every hour. That is 17,897 total print jobs on a print spooler that's been up for about 691 hours. You can calculate this by dividing the Total Jobs Printed value by the System Up Time value (expressed as a number of hours rather than seconds).

- The average print job is about two pages long. You can calculate this by dividing the total pages printed by the total number of print jobs.
- Currently, the print server is fairly active with 17 jobs being spooled, 12 jobs in the queue, and a peak number of jobs being spooled of 39.

If you examine the usage statistics for PrintServer34 as shown in the sample output, you find the following to be true:

- On average, the server prints about 19 jobs every hour. That is 514 total print jobs on a print spooler that's been up for about 27 hours. You can calculate this by dividing the Total Jobs Printed value by the System Up Time value (expressed as a number of hours rather than seconds).
- The average print job is about 11.25 pages long. You can calculate this by dividing the total pages printed by the total number of print jobs.
- Currently, the print server is fairly active with two jobs being spooled, three jobs in the queue, and a peak number of jobs being spooled of seven.

Here, you have a busy print environment that is taking a heavy load. If you examined the printer statistics over several intervals and after several restarts of the printers/spoolers and found the same usage, you would have several causes for concern, because the printers are very busy, especially considering that most workplace printers are only used when people are in the office, which typically is a 12-hour window of time even in an 8-hour work environment.

With this level of usage, you would want to monitor the server's usage and performance closely, as discussed in Chapter 7, "Monitoring Processes and Maintaining Performance." You would want to dig deeper into the usage statistics, looking at details for each printer configured. After monitoring the system's performance and usage over a sufficient interval, you might find the following to be true:

- Additional memory in the server is required because of the large number of print jobs being spooled at any given time.
- Additional processing power is required because of the high number of jobs handled on average.
- Additional disk space is required or a dedicated disk drive for the spooler folder is needed.

The Print Queue object has several additional performance counters that can help with routine monitoring, including:

- **Job Errors** Lists the total number of job errors in a print queue since the last restart. Job errors can occur in the event of problems transferring print jobs to the printer. A relatively high number of job errors can indicate networking problems or problems with network cards.

- **Not Ready Errors** Lists the total number of printer-not-ready errors in a print queue since the last restart. These errors occur if the printer is waiting for user input or otherwise not ready for printing.
- **Out Of Paper Errors** Lists the total number of out-of-paper errors in a print queue since the last restart. If a printer is frequently running out of paper, paper might not be getting refilled properly or you might need an additional paper tray.

You also might find that this system is simply one that you should routinely monitor to help ensure smooth print services operations. You could easily automate the monitoring by creating a script that writes the usage statistics to a log file and then scheduling the script to run on a periodic basis, as discussed in Chapter 9, "Scheduling Tasks to Run Automatically."

Keep in mind that you usually want to monitor printer usage over several days to evaluate any upgrades or changes that might be required. During that time, you might want to stop and then start the spooling to reset the statistics.

Managing Printers

From the command line, you can install and manage printers using the Prnmngr utility. With Prnmngr, you can work with print devices that are physically attached to a computer and employed only by the user who logs on to that computer, called *local print devices*, and print devices that are set up for remote access over the network, called *network print devices*. The key difference between a local printer and a network printer is that local printers aren't shared. When you share printers over the network, you use a computer to host the necessary print services. This computer is called a *print server*.

The primary job of a print server is to share the print device out to the network and to handle print spooling. Using a printer server gives you a central print queue that you can manage easily and saves you the task of installing printer drivers on client systems. You don't have to use a print server, however. Users can connect directly to a network-attached printer, and in this case the network-attached printer is handled much like a local printer attached directly to the user's computer. Users connect to the printer and each user has a different print queue that must be managed separately.

When you install a printer on a computer, you are actually configuring a print queue so that it can be used to route print jobs to the physical print device. So when we talk about installing a printer or configuring a printer, we are really talking about installing and configuring a print queue so that it can be used to route jobs to the physical print device.

If you want to install or configure printers, you'll need the appropriate administrator privileges. In a domain, this means you must be a member of the Administrators, Print

Operators, or Server Operators group. To connect to and use a printer, you don't have to be an administrator. You only need the appropriate access permissions.

Installing Physically Attached Print Devices

Physically attached print devices are connected to a computer directly and can be configured as local print devices or as network print devices. Although a local print device is only available to users logged on to the computer, a network device is accessible to any network users as a shared print device. To get started, connect the print device to the server using the appropriate serial, parallel, or USB cable and then turn on the printer. If you are configuring a network printer, this computer will act as the print server. With Plug and Play printers, simply plugging in the printer will start the automatic installation and configuration process if someone is logged on to the computer.

You can install a local printer manually using Prnmngr and the following parameters:

- **–A AddPrinter** Specifies that you want to add or install a local printer.
- **–P PrinterName** Assigns a name to the printer. This is the name you'll see whether you're working with the Printers page in Control Panel or with the command line.
- **–M PrinterModel** Specifies the model of the printer. This must be the exact model as specified by the manufacturer. The model name determines the printer driver used.
- **–R PrinterPort** Sets the port to which the printer is connected. This can be a parallel port, such as LPT1:, LPT2:, or LPT3:; a serial port, such as COM1:, COM2:, or COM3:; or a USB port, such as USB001.

> **Note** The case you use when setting the printer name and model is the case that is displayed at the command prompt and in dialog boxes. However, although these names are case-aware, they aren't case-sensitive. This means that as far as Windows is concerned, centralcolorlaser is the same as CentralColorLaser.

To configure physically attached printers, you don't have to be logged on to the computer locally. You can also remotely install this type of printer. To do this, use the –S parameter to specify the name of the remote computer to which you want to add a local printer. If necessary, use the –U and –W parameters to specify the user name and password to use when connecting to a remote computer.

> **Note** You cannot specify a user name and password when working at a local command prompt, whether physically logged on or remotely connected. If you try to do this, you will get an error that states, "User credentials cannot be used for local connections."

To see how Prnmngr is used, consider the following examples:

Configure an HP 5500 Series InkJet printer on USB001:

```
prnmngr -a -p "OfficeJetPrinter" -m "hp officejet 5500 series"
-r USB001
```

Configure an HP 1100 DN Series InkJet printer on LPT1:

```
prnmngr -a -p "BusinessJetPrinter" -m "hp businessjet 1100 series DN"
-r LPT1:
```

Configure an Epson Stylus Photo printer on cdesign09 using USB001:

```
prnmngr -a -p "PhotoPrinter" -m "epson stylus photo 1270 esc/p 2"
-r USB001 -s cdesign09
```

Configure an Epson Stylus Color printer on mteam06 using LPT1:

```
prnmngr -a -p "ColorPrinter" -m "epson stylus color esc/p 2"
-r LPT1: -s mteam06 - u wrstanek -w goldfish
```

If a printer is installed successfully, Prnmngr will report "Added printer". Otherwise, it will report "Unable to add printer" and describe the error that occurred. The most common error is the result of a misentered or unknown device model, which causes Prnmngr to report that the printer driver is unknown. Ensure that you are using the correct model name.

Note If this is the first printer installed on a computer, it will be set as the default printer. The printer will not be shared, however. If you want to share the printer so that others can use it, see the section titled "Sharing Printers" later in this chapter.

Tip You can create additional printers for the same print device. The only requirements are that the printer name and the share name be unique. Having additional printers for the same print device allows you to set different properties to serve different needs. You can, for example, have one configuration for low-priority print jobs and another for high-priority print jobs.

Installing Network-Attached Print Devices

Network-attached print devices are attached directly to the network through a network adapter card and are typically configured as network print devices so that they are accessible to network users as shared print devices. To get started, connect the printer to the network and configure it to use an appropriate IP address or obtain an IP address from a DHCP server. Follow the steps as discussed in the printer manual from the manufacturer.

After you configure TCP/IP on the printer, you will need to create a TCP/IP port on the computer that will act as the print server for the printer. The port is used to make a connection over the network to the printer. You can then install the printer as you would install a physically attached print device. The only difference is that you use –R to specify the TCP/IP port you created rather than specifying an LPT, COM, or USB port. For example, if you create a TCP/IP port called IP_192.168.10.15, you can add a printer that uses the port using the following command line

```
prnmngr -a -p "CentralColorLaser" -m "magicolor 2300 dl" -r
IP_192.168.10.15 -s corpsvr03
```

Here, you install a Minolta QMS Magicolor color laser printer so that it uses a TCP/IP port. Because the printer is configured on CorpSvr03, that computer will act as the printer server for this device. The printer will not be set as the default printer for any users, nor will it be shared. If you want to share the printer so that others can use it, see the section titled "Sharing Printers" later in this chapter.

Listing Printers Configured on a Computer

You can list all the printers that are configured on the local computer by typing **prnmngr –l**. If you want to view this information for a remote computer, add the –S parameter followed by the computer name, such as **prnmngr –l –s corpsvr03**. As necessary, you can use the –U and –W parameters to set the user name and password of the logon account to use as well.

The output shows the name of the print server (or is blank if you are working on a local computer) as well as other important information about each printer that is configured. Here is an example:

```
Server name corpsvr03
Printer name magicolor 2300 main for 5th floor
Share name magicolor
Driver name magicolor 2300 DL
Port name 192.168.1.92
Comment Main printer for the fifth floor.
Location 5/ne
Print processor MIMFPR_B
Data type IMF
Parameters
```

```
Attributes 2629
Priority 1
Default priority 0
Status Idle
Average pages per minute 8
Printer status Idle
Extended printer status Unknown
Detected error state Unknown
Extended detected error state Unknown
Number of printers enumerated 1
```

The printer, driver, and port names were set when the printer was installed. The printer is shared as well, making it available to users in the domain for printing. If you wanted to move the printer to a new print server, the only information you really need to note is the driver name, which in most cases is the same as the printer's model.

Viewing and Setting the Default Printer

You can display the default printer for the current logged on user by typing **prnmngr -g** at the command prompt. If you want the user to have a different default printer, you can type **prnmngr -t -p** followed by the name of the printer that should be the default, such as

```
prnmngr -t -p "magicolor 2300 DL"
```

If successful, Prnmngr will report that the printer is now set as the default. Otherwise, Prnmngr will report an error. Typically, a "Not Found" error means that you entered an invalid printer name.

Renaming Printers

Renaming printers is one printer task that you can't perform with Prnmngr. The command utility that you use for this task is Prncnfg. The syntax for renaming printers is

```
prncnfg -x -p CurrentPrinterName -z NewPrinterName
```

Here, you use Prncnfg with the –X parameter to indicate that you want to rename a printer. Then specify the current printer name with the –P parameter and set the new printer name with the –Z parameter, such as

```
prncnfg -x -p "CentralColorLaser" -z "EngineeringPrinter"
```

If the printer exists, Prncnfg will report that it has renamed the printer and set the new printer name.

You can also rename printers that are on remote computers. To do this, use the –S parameter to specify the name of the remote computer, such as

```
prncnfg -x -s corpsvr03 -p "CentralColorLaser" -z "EngineeringPrinter"
```

Here, you are renaming a printer on CorpSvr03. This command doesn't let you set the account for logon, however.

Deleting Printers

Prnmngr provides two ways to delete printers that you no longer want to be available on a particular computer. You can delete individual printers using the following command:

```
prnmngr -d -p PrinterName
```

such as

```
prnmngr -d -p "magicolor 2300 DL"
```

If you enter an invalid printer name, Prnmngr will report that it is unable to delete the printer because the printer wasn't found. If you do not have permission to delete the printer, Prnmngr will report that it is unable to enumerate printers because of the user credentials. You'll need to log on with an account that has the appropriate administrator privileges. Note that this isn't the case when you work with remote computers. When you work with remote computers, you can specify the logon account using the –U and –W parameters, such as

```
prnmngr -d -p "magicolor 2300 DL" -s corpsvr03 -u wrstanek
-p goldfish
```

You can delete all printers from a computer using the following command:

```
prnmngr -x
```

Prnmngr won't prompt you to confirm this action, but it will tell you about each printer deleted, such as

```
Deleted printer OfficeJet
Deleted printer CentralPrinter

Number of local printers and connections enumerated 2
Number of local printers and connections deleted 2
```

Managing TCP/IP Ports for Network-Attached Printers

You use TCP/IP ports to make connections to network-attached printers. You create and manage TCP/IP ports using Prnport. Like Prnmngr, Prnport is a Windows script that you must run using the command-line script host.

Creating and Changing TCP/IP Ports for Printers

You tell Prnport that you want to add a TCP/IP port by using the –A parameter. Then you specify the port name using the –R parameter and specify the printer's IP address using the –H parameter. It is common to base the port name on the IP address for the printer to which you are connecting. For example, if you are configuring a port for a printer on IP address 192.168.10.15, you might use a port name of IP_192.168.10.15.

You must also specify the output protocol that the port should use. The output protocol is set with the –O parameter and is either **raw** or **lpr**. Most printers use the Raw protocol. With Raw, data is sent unmodified over the port to the printer using a designated port number. In most cases, this is port 9100, which is why this is used as the default value. You can set the port number to a different value using the –N parameter. With LPR, the port is used in conjunction with an LPD (line printer daemon) print queue. You set the print queue name using the –Q parameter.

As with most printer configuration commands, you don't have to be logged on to the computer locally to configure ports. If you want to configure ports on a remote computer, use the –S parameter to specify the name of the remote computer to work with. As necessary, use the –U and –W parameters to specify the user name and password to use when connecting to the remote computer. The user name can be specified as *Domain\Username* if the logon domain is different from the current domain.

Consider the following examples:

Add a port to use TCP Raw and connect to 192.168.10.15 over port 9100:

```
prnport -a -r IP_192.168.10.15 -h 192.168.10.15 -o raw
```

Add a port to use Raw output and connect to 10.10.1.50 over port 9500:

```
prnport -a -r IP_192.168.10.15 -h 10.10.1.50 -o raw -n 9500
```

Add a port to use LPR output and connect to 172.20.18.2. Set the queue name to LPRQUEUE:

```
prnport -a -r IP_192.168.10.15 -h 172.20.18.2 -o lpr -q lprqueue
```

Add a port on CORPSVR03 to use TCP Raw and connect to 192.168.10.15 over port 9100:

```
prnport -a -r IP_192.168.10.15 -h 192.168.10.15 -o raw -s corpsvr03
```

If a port is created successfully, Prnport will report "Created/updated port." Otherwise, it will report "Unable to create/ update port" and describe the error that occurred.

Most network-attached printers also support the Simple Network Management Protocol (SNMP). To allow the printer to use this protocol, you must enable SNMP using the –Me parameter, and then set an SNMP community name using the –Y parameter and SNMP device index using the –I parameter. Typically, the community name is set to *public*, which indicates the print device is available for use and management by anyone on the network. The device index is used to designate a particular device in an SNMP community. The first device has an index of 1, the second an index of 2, and so on.

Consider the following example:

```
prnport -a -r IP_192.168.10.15 -h 192.168.10.15 -o raw -me -y public -i 1
```

Note You can specifically disable SNMP using the –Md parameter.

Here you configure a port to use TCP Raw and connect to 192.168.10.15 over Port 9100. You also enable SNMP and configure the SNMP community name as *public* and the device index as *1*.

If you want to change the TCP/IP port configuration later, you can do this using Prnport with the –T parameter. Here, you use the –R parameter to specify the port you want to work with, and any other parameters to set the related property values. Consider the following example:

```
prnport -a -r MainPrinter -h 10.10.12.50 -o raw -md
```

Here, you specify that you want to change the MainPrinter TCP/IP port. You set 10.10.12.50 as the IP address, the output protocol as Raw, and disable SNMP.

Listing Information About TCP/IP Ports Used by Printers

You can list all the printer TCP/IP ports that are configured on the local computer by typing **prnport –l**. If you want to view this information for a remote computer, add the –S parameter followed by the computer name, such as **prnport –l –s corpsvr03**. As necessary, you can use the –U and –W parameters to set the user name and password of the logon account to use as well.

The output shows the name of the print server (or is blank if you are working a local computer) as well as other important information about each port that is configured. Here is an example of the information provided for a RAW port:

```
Server name
Port name IP_192.168.1.101
Host address 192.168.1.101
Protocol RAW
Port number 9100
SNMP Enabled
Community public
Device index 1
```

Here is an example of the information provided for an LPR port:

```
Server name
Port name IP_192.168.1.101
Host address 192.168.1.101
Protocol LPR
Queue crownnet
Byte Count Enabled
SNMP Enabled
Community public
Device index 1
```

> **Note** The LPR port information may show incorrectly that byte counting is enabled. When enabled, the computer counts the number of bytes in a document before sending it to the printer. Most printers do not require byte counting, which slows performance because it is very time-consuming to count each byte in documents when printing.

Deleting TCP/IP Ports Used by Printers

You can delete individual ports used by printers with the following syntax:

```
prnport -d -r PortName
```

such as

```
prnport -d -r IP_192.168.1.101
```

If you enter an invalid printer name, Prnport will report that it is unable to delete the port because it wasn't found. If you do not have permission to delete the printer, Prnport will report that it is unable to enumerate printers because of the user credentials. You'll need to log on with an account that has the appropriate administrator privileges. Note that this isn't the case when you work with remote computers. When you work with remote computers, you can specify the logon account using the –U and –W parameters, such as

```
prnport -d -r IP_192.168.1.101 -s corpsvr03 -u wrstanek -p goldfish
```

Configuring Printer Properties

You can view and configure printer properties using the Prncnfg script with the –T parameter. Regardless of which property you are working with, Prncnfg expects you to use the –P parameter to specify the name of the printer you want to work with. As with most printer configuration commands, you don't have to be logged on to the computer locally to configure printer properties. If you want to change printer properties for remote computers (other than the printer name), you can use the –S parameter to specify the name of the remote computer. As necessary, use the –U and –W parameters to specify the user name and password to use when connecting to the remote computer. The user name can be specified as *Domain\Username* if the logon domain is different from the current domain.

Adding Comments and Location Information

You can make it easier for users to determine which printer to use by adding comments and location information to printers. Comments provide general information about the printer, such as the type of print device and who is responsible for it. Location describes the actual physical location of the print device. When you provide these values, they are displayed on the General tab in the printer's Properties dialog box, as well as in the Print dialog box that is displayed after the Print command is selected in most applications.

The syntax for adding comments and location information to printers is

```
prncnfg -t -p PrinterName -m "Comment" -l "Location"
```

Here, you use Prncnfg with the –T parameter to indicate that you want to change printer properties. Then specify the comment text with the –M parameter and set the printer location information with the –L parameter, such as

```
prncnfg -t -s corpsrv03 -p "CentralColorLaser" -m "Main Engineering
Printer" -l "5th Floor SE"
```

Prncnfg should report that it configured the printer. If it doesn't, you probably forgot a double quotation mark or one of the parameter switches. Of course, you don't have to set both a comment and a location. You can set these values separately as well.

Sharing Printers

Printers you add at the command line aren't automatically shared for others to use. If you want to share such a printer, you must specifically configure it using Prncnfg. Use the –T parameter to specify that you are setting or changing a printer property and the –P parameter to specify the printer to work with. Then use the –H parameter to set the share name and the +Shared parameter to enable sharing. For compatibility with pre–Windows 2000 computers, the share name should be only eight characters in length and should not contain spaces.

Because the location information might not always be available, you might want the printer share name to indicate where the printer is located to save users from having to examine the printer properties. For example, if a printer were located in the southeast corner of the fifth floor, you might want to name the printer share FifthSE. Consider the following example:

```
prncnfg -t -s corpsrv03 -p "CentralColorLaser" -h "FifthSE" +shared
```

Here you are configuring the CentralColorLaser printer on CorpSrv03 to be shared as FifthSE.

To remove printer sharing, you use the –Shared parameter. In the following example, you are removing printer sharing from the printer configured in the previous example:

```
prncnfg -t -s corpsrv03 -p "CentralColorLaser" -shared
```

Publishing Printers in Active Directory

You can make it easier for users to find printers that are available by publishing their information in Active Directory. Once a printer is published, users can search for it based on its location and capabilities, such as whether it is on the fifth floor or whether it can print in color.

You configure printer publishing using Prncnfg. If you want to publish a printer in Active Directory, you use the –T parameter to specify that you are setting or changing a printer property and –P to specify the printer to work with. Then use the +Published parameter to specify that the printer should be published or the –Published parameter to specify that the printer should be removed from the directory.

Consider the following examples:

Publish the CentralColorLaser printer on CorpSrv03 in Active Directory:

```
Prncnfg -t -s corpsrv03 -p "CentralColorLaser" +published
```

Remove the local printer named OfficeJet from Active Directory:

```
Prncnfg -t -p "OfficeJet" -published
```

In either case, Prncnfg should report that it configured the printer. It won't report an error, however, if the printer was already published or removed.

Setting a Separator Page and Changing Print Device Mode

Separator pages can be used at the beginning of a print job to make it easier to find a document on a busy print device. They can be used to change the print device mode, such as whether the print device uses PostScript or Printer Control Language (PCL).

Separator pages are stored in the %SystemRoot%\System32 folder. Four default separator pages are defined on Windows systems:

- **pcl.sep** Switches the print device to PCL mode and prints a separator page before each document.
- **pscript.sep** Switches the print device to PostScript mode but doesn't print a separator page.
- **sysprint.sep** Switches the print device to PostScript mode and prints a separator page before each document.
- **sysprintj.sep** Switches the print device to PostScript mode and prints a separator page before each document. This is essentially an alternate version of Sysprint.sep that uses a different version of the banner text.

You can specify that a printer should use one of these separator pages or any other separator page that is in the %SystemRoot%\System32 folder by using Prncnfg. Use the –T parameter to specify that you are setting or changing a printer property and the –P parameter to specify the printer to work with. Then use the –F parameter to specify the separator page to use.

Consider the following example:

```
Prncnfg -t -s corpsrv03 -p "CentralColorLaser" -f sysprint.sep
```

Here you configure the CentralColorLaser printer on CorpSrv03 to use sysprint.sep.

To stop using the separator page, use the –F parameter with the value " ", such as

```
Prncnfg -t -s corpsrv03 -p "CentralColorLaser" -f " "
```

Scheduling and Prioritizing Print Jobs

You can use Prncnfg to manage print job priorities and scheduling from the command line. Print jobs always print in order of priority, with 1 being the lowest priority and 99 being the highest priority. Jobs with higher priority print before jobs with lower priority. Thus if a physical print device has several printers (print queues), any print job with a higher priority will print before a print job with lower priority. Use the –T parameter to specify that you are setting or changing a printer property and the –P parameter to specify the printer to work with. Then use the –O parameter to set the priority, such as

```
prncnfg -t -p "EngineeringPrinter" -o 50
```

Here you specify that print jobs using the EngineeringPrinter to route print jobs to the related printer have a priority of 50. If, for example, a Marketing Printer was also configured to use the same physical print device but had a lower priority, engineering print jobs would always print first.

Printers are either always available or available only during the hours specified. You set printer availability using the –St parameter to specify the time of day after which the printer is available and the –Ut parameter to specify the time of day after which the printer is no longer available. Times are set using a 24-hour clock, such as

```
prncnfg -t -p "EngineeringPrinter" -st 0530 -ut 1930
```

Here you specify that the printer is available from 5:30 A.M. to 7:30 P.M. each day.

Configuring Spooling and Other Advanced Printer Options

For print devices attached to the network, you'll usually want the printer to spool files rather than print files directly. Print spooling makes it possible to use a printer (print queue) to manage print jobs. You can configure spooling using the following Prncnfg options:

- **+Direct** With +Direct, you configure the printer to print directly rather than spool. Use +Direct if you cannot print using any of the spooling options.
- **–Direct** With –Direct, you spool print documents so that programs finish printing faster rather than printing directly. This is the default.
- **+Queued** With +Queued, you start printing after the last page of the document is spooled. Select this option if you want the entire document to be spooled before printing begins. This option ensures that the entire document makes it into the print queue before printing begins. If for some reason printing is canceled or not completed, the job won't be printed.
- **–Queued** With –Queued, you start printing as soon as the document begins spooling. Select this option if you want printing to begin immediately when the print device isn't already in use. This option is preferable when you want print jobs to be completed faster or when you want to ensure that the application returns control to users as soon as possible. This is the default.

- **+Enabledevq** With +Enabledevq, the spooler checks the printer setup and matches it to the document setup before sending the document to the print device. In the event of a mismatch, the spooler holds the print job but allows correctly matched documents to keep printing. Selecting this option is a good idea if you frequently have to change printer form or tray assignments.
- **–Enabledevq** With –Enabledevq, the spooler doesn't check the printer setup before sending documents to the print device. In the event of a mismatch, the printer will usually stop printing and wait for a user to cancel the print job, change printer form, or insert a paper tray with the necessary paper type. This is the default.

Other advanced Prncnfg options that you can configure include the following:

- **+Keepprintedjobs** With +Keepprintedjobs, jobs aren't deleted from the queue after they've printed. Use this option if you're printing files that can't easily be re-created. You can reprint the document without having to re-create it.
- **–Keepprintedjobs** With –Keepprintedjobs, jobs are deleted from the queue after they've printed. This frees the disk space being used by the print job but doesn't allow you to reprint the document from the print queue. This is the default.
- **+Docompletefirst** With +Docompletefirst, jobs that have completed spooling will print before jobs in the process of spooling—regardless of whether the spooling jobs have higher priority. This is the default.
- **–Docompletefirst** With –Docompletefirst, jobs with higher priority will preempt jobs with lower priority. Thus if a higher-priority job comes into the queue, a lower-priority job stops printing and the higher-priority job starts printing.
- **+Enablebidi** With +Enablebidi, you enable metafile spooling and turn on advanced printing features if they are supported, such as page order, booklet printing, and pages per sheet. If you note compatibility problems when using +Enablebidi, you should disable this feature. This is the default.
- **–Enablebidi** With –Enablebidi, you disable metafile spooling and turn off advanced printing features. Use this option if you experience compatibility problems with the printer.

To see how you can use these options, consider the following examples:

Configure SalesPrinter on sales06 to print directly and keep printed jobs:

```
prncnfg -t -s sales06 -p "SalesPrinter" +direct +keepprintedjobs
```

Configure MainPrinter on the local computer to start printing after the last page is spooled:

```
prncnfg -t -p "MainPrinter" -queued
```

Configure HPLaserJet on corpsvr09 to hold mismatched documents and disabled metafile spooling:

```
prncnfg -t -s corpsvr09 -p "HPLaserJet" +enabledevq -enablebidi
```

Solving Spooling Problems

Windows uses the Print Spooler service to control the spooling of print jobs. If this service isn't running, print jobs can't be spooled.

Checking the Print Spooler Service

You can check the status of the Print Spooler service on a local computer by typing

```
sc query spooler
```

For a remote computer, you specify the UNC server name, such as

```
sc \\Engsvr04 query spooler
```

Either way, the output should have a section for the spooler, which will look similar to this:

```
SERVICE_NAME: spooler
TYPE               : 110  WIN32_OWN_PROCESS  (interactive)
STATE              : 4  RUNNING
                        (STOPPABLE, NOT_PAUSABLE, ACCEPTS_SHUTDOWN)
WIN32_EXIT_CODE    : 0  (0x0)
SERVICE_EXIT_CODE  : 0  (0x0)
CHECKPOINT         : 0x0
WAIT_HINT          : 0x0
```

This tells you that the Print Spooler service is running. If it was stopped, you might want to check the service configuration. You could do this by typing

```
sc qc spooler
```

or

```
sc \\Engsvr04 qc spooler
```

Among other things, the output tells you the startup setting for the Print Spooler, as shown here:

```
[SC] QueryServiceConfig SUCCESS

SERVICE_NAME: spooler
        TYPE    : 110    WIN32_OWN_PROCESS (interactive)
        START_TYPE    : 2    AUTO_START
        ERROR_CONTROL    : 1    NORMAL
        BINARY_PATH_NAME    : C:\Windows\System32\spoolsv.exe
        LOAD_ORDER_GROUP    : SpoolerGroup
        TAG    : 0
        DISPLAY_NAME    : Print Spooler
        DEPENDENCIES     : RPCSS
                         : http
        SERVICE_START_NAME    : LocalSystem
```

The start_type should be AUTO_START, which indicates Print Spooler is set to start automatically.

Fixing a Corrupted Spooler

Spoolers can also become corrupted. If this happens, you'll find that the printer freezes or doesn't send jobs to the print device. Sometimes the print device may print pages of garbled data. In most of these cases, stopping and starting the Print Spooler service will resolve the problem. You can stop Print Spooler by typing

```
sc stop spooler
```

After the spool stops, restart it by typing

```
sc start spooler
```

If you are working with a remote computer, you can enter the computer name you want to work with as well, such as

```
sc \\Engsvr04 stop spooler
sc \\Engsvr04 start spooler
```

> **Note** Some spooling problems can be related to permissions. You'll also want to check the printer access permissions and the permissions on the %SystemRoot%\System32\Spool folder.

Managing Print Queues and Individual Print Jobs

Several Windows scripts are available for working with print queues and the print jobs they contain. You use the Prnqctl utility to start, stop, or pause the printing of all documents in a printer queue. You use the Prnjobs utility to work with print jobs.

Viewing Jobs in the Queue

You can view jobs in print queues using Prnjobs. If you want to view all jobs for all printers on the local computer, type **prnjobs –l**. To view the jobs for a particular printer use the –P parameter to specify the printer name. For a remote computer, you can use the –S parameter to specify the remote computer you want to work with and if necessary use the –U and –W parameters to provide the user name and password required for access to the remote computer.

Consider the following examples:

View all print jobs on CorpSrv03:

```
prnjobs -l -s corpsrv03
```

View all print jobs for MainPrinter on the local computer:

```
prnjobs -l -p MainPrinter
```

The output for an individual job can help you determine the following:

- **Job ID** The job identification number, which is needed when you want to work with individual print jobs.
- **Printer** The name of the printer.
- **Document** The document filename, which can include the name of the application that printed it.
- **Data Type** The printer data type.
- **Driver Name** The name of the print driver, which indicates the model of the printer.
- **Description** The description of the printer.
- **Elapsed Time** The length of time the document has been printing.
- **Job Status** The status of the print job. Entries you'll see include Printing, Spooling, Paused, Deleting, and Restarting.
- **Notify** The person notified when the print job is complete (if notification is configured).
- **Owner** The document's owner.
- **Pages Printed** The number of pages printed so far (if any).
- **Size** The document size in bytes.

- **Time Submitted** The time and date the print job was submitted.
- **Total Pages** The total number of pages in the document.

Pausing the Printer and Resuming Printing

From time to time, you might need to pause a printer so that you can work with the physical print device or troubleshoot a problem. When you pause printing, the printer completes the current job and then halts all other jobs. You pause printing using Prnqctl. For a local printer, type **prnqctl –z**, using the –P parameter to set the name of the printer you want to pause. For a remote computer, you can use the –S parameter to specify the remote computer you want to work with and if necessary use the –U and –W parameters to provide the user name and password required for access to the remote computer.

To resume printing, use the –M parameter instead of the – Z parameter. This should restart printing of all documents in the print queue.

Consider the following examples:

Pause printing for EngineeringPrinter on CorpSrv03:

```
prnqctl -z -s corpsrv03 -p EngineeringPrinter
```

Pause print jobs for 5thfloorPrinter on the local computer:

```
prnqctl -z -p 5thfloorPrinter
```

Resume printing for EngineeringPrinter on CorpSrv03:

```
prnqctl -m -s corpsrv03 -p EngineeringPrinter
```

Emptying the Print Queue

You can use Prnqctl to empty a print queue and delete all of its contents. For a local printer, type **prnqctl –x**, using the –P parameter to set the name of the printer whose print queue you wish to empty. For a remote computer, you can use the –S parameter to specify the remote computer you want to work with and if necessary use the –U and –W parameters to provide the user name and password required for access to the remote computer.

Consider the following examples:

Empty the print queue for SalesPrinter on salespc06:

```
prnqctl -x -s salespc06 -p SalesPrinter
```

Empty the print queue for TempPrinter on the local computer:

```
prnqctl -x -p TempPrinter
```

If successful, Prnqctl reports that it successfully purged documents from the print queue. It will do so even if no documents are in the print queue initially.

Pausing, Resuming, and Restarting Individual Document Printing

You use Prnjobs to pause or resume printing of individual jobs. When you pause a job, you halt the printing of that document and let other documents print. When you resume a job, you tell the printer to resume printing the document from the point at which it was halted.

To pause a print job, you use the following syntax:

`prnjobs -z -p` *`PrinterName`* `-j` *`JobID`*

where *PrinterName* is the name of the printer you want to work with and *JobID* is the ID number of the print job to pause.

To resume a print job, you use the following syntax:

`prnjobs -m -p` *`PrinterName`* `-j` *`JobID`*

where *PrinterName* is the name of the printer you want to work with and *JobID* is the ID number of the print job to resume.

In either case, you work with printers on the local computer by default. For print queues on remote computers, you can use the –S parameter to specify the remote computer you want to work with and if necessary use the –U and –W parameters to provide the user name and password required for access to the remote computer.

Consider the following examples:

Pause printing job number 6 for EngineeringPrinter on CorpSrv03:

```
prnjobs -z -s corpsrv03 -p EngineeringPrinter -j 6
```

Pause printing job number 17 for 5thfloorPrinter on the local computer:

```
prnjobs -z -p 5thfloorPrinter -j 17
```

Resume printing job number 6 for EngineeringPrinter on CorpSrv03:

```
prnjobs -m -s corpsrv03 -p EngineeringPrinter -j 6
```

Prnjobs should report that it successfully paused or resumed printing of that job ID. If you use an invalid job ID, Prnjobs will report "Unable to set the print job".

Removing a Document and Canceling a Print Job

You can use Prnjobs to cancel an individual print job and delete it from a print queue. For a local printer, type **prnjobs -x**, using the –P parameter to set the name of the printer and –J to specify the ID number of the document to be deleted. For a remote computer, you can use the –S parameter to specify the remote computer you want to work with and if necessary use the –U and –W parameters to provide the user name and password required for access to the remote computer.

Cancel printing job number 12 for MainPrinter on the local computer:

```
prnjobs -x -p MainPrinter -j 12
```

Cancel printing job number 9 for EngineeringPrinter on CorpSrv03:

```
prnjobs -x -s corpsrv03 -p EngineeringPrinter -j 9
```

If successful, Prnjobs reports that it successfully canceled the print job. If you use an invalid job ID, Prnjobs will report "Unable to set the print job".

> **Note** If a document is printing when you cancel it, the print device may continue to print part or all of the document. This is because most print devices cache documents in an internal buffer, and the print device may continue to print the contents of this cache.

Backing Up and Restoring Print Server Configurations

As part of your routine planning for outages, you should consider how you are going to handle printer and print server failure. To prepare for potential printer problems, you'll ideally have spare parts or a spare printer to repair or replace a failed printer. If you don't, you should have ready instructions to help users make use of alternate printers or already have a second printer added for use on their computers as a backup in case the primary printer fails.

Backing Up Print Server Configurations

To prepare for potential print server problems, you should have a secondary print server available or have identified a computer you can use as a print server. As part of periodic backups, you should also back up the printer configuration of your print servers using the PrintBrm utility. You back up printer configuration using the following command:

```
printbrm -b -f SaveFile
```

where *SaveFile* is the name or full file path for the printer configuration file with the .printerexport extension. You can specify a remote computer to work with using the –S parameter. In the following example, you back up the printer configuration to the PrintServer12_Config.printerexport file:

```
printbrm -b -f PrintServer12_Config.printerexport
```

As Printbrm backs up the printer configuration, it lists a summary of the current configuration and then lists the tasks it is performing step by step, as shown in this example:

```
Operation mode: backup
Target server: local machine
Target file path: c:\Windows\printserver12_config.printerexport.
Queue publish mode: none
Overwrite Mode: keep existing settings

LISTING PRINT QUEUES
OfficeJetPrinter
HP Color LaserJet 9500 main
magicolor 2300 DL
Adobe PDF
LISTING PRINTER DRIVERS
hp officejet 5500 series, Windows NT x86, LIDIL hpzlllhn
HP Color LaserJet 9500 PS, Windows NT x86, None
magicolor 2300 DL, Windows NT x86, MLMON__B.DLL
Adobe PDF Converter, Windows NT x86, None
LISTING PRINT PROCESSORS
hpzpplhn Windows NT x86 hpzpplhn.dll
MIMFPR_B Windows NT x86 MIMFPR_B.DLL
LISTING PRINTER PORTS
192.168.0.90, TCP
192.168.1.90, TCP
192.168.10.150, TCP
```

```
Saving Print Queues...
Saved print queue OfficeJetPrinter
Saved print queue HP Color LaserJet 9500 main
Saved print queue magicolor 2300 DL
Saved print queue Adobe PDF
Saving Print Processors...
Saved print processor hpzpplhn, Windows NT x86, hpzpplhn.dll
Saved print processor MIMFPR_B, Windows NT x86, MIMFPR_B.DLL
Saving Printer Drivers...
Saved printer driver hp officejet 5500 series, Windows NT x86, 3
Saved printer driver HP Color LaserJet 9500 PS, Windows NT x86, 3
Saved printer driver magicolor 2300 DL, Windows NT x86, 3
Saved printer driver Adobe PDF Converter, Windows NT x86, 3
Saving Printer Ports...
Saved printer port 192.168.0.90, TCP
Saved printer port 192.168.1.90, TCP
Saved printer port 192.168.10.150, TCP
************ 100% Complete ************

Successfully finished operation.
```

If you note any errors in the output, be sure to resolve any issues and then use Printbrm to back up the configuration again. To ensure that the configuration backup is available in case of a total server outage, you should copy the configuration file to a secure network folder on another computer.

Restoring Print Server Configurations

Once you have a printer configuration backup, you can use the backup in several ways. In the event that the print server fails, you can disconnect the server from the network and then use Printbrm to restore the printer configuration on a new print server. You then change the secondary print server's IP address and computer name to match that of the original print server. Users can then access printers and resume printing.

The syntax for restoring a saved printer configuration is:

```
printbrm -r -f ConfigFileToRestore
```

where *ConfigFileToRestore* is the name or full file path of the saved printer configuration file with the .printerexport extension. In the following example, you restore the printer configuration using the PrintServer12_Config.printerexport file:

```
printbrm -r -f PrintServer12_Config.printerexport
```

As Printbrm restores the printer configuration, it lists a summary of its settings and actions, as shown in this example:

```
Operation mode: restore
Target server: local machine
Target file path: c:\Windows\printserver12_config.printerexport.
Queue publish mode: none
Overwrite Mode: keep existing settings
```

```
Restoring Printer Drivers…
Restoring Printer Ports…
Restoring Print Processors…
Restoring Print Queues…
************ 0% ************

Successfully finished operation.
```

If you note any errors in the output, be sure to resolve any issues and then use Printbrm to restore the configuration again. By default, Printbrm will not overwrite the settings of any existing print queues. This is useful in cases where you are restoring print queues on a different computer and that computer already has its own print queues. This is also useful if someone inadvertently deletes print queues from a print server and you want to use Printbrm to restore only the deleted print queues.

To force Printbrm to perform a restore and overwrite settings in existing print queues, add –O FORCE to the command text, such as:

```
printbrm -r -f PrintServer12_Config.printerexport -o force
```

If you ever have questions about the contents of a saved printer configuration file, you can query the file and list its contents using the following syntax:

```
printbrm -q -f ConfigFileToQuery
```

where *ConfigFileToQuery* is the name or full file path of the saved printer configuration file to examine.

Migrating Printers and Print Queues

You can use Printbrm to move printers and their print queues from one print server to another. This is an efficient way to consolidate multiple print servers or replace an older print server.

When you move printers, the server on which the printers are currently located is the source server, and the server to which you want to move the printers is the destination server. With this in mind, you can move printers to a new print server by following these steps:

1. At the command line, create a printer configuration file for the source server by typing **Printbrm –b –s *ServerName* –f *SaveFile***, where *ServerName* is the name or IP address of the source server and *SaveFile* is the name of the .printerexport file.
2. At the command line, restore the printer configuration backup on the destination server by typing **Printbrm –r –s *ServerName* –f *RestoreFile***, where *ServerName* is the name or IP address of the destination server and *RestoreFile* is the name of the .printerexport file to use for the restore.

If the destination server has existing print queues with the same name as those from the source server, you can use –O FORCE to overwrite existing print queue settings with those in the restore file.

Chapter 17

Configuring, Maintaining, and Troubleshooting TCP/IP Networking

Being able to configure, maintain, and troubleshoot Transmission Control Protocol/Internet Protocol (TCP/IP) networking is a vital part of every administrator's job. This chapter starts with a discussion of the command-line tools available for performing these tasks and then delves into each area separately, giving you the knowledge and techniques you'll need to successfully manage and support TCP/IP networking on Windows Vista and Windows Server 2008 systems.

Using the Network Services Shell

The network services shell (Netsh) is a command-line scripting utility that allows you to manage the configuration of various network services on local and remote computers. Netsh provides a separate command prompt that you can use in either interactive or noninteractive mode.

Working with Netsh Contexts

In interactive mode, you enter the shell by typing **netsh** and then specifying the context name of the network service you want to work with. The contexts and subcontexts available depend on the role services, roles, and features installed on the computer. Key context names and their meanings are as follows:

- **advfirewall** Advanced firewall. The context used to manage and monitor the Windows Firewall with Advanced Security. Windows Firewall with Advanced Security is an enhanced version of the standard Windows Firewall that allows you to define security policies and includes extensions for defining advanced packet filtering rules for both inbound and outbound connections.
- **bridge** Network Bridge. The context used to enable or disable transport layer (OSI model layer 3) compatibility mode for network bridges. Also used to view the configuration settings of network bridges.
- **dhcp** Dynamic Host Configuration Protocol (DHCP). The context used for viewing and managing DHCP servers. You use the DHCP context to assign TCP/IP configuration information dynamically to network clients. This context is only available on Windows Server 2008 when the DHCP Server role service is

installed. If the DHCP Server role service is not installed, the shortcut context name "dhcp" opens the dhcpclient context.

- **dhcpclient** DHCP client. The context used for enabling or disabling tracing of DHCP communications.
- **firewall** Windows Firewall. The context used to manage allowed programs, firewall ports, logging, notification and other aspects of the Windows Firewall.
- **http** Hypertext Transfer Protocol (HTTP). The context used to manage the configuration of HTTP listeners.
- **interface ipv4** Interface IP version 4 (IPv4). The context used to view and manage the IPv4 network configuration of a computer. Many Interface IPv4 Show commands are only available when working locally.
- **interface ipv6** Interface IP version 6 (IPv6). The context used to view and manage the IPv6 network configuration of a computer. Many Interface IPv6 Show commands are only available when working locally.
- **interface portproxy** Interface Port Proxy. The context used to manage proxies for IPv4 networks and IPv6 networks as well as between IPv4 and IPv6 networks.
- **ipsec** Internet Protocol Security (IPsec). The context used to view and configure dynamic and static settings for IPsec.
- **lan** Wired Local Area Network (LAN). The context used to manage wired network profiles and to work with wired interfaces. Most Lan commands make use of the Wired Autoconfig service and you must start this service to use these commands.
- **nap client** Network Access Protection (NAP) client. The context used to manage the NAP client configuration.
- **nap hra** NAP Health Registration Authority (HRA). The context used to manage the NAP HRA configuration. This context is only available on Windows Server 2008 when the Health Registration Authority role service is installed as part of the Network Policy And Access Services role.
- **netio** Network Input/Output (netio). The context allows you to add, delete, and list network binding filters.
- **ras** Remote access server (RAS). The context used to view and manage remote access server configurations.
- **ras aaaa** Authentication, authorization, accounting, and auditing (AAAA). The context used to view and work with the AAAA database. That database is used by the Internet Authentication Service (IAS) and the Routing And Remote Access service.
- **ras diagnostics** RAS diagnostics. The context used to configure diagnostics logging and traces for troubleshooting RAS.

- **routing** Routing. The context used to manage routing servers. Used with Routing And Remote Access server. This context is only available on Windows Server 2008 when the Routing And Remote Access Services role is installed as part of the Network Policy And Access Services role.
- **rpc** Remote procedure call (RPC) helper. The context used to view and manage IP address interface settings as well as IP subnet addresses that are configured on a computer. The commands in this context can only be used when you are working locally.
- **rpc filter** RPC firewall. The context used to create and manage RPC firewall filters and rules. The commands in this context can only be used when you are working locally.
- **winhttp** Windows HTTP (WinHTTP). The context used to manage WinHTTP proxy and tracing settings.
- **wins** Windows Internet Name Service (WINS). The context used to view and manage WINS server settings. You use WINS to resolve NetBIOS computer names to IPv4 addresses for pre–Windows 2000 computers. This context is only available on Windows Server 2008 when the WINS Server feature is installed.
- **winsock** Winsock. The context used to view and manage Winsock communications settings.
- **wlan** Wireless LAN. The context used to view and manage wireless networking settings. On Windows Serer 2008, commands in this context are only available when the Wireless LAN service is installed.

Note As noted, some contexts and commands are only available when you use Netsh on a local computer. The key one you'll notice is RPC, which is only available when you are working locally. In addition, some Netsh contexts and commands require the Routing And Remote Access service to be configured even when you are working with a local computer at the command line. If this is the case, you must set the Connections To Other Access Servers remote access policy to grant remote access permission, and then ensure that the remote access service is running.

In Appendix B you'll find a comprehensive guide to these and other contexts and subcontexts. The context name tells Netsh which helper DLL to load. The helper DLL provides context-specific commands that you can use. For example, if you typed **netsh** to work interactively with Netsh and then typed **rpc** you would enter the RPC context. You could then type **show interfaces** to see the IPv4 address interfaces configured on the computer. As a series of steps, this would look like this:

1. Type **netsh**. The command prompt changes to: **netsh>**.
2. Type **rpc**. The command prompt changes to: **netsh rpc>**.

3. Type **show interfaces**. The IPv4 address interfaces configured on the computer are displayed, such as

```
Subnet            Interface        Status    Description

127.0.0.0         127.0.0.1        Enabled   Software Loopback Interface 1
192.168.1.0      192.168.1.101     Enabled    Intel(R) PRO/1000 PM
Network Connection
```

Each context has a different set of commands available and some of these commands lead to subcontexts that have their own commands as well. Keep in mind the related service for the context must be configured on the computer or in the domain to allow you to do meaningful work within a particular context. Regardless of what context you are working with, you can view the list of available commands by typing **help** or **?**. Similarly, regardless of what context you are in, typing **exit** or **quit** will exit the network services shell, returning you to the Windows command prompt.

To switch to a context regardless of where you are within the network services shell, type the full context name. For example, if you are working with the Interface Ipv6 context and want to switch to the Ras Diagnostics context, simply enter **ras diagnostics**. Finally, regardless of which context you are working with, you can always use the .. command to go up one context level. This means that if you are working with the Netsh Rpc context and later want to switch back to the top-level netsh context, you would type .. to go up one context level.

Well, that's how Netsh works interactively: It's slow and plodding, but it's good for beginners or for digging around to find out what commands are available. Once you grow accustomed to working with Netsh, you'll want to use this utility in noninteractive mode. Noninteractive mode allows you to type in complete command sequences at the command-line prompt or within batch scripts. For example, the previous procedure, which took three steps, can be performed with one command line:

```
netsh rpc show interfaces
```

Whether you insert this line into a script or type it directly at a command-line prompt, the resulting output is the same: a list of interfaces on the computer you are working with. As you can see, typing commands directly is a lot faster.

Working with Remote Computers

You can use Netsh to work with remote computers. To work interactively with a remote computer, you start Netsh with the –R parameter and then specify the IP address or domain name of the computer to which you want to connect, such as

```
netsh -r 192.168.10.15
```

or

```
netsh -r corpsvr02
```

While you work with the remote computer, Netsh will include the computer IP address or name in its command prompt, such as

```
[corpsvr02] netsh>
```

Here you use Netsh to work remotely with CorpSvr02. You can provide any necessary user credentials with the following parameters:

- **-u:** Specifies a different user to log on to a remote computer in the form Domain\User or User. Only applicable when working with a remote computer.
- **-p:** Sets the password for the specified user. If you don't specify a password, or if you use "*", you are prompted to enter a password. Only applicable when a different log-on user is specified when working with a remote computer.

In the following example, you work with Netsh on FileServer25 and use the CPANDL\WilliamS account to log on:

```
netsh -r fileserver25 -u cpandl\williams -p *
```

If you want to work noninteractively with remote computers, you must use the following syntax:

```
netsh -c Context -r RemoteComputer Command
```

where *Context* is the identifier for the context you want to work with, *RemoteComputer* is the name or IP address of the remote computer, and *Command* is the command to execute. Consider the following example:

```
netsh -c "interface ipv4" -r corpsvr02 show interfaces
```

In this example, you use the Interface IPv4 context to obtain a list of interfaces configured on CorpSvr02. Here, you cannot use the RPC context to perform this task, because this context is only available on a local computer.

> **Real World** To use Netsh to interact with a remote computer, the Routing And Remote Access service must be configured on the network. Specifically, you must set the Connections To Other Access Servers remote access policy to grant remote access permission. Then, ensure that the remote access service is running.

Working with Script Files

As discussed previously, you can type in complete Netsh command sequences at the command line or within batch scripts. The catch is that you must know the complete command line you want to use and cannot rely on Netsh for help. Some command lines can be very long and complex. For example, the following commands connect to a DHCP server, configure a DHCP scope, and then activate the scope:

```
netsh dhcp server \\corpsvr02 add scope 192.168.1.0 255.255.255.0 MainScope
PrimaryScope
```

```
netsh dhcp server \\corpsvr02 scope 192.168.1.0 add iprange 192.168.1.1
192.168.1.254

netsh dhcp server \\corpsvr02 scope 192.168.1.0 add excluderange 192.168.
1.1 192.168.1.25

netsh dhcp server \\corpsvr02 scope 192.168.1.0 set state 1
```

If you save these commands to a batch script, you can run the script just as you would any other batch script. For example, if you named the script dhcpconfig.bat, you would type **dhcpconfig** to run the script.

When working with remote computers, you can place the script on a network share accessible from the remote computer and then log on remotely to execute the script. Or you can copy the script directly to the remote computer and then log on to execute it remotely. Either way works, but both involve a couple of extra steps. Fortunately, there's a faster way to run a script on a remote computer. To do this, you must change the script a bit and use the following syntax:

```
netsh -c Context -r RemoteComputer -f Script
```

where *Context* is the identifier for the context you want to work with, *RemoteComputer* is the name or IP address of the remote computer, and *Script* is the file or network path to the script to execute. Consider the following example:

```
netsh -c "dhcp server" -r corpsvr02 -f dhcpconfig.bat
```

In this example, you run a Netsh script called dhcpconfig.bat on CorpSvr02 using the DHCP Server context. Note that Server is a subcontext of the DHCP context. The script contains the following commands:

```
add scope 192.168.1.0 255.255.255.0 MainScope PrimaryScope
scope 192.168.1.0 add iprange 192.168.1.1 192.168.1.254
scope 192.168.1.0 add excluderange 192.168.1.1 192.168.1.25
scope 192.168.1.0 set state 1
```

These commands create, configure, and then activate a DHCP scope on the designated DHCP Server, CorpSvr02. Because you are already using the DHCP Server context on CorpSvr02, you don't need to type **netsh dhcp server \\corpsvr02** at the beginning of each command.

Managing TCP/IP Settings

Computers use IP addresses to communicate over TCP/IP. Windows Vista and Windows Server 2008 have a dual IP layer architecture in which both Internet Protocol version 4 (IPv4) and Internet Protocol version 6 (IPv6) are implemented and share common Transport and Frame layers. IPv4 and IPv6 are used in very different ways. IPv4 has 32-bit addresses and is the primary version of IP used on most networks, including the Internet. IPv6 has 128-bit addresses and is the next generation version of IP.

When networking hardware is detected during installation of the operating system, both IPv4 and IPv6 are enabled by default and you don't need to install a separate component to enable support for IPv6. IP addressing can be configured manually or dynamically at the command line. With a manual configuration, you assign the computer a static IP address. Static IP addresses are fixed and don't change unless you change them. With a dynamic configuration, you configure the computer to get its IP address assignment from a DHCP server on the network. This IP address is assigned when the computer starts and might change over time. In domains, Windows servers typically use static IP addresses and Windows workstations typically use dynamic IP addresses.

Configuring IPv4

IPv4's 32-bit addresses commonly are expressed as four separate decimal values, such as 127.0.0.1 or 192.168.10.50. The four decimal values are referred to as octets because each represents 8 bits of the 32-bit number. (Using 8 bits for each decimal number limits the range of possible values to zero through 255.) With standard unicast IPv4 addresses, a variable part of the IP address represents the network ID and a variable part of the IP address represents the host ID. There is no correlation between a host's IPv4 address and the internal machine (MAC) address used by the host's network adapter.

Setting a Static IPv4 Address

When you set a static IPv4 address, you tell the computer the IPv4 address to use, the subnet mask for this IPv4 address, and, if necessary, the default gateway to use for internetwork communications. After you configure these IPv4 settings, you will also need to configure name-resolution settings for Domain Name System (DNS) and possibly WINS.

You assign a static IPv4 address using the Netsh Interface IPv4 context. The command is SET ADDRESS and its syntax is

```
set address [name=]InterfaceName source=static address=IPAddress
mask=SubnetMask [gateway={none | DefaultGateway
[[gwmetric=]GatewayMetric]}
```

> **Note** If the computer already had an IPv4 address configuration on the specified interface, using SET ADDRESS replaces the existing values. To add to the existing settings instead of replacing them, use the ADD ADDRESS command.

You can check to see the available interfaces and their current configuration by typing **netsh interface ipv4 show addresses** at the command prompt or, if you are in the Netsh Interface IPv4 context, by typing **show addresses**. As shown in the following example, the output specifies the name of the interfaces available and their current configuration:

```
Configuration for interface "Local Area Connection"
    DHCP enabled:                         Yes
    IP Address:                           192.168.1.101
    Subnet Prefix:                        192.168.1.0/24 (mask 255.255.255.0)
    Default Gateway:                      192.168.1.1
    Gateway Metric:                       0
    InterfaceMetric:                      10

Configuration for interface "Loopback Pseudo-Interface 1"
    DHCP enabled:                         No
    IP Address:                           127.0.0.1
    Subnet Prefix:                        127.0.0.0/8 (mask 255.0.0.0)
    InterfaceMetric:                      50
```

In most cases, the interface name you want to work with is "Local Area Connection." The pseudo interface listed in this example is used for local loopback communications. The IPv4 address you assign to the computer must not be used anywhere else on the network. The subnet mask field ensures that the computer communicates over the network properly. If the network uses subnets, the value you use may be different on each network segment within the company. If the computer needs to access other TCP/IP networks, the Internet, or other subnets, you must specify a default gateway. Use the IPv4 address of the network's default router.

The gateway metric indicates the relative cost of using a gateway. If multiple default routes are available for a particular IPv4 address, the gateway with the lowest cost is used first. If the computer can't communicate with the initial gateway, Windows tries to use the gateway with the next lowest metric. Unlike the GUI, Windows doesn't automatically assign a metric to the gateway. You must assign the metric manually.

Consider the following example:

```
set address name="Local Area Connection" source=static
address=192.168.1.50 mask=255.255.255.0 gateway=192.168.1.1
gwmetric=1
```

Here you specify that you are working with the "Local Area Connection" interface, setting a static IPv4 address of 192.168.1.50 with a network mask of 255.255.255.0. The default gateway is 192.168.1.1 and the gateway metric is 1.

> **Tip** You can confirm the settings you just made by typing **netsh interface ipv4 show addresses** at the command prompt or, if you are in the Netsh Interface IPv4 context, by typing **show addresses**. Because many Interface IPv4 and Interface IPv6 Show commands are only available when working locally, including Show Addresses, you must be logged on locally to use this command.

Setting a Dynamic IPv4 Address

You can assign a dynamic IPv4 address to any of the network adapters on a computer, provided that a DHCP server is available on the network. Then you rely on the DHCP server to supply the necessary IPv4 addressing information. Because the dynamic IPv4 address can change, you normally don't use a dynamic IPv4 address for servers running Windows Server 2008.

You assign a dynamic IPv4 address using the Netsh Interface IPv4 context. The command is SET ADDRESS and its syntax is

```
set address name=InterfaceName source=dhcp
```

Consider the following example:

```
set address name="Local Area Connection" source=dhcp
```

Here you are working in the Netsh Interface IPv4 context and specify that you want to set a dynamic IPv4 address for the "Local Area Connection" interface.

Adding IPv4 Addresses and Gateways

Both Windows Vista and Windows Server 2008 systems can have multiple IPv4 addresses, even if the computer only has a single network adapter. Multiple IPv4 addresses are useful if you want a single computer to appear as several computers or your network is divided into subnets and the computer needs access to these subnets to route information or provide other internetworking services.

> **Note** Keep in mind that when you use a single network adapter, IPv4 addresses must be assigned to the same network segment or segments that are part of a single logical network. If your network consists of multiple physical networks, you must use multiple network adapters, with each network adapter being assigned an IPv4 address in a different physical network segment.

You assign multiple IPv4 addresses and gateways to a single network adapter using the ADD ADDRESS command of the Netsh Interface IPv4 context. The syntax for this command is similar to that of SET ADDRESS. It is

```
add address [name=]InterfaceName address=IPAddress mask=SubnetMask
[[gateway=]DefaultGateway [gwmetric=]GatewayMetric]
```

Consider the following example:

```
add address name="Local Area Connection" address=192.168.2.12
mask=255.255.255.0 gateway=192.168.2.1 gwmetric=1
```

> **Note** If you specify a gateway, you must also specify the gateway metric. As before, you can confirm the settings you just made by typing **show addresses**.

Here you specify that you are working with the "Local Area Connection" interface and adding the IPv4 address of 192.168.2.12 with a network mask of 255.255.255.0. The default gateway for this IPv4 address is 192.168.2.1 and the gateway metric is 1.

Setting DNS Servers to Use for IPv4

Computers use DNS to determine a computer's IP address from its host name or its host name from an IP address. For computers using static IPv4 addresses, you must tell them which DNS servers to use; you can do this using the Netsh Interface IPv4 context. The syntax for setting a specific DNS server to use is

```
set dnsserver name=InterfaceName source=static address=DNSAddress
```

Consider the following example:

```
set dnsserver name="Local Area Connection" source=static
address=192.168.1.56
```

Here you specify that you are working with the "Local Area Connection" interface and specifying the DNS server address as 192.168.1.56.

When you are configuring a static DNS server address, you can use the optional register parameter to control DNS registration. Keep the following in mind:

- By default, all IP addresses for interfaces are registered in DNS under the computer's fully qualified domain name. This automatic registration uses the DNS dynamic update protocol. If you want to disable this behavior, use **register=none**.
- By default, the computer's full name is registered only in its primary domain as set by the default value **register=primary**. When using dynamic DNS, you can also specify that the connection-specific DNS name should be registered with DNS. To do this, use **register=both**. This allows for occasions when the computer has multiple network adapters that connect to multiple domains.

If a computer is using DHCPv4 and you want DHCPv4 to provide the DNS server address, you can provide the DNS server address as well or specify that the IPv4 address should be obtained from DHCPv4. You tell the computer to get the DNS server settings from DHCPv4 by typing

```
set dnsserver name=InterfaceName source=dhcp
```

Consider the following example:

```
set dnsserver name="Local Area Connection" source=dhcp
```

Here you specify that the "Local Area Connection" interface should get its DNS server address settings from DHCPv4.

> **Note** If the computer already had DNS server IPv4 addresses set, using SET DNSSERVER replaces the existing values. To add DNS server IPv4 addresses instead of replacing them, use the ADD DNSSERVER command. You can confirm the DNS server settings by typing **show dnsservers**.

Specifying Additional DNS Servers to Use

Most networks have multiple DNS servers that are used for resolving domain names. This allows for name resolution if one DNS server isn't available. When you use DHCPv4 to specify the DNS servers, it can automatically tell computers about other DNS servers that may be available. This isn't the case when you manually specify DNS servers to be used.

To tell a computer about other DNS servers that may be available in addition to the primary DNS server specified previously, you can use the Netsh Interface IPv4 context and the ADD DNSSERVER command. The syntax is

```
add dnsserver name=InterfaceName address=DNSAddress
```

Consider the following example:

```
add dnsserver name="Local Area Connection" address=192.168.1.75
```

Here you specify that you are working with the "Local Area Connection" interface and designating an alternate DNS server with an IP address of 192.168.1.75.

By default, a DNS server is added to the end of the DNS server's list in the TCP/IP configuration. If you want the DNS server to be in a specific position in the list use the Index= parameter. For example, if you wanted an additional server to be listed first (making it the primary) you'd set an index of 1, such as:

```
add dnsserver name="Local Area Connection" address=192.168.1.75 index=1
```

Setting WINS Servers to Use

WINS is used to resolve NetBIOS computer names to IP addresses. You can use WINS to help computers on a network determine the address of pre-Windows 2000 computers on the network. Although WINS is supported in all versions of Windows, Windows Server 2008 primarily uses WINS for backward compatibility.

For computers using static IP addresses, you must specify which WINS servers are to be used. Within the Netsh Interface IPv4 context, the syntax for specifying the use of a specific WINS server is

```
set winsserver name=InterfaceName source=static address=WINSAddress
```

Consider the following example:

```
set winsserver name="Local Area Connection" source=static
address=192.168.1.64
```

Here you specify that you are working with the "Local Area Connection" interface and specifying the WINS server address as 192.168.1.64.

If a computer is using DHCP and you want DHCP to provide the WINS server address, you can provide the WINS server address as well or specify that the IP address should be obtained from DHCP. You tell the computer to get the WINS server settings from DHCP by typing

```
set winsserver name=InterfaceName source=dhcp
```

Consider the following example:

```
set winsserver name="Local Area Connection" source=dhcp
```

Here you specify that the "Local Area Connection" interface should get its WINS server address settings from DHCP.

> **Note** If the WINS server IP addresses were already set, using SET WINSSERVER replaces the existing values. To add WINS server IP addresses instead of replacing them, use the ADD WINSSERVER command. You can confirm the WINS server settings by typing **show winsservers**.

Specifying Additional WINS Servers to Use

Most networks have a primary and a backup WINS server. This allows for name resolution if one WINS server isn't available. If you use DHCP to specify the WINS servers, DHCP can automatically tell computers about other WINS servers that may be available. This isn't the case when you manually specify which WINS servers to use.

To tell a computer about other WINS servers that may be available in addition to the primary WINS server specified previously, you can use the Netsh Interface IPv4 context and the ADD WINSSERVER command. The syntax is

```
add winsserver name=InterfaceName address=WINSAddress
```

Consider the following example:

```
add winsserver name="Local Area Connection" address=192.168.1.155
```

Here you specify that you are working with the "Local Area Connection" interface and designating an alternate WINS server with an IP address of 192.168.1.155.

By default, a WINS server is added to the end of the WINS server's list in the TCP/IP configuration. If you want a WINS server to be in a specific position in the list use the Index= parameter. For example, if you wanted an additional server to be listed first (making it the primary) you'd set an index of 1, such as

```
add winsserver name="Local Area Connection" address=192.168.1.155 index=1
```

Deleting IPv4 Address Resolution Protocol Cache

When computers look up domain name information for IPv4 addresses, the related information is stored in the Address Resolution Protocol (ARP) cache so that the next time the information is needed no name lookup is necessary. The address resolution information expires according to a time-to-live (TTL) value set when the information was received, after which time it must again be looked up to get current information and a new TTL. In general, this automated system of obtaining, clearing out, and renewing name information works well. Sometimes, however, old name-resolution information on a system will cause problems before the information is purged. For example, if a computer changes its name information and the TTL hasn't expired on a previous lookup, temporarily you won't be able to find the computer.

DNS administrators have several tricks they can use to reduce the impact of name changes, such as setting an increasingly shorter TTL just prior to a name change to ensure that old information is deleted more quickly and doesn't cause a problem. However, you may find that it's easier just to get rid of the old information and force a computer to make new DNS lookups. You can do this by typing **netsh interface ipv4 delete arpcache** at the command prompt or, if you are in the Netsh Interface IPv4 context, by typing **delete arpcache**. This deletes name information for all interfaces configured on the computer you are working with. When there are multiple interfaces and you only want name-resolution information purged for one interface, you can name the interface to work with by including **name=InterfaceName**, such as

```
delete arpcache name="Local Area Connection"
```

Deleting TCP/IPv4 Settings

Using the Netsh Interface IPv4 context, you can delete TCP/IPv4 configuration settings as well. Table 17-1 summarizes the available commands according to the task to be performed.

Table 17-1 Netsh Interface IPv4 Commands for Deleting TCP/IPv4 Settings

Task	Syntax	Example
Delete a designated IPv4 address from the named interface.	`delete address name=`*`InterfaceName`* `address=`*`IPAddress`*	`delete address name= "Local Area Network" address=192.168.1.5 6`
Delete a static gateway IPv4 address from the named interface.	`delete address name=`*`InterfaceName`* `gateway=`*`GatewayAddress`*	`delete address name= "Local Area Network" gateway=192.168.1.1`
Delete all static gateway IPv4 addresses from the named interface.	`delete address name=`*`InterfaceName`* `gateway=all`	`delete address name= "Local Area Network" gateway=all`

Table 17-1 Netsh Interface IPv4 Commands for Deleting TCP/IPv4 Settings

Task	Syntax	Example
Delete a DNS server from the named interface.	`delete dnsserver name=`*`InterfaceName`* `address=`*`IPAddress`*	`delete dnsserver name= "Local Area Network" address=192.168.1.5 6`
Delete all DNS servers from the named interface.	`delete dnsserver name=`*`InterfaceName`* `address=all`	`delete dnsserver name= "Local Area Network" address=all`
Delete a WINS server from the named interface.	`delete winsserver name=`*`InterfaceName`* `address=`*`IPAddress`*	`delete winsserver name= "Local Area Network" address=192.168.1.5 6`
Delete all WINS servers from the named interface.	`delete winsserver name=`*`InterfaceName`* `address=all`	`delete winsserver name= "Local Area Network" address=all`

Configuring IPv6

IPv6's 128-bit addresses are divided into eight 16-bit blocks delimited by colons. Each 16-bit block is expressed in hexadecimal form. With standard unicast IPv6 addresses, the first 64 bits represent the network ID and the last 64 bits represent the network interface. An example of an IPv6 address is FEC0:0:0:02BC:FF:BECB:FE4F:961D. Because many IPv6 address blocks are set to 0, a contiguous set of 0 blocks can be expressed as "::", a notation referred to as the double-colon notation. Using double-colon notation, the two 0 blocks in the previous address are compressed as FEC0::02BC:FF:BECB:FE4F:961D. Three or more 0 blocks would be compressed in the same way. For example, FFE8:0:0:0:0:0:0:1 becomes FFE8::1.

Setting IPv6 Addresses

By default, computers have their IPv6 configuration automatically assigned. When a computer using IPv6 connects to the network, it sends a link-local multicast request to retrieve configuration settings. Computers using IPv6 can also use DHCPv6 to obtain IPv6 configuration information from a DHCPv6 server. When you configure DHCPv6 servers on a network, you specify how DHCPv6 works for clients and do not need to modify dynamic client configurations to support this. Automatically assigned IPv6 addresses typically are link-local addresses that are accessible only on the local network.

For computers that require routable IPv6 addresses, you'll need to assign a static IPv6 address. When you set a static IPv6 address, you tell the computer the IPv6 address to use and specify whether the address is unicast or anycast. Unicast addresses are the default, and you'll assign two main variations of unicast addresses: unique local unicast and global unicast. Unique local IPv6 unicast addresses are routable on your internal network but not accessible from the Internet. Global unicast addresses, on the other hand, can be routed to the Internet, such as may be required for external servers. Anycast addresses are addresses that can be assigned to multiple interfaces, such as a single IPv6 address for all the interfaces on a computer.

You assign a static IPv6 address using the Netsh Interface IPv6 context. The command is SET ADDRESS and its syntax is

```
set address [interface=]InterfaceName address=IPAddress
type=AddressType
```

> **Note** If the computer already had an IPv6 address configuration on the specified interface, using SET ADDRESS replaces the existing values. To add to the existing settings instead of replacing them, use the ADD ADDRESS command.

You can check to see the available interfaces and their current configuration by typing **netsh interface ipv6 show addresses** at the command prompt or, if you are in the Netsh Interface IPv6 context, by typing **show addresses**. As shown in the following example, the output specifies the name of the interfaces available and their current configuration:

```
Interface 1: Loopback Pseudo-Interface 1

Addr Type  DAD State   Valid Life Pref. Life Address
---------  ----------- ---------- ---------- ------------------------
Other      Preferred     infinite   infinite ::1

Interface 7: Local Area Connection

Addr Type  DAD State   Valid Life Pref. Life Address
---------  ----------- ---------- ---------- ------------------------
Other      Preferred     infinite   infinite fe80::6712:1345:cc87:3820%7

Interface 11: Local Area Connection* 8

Addr Type  DAD State   Valid Life Pref. Life Address
---------  ----------- ---------- ---------- ------------------------
Other      Preferred     infinite   infinite fe80::5efe:192.168.1.101%11
```

> **Note** Computers running IPv6 use the fe80::/64 link-local network address for network adapters connected to networks without IPv6 routers or DHCPv6 servers. When a computer has multiple network adapters configured, it adds a numeric identifier following a percent sign to the IP address in the output. In the example, %7 is added to the output for Interface 7 and %11 is added to the output for Interface 11.

Consider the following example:

```
set address interface="Local Area Connection"
address= 2001:1cb7::2b58:02bb:00ff:fe45:bc7d type= unicast
```

Here you specify that you are working with the "Local Area Connection" interface, setting a static unicast IPv6 address of 2001:1cb7::2b58:02bb:00ff:fe45:bc7d.

> **Tip** You can confirm the settings you just made by typing **netsh interface ipv6 show addresses** at the command prompt or, if you are in the Netsh Interface IPv6 context, by typing **show addresses**. Because many Interface IPv6 and Interface IPv6 show commands are only available when working locally, including show addresses, you must be logged on locally to use this command.

You can assign additional IPv6 addresses to a network adapter using the ADD ADDRESS command of the Netsh Interface IPv6 context. The syntax for this command is similar to that of SET ADDRESS. It is

```
add address [interface=]InterfaceName address=IPAddress
type=AddressType
```

Setting DNS Servers to Use for IPv6

For computers using static IPv6 addresses, you must tell them which DNS servers to use; you can do this using the Netsh Interface IPv6 context. The syntax for setting a specific DNS server to use is

```
set dnsserver name=InterfaceName source=static address=DNSAddress
register=
```

Consider the following example:

```
set dnsserver name="Local Area Connection" source=static
address=fec0:0:0:ffff::1
```

Here you specify that you are working with the "Local Area Connection" interface and specifying the DNS server address as fec0:0:0:ffff::1.

When you are configuring a static DNS server address, you can use the optional register parameter to control DNS registration. Use **register=none** to disable dynamic DNS updates. Use **register=primary** to register the computer's full name in its primary domain (as per the default setting). Use **register=both** to specify that the connection-specific DNS name should be registered with DNS as well as the primary DNS suffix.

If a computer is using DHCPv6 and you want DHCPv6 to provide the DNS server address, you can provide the DNS server address as well or specify that the IPv6 address should be obtained from DHCPv6. You tell the computer to get the DNS server settings from DHCPv6 by typing

```
set dnsserver name=InterfaceName source=dhcp
```

Consider the following example:

```
set dnsserver name="Local Area Connection" source=dhcp
```

Here you specify that the "Local Area Connection" interface should get its DNS server address settings from DHCP.

> **Note** If the computer already had DNS server IPv6 addresses set, using SET DNSSERVER replaces the existing values. To add DNS server IPv6 addresses instead of replacing them, use the ADD DNSSERVER command. You can confirm the DNS server settings by typing **show dnsservers**.

To tell a computer about other DNS servers that may be available in addition to the primary DNS server specified previously, you can use the Netsh Interface IPv6 context and the ADD DNSSERVER command. The syntax is

```
add dnsserver name=InterfaceName address=DNSAddress
```

Consider the following example:

```
add dnsserver name="Local Area Connection" address=fec0:0:0:ffff::2
```

Here you specify that you are working with the "Local Area Connection" interface and designating an alternate DNS server with an IP address of fec0:0:0:ffff::2.

By default, a DNS server is added to the end of the DNS server's list in the TCP/IP configuration. If you want the DNS server to be in a specific position in the list, use the Index= parameter. For example, if you wanted an additional server to be listed first (making it the primary) you'd set an index of 1, such as:

```
add dnsserver name="Local Area Connection" address= fec0:0:0:ffff::2
index=1
```

Deleting TCP/IPv6 Settings

Using the Netsh Interface IPv6 context, you can delete TCP/IPv6 configuration settings as well. Table 17-2 summarizes the available commands according to the task to be performed.

Table 17-2 Netsh Interface IPv6 Commands for Deleting TCP/IPv6 Settings

Task	Syntax	Example
Delete a designated IPv6 address from the named interface.	delete address name=*InterfaceName* address=*IPAddress*	delete address name="Local Area Network" address=2001:1cb7::2b58:02bb:00ff:fe45:bc7d
Delete a DNS server from the named interface.	delete dns name=*Interface-Name* address=*IPAddress*	delete dns name="Local Area Network" address= fec0:0:0:ffff::2
Delete all DNS servers from the named interface.	delete dns name=*Interface-Name* address=all	delete dns name="Local Area Network" address=all

Supporting TCP/IP Networking

The Netsh shell provides two contexts for working with TCP/IP. You use the Interface IPv4 context to view TCP/IPv4 statistics and to change settings. You use the Interface IPv6 context to view TCP/IPv6 statistics and to change settings. The use of these contexts assumes that the necessary TCP/IP network components are already installed on the computer you are working with. If TCP/IP network components aren't installed, you'll need to install them.

Obtaining and Saving the TCP/IP Configuration

If you've worked with Windows for a while, you probably know that you can type **ipconfig** at a command prompt to get basic configuration information for IPv4 and IPv6, such as

```
Windows IP Configuration
Ethernet adapter Local Area Connection:
   Connection-specific DNS Suffix  . :
   Link-local IPv6 Address . . . . . : fe80::6712:1345:cc87:3820%7
   IPv4 Address. . . . . . . . . . . : 192.168.1.101
   Subnet Mask . . . . . . . . . . . : 255.255.255.0
   Default Gateway . . . . . . . . . : 192.168.1.1

Tunnel adapter Local Area Connection* 2:

   Media State . . . . . . . . . . . : Media disconnected
   Connection-specific DNS Suffix  . :

Tunnel adapter Local Area Connection* 8:

   Connection-specific DNS Suffix  . :
   Link-local IPv6 Address . . . . . : fe80::5efe:192.168.1.101%11
   Default Gateway . . . . . . . . . :
```

As you can see, this information shows the IPv6 link local address as well as the IPv4 address, subnet mask, and default gateway being used for the Local Area Connection Ethernet adapter. When you want more details, you type **ipconfig /all** to display additional information including the physical (MAC) address of the adapter, DHCP status, DNS servers used, and host information, such as

```
Windows IP Configuration

    Host Name:    salespc09
    Primary Dns Suffix:    cpandl.com
    Node Type:    Hybrid
    IP Routing Enabled:    No
    WINS Proxy Enabled:    No
```

```
Ethernet adapter Local Area Connection:
   Connection-specific DNS Suffix  . :
   Description . . . . . . . . . . . : Intel(R) PRO/
1000 PM Network Connection
   Physical Address. . . . . . . . . : EA-BF-C2-D4-EF-12
   DHCP Enabled. . . . . . . . . . . : Yes
   Autoconfiguration Enabled . . . . : Yes
   Link-local IPv6 Address . . . . . : fe80::6712:1345:cc87:3820%7(Preferred)
   IPv4 Address. . . . . . . . . . . : 192.168.1.35(Preferred)
   Subnet Mask . . . . . . . . . . . : 255.255.255.0
   Lease Obtained. . . . . . . . . . : Friday, April 04, 2009 9:37:43 AM
   Lease Expires . . . . . . . . . . : Saturday, April 05, 2009 12:05:32 PM
   Default Gateway . . . . . . . . . : 192.168.1.1
   DHCP Server . . . . . . . . . . . : 192.168.1.50
   DHCPv6 IAID . . . . . . . . . . . : 128384737
   NetBIOS over Tcpip. . . . . . . . : Enabled
```

Here a computer with the fully qualified DNS name salespc09.cpandl.com is configured to use DHCP and has an IP address of 192.168.1.35 with subnet mask 255.255.255.0. Because the IP address was dynamically assigned, it has specific Lease Obtained and Lease Expiration date and time stamps.

If you type **netsh interface ipv4 show config** at a command prompt, you can obtain similar, albeit abbreviated, configuration information for IPv4, such as

```
Configuration for interface "Local Area Connection"
    DHCP enabled:     No
    IP Address:     192.168.1.50
    Subnet Prefix:     192.168.1.0/24 (mask 255.255.255.0)
    Default Gateway:     192.168.1.50
    GatewayMetric:     256
    InterfaceMetric:     20
    Statically Configured DNS Servers:     127.0.0.1
    Register with which suffix:     Primary only
    Statically Configured WINS Servers:     None
```

You can examine basic IPv6 configuration information by typing **netsh interface ipv6 show addresses** and **netsh interface ipv6 show dnsservers**. As you can see, these are all ways to obtain similar information about the TCP/IP configuration.

Netsh also gives you the means to save the IPv4 and IPv6 configuration so that the settings can be recreated simply by running a Netsh script. If you want to save the IPv4 settings to a file, type:

```
netsh interface ipv4 dump > FileName
```

where *FileName* is the name of the file to which you want to write the IPv4 configuration information. Listing 17-1 shows an example of an IPv4 configuration file.

Listing 17-1 IPv4 Configuration Script

```
# ----------------------------------
# IPv4 Configuration
# ----------------------------------
pushd interface ipv4


set address name="Local Area Connection" source=static
address=192.168.1.50 mask=255.255.255.0
set address name="Local Area Connection" gateway=192.168.1.1
gwmetric=1
set dnsserver name="Local Area Connection" source=static address=192.
168.1.56 register=primary
set winsserver name="Local Area Connection" source=static address=none

popd
# End of interface IPv4 configuration
```

Listing 17-1 is a Netsh script that you can run using the following syntax:

```
netsh -c "interface ipv4" -f FileName
```

Consider the following example:

```
netsh -c "interface ipv4" -f corpsvr02-ipconfig.txt
```

In this example, you run a Netsh script called corpsvr02-ipconfig.txt using the Interface IPv4 context to apply the IPv4 configuration defined in the script. One of the key reasons for creating a configuration dump is so that you have a backup of the IP configuration. If the configuration is altered incorrectly in the future, you can restore the original configuration from the script.

Examining IP Address and Interface Configurations

The Netsh Interface IPv4 and Netsh Interface IPv6 contexts provide several commands for viewing IP address and interface configurations. Here, an interface refers to a network adapter used by a computer to communicate over TCP/IP. Most computers have two interfaces: a local loopback interface and a Local Area Connection interface.

For IPv4, the local loopback interface is a pseudo-interface that uses the IPv4 address 127.0.0.1 and a network mask of 255.0.0.0. All IPv4 messages sent over this interface are looped back to the computer and are not sent out over the network.

For IPv6, the local loopback interface uses the IPv6 address ::1. All IPv6 messages sent over this interface are looped back to the computer and are not sent out over the network.

The Local Area Connection interface is created automatically when you install TCP/IP networking. Each network adapter will have one such interface. By default the first interface is named Local Area Connection, the second is Local Area Connection 2, and so on.

At the Windows command line, you can view global configuration information for IPv4 by typing **netsh interface ipv4 show global**. The output should be similar to the following:

```
General Global Parameters
---------------------------------------------
Default Hop Limit                      : 128 hops
Neighbor Cache Limit                   : 256 entries per interface
Route Cache Limit                      : 128 entries per compartment
Reassembly Limit                       : 27229728 bytes
ICMP Redirects                         : enabled
Source Routing Behavior                : dontforward
Task Offload                           : enabled
Dhcp Media Sense                       : enabled
Media Sense Logging                    : enabled
MLD Level                              : all
MLD Version                            : version3
Multicast Forwarding                   : disabled
Group Forwarded Fragments              : disabled
Randomize Identifiers                  : enabled
Address Mask Reply                     : disabled

Current Global Statistics
---------------------------------------------
Number of Compartments                 : 1
Number of NL clients                   : 7
Number of FL providers                 : 4
```

This information lists the global status of IPv4 for all interfaces configured on the computer. The Default Hop Limit lists the default maximum hops that are allowed for packets routed over the network. The reassembly limit indicates the maximum reassembly size of IP datagrams. Here, this means IP datagrams sent or received using this interface can have a maximum size of 27,229,728 bytes. Blocks of data aren't usually sent in this size, however. Instead, they are separated into fragments, which are reassembled upon receipt into a complete IP datagram. We'll discuss IP datagram fragmentation in more detail in a moment.

Using **netsh interface ipv4 show interfaces**, you can view summary information regarding a computer's network interfaces. Consider the following example output:

```
Idx  Met   MTU          State          Name
---  ---   -----        -----------    -------------------
  1   50   4294967295   connected      Loopback Pseudo-Interface 1
  7   10   1500         connected      Local Area Connection
```

Here, the computer has two network interfaces. Loopback Pseudo-Interface 1 is connected, has an interface index of 1, has an interface metric of 50, and has an Ethernet maximum transmission unit (MTU) of 4,294,967,295 bytes. Local Area Connection is connected, has an interface index of 7, has an interface metric of 10, and has an MTU of 1,500 bytes.

When using Ethernet II encapsulation, an MTU of 1500 means each block of data transmitted is 1,500 bytes in length, with 20 bytes of this data block used for the IP header. The remaining 1,480 bytes are used as the IP payload for the data block. Thus, an IP datagram of 65,535 bytes would need to be fragmented into many smaller data blocks for transmission. These fragments would then be reassembled on the destination node.

The status of the interface usually reads as Connected when both ends of the computer's network cable are plugged in and Disconnected when either or both ends of the network cable are unplugged.

Working with TCP Internet Control and Error Messages

Each packet sent over IP is a datagram, meaning that it is an unacknowledged and nonsequenced message forwarded by routers to a destination IP address. Each router receiving a datagram decides how best it should be forwarded. This means different datagrams can take different routes between the sending IP address (the source node) and the destination IP address (the destination node). It also means the return route for individual datagrams can be different as well.

Although IP provides end-to-end delivery capabilities for IP datagrams, it does not provide any facilities for reporting routing or delivery errors encountered. Errors and control messages are tracked by the Internet Control Message Protocol (ICMP). You can view ICMP statistics by typing **netsh interface ipv4 show icmp**. The output from this command looks like this:

```
MIB-II ICMP Statistics
------------------------------------------------------
INPUT
Messages:    20302
Errors:    120
Destination Unreachable:    45
Time Exceeded:    88
Parameter Problems:    0
Source Quench:    4
Redirects:    6
Echo Requests:    966
Echo Replies:    966
Time Stamp Requests:    0
Time Stamp Replies:    0
Address Mask Requests:    0
```

```
Address Mask Replies:    0

OUTPUT
Messages:    20302
Errors:    120
Destination Unreachable:    45
Time Exceeded:    88
Parameter Problems:    0
Source Quench:    4
Redirects:    6
Echo Requests:    966
Echo Replies:    966
Time Stamp Requests:    0
Time Stamp Replies:    0
Address Mask Requests:    0
Address Mask Replies:    0
```

> **Tip** For Interface IPv4 and IPv6 SHOW commands that provide summary statistics, you can set the Rr= parameter to the number of seconds to use as a refresh interval. For example, if you wanted the interface statistics to be refreshed automatically every 30 seconds you would type **netsh interface ipv4 show icmp rr=30**. Once you set a refresh rate, you press Ctrl+C to exit the command so that no more updates are made.

In the preceding example, you see detailed statistics on IP datagram messages being received (input messages) and those being sent (output messages). Decoding these statistics is easy if you know what you are looking for. The most basic type of IP datagram message is *Echo*. It is used to send a simple message to an IP node and have an *Echo Reply* echoed back to the sender. Many TCP/IP network commands use Echo and Echo Reply to provide information about the reachability and the path taken to a destination IP node.

Any error that occurs during transfer of an IP datagram, in or out, is recorded as an error. IP attempts a best-effort delivery of datagrams to their destination IP nodes. If a routing or delivery error occurs along the transmission path or at the destination, a router or the destination node discards the problem datagram and tries to report the error by sending a "Destination Unreachable" message.

A time-to-live (TTL) value is set in an IP datagram before it is sent. This value represents the maximum number of hops to use between the source and the destination nodes. "Time exceeded" messages are sent back to the IP datagram originator when the TTL value of the datagram expires. Typically this means there are more links than expected between the source and the destination node. Here, you'd need to increase the TTL value to successfully send traffic between the source and destination node. An expired TTL could also be an indicator of a routing loop in the network. Routing loops occur when routers have incorrect routing information and forward IP datagrams in such a way that they never reach their destinations.

A router or destination node sends a "Parameter Problem" message when an error occurs while processing in the IP header within an IP datagram. The IP header error causes the IP datagram to be discarded, and if no other ICMP messages can be used to describe the error that occurred, the "Parameter Problem" message is sent back to the source node. Typically this indicates an incorrect formatting of the IP header or incorrect arguments in IP option fields.

When a router becomes congested–whether because of a sudden increase in traffic, a slow or sporadic link, or inadequate resources–it will discard incoming IP datagrams. When it does this, the router might send a "Source Quench" message back to the originator of the IP datagram telling the originator that datagrams are arriving too quickly to be processed. The destination node can also send "Source Quench" messages back to the originator for similar reasons. This isn't done for each datagram discarded; rather, it is done for segments of messages or not all. The Internet Engineering Task Force's (IETF) RFC 1812 recommends that "Source Quench" messages not be sent at all because they create more traffic on an already crowded circuit. If "Source Quench" messages are received, however, the originator will resend the related TCP segment at a slower transmission rate to avoid the congestion.

When subnetting is used, the first part of the IP address cannot be used to determine the subnet mask. To discover its subnet mask, an IP node sends an "Address Request" message to a known router or uses either an all-subnets-directed broadcast or a limited broadcast IP address. A router responding to the message sends an "Address Reply" message, which contains the subnet mask for the network segment on which the "Address Request" message was received. If an IP node doesn't know its IP address, it can also send an "Address Request" message with a source IP address of 0.0.0.0. The receiver of this message assumes the source IP node uses a class-based subnet mask and responds accordingly using a broadcast.

Before data is transmitted over TCP, the receiver advertises how much data it can receive at one time. This value is called the TCP window size. When transferring data, the TCP window size determines how much data can be transmitted before the sender has to wait for an acknowledgment from the receiver. The TCP window size is a 16-bit field, allowing for a maximum receive window size of 65,535 bytes. This means that a source node could send up to that amount of data in a single TCP window. Using the TCP window scale option, a receiver can advertise a larger window size of up to approximately 1 gigabyte (GB).

To calculate the retransmission time-out (RTO) value to use, TCP tracks the round-trip time (RTT) between TCP segments on an ongoing basis. Normally, the RTO is calculated once for every full window of data sent. In many network environments, this approach works well and prevents having to retransmit data. However, in a high-bandwidth environment or if there are long delays in any environment, this technique doesn't work so well. One sampling of data for each window cannot be used to determine the current RTO correctly and prevent unnecessary retransmission of data.

To allow for calculating the RTT and in turn the RTO on any TCP segment, a timestamp value based on the local clock is sent in a Timestamp Request message. The acknowledgment for the data on the TCP segment echoes back the timestamp, which allows the RTT to be calculated using the echoed timestamp and the time that the segment's acknowledgment arrived. These messages are recorded as Timestamp Requests and Timestamp Replies.

The final type of ICMP message of import in troubleshooting is the Redirect message. Redirect messages are used to tell the senders of IP datagrams about a more optimal route from the sender to the destination node. Because most hosts maintain minimal routing tables, this information is used to improve message routing while decreasing transfer times and errors. So when you see Redirect messages, you know traffic is being rerouted to a destination node.

Examining Fragmentation, Reassembly, and Error Details

To dig deeper into IP datagram fragmenting and reassembly, you can type **netsh interface ipv4 show ipstats**. The output should look similar to the following:

```
MIB-II IP Statistics
------------------------------------------------------

Forwarding is:     Enabled
Default TTL:    128
In Receives:    24219
In Header Errors:     0
In Address Errors:     250
Datagrams Forwarded:     0
In Unknown Protocol:     0
In Discarded:     0
In Delivered:     23969
Out Requests:     20738
Routing Discards:     0
Out Discards:     0
Out No Routes:     0
Reassembly Timeouts:     60
Reassembly Required     0
Reassembled Ok:     0
Reassembly Failures:     0
Fragments Ok:     0
Fragments Failed:     0
Fragments Created:     0
```

> **Tip** You can refresh these statistics automatically. Add the **Rr=***RefreshRate* parameter, where *RefreshRate* is the number of seconds to use as the refresh interval.

As you can see the IP statistics show the default TTL value for outbound packets created on this computer for transmission. Here, the TTL value is 128. This means that there can be up to 128 links between this computer and the destination computer. If packets use more hops than that, the packets would be discarded and a "Time Exceeded" message would be sent back to the computer.

The In Receives value specifies how many inbound packets have been received. The actual number of packets used is represented by the In Delivered value, and the difference between these values is the result of *inbound packets* that are:

- Received with errors, designated as either In Header Errors or In Address Errors
- Forwarded to other IP nodes, designated as Datagrams Forwarded
- Using an unknown protocol, designated as In Unknown Protocol
- Discarded, such as when a packet's TTL is exceeded, designated as In Discarded

In this example there is a 250-datagram difference between the In Receives and In Delivered values, because of 250 inbound packets with addressing errors.

The number and disposition of outbound packets is also recorded. The number of packets being transmitted out is listed as Out Requests. Any errors coming back as a result of those transmissions are recorded according to type. If a router or other node sends back a "Destination Unreachable" message, this is usually recorded as a Routing Discard. Other types of error messages, such as "Parameter Problem" or "Source Quench" messages, might be recorded as Routing Discards or Out Discards. If there is no route out or if a "No Route" message is returned, the packets might be recorded as Out No Routes.

When data is transmitted outside the local network over routers, it is typically fragmented and reassembled as mentioned previously. Statistics for the reassembly of the original datagrams is recorded and so is the status of received fragments.

Examining Current TCP and UDP Connections

Firewalls and proxy servers can affect the ability to connect a system on the local network to systems on remote networks. Typically, an administrator will have to open TCP or UDP ports to allow remote communications between a computer on the local network and the remote computer or network. Each type of application or utility that you use may require different ports to be opened. A complete list of TCP and UDP ports used by well-known services is stored in *%SystemRoot%*\System32\Drivers\Etc\Services.

Sometimes, however, the tool you want to work with won't have a well-known service associated with it and you may need to experiment a bit to find out what TCP or UDP ports it works with. One way to do this is to start the tool and use a TCP or UDP listener to see what ports become active.

Working with TCP

TCP ports are made available using a passive open, which basically says the port is available to receive requests. When a client wants to use an available port, it must try to establish a connection. A TCP connection is a two-way connection between two clients using Application Layer protocols on an IP network. The TCP endpoints are identified by an IP address and TCP port pair. There is a local TCP endpoint and a remote TCP endpoint, which can be used to identify loopback connections from the local computer to the local computer as well as standard connections from the local computer to a remote computer somewhere on the network. TCP connections are established using a three-way handshake. Here's how that works:

1. A client wanting to use a port sends an active open request (SYN).
2. The local client acknowledges the request, sending a SYN-ACK.
3. To which the client wanting to use the port sends a final acknowledgment (ACK).

Data passed over a TCP connection is apportioned into segments. Segments are sent as IP datagrams that contain a TCP header and TCP data. When a connection is established, the maximum segment size (MSS) is also set. Typically, the maximum value for the MSS is 65,495 bytes, which is 65,535 bytes for the IP datagram minus the minimum IP header (20 bytes) and the minimum TCP header (20 bytes). Technically speaking, SYN, SYN-ACK, and ACK messages are SYN, SYN-ACK, and ACK segments.

You can view current TCP connection statistics by typing **netsh interface ipv4 show tcpconn**. Refresh the statistics automatically by adding the Rr=*RefreshRate* parameter. The output shows you which TCP ports are being listened on, which TCP ports have established connections, and which ports are in a wait state, as shown in this example:

```
MIB-II TCP Connection Entry
Local Address       Local Port  Remote Address     Remote Port  State
-------------------------------------------------------------------------
    0.0.0.0                 42  0.0.0.0            18520        Listen
    0.0.0.0                 53  0.0.0.0            16499        Listen
    0.0.0.0                 88  0.0.0.0            45165        Listen
    0.0.0.0                135  0.0.0.0             2176        Listen
    0.0.0.0                389  0.0.0.0             2256        Listen
    0.0.0.0               1025  0.0.0.0            43054        Listen
    0.0.0.0               1026  0.0.0.0            35016        Listen
    0.0.0.0               1028  0.0.0.0            53398        Listen
    0.0.0.0               3069  0.0.0.0            43189        Listen
    0.0.0.0               3268  0.0.0.0            43230        Listen
    0.0.0.0               3269  0.0.0.0            36957        Listen
    127.0.0.1              389  127.0.0.1           1033        Established
    127.0.0.1              389  127.0.0.1           1034        Established
    127.0.0.1              389  127.0.0.1           1035        Established
    127.0.0.1              389  127.0.0.1           1039        Established
    127.0.0.1             1033  127.0.0.1            389        Established
    127.0.0.1             1034  127.0.0.1            389        Established
    127.0.0.1             1035  127.0.0.1            389        Established
    127.0.0.1             1039  127.0.0.1            389        Established
```

```
127.0.0.1         3073  0.0.0.0          10251    Listen
192.168.1.50       135  192.168.1.56      1040    Listen
192.168.1.50       139  0.0.0.0          12369    Listen
192.168.1.50       389  192.168.1.50      3287    Established
192.168.1.50      3287  192.168.1.50       389    Established
192.168.1.50      3289  192.168.1.50       135    Wait
192.168.1.50       290  192.168.1.50      1025    Wait
```

Entries for 0.0.0.0 represent TCP broadcasts. Entries for 127.0.0.1 represent local loopback ports used by the local computer. You'll also see entries on the physical IP address used by the computer back to the computer. Here, these are shown with the local and remote IP address set to 192.168.1.50. The entries you are most interested in are those in which the remote IP address is different from the local IP address; these represent connections to other systems and networks.

The Local Port and Remote Port columns show you how local TCP ports are mapped to remote TCP ports. For example, in this output local port 135 on IP address 192.168.1.50 is mapped to the remote port 1040 on IP address 192.168.1.56. Each TCP connection also has a state. The most common state values are summarized in Table 17-3.

Table 17-3 TCP Connection States

State	Description
Closed	No TCP connection currently exists.
Listen	An Application Layer protocol has issued a passive open function call to permit incoming connection requests on the specified port. This doesn't create any TCP traffic.
Syn Sent	A client using an Application Layer protocol has issued an active open function call (SYN), which creates and sends the first segment of the TCP three-way handshake.
Syn Rcvd	A client using an Application Layer protocol has received the SYN and sent back an acknowledgment (SYN-ACK).
Established	The final ACK has been received and the TCP connection is established. Data can be transferred in both directions.
Wait	The TCP connection has been terminated and this has been acknowledged by both the local and remote client (FIN-ACK).

You can view additional TCP statistics by typing **netsh interface ipv4 show tcpstats**. The output should be similar to the following:

```
MIB-II TCP Statistics
------------------------------------------------------
Timeout Algorithm:                Van Jacobson's Algorithm
Minimum Timeout:                  10
Maximum Timeout:                  4294967295
```

```
Maximum Connections:                 Dynamic
Active Opens:                        182
Passive Opens:                       174
Attempts Failed:                     6
Established Resets:                  226
Currently Established:               46
In Segments:                         410814
Out Segments:                        410448
Retransmitted Segments:              2811
In Errors:                           0
Out Resets:                          171
```

The TCP statistics detail the following:

- Minimum and maximum timeout values in use
- Total number of active and passive opens since TCP/IP networking was started on the computer
- Any connections that were attempted but failed
- Any connections that were established and then reset
- The total number of connections currently established
- The number of TCP segments sent (in segments) and received (out segments)
- The number of segments that had to be retransmitted
- The number of segments with errors that were received (in errors)

Working with UDP

Unlike TCP, which is connection-oriented, UDP is connectionless, meaning that UDP messages are sent without negotiating a connection. UDP ports are completely separate from TCP ports, even for the same port number. Because UDP messages are sent without sequencing or acknowledgment, they are unreliable, in stark contrast to TCP, which is very reliable. When you work with UDP, you have only a local address and local port pair, which represent the ports being listened on. You can view the related listener entries by typing **netsh interface ipv4 show udpconn**. The output will be similar to the following:

```
MIB-II UDP Listener Entry
Local Address          LocalPort
-----------------------------------------------------

    0.0.0.0          42
    0.0.0.0          445
    0.0.0.0          500
    0.0.0.0          1030
    0.0.0.0          1032
    0.0.0.0          1701
    0.0.0.0          3002
    0.0.0.0          3103
```

```
0.0.0.0          3114
0.0.0.0          4500
127.0.0.1          53
127.0.0.1          123
127.0.0.1          1036
127.0.0.1          3101
127.0.0.1          3102
192.168.1.50          53
192.168.1.50          67
192.168.1.50          137
192.168.1.50          138
192.168.1.50          389
192.168.1.50          464
192.168.1.50               2535
```

Entries for 0.0.0.0 represent UDP broadcast ports. Entries for 127.0.0.1 represent local loopback ports used by the local computer. Entries on the physical IP address for a network adapter are ports which are listening for connections.

UDP messages are sent as IP datagrams and consist of a UDP header and UDP message data. You can view additional UDP statistics by typing **netsh interface ipv4 show udpstats**. The output should be similar to the following:

```
MIB-II UDP Statistics
---------------------------------------
In Datagrams:     42640
In Invalid Port:     732
In Erroneous Datagrams:     20
Out Datagrams:     72217
```

The UDP statistics detail the following information:

- The total number of datagrams received on UDP ports
- The number of datagrams received on invalid ports and discarded
- The number of erroneous datagrams that were received and discarded
- The number of datagrams sent over UDP ports

Troubleshooting TCP/IP Networking

Problems with TCP/IP networking can be difficult to track down, which is why so many tools exist to help you try to determine what's happening. As you start to troubleshoot, make sure you have a clear understanding of the concepts and procedures discussed in the section titled "Supporting TCP/IP Networking" earlier in this chapter. The tools and techniques discussed there will help you uncover and diagnose some of the most complex TCP/IP networking problems. In addition to that discussion, you can use the discussion in this section to troubleshoot connectivity and configuration issues.

Viewing Diagnostic Information

Many TCP/IP networking problems relate to incorrect configuration of networking components and you'll find that one of the fastest and easiest ways to get a complete snapshot of a computer's network configuration and workload is to use the commands available in the Netsh Ras Diagnostics context. Although these commands are meant for troubleshooting remote access, they are also useful in troubleshooting networking in general.

Netsh Ras Diagnostics provides different Show commands that allow you to work with specified types of diagnostics information and different Set commands to allow you to configure diagnostic logging, tracing, and reporting. However, rather than working with individual diagnostics areas, you'll often want to have Netsh Ras Diagnostics generate a comprehensive report for all diagnostics areas. You can create a comprehensive report for diagnostics by typing **netsh ras diagnostics show all type= file destination=** ***FileName*** **verbose= enabled** where *FileName* is the name of the HTML file to generate.

If you then view the report in Internet Explorer, you'll see the contents of several logs, including remote access trace logs, modem tracing logs, Connection Manager logs, IPsec tracing logs, and the Remote Access event logs. You'll also see an installation check of components required for Remote Access and networking in general, a detailed listing of all installed networking components, and the current values of all registry keys used with Remote Access. But the information you want to focus on is the output from the command-line utilities, including:

- arp.exe -a, which displays Address Resolution Protocol entries.
- ipconfig.exe /all, which displays the configuration of all network interfaces.
- ipconfig.exe /displaydns, which displays the contents of the DNS resolver cache.
- route.exe print, which prints contents of the IPv4 and IPv6 routing tables.
- net.exe start, which lists all running Windows services.
- netstat.exe -e, which lists network interface statistics for packet transmissions.
- netstat.exe -o, which lists active connections by protocol, including those for both TCP and UDP connections.
- netstat.exe -s, which lists summary statistics for IPv4, IPv6, ICMPv4, ICMPv6, TCP for IPv4, TCP for IPv6, UDP for IPv4, and UDP for IPv6.
- netstat.exe -n, which lists active connections by address and port, including those for both TCP and UDP connections.
- nbtstat.exe -c, which lists the contents of the cache for NetBIOS over TCP/IP.
- nbtstat.exe -n, which lists local NetBIOS names.
- nbtstat.exe -r, which lists names resolved by broadcast and WINS.

- nbtstat.exe -S, which lists NetBIOS session tables with the destination IP addresses.
- netsh.exe dump, which performs a complete dump of the network configuration. You can use this dump to review the network configuration or to re-create the network configuration in the future.

Note While you could run each of these commands yourself, don't overlook how useful Netsh can be to remotely troubleshoot problems. With Netsh, you don't need to sit at the user's computer or log on remotely using Remote Desktop. You simply start Netsh with the –R parameter to provide the name of the remote computer you want to work with and then go about diagnosing the problem at hand.

Diagnosing General Computer Configuration Issues

As part of diagnostic troubleshooting, you may want to view detailed configuration information for the computer and the operating system, and one of the best ways to do this is to access the Windows Management Instrumentation (WMI) objects that track the related configuration settings. The WMI object that tracks overall computer configuration is the Win32_ComputerSystem object. The WMI object that tracks overall operating system configuration is the Win32_OperatingSystem object.

One way to work with WMI is to use Windows PowerShell. In Windows PowerShell, you can use the Get-WMIObject cmdlet to get the WMI object you want to work with. By redirecting the object to Format-List * you can list all of the properties of the object and their values. When working with WMI, you'll want to work with the root namespace, as specified by setting the –Namespace parameter to root/cimv2. Using the –Computer parameter, you can specify the computer you want to work with. If you want to work with the local computer, use a dot (.) instead of a computer name.

You can thus examine the Win32_ComputerSystem object and its properties to obtain summary information regarding a computer's configuration by entering the following command at the Windows PowerShell prompt:

```
Get-WmiObject -Class Win32_ComputerSystem -Namespace root/cimv2
-ComputerName . | Format-List *
```

If you want to save the output in a file, simply redirect the output to a file. In the following example, you redirect the output to a file in the working directory called computer_save.txt:

```
Get-WmiObject -Class Win32_ComputerSystem -Namespace root/cimv2
-ComputerName . | Format-List * > computer_save.txt
```

The detailed computer information, obtained by using this command, is shown in Listing 17-2.

Listing 17-2 Computer Configuration Information

```
AdminPasswordStatus          : 1
BootupState                  : Normal boot
ChassisBootupState           : 3
KeyboardPasswordStatus       : 2
PowerOnPasswordStatus        : 1
PowerSupplyState             : 3
PowerState                   : 0
FrontPanelResetStatus        : 2
ThermalState                 : 3
Status                       : OK
Name                         : MAILSERVER25
PowerManagementCapabilities :
PowerManagementSupported     :
__GENUS                      : 2
__CLASS                      : Win32_ComputerSystem
__SUPERCLASS                 : CIM_UnitaryComputerSystem
__DYNASTY                    : CIM_ManagedSystemElement
__RELPATH                    : Win32_ComputerSystem.Name="MAILSERVER25"
__PROPERTY_COUNT             : 58
__DERIVATION                 : {CIM_UnitaryComputerSystem,
CIM_ComputerSystem, CIM_System,CIM_LogicalElement...}
__SERVER                     : MAILSERVER25
__NAMESPACE                  : root\cimv2
__PATH                       : \\MAILSERVER25\root\
cimv2:Win32_ComputerSystem.Name="MAILSERVER25"
AutomaticManagedPagefile     : True
AutomaticResetBootOption     : True
AutomaticResetCapability     : True
BootOptionOnLimit            :
BootOptionOnWatchDog         :
BootROMSupported             : True
Caption                      : MAILSERVER25
CreationClassName            : Win32_ComputerSystem
CurrentTimeZone              : -420
DaylightInEffect             : True
Description                  : AT/AT COMPATIBLE
DNSHostName                  : MAILSERVER25
Domain                       : cpandl.com
DomainRole                   : 5
EnableDaylightSavingsTime    : True
InfraredSupported            : False
InitialLoadInfo              :
InstallDate                  :
LastLoadInfo                 :
Manufacturer                 : Dell Inc.
Model                        : Dimension XPS
NameFormat                   :
```

```
NetworkServerModeEnabled     : True
NumberOfLogicalProcessors    : 2
NumberOfProcessors           : 1
OEMLogoBitmap                :
OEMStringArray               : {www.dell.com}
PartOfDomain                 : True
PauseAfterReset              : -1
PCSystemType                 : 5
PrimaryOwnerContact          :
PrimaryOwnerName             : Windows User
ResetCapability              : 1
ResetCount                   : -1
ResetLimit                   : -1
Roles                        : {LM_Workstation, LM_Server,
Primary_Domain_Controller, Timesource...}
SupportContactDescription    :
SystemStartupDelay           :
SystemStartupOptions         :
SystemStartupSetting         :
SystemType                   : x64-based PC
TotalPhysicalMemory          : 3755343872
UserName                     : CPANDL\williams
WakeUpType                   : 6
Workgroup                    :
Scope                        : System.Management.ManagementScope
Path                         : \\Server52\root\cimv2:
Win32_ComputerSystem.Name="Server52"
Options                      : System.Management.ObjectGetOptions
ClassPath                    : \\Server52\root\cimv2:Win32_ComputerSystem
Properties                   : {AdminPasswordStatus...}
SystemProperties             : {__GENUS, __CLASS, __SUPERCLASS...}
Qualifiers                   : {dynamic, Locale, provider, UUID}
Site                         :
Container                    :
```

A summary of the computer configuration entries and their meaning is provided in Table 17-4.

Table 17-4 Computer Configuration Entries and Their Meaning

Property	Description
AdminPasswordStatus	Status of the Administrator password. Values are: 1 = Disabled, 2 = Enabled, 3 = Not Implemented, 4 = Unknown.
AutomaticManagedPagefile	Indicates whether the computer's page file is being managed by the operating system.

Table 17-4 Computer Configuration Entries and Their Meaning

Property	Description
AutomaticResetBootOption	Indicates whether the automatic reset boot option is enabled.
AutomaticResetCapability	Indicates whether the automatic reset is enabled.
BootOptionOnLimit	System action to be taken when the ResetLimit value is reached. Values are: 1 = Reserved, 2 = Operating system, 3 = System utilities, 4 = Do not reboot.
BootOptionOnWatchDog	Reboot action to be taken after the time on the watchdog timer has elapsed. Values are: 1 = Reserved, 2 = Operating system, 3 = System utilities, 4 = Do not reboot.
BootROMSupported	Indicates whether a boot ROM is supported.
BootupState	Indicates how the system was started. Values are: "Normal boot", "Fail-safe boot", and "Fail-safe with network boot".
Caption	System name.
ChassisBootupState	Bootup state of the system chassis. Values are: 1 = Other, 2 = Unknown, 3 = Safe, 4 = Warning, 5 = Critical, 6 = Nonrecoverable.
ClassPath	The Windows Management Instrumentation (WMI) object class path.
Container	The container associated with the object.
CreationClassName	Name of class from which object is derived.
CurrentTimeZone	Number of minutes the computer is offset from Coordinated Universal Time.
DaylightInEffect	Indicates whether daylight savings mode is on.
Description	Description of the computer.
DNSHostName	Name of the server according to DNS.
Domain	Name of the domain to which the computer belongs.
DomainRole	Domain role of the computer. Values are: 0 = Standalone Workstation, 1 = Member Workstation, 2 = Standalone Server, 3 = Member Server, 4 = Backup Domain Controller, 5 = Primary Domain Controller.
EnableDaylightSavingsTime	Indicates whether Daylight Savings Time is enabled. If TRUE, the system changes to an hour ahead or behind when DST starts or ends. If FALSE, the system does not change to an hour ahead or behind when DST starts or ends.

Table 17-4 Computer Configuration Entries and Their Meaning

Property	Description
FrontPanelResetStatus	Hardware security settings for the reset button on the computer. Values are: 0 = Disabled, 1 = Enabled, 2 = Not Implemented, 3 = Unknown.
InfraredSupported	Indicates whether an infrared (IR) port exists on the computer system.
InitialLoadInfo	Data needed to find either the initial load device (its key) or the boot service to request the operating system to start up.
InstallDate	When the computer was installed.
KeyboardPasswordStatus	Indicates the keyboard password status. Values are: 0 = Disabled, 1 = Enabled, 2 = Not Implemented, 3 = Unknown.
LastLoadInfo	Array entry of the InitialLoadInfo property, which holds the data corresponding to booting the currently loaded operating system.
Manufacturer	Computer manufacturer name.
Model	Product name given by the manufacturer.
Name	The computer name.
NameFormat	Identifies how the computer system name is generated.
NetworkServerModeEnabled	Indicates whether Network Server Mode is enabled.
NumberOfLogicalProcessors	Number of processor cores. If the computer has two processors with four cores each, the number of logical processors is eight. If the computer has hyperthreading architecture, the number of logical processors may also be higher than the number of physical processors.
NumberOfProcessors	Number of enabled processors on the computer.
OEMLogoBitmap	Identifies the bitmap for the OEM's logo.
OEMStringArray	List of descriptive strings set by the OEM.
PartOfDomain	Indicates whether the computer is part of a domain. If TRUE, the computer is a member of a domain. If FALSE, the computer is a member of a workgroup.
Options	Lists the management object options.
Path	Identifies the full WMI path to the object class.

Table 17-4 Computer Configuration Entries and Their Meaning

Property	Description
PauseAfterReset	Time delay in milliseconds before a reboot is initiated after a system power cycle or reset. A value of -1 indicates there is no time delay.
PCSystemType	Indicates the type of computer. Values are: 0 = Unspecified, 1 = Desktop, 2 = Mobile, 3 = Workstation, 4 = Enterprise Server, 5 = SOHO Server, 6 = Appliance PC, 7 = Performance Server, 8 = Role Maximum.
PowerManagementCapabilities	Power management capabilities of a logical device. Values are: 0 = Unknown, 1 = Not Supported, 2 = Disabled, 3 = Enabled, 4 = Power Saving Modes Entered Automatically, 5 = Power State Settable, 6 = Power Cycling Supported, 7 = Timed Power On Supported.
PowerManagementSupported	Indicates whether the device's power can be managed.
PowerOnPasswordStatus	Power on password status. Values are: 0 = Disabled, 1 = Enabled, 2 = Not Implemented, 3 = Unknown.
PowerState	Indicates the current power state of the computer. Values are: 0 = Unknown, 1 = Full Power, 2 = Power Save – Low Power Mode, 3 = Power Save – Standby, 4 = Power Save – Unknown, 5 = Power Cycle, 6 = Power Off, 7 = Power Save – Warning.
PowerSupplyState	State of the enclosure's power supply when last booted. Values are: 1 = Other, 2 = Unknown, 3 = Safe, 4 = Warning, 5 = Critical, 6 = Nonrecoverable.
PrimaryOwnerContact	Contact information for the computer's owner.
PrimaryOwnerName	Name of the system owner.
Properties	Lists all the properties of the object.
Qualifiers	Lists any qualifiers for the object.
ResetCapability	Value indicates whether a computer can be reset using the Power and Reset buttons (or other hardware means). Values are: 1 = Other, 2 = Unknown, 3 = Disabled, 4 = Enabled, 5 = Nonrecoverable.
ResetCount	Number of automatic resets since the last intentional reset. A value of -1 indicates that the count is unknown.
ResetLimit	Number of consecutive times a system reset will be attempted. A value of -1 indicates that the limit is unknown.

Table 17-4 Computer Configuration Entries and Their Meaning

Property	Description
Roles	System roles.
Scope	Lists the management object scope.
Site	The site associated with the object.
Status	Current status of the computer. Values are: "OK", "Error", "Degraded", "Unknown", "Pred Fail", "Starting", "Stopping", "Service".
SupportContactDescription	List of the support contact information for the computer.
SystemProperties	Lists the system properties.
SystemStartupDelay	The startup delay in seconds.
SystemStartupOptions	List of the startup options for the computer.
SystemStartupSetting	Index of the default start profile.
SystemType	System architecture type, such as "X86- based PC" or "64-bit Intel PC".
ThermalState	Thermal state of the system chassis when last booted. Values are: 1 = Other, 2 = Unknown, 3 = Safe, 4 = Warning, 5 = Critical, 6 = Nonrecoverable.
TotalPhysicalMemory	Total byte size of physical memory.
UserName	Name of the currently logged-on user.
WakeUpType	Event that caused the system to power up. Values are: 0 = Reserved, 1 = Other, 2 = Unknown, 3 = APM Timer, 4 = Modem Ring, 5 = LAN Remote, 6 = Power Switch, 7 = PCI PME#, 8 = AC Power Restored.
Workgroup	When a computer is a member of a workgroup, the workgroup name is listed here.

As you can see, the detailed configuration information tells you a great deal about the computer's configuration. The same is true for the operating system details, which can be obtained by entering the following command at a Windows PowerShell prompt:

```
Get-WmiObject -Class Win32_OperatingSystem -Namespace root/cimv2
-ComputerName . | Format-List *
```

Listing 17-3 provides an example of the output from this command. As discussed previously, you can redirect the output to a save file.

Listing 17-3 Verbose Operating System Configuration Output

```
Status                                      : OK
Name                                        : Microsoft® Windows Server
® 2008 Enterprise |C:\Windows|\Device\Harddisk1\Partition1
FreePhysicalMemory                          : 679172
FreeSpaceInPagingFiles                      : 3749368
FreeVirtualMemory                           : 2748020
__GENUS                                     : 2
__CLASS                                     : Win32_OperatingSystem
__SUPERCLASS                                : CIM_OperatingSystem
__DYNASTY                                   : CIM_ManagedSystemElement
__RELPATH                                   : Win32_OperatingSystem=@
__PROPERTY_COUNT                            : 65
__DERIVATION                                : {CIM_OperatingSystem, CIM
_LogicalElement, CIM_ManagedSystemElement}
__SERVER                                    : MAILSERVER25
__NAMESPACE                                 : root\cimv2
__PATH                                      : \\MAILSERVER25\root\cimv2
:Win32_OperatingSystem=@
BootDevice                                  : \Device\HarddiskVolume1
BuildNumber                                 : 6001
BuildType                                   : Multiprocessor Free
Caption                                     : Microsoft® Windows
Server® 2008 Enterprise
CodeSet                                     : 1252
CountryCode                                 : 1
CreationClassName                           : Win32_OperatingSystem
CSCreationClassName                         : Win32_ComputerSystem
CSDVersion                                  : Service Pack 1, v.745
CSName                                      : MAILSERVER25
CurrentTimeZone                             : -420
DataExecutionPrevention_32BitApplications : True
DataExecutionPrevention_Available           : True
DataExecutionPrevention_Drivers             : True
DataExecutionPrevention_SupportPolicy       : 3
Debug                                       : False
Description                                 :
Distributed                                 : False
EncryptionLevel                             : 256
ForegroundApplicationBoost                  : 2
InstallDate                                 : 20080917143704.000000-480
LargeSystemCache                            :
LastBootUpTime                              : 20080804124518.375199-420
LocalDateTime                               : 20080804183034.619000-420
Locale                                      : 0409
Manufacturer                                : Microsoft Corporation
MaxNumberOfProcesses                        : 4294967295
MaxProcessMemorySize                        : 8589934464
```

```
MUILanguages                                 : {en-US}
NumberOfLicensedUsers                        :
NumberOfProcesses                            : 95
NumberOfUsers                                : 3
OperatingSystemSKU                           : 10
Organization                                 :
OSArchitecture                               : 64-bit
OSLanguage                                   : 1033
OSProductSuite                               : 274
OSType                                       : 18
OtherTypeDescription                         :
PAEEnabled                                   :
PlusProductID                                :
PlusVersionNumber                            :
Primary                                      : True
ProductType                                  : 2
QuantumLength                                : 1
QuantumType                                  : 1
RegisteredUser                               : Windows User
SerialNumber                                 :
ServicePackMajorVersion                      : 1
ServicePackMinorVersion                      : 0
SizeStoredInPagingFiles                      : 3974528
SuiteMask                                    : 274
SystemDevice                                 : \Device\HarddiskVolume2
SystemDirectory                              : C:\Windows\system32
SystemDrive                                  : C:
TotalSwapSpaceSize                           :
TotalVirtualMemorySize                       : 7591744
TotalVisibleMemorySize                       : 3667328
Version                                      : 6.0.6001
WindowsDirectory                             : C:\Windows
Scope                            : System.Management.ManagementScope
Path                             : \\Server52\root\cimv2:
Win32_OperatingSystem=@
Options                          : System.Management.ObjectGetOptions
ClassPath                        : \\CorpServer52\root\cimv2:
Win32_OperatingSystem
Properties                       : {BootDevice...}
SystemProperties                 : {__GENUS, __CLASS, __SUPERCLASS...}
Qualifiers                       : {dynamic, Locale, provider, Singleton...}
Site                             :
Container                        :
```

A summary of the operating system entries and their meanings is provided in Table 17-5.

Table 17-5 Operating System Configuration Entries and Their Meanings

Property	Description
BootDevice	Disk drive from which the Win32 operating system boots.
BuildNumber	Build number of the operating system.
BuildType	Type of build used for the operating system, such as "retail build", "checked build", or "multiprocessor free".
Caption	Operating system name.
ClassPath	The Windows Management Instrumentation (WMI) object class path.
CodeSet	Code page value used by the operating system.
Container	The container associated with the object.
CountryCode	Country code used by the operating system.
CreationClassName	Name of class from which the object is derived.
CSCreationClassName	Name of class from which computer system object is derived.
CSDVersion	Indicates the latest Service Pack installed on the computer. Value is NULL if no Service Pack is installed.
CSName	Name of the computer system associated with this object class.
CurrentTimeZone	Number of minutes the operating system is offset from Greenwich Mean Time. The value is positive, negative, or zero.
DataExtraction-Prevention_32BitApplications	Indicates whether Data Execution Prevention (DEP) is enabled for 32-bit applications.
DataExtraction-Prevention_Available	Indicates whether Data Execution Prevention (DEP) is supported by the system hardware.
DataExtraction-Prevention_Drivers	Indicates whether Data Execution Prevention (DEP) is enabled for device drivers.
DataExtraction-Prevention_SupportPolicy	Specifies the DEP support policy being used. Values are: 0 = none, 2 = on for essential Windows programs and services only, 3 = on for all programs except those specifically excluded.
Debug	Indicates whether the operating system is a checked (debug) build. If TRUE, the debugging version of User.exe is installed.
Description	Description of the Windows operating system.

Table 17-5 Operating System Configuration Entries and Their Meanings

Property	Description
Distributed	Indicates whether the operating system is distributed across multiple computer system nodes. If so, these nodes should be grouped as a cluster.
EncryptionLevel	The level of encryption for secure transactions as 40-bit, 128-bit, or *n*-bit.
ForegroundApplicationBoost	Sets the priority of the foreground application. Application boost is implemented by giving an application more processor time. Values are: 0 = None, 1 = Minimum, 2 = Maximum (Default).
FreePhysicalMemory	Physical memory in kilobytes currently unused and available.
FreeSpaceInPagingFiles	Amount of free space in kilobytes in the operating system's paging files. Swapping occurs when the free space fills up.
FreeVirtualMemory	Virtual memory in kilobytes unused and available.
InstallDate	When the operating system was installed.
LargeSystemCache	Indicates whether memory usage is optimized for program or the system cache. Values are: 0 = memory usage is optimized for programs, 1 = memory usage is optimized for the system cache.
LastBootUpTime	When the operating system was last booted.
LocalDateTime	Local date and time on the computer.
Locale	Language identifier used by the operating system.
Manufacturer	Operating system manufacturer. For Win32 systems, this value will be "Microsoft Corporation".
MaxNumberOfProcesses	Maximum number of process contexts the operating system can support. If there is no fixed maximum, the value is 0.
MaxProcessMemorySize	Maximum memory in kilobytes that can be allocated to a process. A value of zero indicates that there is no maximum.
MUILanguages	User interface languages supported.
Name	Name of the operating system instance.
NumberOfLicensedUsers	Number of user licenses for the operating system. A value of 0 = unlimited, a value of –1 = unknown.
NumberOfProcesses	Current number of process contexts on the system.
NumberOfUsers	Current number of user sessions.

Table 17-5 Operating System Configuration Entries and Their Meanings

Property	Description
OperatingSystemSKU	Operating system product type indicator.
Options	Lists the management object options.
Organization	Company name set for the registered user of the operating system.
OSArchitecture	The operating system architecture as 32-bit or 64-bit.
OSLanguage	Language version of the operating system installed.
OSProductSuite	Operating system product suite installed.
OSType	Type of operating system. Values include: 1 = Other, 18 = Windows NT or later.
OtherTypeDescription	Sets additional description; used when OSType = 1.
Path	Identifies the full WMI path to the object class.
PAEEnabled	Indicates whether physical address expansion (PAE) is enabled.
PlusProductID	Product number for Windows Plus! (if installed).
PlusVersionNumber	Version number of Windows Plus! (if installed).
Primary	Indicates whether this is the primary operating system.
ProductType	The operating system product type. Values are: 1 = workstation, 2 = domain controller, 3 = server.
Properties	Lists all the properties of the object.
Qualifiers	Lists any qualifiers for the object.
QuantumLength	Number of clock ticks per unit of processor execution. Values are: 1 = Unknown, 2 = One tick, 3 = Two ticks.
QuantumType	Length type for units of processor execution. Values are: 1 = Unknown, 2 = Fixed, 3 = Variable. With variable length, foreground and background applications can have different values. With fixed length, the foreground and background values are the same.
RegisteredUser	Name set for the registered user of the operating system.
Scope	Lists the management object scope.
SerialNumber	Operating system product serial number.
ServicePackMajorVersion	Major version number of the service pack installed on the computer. If no service pack has been installed, the value is zero or NULL.

Table 17-5 Operating System Configuration Entries and Their Meanings

Property	Description
ServicePackMinorVersion	Minor version number of the service pack installed on the computer. If no service pack has been installed, the value is zero or NULL.
Site	The site associated with the object.
SizeStoredInPagingFiles	Total number of kilobytes that can be stored in the operating system's paging files. A value of zero indicates that there are no paging files.
Status	Current status of the object. Values include: "OK", "Error", "Unknown", "Degraded", "Pred Fail", "Starting", "Stopping", and "Service".
SuiteMask	Bit flags that identify the product suites available on the system.
SystemDevice	Physical disk partition on which the operating system is installed.
SystemDirectory	System directory of the operating system.
SystemDrive	The physical disk partition on which the operating system is installed.
SystemProperties	Lists the system properties.
TotalSwapSpaceSize	Total swap space in kilobytes. This value may be unspecified (NULL) if swap space is not distinguished from page files.
TotalVirtualMemorySize	Virtual memory size in kilobytes.
TotalVisibleMemorySize	Total amount of physical memory in kilobytes that is available to the operating system.
Version	Version number of the operating system.
WindowsDirectory	Windows directory of the operating system.

Diagnosing IP, DNS, and WINS Configuration Issues

The Netsh Interface IPv4 context provides commands for viewing the IP, DNS, and WINS configuration on a computer. These commands, with example output, are as follows:

- **Netsh interface ipv4 show addresses** Shows the IP addresses used by network adapters on the computer, as in the following example:

```
Configuration for interface "Local Area Connection"
    DHCP enabled:                         Yes
    IP Address:                           192.168.1.101
    Subnet Prefix:                        192.168.1.0/
24 (mask 255.255.255.0)
```

```
    Default Gateway:                          192.168.1.1
    Gateway Metric:                           0
    InterfaceMetric:                          5

Configuration for interface "Local Area Connection 2"
    DHCP enabled:                             Yes
    IP Address:                               192.168.5.42
    Subnet Prefix:                            192.168.51.0/
24 (mask 255.255.255.0)
    Default Gateway:                          192.168.5.1
    Gateway Metric:                           0
    InterfaceMetric:                          5

Configuration for interface "Loopback Pseudo-Interface 1"
    DHCP enabled:                             No
    IP Address:                               127.0.0.1
    Subnet Prefix:                            127.0.0.0/8
(mask 255.0.0.0)
    InterfaceMetric:                          50
```

Each network adapter is listed in order. Because this computer has two network adapters, there are two entries in addition to the entry for the loopback interface. Any network adapter that is disabled or otherwise unavailable won't be listed.

Each gateway is listed on a per-adapter basis in the order it is used. If a computer has multiple network adapters, each network adapter that is configured and used should have an entry. There is no notation for an incorrectly configured gateway (that is, one that isn't on the same subnet).

- **Netsh interface ipv4 show dnsservers** Shows the DNS servers defined for network adapters on the computer, as in the following example:

```
Configuration for interface "Local Area Connection"
    DNS servers configured through DHCP:  192.168.1.120
                                          192.168.1.225
    Register with which suffix:           Primary only

Configuration for interface "Local Area Connection2"
    DNS servers configured through DHCP:  192.168.5.86
                                          192.168.5.124
    Register with which suffix:           Primary only

Configuration for interface "Loopback Pseudo-Interface 1"
    Statically Configured DNS Servers:    None
    Register with which suffix:           Primary only
```

Each DNS server configured is shown in the search order used. Confirm that the correct IP addresses are used and that the search order is correct.

- **Netsh interface ipv4 show winsservers** Shows the WINS servers defined for network adapters on the computer, as in the following example:

  ```
  Configuration for interface "Local Area Connection"
      WINS servers configured through DHCP: 192.168.1.128
                                            192.168.1.144

  Configuration for interface "Local Area Connection 2"
      WINS servers configured through DHCP: 192.168.5.45
                                            192.168.5.67

  Configuration for interface "Loopback Pseudo-Interface 1"
      Statically Configured WINS Servers:   None
  ```

  Each WINS server configured is shown in the search order used. Confirm that the correct IP addresses are used and that the search order is correct.

As discussed previously, you can also type **Ipconfig /all** at a command prompt to display all TCP/IP configuration information at once. With DHCPv4, you can release and then renew the IPv4 configuration by typing the following commands at a command prompt:

```
ipconfig /release
ipconfig /renew
```

With DHCPv6, you can release and then renew the IPv6 configuration by entering the following commands at a command prompt:

```
ipconfig /release6
ipconfig /renew6
```

If you suspect a computer has problems with DNS, you may also want to display the contents of the DNS resolver cache by typing **ipconfig /displaydns** at a command prompt. You can purge the contents of the DNS resolver cache by typing **ipconfig / flushdns** at a command prompt. To refresh all DHCP leases and re-register DNS names, type **ipconfig /registerdns** at a command prompt.

Other commands you can use for troubleshooting TCP/IP configuration and connectivity include the following:

- **Tracert** Traces connections along the path between computers
- **Ping** Determines whether a network connection can be established
- **Pathping** Combines features of Tracert and Ping to trace routes and provide packet loss information

To check connectivity, you can use any of these commands. In the event of a connectivity problem, the output will confirm this. In the following example, the computer is unable to connect to the specified IP address:

```
Pinging 192.168.1.1 with 32 bytes of data:

Request timed out.
Request timed out.
```

```
Request timed out.
Request timed out.

Ping statistics for 192.168.1.1:
    Packets: Sent = 4, Received = 0, Lost = 4 (100% loss),
```

Here, the computer might not have connectivity to the network or the network configuration may be incorrect. Keep in mind that Windows Firewall and other firewalls on both the source computer and the destination node may block these activities.

To see how you can check connections to specific hosts, consider the following examples:

Trace the route to 192.168.1.100:

```
tracert 192.168.1.100
```

Try to estalish a connection to Mailsever23 by its host name:

```
ping mailserver23
```

Trace the route to Mailserver23.cpandl.com and provide packet loss information:

```
pathping mailserver23.cpandl.com
```

To attempt to verify connectivity to various remote hosts and the TCP/IP configuration, you can do one of the following:

- **Ping the IP address, computer name and fully qualified domain name of a host** Verifies connectivity and name resolution with regard to a remote host according to IP address, computer name, or fully qualified domain name
- **Ping the computer's local loopback address** Verifies that the network adapter and TCP/IP in general is installed and enabled
- **Ping the DHCP, DNS, and WINS servers** Verifies the DHCP, DNS, and WINS server settings of network adapters
- **Ping gateways** Verifies the default gateways settings of network adapters

When a computer is having possible connectivity or configuration problems, you should immediately ask yourself and verify the following questions:

- **Is the computer connected to the network?** If the computer can connect to one of its default gateways (and that gateway isn't configured on the same IP address as one of the computer's IP addresses), the computer is able to connect to the network. If the computer can't connect to any of its gateways, its network cable may be disconnected or it may have a bad network adapter.

- **Does the computer have a bad network adapter?** If the computer can't connect to any of its gateways, it may have a bad network adapter. Try pinging the local loopback address.

Seeing problems connecting to DHCP, DNS, and WINS is also a concern. You troubleshoot problems connecting to a designated server in a similar way. If the computer can connect to the default gateway but can't get to a DNS, DHCP, or WINS server, the server may be down, the IP address in the configuration may be incorrect, or another interconnection between the computer you are working with and the target server may be down. Don't forget, you can use **netsh interface ipv4 show interfaces** and **netsh interface ipv6 show interfaces** to check adapter connection states.

Appendix A

Essential Command-Line Tools Reference

In this book, I've discussed many command-line tools and scripts. This appendix is intended to provide a quick reference to the syntax and usage of these tools as well as other commands and utilities that you may find helpful. These tools are listed alphabetically by tool name. Unless otherwise noted, these tools work the same way on both Windows Server 2008 and Windows Vista. In addition, if a tool is not included in both operating systems, the source of the tool is listed, such as "Windows Server 2008 only" for the tools available only on Windows Server 2008 by default.

ARP

Displays and modifies the IP-to-physical address translation tables used by the address resolution protocol (ARP).

```
arp -a [inet_addr] [-N if_addr]
arp -d inet_addr [if_addr]
arp -s inet_addr eth_addr [if_addr]
```

ASSOC

Displays and modifies file extension associations.

```
assoc [.ext[=[fileType]]]
```

ATTRIB

Displays and changes file attributes.

```
attrib [+r|-r] [+a|-a] [+s|-s] [+h|-h] [+i|-i]
[[drive:] [path] filename] [/s [/d] [/l]]
```

BCDEDIT

Displays and manages the boot configuration data (BCD) store.

```
bcdedit /command [options]
bcdedit [/v]
```

With Bcdedit, you can use the following commands:

- **/bootdebug** Enables or disables boot debugging for a boot application.
- **/bootems** Enables or disables Emergency Management Services for a boot application.
- **/bootsequence** Sets a one-time boot sequence for the boot manager.
- **/copy** Makes copies of entries in the BCD store.
- **/create** Creates new entries in the BCD store.
- **/createstore** Creates a new and empty boot configuration data store.
- **/dbgsettings** Sets global debugger parameters.
- **/debug** Enables or disables kernel debugging for an operating system entry.
- **/default** Sets the default entry for the boot manager.
- **/delete** Deletes entries from the BCD store.
- **/deletevalue** Deletes entry options from the BCD store.
- **/displayorder** Sets the order in which the boot manager displays available operating systems.
- **/ems** Enables or disables Emergency Management Services for an operating system entry.
- **/emssettings** Sets the global Emergency Management Services parameters.
- **/enum** Lists entries in the store.
- **/export** Exports the contents of the system store to a file. This file can be used later to restore the state of the system store.
- **/import** Restores the state of the system store using a backup file created with the /export command.
- **/set** Sets entry option values in the BCD store.
- **/timeout** Sets a time-out value for the boot manager.
- **/toolsdisplayorder** Sets the order in which the boot manager displays the tools menu.

CACLS

This command is deprecated. See ICACLS.

CALL

Calls a script or script label as a procedure.

```
call [drive:][path]filename [batch-parameters]
call :label [args]
```

CD

Displays the name of or changes the current directory.

```
chdir [/d] [drive:][path]
chdir [..]
cd [/d] [drive:][path]
cd [..]
```

CHDIR

See **CD**.

CHKDSK

Checks a disk for errors and displays a report.

```
chkdsk [drive:][[path]filename]
[/f][/v][/r][/x][/i][/c][/l[:size]] [/b]
```

CHKNTFS

Displays the status of volumes. Sets or excludes volumes from automatic system checking when the computer is started.

```
chkntfs [/x | /c] volume: [...]
chkntfs /t[:time]
chkntfs /d
```

CHOICE

Creates a selection list from which users can select a choice in batch scripts.

```
choice [/c choices] [/n] [/cs] [/t nnnn /d choice] [/m "text"]
```

CIPHER

Displays current encryption status or modifies folder and file encryption on NTFS volumes.

```
cipher [/e | /d | /c] [/s:dir] [/b]
       [/h] [[path]filename [...]]
cipher [/k | /r:filename | /w:dir]
cipher /u [/n]
cipher /x[:efsfile] [filename]
cipher /y
cipher /adduser [/certhash:hash | /certfile:filename]
       [/s:dir] [/b] [/h] [pathname [...]]
cipher /removeuser /certhash:hash
       [/s:dir] [/b] [/h] [pathname [...]]
cipher /rekey [pathname [...]]
```

CLIP

With piping, redirects output of command-line tools to the Windows clipboard.

```
[command |] clip
clip < filename.txt
```

Note In this instance, the symbol "|" is the pipe symbol.

CLS

Clears the console window.

```
cls
```

CMD

Starts a new instance of the command shell.

```
cmd [/a | /u] [/q] [/d] [/e:on | /e:off] [/t:{bf | f}]
[/f:on | /f:off] [/v:on | /v:off]
[[/s] [/c | /k] string]
```

CMDKEY

Creates and manages stored user names and passwords.

```
cmdkey [{/add | /generic}:targetname
{/smartcard | /user:user@domain
{/pass{:pwd}}} | /delete{:targetname}
| /ras | /list{:targetname}]
```

COLOR

Sets the colors of the command-shell window.

```
color [[b]f]
```

COMP

Compares the contents of two files or sets of files.

```
comp [data1] [data2] [/d] [/a] [/l]
[/n=number] [/c] [/offline]
```

COMPACT

Displays or alters the compression of files on NTFS partitions.

```
compact [/c | /u] [/s[:dir]] [/a] [/i] [/f]
[/q] [filename [...]]
```

CONVERT

Converts FAT and FAT32 volumes to NTFS.

```
convert volume /fs:NTFS [/v] [/x]
[/cvtarea:filename] [/nosecurity]
```

COPY

Copies or combines files.

```
copy [/d] [/v] [/n] [/y|/-y] [/z] [/l] [/a|/b] source [/a | /b]
[+ source [/a | /b] [+ ...]][destination [/a | /b]]
```

DATE

Displays or sets the system date.

```
date [/T | mm-dd-yy]
```

DCDIAG

Performs diagnostics testing on a domain controller.

```
dcdiag [/s:Server[:LDAPPort]] [/u [Domain\]UserName]
[/p {Password | * | ""}] [/h | /?] [/xsl] [/a | /e] [/I] [/fix] [/c]
[/q | /v] [/n:NamingContext] [/skip:TestName] [/test:TestName]
[/f:textlogname] [/x:xmllogname]
```

This command applies only to Windows Server 2008.

DCGPOFIX

Restores default group policy objects.

```
dcgpofix [/ignoreschema]
[/target: {domain | dc | both}]
```

This command applies only to Windows Server 2008.

DEFRAG

Defragments hard drives.

```
defrag volume [/a] [/v]
defrag [volume | -c] [{-r | -w}] [-f] [-v]
```

You must run this command using an administrator command prompt.

DEL

Deletes one or more files.

```
del [/p] [/f] [/s] [/q] [/a[[:]attributes]]
[drive:][path]filename[...]
```

DIR

Displays a list of files and subdirectories within a directory.

```
dir [drive:][path][filename] [/a[[:]attributes]] [/b] [/c] [/d]
[/l] [/n] [/o[[:]sortorder]] [/p] [/q] [/r] [/s] [/t[[:]timefield]]
[/w] [/x] [/4]
```

DISKCOMP

Compares the contents of two floppy disks.

```
diskcomp [drive1: [drive2:]]
```

DISKCOPY

Copies the contents of one floppy disk to another.

```
diskcopy [drive1: [drive2:]] [/v]
```

DISKPART

Invokes a text-mode command interpreter so that you can manage disks, partitions, and volumes using a separate command prompt and commands that are internal to DISKPART.

```
diskpart
```

More Info Techniques for working with DISKPART are covered in Chapter 10, "Configuring and Maintaining Disks," Chapter 11, "Partitioning Basic Disks," and Chapter 12, "Managing Volumes and RAID on Dynamic Disks." If you run DISKPART in a nonadministrative command prompt, you'll be prompted for consent or permission to run DISKPART in a separate administrative command prompt. DISKPART for Windows Vista SP1 and Windows Server 2008 RTM is a revision to the version of DISKPART for Windows Vista RTM. This revision includes two additional commands: SAN and UNIQUEID.

DOSKEY

Edits command lines, recalls Windows commands, and creates macros.

```
doskey [/reinstall] [/listsize=size]
[/macros[:all | :exename]]
[/history] [/insert | /overstrike]
[/exename=exename]
[/macrofile=fname] [macroname=[text]]
```

DRIVERQUERY

Displays a list of all installed device drivers and their properties.

```
driverquery [/s computer [/u [domain\]user [/p [pwd]]]]
[/fo {table|list|csv}] [/nh] [/v] [/si]
```

DSADD COMPUTER

Creates a computer account in the Active Directory directory service.

```
dsadd computer ComputerDN [-samid SAMName] [-desc Description]
[-loc Location] [-memberof GroupDN ...] [{-s Server | -d Domain}]
[-u UserName] [-p {Password | *}] [-q] [{-uc | -uco | -uci}]
```

This command is available in Windows Vista Business or later if Windows Server 2008 Administration Tools Pack has been installed.

DSADD GROUP

Creates a group account in Active Directory.

```
dsadd group GroupDN [-secgrp {yes | no}] [-scope {l | g | u}]
[-samid SAMName] [-desc Description] [-memberof Group ...]
[-members Member ...] [{-s Server | -d Domain}] [-u UserName]
[-p {Password | *}] [-q] [{-uc | -uco | -uci}]
```

This command is available in Windows Vista Business or later if Windows Server 2008 Administration Tools Pack has been installed.

DSADD USER

Creates a user account in Active Directory.

```
dsadd user UserDN [-samid SAMName] [-upn UPN] [-fn FirstName]
[-mi Initial]  [-ln LastName] [-display DisplayName]
[-empid EmployeeID] [-pwd {Password | *}] [-desc Description]
[-memberof Group ...] [-office Office] [-tel PhoneNumber]
[-email EmailAddress] [-hometel HomePhoneNumber]
[-pager PagerNumber] [-mobile CellPhoneNumber] [-fax FaxNumber]
[-iptel IPPhoneNumber] [-webpg WebPage] [-title Title]
[-dept Department] [-company Company] [-mgr Manager]
[-hmdir HomeDirectory] [-hmdrv DriveLetter:] [-profile ProfilePath]
[-loscr ScriptPath] [-mustchpwd {yes | no}] [-canchpwd {yes | no}]
[-reversiblepwd {yes | no}] [-pwdneverexpires {yes | no}]
[-acctexpires NumberOfDays] [-disabled {yes | no}]
[{-s Server | -d Domain}] [-u UserName] [-p {Password | *}]
[-q] [{-uc | -uco | -uci}] [-fnp FirstNamePhonetic]
[-lnp LastNamePhonetic] [-displayp DisplayNamePhonetic]
```

This command is available in Windows Vista Business or later if Windows Server 2008 Administration Tools Pack has been installed.

DSGET COMPUTER

Displays the properties of a computer account using one of two syntaxes. The syntax for viewing the properties of multiple computers is

```
dsget computer ComputerDN ... [-dn] [-samid] [-sid] [-desc] [-loc]
[-disabled] [{-s Server | -d Domain}] [-u UserName]
[-p {Password | *}] [-c] [-q] [-l]  [{-uc | -uco | -uci}]
[-part PartitionDN [-qlimit] [-qused]]
```

The syntax for viewing the membership information of a single computer is

```
dsget computer ComputerDN [-memberof [-expand]]
[{-s Server | -d Domain}] [-u UserName] [-p {Password | *}] [-c]
[-q] [-l] [{-uc | -uco | -uci}]
```

This command is available in Windows Vista Business or later if Windows Server 2008 Administration Tools Pack has been installed.

DSGET GROUP

Displays the properties of group accounts using one of two syntaxes. The syntax for viewing the properties of multiple groups is

```
dsget group GroupDN ... [-dn] [-samid] [-sid] [-desc] [-secgrp]
[-scope] [{-s Server | -d Domain}] [-u UserName] [-p {Password | *}]
[-c] [-q] [-l] [{-uc | -uco | -uci}] [-part PartitionDN [-qlimit]
[-qused]]
```

The syntax for viewing the group membership information for an individual group is

```
dsget group GroupDN [{-memberof | -members} [-expand]]
[{-s Server | -d Domain}] [-u UserName] [-p {Password | *}]
[-c] [-q] [-l]  [{-uc | -uco | -uci}]
```

This command is available in Windows Vista Business or later if Windows Server 2008 Administration Tools Pack has been installed.

DSGET SERVER

Displays the various properties of domain controllers using any of three syntaxes. The syntax for displaying the general properties of a specified domain controller is

```
dsget server ServerDN ... [-dn] [-desc] [-dnsname] [-site]
[-isgc] [{-s Server | -d Domain}] [-u UserName] [-p {Password | *}] [-c]
[-q] [-l] [{-uc | -uco | -uci}]
```

The syntax for displaying a list of the security principals who own the largest number of directory objects on the specified domain controller is

```
dsget server ServerDN [{-s Server | -d Domain}] [-u UserName]
[-p {Password | *}] [-c] [-q] [-l] [{-uc | -uco | -uci}]
[-topobjowner NumbertoDisplay]
```

The syntax for displaying the distinguished names of the directory partitions on the specified server is

```
dsget server ServerDN [{-s Server | -d Domain}] [-u UserName]
[-p {Password | *}] [-c] [-q] [-l] [{-uc | -uco | -uci}] [-part]
```

This command is available in Windows Vista Business or later if Windows Server 2008 Administration Tools Pack has been installed.

DSGET USER

Displays the properties of user accounts using one of two syntaxes. The syntax for viewing the properties of multiple users is

```
dsget user UserDN ... [-dn] [-samid] [-sid] [-upn] [-fn] [-mi]
[-ln] [-display] [-fnp] [-lnp] [-displayp] [-effectivepso]
[-empid] [-desc] [-office] [-tel] [-email] [-hometel] [-pager]
[-mobile] [-fax] [-iptel] [-webpg] [-title] [-dept] [-company]
[-mgr] [-hmdir] [-hmdrv] [-profile] [-loscr] [-mustchpwd] [-canchpwd]
[-pwdneverexpires] [-disabled] [-acctexpires] [-reversiblepwd]
[{-uc | -uco | -uci}] [-part PartitionDN [-qlimit] [-qused]]
[{-s Server | -d Domain}] [-u UserName] [-p {Password | *}] [-c] [-q]
[-l]
```

The syntax for viewing the group membership for users is

```
dsget user UserDN [-memberof [-expand]] [{-uc | -uco | -uci}]
[{-s Server | -d Domain}] [-u UserName] [-p {Password | *}] [-c]
[-q] [-l]
```

This command is available in Windows Vista Business or later if Windows Server 2008 Administration Tools Pack has been installed.

DSMGMT

Invokes a text-mode command interpreter so that you can manage directory services using a separate command prompt and commands that are internal to DSMGMT.

```
dsmgmt
```

DSMOD COMPUTER

Modifies attributes of one or more computer accounts in the directory.

```
dsmod computer ComputerDN ... [-desc Description] [-loc Location]
[-disabled {yes | no}] [-reset] [{-s Server | -d Domain}] [-u UserName]
[-p {Password | *}] [-c] [-q] [{-uc | -uco | -uci}]
```

This command is available in Windows Vista Business or later if Windows Server 2008 Administration Tools Pack has been installed.

DSMOD GROUP

Modifies attributes of one or more group accounts in the directory.

```
dsmod group GroupDN ... [-samid SAMName] [-desc Description]
[-secgrp {yes | no}] [-scope {l | g | u}]
[{-addmbr | -rmmbr | -chmbr} MemberDN ...] [{-s Server | -d Domain}]
[-u UserName] [-p {Password | *}] [-c] [-q] [{-uc | -uco | -uci}]
```

This command is available in Windows Vista Business or later if Windows Server 2008 Administration Tools Pack has been installed.

DSMOD SERVER

Modifies properties of a domain controller.

```
dsmod server ServerDN ... [-desc Description] [-isgc {yes | no}]
[{-s Server | -d Domain}] [-u UserName] [-p {Password | *}] [-c]
[-q] [{-uc | -uco | -uci}]
```

This command is available in Windows Vista Business or later if Windows Server 2008 Administration Tools Pack has been installed.

DSMOD USER

Modifies attributes of one or more user accounts in the directory.

```
dsmod user UserDN ... [-upn UPN] [-fn FirstName] [-mi Initial]
[-ln LastName] [-display DisplayName] [-empid EmployeeID]
[-pwd {Password | *}] [-desc Description] [-office Office]
[-tel PhoneNumber] [-email EmailAddress] [-hometel HomePhoneNumber]
[-pager PagerNumber] [-mobile CellPhoneNumber] [-fax FaxNumber]
[-iptel IPPhoneNumber] [-webpg WebPage] [-title Title]
[-dept Department] [-company Company] [-mgr Manager]
```

```
[-hmdir HomeDirectory] [-hmdrv DriveLetter:] [-profile ProfilePath]
[-loscr ScriptPath] [-mustchpwd {yes | no}] [-canchpwd {yes | no}]
[-reversiblepwd {yes | no}] [-pwdneverexpires {yes | no}]
[-acctexpires NumberOfDays] [-disabled {yes | no}]
[{-s Server | -d Domain}] [-u UserName] [-p {Password | *}] [-c] [-q]
[{-uc | -uco | -uci}] [-fnp FirstNamePhonetic]
[-lnp LastNamePhonetic] [-displayp DisplayNamePhonetic]
```

This command is available in Windows Vista Business or later if Windows Server 2008 Administration Tools Pack has been installed.

DSMOVE

Moves or renames Active Directory objects.

```
dsmove objectdn [-newname newname] [-newparent parentdn]
[{-s server | -d domain}] [-u username] [-p {password | *}] [-q]
[{-uc | -uco | -uci}]
```

This command is available in Windows Vista Business or later if Windows Server 2008 Administration Tools Pack has been installed.

DSQUERY COMPUTER

Searches for computer accounts matching criteria.

```
dsquery computer [{startnode | forestroot | domainroot}]
[-o {dn | rdn | samid}] [-scope {subtree | onelevel | base}] [-name name]
[-desc description] [-samid samname] [-inactive numberofweeks]
[-stalepwd numberofdays] [-disabled] [{-s server | -d domain}]
[-u username] [-p {password | *}] [-q]   [-r] [-gc]
[-limit numberofobjects]
[{-uc | -uco | -uci}]
```

This command is available in Windows Vista Business or later if Windows Server 2008 Administration Tools Pack has been installed.

DSQUERY CONTACT

Searches for contacts matching criteria.

```
dsquery contact [{startnode | forestroot | domainroot}]
[-o {dn | rdn}] [-scope {subtree | onelevel | base}] [-name name]
[-desc description] [{-s server | -d domain}] [-u username]
[-p {password | *}] [-q] [-r] [-gc] [-limit numberofobjects]
[{-uc | -uco | -uci}]
```

This command is available in Windows Vista Business or later if Windows Server 2008 Administration Tools Pack has been installed.

DSQUERY GROUP

Searches for group accounts matching criteria.

```
dsquery group [{startnode | forestroot | domainroot}]
[-o {dn | rdn | samid}] [-scope {subtree | onelevel | base}]
[-name name] [-desc description] [-samid SAMName]
[{-s server | -d domain}] [-u username] [-p {password | *}] [-q]
[-r] [-gc] [-limit numberofobjects] [{-uc | -uco | -uci}]
```

This command is available in Windows Vista Business or later if Windows Server 2008 Administration Tools Pack has been installed.

DSQUERY PARTITION

Searches for Active Directory partitions matching criteria.

```
dsquery partition [-o {dn | rdn}] [-part filter] [-desc description]
[{-s server | -d domain}] [-u username] [-p {password | *}] [-q]
[-r] [-limit numberofobjects] [{-uc | -uco | -uci}]
```

This command is available in Windows Vista Business or later if Windows Server 2008 Administration Tools Pack has been installed.

DSQUERY QUOTA

Searches for disk quotas matching criteria.

```
dsquery quota {domainroot | objectdn} [-o {dn | rdn}] [-acct name]
[-qlimit filter] [-desc description] [{-s server | -d domain}]
[-u username] [-p {password | *}] [-q] [-r] [-limit numberofobjects]
[{-uc | -uco | -uci}]
```

This command is available in Windows Vista Business or later if Windows Server 2008 Administration Tools Pack has been installed.

DSQUERY SERVER

Searches for domain controllers matching criteria.

```
dsquery server [-o {dn | rdn}] [-forest] [-domain domainname]
[-site sitename] [-name name] [-desc description]
[-hasfsmo {schema | name | infr | pdc | rid}] [-isgc]
[-isreadonly] [{-s server | -d domain}] [-u username]
[-p {password | *}] [-q] [-r] [-gc] [-limit numberofobjects]
[{-uc | -uco | -uci}]
```

This command is available in Windows Vista Business or later if Windows Server 2008 Administration Tools Pack has been installed.

DSQUERY SITE

Searches for Active Directory sites matching criteria.

```
dsquery site [-o {dn | rdn}] [-name name] [-desc description]
[{-s server | -d domain}] [-u username] [-p {password | *}] [-q]
[-r] [-gc] [-limit numberofobjects] [{-uc | -uco | -uci}]
```

This command is available in Windows Vista Business or later if Windows Server 2008 Administration Tools Pack has been installed.

DSQUERY USER

Searches for user accounts matching criteria.

```
dsquery user [{startnode | forestroot | domainroot}]
[-o {dn | rdn | upn | samid}] [-scope {subtree | onelevel | base}]
[-name name] [-namep namephonetic] [-desc description] [-upn upn]
[-samid samname] [-inactive numberofweeks] [-stalepwd numberofdays]
[-disabled] [{-s server | -d domain}] [-u username]
[-p {password | *}] [-q] [-r] [-gc] [-limit numberofobjects]
[{-uc | -uco | -uci}]
```

This command is available in Windows Vista Business or later if Windows Server 2008 Administration Tools Pack has been installed.

DSQUERY *

Searches for any Active Directory objects matching criteria.

```
dsquery * [{startnode | forestroot | domainroot}]
[-scope {subtree | onelevel | base}] [-filter ldapfilter]
[-attr {attributelist | *}] [-attrsonly] [-l]
[{-s server | -d domain}] [-u username] [-p {password | *}] [-q]
[-r] [-gc]  [-limit numberofobjects] [{-uc | -uco | -uci}]
```

This command is available in Windows Vista Business or later if Windows Server 2008 Administration Tools Pack has been installed.

DSRM

Deletes Active Directory objects.

```
dsrm objectdn ... [-subtree [-exclude]] [-noprompt]
[{-s server | -d domain}] [-u username] [-p {password | *}] [-c]
[-q] [{-uc | -uco | -uci}]
```

This command is available in Windows Vista Business or later if Windows Server 2008 Administration Tools Pack has been installed.

ECHO

Displays messages or turns command echoing on or off.

```
echo [on | off]
echo [message]
```

ENDLOCAL

Ends localization of environment changes in a batch file.

```
endlocal
```

ERASE

See **DEL**.

ESENTUTL

Manages Extensible Storage Engine (ESE) databases, including those used by Active Directory Domain Services (ADDS).

Syntax for defragmentation:

```
esentutl /d databasename /s [streamingfilename] /t [tempdbname]
/f [tempstreamingfilename] /i /p /b [backupfilename] /8 /o
```

Syntax for recovery:

```
esentutl /r logfilebasename /l [logdirectory]
/s [systemfilesdirectory]
/i /t /u [log] /d [dbfiledirectory] /n path1[:path2] /8 /o
```

Syntax for checking integrity:

```
esentutl /g databasename /s [streamingfilename] /t [tempdbname]
/f [tempstreamingfilename] /i /8 /o
```

Syntax for performing a checksum:

```
esentutl /k filetocheck /s [streamingfilename]
/t [tempdbname] /p nn
/e /i /8 /o
```

Syntax for repair:

```
esentutl /p databasename /s [streamingfilename] /t [tempdbname]
/f [reportprefix] /i /g /createstm /8 /o
```

Syntax for dumping a file:

```
esentutl /m [h|k|l|m|s|u] filename /p pagenumber
/s [streamingfilename] /t tablename /v /8 /o
```

Syntax for copying a file:

```
esentutl /y sourcefile /d destinationfile /o
```

EVENTCREATE

Creates custom events in the event logs.

```
eventcreate [/s computer [/u domain\user [/p password]]
[/l {application | system}] | [/so srcname]
/t {success | error | warning | information} /id eventid
/d description
```

EXIT

Exits the command interpreter.

```
exit [/b] [exitcode]
```

EXPAND

Uncompresses files.

```
expand [-r] source destination
expand -r source [destination]
expand -d source.cab [-f:files]
expand source.cab -f:files destination
```

FC

Compares files and displays differences.

```
fc [/a] [/c] [/l] [/lbn] [/n] [/t] [/u] [/w]
   [/nnnn][/offline][drive1:][path1]filename1
   [drive2:][path2]filename2
fc /b [drive1:][path1]filename1
   [drive2:][path2]filename2
```

FIND

Searches for a text string in files.

```
find [/v] [/c] [/n] [/i] [/offline] "string"
[[drive:][path]filename[ ...]]
```

FINDSTR

Searches for strings in files using regular expressions.

```
findstr [/b] [/e] [/l] [/r] [/s] [/i] [/x] [/v] [/n]
[/m] [/o] [/p] [/f:file] [/a:attr] [/c:string]
[/d:dir] [/g:file] [/offline] [strings]
[[drive:][path]filename[ ...]]
```

FOR

Runs a specified command for each file in a set of files.

Command-line FOR looping:

```
for %variable in (set) do command [parameters]
for /d %variable in (set) do command [parameters]
for /r [[drive:]path] %variable in (set) do command [parameters]
for /l %variable in (start,step,end) do command [parameters]
for /f ["options"] %variable in (set) do command [parameters]
```

Script FOR looping:

```
for %%variable in (set) do command [parameters]
for /d %%variable in (set) do command [parameters]
for /r [[drive:]path] %%variable in (set) do command [parameters]
for /l %%variable in (start,step,end) do command [parameters]
for /f ["options"] %%variable in (set) do command [parameters]
```

FORFILES

Selects one or more files and executes a command on each file.

```
forfiles [/p pathname] [/m searchmask] [/s] [/c command]
[/d [+ | -] {mm/dd/yyyy | dd}]
```

FORMAT

Formats a floppy disk or hard drive.

```
format drive: [/fs:file-system] [/v:label] [/q] [/a:size] [/c]
[/x] [/p:numzerofillpasses]
format drive: [/v:label] [/q] [/f:size | /t:tracks /n:sectors]
[/p:numzerofillpasses]
```

FTP

Transfers files.

```
ftp [-v] [-d] [-i] [-n] [-g] [-s:filename] [-a] [-A] [-x:sendbuffer]
[-r:recvbuffer] [-b:asyncbuffers] [-w:windowsize] [host]
```

The parameters for the FTP command are case-sensitive. You must enter them in the letter case shown.

FTYPE

Displays or modifies file types used in file extension associations.

```
ftype [fileType[=[command]]]
```

GET-EVENTLOG

A Windows PowerShell command for displaying information about event logs or entries stored in event logs.

```
get-eventlog -list
get-eventlog [-logname] logname [-newest nn]
```

GET-PROCESS

A Windows PowerShell command for displaying information about running processes.

```
get-process -id [id1,id2,...]
get-process -inputobject processname1, processname2,... [process ...]
get-process [-name] [processname1, processname2,...]
```

GET-SERVICE

A Windows PowerShell command for displaying information about configured services.

```
get-service [-displayname [servicename1, servicename2,...]]
 -include [servicename1, servicename2,...]
 -exclude [servicename1, servicename2,...]
get-service [-name] [servicename1, servicename2,...]
 -include [servicename1, servicename2,...]
 -exclude [servicename1, servicename2,...]
get-service [-inputobject servicename1, servicename2,...]
 [-include [servicename1, servicename2,...]
 [-exclude [servicename1, servicename2,...]
```

GETMAC

Displays network adapter information.

```
getmac [/s computer [/u [domain]\user [/p [pwd]]]]
[/fo {table|list|csv}] [/nh] [/v]
```

GOTO

Directs the Windows command interpreter to a labeled line in a script.

```
goto :label
goto :EOF
```

GPUPDATE

Forces a background refresh of group policy.

```
gpupdate [/target:{computer | user}] [/force] [/wait:<value>]
[/logoff] [/boot] [/sync]
```

HOSTNAME

Prints the computer's name.

```
hostname
```

ICACLS

Displays or modifies a file's access control list (ACL).

Syntax for storing ACLs for all matching names into an ACL file:

```
icacls name /save aclfile [/t] [/c] [/l] [/q]
```

Syntax for restoring stored ACLs to files in a directory:

```
icacls directory [/substitute sidold sidnew [...]] /restore aclfile
[/c] [/l] [/q]
```

Syntax for changing the owner for all matching names:

```
icacls name /setowner user [/t] [/c] [/l] [/q]
```

Syntax for finding all matching names with a particular SID applied:

```
icacls name /findsid sid [/t] [/c] [/l] [/q]
```

Syntax for granting permissions:

```
icacls name [/grant[:r] sid:perm[...]]
```

Syntax for denying permissions:

```
icacls name [/deny sid:perm [...]]
```

Syntax for removing permissions:

```
icacls name [/remove[:g|:d]] sid[...]] [/t] [/c] [/l] [/q]
```

Syntax for resetting ACLs to inherited values:

```
icacls name /reset [/t] [/c] [/l] [/q]
```

Syntax for setting an integrity level:

```
icacls name [/setintegritylevel level:policy[...]]
```

Syntax for verifying ACLs:

```
icacls name /verify [/t] [/c] [/l] [/q]
```

IF

Performs conditional processing in batch programs.

```
if [not] errorlevel number command
if [not] [/i] string1==string2 command
if [not] exist filename command
```

```
if [/i] string1 compare-op string2 command
if cmdextversion number command
if defined variable command
```

IPCONFIG

Displays TCP/IP configuration.

```
ipconfig [/allcompartments] {/all}
ipconfig [/release [adapter] | /renew [adapter]
        | /release6 [adapter] | /renew6 [adapter]]
ipconfig /flushdns | /displaydns | /registerdns
ipconfig /showclassid adapter
ipconfig /setclassid adapter [classidtoset]]
```

LABEL

Creates, changes, or deletes the volume label of a disk.

```
label [drive:][label]
label [/mp] [volume] [label]
```

MD

Creates a directory or subdirectory.

```
mkdir [drive:]path
md [drive:]path
```

MKDIR

See **MD**.

MORE

Displays output one screen at a time.

```
more [/e [/c] [/p] [/s] [/tn] [+n]] < [drive:][path]filename
more /e [/c] [/p] [/s] [/tn] [+n] [files]
command-name | more [/e [/c] [/p] [/s] [/tn] [+n]]
```

MOUNTVOL

Manages volume mount point.

```
mountvol [drive:]path volumeName
mountvol [drive:]path {/d | /l | /p}
mountvol [/r | /n | /e]
```

MOVE

Moves files from one directory to another directory on the same drive.

```
move [/y] [/-y] source target
```

NBTSTAT

Displays status of NETBIOS.

```
nbtstat [-a remotename] [-A ipaddress] [-c] [-n] [-r] [-R] [-RR]
[-s] [-S] [interval]
```

Note This command uses case-sensitive switches.

NET ACCOUNTS

Manage user account and password policies.

```
net accounts [/forcelogoff:{minutes | no}]
 [/minpwlen:length]
 [/maxpwage:{days | unlimited}]
 [/minpwage:days]
 [/uniquepw:number] [/domain]
```

NET COMPUTER

Adds or remove computers from a domain.

```
net computer \\computername {/add | /del}
```

NET CONFIG SERVER

Displays or modifies configuration of server service.

```
net config server [/autodisconnect:time]
   [/srvcomment:"text"] [/hidden:{yes | no}]
```

NET CONFIG WORKSTATION

Displays or modifies configuration of workstation service.

```
net config workstation [/charcount:bytes]
[/chartime:msec]
[/charwait:sec]
```

NET CONTINUE

Resumes a paused service.

```
net continue service
```

NET FILE

Displays or manages open files on a server.

```
net file [id [/close]]
```

NET GROUP

Displays or manages global groups.

```
net group [groupname [/comment:"text"]]
  [/domain]
net group groupname {/add [/comment:"text"]
  | /delete} [/domain]
net group groupname username [...]
  {/add | /delete} [/domain]
```

NET LOCALGROUP

Displays local group accounts.

```
net localgroup [GroupName [/comment:"Text"]] [/domain]
```

Creates a local group account.

```
net localgroup GroupName {/add [/comment:"Text"]} [/domain]
```

Modifies local group accounts.

```
net localgroup [GroupName Name [ ...] /add [/domain]
```

Deletes a local group account.

```
net localgroup GroupName /delete  [/domain]
```

NET PAUSE

Suspends a service.

```
net pause service
```

NET PRINT

Displays or manages print jobs and shared queues.

```
net print \\computername\sharename
net print [\\computername] job# [/hold | /release | /delete]
```

NET SESSION

Lists or disconnects sessions.

```
net session [\\computername] [/delete]
```

NET SHARE

Displays or manages shared printers and directories.

```
net share [sharename]
net share sharename[=drive:path] [/users:number | /unlimited]
  [/remark:"text"] [/cache:flag]
net share {sharename | devicename | drive:path} /delete
```

NET START

Lists or starts network services.

```
net start [service]
```

NET STATISTICS

Displays workstation and server statistics.

```
net statistics [workstation | server]
```

NET STOP

Stops services.

```
net stop service
```

NET TIME

Displays or synchronizes network time.

```
net time [\\computername | /domain[:domainname] |
 /rtsdomain[:domainname]] [/set]
net time [\\computername] /querysntp
net time [\\computername] /setsntp[:serverlist]
```

NET USE

Displays or manages remote connections.

```
net use [devicename | *] [\\computername\sharename[\volume]
[password | *]] [/user:[domainname\]username]
[/user:[username@domainname]] [[/delete] | [/persistent:{yes | no}]]
[/smartcard] [/savecred]
net use [devicename | *] [password | *]] [/home]
net use [/persistent:{yes | no}]
```

NET USER

Creates local user accounts.

```
net user UserName [Password | *] /add [/active:{no | yes}]
[/comment:"DescriptionText"] [/countrycode:NNN]
[/expires: {{MM/DD/YYYY | DD/MM/YYYY | mmm,dd,YYYY} | never}]
[/fullname:"Name"] [/homedir:Path] [/passwordchg:{yes | no}]
[/passwordreq:{yes | no}] [/profilepath:[Path]] [/scriptpath:Path]
[/times:{Day[-Day][,Day[-Day]] ,Time[-Time][,Time[-Time]]
[;...] | all}] [/usercomment:"Text"]
[/workstations:{ComputerName[,...] | *}] [/domain]
```

Modifies local user accounts.

```
net user [UserName [Password | *] [/active:{no | yes}]
[/comment:"DescriptionText"] [/countrycode:NNN]
[/expires:{{MM/DD/YYYY | DD/MM/YYYY | mmm,dd,YYYY} | never}]
[/fullname:"Name"] [/homedir:Path] [/passwordchg:{yes | no}]
[/passwordreq:{yes | no}] [/profilepath:[Path]] [/scriptpath:Path]
[/times:{Day[-Day][,Day[-Day]] ,Time[-Time][,Time[-Time]]
[;...] | all}] [/usercomment:"Text"]
[/workstations:{ComputerName[,...] | *}]] [/domain]
```

Deletes local user accounts.

```
net user UserName [/delete] [/domain]
```

NET VIEW

Displays network resources or computers.

```
net view [\\computername [/cache] | [/all] |
 /domain[:domainname]]
net view /network:nw [\\computername]
```

NETDOM ADD

Adds a workstation or server account to the domain.

```
netdom add computer [/domain:domain] [/userd:user]
[/passwordd:[password | *]]
[/server:server] [/ou:oupath] [/dc] [/securepasswordprompt]
```

NETDOM COMPUTERNAME

Manages the primary and alternate names for a computer. This command can safely rename a domain controller or a server.

```
netdom computername computer [/usero:user]
[/passwordo:[password | *]]
[/userd:user] [/passwordd:[password | *]] [/securepasswordprompt]
/add:newalternatednsname | /remove:alternatednsname |
    /makeprimary:computerdnsname |
/enumerate[:{alternatenames | primaryname | allnames}] | /verify
```

NETDOM JOIN

Joins a workstation or member server to the domain.

```
netdom join computer /domain:domain [/ou:oupath] [/userd:user]
[/passwordd:[password | *]]
[/usero:user] [/passwordo:[password | *]]
[/reboot[:timeinseconds]]
[/securepasswordprompt]
```

NETDOM MOVE

Moves a workstation or member server to a new domain.

```
netdom move computer /domain:domain [/ou:oupath]
[/userd:user] [/passwordd:[password | *]]
[/usero:user] [/passwordo:[password | *]]
```

```
[/userf:user] [/passwordf:[password | *]]
[/reboot[:timeinseconds]]
[/securepasswordprompt]
```

NETDOM MOVENT4BDC

Moves Windows NT 4.0 backup domain controllers to a new domain.

```
netdom movent4bdc computer [/domain:domain] [/reboot[:timeinseconds]]
```

NETDOM QUERY

Queries a domain for information.

```
netdom query [/domain:domain] [/server:server]
[/userd:user] [/passwordd:[password | *]]
[/verify] [/reset] [/direct] [/securepasswordprompt]
{workstation | server | dc | ou | pdc | fsmo | trust}
```

NETDOM REMOVE

Removes a workstation or server from the domain.

```
netdom remove computer [/domain:domain] [/userd:user]
[/passwordd:[password | *]]
[/usero:user] [/passwordo:[password | *]]
[/reboot[:timeinseconds]] [/force]
[/securepasswordprompt]
```

NETDOM RENAMECOMPUTER

Renames a computer. If the computer is joined to a domain, the computer object in the domain is also renamed. You should not use this command to rename a domain controller.

```
netdom renamecomputer computer /newname:newname
[/userd:user [/passwordd:[password | *]]]
[/usero:user [/passwordo:[password | *]]]
[/force] [/reboot[:timeinseconds]]
[/securepasswordprompt]
```

NETDOM RESET

Resets the secure connection between a workstation and a domain controller.

```
netdom reset computer [/domain:domain] [/server:server]
[/usero:user] [/passwordo:[password | *]] [/securepasswordprompt]
```

NETDOM RESETPWD

Resets the machine account password for the domain controller on which this command is run.

```
netdom resetpwd /server:domaincontroller /userd:user
/passwordd:[password | *]
[/securepasswordprompt]
```

NETDOM TRUST

Manages or verifies the trust relationship between domains.

```
netdom trust trustingdomainname /domain:trusteddomainname [/userd:user]
[/passwordd:[password | *]] [/usero:user] [/passwordo:[password | *]]
[/verify] [/reset] [/passwordt:newrealmtrustpassword]
[/add] [/remove] [/twoway] [/realm] [/kerberos]
[/transitive[:{yes | no}]]
[/oneside:{trusted | trusting}] [/force] [/quarantine[:{yes | no}]]
[/namesuffixes:trustname [/togglesuffix:#]]
[/enablesidhistory[:{yes | no}]]
[/foresttransitive[:{yes | no}]]
[/crossorganization[:{yes | no}]]
[/addtln:toplevelname]
[/addtlnex:toplevelnameexclusion]
[/removetln:toplevelname]
[/removetlnex:toplevelnameexclusion]
[/securepasswordprompt]
```

NETDOM VERIFY

Verifies the secure connection between a workstation and a domain controller.

```
netdom verify computer [/domain:domain] [/usero:user]
   [/passwordo:[password | *]] [/securepasswordprompt]
```

NETSH

Invokes a separate command prompt that allows you to manage the configuration of various network services on local and remote computers.

```
netsh
```

More Info Techniques for working with Netsh are discussed in Chapter 17, "Configuring, Maintaining, and Troubleshooting TCP/IP Networking."

NETSTAT

Displays status of network connections.

```
netstat [-a] [-b] [-e] [-f] [-n] [-o] [-p protocol] [-r] [-s] [-t]
[interval]
```

NSLOOKUP

Shows the status of DNS.

```
nslookup [-option] [computer]
nslookup [-option] [computer server]
```

PATH

Displays or sets a search path for executable files in the current command window.

```
path [[drive:]path[;...][;%PATH%]
path ;
```

PATHPING

Traces routes and provides packet loss information.

```
pathping [-n] [-h maxhops] [-g hostlist]
 [-i address] [-p period]
 [-q numqueries] [-w timeout]
 targetname [-4] [-6]
```

PAUSE

Suspends processing of a script and waits for keyboard input.

```
pause
```

PING

Determines whether a network connection can be established.

```
ping [-t] [-a] [-n count] [-l size] [-f]
 [-i ttl] [-v tos] [-r count] [-s count]
 [[-j hostlist] | [-k hostlist]]
 [-w timeout] [-R} [-S sourceaddress]
 [-4] [-6] destinationlist
```

Note This command uses case-sensitive switches.

POPD

Changes to the directory stored by PUSHD.

```
popd
```

PRINT

Prints a text file.

```
print [/d:device]
[[drive:][path]filename[...]]
```

PROMPT

Changes the Windows command prompt.

```
prompt [text]
```

PUSHD

Saves the current directory then changes to a new directory.

```
pushd [path | ..]
```

RD

Removes a directory.

```
rmdir [/s] [/q] [drive:]path
rd [/s] [/q] [drive:]path
```

RECOVER

Recovers readable information from a bad or defective disk.

```
recover [drive:][path]filename
```

REG ADD

Adds a new subkey or entry to the registry.

```
reg add keyname [/v valuename | /ve] [/t datatype] [/d data] [/f]
[/s separator]
```

REG COMPARE

Compares registry subkeys or entries.

```
reg compare keyname1 keyname2 [/v valuename | /ve] [/s]
[/outputoption]
```

REG COPY

Copies a registry entry to a specified key path on a local or remote system.

```
reg copy keyname1 keyname2 [/s] [/f]
```

REG DELETE

Deletes a subkey or entries from the registry.

```
reg delete keyname [/v valuename | /ve | /va] [/f]
```

REG QUERY

Lists the entries under a key and the names of subkeys (if any).

```
reg query keyname [/v valuename | /ve] [/s]
[/f data [/k] [/d] [/c] [/e]] [/t type] [/z] [/se separator]
```

REG RESTORE

Writes saved subkeys and entries back to the registry.

```
reg restore keyname "filename"
```

REG SAVE

Saves a copy of specified subkeys, entries, and values to a file.

```
reg save keyname "filename" [/y]
```

REGSVR32

Registers and unregisters DLLs.

```
regsvr32 [/u] [/s] [/n] [/i[:cmdline]] dllname
```

REM

Adds comments to scripts.

```
rem [comment]
```

REN

Renames a file.

```
rename [drive:][path]filename1 filename2
ren [drive:][path]filename1 filename2
```

RMDIR

See **RD**.

ROUTE

Manages network routing tables.

```
route [-f] [-p] [-4|-6] command [destination]
[mask netmask] [gateway] [metric metric] [if interface]
```

RUNAS

Runs program with specific user permissions.

Syntax for running with a specified user's credentials:

```
runas [/noprofile | /profile] [/env] [/netonly] [/savecred]
      /user:account program
```

Syntax for running with credential from a smart card:

```
runas [/noprofile | /profile] [/env] [/netonly] [/savecred]
/smartcard [/user:account] program
```

Syntax for showing available trust levels:

```
runas /showtrustlevels
```

Syntax for running a program at a specified trust level:

```
runas /trustlevel:trustlevel program
```

SC CONFIG

Configures service startup and logon accounts.

```
sc [\\ServerName] config ServiceName
  [type= {own | share|{interact type = {own | share}} | kernel |
filesys |rec | adapt}]
  [start= {boot | system | auto | demand | disabled | delayed-auto}]
  [error= {normal | severe | critical | ignore}]
  [binPath= BinaryPathName]
  [group= LoadOrderGroup]
  [tag= {yes | no}]
  [depend= Dependencies]
  [obj= {AccountName | ObjectName}]
  [DisplayName= displayname]
  [password= password]
```

SC CONTINUE

Resumes a paused service.

```
sc [\\ServerName] continue ServiceName
```

SC FAILURE

Views the actions that will be taken if a service fails.

```
sc [\\ServerName] failure ServiceName [reset= ErrorFreePeriod]
   [reboot= BroadcastMessage] [command= CommandLine]
   [actions= FailureActionsAndDelayTime]
```

SC PAUSE

Pauses a service.

```
sc [\\ServerName] pause ServiceName
```

SC QC

Displays configuration information for a named service.

```
sc [\\ServerName] qc ServiceName [BufferSize]
```

SC QFAILURE

Sets the action to take upon failure of a service.

```
sc [\\ServerName] qfailure ServiceName [BufferSize]
```

SC QUERY

Displays the list of services configured on the computer.

```
sc [\\ServerName] query ServiceName
  [type= {driver | service | all}]
  [type= {own|share|interact|kernel|filesys|rec|adapt}]
  [state= {active | inactive | all}] [bufsize= BufferSize]
  [ri= ResumeIndex]
  [group= GroupName]
```

SC START

Starts a service.

```
sc [\\ServerName] start ServiceName [ServicesArgs]
```

SC STOP

Stops a service.

```
sc [\\ServerName] stop ServiceName
```

SCHTASKS /CHANGE

Changes the properties of existing tasks.

```
schtasks /change /tn taskname [/s system [/u [domain\]user
[/p [password]]]] {[/ru [domain\]user]
[/rp password]  [/tr tasktorun]} [/st starttime] [/ri runintrrval]
[{/et endtime | /du duration} [/k]] [/sd startdate] [/ed enddate]
[enable | disable] [/it] [/z]
```

SCHTASKS /CREATE

Creates scheduled tasks.

```
schtasks /create [/s system [/u [domain\]user [/p [password]]]]
[/ru [domain\]username [rp password]] /tn taskname /tr tasktorun
/sc scheduletype [/mo modifier] [/d day] [/i idletime]
[/st starttime] [/m month [, month [...]]] [/sd startdate]
[/ed enddate] [/ri runintrrval] [{/et endtime | /du duration} [/k]]
[/it | /np] [/z] [/f] [/xml xmlfile]
```

SCHTASKS /DELETE

Removes scheduled tasks that are no longer wanted.

```
schtasks /delete /tn {TaskName | *} [/f] [/s computer
[/u [domain\]user [/p [password]]]]
```

SCHTASKS /END

Stops a running task.

```
schtasks /end /tn taskname [/s computer [/u [domain\]user
[/p [password]]]]
```

SCHTASKS /QUERY

Displays scheduled tasks on the local or named computer.

```
schtasks /query [/s computer [/u [domain\]user [/p [password]]]]
[/fo {table | list | csv} | /xml] [/nh] [/v] [/tn {TaskName]
```

SCHTASKS /RUN

Starts a scheduled task.

```
schtasks /run /tn taskname [/s computer [/u [domain\]user
[/p [password]]]]
```

SERVERMANAGERCMD

Installs and removes roles, role services, and features. Also lists installed roles, role services, and features.

Syntax for queries:

```
servermanagercmd -query [queryfile.xml] [-logPath logfile.txt]
servermanagercmd -version
```

Syntax for installs:

```
servermanagercmd -install component [-resultPath resultfile.xml
[-restart] | [-whatif]] [-logPath logfile.txt] [-allSubFeatures]
```

Syntax for removals:

```
servermanagercmd  -remove component [-resultPath resultfile.xml
[-restart] | [-whatif]] [-logPath logfile.txt]
```

Syntax for installs or removals using an answer file:

```
servermanagercmd -inputPath answerfile.xml
[-resultPath resultfile.xml
[-restart] | [-whatif]] [-logPath logfile.txt]
```

SET

Displays or modifies Windows environment variables. Also used to evaluate numeric expressions at the command line.

```
set [variable=[string]]
set /a expression
set /p variable=[promptstring]
```

SET-SERVICE

A Windows PowerShell command for modifying the configuration of system services.

```
set-service [-name] servicename [-displayname displayname]
 [-description description]
 [-startuptype {Automatic|Manual|Disabled}] [-whatif] [-config]
[parameters]
```

SETLOCAL

Begins localization of environment changes in a batch file.

```
setlocal
setlocal {enableext | disableext}
```

SFC

Scans and verifies protected system files.

```
sfc [/scannow] [/verifyonly] [/scanfile=file] [/verifyfile=file]
[/offwindir=offlinewindowsdirectory /offbootdir=offlinebootdirectory]
```

SHIFT

Shifts the position of replaceable parameters in scripts.

```
shift [/n]
```

SHUTDOWN

Shuts down or restarts a computer.

```
shutdown [/i | /l | /s | /r | /g | /a | /p | /h | /e] [/f]
    [/m \\computerName][/t nn][/d [p|u:]n1:n2 [/c "comment"]]
```

SORT

Sorts input.

```
[command |] sort [/r] [/+n] [/m kb] [/l locale] [/rec recordbytes]
[drive1:][path1]filename1] [/t [drive2:][path2]]
[/o [drive3:][path3]filename3]
```

Note In this instance, the symbol "|" is the pipe symbol.

START

Starts a new command-shell window to run a specified program or command.

```
start ["title"] [/d path] [/i] [/min] [/max] [/separate | /shared]
[/wait] [/b] [/low | /belownormal | /normal | /abovenormal
| /high | /realtime] [/affinity hh] [command/program] [parameters]
```

STOP-PROCESS

A Windows PowerShell command for stopping one or more running processes.

```
stop-process -id [id1,id2,...] [-confirm] [-passthru] [-whatif]
             [parameters]
stop-process -inputobject processname1, processname2,... [-passthru]
             [-whatif] [-config] [parameters]
stop-process -name processname1, processname2,... [-confirm]
             [-passthru] [-whatif] [parameters]
```

STOP-SERVICE

A Windows PowerShell command for stopping one or more running services.

```
stop-service [-displayname [servicename1, servicename2,...]]
 -include [servicename1, servicename2,...]
 -exclude [servicename1, servicename2,...]
stop-service [-name] [servicename1, servicename2,...]
 -include [servicename1, servicename2,...]
 -exclude [servicename1, servicename2,...]
```

> **Note** Windows PowerShell also has commands for starting (start-service), restarting (restart-service), suspending (suspend-service), and resuming (resume-service) services. These commands have the same syntax as stop-service.

SUBST

Maps a path to a drive letter.

```
subst [drive1: [drive2:]path]
subst drive1: /d
```

SYSTEMINFO

Displays detailed configuration information.

```
systeminfo [/s computer [/u [domain\]user [/p [pwd]]]]
[/fo {table|list|csv}] [/nh]
```

TAKEOWN

Allows an administrator to take ownership of one or more files.

```
takeown [/s computer [/u [domain\]user [/p [pwd]]]] /f filename
[/a] [/r [/d prompt]]
```

TASKKILL

Stops running processes by name or process ID.

```
taskkill [/s computer] [/u [domain\]user [/p pwd]]] {[/fi filter1
[/fi filter2 [ ... ]]] [/pid ID|/im imgName]} [/f][/t]
```

TASKLIST

Lists all running processes by name and process ID.

```
tasklist [/s computer [/u [domain\]user [/p [password]]]]
[{/m module | /svc | /v}] [/fo {table | list | csv}] [/nh]
[/fi filtername [/fi filtername2 [ ... ]]]
```

TIME

Displays or sets the system time.

```
time [time | /T]
```

TIMEOUT

Sets a timeout period or waits for key press in batch script.

```
TIMEOUT /t timeout [/nobreak]
```

TITLE

Sets the title for the command-shell window.

```
title [string]
```

TRACERPT

Generates trace reports from trace logs.

```
tracerpt {[-l] logfile1 logfile2 ... | [-o outputfile] |
-rt sessionname1 sessionname2 ...} [-of <CSV | EVTX | XML>]
[-lr] [-summary summaryreportfile] [-report reportfilename]
[-f <XML | HTML>] [-df schemafile] [-int dumpeventfile] [-rts]
[-tmf tracedefinitionfile] [-tp tracefilepath] [-gmt] [-i imagepath]
[-pdb symbolpath] [-rl n] [-export schemaexportfile]
[-config configfile] [-y]
```

TRACERT

Displays the path between computers.

```
tracert [-d] [-h maximumhops] [-j hostlist] [-w timeout]
[-r] [-s sourceaddrress] [-4] [-6] targetname
```

TYPE

Displays the contents of a text file.

```
type [drive:][path]filename
```

TYPEPERF

Displays or logs performance data for specified counts.

```
typeperf {{counter1 counter2 ...} | -cf counterfile} [-sc numsamples]
     [-si {[[hh:]mm:]ss] [-o logfile] [ -f {CSV | TSV | BIN | SQL}]
     [-s server] [-y]
```

```
typeperf {-q object | -qx object} [-sc numsamples ]
     [-si {[[hh:]mm:]ss] [-o logfile] [ -f {CSV | TSV | BIN | SQL}]
     [-s server] [-y]
```

VER

Displays the Windows version.

```
ver
```

VERIFY

Tells Windows whether to verify that your files are written correctly to a disk.

```
verify [on | off]
```

VOL

Displays a disk volume label and serial number.

```
vol [drive:]
```

WAITFOR

Specifies that a computer should wait for a particular signal before continuing.

Send signal syntax:

```
     waitfor [/s computer [/u [domain\]user [/p [pwd]]]] /si signal
```

Wait signal syntax:

```
     waitfor [/t timeout] signal
```

WBADMIN

Performs or schedules backup and recovery operations. This command applies only to Windows Server 2008 and to Windows Vista Business, Enterprise, and Ultimate Editions.

Syntax for enabling backups:

```
wbadmin enable backup
    [-addtarget:{BackupTargetDisk}]
    [-removetarget:{BackupTargetDisk}]
    [-schedule:TimeToRunBackup] [-include:VolumesToInclude]
    [-allCritical] [-quiet]
```

Syntax for disabling backups:

```
wbadmin disable backup [-quiet]
```

Syntax for starting backups:

```
wbadmin start backup
[-backupTarget:{TargetVolume | TargetNetworkShare}]
[-include:VolumesToInclude] [-allCritical]
[-noVerify] [-user:UserName] [-password:Password]
[-noInheritAcl] [-vssFull] [-quiet]
```

Syntax for stopping the current backup job:

```
wbadmin stop job [-quiet]
```

Syntax for listing available disks:

```
wbadmin get disks
```

Syntax for getting the status of current backup job:

```
wbadmin get status
```

Syntax for getting a list of available backups:

```
wbadmin get versions
[-backupTarget:{VolumeName | NetworkSharePath}]
[-machine:BackupMachineName]
```

Syntax for starting a system state backup:

```
wbadmin start systemstatebackup
-backupTarget:{VolumeName} [-quiet]
```

Syntax for starting a system state recovery:

```
wbadmin start systemstaterecovery
-version:VersionIdentifier -showsummary
[-backupTarget:{VolumeName | NetworkSharePath}]
[-machine:BackupMachineName]
[-recoveryTarget:TargetPathForRecovery]
[-authsysvol] [-quiet]
```

Syntax for deleting a system state backup:

```
wbadmin delete systemstatebackup
-keepVersions: NumberCopiesToKeep | -version VersionID |
-deleteOldest
[-backupTarget:{VolumeName}] [-machine:BackupMachineName]
[-quiet]
```

WHERE

Displays a list of files that match a search pattern.

```
where [/r dir] [/q] [/f] [/t] pattern
where [/q] [/f] [/t] $env:pattern
where [/q] [/f] [/t] path:pattern
```

WHOAMI

Displays log on and security information for the current user.

```
whoami [/upn | /fqdn | /logonid]
whoami {[/user] [/groups] [/priv]} [/fo {table|list|csv}] [/nh]
whoami /all [/fo {table|list|csv}] [/nh]
```

Appendix B
Quick Reference for Netsh

As discussed in Chapter 17, "Configuring, Maintaining, and Troubleshooting TCP/IP Networking," the network services shell (Netsh) is a command-line scripting utility that allows you to manage the configuration of various network services on local and remote computers. Netsh provides a separate command prompt that you can use in either interactive or noninteractive mode. Within the Netsh command environment, you can work with a complex maze of contexts and commands.

This appendix provides a quick reference to help you navigate through the available contexts and find commands you want to use. Each of the available contexts is listed in alphabetical order along with an alphabetically sorted list of any applicable subcontexts and commands. Keep in mind that some contexts are only available or only work correctly when you've installed a related role, role service, or feature.

Netsh

The Netsh context is the top-level context within the network services shell. Table B-1 provides a summary of the available commands at this level. Regardless of which context you are working with, you can always use the .. command to go up one context level. If a subcontext is available at the current level, simply type the subcontext name to access the subcontext and its commands. Thus, if you are working with the top-level Netsh context and want to switch to the Advfirewall context, you type **advfirewall**. If you later wanted to switch back to the top-level Netsh context, you type .. to go up one context level.

Table B-1 Commands for the Netsh Context

Command	Description
..	Goes up one context level.
abort	Discards changes made while in offline mode.
add helper	Installs a helper DLL.
advfirewall	Changes to the "netsh advfirewall" context.
alias	Adds an alias.
bridge	Changes to the "netsh bridge" context.
bye	Exits the program.
commit	Commits changes made while in offline mode.
delete helper	Removes a helper DLL.

Table B-1 Commands for the Netsh Context

Command	Description
dhcp	Changes to the "netsh dhcp" context if the DHCP Server role service has been installed. Otherwise, changes to the "netsh dhcpclient" context.
dhcpclient	Changes to the "netsh dhcpclient" context.
dump	Displays a configuration script for settings within the context.
exec	Runs a script file.
exit	Exits the program.
firewall	Changes to the "netsh firewall" context.
http	Changes to the "netsh http" context.
interface	Changes to the "netsh interface" context.
ipsec	Changes to the "netsh ipsec" context.
lan	Changes to the "netsh lan" context.
nap	Changes to the "netsh nap" context.
netio	Changes to the "netsh netio" context.
nps	Changes to the "netsh nps" context.
offline	Sets the current mode to offline.
online	Sets the current mode to online.
p2p	Changes to the "netsh p2p" context.
popd	Pops a context from the stack.
pushd	Pushes current context on stack.
quit	Exits the program.
ras	Changes to the "netsh ras" context.
routing	Changes to the "netsh routing" context.
rpc	Changes to the "netsh rpc" context.
set file	Copy the console output to a file.
set machine	Sets the current machine on which to operate.
set mode	Sets the current mode to online or offline.
show alias	Lists all defined aliases.
show helper	Lists all the top-level helpers.
show mode	Shows the current mode.
unalias	Deletes an alias.

Table B-1 Commands for the Netsh Context

Command	Description
winhttp	Changes to the "netsh winhttp" context.
winsock	Changes to the "netsh winsock" context.
wlan	Changes to the "netsh wlan" context.

Netsh Advfirewall

The Netsh Advfirewall context allows you to view and manage settings for the Windows Firewall with Advanced Security. Table B-2 provides a summary of the available commands for this context and related subcontexts.

Table B-2 Commands and Subcontext Commands for Netsh Advfirewall

Context/Command	Description
netsh advfirewall	
consec	Changes to the "netsh advfirewall consec" context.
dump	Displays a configuration script for settings within the context.
export	Exports the current policy to a file.
firewall	Changes to the "netsh advfirewall firewall" context.
import	Imports a policy file into the current policy store.
monitor	Changes to the "netsh advfirewall monitor" context.
reset	Resets the policy to the default out-of-box policy.
set allprofiles	Sets properties in all profiles.
set currentprofile	Sets properties in the active profile.
set domainprofile	Sets properties in the domain profile.
set global	Sets the global properties.
set privateprofile	Sets properties in the private profile.
set publicprofile	Sets properties in the public profile.
set store	Sets the policy store for the current interactive session.
show allprofiles	Displays properties for all profiles.
show currentprofile	Displays properties for the active profile.
show domainprofile	Displays properties for the domain profile.
show global	Displays the global properties.
show privateprofile	Displays properties for the private profile.
show publicprofile	Displays properties for the public profile.
show store	Displays the policy store for the current interactive session.

Table B-2 Commands and Subcontext Commands for Netsh Advfirewall

Context/Command	Description
netsh advfirewall consec	
add rule	Adds a new connection security rule.
delete rule	Deletes all matching connection security rules.
dump	Displays a configuration script for settings within the context.
set rule	Sets new values for properties of an existing rule.
show rule	Displays a specified connection security rule.
netsh advfirewall firewall	
add rule	Adds a new inbound or outbound firewall rule.
delete rule	Deletes all matching inbound or outbound rules.
dump	Displays a configuration script for settings within the context.
set rule	Sets new values for properties of an existing rule.
show rule	Displays a specified firewall rule.
netsh advfirewall monitor	
delete	Deletes all matching security associations.
dump	Displays a configuration script for settings within the context.
show	Shows all matching security associations.

Netsh Bridge

The Netsh Bridge context allows you to view and manage settings for network bridges. Table B-3 provides a summary of the available commands at this level.

Table B-3 Commands for the Netsh Bridge Context

Command	Description
dump	Displays a configuration script for settings within the context.
install	Installs the component corresponding to the current context.
set adapter	Modifies the bridge configuration for a specified adapter.
show adapter	Shows the adapters configured as a single bridge.
uninstall	Removes the component corresponding to the current context.

Netsh Dhcp

You use the Netsh Dhcp context and related subcontexts to manage the configuration of DHCP servers. Note that these contexts are only available when the DHCP Server role service is installed on a Windows server. Using the Dhcp command when the DHCP Server role service is not installed results in the Dhcpclient context being opened.

The Netsh Dhcp context supports the following commands:

- **server [\\ServerName or \\IPAddress]** Switches the context to the server specified
- **add server** Adds a DHCP server to the list of authorized servers in the directory service
- **delete server** Deletes a DHCP server from the list of authorized servers in the directory service
- **show server** Displays all the DHCP servers in the directory service for the current domain

Tables B-4, B-5, and B-6 provide a summary of the available commands for the Netsh Dhcp Server context, the Netsh Dhcp Server V4 context, and the Netsh Dhcp Server V6 context respectively.

Table B-4 Commands for the Netsh Dhcp Server Context

Command	Description
add class	Adds a class to the server.
add mscope	Adds a multicast scope to the server.
add optiondef	Adds a new option to the server.
add scope	Adds a scope to the server.
backup	Backs up the configuration.
delete class	Deletes a specific class from the server.
delete dnscredentials	Sets the credentials to use for DNS dynamic updates.
delete mscope	Deletes a multicast scope from the server.
delete optiondef	Deletes an option from the server.
delete optionvalue	Deletes an option value from the server.
delete scope	Deletes a scope from the server.
delete superscope	Deletes a superscope from the server.
dump	Dumps the configuration to a text file.
export	Exports the configuration to a file.
import	Imports the configuration from a file.

Table B-4 Commands for the Netsh Dhcp Server Context

Command	Description
initiate auth	Initiates retry authorization with the server.
initiate reconcile	Checks and reconciles the database for all scopes under the server.
mscope <mscope-name>	Switches to the mscope identified by the MScope name.
restore	Restores the configuration.
scope <scope-ip-address>	Switches to the scope identified by the IP address.
set auditlog	Sets audit log parameters for the server.
set bindings	Sets interface bindings for the server.
set databasebackupinterval	Sets the database backup interval of the current server.
set databasebackuppath	Sets the database backup path for the server.
set databasecleanupinterval	Sets the database cleanup interval.
set databaseloggingflag	Sets/resets the database logging flag.
set databasename	Sets the name of the server database file.
set databasepath	Sets the path of the server database file.
set databaserestoreflag	Sets/resets the database restore flag.
set detectconflictretry	Sets the number of conflict detection attempts by the DHCP server.
set dnsconfig	Sets the DNS dynamic update configuration for the server.
set dnscredentials	Sets the credentials to use for DNS dynamic updates.
set napdeffail	Sets the NAP default failure state of the server.
set napstate	Sets the NAP state of the server.
set optionvalue	Sets the global option value for the server.
set server	Sets the current server in the server mode.
set userclass	Sets the global user class name for subsequent operation.
set vendorclass	Sets the global vendor class name for subsequent operation.
show all	Displays all information for the server.
show auditlog	Display audit log parameters for the server.
show bindings	Display interface bindings for the server.
show class	Displays all available classes for the server.

Table B-4 Commands for the Netsh Dhcp Server Context

Command	Description
show dbproperties	Displays server database configuration information.
show detectconflictretry	Displays the detect conflict retry settings.
show dnsconfig	Displays the DNS dynamic update configuration for the server.
show dnscredentials	Displays the currently set DNS credentials.
show mibinfo	Displays MIBInfo for the server.
show mscope	Displays all multicast scopes for the server.
show napdeffail	Displays the NAP default failure state of the server.
show napstate	Displays the NAP state of the server.
show optiondef	Displays all options for the server.
show optionvalue	Displays all option values that are set for the server.
show scope	Displays all available scopes under the server.
show server	Displays the current server.
show serverstatus	Displays the current status for the server.
show superscope	Displays all available superscopes under the server.
show userclass	Displays the currently set user class name.
show vendorclass	Displays the currently set vendor class name.
show version	Displays the current version of the server.
V4	Changes to the "netsh dhcp server v4" context.
V6	Changes to the "netsh dhcp server v6" context.

Table B-5 Commands for the Netsh Dhcp Server V4 Context

Command	Description
add class	Adds a class to the server.
add mscope	Adds a multicast scope to the server.
add optiondef	Adds a new option to the server.
add scope	Adds a scope to the server.
delete class	Deletes a specific class from the server.
delete dnscredentials	Sets the credentials to use for DNS dynamic updates.
delete mscope	Deletes a multicast scope from the server.
delete optiondef	Deletes an option from the server.
delete optionvalue	Deletes an option value from the server.

Table B-5 Commands for the Netsh Dhcp Server V4 Context

Command	Description
delete scope	Deletes a scope from the server.
delete superscope	Deletes a superscope from the server.
dump	Dumps the configuration to a text file.
export	Exports the configuration to a file.
import	Imports the configuration from a file.
set bindings	Set interface bindings for the server.
set detectconflictretry	Sets the number of conflict detection attempts by the DHCP server.
set dnsconfig	Sets the DNS dynamic update configuration for the server.
set dnscredentials	Sets the credentials to use for DNS dynamic updates.
set napdeffail	Sets the NAP default failure state of the server.
set napstate	Sets the NAP state of the server.
set optionvalue	Sets the global option value for the server.
set userclass	Sets the global user class name for subsequent operation.
set vendorclass	Sets the global vendor class name for subsequent operation.
show all	Displays all information for the server.
show bindings	Display interface bindings for the server.
show class	Displays all available classes for the server.
show detectconflictretry	Displays the detect conflict retry settings.
show dnsconfig	Displays the DNS dynamic update configuration for the server.
show dnscredentials	Displays the currently set DNS credentials.
show mibinfo	Displays MIBInfo for the server.
show mscope	Displays all multicast scopes for the server.
show napdeffail	Displays the NAP default failure state of the server.
show napstate	Displays the NAP state of the server.
show optiondef	Displays all options for the server.
show optionvalue	Displays all option values that are set for the server.
show scope	Displays all available scopes under the server.
show superscope	Displays all available superscopes under the server.
show userclass	Displays the currently set user class name.
show vendorclass	Displays the currently set vendor class name.

Table B-6 Commands for the Netsh Dhcp Server V6 Context

Command	Description
add class	Adds a class to the server.
add optiondef	Adds a new DHCPv6 option to the server.
add scope	Adds a scope to the server.
delete class	Deletes a specific class from the server.
delete optiondef	Deletes an option from the server.
delete optionvalue	Deletes an option value from the server.
delete scope	Deletes a scope to the server.
dump	Dumps the configuration to a text file.
export	Exports the configuration to a file.
import	Imports the configuration from a file.
set bindings	Set interface bindings for the server.
set dnsconfig	Sets the DNS dynamic update configuration for the server.
set optionvalue	Sets the global option value for the server.
set preferredlifetime	Sets the preferred lifetime of an issued lease on the DHCP server.
set rapidcommitflag	Sets the global rapid commit flag for the server.
set t1	Sets the value of T1 of an issued lease on the DHCP server.
set t2	Sets the value of T2 of an issued lease on the DHCP server.
set unicastflag	Sets the global unicast flag for the server.
set userclass	Sets the global user class name for subsequent operation.
set vaildlifetime	Sets the valid lifetime of an issued lease on the DHCP server.
set vendorclass	Sets the global vendor class name for subsequent operation.
show bindings	Display interface bindings for the server.
show class	Displays all available classes for the server.
show dnsconfig	Displays the DNS dynamic update configuration for the server.
show mibinfo	Displays MIBInfo for the server.
show optiondef	Displays all DHCPv6 options for the server.
show optionvalue	Displays all option values that are set for the server.
show preferredlifetime	Displays the preferred lifetime.
show rapidcommitflag	Displays the rapid commit flag.

Table B-6 Commands for the Netsh Dhcp Server V6 Context

Command	Description
show scope	Displays all available scopes under the server.
show t1	Displays the T1 value of an issued lease.
show t2	Displays the T2 value of an issued lease.
show unicastflag	Displays the unicast flag.
show userclass	Displays the currently set user class name.
show validlifetime	Displays the valid lifetime.
show vendorclass	Displays the currently set vendor class name.

Netsh Dhcpclient

The Netsh Dchpclient context allows you to enable or disable tracing of DHCP communications. This context supports the following commands:

- **trace enable** Enables tracing for DHCP client and DHCP QEC
- **trace disable** Disables tracing for DHCP client and DHCP QEC

Netsh Firewall

You use the Netsh Firewall context to manage the Windows Firewall. Table B-7 provides a summary of the available commands at this level.

Table B-7 Commands for the Netsh Firewall Context

Command	Description
add allowedprogram	Adds firewall-allowed program configuration.
add portopening	Adds firewall port configuration.
delete allowedprogram	Deletes firewall-allowed program configuration.
delete portopening	Deletes firewall port configuration.
dump	Displays a configuration script for settings within the context.
reset	Resets firewall configuration to default.
set allowedprogram	Sets firewall-allowed program configuration.
set icmpsetting	Sets firewall ICMP configuration.
set logging	Sets firewall logging configuration.
set multicastbroad-castresponse	Sets firewall multicast/broadcast response configuration.
set notifications	Sets firewall notification configuration.

Table B-7 Commands for the Netsh Firewall Context

Command	Description
set opmode	Sets firewall operational configuration.
set portopening	Sets firewall port configuration.
set service	Sets firewall service configuration.
show allowedprogram	Shows firewall-allowed program configuration.
show config	Shows firewall configuration.
show currentprofile	Shows current firewall profile.
show icmpsetting	Shows firewall ICMP configuration.
show logging	Shows firewall logging configuration.
show multicastbroad-castresponse	Shows firewall multicast/broadcast response configuration.
show notifications	Shows firewall notification configuration.
show opmode	Shows firewall operational configuration.
show portopening	Shows firewall port configuration.
show service	Shows firewall service configuration.
show state	Shows current firewall state.

Netsh Http

You use the Netsh Http context to manage the configuration of HTTP listeners. Table B-8 provides a summary of the available commands at this level.

Table B-8 Commands for the Netsh Http Context

Command	Description
add iplisten	Adds an IP address to the IP listen list.
add sslcert	Adds an SSL server certificate binding for an IP address and port.
add timeout	Adds a global timeout to the service.
add urlacl	Adds a URL reservation entry.
delete cache	Deletes entries from the HTTP service kernel URI cache.
delete iplisten	Deletes an IP address from the IP listen list.
delete sslcert	Deletes SSL certificate bindings for an IP address and port.
delete timeout	Deletes a global timeout.
delete urlacl	Deletes a URL reservation.
dump	Displays a configuration script for settings within the context.

Table B-8 Commands for the Netsh Http Context

Command	Description
flush logbuffer	Flushes the internal buffers for the log files.
show cachestate	Lists cached URI resources and their associated properties.
show iplisten	Displays all the IP addresses in the IP listen list.
show servicestate	Shows a snapshot of the HTTP service.
show sslcert	Displays SSL certificate bindings for an IP address and port.
show timeout	Shows the timeout values of the service.
show urlacl	Displays URL namespace reservations.

Netsh Interface

The Netsh Interface context allows you to configure the computers network interfaces and IP addressing. As Table B-9 shows, this context provides access to many related subcontexts.

Table B-9 Commands for the Netsh Interface Context

Command	Description
6to4	Changes to the "netsh interface 6to4" context.
add interface	Adds an interface to the router.
delete interface	Deletes an interface from the router.
dump	Displays a configuration script for settings within the context.
ipv4	Changes to the "netsh interface ipv4" context.
ipv6	Changes to the "netsh interface ipv6" context.
isatap	Changes to the "netsh interface isatap" context.
portproxy	Changes to the "netsh interface portproxy" context.
reset all	Resets information.
set credentials	Sets the credentials used to connect an interface.
set interface	Sets interface parameters.
show credentials	Shows the credentials used to connect an interface.
show interface	Displays interfaces.
tcp	Changes to the "netsh interface tcp" context.
teredo	Changes to the "netsh interface teredo" context.

Tables B-10 and B-11 summarize the commands available for configuring network interfaces for IPv4 and IPv6 respectively. Table B-12 provides a summary for other Netsh Interface subcontexts.

Table B-10 Commands for the Netsh Interface IPv4 Context

Command	Description
add address	Adds a static IP address or default gateway to the specified interface.
add dnsserver	Adds a static DNS server address.
add neighbors	Adds a neighbor address.
add route	Adds a route over an interface.
add winsserver	Adds a static WINS server address.
delete address	Deletes an IP address or default gateway from the specified interface.
delete arpcache	Flushes the ARP cache for one or all interfaces.
delete destinationcache	Deletes the destination cache.
delete dnsserver	Deletes the DNS server from the specified interface.
delete neighbors	Deletes the neighbor cache.
delete route	Deletes a route.
delete winsserver	Deletes the WINS server from the specified interface.
dump	Displays a configuration script for settings within the context.
install	Installs the IP protocol.
reset	Resets the IP configurations.
set address	Sets the IP address or default gateway to an interface.
set compartment	Modifies compartment configuration parameters.
set dnsserver	Sets DNS server mode and addresses.
set dynamicportrange	Modifies the range of ports used for dynamic port assignment.
set global	Modifies global configuration general parameters.
set interface	Modifies interface configuration parameters for IP.
set neighbors	Sets a neighbor address.
set route	Modifies route parameters.
set subinterface	Modifies subinterface configuration parameters.
set winsserver	Sets WINS server mode and addresses.
show addresses	Shows IP address configurations.
show compartments	Shows compartment parameters.
show config	Displays IP address and additional information.

Table B-10 Commands for the Netsh Interface IPv4 Context

Command	Description
show destinationcache	Shows destination cache entries.
show dnsservers	Displays the DNS server addresses.
show dynamicportrange	Shows dynamic port range configuration parameters.
show global	Shows global configuration parameters.
show icmpstats	Displays ICMP statistics.
show interfaces	Shows interface parameters.
show ipaddresses	Shows current IP addresses.
show ipnettomedia	Displays IP net-to-media mappings.
show ipstats	Displays IP statistics.
show joins	Displays multicast groups joined.
show neighbors	Shows neighbor cache entries.
show offload	Displays the offload information.
show route	Shows route table entries.
show subinterfaces	Shows subinterface parameters.
show tcpconnections	Displays TCP connections.
show tcpstats	Displays TCP statistics.
show udpconnections	Displays UDP connections.
show udpstats	Displays UDP statistics.
show winsservers	Displays the WINS server addresses.
uninstall	Uninstall the IP protocol.

Table B-11 Commands for the Netsh Interface IPv6 Context

Command	Description
6to4	Changes to the "netsh interface ipv6 6to4" context.
add address	Adds a static IP address or default gateway to the specified interface.
add dnsserver	Adds a static DNS server address.
add neighbors	Adds a neighbor address.
add potentialrouter	Adds a router to the potential router list on an interface.
add prefixpolicy	Adds a prefix policy entry.
add route	Adds a route over an interface.

Table B-11 Commands for the Netsh Interface IPv6 Context

Command	Description
add v6v4tunnel	Creates an IPv6-in-IPv4 point-to-point tunnel.
delete address	Deletes an IP address or default gateway from the specified interface.
delete destinationcache	Deletes the destination cache.
delete dnsserver	Deletes the DNS server from the specified interface.
delete interface	Deletes an interface from the IPv6 stack.
delete neighbors	Deletes the neighbor cache.
delete potentialrouter	Deletes a router from the potential router list on an interface.
delete prefixpolicy	Deletes a prefix policy entry.
delete route	Deletes a route.
dump	Displays a configuration script for settings within the context.
isatap	Changes to the "netsh interface ipv6 isatap" context.
reset	Resets the IP configurations.
set address	Sets the IP address or default gateway to an interface.
set compartment	Modifies compartment configuration parameters.
set dnsserver	Sets DNS server mode and addresses.
set dynamicportrange	Modifies the range of ports used for dynamic port assignment.
set global	Modifies global configuration general parameters.
set interface	Modifies interface configuration parameters for IP.
set neighbors	Sets a neighbor address.
set prefixpolicy	Modifies prefix policy information.
set privacy	Modifies privacy configuration parameters.
set route	Modifies route parameters.
set subinterface	Modifies subinterface configuration parameters.
set teredo	Sets Teredo state.
show addresses	Shows current IP addresses.
show compartments	Shows compartment parameters.
show destinationcache	Shows destination cache entries.
show dnsservers	Displays the DNS server addresses.

Table B-11 Commands for the Netsh Interface IPv6 Context

Command	Description
show dynamicportrange	Shows dynamic port range configuration parameters.
show global	Shows global configuration parameters.
show interfaces	Shows interface parameters.
show ipstats	Displays IP statistics.
show joins	Displays multicast groups joined.
show neighbors	Shows neighbor cache entries.
show offload	Displays the offload information.
show potentialrouters	Shows potential routers.
show prefixpolicies	Shows prefix policy entries.
show privacy	Shows privacy configuration parameters.
show route	Shows route table entries.
show siteprefixes	Shows site prefix table entries.
show subinterfaces	Shows subinterface parameters.
show tcpstats	Displays TCP statistics.
show teredo	Shows Teredo state.
show udpstats	Displays UDP statistics.

Table B-12 Commands for Other Subcontexts of Netsh Interface

Context/Command	Description
netsh interface 6to4	
dump	Displays a configuration script for settings within the context.
set interface	Sets 6to4 interface configuration information.
set relay	Sets 6to4 relay information.
set routing	Sets 6to4 routing information.
set state	Sets the 6to4 state.
show interface	Shows the 6to4 interface configuration information.
show relay	Shows the 6to4 relay information.
show routing	Shows the 6to4 routing state.
state	Shows the 6to4 state.

Table B-12 Commands for Other Subcontexts of Netsh Interface

Context/Command	Description
netsh interface ipv6 6to4	
dump	Displays a configuration script for settings within the context.
set interface	Sets 6to4 interface configuration information.
set relay	Sets 6to4 relay information.
set routing	Sets 6to4 routing information.
set state	Sets the 6to4 state.
show interface	Shows the 6to4 interface configuration information.
show relay	Shows the 6to4 relay information.
show routing	Shows the 6to4 routing information.
show state	Shows the 6to4 state.
netsh interface ipv6 isatap	
dump	Displays a configuration script for settings within the context.
set router	Sets ISATAP router information.
set state	Sets ISATAP state.
show router	Shows the ISATAP router information.
show state	Shows the ISATAP state.
netsh interface isatap	
dump	Displays a configuration script for settings within the context.
set router	Sets ISATAP router information.
set state	Sets ISATAP state.
show router	Shows the ISATAP router information.
show state	Shows the ISATAP state.
netsh interface portproxy	
add v4tov4	Adds an entry to listen on for IPv4 and proxy connect to via IPv4.
add v4tov6	Adds an entry to listen on for IPv4 and proxy connect to via IPv6.
add v6tov4	Adds an entry to listen on for IPv6 and proxy connect to via IPv4.

Table B-12 Commands for Other Subcontexts of Netsh Interface

Context/Command	Description
add v6tov6	Adds an entry to listen on for IPv6 and proxy connect to via IPv6.
delete v4tov4	Deletes an entry to listen on for IPv4 and proxy connect to via IPv4.
delete v4tov6	Deletes an entry to listen on for IPv4 and proxy connect to via IPv6.
delete v6tov4	Deletes an entry to listen on for IPv6 and proxy connect to via IPv4.
delete v6tov6	Deletes an entry to listen on for IPv6 and proxy connect to via IPv6.
dump	Displays a configuration script for settings within the context.
reset	Resets portproxy configuration state.
set v4tov4	Updates an entry to listen on for IPv4 and proxy connect to via IPv4.
set v4tov6	Updates an entry to listen on for IPv4 and proxy connect to via IPv6.
set v6tov4	Updates an entry to listen on for IPv6 and proxy connect to via IPv4.
set v6tov6	Updates an entry to listen on for IPv6 and proxy connect to via IPv6.
show all	Shows all port proxy parameters.
show v4tov4	Shows parameters for proxying IPv4 connections to another IPv4 port.
show v4tov6	Shows parameters for proxying IPv4 connections to IPv6.
show v6tov4	Shows parameters for proxying IPv6 connections to IPv4.
show v6tov6	Shows parameters for proxying IPv6 connections to another IPv6 port.
netsh interface tcp	
add chimney-application	Adds an application to the TCP Chimney offload table.
add chimneyport	Adds a port filter to the TCP Chimney offload table for the specified local source port and the specified remote destination port.
delete chimneyapplication	Deletes a TCP chimney application from the offload table.
delete chimneyport	Deletes a TCP chimney port entry from the offload table.

Table B-12 Commands for Other Subcontexts of Netsh Interface

Context/Command	Description
dump	Displays a configuration script for settings within the context.
reset	Resets all TCP parameters to their default values.
set global	Sets global TCP parameters.
show chimney-applications	Shows applications in the TCP chimney offload table.
show chimneyports	Shows ports in the TCP chimney offload table.
show global	Shows global TCP parameters.
netsh interface teredo	
dump	Displays a configuration script for settings within the context.
set state	Sets Teredo state.
show state	Shows Teredo state.

Netsh Ipsec

You use the Netsh Ipsec context and its related subcontexts to configure Internet Protocol Security (IPsec). Table B-13 provides a summary of the available commands for this context and all related subcontexts.

Table B-13 Commands for Netsh Ipsec, Netsh Ipsec Dynamic, and Netsh Ipsec Static

Context/Command	Description
netsh ipsec	
dump	Displays a configuration script for settings within the context.
dynamic	Changes to the "netsh ipsec dynamic" context.
static	Changes to the "netsh ipsec static" context.
netsh ipsec dynamic	
add mmpolicy	Adds a main-mode policy to SPD.
add qmpolicy	Adds a quick-mode policy to SPD.
add rule	Adds a rule and associated filters to SPD.
delete all	Deletes all policies, filters, and actions from SPD.
delete mmpolicy	Deletes a main-mode policy from SPD.
delete qmpolicy	Deletes a quick-mode policy from SPD.
delete rule	Deletes a rule and associated filters from SPD.
delete sa	Deletes a security association.

Table B-13 Commands for Netsh Ipsec, Netsh Ipsec Dynamic, and Netsh Ipsec Static

Context/Command	Description
dump	Displays a configuration script for settings within the context.
set config	Sets the IPsec configuration and boot time behavior.
set mmpolicy	Modifies a main-mode policy in SPD.
set qmpolicy	Modifies a quick-mode policy in SPD.
set rule	Modifies a rule and associated filters in SPD.
show all	Displays policies, filters, SAs, and statistics from SPD.
show config	Displays IPsec configuration.
show mmfilter	Displays main-mode filter details from SPD.
show mmpolicy	Displays main-mode policy details from SPD.
show mmsas	Displays main-mode security associations from SPD.
show qmfilter	Displays quick-mode filter details from SPD.
show qmpolicy	Displays quick-mode policy details from SPD.
show qmsas	Displays quick-mode security associations from SPD.
show rule	Displays rule details from SPD.
show stats	Displays IPsec and IKE statistics from SPD.
netsh ipsec static	
add filter	Adds a filter to filter list.
add filteraction	Creates a filter action.
add filterlist	Creates an empty filter list.
add policy	Creates a policy with a default response rule.
add rule	Creates a rule for the specified policy.
delete all	Deletes all policies, filter lists, and filter actions.
delete filter	Deletes a filter from a filter list.
delete filteraction	Deletes a filter action.
delete filterlist	Deletes a filter list.
delete policy	Deletes a policy and its rules.
delete rule	Deletes a rule from a policy.
dump	Displays a configuration script for settings within the context.
exportpolicy	Exports all the policies from the policy store.

Table B-13 Commands for Netsh Ipsec, Netsh Ipsec Dynamic, and Netsh Ipsec Static

Context/Command	Description
importpolicy	Imports the policies from a file to the policy store.
set batch	Sets the batch update mode.
set defaultrule	Modifies the default response rule of a policy.
set filteraction	Modifies a filter action.
set filterlist	Modifies a filter list.
set policy	Modifies a policy.
set rule	Modifies a rule.
set store	Sets the current policy store.
show all	Displays details of all policies and related information.
show filteraction	Displays filter action details.
show filterlist	Displays filter list details.
show gpoassignedpolicy	Displays details of a group assigned policy.
show policy	Displays policy details.
show rule	Displays rule details.
show store	Displays the current policy store.

Netsh Lan

When the Wired AutoConfig Service is enabled, the Netsh Lan context allows you to view and manage automatically configured wired interfaces and their related profiles and settings. Table B-14 provides a summary of the available commands at this level.

Table B-14 Commands for the Netsh Lan Context

Command	Description
add profile	Adds a LAN profile to specified interface on the computer.
delete profile	Deletes a LAN profile from one or multiple interfaces.
dump	Displays a configuration script for settings within the context.
export	Saves LAN profiles to XML files.
reconnect	Reconnects on an interface.
set autoconfig	Enables or disables auto-configuration on an interface.
set profileparameter	Configure authentication and sign on settings for wireless profiles.
set tracing	Enables or disables tracing.
show interfaces	Shows a list of the current wired interfaces on the system.

Table B-14 Commands for the Netsh Lan Context

Command	Description
show profiles	Shows a list of wired profiles currently configured on the computer.
show settings	Shows the current global settings of wired LAN.
show tracing	Shows whether wired LAN tracing is enabled or disabled.

Netsh Nap

You use the Netsh Nap context to manage the Network Access Protection (NAP) configuration. Table B-15 provides a summary of the available commands at this level and for the related Client and Hra subcontexts.

Table B-15 Commands for Netsh Nap and Related Subcontexts

Command	Description
netsh nap	
client	Changes to the "netsh nap client" context.
dump	Displays a configuration script for settings within the context.
hra	Changes to the "netsh nap hra" context.
reset configuration	Resets the NAP configuration.
show configuration	Shows the NAP configuration.
netsh nap client	
add server	Adds trusted server configuration.
add trustedservergroup	Adds trusted server group configuration.
delete server	Deletes trusted server configuration.
delete trustedservergroup	Deletes trusted server group configuration.
dump	Displays a configuration script for settings within the context.
export	Exports configuration settings.
import	Imports configuration settings.
rename server	Renames the URL of an existing trusted server in a trusted server group.
rename trustedservergroup	Renames a trusted server group.
reset configuration	Resets the NAP client configuration.
reset csp	Resets the CSP configuration.

Table B-15 Commands for Netsh Nap and Related Subcontexts

Command	Description
reset enforcement	Resets the enforcement configuration.
reset hash	Resets the hash configuraiton.
reset server	Resets the trusted server configuration.
reset trustedserver-group	Resets the trusted server group configuration.
reset userinterface	Resets the user interface configuration.
set csp	Sets CSP configuration.
set enforcement	Sets enforcement configuration.
set hash	Sets hash configuration.
set server	Sets trusted server configuration.
set tracing	Sets tracing configuration.
set userinterface	Sets user interface configuration.
show configuration	Shows configuration.
show csps	Shows CSP configuration.
show grouppolicy	Shows Group Policy configuration.
show hashes	Shows hash configuration.
show state	Shows state.
show trustedserver-group	Shows all trusted server groups.
netsh nap hra	
add asymmetrickey	Adds asymmetric key configuration.
add caserver	Adds CA server configuration.
add csp	Adds CSP configuration.
add hash	Adds hash configuration.
add useragent	Adds user agent configuration.
delete asymmet-rickey	Deletes asymmetric key aconfiguration.
delete caserver	Deletes CA server configuration.
delete csp	Deletes CSP configuration.
delete hash	Deletes hash configuration.
delete useragent	Deletes a user agent.

Table B-15 Commands for Netsh Nap and Related Subcontexts

Command	Description
dump	Displays a configuration script for settings within the context.
export	Exports configuration settings.
import	Imports configuration settings.
rename caserver	Renames CA server configuration.
reset asymmetrickey	Resets asymmetric key configuration.
reset caserver	Resets CA server configuration.
reset configuration	Resets configuration.
reset csp	Resets CSP configuration.
reset hash	Resets hash configuration.
reset opmode	Resets current mode of HRA.
reset templates	Resets HRA Certificate Template Configurations.
reset timeout	Resets timeout configuration.
reset usepolicyOIDs	Resets Policy OIDs configuration.
reset useragent	Resets user agent configuration.
reset validityperiod	Resets HRA Validity Period.
set caserver	Sets CA server configuration.
set opmode	Sets HRA mode.
set templates	Sets HRA Certificate Template Configurations.
set timeout	Sets timeout configuration.
set usepolicyOIDs	Sets Policy OIDs configuration.
set validityperiod	Sets how long a certificate is good for in minutes.
show asymmetrick-eys	Shows asymmetric keys.
show configuration	Shows configuration.
show csps	Shows CSPs.
show hashes	Shows hashes.

Netsh Netio

The Netsh Netio context allows you to add, delete, and list network binding filters. The available commands are:

- **add bindingfilter** Adds a binding filter
- **delete bindingfilter** Deletes a binding filter

- **dump** Displays a configuration script
- **show bindingfilters** Shows all binding filters

Netsh Nps

You use the Netsh Nps context to manage the configuration of a Network Policy Server (NPS). In Windows Server 2008, NPS replaces Internet Authentication Service (IAS) in Windows Server 2003. Table B-16 provides a summary of the available commands at this level.

Table B-16 Commands for Netsh Nps

Command	Description
add client	Adds client configuration.
add crp	Adds connection request policy configuration.
add np	Adds network policy configuration.
add registeredserver	Registers an NPS Server in Active Directory.
add remediationserver	Adds remediation server configuration.
add remediationserver-group	Adds remediation server group configuration.
add remoteserver	Adds remote server configuration.
add remoteservergroup	Adds remote server group configuration.
add shvtemplate	Adds health policy configuration.
delete client	Deletes client configuration.
delete crp	Deletes connection request policy configuration.
delete np	Deletes network policy configuration.
delete registeredserver	Unregisters an NPS Server in Active Directory.
delete remediationserver	Deletes remediation server configuration.
delete remediationserver-group	Deletes remediation server group configuration.
delete remoteserver	Deletes remote server configuration.
delete remoteservergroup	Deletes remote server group configuration.
delete shvtemplate	Deletes health policy configuration.
dump	Displays a configuration script for settings within the context.
export	Exports configuration.
import	Imports configuration.

Table B-16 Commands for Netsh Nps

Command	Description
rename client	Renames client configuration.
rename crp	Renames connection request policy configuration.
rename np	Renames network policy configuration.
rename remediationserver	Renames remediation server configuration.
rename remediationserver-group	Renames remediation server group configuration.
rename remoteserver	Renames remote server configuration.
rename remoteservergroup	Renames remote server group configuration.
rename shvtemplate	Renames health policy configuration.
reset client	Resets client configuration.
reset config	Resets configuration.
reset crp	Resets connection request policy configuration.
reset eventlog	Resets event log configuration.
reset filelog	Resets file log configuration.
reset np	Resets network policy configuration.
reset ports	Resets port configuration.
reset remediationserver	Resets remediation server configuration.
reset remediationserver-group	Resets remediation server group configuration.
reset remoteserver	Resets remote server configuration.
reset remoteservergroup	Resets remote server group configuration.
reset shv	Resets system health validator configuration.
reset shvtemplate	Resets health policy configuration.
reset sqllog	Resets SQL log configuration.
set client	Sets client configuration.
set crp	Sets connection request policy configuration.
set eventlog	Sets event log configuration.
set filelog	Sets file log configuration.
set np	Sets network policy configuration.
set ports	Sets port configuration.
set remediationserver	Sets remediation server configuration.

Table B-16 Commands for Netsh Nps

Command	Description
set remoteserver	Sets remote server configuration.
set shv	Sets system health validator configuration.
set shvtemplate	Sets health policy configuration.
set sqllog	Sets SQL log configuration.
show client	Shows client configuration.
show config	Shows configuration.
show crp	Shows connection request policy configuration.
show crpconditionattributes	Shows all available connection request policy condition attributes.
show crpprofileattributes	Shows all available connection request policy profile attributes.
show eventlog	Shows event log configuration.
show filelog	Shows file log configuration.
show napserverinfo	Shows NAP server information.
show np	Shows network policy configuration.
show npconditionattributes	Shows all available network policy condition attributes.
show npprofileattributes	Shows all available network policy profile attributes.
show ports	Shows port configuration.
show registeredserver	Shows the registration of an NPS Server in Active Directory
show remediationserver	Shows remediation server configuration.
show remediationserver-group	Shows remediation server group configuration.
show remoteserver	Shows remote server configuration.
show remoteservergroup	Shows remote server group configuration.
show shv	Shows system health validator configuration.
show shvtemplate	Shows health policy configuration.
show sqllog	Shows SQL log configuration.
show vendors	Shows all available vendors.

Netsh P2p

You use the Netsh P2p context and its related subcontexts to manage the Peer-To-Peer (P2P) networking configuration. Table B-17 provides a summary of the available commands at this level and for the many related subcontexts.

Table B-17 Commands for Netsh P2p and Related Subcontexts

Context/Command	Description
netsh p2p	
collab	Changes to the "netsh p2p collab" context.
dump	Displays a configuration script for settings within the context.
group	Changes to the "netsh p2p group" context.
idmgr	Changes to the "netsh p2p idmgr" context.
pnrp	Changes to the "netsh p2p pnrp" context.
netsh p2p collab	
contact	Changes to the "netsh p2p collab contact" context.
dump	Displays a configuration script for settings within the context.
netsh p2p collab contact	
delete	Deletes a contact from the contact store.
dump	Displays a configuration script for settings within the context.
export	Exports the Me contact (representing the current user) to a file.
import	Imports a contact to the contact store.
set	Changes contact data.
show contacts	Shows contact data.
show xml	Shows content of contact XML file.
netsh p2p group	
database	Changes to the "netsh p2p group database" context.
dump	Displays a configuration script for settings within the context.
gping	Checks for connectivity to the remote group port.
resolve	Resolves a participant in the group and lists its address.
show acl	Lists access control list (ACL) information.
show address	Resolves a participant in the current node and lists its address.

Table B-17 Commands for Netsh P2p and Related Subcontexts

Context/Command	Description
netsh p2p group database	
dump	Displays a configuration script for settings within the context.
show statistics	Lists database stats for given <identity P2PID> <group P2PID>.
netsh p2p idmgr	
delete group	Deletes groups from identities.
delete identity	Deletes identities.
dump	Displays a configuration script for settings within the context.
show groups	Displays identities and group list.
show identities	Displays identity list.
show statistics	Displays identity statistics.
netsh p2p pnrp	
cloud	Changes to the "netsh p2p pnrp cloud" context.
diagnostics	Changes to the "netsh p2p pnrp diagnostics" context.
dump	Displays a configuration script for settings within the context.
peer	Changes to the "netsh p2p pnrp peer" context.
netsh p2p pnrp cloud	
dump	Displays a configuration script for settings within the context.
flush	Flushes cache entries.
repair	Starts split detection and repair.
set pnrpmode	Modifies PNRP mode configuration parameter.
set seed	Modifies PNRP SeedServer configuration parameter.
show initialization	Displays cloud bootstrap configuration/status.
show list	Displays list of clouds.
show names	Displays locally registered names.
show pnrpmode	Displays PNRP mode configuration parameter.
show seed	Displays PNRP SeedServer configuration parameter.
show statistics	Displays cloud statistics.
start	Starts a P2P networking cloud
synchronize host	Synchronizes a cloud with a specified host.

Table B-17 Commands for Netsh P2p and Related Subcontexts

Context/Command	Description
synchronize seed	Synchronizes a cloud with its seed server.
netsh p2p pnrp diagnostics	
dump	Displays a configuration script for settings within the context.
ping	Pings PNRP nodes.
netsh p2p pnrp peer	
add registration	Registers a peer name.
delete registration	Unregisters peer names.
dump	Displays a configuration script for settings within the context.
enumerate	Enumerates a peer name in the specified cloud.
resolve	Resolves a peer name.
set machinename	Sets configuration information for the PnrpAutoReg service.
show convertedname	Converts from peer names to DNS names and vice versa.
show machinename	Shows configuration information for the PNRP machine name publication service.
show registration	Lists registered peer names.
traceroute	Resolves a peer name with path tracing.

Netsh Ras

You use the Netsh Ras context to manage the configuration of the Remote Access Service (RAS) and the Routing And Remote Access Service (RRAS). Table B-18 provides a summary of the available commands at this level.

Table B-18 Commands for the Netsh Ras Context

Command	Description
aaaa	Changes to the "netsh ras aaaa" context.
add authtype	Adds types of authentication the Remote Access server will negotiate.
add link	Adds to the list of link properties PPP will negotiate.
add multilink	Adds to the list of multilink types PPP will negotiate.
add registered-server	Registers the given Windows computer as a Remote Access server in the Active Directory of the given domain.
delete authtype	Deletes an authentication type from the Remote Access server.
delete link	Deletes from the list of link properties PPP will negotiate.

Table B-18 Commands for the Netsh Ras Context

Command	Description
delete multilink	Deletes from the list of multilink types PPP will negotiate.
delete regis-teredserver	Unregisters the given Windows computer as a Remote Access server in the Active Directory of the given domain.
demanddial	Changes to the "netsh ras demanddial" context.
diagnostics	Changes to the "netsh ras diagnostics" context.
dump	Displays a configuration script for settings within the context.
ip	Changes to the "netsh ras ip" context.
ipv6	Changes to the "netsh ras ipv6" context.
set authmode	Sets the authentication mode.
set client	Reset the statistics or disconnect a Remote Access client.
set conf	Sets the configuration state of the server.
set portstatus	Resets the statistics information of RAS ports.
set type	Sets the Router and RAS functionalities of the computer.
set user	Sets the Remote Access properties of a user.
show activeservers	Shows active RAS servers by listing for Remote Access Server advertisements.
show authmode	Shows the authentication mode.
show authtype	Displays the authentication types currently enabled.
show client	Shows Remote Access clients connected to this computer and their status.
show conf	Shows the configuration state of the server.
show link	Shows the link properties PPP will negotiate.
show multilink	Shows the multilink types PPP will negotiate.
show portstatus	Shows the current status of RAS ports.
show regis-teredserver	Displays whether a computer is registered as a Remote Access server in the Active Directory of the given domain.
show status	Shows the status of the Routing And Remote Access Server.
show type	Shows the router and RAS functionalities of the computer.
show user	Displays Remote Access properties for a user(s).

Tables B-19, B-20, and B-21 provide a summary of the available commands for the Netsh Ras Aaaa context, the Netsh Ras Demanddial context, and the Netsh Ras Diagnostics context, respectively. Two additional contexts, Netsh Ras Ip and Netsh Ras Ipv6, are summarized in Table B-22.

Table B-19 Commands for the Netsh Ras Aaaa context

Command	Description
add acctserver	Adds a RADIUS accounting server.
add authserver	Adds a RADIUS authentication server.
delete acctserver	Deletes a RADIUS accounting server.
delete authserver	Deletes a RADIUS server.
dump	Displays a configuration script for settings within the context.
set accounting	Sets the accounting provider.
set acctserver	Sets properties of an accounting server.
set authentication	Sets the authentication provider.
set authserver	Sets properties of an authentication server.
set ipsecpolicy	Sets the IPsec policy for L2TP connection.
show accounting	Displays the current accounting provider.
show acctserver	Displays the RADIUS server(s) used for accounting.
show authentication	Displays the current authentication provider.
show authserver	Displays the RADIUS server(s) used for authentication.
show ipsecpolicy	Shows the IPsec policy for L2TP connection.

Table B-20 Commands for the Netsh Ras Demanddial context

Command	Description
add interface	Adds a new demand dial interface.
delete interface	Deletes a demand dial interface.
dump	Displays a configuration script for settings within the context.
set callbackdevice	Sets the callback number of the callback device for demand dial interfaces.
set credentials	Sets the dial out credentials for a demand dial interface.
set interface	Sets the option settings for a demand dial interface.
set ppp	Sets the PPP options for a demand dial interface.
set security	Sets the security options for a demand dial interface.
show callback-device	Shows the callback number of the callback device for demand dial interfaces.
show interface	Shows the settings for a demand dial interface.
show ppp	Shows the PPP options for a demand dial interface.
show security	Shows the security options of a demand dial interface.

Table B-21 Commands for the Netsh Ras Diagnostics context

Command	Description
dump	Displays a configuration script for settings within the context.
set cmtracing	Enables/disables Connection Manager logging.
set loglevel	Sets the global log level for RRAS.
set modemtracing	Enables or disables tracing of modem settings and messages during a network connection.
set rastracing	Enables/disables extended tracing for a component.
set security-eventlog	Enables or disables Security Event logging. You can view Security Event logs using Event Viewer.
set trace-facilities	Enables/disables extended tracing for all components.
show all	Generates an extensive Remote Access diagnostics report.
show cmtracing	Shows whether Connection Manager logging is enabled.
show configuration	Displays configuration information.
show installation	Displays installation information.
show loglevel	Shows the global log level for RRAS
show logs	Shows all logs.
show modemtracing	Shows whether tracing of modem settings and messages during a network connection is enabled.
show rastracing	Shows whether extended tracing is enabled for components.
show securityeventlog	Shows whether Security Event logs are enabled.
show tracefacilities	Shows whether extended tracing is enabled for all components.

Table B-22 Commands for the Netsh Ras Ip and Netsh Ras Ipv6 contexts

Context/Command	Description
netsh ras ip	
add range	Adds a range to the static IP address pool.
delete pool	Deletes all ranges from the static IP address pool.
delete range	Deletes a range from the static IP address pool.
dump	Displays a configuration script for settings within the context.
set access	Sets whether clients are given access beyond the remote access server.

Table B-22 Commands for the Netsh Ras Ip and Netsh Ras Ipv6 contexts

Context/Command	Description
set addrassign	Sets the method by which the Remote Access server assigns IP addresses to its clients.
set addrreq	Sets whether clients can request their own IP addresses.
set broadcastnameresolution	Sets whether to enable or disable broadcast name resolution using NetBIOS over TCP/IP.
set negotiation	Sets whether IP is negotiated for client Remote Access connections.
set preferredadapter	Specifies the preferred adapter for Routing And Remote Access Service.
show config	Displays current Remote Access IP configuration.
show preferredadapter	Shows the preferred adapter for Routing And Remote Access Service.
netsh ras ipv6	
dump	Displays a configuration script for settings within the context.
set access	Sets whether clients are given access beyond the remote access server.
set negotiation	Sets whether IPv6 is negotiated for client Remote Access connections.
set prefix	Sets the prefix that RAS server uses.
show config	Displays current Remote Access IPv6 configuration.

Netsh Routing

You use the Netsh Routing context to manage the configuration of IP routing when you configure a software router as part of the Routing And Remote Access Service (RRAS). Table B-23 provides a summary of the available commands at this level and for the Routing Demanddial subcontext. Table B-24 summarizes the Routing Ip subcontext.

Table B-23 Commands for Netsh Routing and Netsh Routing Demanddial

Context/Command	Description
netsh routing	
demanddial	Changes to the "netsh routing demanddial" context.
dump	Displays a configuration script for settings within the context.
Ip	Changes to the "netsh routing ip" context.
ipv6	Changes to the "netsh routing ipv6" context.
reset	Resets IP routing to a clean state.

Table B-23 Commands for Netsh Routing and Netsh Routing Demanddial

Context/Command	Description
netsh routing demanddial	
add interface	Adds a new demand dial interface.
delete interface	Deletes a demand dial interface.
dump	Displays a configuration script for settings within the context.
set callbackdevice	Sets the callback number of the callback device for demand dial interfaces.
set credentials	Sets the dial out credentials for a demand dial interface.
set interface	Sets the option settings for a demand dial interface.
set ppp	Sets the PPP options for a demand dial interface.
set security	Sets the security options for a demand dial interface.
show callbackdevice	Shows the callback number of the callback device for demand dial interfaces.
show interface	Shows the settings for a demand dial interface.
show ppp	Shows the PPP options for a demand dial interface.
show security	Shows the security options of a demand dial interface.

Table B-24 Commands for the Netsh Routing Ip Context

Command	Description
add boundary	Adds a multicast scope boundary on an interface.
add filter	Adds a packet filter to a specified interface.
add interface	Enables IP forwarding on an interface.
add persistentroute	Adds a persistent static route.
add preferenceforprotocol	Adds a preference level for a routing protocol.
add rtmroute	Adds a nonpersistent (NetMgmt) route.
add scope	Adds a multicast scope.
autodhcp	Changes to the "netsh routing ip autodhcp" context.
delete boundary	Deletes a multicast scope boundary from an interface.
delete filter	Deletes a filter from a specified interface.
delete interface	Deletes IP forwarding on a specified interface.
delete persistentroute	Deletes a persistent static route.

Table B-24 Commands for the Netsh Routing Ip Context

Command	Description
delete preferencefor-protocol	Deletes preference for a specified protocol.
delete rtmroute	Deletes a nonpersistent route used for network management.
delete scope	Deletes a multicast scope.
dnsproxy	Changes to the "netsh routing ip dnsproxy" context.
dump	Displays a configuration script for settings within the context.
igmp	Changes to the "netsh routing ip igmp" context.
nat	Changes to the "netsh routing ip nat" context.
relay	Changes to the "netsh routing ip relay" context.
reset	Resets IP routing to a clean state.
rip	Changes to the "netsh routing ip rip" context.
routerdiscovery	Changes to the "netsh routing ip routerdiscovery" context.
set filter	Changes filter attributes on the specified interface.
set interface	Sets the interface state.
set loglevel	Sets the global logging level.
set persistentroute	Modifies a persistent static route.
set preferenceforprotocol	Sets the preference level for the specified protocol.
set rtmroute	Modifies a nonpersistent netmgmt route.
set scope	Sets the name of a multicast scope.
set updateroutes	Updates the Routing information for a specified or all interfaces.
show boundary	Displays the configured multicast scope boundaries.
show boundarystats	Displays IP multicast boundaries
show filter	Displays packet filter information.
show interface	Displays interface information.
show loglevel	Displays the global logging level.
show mfe	Displays multicast forwarding entries
show mfestats	Displays multicast forwarding entry statistics
show persistentroutes	Displays persistent static routes.
show preferencefor-protocol	Displays preference levels for all protocols.
show protocol	Displays all configured IP protocols.

Table B-24 Commands for the Netsh Routing Ip Context

Command	Description
show rtmdestinations	Displays destinations in the routing table.
show rtmroutes	Displays routes in the routing table.
show scope	Displays the multicast scopes configured on the router.
update	Updates auto-static routes on an interface.

Tables B-25, B-26, B-27, and B-28 provide a summary of the available commands for additional subcontexts of Netsh Routing Ip. Table B-25 summarizes the Netsh Routing Ip Autodhcp and Netsh Routing Ip Dnsproxy contexts. Table B-26 summarizes the Netsh Routing Ip Igmp and Netsh Routing Ip Nat contexts. Table B-27 summarizes the Netsh Routing Ip Relay and Netsh Routing Ip Rip contexts. Table B-28 summarizes the Netsh Routing Ip Routerdiscovery, Netsh Routing Ipv6, and Netsh Routing Ipv6, Relayv6 contexts.

Table B-25 Commands for Netsh Routing Ip Autodhcp and Netsh Routing Ip Dnsproxy

Context/Command	Description
netsh routing ip autodhcp	
add exclusion	Adds an exclusion to the DHCP allocator scope.
delete exclusion	Deletes an exclusion from the DHCP allocator scope.
dump	Displays a configuration script for settings within the context.
install	Installs the routing protocol corresponding to the current context.
set global	Changes global DHCP allocator parameters.
set interface	Changes DHCP allocator parameters for an interface.
show global	Shows DHCP allocator configuration.
show interface	Shows DHCP allocator configuration for the specified interface.
uninstall	Removes the routing protocol corresponding to the current context.
netsh routing ip dnsproxy	
dump	Displays a configuration script for settings within the context.
install	Installs the routing protocol corresponding to the current context.
set global	Sets global DNS proxy parameters.
set interface	Sets DNS proxy parameters for an interface.

Table B-25 Commands for Netsh Routing Ip Autodhcp and Netsh Routing Ip Dnsproxy

Context/Command	Description
show global	Show DNS proxy configuration.
show interface	Shows DNS proxy configuration for the specified interface.
uninstall	Removes the routing protocol corresponding to the current context.

Table B-26 Commands for Netsh Routing Ip Igmp and Netsh Routing Ip Nat

Context/Command	Description
netsh routing ip igmp	
add interface	Configures IGMP on the specified interface.
delete interface	Removes IGMP router/proxy from the specified interface.
dump	Displays a configuration script for settings within the context.
install	Installs IGMP router/proxy and sets global logging.
set global	Sets IGMP global parameters.
set interface	Changes interface configuration parameters.
show global	Displays the global IGMP parameters.
show grouptable	Shows IGMP hosts group table for a multicast group.
show ifstats	Shows IGMP statistics for a specified interface.
show iftable	Shows IGMP host groups for a specified interface.
show interface	Displays the interface IGMP configuration.
show proxygrouptable	Shows IGMP hosts group table for an IGMP Proxy interface.
show rasgrouptable	Shows hosts group table for a Remote Access client interface.
uninstall	Removes the routing protocol corresponding to the current context.
netsh routing ip nat	
add addressmapping	Adds an IP address mapping to the NAT interface address pool.
add addressrange	Adds an address range to the NAT interface address pool.
add ftp	Enables the FTP proxy.
add interface	Configures NAT on the specified interface.
add portmapping	Adds a protocol port mapping on the NAT interface.
delete addressmapping	Deletes an address mapping from the NAT interface address pool.

Table B-26 Commands for Netsh Routing Ip Igmp and Netsh Routing Ip Nat

Context/Command	Description
delete addressrange	Deletes an address range from the NAT interface address pool.
delete ftp	Disables the FTP proxy.
delete interface	Removes NAT from the specified interface.
delete portmapping	Deletes a protocol port mapping from a NAT-enabled interface.
dump	Displays a configuration script for settings within the context.
install	Installs the routing protocol corresponding to the current context.
set global	Sets global NAT parameters.
set interface	Changes NAT parameters for an interface.
show global	Shows NAT configuration.
show interface	Shows NAT configuration for the specified interface.
uninstall	Removes the routing protocol corresponding to the current context.

Table B-27 Commands for Netsh Routing Ip Relay and Netsh Routing Ip Rip

Context/Command	Description
netsh routing ip relay	
add dhcpserver	Adds DHCP servers to the global list of DHCP servers.
add interface	Enables DHCP Relay Agent on the interface.
delete dhcpserver	Deletes DHCP servers from the global list of DHCP servers.
delete interface	Disables DHCP Relay Agent on the interface.
dump	Displays a configuration script for settings within the context.
install	Installs the routing protocol corresponding to the current context.
set global	Sets global parameters for DHCP Relay Agent configuration.
set interface	Updates the DHCP relay agent configuration on the interface.
show global	Shows DHCP Relay Agent global configuration.
show ifbinding	Shows IP address bindings for interfaces.
show ifconfig	Shows DHCP Relay Agent per-interface configuration.
show ifstats	Shows per-interface DHCP Relay Agent statistics.

Table B-27 Commands for Netsh Routing Ip Relay and Netsh Routing Ip Rip

Context/Command	Description
show interface	Shows interface-specific DHCP Relay Agent configuration.
uninstall	Removes the routing protocol corresponding to the current context.
netsh routing ip rip	
add acceptfilter	Adds an acceptance filter for routes received on an interface.
add announcefilter	Adds a filter for routes announced on an interface.
add interface	Configures RIP on a specified interface.
add neighbor	Adds a RIP neighbor on an interface.
add peerfilter	Adds a filter for servers that can be accepted as peers.
delete acceptfilter	Deletes an acceptance filter for routes received on an interface.
delete announcefilter	Deletes an announcement filter set for an interface.
delete interface	Removes RIP from the specified interface.
delete neighbor	Deletes a RIP neighbor from an interface.
delete peerfilter	Deletes a filter for an accepted peer server.
dump	Displays a configuration script for settings within the context.
install	Installs the routing protocol corresponding to the current context.
set flags	Sets RIP-related flags for a specified interface.
set global	Sets global RIP parameters.
set interface	Modifies RIP configuration on a specified interface.
show flags	Shows RIP flags set for specified interfaces.
show global	Shows RIP global parameters.
show globalstats	Shows RIP global statistics.
show ifbinding	Shows RIP interface IP address binding.
show ifstats	Shows RIP per-interface statistics.
show interface	Shows RIP configuration for the specified interface.
show neighbor	Shows RIP peer statistics.
uninstall	Removes the routing protocol corresponding to the current context.

Table B-28 Commands for Netsh Routing Ip Routerdiscovery, Netsh Routing Ipv6, and Netsh Routing Ipv6 Relayv6

Context/Command	Description
netsh routing ip routerdiscovery	
add interface	Configures router discovery for the specified interface.
delete interface	Removes router discovery from the specified interface.
dump	Displays a configuration script for settings within the context.
set interface	Updates interface router-discovery configuration.
show interface	Displays router-discovery information.
uninstall	Removes the routing protocol corresponding to the current context.
netsh routing ipv6	
add filter	Adds an IPv6 packet filter to a specified interface.
add persistentroute	Adds a persistent route to a specified interface.
delete filter	Deletes an IPv6 filter from a specified interface.
delete persistentroute	Deletes a persistent static route.
dump	Displays a configuration script for settings within the context.
relayv6	Changes to the "netsh routing ipv6 relayv6" context.
set filter	Changes IPv6 filter attributes on the specified interface.
set persistentroute	Modifies a persistent static route.
show filter	Displays IPv6 packet filter information.
show persistentroutes	Displays persistent static routes.
netsh routing ipv6 relayv6	
add dhcpserver	Adds DHCPv6 server to the global list of DHCPv6 servers.
add interface	Enables DHCPv6 Relay Agent on the interface.
delete dhcpserver	Deletes DHCPv6 server from the global list of DHCPv6 servers.
delete interface	Disables DHCPv6 Relay Agent on the interface.
dump	Displays a configuration script for settings within the context.
install	Installs the routing protocol corresponding to the current context.

Table B-28 Commands for Netsh Routing Ip Routerdiscovery, Netsh Routing Ipv6, and Netsh Routing Ipv6 Relayv6

Context/Command	Description
set global	Sets global parameters for DHCPv6 Relay Agent configuration.
set interface	Updates the DHCPv6 Relay Agent configuration on the interface.
show global	Shows DHCPv6 Relay Agent global configuration.
show interface	Shows interface-specific DHCPv6 Relay Agent configuration.
uninstall	Removes the routing protocol corresponding to the current context.

Netsh Rpc

The Netsh Rpc context and the Netsh Rpc Filter context allow you to work with the Remote Procedure Call (RPC) firewall. Table B-29 provides a summary of the commands available with these contexts.

Table B-29 Commands for the Netsh Rpc and Netsh Rpc Filter Contexts

Context/Command	Description
netsh rpc	
add	Creates an Add list of subnets.
delete	Creates a Delete list of subnets.
dump	Displays a configuration script for settings within the context.
filter	Changes to the "netsh rpc filter" context.
reset	Resets the selective binding settings to "none" (listen on all interfaces).
show	Displays the selective binding state for each subnet on the system.
netsh rpc filter	
add condition	Adds a condition to an existing RPC firewall filter rule.
add filter	Adds an RPC firewall filter.
add rule	Adds an RPC firewall filter rule.
delete filter	Deletes RPC firewall filter(s).
delete rule	Deletes the RPC firewall filter rule.
dump	Displays a configuration script for settings within the context.
show filter	Lists all RPC firewall filters.

Netsh Winhttp

You use the Netsh Winhttp context to manage Windows HTTP (WinHTTP) proxy and tracing settings. The available commands for this context are:

- **dump** Displays a configuration script
- **import** Imports WinHTTP proxy settings
- **reset proxy** Resets the WinHTTP proxy setting to the direct values
- **reset tracing** Resets the WinHTTP trace parameters to their default values
- **set proxy** Configures WinHTTP proxy setting
- **set tracing** Configures WinHTTP tracing parameters
- **show proxy** Displays current WinHTTP proxy setting
- **show tracing** Displays current WinHTTP tracing parameters

Netsh Wins

You use the Netsh Wins context and the Netsh Wins Server context to manage Windows Internet Naming Service (WINS) servers and their configurations. Table B-30 provides a summary of the commands available with these contexts. Note that these contexts are only available when the WINS Server feature is installed on a Windows Server computer. Using the Wins command when the Wins Server feature is not installed results in the Winsock context being opened.

Table B-30 Commands for the Netsh Wins and Netsh Wins Server Contexts

Context/Command	Description
netsh wins	
dump	Dumps configuration to the output.
server [*ServerName* | *IPAddress*]	Switches to the specified server context. If you don't specify a server name or IP address, this implies you want to work with WINS server on the local computer.
netsh wins server	
add name	Adds a name record to the server.
add partner	Adds a replication partner to the server.
add pgserver	Adds a list of Persona Grata Servers for the current server.
add pngserver	Adds a list of Persona Non Grata Servers for the current server.
check database	Checks the consistency of the database.
check name	Checks a list of name records against a set of WINS servers.
check version	Checks the consistency of the version number.

Table B-30 Commands for the Netsh Wins and Netsh Wins Server Contexts

Context/Command	Description
delete name	Deletes a registered name from the server database.
delete owners	Deletes a list of owners and their records.
delete partner	Deletes a replication partner from the list of replication partners.
delete pgserver	Deletes all or selected Persona Grata Servers from the list.
delete pngserver	Deletes all or selected Persona Non Grata Servers from the list.
delete records	Deletes or tombstones all or a set of records from the server.
dump	Dumps configuration to the output.
init backup	Initiates backup of WINS database.
init import	Initiates import from an LMHOSTS file.
init pull	Initiates and sends a pull trigger to another WINS server.
init pullrange	Initiates and pulls a range of records from another WINS server.
init push	Initiates and sends a push trigger to another WINS server.
init replicate	Initiates replication of database with replication partners.
init restore	Initiates restoring of database from a file.
init scavenge	Initiates scavenging of WINS database for the server.
init search	Initiates search on the WINS server database for the specified record.
reset	Resets a configuration entry in a table.
set autopartnerconfig	Sets the automatic replication partner configuration info for the server.
set backuppath	Sets the backup parameters for the server.
set burstparam	Sets the burst handling parameters for the server.
set defaultparam	Sets the default values for the WINS Server configuration parameters.
set logparam	Sets the database and event logging options.
set migrateflag	Sets the migration flag for the server.
set namerecord	Sets Intervals and Timeout values for the server.
set periodicdbchecking	Sets periodic database checking parameters for the server.
set pgmode	Sets the Persona Grata/Non Grata mode.
set pullparam	Sets the default pull partner parameters for the server.
set pullpartnerconfig	Sets the configuration parameters for the specified pull partner.

Table B-30 Commands for the Netsh Wins and Netsh Wins Server Contexts

Context/Command	Description
set pushparam	Sets the default push partner parameters for the server.
set pushpartnerconfig	Sets the configuration parameter for the specified push partner.
set replicateflag	Sets the replication flag for the server.
set startversion	Sets the start version ID for the database.
show browser	Displays all active domain master browser [1Bh] records.
show database	Displays the database and records for all or a list of specified owner servers.
show info	Displays server configuration information.
show name	Displays the detail information for a particular record in the server.
show partner	Displays all or pull or push partners for the server.
show partnerproperties	Displays default partner configuration.
show pullpartnerconfig	Displays configuration information for a pull partner.
show pushpartnerconfig	Displays configuration information for a push partner.
show recbyversion	Displays records owned by a specific server.
show reccount	Displays the number of records owned by a specific owner server.
show server	Displays the currently selected server.
show statistics	Displays the statistics for the WINS server.
show version	Displays the current maximum version counter value for the WINS Server.
show versionmap	Displays the owner ID to Maximum Version Number mappings.

Netsh Winsock

The Netsh Winsock context allows you to manage Winsock communications. The commands available with this context are:

- **audit trail** Shows the audit trail of Layered Service Providers (LSP) that have been installed and uninstalled
- **dump** Displays a configuration script
- **remove provider** Removes a Winsock LSP from the system
- **reset** Resets the Winsock Catalog to a clean state
- **show catalog** Displays contents of Winsock Catalog

Netsh Wlan

The Netsh Wlan context allows you to manage a computer's wireless networking configuration. Table B-31 provides a summary of the commands available with this context.

Table B-31 Commands for the Netsh Wlan Context

Command	Description
add filter	Adds a wireless network into the wireless allowed or blocked list.
add profile	Adds a WLAN profile to specified interface on the system.
connect	Connects to a wireless network.
delete filter	Removes a wireless network from the wireless allowed or blocked list.
delete profile	Deletes a WLAN profile from one or multiple interfaces.
disconnect	Disconnects from a wireless network.
dump	Displays a configuration script for settings within the context.
export	Saves WLAN profiles to XML files.
set autoconfig	Enables or disables auto-configuration logic on interface.
set blockednetworks	Shows or hides the blocked networks in visible network list.
set createalluserprofile	Allows or disallows everyone to create all user profiles.
set profileorder	Sets the preference order of a wireless network profile.
set tracing	Enables or disables tracing.
show all	Shows complete wireless device and networks information.
show autoconfig	Shows whether the auto-configuration logic is enabled or disabled.
show blockednetworks	Shows the blocked network display settings.
show createalluserprofile	Shows whether everyone is allowed to create all user profiles.
show drivers	Shows properties of the wireless LAN drivers on the system.
show filters	Shows the allowed and blocked network list.
show interfaces	Shows a list of the wireless LAN interfaces on the system.
show networks	Shows a list of networks visible on the system.
show profiles	Shows a list of profiles configured on the system.
show settings	Shows the global settings of wireless LAN.
show tracing	Shows whether wireless LAN tracing is enabled or disabled.

Index

Symbols and Numbers

A

D

E

F

K

L

M

Q

S

U

V

W

X

About the Author

William R. Stanek (*http://www.williamstanek.com/*) has more than 20 years of hands-on experience with advanced programming and development. He is a leading technology expert, an award-winning author, and a pretty-darn-good instructional trainer. Over the years, his practical advice has helped millions of programmers, developers, and network engineers all over the world. He has written more than 75 books. Current or forthcoming books include *Microsoft Exchange Server 2007 Administrator's Pocket Consultant*, Second Edition, *Windows Server 2008 Administrator's Pocket Consultant, Microsoft SQL Server 2008 Administrator's Pocket Consultant*, and *Windows Server 2008 Inside Out*.

William has been involved in the commercial Internet community since 1991. His core business and technology experience comes from more than 11 years of military service. He has substantial experience in developing server technology, encryption, and Internet solutions. He has written many technical white papers and training courses on a wide variety of topics. He frequently serves as a subject matter expert and consultant.

William has an MS with distinction in information systems and a BS in computer science, magna cum laude. He is proud to have served in the Persian Gulf War as a combat crewmember on an electronic warfare aircraft. He flew on numerous combat missions into Iraq and was awarded nine medals for his wartime service, including one of the United States of America's highest flying honors, the Air Force Distinguished Flying Cross. Currently he resides in the Pacific Northwest with his wife and children.

What do you think of this book?

We want to hear from you!

Do you have a few minutes to participate in a brief online survey?

Microsoft is interested in hearing your feedback so we can continually improve our books and learning resources for you.

To participate in our survey, please visit:

www.microsoft.com/learning/booksurvey/

...and enter this book's ISBN-10 number or ISBN-13 number (located above barcode on back cover*). As a thank-you to survey participants in the United States and Canada, each month we'll randomly select five respondents to win one of five $100 gift certificates from a leading online merchant. At the conclusion of the survey, you can enter the drawing by providing your e-mail address, which will be used for prize notification only.

Thanks in advance for your input. Your opinion counts!

Microsoft® Press

*** Where to find the ISBN on back cover**

Example only. Each book has unique ISBN.

No purchase necessary. Void where prohibited. Open only to residents of the 50 United States (includes District of Columbia) and Canada (void in Quebec). For official rules and entry dates see:

www.microsoft.com/learning/booksurvey/